P9-ASG-342

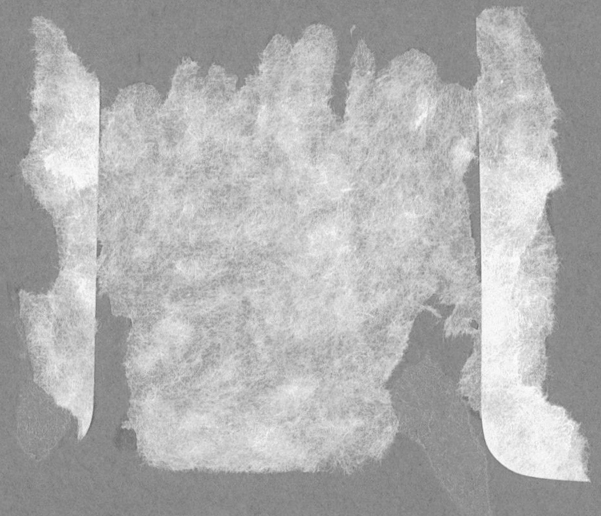

INTELLECTUAL FOUNDATIONS OF AMERICAN EDUCATION

PITMAN EDUCATION SERIES

Rychard Fink, GENERAL EDITOR

THE COST OF EDUCATION INDEX

ELEMENTARY CURRICULUM: A BOOK OF READINGS
Edited by Robert E. Chasnoff

NEW PERSPECTIVES IN READING INSTRUCTION
Edited by Albert J. Mazurkiewicz

SEVEN STORIES FOR GROWTH
Daniel Sugarman and Rolaine Hochstein

INTELLECTUAL FOUNDATIONS OF AMERICAN EDUCATION

Readings & Commentary

EDITED BY

HAROLD J. CARTER

THE CITY COLLEGE
THE CITY UNIVERSITY OF NEW YORK

Pitman Publishing Corporation

NEW YORK/TORONTO/LONDON

Library of Congress Catalog Card Number: 65–10978
Manufactured in the United States of America
DESIGNED BY VINCENT TORRE
1.987654321

For Mildred

FOREWORD

One unfortunate characteristic of certain educators is their inclination to take fundamentally sound ideas and turn them into fads. This is usually accomplished by their writing and talking about an idea with enthusiasm and, in the process, making excessive claims about what it will accomplish. As usually happens, the complexities of teaching and learning keep the idea from achieving as much as the originator expected, and a reaction sets in when that becomes clear. Such reactions are usually attacks; they are seldom efforts to take what is sound in an idea and use it.

The foundations approach to the education of teachers is a case in point. The notion that such subject areas as history, philosophy, sociology, and psychology offered to educators concepts that could inform and inspire them appeared in certain courses at Teachers College, Columbia University, during the 1930's. For well over a decade, teachers like William Heard Kilpatrick, John Childs, George Counts, and, particularly, Harold Rugg taught these courses. It was Rugg who, in 1947, published *The Foundations of American Education* in which he claimed that a series of basic concepts in psychology, sociology, esthetics, and ethics, when known and accepted by teachers, would help them build a "Great School."

Among the most immediate consequences of Rugg's vision that ". . . a sound theory of society, of the nature, behavior, and expression of men, as foundations of education [will turn] teacher-education institutions [into] centers of ideas" were new professional programs of foundations studies at universities in Ohio, Illinois, and Florida. The claims about what would be accomplished by educating teachers through foundations programs expressed the usual enthusiasm: Such courses would turn teachers into formulators of national educational policy, and make them top-level decision-makers who would reconstruct the attitudes and beliefs of Americans.

It is certainly fair to ask, Should teachers do this? It is equally fair to ask, Will any sequence of courses give people such competencies? Naturally, critics asked these and other questions; and when it became clear that foundations courses were not transforming education majors into unusually effective social leaders, a reaction set in. This took the form, most recently, of a blanket rejection by Dr. Conant of the foundations idea.

The idea of foundations for the education of teachers is too sound to be destroyed by such swings of the pendulum of popularity. If it could be agreed that teachers must be among the best-educated people in our nation—which means that they must be sensitive to social issues, and able to understand them and respond to them in terms of our historic democratic aspirations—then the economical use of time in any curriculum for teacher education suggests the continued use of foundations of education courses.

In this volume, *Intellectual Foundations of American Education,* Dr. Carter presents material which, when understood and acted upon, will help teachers to display the characteristics of well-educated and responsible citizens, and also to acquire those specialized understandings they must have in order to perform their chosen roles. These are purposes both modest and manageable, and they deserve approval and support.

Intellectual Foundations of American Education offers to those who are preparing to teach a series of "vestibule" experiences. They should help the student, as he grows older, to progress through the corridors of the human enterprise into the many subject area storerooms where man codifies and stores his knowledge. The material Dr. Carter has selected and edited makes for a fine beginning. But it is only that, a beginning. Rugg's shining image of a "Great School" will be transformed into living fact only if what Dr. Carter has so ably begun inspires teachers to undertake a lifelong search for knowledge.

Rychard Fink

PREFACE

THIS BOOK of readings is designed to give prospective teachers an opportunity to think through some of the most important issues in modern American education. Hopefully, it will also prove useful to citizens who want to understand the purposes, functions, and obligations of America's schools.

The emphasis throughout is on the present. The selections represent the work of scholars in many fields, men and women who have devoted considerable energy and skill to the task of enriching and enhancing what is known about our society, our people, and our educational institutions.

In using the contributions of others, I am fully aware that uniformity of style cannot be achieved. Whatever unity and continuity this book has must depend on the organization of the material, the introductory remarks preceding each section, and the drawing of a composite picture at the conclusion. I have tried to make possible a considerable degree of intellectual cross-fertilization, because the scholars cited have been influenced by the values of our democratic society and have, in many instances, influenced each other. The plan of organization for this volume was adopted because existing books on the subject, although excellent in many respects, tend to emphasize the historical development of American education; and, of greater significance, they tend to minimize the educational values of the interdisciplinary approach.

In selecting material for this book, I was faced with too much worthwhile material, and many important and valuable statements could not be used because space was not available. The selections represent my best judgment about the contributions that will most completely illuminate the thesis and, at the same time, stimulate and encourage the reader to make a creative response.

Harold J. Carter

CONTENTS

PART ONE
Cultural Values and Education

CHAPTER 1 The Ethos of the Democratic Society 13

Democracy and Educational Administration/JOHN DEWEY 15

CHAPTER 2 The Premises Underlying Education 22

The Philosophical Premises Underlying Public Education/ VAN CLEVE MORRIS 23

CHAPTER 3 The Social Milieu and Education 33

Education and the Technological Revolution/ GEORGE S. COUNTS 35

Education and Power/R. BRUCE RAUP 41

CHAPTER 4 The American Paradox 53

The Intellectual in Action/HAROLD TAYLOR 54

Intellectuals and Other People/MERLE CURTI 64

Freedom, Conformity, and Uniformity/GLENN AUSTIN 71

CHAPTER 5 The Scope of Democratic Education 79

Education for Democracy/H. GORDON HULLFISH 80

PART TWO
Moral-Ethical Values, Spiritual Values, and Education

CHAPTER 6 Values and Education 97

Moral Authority and Religious Sanction/R. BRUCE RAUP 97

How Do We Know What Values Are Best?/ GEORGE E. AXTELLE 103

CHAPTER 7 Religion and the State 110

Church and State in American Education/R. FREEMAN BUTTS 111

What Should Be the Relation of Religion and Public Education?/HENRY P. VAN DEUSEN 114

Better Schools for Better Times/ MOST REVEREND JOSEPH M. MARLING, C.P.P.S. 134

Religion in the Public School: A New Approach to the Jewish Position/RABBI ARTHUR T. GILBERT 141

Community Education: A Functional Relationship between School and Church/WESNER FALLAW 149

CHAPTER 8 A Synthesis of Values for Education 160

Education for Religious Quality in Experience/ WARD MADDEN 161

CHAPTER 9 A Basis for the Teaching of Values 180

Toward a Philosophy of Moral Education/ WILLIAM K. FRANKENA 181

PART THREE
Law and Education

CHAPTER 10 Law Insures Stability and Change 197

Stability and Change in Basic Concepts of Law Governing American Education/NEWTON EDWARDS 198

CHAPTER 11 Law Enriches the Curriculum 210

Law and Education/HARRY KALVEN, JR. 211

CHAPTER 12 Law for Educators 215

Essentials of School Law for Educators/E. E. REUTTER, JR. 216

CHAPTER 13 Law to Resolve Issues 226

Education—A Thing Apart?/ERNEST A. ENGELBERT 226

PART FOUR
Finance and Education

CHAPTER 14 Need for a Policy 237
The Shortage of Education/WALTER LIPPMANN 238
CHAPTER 15 General Statistics 245
Progress of Public Education in the United States, 1962–1963/ OFFICE OF EDUCATION, UNITED STATES DEPARTMENT OF HEALTH, EDUCATION AND WELFARE 245
CHAPTER 16 Economics of the Problem 251
Economic Prospects and School Finance/PROCTOR THOMSON 252
CHAPTER 17 Income in Relation to Education 262
Money Value of an Education/HERMAN P. MILLER 263
Education: An Advantage for a Lifetime/HERMAN P. MILLER 273
CHAPTER 18 Federal Aid—Concepts and Issues 278
Report on Federal Responsibility in the Field of Education/ COMMITTEE ON FEDERAL RESPONSIBILITY IN THE FIELD OF EDUCATION 279
Federal Aid to Education: Issues Before Congress/ WILLIAM B. RICH 285
CHAPTER 19 A Proposal for Financing Public Education 295
A Proposal for Financing Tax-Supported Education/ ROBERT HELLER 296

PART FIVE
The Group and Education

CHAPTER 20 Group Values—American Communities 316
American Communities/C. M. ARENSBERG 316
The Characterization of American Culture in Studies of Acculturation/LEONARD MASON 336
CHAPTER 21 Group Values—"Core Culture" 341
The Dominant Value Profile of American Culture/ CORA DU BOIS 342
CHAPTER 22 Group Values—"Status-Glissando" 348
Social Class and the Dynamics of Status in America/ WALTER GOLDSCHMIDT 349

CHAPTER 23 Group Values—"Traditional to Emergent" 353

Education in a Transforming American Culture/ GEORGE D. SPINDLER 354

CHAPTER 24 The Role of Social Class in Education 363

Class, Leisure, and Social Participation/LEONARD REISSMAN 364

CHAPTER 25 The Role of the Family in Education 371

Social Class Factors and School Attendance/JAMES S. DAVIE 372

Educational Attainment and Family Background/ FLORENCE CAMPI 383

Limited Educational Attainment: Extent and Consequences/ E. W. BRICE AND E. E. HUYCK 384

PART SIX
The Individual and Education

CHAPTER 26 Determinants and Components of Personality 392

Culture and Personality: A Conceptual Scheme/ CLYDE KLUCKHOHN AND O. H. MOWRER 393

CHAPTER 27 Function of Experience 413

An Inquiry Concerning the Characteristics of Man/ HADLEY CANTRIL 414

CHAPTER 28 Planned Experiences and Behavior 425

Freedom and the Control of Men/B. F. SKINNER 426

CHAPTER 29 Intelligence, Ideas, and Education 431

Some Prospects of a General Science of Human Relations/ WALTER G. O'DONNELL 432

PART SEVEN
Educational Specifications

CHAPTER 30 Educational Specifications—As Viewed by a Social Scientist 443

The Spirit of American Education/GEORGE S. COUNTS 443

CHAPTER 31 Educational Specifications—As Viewed by a Philosopher 448

What Can Philosophy Contribute to Educational Theory?/ CURT J. DUCASSE 449

CHAPTER 32 Educational Specifications—As Viewed by the National Association of Manufacturers 457

Views on the Curriculum/CHARLES R. SLIGH, JR. 458

CHAPTER 33 Educational Specifications—As Viewed by the AFL-CIO 465

What the Public Schools Should Teach/WALTER P. REUTHER 466

CHAPTER 34 Educational Specifications—As Viewed by the National Education Association 471

The Purposes of Education in American Democracy/ EDUCATIONAL POLICIES COMMISSION, NATIONAL EDUCATION ASSOCIATION 472

CHAPTER 35 Educational Specifications—As Viewed by a Local Board of Education 475

Aims and Objectives of Education/ BOARD OF EDUCATION OF THE CITY OF NEW YORK 475

CHAPTER 36 The Role of the State 477

The State's Responsibility for a Reasonable Educational Program/ALONZO G. GRACE 477

PART EIGHT
Educational Institutions

CHAPTER 37 General Statistics 488

Enrollment, 1962—1963/OFFICE OF EDUCATION, UNITED STATES DEPARTMENT OF HEALTH, EDUCATION AND WELFARE 488

CHAPTER 38 "The Ladder System": The Structure of Education in the United States 495

CHAPTER 39 The Role of Elementary Education 498

Functional Schools for Young Children/OFFICE OF EDUCATION, UNITED STATES DEPARTMENT OF HEALTH, EDUCATION AND WELFARE 499

CHAPTER 40 The Role of the Junior High School 505

The Junior High School Program—Statement of Functions/ THE SOUTHERN ASSOCIATION OF COLLEGES AND SCHOOLS 506

CHAPTER 41 The Role of the Senior High School 516

An Analysis and a Look Ahead/H. H. CUMMINGS, *et. al.* 517

CHAPTER 42 The Role of Higher Education 533
The Happy Crisis in Higher Education/CHARLES FRANKEL 534
CHAPTER 43 The Role of Adult Education 544
The Adult and His Education/HORACE M. KALLEN 545

PART NINE
The Educators and Education

CHAPTER 44 The Challenges in Teacher Preparation 563
Education and Social Class in the United States/W. H. BURTON 564
CHAPTER 45 Professional Preparation—Fundamental Postulates 577
On the Education of Teachers/ROBERT ULICH 578
CHAPTER 46 Professional Preparation—Role of the University 584
Professional Education as University Education/ CHARLES FRANKEL 585
CHAPTER 47 The Prospective Teacher—"Subject of Education" 597
The Student as a Responsible Person/HAROLD TAYLOR 598
CHAPTER 48 The Desirable Personality Traits 606
Emotions and Learning/DANA L. FARNSWORTH 607
CHAPTER 49 Academic Freedom—The Educator's Authorization 616
The Free University in an Open Society/KURT P. TAUBER 617

Some Observations After the Facts 631
Selected Bibliography 635
Index 643

INTELLECTUAL FOUNDATIONS OF AMERICAN EDUCATION

SOME OBSERVATIONS BEFORE THE FACTS

The schools, public and private, secular and sectarian, that make up the enterprise of American education are a creation of that society and are charged with the task of perpetuating its values. As society's surrogate, each school transmits a large part of the culture in the intricate process of socializing and maturing each student. The proper performance of this task requires all kinds of knowledge, especially knowledge identified with the following areas: the goals desired by the society, the current status of the social milieu, the general knowledge deemed essential for each student as a functioning member of society, the specialized knowledge required for economic security, the nature of the learner, the nature of learning, the role of the family, the role of the group, and the role of the school.

This is the intellectual core of American education. It comprises the reflections and inquiries of scholars from many disciplines. The technique of relating knowledge from many subject areas to give substance and design to the study of education is called the interdisciplinary approach. At first glance, such an approach might seem to ask a great deal of students. Actually, all students have, through the years, come to know quite a lot about different subject areas. With this book, they can use what they know and learn even more. The use of an interdisciplinary approach enables those who will soon be teaching to analyze fully and relate adequately a mass of data pertinent to certain educational issues. There is no other way to understand anything as complex as education. As John Dewey pointed out: "The scientific content of education consists of whatever subject-matter, selected from other fields, enables the educator, whether administrator or teacher, to see and to think more clearly and deeply about whatever he is doing."[1]

No teacher can hope to do justice to the educational goals of this society without learning to manage a broad range of concepts and the knowl-

[1] John Dewey, *The Sources of a Science of Education* (New York: H. Liveright, 1929), p. 75.

edge they symbolize. This point is of dramatic import because teaching means accepting responsibility for contributing positively to the intellectual, social, emotional, and physical growth of each student. The identification and definition of the problems encountered in education is the first step toward the knowledge required to solve these problems. This body of knowledge, obtained from various disciplines, constitutes the science of education. In reference to this point, John Dewey stated: "First, educational practices furnish the material that sets the problems of such a science, while sciences already developed to a fair state of maturity are the sources from which material is derived to deal intellectually with these problems. There is no more a special independent science of education than there is of bridge making. But material drawn from *other* sciences furnishes the content of educational science when it is focused on the problems that arise in education."[2]

Certain difficulties are involved in the proposal that the interdisciplinary approach be used by every teacher to manage his professional problems. The inflexibility of the academic mind, as evidenced by the thinking of far too many educators, will cause a number of scholars not only to resist a broad-fields, integrated approach, but to battle earnestly to preserve subject areas and academic disciplines. Actually, the interdisciplinary approach is a threat to no one. In practice, educators have always relied upon, and have utilized to varying degrees, contributions from the various disciplines. Indeed, when people begin to study a complex area through an interdisciplinary approach, the most immediate result is a larger concern with ideas that often leads to the election of course work in the traditional subject areas. As for the thesis that education is a discipline in its own right and should be preserved as such, that remains an interesting claim worth talking about—but not here.

It is hoped that the material presented in this book will do the following: encourage you, the reader, to react critically to the thinking of the scholars cited; stimulate you to investigate further matters that perplex you; and encourage you to continue to formulate a position about education that accepts and uses reliable data and is consistent with the American democratic ideal. The point is that your growth and development are at stake. You should care enough about it to want to use intelligence and not rely excessively upon what is said in a book or by an instructor. All too frequently in teacher education, we have acted as if better teachers would be produced by adding courses to the curriculum and marching students in and out of them. This practice caused H. G. Hullfish and P. G. Smith to remark: "Whatever the public problem, from temperance to thrift, from how to drive a car to how to feed livestock, a course has seemed the ready way to provide an answer, especially when the critic is able to generate considerable pressure on behalf of his special interest. He has been misled by the magic of

[2] *Ibid.*, pp. 35–36.

titles (and some schools seem to have been, also), as other critics, in other times, have been misled by the magic of words."[3]

In relying upon the presence and use of particular courses, we have far too often produced slavish reliance upon what the instructor has to say. One can concede that the instructor has been thinking and has something to say, but it is still necessary to indicate the obvious: The learner should be thinking, also. In far too many American classrooms, teachers over-dominate the learning situations. When this happens, many students learn some interesting things, including how to let others think for them! In commenting on this unhappy reliance upon the words of others, Hullfish and Smith have said: "Too many of us, in school and out, have assumed that the ability of an individual to repeat the thoughts of others provides evidence that he is an independent thinker. We forget that parrots are not notably reflective. Were we to remember this, we might discover that the time for a teacher to be worried, apart from those moments when facts which are beyond dispute are at issue, is when all in a class agree with him. It is a sad fact that classrooms are frequently intimidated by the tyranny of the right answer, *the answer none dare question.*"[4]

For these reasons, the author has resisted the temptation to coax the reader into thinking certain things, and enters the plea that everyone use the material included in this book in order to reflect and think critically. That is said out of the conviction that the initiative and responsibility for learning should rest solely and exclusively with the student. If he cannot support his own development, he must be taught how to do so. The instructor serves the learner most fruitfully as an intelligent guide. In such an educative process, the instructor is a professional thinker who supports the thoughtful student. The success of the process has meaning, at least for Americans, when teachers and students attain and utilize those patterns of behavior that represent democratic living. There are many elements in such behavior, and many ways of talking about them, but those that follow seem most important.

Rationality. We Americans decided a long time ago to rule ourselves. If we are to rule ourselves well, then rationality is essential and we must devote ourselves to the continuous use of intelligence. Our world is growing more complicated day by day, and tomorrow we will have to think more ably than today. We know that the method of intelligence includes: defining with maximum clarity what is at issue, formulating hypotheses related to the definition, obtaining verifiable data from all relevant sources, selecting the most suggestive hypothesis, applying the hypothesis related to the defined issue, evaluating the results, and determining what remains to be accomplished. In daily life, of course, we seldom have a chance to act in terms of

[3] H. G. Hullfish and P. G. Smith, *Reflective Thinking: The Method of Education* (New York: Dodd, Mead, 1961), p. 7.

[4] *Ibid.*, pp. 23–24.

such a checklist. What we do is pick up hints of meaning, leap at a partial, but supportable, generalization, and build a whole response from a sense of what is fit and proper. When we can afford to live at a slower pace, we can conceptualize and think abstractly with greater attention to details. At all times, however, the flood of information that comes from the mass media of communication must be appraised and evaluated, summarized and classified, and stored away until it is needed.

Social Sensitivity. Social sensitivity has been described by Hilda Taba as "an awareness of, and responsiveness to, social and human phenomena." The socially sensitive individual, acting rationally, makes his life part of the lives of others so that, wherever he is present, people have a chance to live more effectively and efficiently. In an ideal sense, and following John Donne's famous thought, a socially sensitive person knows he "is part of the main." This is the kind of person who starts from and moves toward that essential element of the democratic ethos, the idea of individual dignity and worth. He accepts the responsibility of engaging in socially significant activities and tries hard, as hard as he can, not to damage any other person's self-esteem.

Cooperativeness. In our complex industrial-technological society, any man must usually rely upon many others in order to take care of his business. Whatever is done had better be done well, for most activity is reciprocal. It is not a case of living for others, but of knowing that one lives with them. Indeed, as John Dewey observed, the fact is that dependency is a power—the power to rely on others.

Appreciation of Diversity. If Americans live the "good life" by living with and for each other, then each individual is obligated to understand the factors that produce individual differences and to use such differences for the common good. Containing as it does intellectual variety and difference, a society has an inexhaustible storehouse of alternative solutions it can apply to its problems. More than anything else, perhaps, the presence of variety and difference teaches men that they need not be threatened by anything new or strange.

Creativeness. Creativity appears when any person takes care of his business—any kind of business—in any way that had not occurred to him before. It is perfectly safe to assume that each individual is potentially creative and that in the search for the "good life," as we Americans have defined it, this life will become a reality for every person. We have been creative enough to build a remarkable civilization, and that civilization, if we are wise enough to stand back and let it challenge us, can unleash an even greater measure of creativity.

Esthetic Appreciation. Understanding and appreciation of beauty in all its dimensions and manifestations was once the prerogative of aristocrats. Today we could, and sometimes we do, help some individuals to achieve proportion, balance, and perspective in many of their activities. To think, to act, to relate to others, to relate to oneself, to maintain a high level of aspiration for oneself and others, and to do them with taste, judgment, and balance, is to demonstrate the value of esthetic appreciation.

Self-Direction. Implied in each of the previous patterns of behavior is the obligation of each individual to be true to himself, to be as much the architect of his own life as he can. At all times, a democrat reaches out for life in the light of what he knows of himself, what he desires for himself, what he knows of others, and what he desires for others. Today, we speak of such a person as a mature human being.

The physically and mentally normal person can learn to act in accordance with these patterns of behavior. Whether he does or does not depends upon the chance he has to learn them. When he has such a chance, he must find this point of view meaningful and worth doing, and even then he must live his life with his own style and flair. In doing this, he will be like others, part of a grand consensus among reasonable men, but also different.

Nothing of this sort can happen unless the American school makes the fullest possible range of educational opportunities available to each child. With such equality of opportunity, and with teachers who know how to make positive learning take place, each American will know who he is and why life is worth living and will be eager to use the present as a vantage point for changing the future.

Our animal destiny is growth and change. Our destiny as human animals is to work to achieve ends that are generous and humane. Our destiny as teachers for a democratically inclined society is to struggle to make that everyone's chance. Nothing less is worth doing.

PART ONE

Cultural Values and Education

EDUCATIONAL institutions are social inventions used by human groups to perpetuate their commonly accepted beliefs. Schools and teachers are elements of the complex institutional arrangements that contribute to the socialization and maturation of the young. The organization and the purposes of education have always reflected the political, economic, social, and cultural sophistication of society. In relatively unsophisticated societies, formal education is comparatively uncomplicated, for the young learn most important matters through direct participation in everyday affairs. Other things that must be learned are communicated through deliberate teaching, which is a secondary medium of instruction.

As societies grow more sophisticated and knowledge increases, all social agents, including education, display greater complexity because they must now perform more intricate and more numerous functions. This process of change from the (apparently) simple to the (obviously) complex involves an increase in the number of years the young must devote to education. Language rather than direct participation in everyday affairs becomes the primary medium of instruction. The stockpiling of knowledge for future use is held in higher esteem than learning how to use the knowledge in the immediate present. Schools with special concerns are created, and they require procedures through which teachers, who serve as the society's surrogates and mediators, can be selected and trained. As sophistication increases, the further sources of authority that guide all institutions in the performance of their tasks become obscure, and their power to control is expressed in fragmented and impersonal ways.

It is commonly accepted that the United States is the world's most advanced technological society and, in many ways, the most sophisticated. But as American life has grown more complex, the responsibilities involved in the assumption and the utilization of authority for the benefit of all have become confused with issues, politics, expediency, and highly partisan behavior on the part of many individuals. As a result, many citizens have put into places of secondary importance the values and goals that should be the dominating motives for action. The ideas included in the democratic ethos, which should motivate the conduct of all individuals, and all the social agencies of the society, have become rituals, always praised and only occasionally put to work.

The process of education in a democratic social order should encompass the wishes, desires, and needs of both adults and students, who are at different stages of maturity, as well as the talents and skills of educators. Ideally, this relationship should be a transaction among people who place the same value on personality. Practically, this means that every person involved in the processes of education must search out and use all the methods that wit and talent can discern in the values of the democratic ethos. In these terms, and for these reasons, this section begins with an examination of the essential elements of the democratic ethos. It presents considerations about: the premises basic to education in a democratic society; the social setting in which education currently operates; the relevant issues that presently influence the functioning of education; and the forces that seek to curb the full operation of a democratic educative process.

Chapter I

THE ETHOS OF THE DEMOCRATIC SOCIETY

EDUCATION *in the United States, as it guides and influences the growth of individuals, seeks to implement and ultimately to fulfill the ideal aspirations of the people. We refer to these aspirations as the democratic ethos. The ethos can provide three guides: First, the idealistic goals point to the direction in which the society should move and suggest the methods to be used along the way; second, the statement of goals serves as a standard of measurement which discloses what remains to be accomplished by comparing what has been done with what is desired; third, such goals, which pervade all aspects of American life, establish the frame of reference in which education operates, and offer definition and direction for the practical activities of education.*

As they perform their functions, educators must accept and try to resolve many serious problems in accordance with the ideal possibilities of the democratic ethos. One such problem is: Should education prepare individuals to meet and accept opportunities and responsibilities in the future or in the present? The issue raised here is not necessarily a conflict between the ideal and the practical or between long-term aspirations and immediate behavior. A person learns democratic techniques and ideals in order to use the techniques in the present, and this accomplishment confirms the validity of the ideals.

In the following excerpt the philosopher John Dewey indicates: (a) the idealized values of democracy as a way of life; (b) the methodological possibilities of democracy as a way of life, and (c) the responsibilities of educators, who serve as society's agents for the achievement, utilization, and perpetuation of the democratic ethos.

Democracy as a way of life requires that each individual display initiative and responsibility for its continuous use and refinement. Such action means that each individual accepts himself and all other individuals as persons of inestimable dignity and worth. This affirmation makes irrational any social policy that categorizes individuals on the basis of physical characteristics, patterns of speech, and so on. Men have lived with one another from the moment they appeared in nature as human animals. In the democratic form of living, the individual-group reciprocal relationship is the basis for individual and group conduct. Each individual exists simultaneously as an individual and as a member of many groups. The individual accepts responsibility for demonstrating that he has worth by actively working for the enrichment of the quality and significance of his experiences and of the experiences of others. This process, in which each individual participates in the formulation and implementation of standards that regulate the conduct of all, is best described as cooperative interaction. Each individual is continuously aware of the impact of his conduct upon the welfare of others. The guiding force is always the advancement of all (the group) and never the enhancement of an individual to the detriment of the group (everyone else). Each individual, and each group in which the individual claims membership, is obliged to maintain the environment that enables individuals and groups to demonstrate their worth. The idea of individual worth presumes that all persons are intelligent to varying degrees and, therefore, each man is capable of acting intelligently in his own behalf. The group has the responsibility of making it possible for each human being to make the best contribution he can. This, in turn, requires equality of opportunity, for without total support of the group as he develops, no individual can become all he is capable of being.

The methodological possibilities of democracy as a way of life urge us to seek out and affirm democratic processes within the complex organization of government, just as we do in face-to-face relationships. Thus, the consent of the governed demands the broadest possible uses of intelligence and the enjoyment of the moral, political, and social consequences that accompany them.

As they work, educators must be responsible for the development of the personalities of the children and youth they teach. The methods they use to support the intellectual, social, psychological, and physical maturation of each individual are of strategic importance. Whatever may be the case in other institutions, the tenets upon which each school is organized and the manner in which educators conduct themselves must be consistent with the ethos of the society. Schools in a society with democratic aspirations can contribute to the development of democratic personalities only to the degree that the ethos is part of the character of all the individuals who staff and manage the school. A democratically organized society requires a distinctive program for the education of its members, one that reflects an understanding of the learner and of the culture in which he lives, grows, and functions. Only through constant practice will the values sought by a democratically inspired people be achieved.

DEMOCRACY AND EDUCATIONAL ADMINISTRATION

John Dewey

In the first place, democracy is much broader than a special political form, a method of conducting government, of making laws, and carrying on governmental administration by means of popular suffrage and elected officers. It is that, of course. But it is something broader and deeper than that. The political and governmental phase of democracy is a means, the best means so far found, for realizing ends that lie in the wide domain of human relationships and the development of human personality. It is, as we often say, though perhaps without appreciating all that is involved in the saying, a way of life, social and individual. The key-note of democracy as a way of life may be expressed, it seems to me, as the necessity for the participation of every mature human being in formation of the values that regulate the living of men together: which is necessary from the standpoint of both the general social welfare and the full development of human beings as individuals.

Universal suffrage, recurring elections, responsibility of those who are in political power to the voters, and the other factors of democratic government are means that have been found expedient for realizing democracy as the truly human way of living. They are not a final end and a final value. They are to be judged on the basis of their contribution to end. It is a form of idolatry to erect means into the end which they serve. Democratic political forms are simply the best means that human wit has devised up to a special time in history. But they rest back upon the idea that no man or limited set

Reprinted from *School and Society*, Vol. 45, No. 1162 (April 3, 1937), pp. 457–462.

of men is wise enough or good enough to rule others without their consent; the positive meaning of this statement is that all those who are affected by social institutions must have a share in producing and managing them. The two facts that each one is influenced in what he does and enjoys and in what he becomes by the institutions under which he lives, and that therefore he shall have, in a democracy, a voice in shaping them, are the passive and active sides of the same fact.

The development of political democracy came about through substitution of the method of mutual consultation and voluntary agreement for the method of subordination of the many to the few enforced from above. Social arrangements which involve fixed subordination are maintained by coercion. The coercion need not be physical. There have existed, for short periods, benevolent despotisms. But coercion of some sort there has been; perhaps economic, certainly psychological and moral. The very fact of exclusion from participation is a subtle form of suppression. It gives individuals no opportunity to reflect and decide upon what is good for them. Others who are supposed to be wiser and who in any case have more power decide the question for them and also decide the methods and means by which subjects may arrive at the enjoyment of what is good for them. This form of coercion and suppression is more subtle and more effective than is overt intimidation and restraint. When it is habitual and embodied in social institutions, it seems the normal and natural state of affairs. The mass usually become unaware that they have a claim to a development of their own powers. Their experience is so restricted that they are not conscious of restriction. It is part of the democratic conception that they as individuals are not the only sufferers, but that the whole social body is deprived of the potential resources that should be at its service. The individuals of the submerged mass may not be very wise. But there is one thing they are wiser about than anybody else can be, and that is where the shoe pinches, the troubles they suffer from.

The foundation of democracy is faith in the capacities of human nature; faith in human intelligence and in the power of pooled and cooperative experience. It is not belief that these things are complete but that if given a show they will grow and be able to generate progressively the knowledge and wisdom needed to guide collective action. Every autocratic and authoritarian scheme of social action rests on a belief that the needed intelligence is confined to a superior few, who because of inherent natural gifts are endowed with the ability and the right to control the conduct of others; laying down principles and rules and directing the ways in which they are carried out. It would be foolish to deny that much can be said for this point of view. It is that which controlled human relations in social groups for much the greater part of human history. The democratic faith has emerged very, very recently in the history of mankind. Even where democracies now exist, men's minds and feelings are still permeated with ideas about leadership imposed from above, ideas that developed in the long early history of mankind. After democratic political institutions were nominally established, beliefs and ways of looking at life and of acting that originated when men and women were externally controlled and subjected to arbitrary power, persisted in the family, the church, business, and the school, and experience shows that as long as they persist there, political democracy is not secure.

Belief in equality is an element of the democratic credo. It is not, however, belief in equality of natural endowments. Those who proclaimed the idea of equality did not suppose they were enunciating a psychological doctrine, but a legal and political one. All individuals are entitled to equality of treatment by law and in its administration. Each one is affected equally in quality if not in quantity by the institutions under which he lives and has an equal right to express his judgment, although the weight of his judgment may not be equal in amount when it enters into the pooled result to that of others. In short, each one is equally an individual and entitled to equal opportunity of development of his own capacities, be they large or small in range. Moreover, each has needs of his own, as significant to him as those of others are to them. The very fact of natural and psychological inequality is all the more reason for establishment by law of equality of opportunity, since otherwise the former becomes a means of oppression of the less gifted.

While what we call intelligence be distributed in unequal amounts, it is the democratic faith that it is sufficiently general so that each individual has something to contribute, whose value can be assessed only as enters into the final pooled intelligence constituted by the contributions of all. Every authoritarian scheme, on the contrary, assumes that its value may be assessed by some *prior* principle, if not of family and birth or race and color or possession of material wealth, then by the position and rank a person occupies in the existing social scheme. The democratic faith in equality is the faith that each individual shall have the chance and opportunity to contribute whatever he is capable of contributing and that the value of his contribution be decided by its place and function in the organized total of similar contributions, not on the basis of prior status of any kind whatever.

I have emphasized in what precedes the importance of the effective release of intelligence in connection with personal experience in the democratic way of living. I have done so purposely because democracy is so often and so naturally associated in our minds with freedom of *action*, forgetting the importance of freed intelligence which is necessary to direct and to warrant freedom of action. Unless freedom of individual action has intelligence and informed conviction back of it, its manifestation is almost sure to result in confusion and disorder. The democratic idea of freedom is not the right of each individual to *do* as he pleases, even if it be qualified by adding "provided he does not interfere with the same freedom on the part of others." While the idea is not always, not often enough, expressed in words, the basic freedom is that of freedom of *mind* and of whatever degree of freedom of action and experience is necessary to produce freedom of intelligence. The modes of freedom guaranteed in the Bill of Rights are all of this nature: Freedom of belief and conscience, of expression of opinion, of assembly for discussion and conference, of the press as an organ of communication. They are guaranteed because without them individuals are not free to develop and society is deprived of what they might contribute.

What, it may be asked, have these things to do with school administration? There is some kind of government, of control, wherever affairs that concern a number of persons who act together are engaged in. It is a superficial view that holds government is located in Washington and Albany. There is government in the family, in business, in the church, in every social group. There are regulations, due to custom if not to enactment, that settle how individuals in a group act in connection with one another.

It is a disputed question of theory and practice just how far a democratic political government should go in control of the conditions of action within special groups. At the present time, for example, there are those who think the federal and state governments leave too much freedom of independent action to industrial and financial groups, and there are others who think the government is going altogether too far at the present time. I do not need to discuss this phase of the problem, much less to try to settle it. But it must be pointed out that if the methods of regulation and administration in vogue in the conduct of secondary social groups are non-democratic, whether directly or indirectly or both, there is bound to be an unfavorable reaction back into the habits of feeling, thought and action of citizenship in the broadest sense of that word. The way in which any organized social interest is controlled necessarily plays an important part in forming the dispositions and tastes, the attitudes, interests, purposes and desires, of those engaged in carrying on the activities of the group. For illustration, I do not need to do more than point to the moral, emotional, and intellectual effect upon both employers and laborers of the existing industrial system. Just what the effects specifically are is a matter about which we know very little. But I suppose that every one who reflects upon the subject admits that it is impossible that the ways in which activities are carried on for the greater part of the waking hours of the day; and the way in which the share of individuals are involved in the management of affairs in such a matter as gaining a livelihood and attaining material and social security, can not but be a highly important factor in shaping personal dispositions; in short, forming character and intelligence.

In the broad and final sense all institutions are educational in the sense that they operate to form the attitudes, dispositions, abilities and disabilities that constitute a concrete personality. The principle applies with special force to the school. For it is the main business of the family and the school to influence directly the formation and growth of attitudes and dispositions, emotional, intellectual, and moral. Whether this educative process is carried on in a predominantly democratic or non-democratic way becomes, therefore, a question of transcendent importance not only for education itself but for its final effect upon all the interests and activities of a society that is committed to the democratic way of life. Hence, if the general tenor of what I have said about the democratic ideal and method is anywhere near the truth, it must be said that the democratic principle requires that every teacher should have some regular and organic way in which he can, directly or through representatives democratically chosen, participate in the formation of the controlling aims, methods, and materials of the school of which he is a part. Something over thirty years ago, I wrote: "If there is a single public-school system in the United States where there is official and constitutional provision made for submitting questions of methods of discipline and teaching, and the questions of the curriculum, text-books, etc., to the discussion and decision of those actually engaged in the work of teaching, that fact has escaped my notice." I could not make that statement to-day. There has been in some places a great advance in the democratic direction. As I noted in my earlier article there were always in actual fact school systems where the practice was much better than the theory of external control from above: for even if there were no authorized regular way in which the intelligence and experience of the teaching corps was consulted and utilized, administrative officers accomplished that end in informal ways. We may hope this extension of democratic methods has not endured but has expanded. Nevertheless, the issue of authoritarian versus democratic methods in administration remains with us and demands serious recognition.

It is my impression that even up to the present democratic methods of dealing with pupils have made more progress than have similar methods of dealing with members of the teaching staff of the classroom. At all events, there has been an organized and vital movement in the first matter while that in the second is still in its early stage. All schools that pride themselves upon being up-to-date utilize methods of instruction that draw upon and utilize the life-experience of students and strive to individualize treatment of pupils. Whatever reasons hold for adopting this course with respect to the young certainly more strongly hold for teachers, since the latter are more mature and have more experience. Hence the question is in place: What are the ways by which can be secured more organic participation of teachers in the formation of the educational policies of the school?

Since, as I have already said, it is the problem I wish to present rather than to lay down the express ways in which it is to be solved, I might stop at this point. But there are certain corollaries which clarify the meaning of the issue. Absence of participation tends to produce lack of interest and concern on the part of those shut out. The result is a corresponding lack of effective responsibility. Automatically and unconsciously, if not consciously, the feeling develops, "This is none of our affair; it is the business of those at the top; let that particular set of Georges do what needs to be done." The countries in which autocratic government prevails are just those in which there is least public spirit and the greatest indifference to matters of general as distinct from personal concern. Can we expect a different kind of psychology to actuate teachers? Where there is little power, there is correspondingly little sense of positive responsibility. It is enough to do what one is told to do sufficiently well to escape flagrant unfavorable notice. About larger matters, a spirit of passivity is engendered. In some cases, indifference passes into evasion of duties when not directly under the eye of a supervisor; in other cases, a carping, rebellious spirit is engendered. A sort of game is instituted between teacher and supervisor like that which went on in the old-fashioned schools between teacher and pupil. Other teachers pass on, perhaps unconsciously, what they feel to be arbitrary treatment received by them to their pupils.

The argument that teachers are not prepared to assume the responsibility of participation deserves attention, with its accompanying belief that natural selection has operated to put those best prepared to carry the load in the positions of authority. Whatever the truth in this contention, it still is also true that incapacity to assume the responsibilities involved in having a voice in shaping policies is bred and increased by conditions in which that responsibility is denied. I suppose there has never been an autocrat, big or little, who did not justify his conduct on the ground of the unfitness of his subjects to take part in government. I would not compare administrators to political autocrats. Upon the whole, what exists in the schools is more a matter of habit and custom than it is of any deliberate autocracy. But, as was said earlier, habitual exclusion has the effect of reducing a sense of responsibility for what is done and its consequences. What the argument for democracy implies is that the best way to produce initiative and constructive power is to exercise it. Power, as well as interest, comes by use and practice. Moreover, the argument from incapacity proves too much. If it is so great as to be a permanent bar, then teachers can not be expected to have the intelligence and skill that are necessary to execute the directions given them. The delicate and difficult task of developing character and good judgment in the young needs every stimulus and inspiration possible. It is impossible that the work should not be better done when teachers have that understanding of what they are doing that comes from having shared in forming its guiding ideas.

Classroom teachers are those who are in continuous direct contact with those taught. The position of administrators is at best indirect by comparison. If there is any work in the world that requires the conservation of what is good in experience so that it may become an integral part of further experience, it is that of teaching. I often wonder how much waste there is in the traditional system. There is some loss even at the best of the potential capital acquired by successful teachers. It does not get freely transmitted to other teachers who might profit by it. Is not the waste very considerably increased when teachers are not called upon to communicate their successful methods and results in a form by which it would have organic effect upon general school policies? Add to this waste that results when teachers are called upon to give effect in the classroom to courses of study they do not understand the reasons for, and the total loss mounts up so that it is a fair estimate that the absence of democratic methods is the greatest single cause of educational waste.

I conclude by saying that the present subject is one of peculiar importance at the present time. The fundamental beliefs and practices of democracy are now challenged as they never have been before. In some nations they are more than, challenged. They are ruthlessly and systematically destroyed. Everywhere there are waves of criticism and doubt as to whether democracy can meet pressing problems of order and security. The causes for the destruction of political democracy in countries where it was nominally established are complex. But of one thing I think we may be sure. Wherever it has fallen, it was too exclusively political in nature. It had not become part of the bone and blood of the people in daily conduct of its life. Democratic forms were limited to Parliament, elections, and combats between parties. What is happening proves conclusively, I think, that unless democratic habits of thought and action are part of the fiber of a people, political democracy is insecure. It can not stand in isolation. It must be buttressed by the presence of democratic methods in all social relationships. The relations that exist in educational institutions are second only in importance in this respect to those which exist in industry and business, perhaps not even to them.

I recur then to the idea that the particular question discussed is one phase of a wide and deep problem. I can think of nothing so important in this country at present as a rethinking of the whole problem of democracy and its implications. Neither the rethinking nor the action it should produce can be brought into being in a day or year. The democratic idea itself demands that the thinking and activity proceed cooperatively. My utmost hope will be fulfilled if anything I have said plays any part, however small, in promoting cooperative inquiry and experimentation in this field of democratic administration of our schools.

Chapter 2

THE PREMISES UNDERLYING EDUCATION

WHENEVER *any group dominates an educational institution, the institution will, of course, reflect the social policy of that group. From Colonial times, America has had public and private groups whose interests required them to establish and manage schools of their own. Many justifications for the existence of publicly and privately endowed education have appeared throughout the years. Almost all present-day justifications are based upon agreements used in the past. For our purpose, the thesis offered by Van Cleve Morris, a philosopher, clarifies the relationship of education as a socializing institution of the democratic ethos.*

Morris suggests that there are two sets of premises upon which contemporary education, both private and public, rests. The first set accounts for the existence of all forms of public and private education. According to Morris, "Education makes a difference in the development and destiny of a human individual." A group with strong religious or moral convictions wants its children to learn and live by them. Such a group often builds its own schools. Since individuals must live in groups to become human, it follows that "education makes a difference in the development and destiny of the human group." The public welfare is determined by the achievements of each individual, and consequently, a society is obligated to create and maintain agencies to educate its people.

The second set of premises moves from these generalities to a discussion of the educational needs of a democratic society. These premises conclude that "democracy rests upon an enlightened citizenry" and "democracy as a way of life (rather than a political system) requires the widest possible degree of shared concerns among its people." Furthermore, the shifting role of the family in contemporary American society has produced sharp changes in the nature of parental responsibility. Since many families no longer accept certain responsibilities, "the family as a social institution has surrendered its educational capabilities to the state." Present-day thinking about the democratic way of life reflects the historic experience of Americans. "Education has always been public; it is the only kind of education there is; and it is therefore the only design for education to take."

THE PHILOSOPHICAL PREMISES UNDERLYING PUBLIC EDUCATION

Van Cleve Morris

The public school of our time stands beleagured behind a frail fortress. Constantly embattled by a critical public, it finds itself a great share of the time on the psychological defensive. It is in desperate need of a theoretic justification of its existence stated in cultural, political, and social terms. What educators everywhere must now boldly assert and explain to the lay community is a working rationale for the rise and widespread establishment of education as a public function in the modern civilized world. If this rationale can be laid out, if it can be shown that modern civilization depends in a special and peculiar way upon the public-izing of this well-known human activity, we may be on our way to a clearer grasp of the troubles that beset us with respect to the jeopardy in which the public school finds itself today.

Whatever the philosophical premises of public education may be, some of them necessarily refer to cultures and political systems of all types and not simply to Western cultures or to societies which call themselves democratic. By this I mean that some of the philosophical premises upon which *public* (as against private) education stands do not limit themselves to democratic ideologies, even though we know that in these ideologies, public education has found its strongest friends and consequently its most rapid growth. There are, however, other premises that have special application to free and open societies. And since we live and have our political and social being in such a society, this essay shall consider these also.

Reprinted from *Progressive Education,* Vol. 34, No. 3 (1957), pp. 69–74.

TWO KINDS OF PREMISES

This paper, then, takes up two groups of premises which underlie public (and, by association or contrast, private) education. The first group, consisting of two, relates to general assumptions underlying education itself, and I shall try to show that one of these assumptions seems related to private education, the other providing a basis for public education. The second group, consisting of four, relates more specifically to education in democratic communities.

In attempting to open discussion and to focus initial attention upon those premises which support education in general, it is appropriate to refer to Professor John Childs. His clear and persuasive book *Education and Morals* lays down the bedrock ideas upon which all teaching and learning eventually rest. He supplies both of the premises in our first group: first, that education makes a difference in the development and destiny of a human individual, and second, that education makes a difference in the development and destiny of a human group.

> . . . men everywhere reveal by their actual deeds that they regard the immature human being as the kind of creature who should go to school. This universal tendency to organize and support schools is a concrete expression of the basic human conviction that patterns of conduct and personality are not wholly predetermined, but are created, at least in some significant sense, by experience. . . .[1]

What happens to human beings, what they do, and what they undergo, in some measurable and significant manner, conditions what they become. It is because men everywhere believe this that they send their youngsters to places called schools.

But:

> Schools are also public testimony to man's faith in the possibility of control over his own destiny. They are founded because man believes that he has some measure of power to shape the course of his own ways of living. A school system is organized whenever a human group begins to become conscious of its own experience, and desires to select from the totality of its beliefs and practices certain things which it is concerned to preserve and foster by reproducing them in the lives of its young. In other words, the organization of a system of schools signifies the deliberate attempt of a human group to control the pattern of its own evolution.[2]

And finally to sum up, Professor Childs says:

> In fine, the enterprise of education is founded in two basic and interrelated faiths—faith in the modifiability of the human form, and faith in the possibility of controlling the human enterprise in the interest of cherished ends, or values.[3]

[1] New York, Appleton-Century-Crofts, 1950, p. 5.
[2] *Ibid.*, p. 5–6. [3] *Ibid.*, p. 6.

These two basic premises, so deeply rooted in the modern mind as to be almost too obvious to mention, support what we attempt to do in educating the human person. But there is more to it than this, for it is possible to connect the phenomenon of public education much more intimately to the meaning of these premises.

EDUCATION AND HUMAN DEVELOPMENT

We assume in the first instance that it is possible to modify the human form. And we all know that to modify, in any intelligent sense, means to improve, and there is plenty of room for improvement in this human animal. But the improvement and development of any given human being is pretty much a concern of that individual himself or the family which is raising him. Developing that particular individual is not ultimately required for the on-going life of society. Of course, in the Christian ethic there is a well-known injunction to concern oneself with the fulfillment of the needs of others, and the democratic tradition speaks in similar language. But at root this first premise makes no special demands and does not indicate whether education should be formal or informal, public or private.

The point is that this first premise—that education makes a difference in the development and destiny of the human person—if anything, gives support to private education. Each individual is his own master; each should be the architect of his own character; and thus each should be free to seek or not to seek education. In a strict and abstract sense, the *Public* (with a capital P) is indifferent to the fortunes of any given individual, except where its own welfare is involved, and is therefore unconcerned with whether that individual educates himself or not.

EDUCATION CAN CHANGE HISTORY

Now the proviso above, "except where its own welfare is involved," is the key to the second premise and to the subsequent rationale for public education. For the welfare of the Public is inextricably interwoven with the welfare of individuals, their state of enlightenment, their condition; in short, with the quality of their total experience. The Public fortunes, therefore, rest ultimately upon the fortunes of the members of the body politic, and it therefore becomes prudent, indeed mandatory, for the Public to take measures to see to it that each individual educates himself as fully as possible. It is only when these measures are taken that the second premise takes on operational meaning; a culture becoming conscious of its own experience employs the instrument of education to perpetuate its values and to render its future less precarious than it would otherwise be. A culture takes hold of its own experience, fortifies it, re-charges it, and transmits it to oncoming generations, having faith that through educational means its future will consist of that which is consciously and deliberately achieved rather than that which is haphazardly and accidentally fallen into.

We all have these two faiths about education—that it can change people and that it can change history. If we didn't, it is doubtful we would spend so much time, energy, and treasure on it. And we can discern in the second premise that the Public has a vital concern in this undertaking. It is not correct to say, therefore, that we have public-ized education in America out of some socialistic impulse to save money or equalize wealth. We have socialized education because we realize our national destiny is dependent upon it; we have understood from the beginning that without an enlightened people we cannot become an enlightened civilization.

PREMISES OF DEMOCRATIC EDUCATION

Now when it comes to education as an instrument of a *democratic* culture, the premises narrow themselves considerably. Of course, there has always been a kinship between politics and education, but this is particularly so in a democratic community, and the kinship is especially intimate. At this point it is necessary to shift terminology slightly, and we are now to speak of universal education rather than public education. Since universal education is almost always public it is doubtful there will be any danger of misinterpretation.

Premise No. 3 can be stated as follows: Democracy rests upon an enlightened citizenry. By way of analyzing this premise and showing its modern application, it should be helpful to recall that this premise has not always held as special a place in men's minds as it apparently does today.

There have always been two more or less antithetical theories with respect to the survival of the democratic state. One view, the Platonic view, holds that what democracy needs to insure its perpetuity is enlightenment at the "top," among the ranks of leadership. Indeed, the common man is incapable of enlightenment; he must depend upon the enlightened leader whose cares and concerns embrace those of the common citizen. Only in this way can a free and democratic society sustain itself. We know, of course, that the educational and political design for such a society was first put together by Plato in *The Republic*. Although never spelled out in detail, the plan was to provide a general education for all youngsters of the state early in childhood so as to uncover gifts and talents which further education might reasonably exploit. The individuals sifted out in this manner and surviving through several educational steps, some of which would correspond to our "on-the-job" training, would finally emerge at the age of fifty as philosopher-kings. These individuals were the guardians of the state constituting the liberal and enlightened leadership upon which democratic institutions would depend for growth and survival.

Thomas Jefferson became enraptured with this general view, evidently, for he envisioned a very similar arrangement for education in America. Of course, he was intensely sensitive to the strategic role that education plays in social life as is revealed by his oft-quoted dictum: "If a nation expects to be ignorant and free, in a state of civilization, it expects what never was and never will be."[4] And it is true that he was a vigorous champion of wider public access to channels of information and instruction:

> No one more sincerely wishes the spread of information among mankind than I do, since none has greater confidence in its effect towards supporting free and good government.[5]

JEFFERSON PLATONIC OUTLOOK

But Jefferson nevertheless still lived in the shadow of an aristocratic look at life, and his politics as well as his education assumed an aristocratic shape. He distinguished between an artificial aristocracy which characterized Europe and the natural aristocracy—the aristocracy of "virtue and talents"—which he felt was democratic, and it was one of his primary political doctrines that only the wise and prudent, the talented and gifted, should find their way into government. In consequence, any educational system which managed to sift out and train the natural, intellectual aristocracy was a system consistent with democratic ideals. For this reason, we can say that, with the exception of politically inspired preachments of a popular nature sloganizing in favor of general and universal education, most of Jefferson's educational ideas had to do with the training of this intellectual elite and to the raising up of a corps of civil servants whose depth of understanding and grasp of political and social problems would equip them for leadership in this republic.

The result of all this was that the founding fathers, in the thralls of Jeffersonian-Platonic thinking, believed that a free society must ultimately rest upon an enlightened ruling class rather than an enlightened populace. Consequently the educational forms which have grown up in the United States since the founding of the Republic have generally been Jeffersonian forms, i.e., principally devoted to the abler group of youngsters.

CONFLICT BETWEEN JACKSONIAN AND JEFFERSONIAN PREMISES

But about mid-way in the nineteenth century there was an important shift in popular thought with respect to the nature of government. This shift, sometimes attributed to the influence of Andrew Jackson, was manifest in a

[4] *Democracy*, Thomas Jefferson, Saul K. Padover, ed. (New York: Appleton-Century Co., Inc., 1939), p. 137. (In a letter to Colonel Yancey, 1816.)

[5] *Ibid.*, p. 231. (In a letter to Hugh L. White, 1810.)

growing belief that what democracy needed was not a ruling class of special talent and ability but an enlightened electorate, a people with enough political sensitivity to recognize civic competence when they saw it. Slowly, this attitude took hold, and the nineteenth century was an era of widening the sources of education and extending the instruments of political privilege to the masses of the American people. One of the greatest contributions to this movement, as we know, was the public school, locally controlled, and supported by taxes levied against the general population. Especially at the secondary level was the rise of the universal school so remarkable, and today upwards of ninety percent of our high-school-age citizens attend school. Jefferson could not be expected to have anticipated such a thing.

But the Jeffersonian and the Jacksonian conceptions of education, "the one valuing opportunity as the nurse of excellence, the other as the guard of equity,"[6] have been and are today in constant conflict in the mind of the American educator, and many if not most of our educational ailments in America can be traced to this fundamental division in educational and political philosophy. Nevertheless, Premise No. 3 has been stated in Jacksonian terms, and advisedly, for although secondary and higher education in the United States are still operating on Jeffersonian policies, the current of theory and practice at the elementary level is definitely Jacksonian and the mood of the educational community seems to me to favor the Jacksonian emphasis upon educating *all* American youth. Of course, the big question is whether these two ideas must necessarily be incompatible. Can the American school do both jobs simultaneously? We shall probably have to wait to see.

We have been speaking largely in political terms, in terms which indicate that a political system which calls itself democratic necessarily relies heavily upon the formal and legal institutionalization of instruments for disseminating information. Since the school is especially qualified for this work, its alliance with democratic political systems is seen to be quite necessary. But there is perhaps a wider and more profound attachment that any democratic community has to universal education, and it may be more appropriately suggested by the word "social" or "sociological" in place of the word "political." Democracy is not only a political mechanism; it is also a way of life. It is an ethos of human relationships, a special social climate in which free and responsible human desires can find fulfillment. Democracy in this sense is extremely difficult to define or describe, but one of its basic necessities is what we might call "the sharing of experience."

DEVELOPING SHARED CONCERNS

With this introduction we can now state Premise No. 4: Democracy as a way of life (rather than a political system) requires the widest possible

[6] Harvard Committee, *General Education in a Free Society* (Cambridge: Harvard University Press, 1948), p. 34.

degree of shared concerns among its people. Educators hear a lot these days about "sharing." It has become a standard cliché in the professional lexicon. But in a deeper and more critical meaning, the idea of sharing has considerable philosophic significance. Dewey, in his *Democracy and Education*, devotes a full chapter entitled "The Democratic Conception of Education" to the elaboration of this idea, and in substance his point is this:

> . . . [Democracy] is primarily a mode of associated living, of conjoint communicated experience. The extension in space of the number of individuals who participate in an interest so that each has to refer his own action to that of others, and to consider the action of others to give point and direction to his own, is equivalent to the breaking down of those barriers of class, race, and national territory which kept men from perceiving the full import of their activity. These more numerous and more varied points of contact denote a greater diversity of stimuli to which an individual has to respond; they consequently put a premium on variation in his action.[7]

What this tight and compact terminology means of course is that only through the widest possible exposure to the concerns of others, can the individual gather the fuel to fashion his own behavior and build his own life. If self-realization is a defensible object of a human life, then the wider an individual can share in the experiences of other human lives the deeper and richer will be his experience. It is because modern democratic culture (particularly the American variety) has contrived the most efficient technological and social mechanisms for the dissemination and sharing of experience that we believe we live fuller lives than primitive, isolationist man. And one of the finest of these mechanisms is the universal public school. What Dewey is saying is simply that isolationism, *per se* and of whatever type, is antithetical to the meaning of democracy; education, universal public education, is its most effective antidote.

It is perhaps appropriate at this point to summarize what we have done. We have dealt with four philosophical premises underlying public education. We might give them labels:

1. The psychological premise—education can make a difference in the shaping of human personality and character.
2. The cultural premise—education can make a difference in the historical destiny of a human group.
3. The political premise—democratic self-government requires an enlightened and educated electorate.
4. The sociological premise—the democratic way of life demands open channels of communication and widespread sharing of life's concerns among individuals.

What remains to be done?

[7] New York, Macmillan, 1916, p. 101.

FAMILY DISINTEGRATION

At a somewhat more immediate level, there may be mentioned a couple of other premises which might require our attention. They refer to the adjective "public" in its more literal sense. Premise No. 5 therefore is as follows: The family as a social institution has surrendered its educational capabilities to the state. Whether we like it or not, to me it is irrefutable that the family in American life is no longer capable of the educative function. This is so for a great number of reasons; we cannot go into all of these here, but a few observations may help to document it.

The educative function in the first place has been enormously confounded by the mere quantitative growth of knowledge and by the ever-increasing complexity of our knowledge. Not only that but the period of infancy has been constantly lengthening and the variety of educational experiences available to youth is practically without number. But more important than any of these perhaps is the changing character of the family itself. No longer the producing unit of society, the family is a loose-knit arrangement of individuals who have no genuine *group* function other than co-habitation. There is no corporate purpose, no associated interest around which their educational lives might possibly develop. The bread-winner is at a distant location performing operations generally quite mysterious to the children and oft-times to the spouse. The wife, a manual laborer for a good part of the day, finds little stimulation in the routine tasks of modern housekeeping. We see therefore in our day the disintegration of the family not only as an educational unit but as a recreational and social and religious unit as well.

Of course, candor requires us to recognize that our new-found devotion to public education is the result not only of our recognition that as parents we are very poor teachers but also the somewhat uglier discovery that in this sophisticated, well-ordered and antiseptic age we do not cherish the company of children as much as we used to. Since the rough-and-tumble frontier days, adults have changed, children have not, and we are just as glad that the public school can take them off our hands for the major part of the day.

EDUCATION IS PUBLIC

We turn now to a final premise, one which unfortunately is more difficult to distill out of the many practices today which indicate its presence. Maybe it is difficult to locate and identify because it is after all not a premise which helps to rationalize our commitment to public education but only a habit of thought we have gotten into. If the above can be called rational rationalizations, we have now to examine an "unrational rationalization." I refer to a tentative Premise No. 6 which might be stated as follows: Education has always been public; it is the only kind of education there is; and it is therefore the only design for education to take.

This popular and widespread layman's notion is deliberately included here, even though it is hopelessly incorrect and erroneous, because much of the strength of public education in America is founded on this blind and uncritical mentality which, viewing things as they are, concludes that that is what they ought to be.

This is not mere facetiousness, even of a scholarly sort. American life embraces many peculiar paradoxes which can be explained in no other way. Take for instance, the problem of public medicine. All of the previous five premises, if applied to man's physical rather than psychic being, would hold for *public* medicine equally as well as for public education. But we know that one of the biggest political squabbles of our day is the attempt to public-ize our medical institutions. We still take the position that health is a private, individual affair, while education is a public, group affair—a most unrational, unscientific, and, to many people, undemocratic point of view. It is difficult to explain this peculiar paradox except to lay it to the psychic habits of a cultural group. We have simply gotten into the habit of viewing medicine as private and education as public, and that's about the size of it.

One doesn't have to look very far to see other examples of habitual unrationality. In a recent pamphlet on education published by the National Association of Manufacturers the following appears:

> With governmental support and control there is inclined to be less consideration of minority wishes by the majority, more dependence on the advice of professional experts than on purely local considerations, and more inclination to follow current political and sociological ideologies which may not be approved by some individualists.[8]

It is clear the author of this sentence has never been to his local school; for if he had made the visit he would find quite the opposite. At that school which is governmentally supported and controlled he would find all kinds of minorities, even the minorities of one, being soothed and placated by the agent of the majority, the principal; instead of experts in every corner, he would find just ordinary folks (probably arranged in discussion groups!) trying honestly to solve the troublesome problems of teaching boys and girls; and, to crown all, instead of visionary ideologies clogging the educative process, he would discover a group of timid and frightened teachers who would hesitate to admit even a membership in the League of Women Voters; if, of course, they were members; which, of course, they are not.

[8] Educational Advisory Committee and the Educational Advisory Council of the N.A.M., *This We Believe About Education* (New York: The National Association of Manufacturers, 1954), p. 12.

What the public-izing of education has done to the teaching profession is not at all lovely to behold, and educators may be able to understand though not support the medical profession when it fights the public medicine movement as vigorously as it does. All the doctors have to do is look around the corner to see how the socialized profession of teaching is making out.

But, while *un*reason may have taken hold in many departments of our social life, there is fortunately enough reason left to give support and purpose to the idea that education is and must continue to be public in both outlook and practice. Education takes pride, the medical profession (and others) notwithstanding, in its socialized character. It was built deliberately and with farseeing intention as a social instrument. Its primary raison d'etre is to serve the larger community. The premises which rationalize its work are the premises which support every effort of man to civilize himself and to render corporate social life both creative and humane. Any movement toward these ends is undertaken in the name of fulfilling its public and social purpose.

Chapter 3

THE SOCIAL MILIEU AND EDUCATION

THE *central purpose of American education is to provide individuals with the theoretical and practical knowledge they need to live democratically in the national and international communities. Students must learn as much as they can understand of the ramifications and nuances of the political, economic, social, and cultural forces in the world. The world today is divided among societies striving to achieve, in their own ways, positions of strength and power. The roles and responsibilities of the individual are complicated and intensified by man's conquest of time and space, which forces very different kinds of societies to live close together. For instance, today even modest expressions of nationalism and patriotism cause reactions across the world—and such conceptions are seldom expressed modestly.*

During the last few hundred years, historical epochs have been described in such terms as "The Industrial Civilization," "The Technological Revolution," "The Atomic Age," and "The Age of Anxiety." It could not be otherwise, for science and technology have remade a large part of man's traditional culture. However, the point is that only part of American culture has been changed. Influences from our rural, agrarian past coexist with the conditions of a mass, industrial, urban present, and thoughtful men, particularly educators, must think long and hard about the resulting problems. These are aggravated and intensified by the complex ties that bind this society to diverse societies across the world. The need to maintain communication among all the citizens of our society, and with democratic and nondemocratic nations elsewhere, has produced complicated problems for the educator—problems that do not lend themselves to easy, logical analysis and readily formulated solutions.

The attainment of the democratic ethos as a way of life is not only a "good" for Americans, but is also a "good" for all people. While that is certainly a presumption, it has considerable historical and psychological support. Unfortunately, this political ideal has been and is being subverted by advocates of expediency—some of them inheritors of the democratic dream—who work with limited objectives and questionable standards of value. It is important to emphasize that the most serious problems faced by democracy center upon man's relation to man. These problems force us to study how and why any individual interacts with all the possibilities of an evolving present. The quality of this interaction influences the climate of the learning environment for students and educators, and consequently affects thinking and personality. Educators, as mediators of the culture, are required to help students find values that will stabilize and clarify their activities.

In tracing the influence the scientific-technological revolution has had upon our culture, George S. Counts, a social scientist, delineates "seven stark realities" that require immediate attention: (1) time and distance have been conquered to the extent that the entire world may now be regarded as a neighborhood in which all individuals and groups are forced by circumstance to interact with each other; (2) the colonial peoples of the world, especially people of color, are now seeking equal status and will not rest until they attain first-class status; (3) the locus of economic, technological, military, and political power has shifted from western Europe to Russia and the United States and there is every indication that an additional shift will take place; (4) totalitarianism in the form of communism is effectively challenging the role of democracy; (5) because of technological advances, war today threatens the existence of world civilization and this threat hinders the establishment of a viable world community; (6) scientific and technological advances have given people power over material things, over the human mind, and over the life process itself sufficient to enable men to control all aspects of living; and (7) the cultural lag in our society has produced many intense conflicts.

EDUCATION AND THE TECHNOLOGICAL REVOLUTION

George S. Counts

In the first place, the whole earth has been reduced to the dimensions of a little neighborhood. As a result of this development we may say that a major cycle in the life of man is closing in our time—a cycle which embraces hundreds of thousands, possibly a million years. It opened in that long-forgotten age, aeons before the dawn of recorded history, when man moved out from his place of origin, from some Garden of Eden, to occupy and sustain himself in practically all parts of the earth. In the process of migration, settlement, and adaptation, combined with the operation of factors of geographical barriers, great distances, and isolation, the several races and varieties of the human species, the many languages, religions, cultures, and political systems were formed.

For some time now, probably since the voyages of Columbus and Vasco da Gama, and particularly during the present epoch, this ancient tendency toward separation and differentiation has been reversed. In terms of means of communication and life conditions that bind men together into communities and societies, the whole earth is no larger than that tiny Garden in which man first ate of the fruit of the tree of knowledge of good and evil, and thus became man. And the divers members of the human family, with their long heritage of rivalry and conflict, of prejudice and hatred, are being pressed together in this tiny garden. As a consequence, the lot of each, including ourselves, is being joined in ever-growing measure with the lot of all. From this condition there is no retreat. We in the Americas in particular must realize that the great oceans, east and west, that protected us for centuries do so no longer.

In the second place, the colored peoples of the earth are rising everywhere, from Harlem to Tokyo and Timbuktu. So, a second great cycle, embracing approximately five hundred years, is passing into history. At the beginning of this period the light-skinned peoples of Europe were in imminent danger. Indeed, to the mythical visitor from Mars it might have appeared at the time that they stood a good chance of being either enslaved or driven into the sea. The Tartars still occupied much of Russia; the Moors were still en-

Reprinted from *Teachers College Record,* Vol. 59, No. 2 (March 1958), pp. 314–318.

trenched in Spain; and the Ottoman Turks were striking boldly and powerfully at the southeastern gates of Europe. Then, owing to a number of factors, one of which was certainly revolutionary inventions in the modes of warfare and another the advance of nautical science, the tables were turned. These Europeans took the offensive. They threw off the Tartar yoke, expelled the Moors, halted the advance of the Turks, discovered and conquered the New World, took possession of the islands of the eastern seas, swept over the Dark Continent, and penetrated the vast expanses of Asia. By the end of the nineteenth century they held nine-tenths of the land surface of the globe and dominated the remainder. As a result of their fabulous successes, they developed a sense of unqualified superiority, identified themselves with the advance of civilization, and assumed that they were destined by their own nature to rule the "lesser breeds" of man forever.

Again the tables are turning. The surviving colonial empires of the eighteenth and nineteenth centuries, the British, the French, and the Dutch, are in process of dissolution. And the colored peoples will not be satisfied until they have achieved equal status among the nations. Nor will they be satisfied until they have removed the last vestige of imputed inferiority which the power of the white man forced upon them.

In the third place, the center of gravity of industrial, military, and political power has already shifted from Western Europe, where it had rested during the modern period down to the end of the nineteenth century. It has shifted east and west, to Russia and the United States. Six of the eight so-called great powers which ruled the world fifty years ago have been reduced to the status of secondary powers by the wars of our period. The fiasco of the British and French attack on Egypt in the autumn of 1956 reveals to all eyes how the mighty have fallen. At present only two great powers remain. If they were alike in their traditions, institutions, and basic values, the situation would be critical, as any student of history would know. Thus, Charles A. Beard, the great historian, wrote to me on July 13, 1945, before the war was over in the east: "The sky is clear and ominous: only two mighty armed powers are on the horizon. What impends and with what portents? Day and night, I wonder and tremble for the future of my country and mankind." We have reached the point in history foreseen by Alexis de Tocqueville in 1835. Speaking of the Russians and the Americans, he wrote: "Their starting points are different, and their courses are not the same; yet each of them seems marked out by the will of Heaven to sway the destinies of half the globe."

That this situation will change in the decades ahead is clear. We may expect to see the renewal of the British Commonwealth, the integration of the West European states, and the rise of new great powers perhaps in China, India, Brazil, and possibly in other regions of the earth.

In the fourth place, the whole world is threatened by a powerful and ruthless totalitarian movement—Soviet Communism. Stemming from the Russian Revolution of 1917, this movement constitutes a strange and dynamic synthesis of an old Russian revolutionary tradition, out of which Bolshevism came, and Marxian doctrines, Russian expansionism, and Russian Messianism. With a sense of mission rarely equalled in history, the Soviet leaders see the eventual spread of Communism over the entire earth under their inspired guidance and through the extension of Soviet power. Their triumphs during and following the war in advancing their dominion in eastern Europe and Asia confirm these men in their doctrines. The death of Stalin and the rise of Khrushchev to power should deceive no one on this point.

Today the members of the tiny oligarchy in the Kremlin, which holds sway over practically one-third of the human race, believe with the fanaticism of religious conviction that the forces of history are working swiftly and inexorably on their side. They are profoundly convinced that "all roads today lead to Communism." Through their own Communist Party of the Soviet Union and the network of Communist Parties embracing practically all countries they are subjecting to implacable and pitiless attack the liberal and democratic forces of the world. With cold and careful calculation and guided by the ethics of battle they are promoting strife and unrest everywhere beyond the borders of their own domain. And as they excoriate the decaying imperialisms of the past they seek to fasten on mankind a new imperialism far surpassing in rigor and ruthlessness the colonial systems of the nineteenth century. In Hungary in October and November, 1956, they presented to the world a perfect exhibit of their methods, morals, and purposes.

In the fifth place, war threatens the very survival of civilization. Here is the supreme question confronting mankind in the second half of the twentieth century. While in the past the great destroyer has devoured and enslaved many tribes and peoples, today it places in jeopardy the entire human adventure. We know that total war, waged with the rapidly advancing military technology and with that spirit of ruthlessness which in our lifetime has greatly weakened the sense of mercy and humanity, threatens all the ways and values of civilized life. We know that it constitutes the most dangerous threat to the survival of civilization that mankind as a whole has ever encountered. We must remember that the earth today is a little neighborhood.

Unless this terrible scourge is driven from the earth, no civilization worthy of the name can be expected to endure. Otherwise, with the earth growing ever smaller and the engines of death ever more destructive, preparation for war may become the all-absorbing interest of mankind until the arrival of that fateful day when time shall be no more. A few short years ago we were contemplating the awful moment when, perhaps without warning, great cities would be consumed in the purple and orange holocaust of atomic explosion. Now we have the so-called hydrogen bomb, which, if let loose in the world, might exterminate the entire population of the earth and render it uninhabitable for centuries. As to what dreadful weapons may lie beyond the veil that mercifully shrouds the future, even distinguished scientists can only speculate. During the present respite, how long or short we know not, we have our chance of building a just and lasting peace.

In the sixth place, the advance of science and technology has put in the hands of men fabulous power for peaceful uses—power over material things, power over the life process, power over the human mind. In 1835, according to the German engineer and economist Leo Hausleiter, the total capacity of machines in the world was approximately 650,000 horsepower. By 1900 in the United States alone the figure stood at 70 million, and by 1935 at over 1 billion. Today it cannot be far from 2 billion. If one horsepower is reckoned as equal to the power of twelve men, this means that the American people have working for them over 20 billion mechanical slaves, almost ten times the total population of the earth. And Leland Olds, formerly chairman of the Federal Power Commission and a life-time student of mechanical power, has recently predicted that power consumption in the United States "might increase six to eight times by 1970." When we consider that the age of atomic energy, electronics, and automation is upon us, we can see that not only the contours of the economy, but also the contours of labor and leisure, of our whole way of life are certain to be radically transformed. At this point we are reminded of the observation of Aristotle: "If every tool when summoned could work of its own accord, as the creations of Daedalus moved of themselves or the tripods of Hephaestus went of themselves about their sacred work; if the weavers' shuttles could weave of themselves; then the master workers would need no apprentices, and the landlords would need no slaves." Today, of course, in many respects we are far beyond the vision of the ancient philosopher.

Power over the life process is almost equally impressive. Unquestionably the advance and application of medical science constitute one of the glories of our civilization. Our fathers and mothers of the eighteenth and early nineteenth century had little more control over the life process than the people of antiquity. They multiplied without restraint, they lived on a monotonous and badly balanced diet, they were mowed down by disease, and they grew old in middle age. The average expectation of life in the most advanced communities and regions was between thirty and thirty-five years. Today most of the dread diseases of the past have been banished, control over births is widely practiced, and the life span has been raised to seventy years. With further developments in chemistry and the biological sciences, the time may not be far distant when man will be able to fashion himself into whatever image may strike his fancy. Given the present level of our ethics and our social organization we can view such a possibility only with deep misgivings.

The increase of power over the human mind constitutes, from the standpoint of free society, one of the most crucial problems of the age. Such a society rests not only on guarantees of individual security from the violence of mobs and the arbitrary acts of government, but also on general conditions of life that make possible the development of informed and independent judgment. The advance of technology has created new and powerful instruments of mind control; and the entire process of mind-forming has become more and more organized, or at least subject to organization. The individual has become increasingly dependent for information, political ideas, and social attitudes, upon organized education and the new media of mass communication, particularly the daily press, the comic, the movie, the radio, the television. That these new agencies have enormous power has been demonstrated in our time by both advertising agencies and totalitarian states. If conducted with a high sense of public duty, personal integrity, and devotion to truth, they may serve mightily to promote enlightenment, understanding, and good will within the nation and throughout the earth. In a world as vast in its reaches, as complicated in its structure, and as dynamic in its movements as ours, they are indispensable to the successful functioning and perhaps the very survival of a democratic society. They are also equally indispensable to the totalitarian state.

We enter the atomic age with minds formed largely in pre-industrial times. And the fact must be emphasized repeatedly that the strange technological civilization which has burst upon mankind so suddenly and which is sweeping across the world so swiftly is still in its early stages. In certain of its phases it is far more advanced than in others. Our functional ideas, our moral conceptions, and our social organization lag seriously behind our modes of livelihood, forms of communication, use of mechanical energy, and scientific knowledge. This lag is doubtless responsible for many of the troubles and conflicts of our time. It is certainly the underlying source of the more powerful and disrupting tensions to be observed within our domestic society and among the nations of the world. Today a great gulf stands between many of the stubborn realities of our emerging industrial civilization and our customs, loyalties, understandings, and outlooks. It has been said that "distance has been annihilated, but the sense of distance remains." This could be said of so many things in the world today. The task of bringing our old minds into accord with the facts of the new world is a gigantic and urgent educational undertaking. Indeed, we shall not know peace and serenity until this is accomplished.

The possibility that democratic values will be used to resolve the problems described as the "seven stark realities" assumes that students can become the kind of people who are able to act like democrats. Full participation as citizens requires that, on the basis of formal education and other experiences, individuals display initiative, wisdom, judgment, insight, and perspective in a manner consistent with the democratic ethos.

R. Bruce Raup, a philosopher, phrases the central problem confronting educators thus: "Can democracy generate enough effective power with people—with the peoples of the world—to compete successfully with the demonstrated power of totalitarian regimes?" The proponents of democracy are obligated, in order to achieve success, to utilize human power to "become a democratically power-wise people." In support of this thesis, Raup offers a definition of the power of democratic people in which anti-democratic behavior is characterized as low-power and democratic behavior as "high octane." The essential elements of the democratic ethos require men to use their strength for the welfare of the community. This has not yet been done. People are still unable to deal effectively and realistically with what Raup describes as the "short circuits of human power" and the factors that cause them. He believes that if we understood our inadequacies, we would formulate and implement a democratically viable program of education.

In viewing the inadequacies of the American social scene, Raup argues that the following "short circuits in the human power relation" may well destroy democracy: (a) "the complexity of public affairs and the gulf between the public and the public leader"; (b) "the availability of instruments of compulsion by force—military devices, means of torture, and secret police methods"; (c) "the gigantic competition of powerful interests (national, religious, and economic, particularly) for the power that inheres only in the people's community of persuasion, and the consequent fear of each that the other will get there first"; (d) "the susceptibility of the public to appeals couched in over-simplified, stereotyped, emotional language"; (e) "the maladjustment, ranging from egomania to social cowardice, that warps the personalities of individuals"; (f) "the 'Esau' temptation"; and (g) "the lack of effective ways and means for public deliberation on matters in which action is being taken." Raup suggests that the task of the educator is two-fold: (1) to assist individuals in the resolution of the problems imposed by the "short circuits"; and (2) to develop personalities mature enough to undertake positive action in the interest of the community.

EDUCATION AND POWER

R. Bruce Raup

First, the term "power" for present purposes has very definite limits. I am not speaking of physical forces, often called, interchangeably, the forces of nature and the powers of nature—electrical power, steam power, motive power. I am dealing rather with human power, with power as it appears in the relations of man with man—the phenomena of power in persons, in groups, in peoples. It is in this connection that there is a revival of interest today and that education builds upon important assumptions.

In the background of all we can say or do today in regard to human power is one dominating issue. I put it in the form of a question: Can democracy generate enough effective power with people—with the peoples of the world—to compete successfully with the demonstrated power of totalitarian regimes? This is a pervasive source of tension. Almost every phase of our lives is actually or potentially affected by the strain it is producing. All of our current public efforts (and many private ones), including our education, are colored by uncertainties that arise from this underlying issue. I am convinced that democracy cannot meet this challenge while it continues merely to *play* at the serious business of human power. It can succeed only if it will make it its business to understand the nature of human power, the conditions of its adequacy, and the means of its achievement. We must, deliberately and with no false modesty, become a democratically power-wise people.

DEMOCRATIC POWER DEFINED

Charles E. Merriam writes:

> . . . in the new world into which we are madly rushing no single factor in life will be more important than the composition and incidence of political power, and no task more urgent than the understanding and utilization of a force whose mastery may mean light or darkness for individuals and for civilization.[1]

Merriam, after many years of studying what thinkers had written about human power (especially political power), thought it best not to venture a nice definition of the term. Better, he thought, just to locate typical phe-

Reprinted from *Teachers College Record*, Vol. 51, No. 8 (May 1950), pp. 500–511.

[1] Charles E. Merriam, *Political Power* (New York: Whittlesey House, McGraw-Hill Book Company, Inc., 1934), p. 14.

nomena of power and describe them. But as he went on writing he did tend to do a bit of defining. He says:

> . . . power does not lie in the guns, or the ships, or the walls of stone, or the lines of steel. Important as these are, the real political power lies in a definite common pattern of impulse. If the soldiers choose to disobey or even shoot their officers, if the guns are turned against the government, if the citizenry connives at disobedience of the law, and makes it even a virtue, then authority is impotent and may drag its bearer down to doom. Power withdraws from its physical externals, beyond its symbols, lurking somewhere behind its material defenses. It is a creature of habits, of culture patterns woven deeply into the lives of men. . . .[2]

Here, an effort to *locate* power merges into something approaching a definition. Power is the effectiveness of a commonly persuaded group. This is of utmost importance as a near definition of power.

Bertrand Russell, equally a student of the literature on human power, is more bold. He does frankly venture a definition. Power, he says, is "the production of intended effects." While this may be a bit too refined for my present purposes, I hold it to be most helpful and suggestive. Russell is saying that power is analogous to what the physicist calls energy. We do not *see* the energy; we see "work" done, and this is as close as we can come to defining it. So he says, of human power, that we see something of a kind that is done, and this is as close as we can come to defining human power. It is "the production of intended effects." Now this is close to what Merriam says. If anyone tries to produce something with people, he will find that he can be effective only if that something is in line with patterns deep within the common, habitual structure of the people's characters. Emphasis is upon the word "common."

Thus, a definition of power, as applied to man's relations with man—following the suggestions of these two authors and putting it satisfactorily to myself—comes to be: *Power is effectiveness in producing intended results with people.*

Another writer, Harold Lasswell, suggests a further point to be added to a working definition of power. He says: "The degree to which 'x' influences a decision measures the power of 'x'." (*Power and Personality*, p. 18) He emphasizes the phenomenon of human power as it appears closer to the scene of action, that is, in connection with decision. Lasswell encourages me, therefore, to add something to our definition: *Power is effectiveness in producing intended public choices and decisions.*

Now, with this definition in mind, let us ask: What of our assumption that power can be more democratic and more effective at the same time? For, as believers in democracy this must be our assumption. This locates what we most need to know. How can a people with the ideals of democracy

[2] *Ibid.*, pp. 7–8.

realize the power they need in the world today and tomorrow? Merriam set us well on the way to an answer to this question. Since power, as he indicates, is in the deep common persuasions of the people who are controlled and directed by it, the measure of the power in any case is in the degree to which these persuasions *are* deep and common. We have more popular ways of saying this. For example, we say that if a leader is finally to get something done in society, he has to have the people back of him. But while this popular way of speaking has its values, the more considered definition will be better for our purposes. It will serve as a criterion. It is a way of telling whether the power relation at any point needs to be corrected in order to reach its maximum. And it does more than this. It indicates how the corrections may be made. It also suggests what maximum power would be in any case and where something might be done to move toward that maximum.

By our definition, there are two chief actors in the power relation: (1) the instigator of what is intended, and (2) the people concerned in what is intended. The first might be called the leader. The second the public. The noting of these two actors gives us a clue. We can ask what the behavior of each should be if a maximum of power is to be realized, that is, a maximum of effectiveness in the production of intended public choices and policies and decisions. And we have seen that this means how each should behave in order to achieve a maximum of *common* public persuasion and intention in what is chosen and decided upon. For we must keep in mind that the degree of this community of intention is the measure of the power. In the "mathematics" of power, the denominator of the fraction is always this community of persuasion and intention. The numerator always indicates the degree to which in any case there is an approach to maximum power.

Let us say that the denominator is 100. It is clear that public decision can be and often is made at a low fraction of maximum power. In a "prison" state, the instigator is largely indifferent to the degree of community of intention. He makes the rules. His public accepts or else. It must do or die. Even in this case, however, there is *some* fraction. It may be 5/100. In a prison there are limits to which the rulers can go without the consent of the ruled. In the most dictatorial political regimes, this fraction is usually much higher. Merriam emphasized this point. Dictators must get their power from the deep habitual patterns woven into the lives and characters of people. So much is this the case, that it presents a fruitful way to think about power. The power of even the most absolute of rulers is just whatever this community allows him. But this community may not be a community of intention. This means that people might acquiesce, while if left to their own preferences they would not go the same way. All of us know Germans who went along with the Nazi rulers but who would not, of their own accord, have chosen to go the same way. Thus we often have a conformity with only a small fraction of common intention. Assent, acquiescence, conformity without community of intention mean low-level power. Consent with community of intention is "high octane."

It is clear that democracy is ideally conceived to run on high octane—high community of persuasion and intention. Then why be concerned? The answer to this is that in the field of human power there are some extremely difficult obstacles to the realization of a high octane status. We have not learned to realize the power potential of democracy. I am proposing that we can overcome the obstacles and actualize this power potential only if we will keep clearly in mind just what it is—the community of persuasion and intention of those controlled by it. Confusion on this point weakens us. Concentration upon it, I believe, is the real "atomic" secret of the success of democracy in the world.

SHORT CIRCUITS OF HUMAN POWER

In our confusion, we run after false gods and up blind alleys. We are lured by short cuts to power. Instead of generating and channeling power directly, we work a strange wizardry of criss-cross devices and continually make ourselves liable to the power-sapping effect of short circuits and to the conflagrations that often result therefrom.

From this viewpoint, study the great variety of instigators of public policy—leaders, if you wish—note the pressures upon them, and the temptations they suffer to short-cut the route to genuine power. The short cuts most commonly taken are exploitation through deceit, and compulsion by force. The principal motivations are fear and the love of possession and power. The conditions which make such exploitation and compulsion possible are: (1) the complexity of public affairs and the consequent distance between the public and the public leader; (2) the readiness to hand of the instruments of compulsion by force—military devices, means of torture, and secret police methods; (3) the gigantic competition of powerful interests (national, religious, and economic particularly) for the power that inheres only in the people's community of persuasion, and the consequent fear of each that the other will get there first; (4) the susceptibility of the public to appeals couched in oversimplified, stereotyped, emotional language; (5) the maladjustment, ranging from egomania to social cowardice, that warps the personalities of individuals; (6) the "Esau" temptation (the mess of pottage); (7) the lack of effective ways and means for public deliberation on matters in which public action is being taken.

We have, thus, three areas of inadequacy to understand and to do something about if we would realize the potential power of democracy: (*a*) the principal short cuts to power, (*b*) the motivations to their use, (*c*) the conditions which are conducive to these short cuts and motivations.

The following diagram should help to keep in focus these several important parts in the dynamics of democratic power. With it before us, several of the conditions named under (*b*) and (*c*) will be taken up to see how they appear in the experiences of everyday life.

It is important to remember that intended public choices and decisions *can* be produced at almost any level on this scale. The conditions to be taken up are those which today operate most seriously to keep us functioning at a low level and which must be reckoned with if high-level democratic power is to be realized.

DYNAMICS OF DEMOCRATIC POWER

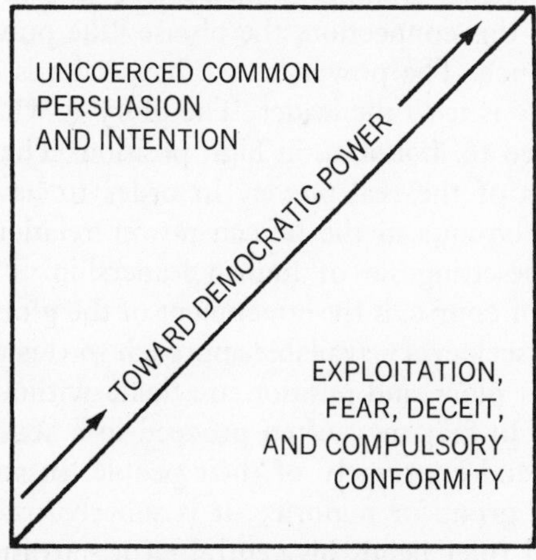

First, note the pervasiveness of fear. Fear is an emotional state we get into when forces beyond our control threaten to do us injury of some kind. The depth psychologists know how deep, subtle, pervasive, and often senselessly exaggerated fear becomes in the personalities of people. In a condition of fear we are apt to become even less able to control the forces and avoid the threats. We do irrational things. We take short cuts to safety. We misconstrue the threatening force. Carefully considered conduct becomes more and more difficult.

In the world today there are so many forces that threaten—forces beyond any present means of control—that the irrationalities of fear assert themselves and intensify our susceptibility to low-grade power. We use every device to run to cover, to protect our possessions, our ways of living, our lives. We respond to the unknown, the unfamiliar, with diseased imagination. We have been told that the reason horses shy off the road at the appearance of some small object on the side is that such an object takes on enormous proportions in horses' vision. I do not know whether this has been verified about horses, but I do know that fear transforms unfamiliar objects in the environment of men into ogres. And man responds as to an ogre. This is one of the chief motivations of resort to force, compulsion, deceit—to low-grade ways of getting the power of the united public on our side.

The other principal motivation to short cuts is the love of possession and power. Probably these two—love of possession and love of power—are eventually reducible to love of power. Both possession and power establish the possessor in a position in which he can work his will and make his choices with the backing of the public concerned. So sweet is this power that men will do strange and dangerous things to gain it and keep it. As I look at what happens to leaders in this connection, the phrase "the power and the glory" gains a new significance. The power, as we have said, is just the degree to which the community is *with* the leader. The glory is what goes with being the central one looked to, honored, in high position. The glory of position is often far in excess of the real power. In order to have the glory, men often contrive short circuits in the human power relation. Glory on short human power is a besetting sin of human leadership. The relation at the "high-octane" level, of course, is the attachment of the glory to the maximum power. *Great* leaders seek every available approach to this maximum relationship. They know that glory and position are fickle without it. They seldom seek the glory itself. In fact they often proceed in a way which elicits the hysterical resistance and contumely of their people. In an individual leader or in a leading small group or minority, it is soberly true that power corrupts. Every rightful ruler bends his central efforts to the establishment of the conditions of his own eventual abdication. I believe it is impossible for a person or a minority to stay in power for long without so short-circuiting the power relation as to sap and drain it. The relation will move downward. I believe it is in the nature of the case that power in society held by an individual or a minority over a long period of time will turn corrupt when by corrupt is meant the position of glory and control at a low level of power. Even the most rigorous self-criticism and the most open and good-willed mind and character are incapable of long sustained adequacy in being the chief instigator or clearing house of the policies and decisions and choices a people make.

Power at a low level often is achieved through wealth and possession. By means of such possession the consent of more people to one's own wishes and proposals is made available. The possessor can be more effective in producing public choices and decisions. This motivation is so well known for its production of power at a low level that I need little more than mention it. It induces men to resort to deceit, exploitation, and force to keep what they have. Wealth, possession on a level higher than that of others, makes the others always a threat. Men fear this threat. They are uneasy. There is no one quite so insecure as those who *have* when surrounded by those who have not. The Marxist has made this observation into an inevitable course of events. The *haves*, he says, will fight, destroy before they yield to the threats of the *have nots*. How many of our customs and laws have grown up to protect the *haves* from the *have nots?* Penalties for stealing property are extremely severe.

And men will resort to deceit and exploitation through propaganda, advertising, sharp practices, armies, navies, wars—to protect themselves in the having and holding. Thus the great web of low-level lines of power over the choices and decisions the public makes.

LOW MOTIVES MADE EASY

We turn now to some of the chief conditions which make men so susceptible to the low-power behavior that is motivated by fear and the passion for possession and power. First is what we might call the *distance* between the people and the leader, between the public which is involved in the decisions and the leaders who instigate them. This works two ways. The leader cannot possibly know and have a feeling for the human conditions surrounding the policy or decision he is proposing, and the public generally, incapable of working the matter through, just goes about its familiar affairs and is in effect indifferent. This is often called public apathy. Whatever we name it, there is such a distance between the leader and the public that there is almost unlimited opportunity and temptation to short-cut the power relation. Men do this and then rationalize it. They say the mass of the people is incapable; leaders will just have to keep people satisfied with slogans and sops while they go about what they want to do. This procedure is low enough in the power scale, even when the principles of the leader are otherwise high. But the depth becomes serious when this distance is taken advantage of to serve some personal privilege or to favor some exploiting interest.

It is not necessary to go into national or international relations to discover this condition. It can be found in a state, a city, a county, a rural village, a society, a club, a school system, a school, a home. The increasing complexity of the human situation makes achievement of needed understanding a gigantic task, even in one locality. The constantly more refined division of labor makes the preoccupation of people with their little jobs so absorbing that the larger scope of the power relation becomes a foreign domain. So long as this condition is unresolved, the power relation is destined to be maintained on a low level. The public's policies and decisions will be wrought with limited and unconsidered public consent. The small interested group and the unprincipled political person can work to deceive and exploit the public in the policies made and carried out. And the policies made will have police powers of the state back of them. This is far down the scale in power.

The second condition is the existence of armies, military systems, and highly effective secret police systems. After World War I, a group of public-spirited people created a committee to study and report on the Causes and Cure of War. This committee's chairman, Carrie Chapman Catt, stated that while the causes of war were discovered to be many and various—more than one hundred and fifty were listed—all seemed, upon closer analysis, to reduce to one—the existence of big military systems in the countries concerned. Even though this statement must be considered extreme and oversimplified, its emphasis cannot be ignored. The claims of military maintenance upon the economic, political, occupational, and general social and ideational structure of a society are wide, deep, and persistent; they are strengthened by a rationale of threatened emergency and by the coercive power of the state; they tend to be guaranteed by interests of all kinds which become vested in their fulfillment. And the only business which can ever justify this octopus is war or the threat of war. The outbreak of war throws it into high gear.

Although conditions in the world today may make us feel the need for keeping ourselves armed heavily for defense, under such circumstances it is even more important to be alert to the potentialities of armed systems for *creating* wars. My chief point is that militarism has a meaning in the human power relation which requires eternal vigilance. The public's deep involvement in the means of war leads the public to be more ready to resort to war than to deliberative means of settling disputes. It is from this very real succession of events and not from some other-worldly source of truth that man gathers the wisdom of the saying, "He that taketh the sword shall perish by the sword." We cannot hope to succeed if we seek to resolve all other causes of war first and then remove the military systems, for the latter are *a*, if not *the*, chief cause. The vicious necessity for their continuation intrenches conditions which compound to hold human power at its lowest level. Ready resort to violence is man's power enemy number one.

The third condition which creates fears and compulsions by force, and thus leads to taking short cuts to power, is the existence of deep cleavages within a people or between peoples. In the world today the parties to such a cleavage know that they must have the support of the world community. This is true whether the cleavage is nationalistic or economic class or religious or ethnic or racial. There is, therefore, a mad scramble for power; to get there first. But what does *there* mean? It means the assent of the peoples of the world. And if that assent cannot be had one way, it will be sought in another. The winner must have it. Thus, world-shaking bets are being made: totalitarian dictatorship on the one extreme; blithe trust in laissez faire on the other. The lesson of the past twenty-five years is that totalitarianism has enormous capacity for creating effectual, low-level power; that is, for getting a public to the point of readiness for making decisions intended by its leaders. Must other peoples, those who have rejected dictatorships and aimed toward democracy, resort to the same totalitarian strategy in the great struggle today for the assent of the peoples of the world? This is an unsolved problem. Democracies can no longer be indifferent to the meaning and cultivation of power. The cleavage conditions in the world are leading to the invention of short cuts to power which will be the curse of man for centuries to come unless something is done about them. I do not propose particular solutions. I am only seeking a clearer viewpoint from which to work at the problem. We should not be blind to the claims of the ascending scale of human power upon any decision of the moment. Each new decision should find us as peoples able to operate a notch farther up toward the higher levels.

A fourth condition is public susceptibility to stereotypes and the staggering extent to which the agency of propaganda has been developed. In order to think about things and events which are widely inclusive and distant, we have to generalize, simplify, and symbolize. But symbols—verbal symbols—easily become stereotypes, and can be used as agencies of the greatest misdirection and human cruelty. This is so well known that I need do little more than mention it. Leaders have found that they can produce a people who will, even contrary to their own good, make the very public decisions and choices they as leaders want. They do it with words that make up minds and release directed action. They deceive, exploit, and, as dictators, reduce the ugliness of physical enforcement by a synthetic production of a mind that "elects" to do their will. This is one of the chief agencies of cold war. In recent decades it has assumed proportions which rank it among the foremost resorts ready at hand for those who are moved to short-cut the human power relation. It gets superficial common assent—conformity—not the informed, considered common persuasion and intention which mark the choices at the higher levels of the power scale. It is common action without a foundation in genuine communication. In fact, it can be achieved only by studied prevention of thorough and basic communication.

This refinement of the means of dictatorship and coercion presents to the educator of democracy an unprecedented task. The individualism of our tradition is not a complete answer to this new means of public development. Deliberate thought control on a public-wide basis will not die out. It is a power device which we can assume has come to stay. The corrective of it does not lie solely in the reassertion of individual critical-mindedness, essential as this still is, but also directly in the field of the common public mind itself. In brief, it has become imperative to learn as educators how positively and most effectively to further the development of the kind of common persuasions which are found toward the top of the scale of power. This task will have a terminology peculiar to it, one different in some respects from the wording of our aims and methods in cultivating critical-mindedness in the individual. The purposes of public education need appropriate restatement. The goals of citizenship, the conceptions of desirable personal character and of effective intelligence—these are already yielding here and there to the requirements of a more adequate attainment of human power. And this translation into the language of a thoroughgoing democratic authority has only begun.

The fifth of the conditions to be noted as generating short circuits in the human power relation is man's proneness to warping depth-disturbances in personality. With all of the valid emphasis upon the social determiners of self and personality, and again, giving full and due weight to the claims of the community upon the individual, it is well to keep in mind that once formed the self *is* a self, the personality *is* an individual personality, and that as such the individual can have a tremendous generative influence in the reconstruction of the common persuasions which make up the public of which he is a member. Things crystallize in him. What he gathers into himself he makes over into an image peculiar and unique. In self-defense or in self-realization he tends to reshape the human medium, to make it more congenial to himself.

When this individual personal character gets badly misshapen within, we now well know that it strains and pushes, irrationally, often entirely unbeknown to itself, to reconstitute the community of its fellows into forms in which it hopes for better satisfaction. This is one way to understand the individual's hunger for power in his own right. He gains personally by being effective in shaping things and people to his own patterns of liking. He idealizes the kind of community in which *he* would be better satisfied. The power of one person thus for good or harm should never be underestimated. In the present setting, it should be noted as another of the chief causes of dangerous short cuts in the human power relation.

One illustration may well be both clarifying and sobering. Can anyone doubt that great evil would have been spared all mankind if some well-informed and wise teacher of young children and youth, somewhere during the school years of young Schicklgruber in Austria, had discovered the quirks of maladjustment deep in his personal character and set in motion the correctives that were needed? But *every* individual personality is in his own measure an influence projected into his community, eliciting that which is required for the satisfaction of his urges and preferences. He tends to create a community in his own image. What a person *is* by way of conduct, quality, and emphasis serves to elicit some responses, not others, from his fellows. Nazi Germany was not inevitable; it was just *possible*. If someone other than Hitler, or if a readjusted Hitler had called to Germany, another Germany, also potentially there, would have responded. Never underestimate the resources in an individual either to short-cut or to raise the level of human power.

Granting all the differences of view today in this field of depth-psychology, there is still great hope to be placed in the understanding it can put at the educator's disposal. And if we are going to be intelligent about education and human power, we have no reasonable choice but to avail ourselves and our schools of these understandings.

There is a sixth condition which encourages resort to power short cuts—man's susceptibility to the "Esau" temptation. Esau was hungry. As the elder son he had a right to inherit the holdings of his father. Jacob wanted this property. He knew Esau was hungry. He got Esau to sell to him his birthright for a mess of pottage. The immediate need and the present though short-sighted interest gave the trickster his chance. Jacob got the power. Esau got the mess of pottage. Esau was then soon without power to claim for himself more pottage to meet his continuing and mounting need. Jacob's achievement was far down indeed on the scale of human power.

Peoples are being promised economic sufficiency if they will just yield the control of their lives and their destiny to the promising leaders. We in America have in a most distinctive way the birthright of democratic power, a right of choosing, selecting, and deciding upon the course of our lives—a function which we may never fully or irrevocably delegate to any ruler or rulers. The satisfaction of a need of the moment, the preciousness of material gain, the promise of security, of equal distribution of wealth and advantage, of collective power—these too readily make Esaus of us all. Americans today have a pressing responsibility to protect their birthright of democratic power and to project it with added effectiveness into the patterns of power that are being worked out by the peoples of the world. From the nursery school through the university we need to be learning how to cultivate this birthright and protect it against the bribe of ready economic advantage.

The seventh of the things that make us too ready for power short cuts is our present incompetence for realizing the fuller measure of power. There is much that we do not know about how to achieve the higher levels of performance. We can study and work to curb and correct the corruption of power that comes from the six sources named. This is an important beginning, but only a beginning. For study of each of these ways in which power "goes wrong" has served by contrast to emphasize what the course of a healthy power would be. This is the educator's chief clue to his task. His work is not primarily therapeutic; it is positive and preventive. Acting with and for his whole people, he will seek to institute these positive measures with a momentum sufficient to carry them forward in their own right.

We can simplify the thought of this complicated task and get it into a manageable pattern for directing action by remembering always that its great common denominator is thoroughgoing communication. The power that is greatest of all is in the common persuasion of people who are free and equipped to conclude and decide for themselves. Community of this basic kind is dynamic; it is always a composite of different stages in the untiring process of coming to have and to maintain important things in common. The seven noted enemies of this process point us to their opposites, which outline a positive program of education in power.

Chapter 4

THE AMERICAN PARADOX

DEMOCRACY *works when each citizen, acting as an individual and as a member of various groups, understands what knowledge is of most worth and struggles to live by it. This behavior places a premium upon many skills and abilities. The citizen must be able to use all available pertinent data in defining issues. He must be able to design and apply solutions, to appraise the results obtained, and to derive new ideas from what he has done. When this happens, both individual and group living are enriched and enhanced. A humanitarian frame of reference and the skilled use of related and relevant knowledge are basic to such action.*

All men can act this way, not just a select few. A rational human being, with the passion and courage to use ideas on behalf of individual well-being and for the general welfare, is a proper goal of education. Although American educators are supposed to teach everyone how to think, and to base action on thinking, society has often been hostile toward those who strive to solve political, economic, social, and cultural problems in rational ways. Despite this animosity, America continues to produce a full quota of intellectuals who demonstrate quite clearly the values to be derived from the practical applications of ideas. This conflict between theory and practice, described by Merle Curti as the "American paradox," is commonly referred to as "anti-intellectualism." Often a brake on the development of creative intelligence, it continues to weaken the contributions that education and educators can make to human welfare.

Harold Taylor, a philosopher, is concerned with the role of ideas in the daily life of the citizen and the significance of ideas in the educative process. He believes that ideas are the basis for action and postulates that there are two types of individuals in American society: (1) the man of practice who is concerned with the development, refinement, and application of knowledge without concern for the undergirding ideas, and (2) the man of ideas, who devotes all his time and energy to developing new concepts for the public good. Of special significance to American students and teachers are these three ideas: The intellectual life is justified by the democratic ethos; intellectuals can rise from any group in the society; through intellectual activity America can continue to achieve a more rewarding way of life for its citizens and for the rest of the world. In elaborating upon his thesis, Harold Taylor raises and answers the following questions: "What is an intellectual?" "What are the responsibilities of the intellectual?" "What functions can the intellectual perform for society?"

THE INTELLECTUAL IN ACTION

Harold Taylor

I begin with a comment by the Greek citizen Pericles, who had so much to do with the public life of Athens.

> Unlike other cities, Athens expects every citizen to take an interest in public affairs; and, as a matter of fact, most Athenians have some understanding of public affairs. We do believe in knowledge as a guide to action; we have a power of thinking before we act, and of acting too, whereas many peoples can be full of energy if they do not think, but when they reflect they begin to hesitate. We like to make friends abroad by doing good and giving help to our neighbors; and we do this not from some calculation of self-interest but in the confidence of freedom in a frank and fearless spirit. I would have you fix your eyes upon Athens day by day, contemplate her potentiality—not merely what she is but what she has the power to be, until you become her lovers. Reflect that her glory has been built up by men who knew their duty, and had the courage to do it. Make them your examples and learn from them that the secret of happiness is freedom, and the secret of freedom, courage.

This is also the secret of Athens' greatness in the greatest days of Greek civilization. I believe that what Pericles has said is profoundly true. We all know what he means when he says that people can be full of energy when they do not think, but when they reflect they begin to hesitate. The man of action, or the man who is doing well and who feels happy with things as

"The Intellectual in Action," by Harold Taylor, is reprinted with permission from the September 1958 issue of the *Bulletin of the Atomic Scientists*. Copyright September 1958 by the Educational Foundation for Nuclear Science, Inc., 935 East 60th Street, Chicago 37, Illinois.

they are, is annoyed to be asked to reflect on himself, or he senses danger to his own situation in the possibility that he may be wrong.

This in a real sense is the reason for the suspicion held in some quarters of America for the intellectual. The intellectual, the social critic, the thoughtful citizen, put things in doubt. They question what exists, and make anxious those who have adapted themselves fully to what exists. The kind of self-confidence needed by a person or a country is the kind which has a frank and fearless spirit, which has no fear of being questioned or criticized. There is a difference, of course, between self-confidence and complacency. Complacency wishes to ignore criticism, to prevent it, or to explain it away. It is thoughtless and mindless, and it is based on self-interest.

WHAT IS AN INTELLECTUAL?

Self-confidence is built upon an honest appraisal of the reality of things. It is based on the belief in knowledge as a guide to action. The union of thought and action, the creation of the ideal from the materials of the real, the desire to imagine what *can* be in place of what *is*—these are the elements of a philosophy which defines the true intellectual in action.

We have no separate intellectual class in this country, and it is my hope that we never will. The ideal society is one in which the citizens think for themselves and do not want others to do their thinking for them. There are, of course, intellectuals in every society, and there are intellectuals in America. But in America they do not form a class of political or social leaders whose function it is to think for the rest. Many of our political leaders take pride in not being intellectuals and take pains to make it clear that they are regular Americans without any intellectual connections. The intellectual in America is tested by his society in the same way as anyone else—by his ability to perform the tasks he undertakes. If he is a novelist, can he write books which are interesting, which have in them the ring of truth, which compel the attention of the reader to the image of human life which they proclaim? If he is a newspaper writer, can he get down the facts, can he perform his task of informing the reader? If he is a composer, can his music command the attention of musicians, can he write for opera, for full orchestra, for dancers? If he is an educator, has he anything to say which can persuade his listener or evoke a response toward the ideas he advocates?

In that case, who is the American intellectual? He is to be found in many areas of American society. The writer, certainly, the novelist, the editor, the poet, the playwright, the movie and television writer, the teacher, the government official, the scientist. But every scientist and every teacher, for example, is not an intellectual. A person who teaches or who carries out research may perform his task without a serious interest in the ideas with which he operates. An intellectual, in other words, is a person who is interested in ideas and carries on a serious intellectual life of his own. If he has no private world of ideas, he is merely a practitioner or a technician in the field of ideas.

There are corporation executives who are seriously interested in the theory and practice of corporate enterprise, in economics, in political philosophy, in public affairs, and are among the American intellectuals. I submit that the man who wishes to make a contribution to his society, whether as an office-worker, a carpenter, or a college professor, must have some degree of interest in ideas and some degree of ability to deal with them. Otherwise, he has eliminated the dimension of his life which has to do with himself as a person, his citizenship, his sense of public responsibility, his relation to his own time. It is for this reason that I believe that every boy and girl must have a full opportunity for education, not merely for vocational training, but for sharing in the intellectual life of his society, in whatever degree his capacities and interests may allow.

The ideal for American society is therefore one in which the intellectual and aesthetic interests of the citizens are an element in the daily life of the country. For this reason I welcome the mass culture which is so often despised by our social critics, and I believe that the spread of mass culture through television, radio, magazines, and newspapers and every part of the mass media is a significant part of the development of America as a civilization. For a similar reason I welcome the impending expansion of our college population, without fear that in such an expansion our intellectual standards will be lowered and our educational system debased.

This is not to say that I look to a time when the interests of our most advanced intellectuals—research scientists, historians, poets, philosophers, or writers—will be shared by the entire population. This is not a natural or attainable goal, since those who are at work in particular areas of intellectual advancement must by definition be involved with ideas which will not be immediately available to everyone. It is to say that the dissemination of ideas and the enjoyment of art on a mass scale has a positive effect on raising the level of intellectual interest and information by the total population. By putting more of our young people and the adult population into the stream of mass culture we do not debase standards, we create new possibilities for the development of higher standards. It is the responsibility of the rest of us who already make some claim to intellectual interests and values to seize every opportunity to encourage the spread of thinking, whether this be carried out in the home, in the community, at PTA meetings, in the school, in adult education courses, in television, radio, magazines, or college.

RESPONSIBILITIES OF THE INTELLECTUAL

Education, today, is being talked about, debated, discussed, argued, and even advertised in such volume that sheer weight of attention is bound to bring reforms in a positive direction. If we, as interested citizens, intellectuals, and educators, do not add our voices to those now being heard, it is our own fault. We have been given the opportunity. It is up to us to take part, to speak up, to express conviction. If we do not speak up, it must be either that we are afraid to, or that we have nothing to say. I have little patience with the argument that this country is anti-intellectual. What country is not, merely by the fact that no country as yet has a system of public education which can involve all of its citizens in an interest in ideas and cultural values? Of course, there is anti-intellectualism. But it is not to be overcome by a retreat from the issues, nor by condemning mass culture and the sins of the advertisers.

Let me turn for a moment to one sector of the educational front—the sector occupied by college professors. We hear more about their salaries than about their ideas, although, of course, we must speak fiercely and urgently about salaries. But, at the present time, money is what college presidents and college professors talk about, while businessmen, admirals, and bankers talk about education.

"The function of a teacher," says Alexander Meiklejohn, "is to stand before his pupils and before the community at large as the intellectual leader of his time. If he is not able to take this leadership, he is not worthy of his calling."

If a teacher allows that leadership to be taken away from him by others—by politicians investigating colleges, by pressure groups who try to silence him, by those who speak more loudly outside the schools and colleges—this means simply that he is not fulfilling his mission as a teacher and an educator. It is the task of the intellectual to express his view of the world in his own way and to celebrate the possibilities in human existence. I believe that it is because teachers in the colleges have not considered their task to be that of exercising intellectual, social, or cultural leadership before their pupils and before the community at large that their pupils and the community at large have become content with what they find around them, have accepted the values of their own society, and have sought success in material terms.

OUR CULTURE—AS THE YOUNG SEE IT

"Success for me," says one student who speaks for many of his contemporaries, "would mean a job I could leave after eight hours and that would provide for self-fulfillment within a framework of inconspicuous luxury."

Now surely this is an over-modest demand, and much less a demand than the young should be making. The demands are not less because this generation is less idealistic than its predecessors. It is more talented, better educated, better able to handle its problems, and is genuinely concerned with human values. But it has been taught by its society to recognize the advantages of material success and personal security, but not the means of translating idealism into productive action. This seems to me to be the responsibility of the contemporary teacher.

I turn to another student, with a different view of life and a different view of his society. He is speaking of the culture he finds around him, in his university and in his country.

Everywhere is blah, and when our own blah stops like a toy that has run down, we turn on television and the phonograph to stuff the void. Everywhere, in the subway, in the airport waiting-room, in rest rooms even, the music plays and races through our veins like a file of ants—but only while the Wurlitzer whirls. When we run out of dimes, when the joint closes up for the night, not one beat remains in our bones. Only a pre-dawn inquietude. But, happy to report, we are slowly erasing this unpleasantness from our daily schedule: with the pocket-sized radio, we soon will never walk alone.

We have no other-rooms, no private dens, we do not have the back-shops Montaigne advised all men to keep: our hearts are public houses. . . .

Wine needs time and the darkness of a cellar. But the minute we receive any juice at all, we spill it out before it can assume an intoxicating dimension: hence the flatness of our speech and of our lives. . . .

If this is the character of our culture, as seen by the young, if, in fact, all the generalizations about conformity, security-mindedness, complacency, and banality are true—what is the solution? How do we get nonconformity, boldness, daring, excitement, flavor, freshness, originality?

Again, it would be easy to condemn. But we have had much of that. It is a negative time. But the question is, What do we do?

LET THE POEM SPEAK FOR ITSELF!

One thing we who are in the colleges can do is to concern ourselves with the life of the intellect and the imagination again, and remind ourselves *and* the public that the purpose of education is to develop people who can think and act for themselves. We have become so engrossed in the practical problems of education and the culture that we find our teachers talking only of "problems"; we have become lobbyists for the intellect, full of promotional devices for advertising the virtues of the humanities, the sciences, or foreign languages. Even in our teaching we have been pressing for attention to cultural and aesthetic values rather than allowing the values to be seen, enjoyed, and savored by ourselves and our students. We must let the poem speak for itself, in its own purity and enchantment, without our eternal explanations and analysis. Let the music be played and listened to, without explanation, with no set of instructions on how to listen, what to look for. Let the idea generate its own response in the minds of our listeners, let them see for themselves that the idea itself is passionately held by the man who proposes it. There is too much concern for classifying, and thus defeating, the new. When a few young Englishmen say bitter things about their own society and the place of the intellectual in it, they are immediately classified as Angry Young Men, who, in fact, are less angry than unhappy and complaining. When a group of American writers and poets give us a model for a life of drugs, travel, jazz, and mystic experience, we confuse and elevate their meaning by classifying them as a Beat Generation. This is intellectual promotional work, not creative thought or contemporary literature.

W. H. Auden spoke in his poetry lecture last year at Oxford of a teacher of Anglo-Saxon who had lectured to him.

"I do not remember a single word he said, but at a certain point he recited, and magnificently, a long passage of *Beowulf*. I was spellbound."

I think we need to have more people spellbound, entranced, joyful, enchanted. They need not stay that way permanently, but they need to know from direct experience what it means to be captured by a feeling or an idea. If we are overimpressed by money and material values, if our culture is lacking in spiritual content, then is it not the task of the artist, the architect, the dancer, the playwright, the philosopher, the composer, the social thinker, the scientist to show us what he can do and to have enough confidence in what he is doing to work in his own way without regard to the number of people he influences or even reaches? With the present resources of the mass media, the present demand for more ideas and more talent will leave few who have such talent alone in obscurity.

HOW DO WE BREAK OUT OF THE CONFORMIST CIRCLE?

I would like to look further at the idea of nonconformity, a virtue widely celebrated but rarely visible. How do we get it? Certainly not by trying to nonconform. Deliberately to cultivate nonconformity is to act falsely and hypocritically. The conformist can very well ask, If a situation is a good one why change it? If teenagers speak the same language, dress the same way, think the same thoughts, or if their mothers and fathers in the suburbs of Chicago, San Francisco, Cleveland, New York, and Boston all have the same kind of houses, cars, and ideas, how do they break out? Should they move to the city? Read only James Joyce? All switch to MGs in place of those fin-tailed, gas-burning monsters of the automobile industry? Should they drop John Foster Dulles in favor of Mendes-France? The classical ballet for Martha Graham?

I can't imagine that this would give us anything but new forms of conformity. Already there is a standard liberal stance, and modern art itself has a grip on modern taste from which only a few can depart. Those who are influential in creating standards of aesthetic taste are themselves continually searching for new forms.

What has happened is that the concept of opinion-makers has transferred itself from business with its advertising and promotional instruments until now it is assumed that there are influential leaders in all fields—from art to politics—who mold the public attitude by their techniques of persuasion and the engineering of mass opinion. The counterpart to this is the public opinion poll which tells the man who is trying to lead opinion what the public thinks on every conceivable issue, so that then he can trim his opinion to suit the people. This is the double-edge of conformity—the conformity of democratic leadership to citizens' opinions, and the conformity of the citizens to the acceptance of brand names attached to public figures and to ideas. People seem to be reading the magazines to see what they should think, while the editors and political leaders anxiously watch the readers and listeners to see what they are thinking. This completes the conformist circle.

Again, how do we break out?

In the first place, I question the concept of the opinion-leader and the masses. I also question the wisdom of wanting to know what other people think before you say what you think. College presidents are, among others, considered to be opinion-leaders, although a great deal of the time they are business managers and administrative experts, busy with the public relations mechanisms of making their institutions attractive to the public and finding money to support them. They therefore do not lead opinion, but follow it in search of funds.

However, college presidents, among hundreds of others, receive through the mail masses of pamphlets, books, circulars, and statements from the United States and foreign governments, businessmen, editors, industrialists, educational organizations, few of which they can possibly read and fewer of which they could use in action, even if they wanted to. As W. H. Whyte's book of several years ago asked, *Is Anybody Listening?*

Certainly there are public figures whose views count and whose opinions are respected. But they "form opinion" because they are thinking freshly and well, independently and soundly. We need to understand that the public consists of individuals, not of masses of subscribers or listeners, and that these individuals are considerably more intelligent than they are assumed to be. That they are on the whole ill-informed, we know from the polls showing, for example, that 79 per cent of Americans in 1953 did not know what the initials NATO stood for, 54 per cent knew nothing about what the United Nations was doing.

But there are reasons for this, deep in the culture and in the educational system. The mistake is to generalize from this, and to say that therefore the American people should be talked down to, should be "sold" ideas like soap, and should be manipulated into holding views which the "opinion-leaders" want them to hold. I do not believe that such efforts to manipulate opinion fall within the ethics of democratic government, but more than this, I do not believe that in the long run they are very successful. Public relations efforts create their own antidotes and create after a while a cynicism about the efforts rather than an acceptance of the propaganda—unless, of course, there is solid truth and sound opinion at the heart of the enterprise, in which case the truth may be believed.

The break with conformity which I propose, therefore, is an old-fashioned remedy and repeats what Pericles, among others, has already suggested. It is the remedy of the nonconformists, Robert Frost, Frank Lloyd Wright, Albert Einstein, Carl Sandburg, Martha Graham. It is to tackle the thing which matters most to oneself, in a frank and fearless spirit, being true to oneself, and refusing to be deflected from that central enterprise either by the attractions of material success or by the disapproval of the public. This is a philosophy of risk, a philosophy of experiment, and of true individualism. The independent man must not be alarmed at where his independence will take him. If it takes him to conservatism, he should accept himself as a conservative and not become an anxious liberal. If he should then become a radical, then that is what he should be, and not a cynical conservative.

THE INTELLECTUAL AND NATIONAL POLICY

Finally, I wish to turn from the intellectual as an individual to questions of national policy. I see an enormous need for the full acceptance of the intellectual and the artist by the United States government. I would like to revert to type for a moment and speak of money. The United States is rich in resources, material resources, human resources, cultural resources—we have them in profusion. Yet we behave toward our cultural resources like niggardly parents of an unwanted child. The simple fact is that America can be better understood both at home and abroad today by the testimony of its writers and its artists than by the threats of military power and the statements of politicians.

When we learn of the reception accorded to our creative artists—Marian Anderson, Leonard Bernstein, the Philadelphia Symphony, the New York City Ballet—and to our intellectuals, whose work abroad is in some cases better known than it is at home, we can regret that the United States government lacks a coherent cultural or educational policy. We have not yet worked out a way in which the creative arts in America can be financially supported. This is true also of science and education, and if we put together the arts, the sciences and education, we can say that most of the sources of American culture are underfinanced.

This is partly because we do not yet realize how great a part can be played by the arts and sciences in our daily lives, and partly because we do not yet realize how important our political and cultural contribution can be to the world at large. Ahmed Bokhari of Pakistan has put it, "East and West can now, for the first time, meet on terms other than conquest and exploitation." We know from our recent experiences with visitors from the Soviet Union, from the exchange of scientists, educators, industrialists, and others between countries, including the United States, that to share in the exchange of ideas is perhaps the most important single factor which can ease the tensions among all countries. Respect for ideas and for intellectual and cultural achievement rises above politics and governments.

It is for this reason that we should be happy that our part in the Brussels Fair is one which is not devoted so much to propaganda as to the presentation of American architecture and American culture in its reality. For this reason we should regret that our government has not seen fit to give more of its support to the artists who could bring the excitement of the American performing arts to Europe if only there were funds to do so.

It is also true that in the new countries in the East where national independence has been late in beginning, those who serve as national leaders are themselves intellectuals and respected as such, among them Premier Nu of Burma, Malik of Lebanon, Nehru of India, Bokhari of Pakistan. We need also to consider the role of intellectuals in European government where Malraux, one of our most distinguished men of contemporary arts and letters, has always been involved in the political and social issues of his society and is now a government official.

Yet our government sends too few books abroad, either in English or in translation, to reach the millions of potential readers in Europe and the East, at a time when the Soviet Union is translating and distributing, at prices ranging from ten cents to eighty cents, millions of textbooks and Russian works in languages ranging from Urdu to English. There is also too great an emphasis in the selection of the books we do send abroad or those which emphasize the American political system. Again, we are not content to allow our arts and culture to speak for themselves at a time when the countries of the world do not wish us to tell them what they should think about us.

This is not an ordinary period in American history. It is the first time in the history of civilization that one country has ever had the chance of leading the whole world in creative and democratic experiments in social planning. It is the first time in history that any country has had the means, both in material wealth and in social structure, to give to every child born an opportunity for education up to the height of his powers. It is the first time that any country has had the economic strength to wipe out entirely the slums, and with them the bad human relations, the juvenile delinquency, and the evils of congestion. It is the first time that it has been possible for the entire resources of Western culture—its music, poetry, drama, literature, ballet, art objects—to be brought to a whole population through television, motion pictures, radio, and the mass magazines.

These possibilities coincide with shortened work hours and higher pay for everyone—everyone, that is, except artists, intellectuals, teachers, and educators.

We in America are at the beginning of what amounts to a cultural revolution made possible by science and education, moving in an incredibly short time from education and culture for the few to universal education and a high level of mass culture for the total population. With the flood of new talent which will be forthcoming from the millions more who will be in our schools and colleges, with the thousands of new writers, artists, architects, planners, builders, composers, playwrights, and scientists, we are now approaching a time when the achievements of the American past can be seen to be just the beginning of a magnificent new era in American culture.

But we could lose the revolution easily by failing to recognize the content of our own tradition. Our tradition is not conservatism, or middle-of-the-roadism, or moderation. It is individualism, liberalism, humanitarian democracy, and it is progressive, stemming from John Locke, John Stuart Mill, Tom Paine, Walt Whitman, William Lloyd Garrison, Woodrow Wilson, William James, John Dewey. There are challenges within our tradition which face us now. They center in the challenge to the American mind to express itself in new forms.

It will be clear, I imagine, that I am among those who believe that we are entering a new era which is full of promise for creative change and for the expansion of new frontiers. It will also be clear that I hold the view that the educated man, the intellectual in action, has a central part to play in the development of original ideas and the solution of social problems. It remains only for me to say that as you reflect, with Pericles, on what your country has the power to be, that you do as he asks, Reflect that her glory has been built, not by the security-minded, not by men in gray flannel suits, but by men and women who used knowledge as a guide to action, and by men and women who knew their duty and had the courage to do it.

Despite the fact that far too many people are suspicious of intellectuals, our society needs them in ever-increasing numbers. The current distrust of intellectuals, the intellectuals' attitude toward non-intellectuals, and the image that intellectuals have of themselves all merit examination.

One might imagine that the method of intelligence would be quickly accepted as an essential element of the democratic ethos. Since it is a public method, always open to scrutiny, it gives every citizen complete access to information. In all instances, it rests its case upon free discussion and open-ended tests. But for some, these strengths are dangerous. They breed skepticism, inquisitiveness that will not take no for an answer, and a love of change that leaves nothing untouched. Some men have such a dread of the method of intelligence that they will oppose it in every way they can. If they had their way, intellectuals would never create the "new forms" referred to by Harold Taylor, and would never have a chance to solve some of our most pressing social problems.

Merle Curti, an historian, has helped explain the historical development of the intellectual–anti-intellectual controversy. Curti believes that anti-intellectualism was caused by the following: hostility toward intellectuals that was brought to this country, with a host of other attitudes, by the first settlers; the belief expressed by Americans, both past and present, that scholarship threatens religion; pragmatic, utilitarian thinking that praises the doer and criticizes the thinker; the tendency on the part of many people to believe that cultural activities are feminine pursuits; the hostility of politicians toward all kinds of intellectualism; the common lack of faith in men of ideas; and the clash of ideas exemplified by the Cold War, which has served to alienate further the masses of the people from the intellectuals.

Of value to the student who wants to function as an intellectual within the democratic frame of reference are the following remarks from Curti's presidential address to the American Historical Association.

INTELLECTUALS AND OTHER PEOPLE

Merle Curti

Both popular distrust of the intellectual and anti-intellectualism among the intellectuals seem to have waxed stronger than ever in recent years. One might have expected popular anti-intellectualism to lessen in the present century, with Jacksonian democracy far in the past, the frontier a memory, and education and research supported as never before. But, despite a few dissenting voices,[1] most observers who have written on the theme agree that popular suspicion on the critical role of intellectuals has increased, that it has become more intense, and that demagogues are exploiting it as never before in our history.[2] The official sanctions given to the attacks on intellectuals and

Reprinted from *American Historical Review*, Vol. lx, No. 2 (January 1959), pp. 274–281.

[1] For example, David Riesman, "Some Observations on Intellectual Freedom," *American Scholar,* XXIII (Winter, 1953–54), 9–26, and Eugene Lyons, "What Reign of Terror Petrifies the Intellectuals?" *Saturday Evening Post,* CCXVI (May 1, 1954), 10.

[2] Aaron Levenstein, "The Demagogue and the Intellectual," *Antioch Review,* XIII (September, 1953), 259–74; Marya Mannes, "Any Resemblance . . . ," *The Reporter,* VIII

on the reasoning process have disturbed not only secular-minded liberals but prominent Catholics as well.[3] Not only the distrust of intellectuals but actual interference with rational inquiry and fact-finding procedures, as in the Bureau of Standards case, have deeply troubled scholars and citizens alike. Anti-intellectualism has also evoked sustained comment in journals of opinion at home and abroad.[4] McCarthyism, a particularly virulent form of anti-intellectualism in the popular sense, has become an international issue. And we recall the attacks on Adlai Stevenson and the scholars and writers who worked for him in 1952. Our common speech in that year took on as a term of opprobrium the curious word egg-head—the overtones of meaning ranged from scrambled to soft-boiled! The memory of the California oath is still fresh. So is the attack the staff of the Reece committee has lately made on the foundations and on a Commission of our own American Historical Association.

The most common, the most obvious, and perhaps the soundest explanation for such a situation is, of course, the climate of opinion created by the cold war in general and the revelation of certain cases of disloyalty in the intellectual community in particular. But our fellows in the social sciences have argued that increase in anti-intellectualism is the product of profound social and cultural changes which have long been under way and have only been accelerated of late. Specialization of functions has, it is said, increased the social distance between intellectuals and the rest of the community to such an extent that viable relations have become all but impossible. How can there be understanding in view of the depersonalized relations between intellectuals and nonintellectuals in the anonymous community of our time?[5]

Still other social scientists contend that the changing American culture favors those who make slogans and write advertisements, who rationalize the interests of government and business, rather than those who inquire and debate.[6] Many, perhaps most who engage in these activities, do not stop to consider that their own thinking is bound to be affected, yes, debased, by the evasions and half-truths that they turn out as information. But this only makes the surrender to anti-intellectualism the more insidious. In short, the intellectual tends to become a mere bureaucrat, a powerless figure, unable to defend reason and the freedom of the mind, perhaps seeing no necessity of so de-

---

(June 23, 1953), 34; the remarks of Senator J. W. Fullbright, February 2, 1954, *Congressional Record,* C (February 2, 1954), 1105–1106. Two examples of anti-intellectualism in more or less formal exposition are William F. Buckley, Jr., *God and Man at Yale* (Chicago, 1951), and Paul Harvey, *Autumn of Liberty* (Garden City, New York, 1954).

[3] *Commonweal,* LVII (November 28, 1952), 218, and LIX (January 15, 1954), 380.

[4] The report in the London *Economist,* CLXVI (March 21, 1953), 802–803, is representative.

[5] Baker Brownell, *The Human Community* (New York, 1950), pp. 20 ff., pp. 219 ff.; C. Wright Mills, *White Collar* (New York, 1951), pp. 142–60.

[6] Eric A. Havelock, *The Crucifixion of Intellectual Man* (Boston, 1950), pp. 74 ff.

fending it, however formidable the assaults to which these are subjected in our "age of unreason and anxiety."[7]

Related to the tendency of many intellectuals to become mere technicians is the contention that the changing American culture also sets high value on the ability to get along with the group and to take cues from it.[8] This is stifling to independent thought and it has promoted a climate in which it is easy to identify nonconformity with subversion and in which it is not easy to think critically. So run the arguments of many of our colleagues in other social disciplines.

The historian might well give serious attention to such analyses as these. It also seems to me highly important to explore the impact of the military on the life of intellectuals. What has been the influence of the habit of obedience and command on the free and inquiring mind? What about psychological warfare? A writer in the London *Economist* thinks it is bad for those who wage it. "On both sides of the iron curtain," he says, "there must be many thousands of unhappy psychological warriors who know, if they ever stop to think, that they are being corrupted by their own daily work."[9]

The arguments of the social scientists have not been sufficiently tested to satisfy the historian. Indeed, they have been challenged by those who hold that the intellectual in contemporary America is no more isolated or frustrated than intellectuals have always been, that the professor now actually rates high on the scale of the public opinion poll, and that the middlebrow has appeared to mediate between lowbrow and highbrow to the advantage of each.[10] The historian might well bring his talents to bear in helping to test these conflicting ideas. In so doing he can and should make use of objective measures of social change such as repeated attitude and public opinion studies, carefully handled according to the newer and more critical statistical methods.

But we do not need to use refined statistical methods to know that fear is abroad in our country and that those who live by ideas are especially subject to hysterical and unwarranted attack. Civil liberties won through centuries of struggle are in danger. Many of us believe that the contemporary attack on

[7] C. Wright Mills argues this point tellingly in more or less these words in *White Collar*, Chapter 7, and elsewhere. It is interesting to note that when the New York edition of Julien Benda's *Treason of the Intellectuals* (New York, 1928) appeared, many reviewers did not seem to attach much importance to Benda's indictment of the intellectuals for their "surrender" to "utilitarianism" and to "power struggles." See, for example, *Nation*, CXXVIII (January 2, 1929), 23–24; *New Republic*, LVII (December 12, 1928), 105–107; and *Saturday Review of Literature*, V (October 27, 1928), 289–90.

[8] David Riesman, *The Lonely Crowd* (New Haven, 1950), *passim.*

[9] London *Economist*, CLXXII (August 14, 1954), 498–99.

[10] Barzun, *God's Country and Mine;* Russell Lynes, "Highbrow, Lowbrow, and Middlebrow," *Harper's Magazine*, CXCVIII (February 1949), 19–28; *Life*, XXVI (April 11, 1949), pp. 99–102.

reason endangers not only the intellectual life but American civilization itself. Believing this despite the assurance from certain quarters that all is well, we are obliged, as intellectuals, not only to promote researches which may further illuminate the problem but also to search for possible alleviations of today's critical tensions.

From at least the mid-nineteenth century to our own day proposals have been made for the recognition of a cultural elite as one way of strengthening the position of the intellectual. These proposals have sometimes been launched with a kind of pride, approaching snobbishness, that Bacon would have called arrogance. The evidence for such "arrogance" is likely to be indirect. It is found, for example, in commencement orations of a hundred years ago which often admonished graduating classes to avoid giving offense by assuming airs.[11] With the spread of college education it is probable that such admonitions came to be less needed. Some intellectuals, however, have continued to invite resentment by the way in which they hold their learning. Somehow the impression is conveyed that they feel a moral superiority to the hillbillies, the masses of common people, because they know that El Greco is better than Gainsborough, Emily Dickinson than James Whitcomb Riley. Psychologists keep telling their fellow intellectuals that high intellectual capacity is not a personal achievement but a gift of nature, widely distributed among all classes. Yet there is a temptation for the "happy few" to be patronizing toward those whose children will some day sit at their desks and speak from their platforms. Sometimes we forget that it was a boy born in a crude log cabin who grew up to write the Gettysburg address, that a humble Massachusetts fish peddler wrote letters that will be long remembered, that the great religious leader of the Western world was a carpenter.

Although the idea of a cultural elite is undeniably attractive today, it is without substantive precedent in this country unless one goes back to the Puritan clergy or, possibly, to Jefferson's University of Virginia. It also defies our democratic tradition of the dignity of all work and the worth of each human being. It is consistent with our democratic institutions to hold that some will be better at certain kinds of work than others, and to respect the methods and honor the achievements of specially gifted or specially trained people. But for any group consciously to set itself up, because of its abilities and training, as superior to other groups in society is inconsistent

[11] Examples are Harvey Curtis, D. D., *Inaugural Address delivered at the Annual Commencement at Knox College* (Chicago, 1858), pp. 6 ff.; John Holmes, *An Address delivered at Waterville, before the Associated Alumni of Waterville College . . .* (Portland, 1831), pp. 21–22; Philip Lindsley, *Speech about Colleges, delivered in Nashville, on Commencement Day . . .* (Nashville, 1848), pp. 24 ff.; L. Carroll Judson, *The Probe . . .* (Philadelphia, 1846), pp. 43–44; Henry Ward Beecher, *Man and His Institutions* (New York, 1856), pp. 9 ff.; Reverend R. H. Bishop, *Address at Miami, September 30, 1830* (Miami, 1830), pp. 46 ff.; and Theodore Parker, *The American Scholar*, George W. Cooke, ed. (Boston, 1907), pp. 1 ff.

with democracy. Thus the elitism implicit or explicit in the writings of Santayana, Babbitt, Mencken, and Hutchins is unrealistic.[12]

The old notion of the scholar as belonging to a class apart from and above the people is also, it seems to me, related to a dualistic tradition that has little place in the world today. We see this dualism reflected in Plato's arguments for the philosopher king, in medieval scholasticism, in the rationalism of many philosophers, and in the faculty psychology of the last century, repudiated by scientific psychologists but still influential. In so far as reason is regarded as "pure" and in so far as it is assumed that thinking can operate without reference to consequences, this dualistic tradition of mind and body, of materialism and idealism, fits in with and reinforces the too-sharp distinction between the man of thought and the man of action.

I am not certain when the first formal rejection of this time-honored position was made. I do know that the academic addresses of a century ago clearly point to such a rejection. For example, a spokesman in a small Ohio college in 1843 maintained that misunderstanding and antagonism on the part of the producing classes and the intellectuals toward each other was neither necessary nor desirable. It was, he urged, rooted in an Old World tradition that drew a curtain between the philosophers who isolated themselves from that useful, everyday knowledge the people possessed; and the producing classes who, destitute of intellectual culture and unable to grasp the relation and meaning of what they saw, failed to contribute to society what they might otherwise have given.[13]

It remained, however, for a philosopher in our time to probe into the traditional dualism between thought and action. John Dewey has given us the fullest and most thoughtful statement of this approach. He maintained that the distrust of intellectuals by the common man and the reservations many intellectuals have about the plain people, are related to the Old World heritage that originated and flourished in class societies.[14]

Dewey's association of dualism with class societies has been questioned and many competent philosophers detect flaws in the instrumentalism that he has offered in place of the doctrines he criticized.[15] I leave to philosophers

[12] David Spitz in *Patterns of Anti-Democratic Thought* (New York, 1949) gives an informative treatment of the general idea of an elite.

[13] Rev. Sherman Canfield, *An Address on the Power and Progressiveness of Knowledge, delivered at the Commencement of Willoughby University, February 22, 1843* (Painesville, Ohio, 1843), pp. 18 ff. Canfield was a Presbyterian minister who, after a residence in Ohio City, was pastor of the First Church in Syracuse from 1854 to 1870.

[14] Dewey developed these ideas in many books and articles, especially in *Experience and Nature* (Chicago, 1925), pp. 21, 37, *Freedom and Culture* (New York, 1939), *Reconstruction in Philosophy* (New York, 1920), and *The Public and Its Problem* (Chicago, 1946), p. 138.

[15] For example, Arthur E. Murphy, *The Uses of Reason* (New York, 1943), pp. 85–95; Max Horkeimer, *Eclipse of Reason* (New York, 1947), pp. 54 ff.; Morris R. Cohen, *American Thought,* pp. 290 ff.; John U. Nef, *The United States and Civilization* (Chicago, 1942), p. 210.

the task of unraveling the more technical aspects of the controversy. But I know that the physiologists and experimental psychologists support Dewey's basic theory that thinking is not sharply set off from action. Thinking indeed *is* activity, symbolic activity, and an idea is an embryonic act. It is true that when theory is too quickly applied in practice, harm or even disaster may result. But to avoid reference to the problems of the day and association with ordinary people, deprives intellectuals of valuable tests for their theories, as well as of stimulating contact with American experience. The ivory tower can become a pretty dull place, and rather unproductive, too.

The historian can call attention to a body of American experience that is in line with Dewey's general position. Benjamin Franklin operated effectively on the assumption that there is no necessary dichotomy between theory and practice. Leading founders of the Republic, notably the framers of the Constitution, were men of action, and also educated men with great respect for learning. I may also refer again to the fairly successful co-operation between intellectuals and people in the great crises of our history, and to the shoulder-to-shoulder partnership intellectuals entered into with farmers and other humble folk for a greater measure of social and economic justice.

The role of intellectuals in the labor movement, a subject that needs further investigation, is illuminating in this connection. In general labor did not ask for guidance[16] though many wage-earners did read *Looking Backward*, *Progress and Poverty*, and the Haldeman-Julius distillations of socialist theory. Even wage-earners who at first pinned much hope to the new interest of the intellectuals in their movement were disillusioned when they found that some brainworkers were patronizing and that others were prone to lead the rank and file into what labor leaders looked on as wild goose chases. In turn, many intellectuals were also disillusioned when they found that trade unions did not always observe the canons of democracy, that the movement was spotted with intra-power struggles, and that it was more concerned with wages than with social justice in the broad sense. In time the intellectuals who stuck with the movement either ceased being intellectuals or learned the folly of trying to lead it too quickly or too far from its mooring, learned to respect "the tough fabric of custom and behavior" which at first they had misunderstood or challenged.[17]

One might also consider the successful experiences of experts in economics, political science, and law at the University of Wisconsin in serving the

[16] Selig Perlman, *Theory of the Labor Movement* (New York, 1928), pp. 5–9, 41–42, 68. Cf. *Industrial and Labor Relations Review*, IV (July 1951), 489–94 and *American Federationist* XXIII (March 1916), 198–99, and XXIX (March 1922), 212–15.

[17] This account is much indebted to George Soule's *The Intellectual and the Labor Movement*, League for Industrial Democracy Pamphlets (New York, 1923). See also Herbert E. Cory, *The Intellectuals and the Wage Earners* (New York, 1919). C. Wright Mills has brilliantly discussed the contemporary aspects of the problem in *The New Men of Power* (New York, 1948), pp. 281 ff.

progressive movement by blueprinting social legislation and by staffing the state commissions.[18] Other examples will come to mind, such as the pioneer work of Thomas Davidson, William Allan Neilson, and Morris Cohen at Breadwinners College and of Charles Beard at Ruskin Hall and, years later, in the Bureau of Municipal Research. In the 1930's this approach received wide implementation in the Federal Arts Projects and in the Tennessee Valley Authority.

One cannot claim that all these experiments were entirely successful. I know that many competent authorities take a less cheerful view than many of us do, and tend rather to agree with an earlier president of this Association who spoke from experience as well as scholarship. Woodrow Wilson maintained that the conflict in America between the man who thinks and the man who does is inevitable.[19] One must admit that his own effort to do both lent a tragic tension to his whole work. But in my view the total record is impressive. Today the intellectual, living in an atmosphere of fear and suspicion, is tempted, especially if he works in the field of the humanities or the social sciences, to seek safety in narrow specialization. But consideration of experiences such as those I have called to mind might well encourage him instead to turn his back on the ivory tower. For they have shown that intellectuals and other people can work together, can understand each other.

Finally, intellectuals must surely give more thought to popular education, both to adult education and to the teaching of the young. Something has been painfully lacking in the education of the American people, something above and beyond the overemphasis on vocationalism. It is clear that Americans have not been taught to understand what critical thinking is. I realize of course that education cannot easily rise above the prevailing cultural level which sets the problems and prescribes much that is done. But in our culture it is possible to teach children as well as adults to avoid falling into the trap of what has been called the undistributed middle—of hearing that X is a communist, knowing that X is an intellectual, and concluding that all intellectuals are communists. We have lately heard a spirited appeal to resist the vocationalism in our schools. To my mind it is much more important for crusaders to bring home to educators the tragic consequences of assuming that vague ideals, indoctrination of moral and political values, or even the discipline of the basic school subjects, are sufficient to develop an ability to resist the emotional appeal of the demagogue.

I said that adults can be taught, too, and modern psychologists assure us that learning is possible at any age. Most people have the ability to understand why it is important, in a democratic and changing society, not to be

[18] Charles McCarthy, *The Wisconsin Idea* (New York, 1912) and Merle Curti and Vernon Carstensen, *The University of Wisconsin: A History* (Madison, 1949–50), II, 3, 109–11, 132–33, 441.

[19] Woodrow Wilson, *Leaders of Men,* T. H. Vail Motter, ed. (Princeton, 1952), pp. 8 ff.

afraid of new ideas. And intellectuals need not always talk down. As Theodore Parker said, the scholar is "to think with the sage and saint, but talk with common men."

Many Americans today want to deny the importance of intellectualism, or avoid it by stressing uniformity and conformity. To some people, the conflict between the forces seeking to extend the method of intelligence and the forces seeking to impose an orthodoxy represents a serious social problem. This conflict is reflected in the operations of all social institutions, and especially so in the operation of the schools.

It is interesting to note that educators are often regarded as the least stable and least reliable of all professionals. People in authority often assume that educators must be stringently supervised and periodically called upon for expressions of loyalty lest their actions weaken society. Whether students and educators are entitled to freedom of thought and freedom of action or whether they must conform to edicts imposed upon them and, in conforming, achieve uniformity of both thought and action is an issue that remains to be resolved.

Glenn Austin, a philosopher, examines the significance of the ideas involved in the concept of democracy as an open society, elaborates upon the basic problem confronting contemporary American society, and offers a number of implications for education. He pleads for the continuation and enlargement of a society dedicated to self-improvement through the method of intelligence. His position requires that we use the traditions of our democratic past, but with such sensitivity as to keep the past from prescribing a rigid pattern for the present. Austin describes mindless conformity and thoughtless uniformity as the forces that will destroy society by destroying individuality.

FREEDOM, CONFORMITY, AND UNIFORMITY

Glenn Austin

Much has been said and written recently concerning the problem of freedom and conformity in American life. There has been, however, a tendency to overlook the fact that the problem is both a social and an educational one,

Reprinted from *Teachers College Record*, Vol. 58, No. 4 (January 1957), pp. 207–212.

and that these two aspects of the problem are closely interrelated. Moreover, there has apparently been either an unawareness of or an unwillingness to recognize the relatedness of conformity and educational uniformity. Yet it is in pressures toward social *and* educational conformity *and* uniformity that we may find the greatest danger to democracy in our time.

DEMOCRACY AS AN OPEN SOCIETY

The many definitions of democracy which have been attempted have served to bring out various aspects of a very complex concept. We seem to be at a stage in our national history when one particular meaning of democracy, that is, democracy as an open society, is of extreme importance. A democratic society needs to be an open society, dedicated to its own self-improvement by peaceful means. This much, of course, seems acceptable to all believers in democracy. But let us fill out this concept of an "open society." The word "open" means that the possible ways of improvement are open also. A democratic society is not one which must conform to any prescribed, predetermined pattern. It is a society which emphasizes participation of all its members in developing the values to be cherished (in that society) and in selecting the most desirable of the alternative directions for social change. And perhaps most important of all, the criteria for what is improvement and what is desirable are determined by the members of the society. A democracy, then, must be vitally concerned with the method or the means by which this open society can continue to be open; can continue to improve itself by peaceful means. This does not mean that we disregard our past, our ideals, or our democratic ancestors and traditions; but it does mean that neither the traditions nor the ancestors prescribe a rigid pattern. This, it seems to me, would make sense to such ancestors as Jefferson, Washington, Lincoln, and Tom Paine.

This conception of an open society means that we must have unfettered expression and communication of opinion and belief. Such freedom is widely accepted in theory but not so widely practiced. We must stop operating on the principle that bad ideas will drive out good. Milton, Jefferson, and Mill all agreed that freedom of expression must be preserved and that if truth and error were both expressed, truth would always win. Censorship, then, it is argued, is evil in a democratic society because it prevents us from discovering what may be *the* truth, under the guise of trying to protect us from error and heresy. This makes an irrefutable argument against censorship and other limitations on freedom of thought and expression. But in an open society, such limitations are an even greater evil because they prevent us from using the method by which the participants in a society, both groups and individuals, become aware of all the possible solutions to social problems coming from the various areas of society, and then work out the *best* truth in light of all these possibilities.

All things which interfere with freedom of thought and expression in an open society are thus chopping away at its self-improvement potentialities. The self-realization of an open society is dependent upon the operation and expression of free intelligence in all areas of living. It should be obvious that in this kind of society diversity is precious. Diversity becomes a value, because from the many diverse individuals and groups and minorities within society we receive more and more ideas as to possible desirable directions of social development. Each group tends to see the social welfare from its own point of view, but out of these various points of view we are able to work out together what is best for our society. The best answers to our problems are not all already known and waiting to be discovered, they are to be worked out in the democratic process. As an open society, democracy cherishes diversity because it recognizes that therein lies its capacity for self-improvement, and in freedom of expression and communication lies our guarantee of *peaceful* change.

In the last few years all of us have become aware of the pressures being exerted against diversity and against the principle that we need free expression of all points of view, that we need a free, critical intelligence exploring all areas of life. We have heard derogatory, derisive comments aimed at many intellectuals in our society, at men of education and ability, men of recognized intellectual achievements who have been maligned and slandered by political and journalistic commentators who seem to believe that higher education, unusual intelligence, humaneness, and good will are undesirable qualities for citizens in a democracy. Much of this contempt has been crystallized into that scorn-filled epithet, "egghead." Throughout our land we have seen much of the attitude displayed in the following lines from an old Jewish poem:

> Leave fantastic dreams alone
> And mind no business but your own,
> For what has been must be.
> Nothing the wisdom of old surpasses.
> Our fathers were wise and their children are asses:
> Eternal *their* laws, beyond question or doubt,
> Our business is only to carry them out.
> For what has been must be.

The causes for these recent pressures against diversity and free intelligence are numerous. Certainly the anxieties and tensions resulting from our trying to live democratically in a world in which there is also a totalitarianism devoted to conflicting values have been responsible for many of those excesses which we have come to label "McCarthyism." As a nation we seem to be partially emerging from the cloud that was cast over our democratic values by the senator from Wisconsin, but there is no guarantee yet that even this particular battle has been won, even though the major figures may change. We are now being very quiet about McCarthy and acting a little sheepish because we feel he made a fool of us in the eyes of the world. Perhaps we have learned something. But we have not yet faced the even greater problem from which this one is only derivative.

THE BASIC PROBLEM

In David Riesman's much discussed book, *The Lonely Crowd*, which has the subtitle, *A Study of the Changing American Character*, there is a fascinating discussion of the change in the American character from the stage of *inner-direction* to the stage of *other-direction*. Other-direction seems on the way to becoming dominant in our country and may perhaps tend to become dominant in all countries as they reach a particular stage in their social development. Riesman's argument is too important and too complex for a hasty summary here. But what he has to say is extremely significant for the problems of uniformity and conformity, both in society and in education.

Increased education, leisure, services, mass communication, the shift from primary to secondary groups, have come with capitalism, industrialism, and urbanization. Out of this complex with its emphasis on socialized behavior and social adjustment has come the other-directed person, who is described in this fashion by Riesman:

> What is common to all other-directeds is that their contemporaries are the source of direction for the individual—either those known to him or those with whom he is indirectly acquainted, through friends and through the mass media. The source is of course "internalized" in the sense that dependence on it for guidance in life is implanted early. The goals toward which the other-directed person strives shift with that guidance; it is only the process of striving itself and the process of paying close attention to the signals from others that remain unaltered throughout life.[1]

We might say he is like a tremendous insect, perhaps like Kafka's great beetle, with extremely long antennae, always feeling his way, sensitive and receptive to every external pressure, so that his every action and thought are determined for him by his constant seeking of approval through conformity.

We need not push Riesman's analysis any further. *If* in a society like ours we are becoming more and more anxious about what all the others think and are trying only to conform to their pattern of expectation for us, then we are tending to become all alike. Such a process would be truly a vicious circle, with every individual trying to conform to a pattern of character

[1] David Riesman, *The Lonely Crowd* (New Haven: Yale University Press, 1950), p. 22.

and thinking dictated by the approval of *all* other individuals. Actually, of course, we would cease to be individuals in the full sense. A society established on this process would surely be doomed to complete uniformity with no individual diversity. Such a society would never produce a Thoreau or an Einstein or even our own ordinary individualities. A society in which everyone is striving to live up (or down) to the common denominator of all other persons' patterns is like a community in which everyone does nothing but take in everyone else's washing, even using the same brand of automatic washer and drier. There would seem little hope for any improvement in such a society, or indeed for *any* rationally directed social change. This, then, could not be an open society, capable of exerting any significant degree of control in the direction of self-improvement. This would be a society of the indiscernible, of the indistinguishable. It would seem to be trying to disprove Leibniz by producing individuals who are exactly alike, but it would ultimately be made up of the same individual, operating under different numbers.

To guard against being misunderstood I should emphasize that when I speak of individuality I am not referring to "individualistic free private enterprise" or to the unlamented "rugged individualism" popular during my youth. To those who insist that these are foundations for all forms of individuality and freedom I can only reply that they apparently are embracing the fallacies of strict economic determinism for which the Communists have been severely and rightly criticized. They are almost out-Marxing the Marxists, and someone might even label them un-American. Nor would I wish to argue that absolutely all conformity is dangerous; but a *reasonless* or *thoughtless* conformity *is* dangerous and is usually coupled with the idea that nonconformity in any form or differences in any degree are subversive and intolerable. I am of course primarily concerned about conformity in the realm of ideas, of beliefs, of values, and of attitudes toward social change. Is not our basic freedom, after all, the freedom to think and to make effective choices?

SOME EDUCATIONAL IMPLICATIONS

Let us turn now to some of the implications of all this for education. Education and society are ceaselessly interacting with each other, each affecting the other. Social change is taking place, and education can react to it in at least three ways: (1) ignore it and thus tacitly approve it; (2) re-enforce social change indiscriminately; or (3) strive to help people to operate with an awareness of the alternatives available and what can be done about them. Today education is being criticized by those who would make a cult of uniformity and conformity. Academic freedom is frequently under fire *not* because it is an academic issue but because it is primarily a *social* issue, the right of free intelligence to explore, to criticize, to evaluate in all areas of life. This is dangerous to conformity of any kind, in education or in society. Loyalty oaths have been experienced almost everywhere. The Fund for the Republic has recently set aside a substantial sum of money for a study of the degree of fear existing among teachers. Lists of *verboten* books have been pushed upon school librarians, as in California, not so long ago. Textbooks have been dropped from use under pressure, or perhaps republished in "safe" conformity editions. We have seen infringements upon the civil liberties of teachers and all other citizens. We have seen anyone whose opinions differed from those of the majority becoming immediately suspect. Honest criticism, instead of being considered desirable, has been labeled disloyal. This story has been told many times; there is no need to repeat its details to any informed group.

Yet when one looks at the pattern of much of American education one is surprised at the extent and the intensity of these attacks. By and large, American education, particularly secondary and higher education, has operated under a philosophy which has emphasized the value of uniformity, of adjustment and conformity. Some have hoped that critical thinking and evaluation would be an automatic and contradictory by-product, perhaps, but seldom has emphasis been placed upon them. Frequently education at all levels has been looked on as simply a matter of acquiring prescribed information. Too often, we teachers pour it in and "pour it on," and our grades merely measure how much of what has been poured into the student he is able to give back to us on our tests. We subject every student to the same standardized once-over-lightly, or not so lightly, treatment. We require the same of everyone. All this information, it is assumed, somehow becomes a part of the student and makes a difference in him. Perhaps it will make the same difference in all the students! Instead of the inquiring mind, then, we thus tend to encourage the merely receptive mind. In all too many institutions throughout the land we have so many students in classes that it is difficult to do anything except to pass out the information and fill their receptacle-like minds as full as possible. A friend once suggested to me this might be the reason some teachers affectionately refer to their students as "jugheads." Perhaps our educational efforts have been more successful than we think; perhaps we are reaping what we have sowed. Those people who are now criticizing education for not teaching enough conformity, along with all those who fail to become concerned about pressures for conformity are, by and large, products of that educational system just described. Perhaps some of education's chickens are coming home to roost.

In a short book, *The Cultivation of Idiosyncrasy* (1949), Harold Benjamin focuses attention on the big problem for education in a democratic society. He points out the absurdity of our idea of education as acquiring, adjusting, conforming. In trying to give everyone exactly the same educational experiences and the same material, testing them to make sure they know the right answers and can hand them back when the appropriate stimulus is presented—in all this, he says, we are in danger of reducing our society to a flat level of conformity and mediocrity. It may work well under totalitarianism, where people are told what to think, or in a society where change is almost nonexistent, but it will certainly not meet the needs of a society made up of individuals who need to think and evaluate for themselves and decide for themselves if, where, what, how, and when social changes should take place.

That kind of society needs citizens with individuality; it will prize diversity and idiosyncrasy. It needs individuals who have a sense of commitment to value systems which have been critically examined and which have stood up under that examination, and who recognize that others may not agree. It needs an educational system which appreciates creativity, individuality, and diversity; which encourages the free-ranging intelligence to examine all areas of life and all points of view. (Freedom of thought need not mean merely that we think as, when, and *if* we please.) It needs an education in which students work on real problems, in which there are genuine alternatives available, and in which students make real choices after a critical evaluation of alternative possibilities. It needs an education in which controversial issues involving conflicting value assumptions are brought out into the open and critically examined. It needs to recognize that anything worth believing in will welcome and survive critical examination. It needs to recognize that anything that will not survive critical examination is not worth believing in.

As Harold Benjamin remarks, our society needs only that conformity which the achievement of our greatest goals requires; ". . . and it requires just as many uniquely developed peaks of ability, just as much idiosyncrasy as the attainment of our goals will allow and need. . . . That society which comes closest to developing every socially useful idiosyncrasy in every one of its members will make the greatest progress toward its goals."[2]

CONFORMITY OR DIVERSITY

As a people we must decide how much conformity is necessary if we are to be strong (admittedly this is a problem) and how much diversity is possible to make for the greatest progress toward the goals we set up. A society which emphasizes diversity has great potentiality for self-improvement; its life has a richer texture, and its future guarantees individuality for all. We can gain only temporary strength through sacrificing diversity to conformity. The pressures of all our mass media toward uniformity and subsequent conformity in a society in which so many of us read the same papers, listen

[2] Harold Benjamin, *The Cultivation of Idiosyncrasy* (Cambridge: Harvard University Press, 1949), pp. 36–37.

to the same radio commentators, watch the same television programs, listen to the same commercials—these pressures are almost overwhelming. Our problem is not one of obtaining conformity, but one of retaining individuality and diversity, even nonconformity, against all these pressures. I see no basis whatever for approaching this problem with a turn-of-the-century attitude of easy optimism, or a ready belief in the inevitability of progress and a guaranteed happy resolution of our difficulty. Education at all levels faces a serious challenge—the call to revise many of its practices in light of this long-range social need. If those of us who are aware of the dangers use every opportunity *in society and in education*, we *may* be able to preserve that diversity without which continuous social strength is impossible in a rapidly changing world, and without which individuality must surely disappear. This correlation of individuality and an open society still exists as what William James would call a live option, that is, as a possibility which our strong faith and our determined efforts *may* perhaps make into a reality. The alternative to this is a static, uniform dead-level of conformity and mediocrity, with eventual loss of basic freedoms.

Chapter 5

THE SCOPE OF DEMOCRATIC EDUCATION

THE *guidelines for the operation of American education will emerge from an analysis of the philosophy of democracy. This analysis provides the principles which, in turn, will serve as the standards of evaluation for teaching and learning.*

The most important conclusion to be reached from a study of the development of Western culture—and it is a conclusion that includes an honest appreciation of differences—comes to this: Of all forms of social organization, only democracy, theoretically and practically, offers the greatest good to the greatest number. Schools are designed to support this in as deliberate a way as possible by providing equality of educational opportunity to every person. The motivating force here is faith in the dignity and worth of human beings. The practical task is to offer every person, ignoring time, place, and circumstance, a seat in a schoolroom that has a program that will assure his fullest development.

Each time the school provides the conditions of optimum growth for any individual, it becomes possible for him, deeply conscious of his own worth, to make a positive contribution to the growth of others. In the resulting individual-group relationship, the freedom to find and enjoy success as a learner helps the individual and the group to accept the obligation to maintain conditions that encourage everyone to continue to be free. As individuals and groups learn how to make success bring about more success, they make it possible for learning to become a continuing process. When an individual can behave in this way, his knowledge and his actions enhance his self-understanding, his understanding of others, and his commitment to avoid any violation of freedom for himself or others.

There can be no faith in individual dignity and worth serious enough to make a society offer equality of opportunity in its schools without knowledge of how and why men behave as they do. The task of the democrat, in this instance, is to apply the methods of intelligence to the study of his own nature, and to accept and use all that he learns about himself and others.

H. Gordon Hullfish, a philosopher, elaborates on these matters in the following article.

EDUCATION FOR DEMOCRACY

H. Gordon Hullfish

I know of no simple answer to the question, "What education will best serve a democratic people?" Few problems within a democracy, subject as they are to consideration by all of the people, are readily, or permanently, solved. Education is no exception. The totalitarians face a simpler problem in constructing an appropriate education. They have only to design an educational machine which the machine operators, the teachers, will service. The intricacies of the machine and the resulting character of the service may need to be changed from time to time, but this is a "top office" decision, so to speak, one in which the operators are no more involved than are the machines. A democracy dare not come at its problems in this way, though some of the more fanatical educational critics and, indeed, some educational officials, act on occasion as if theirs were a "top office" responsibility. But this is only to say that one of the luxuries democracies have long indulged in has been to permit some citizens to demonstrate publicly the inappropriateness of their ideas and of their behavior. How far we dare to indulge ourselves in this direction is a pertinent question, though we need not pursue it here.

If there is no simple answer, there are some factors, nevertheless, that may be marked off as elements essential to any full consideration of the problem. And, obvious as it may be to say this, the public school must be noted as the ground in which the democratic aspiration is rooted generation by generation. I will not say that schools other than public fail to provide a ground in which these roots take hold. I must say, however, that were we without public schools the tendencies among us toward divisiveness would be accentuated dangerously. We should have to find a way to invent such schools. Fortunately for us, our forebears wanted no man to have an un-

Reprinted from *American Association of University Professors, Bulletin,* Vol. 41 (June 1955), pp. 253–267.

warranted advantage over others, on education or any other score, and in their wisdom they evolved a public instrument of enlightenment and, significantly, of association. I can point to no charts, to no statistical tables, to prove the point; yet a claim that our public schools, opening their doors as they do year in and year out to the children of each neighborhood, asking only that residence as of the moment be established, have been the greatest single force in building whatever sense of oneness, of togetherness, we have achieved, is hardly open to challenge.

I can point, of course, to our failure, in some neighborhoods, to be neighborly. Some of our children have been denied the enriching experience (or better, perhaps, the democratic right) of maturing in situations where they could share their interests and emerging values freely with the interests and values of all of the children of the neighborhood. The Supreme Court has now made this denial a matter of public record, labelling it for what it has always been, a failure to live up to the commitment of our heritage, a failure to educate for democracy. But there is another side of this situation which is not so obvious, one not dramatized by court decision. The deprivation of some children of a freely shared experience with others in any neighborhood, from small town to the nation as a whole, is, in fact, a deprivation of all children. Our chance of living together with understanding in our adult years is directly proportionate to the opportunity afforded us to develop a sense of togetherness as we mature. Private and parochial schools, while they may not be undemocratic, either in conception or in practice, will have more difficulty than do public schools in meeting the responsibility for combatting divisive tendencies which both schools share. What all of us need to remember is that children in a democracy should share their growth as they share the sidewalks, as pathways to common adventures—where they may meet to play together and to plan together; where they may jostle one another as pathways cross; where they may go their separate ways; where they may deny to none the right of use.

Woodrow Wilson was not thinking primarily about public education, though he was thinking deeply about the future of democracy, when he remarked, "We overlook the fact that the real source of strength in the community comes from the bottom." Pursuing this thought, he asked,

> Do you find democracy renewing itself from the top? Don't you find society renewing itself from the ranks of unknown men? Do you look to the leading families to go on leading you? Do you look to the ranks of men already established in authority to contribute sons to lead the next generation? They may, sometimes they do, but you can't count on them; and what you are constantly depending on is the rise out of the ranks of unknown men, the emergence of somebody from some place of which you had thought the least, of some man unanointed from on high, to do the thing that the generation calls for. Who would have looked

to see Lincoln save a nation? . . . All the while there was springing up in him, as if he were connected with the very soil itself, the sap of a nation, the vision of a great people, a sympathy so ingrained and intimate with the common run of men that he was like the people impersonated, sublimated, touched with genius. And it is to such sources that we must always look.[1]

But he was thinking of public education when he said,

You know that the great melting-pot of America, the place where we are all made Americans of, is the public school, where men of every race and of every origin and of every station in life send their children, or ought to send their children, and where, being mixed together, the youngsters are all infused with the American spirit and developed into American men and American women.[2]

Before leaving either this point or Woodrow Wilson, we should note that the function of the public school in providing an education for democracy is not restricted to the children, any more than education itself is restricted to the immature years. No society ever suffered from an excess of knowledge or intelligence, or from an over-supply of understanding shared by its citizens. A democracy strengthens itself as it makes gains in each of these directions; and the citizens, in the institution which is the public school, possess an instrument that may be used neighborhood by neighborhood to strengthen themselves and their common life. Education, as is true of democracy itself, is never "a thing done, but," as Archibald MacLeish has phrased it, "a thing a-doing." Thus, Woodrow Wilson noted that "When, in addition to sending our children to school to paid teachers, we go to school to one another in those same schoolhouses, then we shall begin more fully to realize than we have ever realized before what American life is."[3] Quite specifically, he pointed to his participation in this Forum as giving him the assurance that this was so. It was against the background of an early experience of his at Cooper Union that he said:

And what I like about this social center idea of the schoolhouse is that there is the place where the ordinary fellow is going to get his innings, going to ask his questions, going to express his opinions, going to convince those who do not realize that the vigor of America pulses in the blood of every true American, and that the only place he can find the true American is in this clearing house of absolutely democratic opinion.[4]

A nation which develops education widely, involving many of its citizens and all of its future citizens in its program, has provided itself with an assurance that it will not stand still, that its life will almost certainly improve. And this is so even when the purpose of education is admittedly to maintain the

[1] *Wilson's Ideals,* S. K. Padover, ed., pp. 18–19. [2] *The New Freedom,* p. 97.
[3] *Ibid.,* p. 98. [4] *Ibid.,* p. 99.

status quo. Ideas beget ideas; they stir the imagination of those who entertain them. Whenever we permit the examination of some ideas, we open the possibility that ideas which hold no permit will confront the thinker and ask to be heard. It is no accident that parents in small and private ways withhold some ideas from their children, being fearful that if certain implications come into view the children will go on to speculate about ideas the parents would like to hold back for a later day, if not forever. Nor is it an accident that organizations and institutions behave identically, on a large scale, and publicly. But over the long haul the censor fights a losing battle. Thus, we may hope that the Communist world presently, if the figure is not inappropriate, has a bear by the tail. If the Communists are to be the force in our time they clearly wish to be, they will need citizens as knowledgeable and as skilled as are citizens in other parts of the world. No other road to survival is open to any nation in our complex scientific and technological present. Every demand upon the Communists, therefore, that they extend their knowledge, in whatever area, is equally a demand that the diligence of the security police be extended. So it is that the purge and the public apology for having thought wrongly are becoming familiar features of Communist life; but, also, so it is that ideas are extended and reconstructed even as the intention is that they remain static until such time as, an order permitting, or demanding, change is given. Our repressive critics are but faint counterparts of these security police and, so long as we retain our devotion to open discussion, to the free examination of ideas, they are reduced to the nuisance level of the horse fly. Yet we had better bestir ourselves whenever the self-appointed censor gains the slightest measure of governmental backing.

It is at this point, of course, that we find the critical test of how well we are doing in educating for democracy. We can put aside for the moment, almost as irrelevant, the many current arguments about what specifically we are teaching, and how well. The anecdotes that the critics regale us with about the young men and women they have met who cannot spell are interesting, yet they are unrelated to the main issue. This is equally true of the counter argument, that test results show present students to be learning the fundamentals as well as did students in an earlier day, and frequently better. I am not suggesting that we should fail to teach well whatever we select as fundamental. Few of us ever know enough. This is true even of those who find it profitable to tell the rest of us of our lacks. What I do wish to suggest is that the critical factor is the atmosphere that pervades and surrounds the learning situation. Democracy makes no gain, no matter how well the basic tools of learning are taught, if teachers and students are caught up in an atmosphere of fear, suspicion, and repression.

That such an atmosphere has prevailed for a number of years, and that it has had serious consequences for education, we well know. Each of us has his anecdotes on this score, too. My latest comes from the chairman of a large department in a liberal arts college in a great university. He was seeking an instructor to add to the staff. One letter, that recommended a young man highly, made note of his years of study and experience, of the character and range of his scholarship, of his personality and of his promise as a teacher. But, then (was he perhaps throwing an anchor to the windward?) the writer said of his candidate that while he had a broad social point of view he was in no sense a radical. We have more than anecdote to go on, however. We have the fact of the harassment of individual teachers and school systems the country over by those who would use the limitations of their own minds as the limits of growth for the minds of others. The atmosphere has not been good; it has not encouraged our best efforts to animate the educative process by keeping always to the fore the spirit of that free-wheeling intelligence on which the democratic aspiration feeds. Yet, in my opinion, the atmosphere is improving. We are getting our second wind. We are discovering that free people will not gain security when they deny, to the institution by which they renew themselves generation by generation, its right to be free.

Democracy is in need of the best-informed thought, and of the best-disposed thought, that the genius of the people can generate. About these ends, when stated thus, little difference arises among us. We find most men to be for the free mind, and for the generous heart, about as readily as Calvin Coolidge found them to be against sin. Differences appear only when we construct the educative means to foster these ends, quite as differences arise when men set out to check sin. Actually, of course, the differences go beyond means, beyond instrumentalities. There are some who are sure that the best-informed thought, and the best-motivated conduct, stand in some duplicating relationship to standards which reside beyond time and place and, thus, beyond man. There are others (John Dewey was one of these) who believe that it is within time and place, and circumstance, that standards for thought and conduct are developed and the tests of their adequacy found. There are those who believe, therefore, that man lives under the guidance of absolute standards and that education ought to bring him to an understanding of this fact. There are others (again, Mr. Dewey was of this company) who believe that men are capable of generating the standards and ideals by which to guide their thought and conduct. And there are those, to narrow this discussion somewhat, who seem to believe that all that is wrong with modern education is that John Dewey lived and, in the living, convinced others that the philosophy he evolved was meaningful for the improvement of life in general and for the improvement of education specifically. Some of those convinced do use what Douglas Bush of Harvard has recently referred to as "John Dewey's philosophy of barbarism,"[5] as a point of orientation, in plan-

[5] "Education for All Is Education for None," *The New York Times Magazine*, January 9, 1955, p. 13.

ning programs for the education of teachers and, in consequence, so it is held, the true purposes of education have been subverted.

It does seem to me at times that some critics of education resemble the habit-ridden citizen who, come what may, is determined to defeat Franklin Delano Roosevelt each time he casts a ballot. But, be this as it may, the differences in outlook are facts of our times. They are not to be laughed away nor, as I see it, are they to be reconciled. I think we have spent enough time trying to find the common elements in our differing views, knowing all the while that the uncommon element, the element that made for the difference in the first instance, would not be under scrutiny. What we have to ask ourselves is whether our differences have brought us to the end of the road, reducing us to the pathetic gesture of calling the other fellow barbaric, while seeing naught but the acme of civilization in our own mirrors.

I do not believe that we are at the end of the road, though I do believe the pathway we have been following leads but to frustration and unnecessary bickering. Our democratic experience ought to be more useful to us than we have permitted it to be. We are not without experience in developing unity as we have clarified differences, even deepened them. Let me be quite specific. On the issue presented above, I stand with John Dewey. I will not say that those of other persuasions are wrong. I will only say that I think they are. In some specific instances I believe that some who differ are ill-informed and I must believe, further, that where this is so the discovery of this fact would have the same impact upon their views as a comparable discovery should have on mine. But where does this leave us? In a democracy, since neither camp has the authority to abolish the other, it should leave each of us, first, with the right to believe as he does and, second, insofar as any one of us has responsibility for the education of others, with the responsibility to gain supporting evidence for the practices he advocates. Nostalgia, we should note, is not a substitute for evidence, nor is the niggling use of anecdote a substitute for reasoned conclusions. Our schools will not become adept in educating for democracy as long as those of us who try to give them direction fail to understand its meaning for our own behavior.

There are several reasons why we have not done better than we have, including the limitation each of us confronts in his own person. Education has changed as the needs of the nation have changed. It has changed as the trend toward urban life made our rural character a thing of the past. It has changed as the nature and character and purposes of those who seek it have changed. It has changed as the nature and character and purposes of those who provide it have changed. It has changed as knowledge—the knowledge the schools are asked to transmit, as well as the knowledge of what is involved in the act of transmission—has changed. It has changed as the place of our nation in a concert of nations has changed and as, in the process, our obligations and the conditions of our security have changed. The wonder is not that education has been under criticism. The wonder is that it gained such obvious vitality while undergoing one growing pain after another.

But there is yet another reason, one that takes me back to my standing ground, my point of difference with those who stand otherwise. Each of us finds his standing ground good and from it expects to give order and meaning to all that he touches, including education. From it we each move toward system, toward substance, labelling the result a philosophy of life, a philosophy of education or, more simply, yet perhaps more forcefully, a way of life. Thus we move toward inclusiveness, preparing ourselves better all the while to fend off those of other persuasions. If we have done our task well, we shall have no difficulty in showing, when we come to education, that whatever the other fellow proposes or does is, on the face, wrong. It is in these terms that one of John Dewey's critics has said, in effect, that even if Mr. Dewey's pedagogical proposals were correct, so far as enhancing learning is concerned, he would reject them. It is paradoxical that the excluding potential of each point of view is raised as each advances toward inclusiveness. I am reminded of a favorite remark of my former colleague, Boyd H. Bode, "The trouble with the university professor is that he identifies the university with the universe."

As soon as we turn to the social scene, and all who think about education must do this, the problem appears in clearer focus, though the difficulty of dealing with it is perhaps increased. Many who would lay no claim to having a philosophy, or to having formulated a philosophy of education, would tend to recognize a personal commitment in the phrasing, "the democratic way of life," and would anticipate, now that they feel themselves to be aware of competing ways of life, that our schools should advance the democratic way. This seems reasonable, and many have been and are involved in setting forth its pattern, at ease with their conviction that in doing so they will put the schools on the right track. Boyd Bode gave this conviction support when, in discussing fascism and communism in *Democracy as a Way of Life,* he said, of these doctrines, that each provided "a comprehensive plan for the organization of both individual and collective conduct, which is essentially what is meant when we speak of *a way of life*."[6] The title of this volume gives evidence that its author, devoted as he was to the rights of free men, was concerned to show the superiority of the democratic way of life, in contrast to the patterns of fascism and communism. He did show this, yet he left a question with me that I still find bothersome.

In what sense is democracy a way of life? In what sense, indeed, is communism a way of life? In what sense is the latter more than the lengthened shadow of the leader's whip? Do we mean that each has an internal substance that all who live in relationship to it grasp and understand? If so, neither

[6] P. 7 (italics in original).

qualifies as a way of life. Was communism equally communism under Lenin and Stalin? Is it now the same way of life under Malenkov? Was democracy not democracy before women were granted the vote? And what of our way of life when it was legal to conduct segregated schools? Was our way of life more in evidence on the frontier, when the individual took the law in his own hands? At what point do we stop and say, "There it is; have a go at it"? Was democracy non-existent when unions were unheard of? Is our way of life more in evidence now that the stockmarket is watched by government than when bullish and bearish movements were its private business? And who among us is our authority—historian, politician, businessman, churchman, educator, farmer, miner, or factory worker? What, then, is in conflict when we speak of competing and conflicting ways of life? Do we select a single feature (say, the two-party system) or a central tendency (say, belief in a divine being) or an historic fact (say, a general dependence on individual initiative in economic matters) as our point of contrast?

Now, I recognize that our past has given us preferences in the realms of social and individual values. It has given us opportunities, too. I can swell with appropriate pride when I think of these. I recognize further that some of these values are not prized by all others in the world, and that when others threaten them we value them more intensely. This latter fact is inescapable, and it is good that this is so. Bode was not wrong in insisting that the commonly shared values in a culture give life its meaning and purpose. I am not happy over the prospect, however, that some among us may come up with a delineation of *the* democratic way of life at a moment when a pervading anxiety provides a power opportunity which will end speculation for the rest of us. If this happens, the problem of educating for democracy will be solved. Schools will be used to assure continuity for the newly developed power and, while a way of life may seem to prevail, democracy will be but a façade for authoritarianism, obscuring the motives of those who manipulate the controls in the back room.

This sad ending was not envisioned by Boyd Bode. Far from it. His was a blow struck against authoritarianism, against, so far as schools were concerned, indoctrination in any form. As he put it,

> Democratic education is obliged to stake everything on a program for the liberation of intelligence. It need not, and must not, demand uniformity of belief. Pupils come to school with all kinds of backgrounds; it is hardly conceivable that they should all emerge with the same set of conclusions. It is not to such uniformity of conclusions, but to certain habits of thinking and feeling and acting, that democracy must look as its hope for the future.[7]

He held that the democratic school could make "an honest disclaimer of any intention of predetermining the patterns"[8] of belief young people would

[7] *Ibid.*, p. 106. [8] *Ibid.*, p. 97.

achieve in an education appropriate to the democratic way of life. He equally held, however, that the democratic school should help young people achieve understanding of the values they hold simply by having been born among us, that it should help them think through the conflicts which arise when such values are compared and contrasted, and that its continuing obligation was to help the young person at each stage of his development advance his understanding of that which was distinctively democratic in the human relationship. "Unless the next generation can do a better job than we have done," he insisted, "the values of our civilization will be seriously endangered. He [the student] is entitled to have all the light that the school can furnish on underlying issues and he should have the opportunity for the exercise of enlightened and independent judgment."[9]

My question arises because the phrasing, *a way of life*, is used loosely. At times we refer to a belief which holds that each individual should develop his own values and learn to use them as the means of gaining meaning and purpose for his daily living. We recognize that this is an individual matter, that democracy provides each individual with this opportunity and privilege. At other times, however, what we refer to is an individual perception of democracy that we have staked out as a way of life into which the immature individual should be inducted. I don't believe we can have it both ways. If the latter meaning is at issue, the former meaning is denied. If we know in advance what the democratic way of life is, we are acting wastefully, if not dangerously, when we permit each individual to formulate his *Weltanschauung* independently. Moreover, if we know in advance what this way of life is, we shall have little further need for the free-ranging intelligence, the play of idea upon idea, the give and take of discussion and conference as differences are explored, or the achievement of compromises as understanding is substituted for force—all qualities which have characterized our past.

For my own part I prefer to leave the problem of a way of life in the hands of each individual, helping him, to be sure, but leaving up to him the choosing, the judging, the reflection which give him his personal character. This, I am sure, was finally Bode's position, despite an emphasis that some might misuse in their anxiety to assure democracy's survival. I believe, too, it was John Dewey's position, though the emphasis in the first sentence that follows may cast a doubt: "We have advanced far enough to say that democracy is a way of life. We have yet to realize that it is a way of personal life and one which provides a moral standard for personal conduct."[10] On the personal level we can discuss our differences. We can accommodate ourselves one to the other in terms of our dispositions and our tolerances. We can create the social instruments, as we have already done in part, to

[9] *Ibid.*, p. 98. [10] *Freedom and Culture*, p. 130.

facilitate our relationships and to extend the range of our common interests and understandings. We can, in short, come at life in ways that involve each of us responsibly in determining the shape of things to come, without giving to any of us the privilege of doing the final shaping.

Democratic principles are involved, of course, in what is here suggested; and these did not come out of the blue. They have been developed over the years as men have struggled with others, and with themselves, to find and to maintain ways of living together that would make the burdens of life more tolerable. To question the usefulness of referring to democracy as a way of life, so far as the conduct of education is concerned, is not to question the distinctiveness of democracy. Ways of life are surely involved in democracy; a way of life is not.

What we need to emphasize is the quality that pervades the human relationship because certain *principles of relationships* are at issue. Respect for the individual person; respect for ideas that individuals generate; respect for decisions taken jointly; respect for law as this is hammered out on the anvils of interpretation that respect both the individual and the need for social controls in order that individual respect may be maintained; respect for legislation that seeks to equalize opportunity both at the beginning and at the end of life—these are among the working principles of those who take democracy seriously. As principles they help men discover ways, better ways, of conducting the human relationship. They do not, being principles, underwrite what the specific ways are to be. It is the function of shared intelligence to make this discovery as we move from situation of relationship to situation of relationship. Our principles help us in our valuing; they provide us with bases of judging how better to organize our lives; they function as dynamic instruments that keep us coming at life democratically. What they add up to, indeed, is a way of coming at life. And this, as I see it, is just what democracy, over and beyond its more limited political meaning, connotes: *a way of coming at life so that each individual and each idea may have an opportunity to be heard in situations of tolerance and understanding, providing us thus with a normal means of progressively extending the base line of our common interests, the ever-present democratic concern.*

An education designed for democracy, then, should exemplify all of the flexibility, all of the tolerance, which democratic principles demand, if it is to be free of dogma or of routine practice. No school of thought has an inherent right to take it over. No specified body of subject matter will guarantee its success. No single methodology will of itself transform it from an authoritarian operation into a democratic one.

We argue over the wrong things. Instead of examining the consequences of our actions to see what qualities of democratic relationships they advance, and in what degree, we quarrel about the validity of the prospectus we propose. Thus, some say that all who believe in absolute standards are undemocratic, that all who believe in organized subject matter are authoritarian. Others reverse the picture, saying that those who do not believe in absolute standards are irresponsible, that those who turn to interest and need in building the curriculum are barbaric. All use labels too freely. The test lies in the consequences of the teacher-student relationship, in the meaningful quality of the learning situation which results, in the spirit that pervades the total undertaking.

I happen to believe, for instance, that men have progressively built up the principles that guide them in their behavior and that this is a never-ending process. Yet I know those who believe our directing principles to be absolute and, though they are surely wrong, they are good men. They believe that life is somehow fulfilled for them by their sense that what they take to be personally true and good has objective status in the universe at large. They believe in democracy, I discover, quite as much as I do, and their desire to achieve it for all men is no less than mine. Are we then to part company when we turn to the task of education? I don't think so. I do think we might properly part company, with the parting being initiated from either quarter, if one were to discover that the other mistreated students by denying them the right to become persons in the only way that they can, by doing their own choosing, judging, thinking.

Life would be simpified if we could tell from the reading of an individual's philosophical and pedagogical credentials what consequences would follow his entry into the classroom. But life is not this neat, and we shall have to continue to reach our judgments by evaluating the quality of the intellectual and human enterprise which results as the teaching-learning act is initiated and maintained. It is here, if any place, that we may gain evidence on which to establish preferences for curricular patterns, for methods of teaching, or for purposes. If we come at education democratically, we shall be patient with those who differ with us, more tolerant of their deviations. If we come at education democratically, we shall share as our common holding the values and the principles by which free men may create an enriched life in which all may participate with dignity and, through education, may create future citizens who possess the techniques and the temper to carry this life forward.

We shall be educating for democracy, it seems to me, when we see, in the need to help the immature grow into the skills, the knowledge and the attitudes needed by free men, an opportunity to educate ourselves concurrently in what it means to come at life democratically. Ralph Barton Perry has said:

> To live appropriately to a democratic society requires that one shall prefer this form of association to the company of the servile and obsequious. It is this inter-

play of freedoms—this living among the free—that creates the zest and exhilaration of democratic social relations.[11]

To grow to prefer the democratic society requires that one shall have the opportunity to live within an educative experience that gains its meaning from those who do their teaching under the spur of the zest and exhilaration which they know will accompany the achievement of democratic social relations.

[11] *Realms of Value*, p. 286.

PART TWO

Moral-Ethical Values, Spiritual Values, and Education

THE DEMOCRATIC ethos provides a rationale for all the activities of the members of society. When the ethos is understood, the value system of the society is made clear. Moral-ethical values and spiritual values, as integral parts of the value system, are deeply rooted convictions that strengthen all other values. Values, as an important part of our social heritage, help men to think and act in ways that tie the present to the past and, in providing a sense of history, strengthen the ethos of the society. For this reason, when values are subverted, the social fabric is weakened.

Today, our society is pluralistic, its institutions complex, its values many and varied. The attempts to allocate spheres of influence and responsibility to secular and sectarian agencies for the inculcation of values have not been too successful. This has caused many people to lose sight of the ideal meaning of democracy. Far too often, there is no connection between the values learned from a sectarian source and the values practiced in a secular setting. The ideal possibilities of democracy will never become actual if moral-ethical and spiritual values remain separated.

There is considerable agreement today that leaders and followers must be more knowledgeable than ever before, and that our values must let us deal successfully with present issues even as they serve as a basis for future actions. Educators, in theory if not in practice, are held responsible for teaching children those values that will let them deal with everyday affairs in a democratically consistent manner. Both secular and sectarian groups want the public schools to accomplish what other socializing agencies have failed to achieve.

This delegation of responsibility for teaching values raises a number of complex issues. Moral-ethical and spiritual standards have been taught by the older generation to the younger generation from time immemorial; today, however, the standards and precepts taught young people do not always help them to make sense of both the difficulties and the opportunities of the present. It seems clear that the teaching, learning, and practicing of democratic values require careful reappraisal. Unfortunately, the pluralism of society makes it hard to take these steps; on the one hand, our value conflicts reduce the chance of effective school-community cooperation; but on the other hand, the school is asked to undertake more tasks than ever.

Chapter 6

VALUES AND EDUCATION

The primary objective of this chapter is to make available to those preparing to teach some concepts and strategies that will clarify democratic values for them.

Many points of view are presented in the literature about the nature and sources of values and to impose on any student still another set of moral-ethical and spiritual standards may not contribute materially to his quest for knowledge. It seems more likely that the true sense and meaning of value conflicts will be understood best when each student learns, under the guidance of his teachers, what previous generations learned. When the young study the past in this way, they can reconsider their heritage and can make its significance available and relevant to present-day conditions.

Several contributions aid our quest for maximum clarity about our historic values. In these writings, the term "moral-ethical" is used since moral and ethical are so intimately related. In so doing, considerations of character are linked to matters of principle. R. Bruce Raup, a philosopher, contends that the moral and the religious are different aspects of human endeavor, and it is misleading to look upon them as dealing with identical values. What is moral originates in the community, and the authority for designating the good and the right is the responsibility of the individuals comprising the community. The sanctions established to uphold the claims as to what is moral are created by human beings and can be changed only by human beings. Raup points out that not all human interests are moral. Each individual has "a domain of privacy," which is potentially moral.

Such moral ideas cannot be realized until individual activities affect the lives of others. In actual practice, individuals are more concerned with matters pertaining to the self-domain than with moral matters affecting the community. Furthermore, a balance should be kept between the realm of the private and the personal and the realm of the public lest an undue emphasis upon the moral diminish the satisfactions to be gained from efforts to live and work with others.

In the realm of the self-domain, religious experience operates as and is identified as a good. Raup suggests that religious experience sustains the individual in his efforts to understand what experience intimates. Religious experience should not be permitted to claim authority over the uncertainties of life and thus lessen the good to be derived from moral activity. As Raup says: "When a religion claims a moral sanction that is eventually over *moral authority, it gets out of its proper dimension and, as history so clearly testifies, it builds the defeat of its own freedom." There is a place for both moral experience and religious experience in the daily activities of each individual. A relationship exists between that which is defined as moral and that which is defined as religious, and the individual should strive to understand how they are related.*

A second philosopher, George E. Axtelle, focuses attention upon these fundamental questions: "How do we know whether a given value statement is true?" "How can we know which values are better?" "Is there a hierarchy of values?" "How can we deal with absolute values?" Axtelle examines democratic values in relation to cultural relativity, democracy and cultural relativity, and democracy and absolutism.

MORAL AUTHORITY AND RELIGIOUS SANCTION

R. Bruce Raup

MORAL AUTHORITY

The distinction between the moral and religious dimensions is seen most clearly as we examine their respective sources of authority. Moral authority takes form eventually in connection with the claims of the community upon the conduct of its members. It is the authority of a people's deep common persuasions of what is acceptable, permissible, required, and expected. The depth to which these community claims penetrate the lives of the people is

Reprinted from *Teachers College Record*, Vol. 54, No. 6 (March 1953), pp. 299–304.

illustrated by the meaning of the word "mores," which comes from the same root. The mores are so integrally a part of the people's minds and characters that they are seldom even thought of; they are just the way the people are, believe, expect, act. Their presence and power are seen in the quick, almost automatic, and often violent rejection and expulsion of those who deviate from them.

When mores are broken and the moral front becomes irregular, and the contention of the deviate is listened to, and community claims of long standing come up for re-examination, then the moral interest has become reflective, deliberate. But it has not changed its base in the community. It only seeks a reconstructed common acceptance, requirement, and expectation, for herein is the eventual arbiter. The moral prophet is confirmed only in the eventual honor of a finally reconstructed community. He may indeed, as a lone individual, have felt deeply convinced that he was right, but among the hundred others who have proposed different reforms and who have felt equally that they were right, he is the only one who eventually survived, as we say, in the hearts of his people. And this, often long after he had been persecuted, even physically destroyed, for his belief. The authority for what is good and right for the human community is in the keeping of the human community. There has been no claimed source of moral authority in all history which has not eventually been compelled to yield to the advancing claims of this community.

By its very nature moral authority can and must be thus humanly established and, when changed, must be thus humanly changed. A people steeps its character in modes and principles of conduct which its members live by. The concern is common because all members may be involved in the consequences when any one or more of them chooses to deviate. We do not let people freely steal, lie, commit murder, hurt others physically or personally, directly or indirectly work harm upon others. These moral requirements of a people are held in many and varying degrees of seriousness. Some of them are sharply defined and embodied in legal institutions. Others are customary and are enforced largely by public opinion or ready individual acceptance or both. Still others are in the form of generalized guides or moral principles which have been formulated over long years to direct conduct in the interest of the human claims upon it. But at whichever of these levels the moral claim is defined, the inevitable conclusion is that it is a human community claim.

We do not speak of moral freedom as readily as we speak of other freedoms. This is probably because the essential character of the moral interest is found in community requirements and community expectations. There *is* moral freedom but it is not freedom *from* the community; it is freedom *within* the community. It is either freedom to act with a wide range of choice, when the public interest does not require strict limits to choice, or freedom to propose or otherwise initiate change in common requirements and standards. It might come to mean partial revolt against community requirements, but such a revolt when justified is not a retreat to chaos. As such it would be immoral. When it is justified it is a step in a daring, vigorous campaign to effect change in the standard requirements of the community.

Not all human interests are moral. We are individuals, unique, self-regarding, each building a domain of privacy. We ask respect for this privacy and in turn give respect to the similar domain in others and to their unique claims as far as we reasonably can. Any part of our individual self-domain is *potentially* moral, as when its effect upon others becomes a matter to consider. But potentially does not mean actually. In most of our pursuit of interest in living, the realm of the personal and private is much more inclusive than our occupation with the moral. This is as it should be. Indeed, conduct becomes immoral when it does not respect and actually further this wide range of rightful privacy. Paradoxically, one of our chief community (moral) attainments is a common, standardized, institutionalized regard for this very individual freedom.

When the active moral interest is made to extend incessantly over every phase of living, it becomes a damper on living; it dulls and warps life. Our use of the word "puritanical" is testimony to the eventual public rejection of such practice. Again, when the moral and the political merge and as such become the all-dominating emphasis in a people's life, we experience what is called totalitarianism. The moral interest, as active, is properly a *limited* part of human life, that part in which we must attend to the wide human claim on our behavior. If we would but realize this limitation, our attention to moral needs would be more definite and more adequate, and the experience of freedom would thereby be more inclusive and more genuine.

In this setting, the nature and the pursuit of the religious interest come into focus. And, again, the distinctive character of the religious interest may well be seen as we note the kind of authority to which it turns.

RELIGIOUS SANCTION

But first, what do we mean by religious experience? To search for a precise definition would not be very rewarding. Better that we point to it, denote it. The assumption that religious experience is a wide if not a universal kind of experience may safely be made. So if we point to it, it will be recognized. It is what happens in us, for example, when we are aware of an ever-receding range of the unknown and the mysterious; when we sense our human inability to understand and to control; when we are humbled by the limits of our wisdom and our power; when the unpredictable and the precarious make us feel our perpetual unreadiness for what may come; when we are confronted by the indeterminacy as well as the ordered and determined nature in our context of living; when we are either cast down or lifted up by the events of the seemingly limitless medium in which our existence and our destiny are wrought; when we feel the depths of human degradation, or the heights of human good and human aspiration; when we partake in the unceasing drama of hate and love, and suffer it and wonder at it so much more than we can understand it; when we move, less than half knowing why, through the gamut of our possibilities, from doubt and despair to faith and courage and even to moments of ecstasy, moments which no one can ever take entirely from us; when we are in the presence of the great crises of life, birth, death, personal devotion and personal separation, calls to greatness in sacrifice, calls to decision where no one of the alternatives is clear and the step is a venture into the largely unkown.

It is in such events as these that we most commonly undergo what we term a "religious experience." On these occasions no feeling is more basic than that of being responsibly involved in what is beyond our understanding and our power. We must act, although we so little know how or why. Yet we try. We must try, for even choosing not to act is a dangerous kind of action. So we do aspire, project a future, plan and proceed. We test the rules, try to keep them or to change them, makes choices and decisions as occasion arises, work with our fellows and work alone. And when we must do all this in a setting the meanings of which we so little grasp, we like to think that the powers and the conditions which are so far out of our ken and our reach are still on our side; that we are not out of harmony with them. Is not this just the setting in which our religious interest directs our pursuit?

We do reach as far as scientifically guided, consistent, tested reasoning can toward the unknown and the mysterious, but we do not and, I believe, should not stop there. We reach in speculative, imaginative construction beyond what we more surely know, often in terms of what we more surely know, and try to picture to ourselves the nature of that which is thus beyond us. We try to conjure some explanatory conditions, some chain of causes for what we see happen to us and around us. Some try to do this with consistency; some make undisciplined leaps in imagination and fill the heavens with persons and powers to their satisfaction. Some become very influential seers and gather great numbers of followers to see with them from where they stand and as they see. Some seers come to claim or to have claimed for them a special access to the great unknown. These become great leaders in vision, and how well we know the influence they have in the thinking and conduct of whole peoples! Systems of observance are instituted in the patterns thus conceived and great populations seek thereby to keep their lives in harmonious relation to that which is ever beyond them.

While thus to pursue the religious interest is one of the deepest of human goods, this pursuit loses its rightful savor and defeats its own best attainments when its tenets and its agents make claim to authority which is more certain than the very admission of uncertainty in which they must venture. When one person conceives a structure of things beyond his actual ken, starting with what he does more surely know, and finds great reward and good in believing and living as nearly as he can in harmony with this vision, he is exercising a privilege and a good to which he has a right, a right which both he and we must cherish. When he gathers a group with him and they freely join in the grounds of confidence thus afforded, this group too, however small or large, must enjoy the right to do so. But when this imaginatively constructed unknown is made into claims of final authority over the minds of people and is promoted itself as the Truth, it steps out of bounds.

It becomes important in this connection to note the distinction between authority and sanction. In the dictionary we find that authority means "power or right to enforce obedience; moral or legal supremacy; the right to command, or give an ultimate decision." And, again, "power over the opinions of others; . . intellectual influence." Evidently the primary medium in which authority is pertinent is one in which there is an implicit claim either upon the social and moral conduct of the people concerned or upon what they intellectually believe and assert as established. Both of these can today be shown to be claims which are valid eventually and only in the freely persuaded common acceptance of the people concerned.

The derivation of the word *sanction* is significant when we compare its meaning with that of authority. The root verb means "to render sacred" and the root noun means "a law or a decree; especially an ecclesiastical decree." As we well know, the word "sanction" in common usage has come to mean practically the same as authority. Originally, the word "sanction" represented people in the pursuit of religious orientation. But then we see the eventual merging of this meaning with that of authority. The two dimensions have come thus to be taken as one.

This merging of meanings has produced confusion in modern thought and action. Moral character and conduct, we are told, are to be had and maintained at a desirable level only through the cultivation of religious experience and the operation of religious sanction. It is at this point that the identification of religious *sanction* with moral *authority* has become seriously misleading. In achieving moral adequacy the basic and eventual authority is acceptance and active promotion in and by the community of the people concerned. Religions may sanction this authority; that is, incorporate it in their great ventured world outlooks, and, for their own adherents, thus render it sacred. This is a deeply human aspiration. It represents a human need. But to confuse this religious sanction with the rightful moral authority is to induce the making of public policies, particularly of political and educational policies, which lead to partial paralysis in both the moral and the religious dimensions of human living.

The surest way to see the ill consequences of this assumption of an unfounded authority is to let a religion thus built up and institutionalized confront a human moral claim to which its God or its gods do not consent. The moral claim *must* be heeded. If, for example, a religion denies the community moral claim to the conditions of health, we in this community must assert and press the moral claim, and the religion must either prove the falsity of the claim on moral grounds, or yield and change. If, again, this world of nations decides to settle its difficulties without resort to the irresponsible use of violence and deceit, then any religion whose God or gods demand and justify these practices has to settle the issue in the moral dimension with other peoples, and the gods may just have to change their demands accordingly.

When a religion claims a moral sanction that is eventually *over* moral authority, it gets out of its proper dimension and, as history so clearly testifies, it builds the defeat of its own freedom. For peoples cannot finally surrender to any other authority their claim to the moral authority by which they live.

There is indeed a vital relation between the moral needs and the religious interests of people. If what is found to be morally good is at the same time believed to be in harmony with what we in our farthest reaches of imaginative construction conceive to be the shape of what is beyond our sure knowledge and power, we may become thereby the stronger exponents of the moral good. We may feel the sanction of the powers that be—that they are on our side.

It is therefore possible that one and the same moral requirement in the world community of peoples may have back of it the spiritual support and sanctions of many otherwise differing religions.

Again, if a minority believes that the common (moral) standards are inadequate and undertakes to bring about a change in them, the conceived sanction of a religious belief may mean the difference between the qualities of character which succeed and those which fail. In fact, more often than not, religions have come into prominence through thus furnishing spiritual orientation and sanction of a militant moral minority.

If the world of peoples would thus give rightful priority to moral claims, to "human rights," and make *only* these claims upon one another, the claims would work their way into the many religions and thus procure unity in a setting of rightful diversity. This, the moral authority, is the only just authority among peoples. They must otherwise be free to chart the unknown, to seek comfort and confidence, sanction, inspiration and faith in their own ways, ten thousand ways—individuals in their own ways, minorities in their own ways, whole peoples in their ways. The moral community of man must support this almost unlimited range of options when people seek the good in their relations with what is beyond anybody's sure knowledge. There is no other reasonable meaning of religious freedom.

HOW DO WE KNOW WHAT VALUES ARE BEST?

George E. Axtelle

DEMOCRATIC VALUES AND CULTURAL RELATIVITY

Cultural subjectivity. It is the peculiarity of each culture, class, institution or occupation that it must view the world through its own perspective, and that it judges others by its own standards. It takes itself for granted. This would be a matter for amusement in a world where cultures, classes, institutions, and occupations were comparatively stable, isolated, and independent. In our world of rapid change and mobility, of cultural association and interdependence, it is no laughing matter. Standards have little value unless they are agreed to by those to whom they apply as well as those who apply them. Cooperative action demands common standards, common objectives, and a common frame of reference. Thus the question of whether democratic values or any other can transcend the cultures in which they originate, and become accepted in a broader field of cutural interaction is one of great importance. Agreement and cooperative relations within and among cultures depends upon a body of common ideals and values. The alternative is "war of all against all," each ready to perish in its own sense of "rightness."

I believe that certain ideals, ideas, and values may transcend the cultures in which they originate and come to achieve universal acceptance.

Science and cultural relativity. Experimental science is the peculiar product of western civilization. In spite of that fact it has had no little difficulty becoming assimilated by that civilization itself. Wherever its results or its method of thought clash with older beliefs and values conflict still occurs. It is now generally accepted and employed in physical and technological areas, less so in biological areas and meets much resistance in social areas. Yet its advance seems to be continuous and cumulative.

In view of the resistance which science has met in the culture of its origin, it is significant that other advanced cultures such as the Russian, Chinese, Indian and others are beginning to assimilate it with great rapidity. Here too it will doubtless meet deep resistances as it clashes with older institutional and class values. There is every reason to believe that it will continue its progressive conquest of the various cultures.

Reprinted from *Progressive Education*, Vol. 27 (April 1950), pp. 191–195.

One reason for this belief is that technology, the child of science, is accepted more readily than science itself. But technology like the proverbial camel's head in the tent, increasingly takes possession of the cultures in which it is introduced. As this happens the demand for science increases, and the expansion of science and technology continues cumulatively.

Here we have a culture trait with a universal character although it is the child of a particular culture. Moreover in its assimilation by the various cultures it creates a common basis of understanding and communication among them. It also creates the social, economic and intellectual conditions from which emerge the values and ideas that are central to democracy. This is not to say that it will produce a uniform world culture or a uniform expression of democracy. It is to suggest rather that within a set of common values and ideas the various cultures will maintain their integrity and that whatever world culture may develop there will be differentiation and variety of expression.

Religion and cultural relativity. It is significant that the original insights of the great world religions express basic democratic values. In their institutional expression these insights are largely overlaid and obscured by their cultural contexts. Dominant power elements in a society jealously guard the character and expression of religious institutions because of their crucial role in shaping social valuations. This has the effect of hardening, or rigidifying, the culture and of accentuating its ethnocentricity and cultural subjectivity. The extreme expression of cultural rigidity, subjectivity, and ethnocentrism occurs when religious beliefs and values of the culture are translated into ontological absolutes.

Yet it must not be forgotten that the original insights of the great world religions have a universal appeal which cuts across cultural frontiers. It is only because of this fact that they are world religions. Since there is no cultural medium through which these insights can be communicated without being reduced to the prevailing culture pattern, religious reformers continue to arise and re-express the earlier insights and values so long as the culture possesses vitality. Thus religion is at once the most conservative force in a culture and at the same time a liberating and progressive force.

The universal appeal of the original insights is rooted in their effort to see man and human values in their generic character cutting across culture frontiers. Christ said that he brought a sword. By this he meant that his vision was one which would eternally attack prevailing ways and institutions in terms of generic and universal values, values springing from what is common among men irrespective of culture. Hence, Christianity and every other world religion in their vital phases have been a profound challenge, a criticism and solvent of prevailing cultures and their values. But, as noted above, this is a two-way process. In dissolving prevailing ways and their values religion has likewise been assimilated by them and to them.

Democracy and cultural relativity. I have suggested that in certain respects both religion and science express something universal and generic about men and values, hence their capacity to transcend their cultural origins. In a similar way we might say that democracy expresses something generic and universal. It is for this reason that all three are both rejected and assimilated by cultures; but neither assimilation nor rejection is complete, but is rather an accommodation. Hence occur periodic revivals which renew and extend earlier insights which act as progressive ferment in the culture. When these revivals fail to occur the culture atrophies and becomes archaic.

It should be noted that in some sense most cultures have certain democratic insights, values and practices. We should beware (in our own cultural subjectivity) of identifying our own culture with democracy. While certainly conditions in our own culture have been favorable to the growth of democratic values and practices, the weight of earlier non-democratic values is yet great. In our own case, as in others, our culture is an inextricable mixture of democratic and other values. Obviously, therefore, we cannot expect to export our culture *in toto* as democracy, nor even that part which we deem democratic.

Our problem is to try to identify values which are common to men whatever their culture, for among these may be found those which more fully express the democratic idea. We must expect democratic values to express themselves differently in different cultures. The recognition of this fact is itself fundamental to the democratic outlook.

Faith in the future of democracy lies in its cultural inclusiveness, in its roots in human nature and in its universal values common to all men. The virtue of democracy lies in its hospitality toward variety and difference and in its capacity to promote cultural synthesis and creativity. It offers the promise of producing a body of overarching or undergirding values for one world culture with the utmost encouragement of cultural variety and cultural differentiation within this common framework.

As with science and religion, democracy is an expression of values common among men. Its future will doubtless be enriched by the contribution of many cultures. Hence, it does not depend merely upon a particular culture pattern transcending its particular origins but upon the creativity of cultural interaction and cultural fusion. The capacity of western democracy to encompass and carry forward this process of fusion is its distinctive contribution to man's future. We may expect democracy along with science and religion to become a major dynamic in cultural change and reconstruction. We may also expect science, religion, and democracy to reinforce each other at those points at which they express common humanity.

Democracy seems to offer the only basis upon which the various cultures can cooperate, at the same time that it stimulates and encourages what is unique and distinctive in each of the several cultures. Democratic values lie at the heart of social and cultural creativity and advance. They respect and preserve the integrity of cultures at the same time that they release the progressive and reconstructive forces essential to their stability and vigor. Nor should we think of a world culture as utopian or romantic. The past has seen several instances approaching such a culture. The Hellenistic and Roman periods are cases in point. Certainly western civilization in many respects tends to become world wide in character. Ultimately, however, we must expect other major cultures to contribute significantly to the larger synthesis.

Democracy and absolutism. We return now to the question: how can groups, institutions or cultures which hold absolute values cooperate in a common world? What does democracy do in the presence of fixed attitudes and coercive power? Can democracy depend upon agreements at the level of action, looking forward to common experiences and cooperative action to build a common body of operational or procedural values sufficient to enable a society to achieve a measure of stability?

We may note that, historically, democracy has emerged precisely at those points in time when dominant powers were effectively challenged. The middle classes in Ancient Greece and in Western Europe were able to challenge the landholding and military classes. Democracy emerged as a *modus vivendi* in the situation. So long as these were the major centers of power the balance was unstable. Democracy has prospered when a variety of independent centers of power have come into being. In this situation procedures have developed which defined the limits within which power could be exercised. This is the meaning of constitutional government. Stability has depended upon the existence of such a variety of centers of power that any single conflict would leave most of them undisturbed. They have remained as a balance wheel, a public, a source of judgment of the controversy.

It is interesting to note that the most absolutistic groups when in a minority role are often the most ardent champions of democratic procedures. Instances of this are the Catholics in colonial America and the communists in America in the 1920's and 1930's. It is also important to note that the most idealistic ideologies become apologies for tyranny in its more extreme forms when they become official. Religious hierarchies and "the party of the working class," when they dominate a society may be most extreme in their tyranny. (The British Labor Party is not an illustration of this point because it actually represents large segments of the middle class and has never proclaimed exclusive right to existence.) It is questionable whether democracy can ever long survive the absence of a plurality of power centers in a society. It would seem to be sound democratic strategy therefore, to encourage the greatest variety of independent centers of power.

THEORETICAL QUESTIONS

How do we know whether a given value statement is true? A value statement has ultimate reference to the life of a community. The community may vary in size and complexity from a family to the community of nations. A community is any group which is aware of common needs. There are two tests of the validity of a value judgment. How effective is it, as a proposal for action, in uniting the parties affected by it? In the long run, how well does it accomplish what it proposes to accomplish?

A community may make two kinds of mistakes in such judgments. It may be swayed by dominant and influential interests to accept as a value a line of action which ignores the needs of other less articulate and influential interests. Or an initial proposal while unifying the community at the time may conceal unexpected contradictions or it may be in error in its assumptions of fact. As a result the course of action fails to do what it proposes, i.e., to advance and prosper the various interests which constitute the community, and to maintain the integrity of the community.

An important function of leadership is to identify those who may be affected by a course of action; to help them express their situation and their interests in such a way that they may be fully incorporated in the value judgment. How well this is done determines how well the community is unified in action. It is also a function of leadership to see that the community has an adequate understanding of the nature of the situation, including the interests involved, and to help the community make a proper estimate of the probable consequences of the various proposals that are considered. It is at this point that the work of science and the expert becomes crucial in the value judgment. The best intentions in the world miscarry when inadequately informed.

How do we know which values are better? We have indicated above the tests of validity of a value judgment: the test of inclusiveness and the test of operation. These criteria apply here. The course of action which most unites a community at the time and which in the long run keeps it united is the better course of action. Those values are better which better organize a community in its cooperative life, which more fully enlist the active energies and interests of the individual or the community in a unified act which results in the continuing integrity of personality or community.

Is there a hierarchy of values? Values are as varied as situations and communities. The value in each situation is that course of action which most fully meets the demands of the situation. The conception of hierarchy among values springs from the idea that means and ends are externally related to one another, that ends can be shaped independently of means and that means can be shaped independently of ends. Since the reality of ends is considered to exist independently from the realm of action—hence in a static and absolute form—these ends may be organized into a logical hierarchy. But this misconceives the valuing situation. It ignores the fact that means and ends are related as part to whole, hence they mutually shape each other. The end is the course of action which unifies the community. The means are the aspects, or steps, or parts of the total course of action. To treat values or ends apart from the concrete situations in which they operate is to deprive judgment and action of flexibility and sensitiveness in the situation. When we conceive value as a course of action appropriate to a situation such external ends lose meaning.

It is true, however, that men have learned through their experience certain principles of social action. They have learned, for example, that truth, intelligence, inclusiveness, creativity, and other qualities are essential to the cooperative act. These are to be thought of as value principles for the guidance of value judgment. We may indeed, as educators, plan to cultivate these qualities in the character of our students. To identify such value principles as absolutes belonging to a hierarchical structure is to give them a static character and isolate them from action; it is to deprive actual situations of the kind of thought and attention essential to their resolution. The hierarchical and absolute conception of values produces a stereotyped and static form of thought which embarrasses it in the presence of concrete situations.

How can we deal with absolute values? Absolute values in effect refer to fixed and stubborn attitudes and beliefs which acknowledge no authority in experience, i.e., in the cooperative act. Absolute values are often the intellectual instruments of sub-groups in a community seeking sanction for interests and attitudes in some metaphysical realm, which they cannot justify in the cooperative act. When such groups possess power their attitudes are accompanied by coercion. Then we are confronted with the question how democracy shall deal with coercion and power. They are recalcitrant and stubborn because they have the power to exercise privileges which the cooperative act cannot justify.

The problem of the rest of the community is to clarify its own common needs and interests. This perception of common interests modifies the attitudes of the community and alters the structure of power. For it must not be forgotten that all power in the last analysis rests upon attitudes. When the community clearly discerns its own interests it deprives recalcitrant groups of the social power to enforce their attitudes. They then have no recourse but their own reconstruction as members of the community in good faith, or futile isolation.

Since the community must always have regard for its own integrity it must try to restore these groups to good membership lest they remain a disintegrative factor. In short, fixed attitudes and coercive power can only be resisted by altering the power structure. Appeasement but strengthens them.

At the same time their reconstruction must always be a concern of the community in the interest of its own unity. Hence, it must use coercion in such a way that hitherto recalcitrant groups can reconstruct their attitudes and become participating members in good faith.

CONCLUSION

Democracy as an expression of the principle of inclusiveness is hospitable to cultural variety and differentiation. It is also the expression of generic human needs common to men in all cultures, particularly the need for cooperation. Hence, if conceived in this way democracy offers a general platform upon which all cultures may cooperate.

The value in any situation is the course of action which most unifies the interests and energies involved in it. Hence the selection and validation of values has reference to such a course of action. It not only unifies the community for the moment but contributes to the continuing integrity of the community. Hence, values are as varied as situations and communities.

To ascribe absolute status to values is to deprive action of flexibility and intelligence. Such conceptions of values frequently serve special national, class, or institutional interests that are unwilling to reconstruct themselves in accordance with the common interests of the community. They can be dealt with only as the community clarifies its common interests to itself and enters upon a course of action appropriate to those interests. Special groups in the interests of their own survival must participate in the life of the community or suffer frustration. The appeal to absolute values is the appeal of those who refuse to enter into full participation in the community for fear of loss of special privileges which cannot be justified on operational or social grounds.

Chapter 7

RELIGION AND THE STATE

Because *the idea of democracy encourages the fullest development of man's potentialities, a democratically inclined society is always pluralistic. When the opportunity to choose among many alternatives is expressed in thoughtful ways, conditions appear which fulfill the Constitution's deep concern with "the general welfare." The fact of cultural pluralism does not mean that any individual accepts and approves all the values that are available, but it does suggest tolerance, understanding, and appreciation. These are the characteristics that lead to a common orientation, to a range of values that have common appeal—what in our case are called American values. In searching for groups of similar values with universal appeal, the idea of the general welfare avoids the limitations of either-or thinking and any off-handed rejection of new value proposals.*

The values that represent a community's consensus must, of necessity, shun reliance on absolutes. By emphasizing orthodoxy and subordinating variety, absolute convictions restrict the efforts a democratically oriented society must make to keep all the possibilities of life open to its citizens. Our schools must help young people learn how broad the spectrum of values is in American society. If the young are well taught, they will appreciate and understand human differences. Many sectarian individuals and groups have contended, and continue to contend strenuously, for the exclusive right to propose a core of basic values for school life. As a result, the concept of the separation of church and state has become a value in itself. Especially relevant is the thesis of R. Freeman Butts, an historian, whose general position was formulated prior to certain recent court decisions, which further clarified the issues involved in the separation of church and state in such matters as reading of the Bible and state-formulated school prayers.

CHURCH AND STATE IN AMERICAN EDUCATION

R. Freeman Butts

Most Americans have long believed that one of the firmly established traditions of our national way of life has been the principle of separation of church and state as defined in the First Amendment to the Constitution in the words, "Congress shall make no law respecting an establishment of religion, or prohibiting the free exercise thereof." There has been little disagreement that the principle of separation has meant the protection of religious freedom and the right of individuals to worship and believe as they see fit according to conscience. This right has been embodied securely in the second clause of the First Amendment, which guarantees "free exercise" of religion, and in the bills of rights of the state constitutions.

In recent years, however, attention has been directed to the other aspect of the principle of the separation of church and state as defined in the First Amendment, namely, the prohibition concerning "an establishment of religion." Two recent Supreme Court decisions in the Everson and McCollum cases, along with their attendant bitter controversies, have made it clear that there is much less common agreement in the public mind concerning the meaning of the first clause of the First Amendment.

It is the meaning of the "establishment of religion" clause that is now being disputed so vigorously with respect to its application to education. Some prominent Roman Catholic and Protestant groups are insisting that this clause means simply that the federal government may not give support or special privileges to a single church in preference to other churches. They thus argue that the federal and state governments *may* properly "cooperate" with many or all churches just so long as the government treats all churches fairly and impartially and does not interfere with the free exercise of religion.

This would mean for education that the state *could* constitutionally promote and even support educational activities designed to help individuals avail themselves of religious instruction. Specifically, some Protestants argue that religious instruction in public schools would be perfectly proper and indeed desirable and necessary, so long as sectarian instruction is not forced

Reprinted from *Teachers College Record*, Vol. 52, No. 31 (December 1950), pp. 145–157.

upon those who do not wish it, thus preserving the principle of freedom of conscience. Likewise, some Catholics argue that the use of public funds for the support of certain activities related to their parochial schools not only would be permissible but would be a wise and desirable public policy. Under this heading would come the use of public funds for the transportation of children to church-controlled schools, free textbooks, school lunches, and health and medical services to these children. In this view any defensible meaning of the principle of separation of church and state would permit "cooperation" between church and state. Such cooperation, they maintain, would not infringe upon religious freedom so long as the state does not give preference to a single "establishment of religion."

ORIGINAL MEANING OF ESTABLISHMENT

It thus becomes necessary for Americans and especially for professional educators to look again at the historical meaning of "an establishment of religion" in order to see what validity these new arguments may have. Let us consider very briefly what the original meaning of "an establishment of religion" was as practiced in some of the American colonies in the seventeenth century. Establishment had two aspects: It meant, first, that the state used the force of law to give *financial support* to the established church. The state levied taxes upon all persons without regard to their religious beliefs, collected taxes for the support of clergymen and for the building and maintaining of churches. The state used its coercive power to punish with fines or imprisonment those who failed to pay their religious taxes.

Establishment meant, secondly, that the state gave *legal and moral support* to the doctrines and public worship of the established churches. The state prohibited by law the free exercise of religion. No religious beliefs except those of the legally approved religion could be publicly stated or taught without danger of legal punishment by the state. Public office holders in the state were required to be religiously orthodox and to take an oath to that effect. Clergymen were required by law to conform to the doctrines and methods of worship of the established church, and all persons, regardless of belief, were compelled by law to attend the public services of the established church and were subject to fines and penalties for failure to do so.

These, then, were the two principal aspects of the original meaning of "an establishment of religion": The financial support of religion by public funds and the legal enforcement of orthodox doctrines and modes of worship.

ORIGINAL MEANING OF "SEPARATION"

It is clear, then, that one of the dominant traditions in early colonial America was the belief that church and state were legitimate partners in the propagation and maintenance of an established religion. It should be noted immediately, however, that a second and equally authentic tradition was present in other colonies almost from their beginnings. This was the tradition of "separatism" which began as a minority viewpoint in the early seventeenth century but which became a majority point of view toward the end of the eighteenth century. As the tradition of separatism won its way in principle, the practice of establishment began to crumble on many fronts, until a high degree of separation was eventually won.

The theory of separation of church and state had its roots in the sixteenth and seventeenth centuries among several Protestant sects of Europe who resisted any civil or ecclesiastical authority that tried to enforce uniformity of belief. Thus, to achieve freedom of conscience for themselves and for others they fought against any union of church and state. They argued that all churches were voluntary associations of believers, and therefore they could brook no interference of the civil power with ecclesiastical affairs. Since religion is an individual relationship between each individual and God, they said, any coercion upon individuals is sinful and useless; the state must confine itself to civil affairs and leave religion to voluntary religious agencies.

One of the most effective early statements of the principle of separation in America was made by Roger Williams, who believed that conflict among various religions could end only when there was complete separation between church and state, when all connections between civil and religious authorities were cut away. Neither should try to control the affairs of the other. All religious beliefs should not only be allowed freedom to exist, but the state must not infringe the *equal* rights of any religious belief, Christian or non-Christian. He even held that freedom of *non-belief* should be allowed by the state. Only in these ways may the true welfare of the state as well as of all religions be achieved.

Needless to say, such "radical" views as those expressed by Roger Williams in the seventeenth century did not immediately change the picture of the dominant outlook toward establishment, but they did take root ever more firmly among larger numbers of people, especially among the non-conformist and dissenting groups that came to America in increasing numbers in the seventeenth and eighteenth centuries. Above all, the most important factor in the growth of freedom was the rapid increase of a wide variety of religious groups which soon began to attack the entrenched establishments.

In the eighteenth century two things happened. The first is very familiar. It was the effort to maintain the public support of a single establishment but at the same time to give greater toleration to non-conformist religious groups. Thus gains were made for the "free exercise" of religion, but the *financial support* of the single establishment was maintained. Even though dissenting groups could practice their own faith in public worship they were still required to pay taxes for the single preferred church.

Then, in several colonies a second thing happened, and this has either been forgotten or purposely overlooked by those who demand more cooperation between church and state today. This was the effort to *recognize several churches as equal members of the established religion* and to give them all *financial support* through the force of law. The term "establishment" came to be applied, not just to *one* church, but to any and all churches that had legal and financial connections with the state. To distinguish this form of establishment from the earlier form I shall call it a *multiple establishment* of religion.

During the eighteenth century the dissenting groups became restless under the financial obligations laid upon them by the standing orders. Despite their greater freedom to organize and to worship they found that "free exercise" was still a shadowy grant of toleration so long as the single establishments had the privileges of tax support. They therefore worked to gain exemption from the religious taxes and then demanded the complete disestablishment of the standing orders. The established churches, for their part, tried to save what they could by persuading the legislatures to open up the tax privileges to those dissenting groups that had grown strong enough to threaten complete disestablishment. By this compromise more and more churches were admitted into the establishment and given the legal right to tax their members for the support of their own clergymen, churches, and public worship.

For example, by laws passed in 1727 in Massachusetts and Connecticut, Episcopalians were given the right to have their local taxes applied to the support of their own clergy, even though the Congregational church was most widely recognized as the established church. But when Episcopalians gained the legal and financial right to support their own churches from tax funds it can truly be said that a multiple establishment had been achieved. By the time of the First Amendment, in 1789, there were no longer single establishments of religion in New England: Massachusetts, New Hampshire, and Connecticut used tax funds for the support of any Protestant minister of whatever denomination who might be elected by a majority of voters in town meeting. This was multiple establishment.

Similarly in the South all remaining single establishments became multiple establishments or were wiped out entirely by the time of the First Amendment. The constitution of Maryland in 1776 and of South Carolina in 1778 contained elaborate provisions for multiple establishment.

A bill introduced into the Virginia legislature in 1779 by conservatives who were trying to defeat Jefferson's Bill for Religious Freedom clearly illustrates the meaning of multiple establishment as favored by conservatives and as opposed by Jefferson and Madison.

> The Christian Religion shall in all times coming be deemed and held to be the established Religion of this Commonwealth; and *all Denominations* of Christians

demeaning themselves peaceably and faithfully, shall enjoy *equal* privileges, civil and Religious. . . .

Whenever free male Persons not under twenty one Years of Age, professing the Christian Religion, shall agree to unite themselves in a Society for the purpose of Religious Worship, they shall be constituted a Church, and esteemed and *regarded in Law as of the established Religion of this Commonwealth,* and on their petition to the General Assembly shall be entitled to be incorporated and shall enjoy *equal Privileges* with any other Society of Christians, and all that associate with them for the purpose of Religious Worship shall be esteemed as belonging to the Society so called.[1]

THE FIRST AMENDMENT

This was the conservatives' definition of "establishment of religion." It plainly meant multiple establishment. It was this meaning that Jefferson had in mind when he wrote in his Bill for Religious Freedom, which was finally passed in Virginia in 1786, "That no man shall be compelled to frequent or *support any religious worship, place, or ministry whatsoever.*" Jefferson also stated that no person ought to be compelled to support even *his own* minister. It was this meaning of establishment that Madison had in mind when he took a leading part in framing the first clause of the First Amendment prohibiting the Congress from making any "law respecting an establishment of religion."

Thus, "estabishment" came to be applied, not just to *one* church, but to any or all churches that had legal and financial connections with the state. This extended meaning of "establishment" was widely recognized at the time of the passing of the First Amendment. *Any* cooperation between the state and any or all churches was considered to be "establishment." It was this expanded meaning of multiple establishment that the First Amendment was designed to prevent on the national level as well as to prevent the narrow establishment of a single church.

It is this meaning of multiple establishment which has been forgotten, conveniently overlooked, or never understood by the various groups today who urge that "cooperation" between church and state is admissible so long as the state treats all religious groups equally and fairly. *That was exactly the purpose* of the several colonial provisions for multiple establishment and it was exactly the purpose of the attempts made in Virginia to achieve multiple establishment. Of course, they would have ruled out some sects which the dominant churches did not consider to be "safe" or legitimate religious groups, but the principle of multiple establishment is the same whether few, many, or all religious groups are taken into it. The state would always have to decide what was and what was not a religious group if it set out to "cooperate" with them all.

[1] H. J. Eckenrode, *Separation of Church and State in Virginia* (Richmond, 1910), pp. 58–59. [Italics added.]

I am convinced, too, that this meaning of multiple establishment was outlawed by the constitutions of the new states of the West when they were admitted to the Union. Note, for example, in the Kentucky constitution of 1792 the prohibition of support for *any* religion (that is, no single or multiple establishment) as well as the guarantee of free exercise of religion:

That all men have a natural and indefeasible right to worship Almighty God according to the dictates of their own consciences; that no man of right can be compelled to attend, erect, *or support any place of worship, or to maintain any ministry* against his consent; that no human authority can in any case whatever control or interfere with the rights of conscience; and that no preference shall ever be given by law to any religious *societies* or *modes* of worship.[2]

A careful inspection of state constitutions will show that virtually every state constitution contains a similar prohibition against support of *any* place of worship or maintenance of *any* ministry of religion. The intention in all these provisions is clearly to prohibit "an establishment of religion," and I am convinced that these state provisions as well as the first amendment were all intended to prohibit multiple establishment as well as single establishment. They are all a part of the same historical process.

THE FOURTEENTH AMENDMENT

The final step in the application of the basic principle of separation on the national level began with the adoption of the Fourteenth Amendment to the United States Constitution in 1868. The first section of the Fourteenth Amendment reads as follows:

No state shall make or enforce any law which shall abridge the privileges or immunities of citizens of the United States; nor shall any state deprive any person of life, liberty, or property, without due process of law; nor deny to any person within its jurisdiction the equal protection of the laws.

Thus were achieved through constitutional amendment those limitations upon the states with respect to civil liberties which the Bill of Rights of the Constitution forbids to the federal government itself. What the federal government cannot do, the states cannot do. The Fourteenth Amendment was in direct line with the principles of the first ten amendments.

During the last twenty-five years the Supreme Court has made the various aspects of the First Amendment applicable to the states by the Fourteenth Amendment. A whole series of cases bearing on freedom of speech, press, assembly, and petition was decided in the 1930's. During the 1940's the Supreme Court made the free-exercise-of-religion clause of the First Amend-

[2] Francis N. Thorpe, *The Constitutional History of the United States* (Chicago: Callaghan & Co., 1901), Vol. III, p. 1274. [Italics added.]

ment applicable to the states through the Fourteenth Amendment. In 1947 the Supreme Court decision in the Everson case took the next logical step and gave the same interpretation to the establishment-of-religion clause of the First Amendment and made *it* applicable to the states through the Fourteenth Amendment. In the Everson case the Supreme Court majority stated the principle (with which the minority agreed) as follows:

> The "establishment of religion" clause of the First Amendment means at least this: Neither a state nor the Federal Government can set up a church. *Neither can pass laws which aid one religion, aid all religions, or prefer one religion over another. . . . No tax in any amount, large or small, can be levied to support any religious activities or institutions, whatever they may be called, or whatever form they may adopt to teach or practice religion. . . .* In the words of Jefferson, the clause against establishment of religion by law was intended to erect "a wall of separation between Church and State."

No clearer statement could be made to show that the principle of separation of church and state as defined in the Everson case is in direct line with the historic meaning of the separation of church and state in America. Thus, the Supreme Court gradually brought its decisions into line with the intent of the framers of the First and Fourteenth Amendments. In order to protect the civil rights of all American citizens, the federal government has the right to enforce separation of church and state upon the several states by prohibiting single or multiple establishments of religion in the states. As indicated throughout this discussion, "establishment of religion" has always implied legal and financial support for religion. State support for one or for many religions, whether preferentially or impartially, is thus prohibited. Far from being a perversion of the original meaning of separation, the *principle* enunciated in the Everson case is the logical culmination of the authentic historical tradition of the principle of separation of church and state as it has developed from 1776 to the present time.

MEANING OF SEPARATION FOR EDUCATION

Now, what does this historical tradition of separation mean for education? The transition from private to public education in America took place in the first half of the nineteenth century *after* the principle of the separation of church and state had been clearly stated on both national and state levels but *before* it had been applied everywhere in practice. Indeed, education is one of the best examples to show how the principle itself came to be applied in practice during the early decades of the new nation. The principle of separation as applied to education was well developed in most states by the Civil War, and by the turn of the twentieth century the principle of separation was widely accepted as applicable to American public education in virtually all states. There were, however, wide variations of interpretation concerning what the principle meant for practice.

During this historical process most of the difficult issues of separation in education have centered around two main problem areas, namely, the use of public funds for religious schools, and religious instruction in the public schools. In its most general form the principle of separation of church and state came to embrace these two propositions:

1. Public funds shall not be used for religious schools.
2. Religious instruction shall not be given in the public schools.

It was a long and painful process to achieve these principles in practice and indeed they have not been uniformly applied everywhere even today, principally because of a lack of understanding of this history or a refusal to accept its meaning. In general, the process of arriving at agreement on these two principles during the nineteenth century went through several stages somewhat similar to the stages through which the principle of separation itself went during the eighteenth century. These stages were, of course, not parallel in time, but the general trend to the end of the nineteenth century is unmistakable.[3]

In general, America moved away from sectarian schools designed to promote established religious doctrines and worship and moved toward a common school supported by public funds, free and available to all, and designed to promote democratic citizenship. The curriculum of American schools moved away from a content permeated with religion toward a content based upon secular knowledge and morality.

When the educational revival of the 1820's to 1850's began to gain momentum, the advocates of a public school system ran head on into the issue of separation. The first attempts of the educational reformers to resolve the issue and to create a common school free to *all* and aimed at creating a democratic citizenry took the form of the non-sectarian religious public school. Horace Mann and other reformers had seen that a common school supported by public taxation could *not* include the teaching of any sectarian doctrines under the principle of separation as they understood it. They, however, believed that the requirements of religious freedom could be maintained if the public school simply divorced itself from *sectarian* religious instruction. But they also believed that the common elements of education should include moral education that would be based upon the common elements of Christianity to which all Christian sects would agree or to which they would take no exception. In general, these "common elements" took two forms; namely, teaching the common Christian, moral virtues of honesty, fairness, and truth, and also reading of the Bible as containing the common elements of Christian morals but reading it with no comment in order not to introduce

[3] For a more extensive discussion of this point see R. Freeman Butts, *The American Tradition in Religion and Education* (Boston: Beacon Press, 1950), Chapter V.

sectarian biases. On this basis, they felt justified in requiring support of the non-sectarian, religious public school by taxation upon all citizens.

NO RELIGIOUS INSTRUCTION IN PUBLIC SCHOOLS

If America had remained an exclusively Protestant country, this solution might have satisfied many people, despite the clear fact that a non-sectarian public school represented a form of cooperation between the state and many religious groups, in effect, a multiple establishment of religion in education. The practical difficulty arose, however, because America became increasingly heterogeneous in religious belief. The great increases in immigration from Ireland and Germany in the period from 1820 to 1860 brought large numbers of Roman Catholics to America. When faced with the prospect of sending their children to the so-called "non-sectarian" public school, they soon raised the objection that what seemed to be "non-sectarian" to Protestants was actually "sectarian" to Catholics. Catholics, therefore, objected to the sectarian quality of the public schools and made two general efforts to remedy the situation. They tried to have the Protestant non-sectarian instruction, including reading of the Bible, removed from the public schools, and they tried to obtain a share of the public funds for their own parochial schools in order that their rights of conscience would not be infringed by being forced to attend a public school where Protestant teachings were presented.

It was this situation which brought about appeal to the principle of separation of church and state and made necessary its application to education. The over-all result, after years of controversy and agitation, was that the majority of Americans decided that the only possible and practicable decision was to follow the principles of Madison and Jefferson that true protection for equal rights of conscience requires that *all* religious instruction be eliminated from the public schools and that no public funds be used for the support of religious schools.

During the second half of the nineteenth century the principle of separation in education spread rapidly through the states and even became a national political issue. In general, the prohibition against use of public funds for sectarian purposes became almost universal among the states by 1900, and the prohibition of religious instruction in the public schools was also widespread.

The one point that remained most in doubt as to *practice* was whether the reading of the Bible in public schools violated the principle of separation. It cannot be blinked that some courts ruled that the Bible was *not* sectarian instruction provided it was read without comment and if students who objected were excused from taking part. These decisions reflected the continuing belief among many persons that multiple establishment in education, if non-sectarian, was perfectly proper and would not violate freedom of worship and conscience. Other courts, however, have held exactly the opposite, that Bible reading *was* sectarian in the eyes of Catholics, Jews, and non-believers and therefore should be prohibited as unconstitutional because it in effect created a multiple establishment of religion.

NO PUBLIC FUNDS FOR RELIGIOUS SCHOOLS

The achievement of complete separation with regard to prohibiting the use of public funds for sectarian schools was even more universally widespread by 1900. The movement gained great headway following the Civil War. One of the reasons for this acceleration was the fact that the Roman Catholic Church redoubled its efforts to achieve a share of the public funds for its own parochial schools. This effort undoubtedly redoubled the efforts of other groups to prevent such outcome. These struggles took place on the national level as well as among the states. Virtually all states included some form of constitutional provision to prohibit tax funds for sectarian purposes. This movement was undoubtedly hastened by the action of the federal government. Congress required that all new states admitted to the Union after 1876 must adopt an irrevocable ordinance that not only guaranteed religious freedom but also required the state to include a provision

> . . . for the establishment and maintenance of a system of public schools, which shall be open to all the children of said State and free from sectarian control.

Congress was thus reflecting the trend that by this time had begun to sweep the country to establish common school systems based upon separation of church and state and it lent the authority of the federal government to that movement.

One other aspect of the national struggle over the religious issue in the nineteenth century should be mentioned. That has to do with the efforts in the Congress to achieve federal aid for education during the 1870's and 1880's. Much of the impetus behind the proposals of the Hoar bill of 1870 and the Blair bills of the 1880's came from Republican desires to promote systems of common schools in the Southern states, but the religious issue was inevitably injected. The Catholic Church opposed federal aid to the states if it was to be confined to public schools, but on occasion favored federal aid if it was to be divided fairly among public and parochial schools. Sufficient support to pass a federal aid bill was never achieved in both houses of Congress at once, so federal aid for general purposes of education had to wait at least until the twentieth century. In its appropriation acts for the District of Columbia in 1896 and 1897, Congress expressed a national policy in conformity with the policy of the vast majority of the states:

> And it is hereby declared to be the policy of the Government of the United States to make no appropriation of money or property for the purpose of founding,

maintaining, or aiding by payment for services, expenses, or otherwise, any church or religious denomination, or any institution or society which is under sectarian or ecclesiastical control. . . .

If this declared policy of the federal government which squares with the no-establishment clause of the First Amendment is maintained when federal aid to general education is finally voted by Congress, the worst dangers of divisive conflicts over religious issues in education will be avoided. The Smith–Hughes Act of 1917 set a desirable pattern when it provided that

No portion of any moneys appropriated under this Act for the benefit of the States shall be applied, directly or *indirectly*, . . . for the support of any religious or privately owned or conducted school or college.

If federal aid is granted directly or indirectly to religious schools, the cruel struggles of the nineteenth century will be repeated many fold, and this time with much more disastrous effect. The safest and the wisest policy both for the civil community and for the various religious communities is to adhere to the principle of separation of church and state defined so clearly in principle in the First Amendment and so nearly achieved in educational practice by 1900. In the course of 125 years of national and state history it had become clear to most Americans that the effort to achieve a common school in a religiously divided society required the giving up of sectarian and religious instruction in the public schools and the founding of public education upon a secular democratic base.

RENEWED DEMANDS FOR ESTABLISHMENT IN RECENT YEARS

Since the beginning of the twentieth century, however, the most noteworthy developments have been the increased efforts to reopen the question of separation and to gain greater "cooperation" between the churches and the state in education. Only the barest mention of a few of these efforts can be made here.

First, with respect to the issue of public funds for sectarian schools the effort is no longer to gain public funds directly. The efforts in the past fifty years, and especially in the past twenty years, have been directed toward gaining *indirect* support. By and large, Catholic groups have been primarily interested in these efforts. When efforts to achieve direct aid have proved unsuccessful, demands have been made for public funds to support educational activities *not directly involving classroom teaching*, such as public funds for transportation of children to parochial schools, providing free textbooks and health services at public expense to children in parochial schools, and the use of parochial school buildings with their religious teachers as public schools. Financial support has been granted by several of the states on some of these issues. These states would also be able to use federal funds for such purposes under present proposals to grant federal funds for any purpose for which the several states grant state funds. This provision was contained in the Taft bill as passed by the Senate in the Eightieth Congress in 1948 and again by the Senate in 1949.

The argument in favor of this practice is that public funds used for these indirect purposes are aids to the children and not aids to the religious schools as such. The opposing position has been that indirect aid which helps children to receive religious instruction in religious schools is just as much aid to the religious school as is direct aid. Without making distinctions that may be necessary in individual cases, the whole meaning of the historic principle of separation of church and state points to the prohibition of indirect aid to religious schools just as fully as it does to direct aid. Both indirect and direct aid would be tantamount to multiple establishment of religion. The principle of separation prohibits multiple establishment as completely as it does single establishment. Any form of legal cooperation is prohibited.

Secondly, with respect to the issue of religious instruction in the public schools the effort is no longer to teach specific sectarian doctrines as a regular part of the school curriculum. That, too, has been effectively prohibited by the first one hundred and twenty-five years of our national history. But since 1900 the demand has grown insistently, largely from Protestant groups, that the Bible should be widely read in the public schools on the ground that it is *not* sectarian instruction. Several states have passed laws making it compulsory or permissible. The courts have been divided but the majority has decided that Bible reading without comment by the teacher is permissible. The latest instance was a decision in New Jersey recently permitting Bible reading in the schools.

Other points of issue have involved the practice of holding religious exercises in the public schools and the employment of public school teachers who wear religious garb. Again the courts have been divided, but often find such practices permissible. The greatest spread of religious instruction has been achieved through the practice of excusing pupils during school hours to attend religious instruction given by their own religious instructors, either within or outside the public school building. This, the so-called "released time" practice, arose when it became clear that the principle of separation prohibited the practice of direct sectarian instruction in the public schools.

Again, without regard to individual variations in practice, it seems evident from the historical principle of separation of church and state, as here described, that such practices as these fall well within the framework of state promotion of religious instruction. To non-Protestants the reading of the King James version of the Bible must indeed seem to be sectarian religious instruction and must come within the meaning of multiple establishment of religion. Likewise, to non-Catholics the use of Catholic parochial school buildings and the employment of Catholic nuns in their religious garb must seem to be state support for sectarian religious instruction. Similarly, to all who may not find their own specific religious beliefs represented in a program of "released time" religious instruction during public school hours, such a practice must seem to be a multiple establishment of religion which violates their own rights of conscience.

SEPARATION DESIRABLE IN FUTURE AS IN PAST

Finally, to all who accept the historical meaning of the separation of church and state as described here, it must be clear that individual practices should be examined in the light of this history. To be sure, we have every right to make common decisions for change in our historic traditions, but the choices before us cannot wisely be made without regard to the traditions that live on in us. If we decide to return to some form of "cooperation" between church and state, we must take responsibility for realizing that we are returning to some form of establishment of religion and we must be prepared for the consequences. We must realize that when we do so we run the risk of stimulating divisive forces in the American community, and the churches must realize that when they ask for any form of cooperation or religious establishment they run the risk of increasing the amount of state control over religion.

To all to whom the meaning of this history is clear such a return becomes a threat to genuine freedom of religion based upon equal rights of conscience, a threat which the members of the First Congress so clearly saw when they framed the First Amendment to the United States Constitution. The best protection for religious freedom is, as they readily saw, to make matters of public policy a matter of common decision among people of all faiths without regard to religious sanctions. This is the essence of the principle of separation of church and state. As the government of the United States rests upon these common secular decisions of the widest possible community, so should the policies and program of public education rest upon similar secular decisions.

In education above all, decisions of public policy should be made in the light of the "general welfare" rather than in the light of religious preferences or religious sanctions. Here, a determination to make such decisions on the basis of the common, secular agreements of a community made up of differing religious orientations is a necessity that need not be a matter of hostility to religion in any form. It is simply a recognition of the realities of the bitter American experience with establishments of religion and the struggles involved in achieving separation of church and state. Neutrality of the state toward religion does not reflect an anti-religious attitude. Neutrality and not "cooperation" is required if America is to achieve genuine equality of religious conscience which is at the heart of our basic civil rights. Neutrality and not "cooperation" of church and state is definitely required if America is to avoid the double pitfalls of the established religions of earlier times and the attacks upon religious freedom of more recent times. Central to this task is the achievement and preservation of a common elementary and secondary school dedicated to the avoidance of these double dangers and dedicated to the fostering of our basic democratic heritage which relies so heavily upon the values of genuine religious freedom.

Although American society is in theory committed to the separation of church and state, the present relationship of religion and publicly sponsored education continues to vex and perplex educators and citizens. The role, function, and contribution of religious education are understood in vastly different ways. Despite recent legal enactments and court decisions, the relation of religion to public education must still be resolved in a satisfactory manner.

In our examination of this problem, the thinking of representatives of three major faiths is presented. In a general sense, the thesis of each of these authors deals with the values that education can obtain from religion.

Another thesis, offered by Wesner Fallaw, a theologian, is designed to perpetuate the values associated with each of the major religions and yet still preserve the concept of the separation of church and state. Fallaw suggests a cooperative community effort in which public school officials, churchmen, parents, and university scholars join forces to achieve a balanced workweek for each student. The balanced workweek will provide opportunities for religious training and other cultural activities without lessening the opportunities of the public schools to fulfill their obligations to the public. Parents will make the final decision concerning the dimensions of the workweek in reference to religious training and other cultural activities.

WHAT SHOULD BE THE RELATION OF RELIGION AND PUBLIC EDUCATION?

Henry P. Van Dusen

Our topic marks the meeting point of two of the most powerful and persistent concerns of the human spirit: the enterprise of *education*, dedicated to the quest for Truth, in the confident assurance that it is Truth which sets

Reprinted from *Teachers College Record*, Vol. 56, No. 1 (October 1954), pp. 1–9.

men free; and the heritage of *religion*, declaring its knowledge, not of all Truth, but of the ground and principle of Truth.

However these two concerns—education and religion—may differ, however far apart their paths may at times appear to diverge, they confess a common allegiance to a single sovereign, Truth. It is obvious that if each rightly apprehends that sovereign and its command upon them, they *should* find themselves yokemates, fellow warriors in a common battle against ignorance and error. That is the ideal, the normative, relation of religion and education—yokemates, fellow warriors in the advance and defense of Truth. The relations between religion and education, therefore, must always be primarily a matter of Truth—the liegelord to whom both profess an absolute allegiance. By the same token, if there be strain or misunderstanding between education and religion, it must be basically because of divergent conceptions of Truth, whether that divergence be overt or hidden.

To suggest that the relation of religion and education has not always been an altogether happy one, that the association of these two great interests in their joint concern for the preparation of youth for life has not always been, especially in these latter years, an easy and cordial partnership, is to state the obvious. That is the position today. Indeed, I think we may say that the two most obvious—and most important—features of the present situation with respect to our topic are just these: (1) increased concern for the role of religion in education, and (2) confusion and uncertainty as to the rightful relation of religion and education. These two features furnish the "existential" setting for our discussion. It is in the hope of casting some light upon that bafflement that, as I understand it, this discussion is taking place.

Parenthetically, may I say that what disturbs some religionists most deeply in the current discussion of the relation of religion and public education in this country is precisely the apparent unwillingness of some educators to examine the issues in the context of Truth; indeed, their seeming indifference, if not unawareness, that this is the only context in which education itself should properly discuss these issues. Religion has multiple masters—Goodness, Beauty, Holiness, as well as Truth; but education is in the simpler and happier situation of acknowledging only one regnant lord—Truth. Indeed, in education's perspective, our topic should really be phrased: "What, if any, is the relation of religion to Truth?"

Now all this may seem an annoyingly abstract introduction. Am I mistaken in sensing some impatience to be done with such theoretical considerations and get on to the concrete issues of our topic in the current American scene? Of course there are two major alternative perspectives in which any such matter may be discussed—in terms of fundamental principle or in terms of concrete situations. Personally, I would prefer at least some attempt to wrestle with the first before tackling the second. But let us accept for the moment the incurably pragmatic thought patterns of the American mentality, especially the American public educator. Nevertheless, we shall be guilty of viewing these issues in an inexcusably shallow perspective unless we bear constantly in mind the issue of Truth which underlies them; and to that issue I shall return later and at the end.

Our first question is, Why should education be concerned with religion at all? At least four independent though not unrelated considerations merit mention.

1. The first is the recognition that religion has been and is one of the most widely prevalent, persistent, and powerful forces in the life of humanity—in all ages, among all peoples, at all stages of cultural development. We speak of three foundation stones in the structure of society as familiarly, as inevitably, as we assume the three R's at the base of education. They are home, school, and church. This triad is not a distinctively American phenomenon. Of the three social institutions, two are primordial and virtually universal—home and church. (As a matter of fact, the third—the school—has been a very late addition, in vast areas of the world an importation from the West through Christian missions.) To be unaware of religion's force in life and to lack some understanding of its variations, history, development, and significance is to be without one of the essential data for intelligent human living; yet that is an illiteracy which the great bulk of the oncoming generation in our land must confess.

2. More specifically, in the society of which we are immediate heirs—both Western civilization in general and American culture in particular—the Judeo-Christian religion has been probably the most pervasive and influential single formative influence upon its literature, its art, its philosophy, its history.

Some years ago a group of young instructors in the various academic departments of one of our Eastern men's colleges fell into the habit of meeting over a cup of coffee when the day's work was ended and discussing their professional problems. Their subjects included the classics, art, literature, history, and philosophy. Quite to their surprise they discovered that it was impossible adequately to teach any one of those subjects unless the students had a prior familiarity with the Jewish-Christian tradition. For it is that heritage which furnishes the groundwork for almost every element in Western civilization and Western culture. The upshot of that discovery was a very impressive report drafted by a special committee of the faculty, pointing out that in that university at that time there was no department of religion or even a single course in religion, and yet, in the view of those who were responsible for teaching subjects other than religion, at least an elementary knowledge of the Jewish-Christian tradition was necessary before they could begin their work. The final outcome was the initiation of a department of religion which has since become one of the strongest in any Eastern university.

In Anglo-Saxon lands, one specific element within the large and complex matrix of the Judeo-Christian heritage has held a uniquely influential role. The Bible, by universal acknowledgment, is the greatest literary monument our language knows. We should hold any educational program inexcusably deficient which did not provide youth with some acquaintance with Shakespeare, not to speak of other masters in our literary heritage. By the same token, it is well-nigh unthinkable that any boy or girl should have passed through the process of education for life without opportunity to gain first-hand acquaintance with the noblest collection of literature in the English tongue. Yet, this too is a lacuna in the schooling of most of us. If I speak strongly, it is as one who has found himself hopelessly handicapped in his education by that specific ignorance, and has had to struggle futilely all through maturity to overcome the deficiency. Moreover, one cannot possibly read intelligently the literature of the English-speaking people, even Shakespeare himself, without knowledge of the Bible.

If it is impossible to achieve even an elementary understanding of the major elements in our Western culture without familiarity with the Judeo-Christian faith and its literature, which have so largely furnished the matrix within which it has developed and its underlying continuum, how much more is this the situation with respect to our national background and culture. Is it not fair to suggest that an intelligent stranger from another planet, or another continent, seeking to comprehend the history, institutions, and tradition—the ways of thought and life—of the American people would quickly recognize that his quest would be doomed to superficiality and futility until he had made acquaintance with the influence of religion upon them? Yet, this is a prerequisite for *self*-understanding largely denied to Americans themselves so far as their formal schooling is concerned.

3. Religion has to do with the most elemental, the most universal, and, in the end, *the most important issues of human existence*—its origin, its nature, its meaning and purpose, its destiny, especially with the determinative and inescapable events which mark and mould each person's life—birth, love, parenthood, death.

Dean Sperry has reminded us:

> The world seeks the church uncritically, habitually at those times when life most matters. Young people who profess to have outgrown religion still enter the church to be made man and wife. Parents who have drifted away from the church still bring their children back for baptism. The last low whispers of the world's dead are uniformly burdened with God's name but the church is always requisitioned to speak that name over those dead. In obedience to some deep unreasoned prompting, men seek churches when life is most real.[1]

[1] Willard L. Sperry, *Reality in Worship* (New York: The Macmillan Company, 1947), p. 30.

That is to say, religion is not only concerned with the great questions of life; it has to do with the fundamental, inexorable, inescapable events which mark and mould every human pilgrimage—birth, love, parenthood, death.

Let it not be said that these are questions and issues which press only on the adult mind and therefore are most appropriately considered in connection with *higher* education, but have no relevance for school-age youth. There may have been a time when that was the situation, but not today. No one acquainted with the present generation of school youngsters can doubt that those who are asking any questions at all, that is to say who are mentally alert, are now discussing precisely these matters. Education which declines to face their queries is as benighted as the obsolete prudery which evaded the no less universal (and closely related) question, Where do babies come from?; and no less without excuse in its evasion.

4. Lastly, there is the more theoretical but even more basic issue of the nature and ground of truth—the elemental recognition that, *if* there be any Power or Powers beyond nature and man, with which religion is concerned, the existence and nature of that Power must have vital bearing upon the very reality, Truth, which education aims to know, to mediate, and to serve. This is not to prejudge the existence of such a Power; it is simply to recognize that the question of its existence is fundamental in the enterprise of truth-seeking.

In summary, education should take cognizance of religion simply because to fail to do so is to condemn its products to illiteracy.

Yes, but at once we confront three complicating factors which bedevil both discussion and practice in this matter at every point. Let us designate them: the duality of religion, the diversity of religions, and the American "tradition" with respect to the relation of government and religion.

The first point to be noted is that religion appears in discussions of education, as indeed it does in the life of the society which education seeks to serve, in not one but two senses.

Religion appears, in the first place, as a general and almost universally present fact in human culture. I am not here acquiescing in the present widely prevalent and, as I think, misguided and muddying practice of identifying religion with any scheme of values (see *The American College Dictionary:* "religion: 1. the quest for the values of the ideal life"), so that one may say, "Music is his religion" or "Golf is his religion" or "Crime is his religion" or "Patriotism is his religion." Throughout this discussion, I am holding to the ancient and, as I believe, only sound meaning of religion as "recognition of a superhuman Power or Powers." As we have said, that recognition, however varied its manifestations, has been well-nigh universal among mankind and is so today, even in the United States. One of the basic premises of religion in that sense is that the Ultimate Reality, God, is also the principle and ground of Truth. And a corollary is that religion, since it has to do with the ground of Truth, should have a determinative role in the educational process as a whole. This corollary is simply the counterpart in the realm of learning of the broader contention that religion, since it has to do with Ultimate Reality, should permeate and direct the whole of life.

But religion appears in society, also, as a quite specific interest within the totality of human interests, distinguishable from and parallel to the others —art, music, science, politics, golf, and so forth. Witness the locus and role of churches within communities. In this second sense, religion has its own history and subject matter and literature and cultus, and practice; as a specific phase of culture, its place within the educational enterprise is alongside the other major academic subjects.

This duality may be defined as the distinction between religion and the several religions. The question may well be put, In which of these two senses, if in either, should education take cognizance of religion and make provision for it?

But the situation is still more complicated by the second factor, the plurality of religions in contemporary American culture. "Religion in education?" someone may protest, "Which religion?" With the population divided in allegiance between three major faiths—Judaism, Roman Catholicism, and Protestantism—and no-faith, and Protestantism further divided into a multitude of sects, how can education, which is the servant of the community as a whole, make provision for religion?

These two complicating factors arise from the current scene. There is a third which descends upon us out of the past. It springs from the fact that public education in this land operates under a system of law which has its basis in the Federal Constitution, and the First Amendment to the Constitution specifies, "Congress shall make no laws respecting an establishment of religion, or prohibiting the free exercise thereof."

Our topic is oriented toward the future—not what has been or what is but what should be the relation of religion and public education. But we shall chart a true course ahead in inexcusably and dangerously superficial fashion unless we recall how we have arrived at our present position. Ideally, that would require us to review at least in broad outline the history of religion in public education in this country. Though time forbids us to trace the pathway by which we have arrived at our present position, at least we should remind ourselves of the starting point from which we have come. This is all the more important in view of the frequent appeals to the "intent of the Founding Fathers" and of the determinative role of their embodiment of their intent in the Federal Constitution.

What was the predominant attitude of the Founding Fathers toward religion and its role in national life? What was their conviction regarding the place, if any, of religion in education? Happily, we are not left in the dark as to the correct answers to those questions, although they may strike with rather startling and blinding illumination some who are perhaps less familiar with national origins and Constitutional history than we would all wish to be.

The Founding Father most frequently invoked in support of the exclusion of religion from public education is Thomas Jefferson; and the favored text is an almost chance phrase in a letter from Jefferson to a group of Connecticut Baptists in 1802, in which he spoke of erecting "a wall of separation between church and state." It is true that Jefferson was more deeply concerned to prevent the control of public education by any particular church than almost any other of the Fathers, but that concern was coupled with this desire for his own beloved University of Virginia:

> It was not, however, to be understood that instruction in religious opinion and duties was meant to be precluded by public authorities, as indifferent to the interests of society. On the contrary, the relations which exist between man and his Maker, and the duties resulting from those relations, are the most interesting and important to every human being, and the most incumbent on his study and investigation. The want of instruction in the various creeds of religious faith existing among our citizens presents, therefore, a chasm in a general institution of the useful sciences.

And Jefferson envisioned that the professor of ethics in the University would "deal with the proof of the being of God and the divine authority of morals."

With respect to the First Amendment, it is, I believe, beyond challenge that it was intended to apply solely to the federal government, and that intention was to prevent the national government from establishing a particular religion. It was not intended to prohibit even the establishment of a particular religion in a state; at the time of its adoption, a particular religion (one of the Christian denominations) was, in fact, established in five states. Some authorities on the Constitution hold that the Amendment was intended, by implication, to safeguard state establishments.

The prevailing viewpoint of the Founding Fathers has been summarized by Justice Story in his authoritative *Commentaries on the Constitution:*

> Probably at the time of the adoption of the Constitution, and of the amendment to it, now under consideration, the general, if not the universal sentiment in America was, that Christianity ought to receive encouragement from the state, so far as was not incompatible with the private rights of conscience, and the freedom of religious worship. An attempt to level all religions, and to make it a matter of state policy to hold all in utter indifference, would have created universal disapprobation if not universal indignation. . . .

It is fair to say that Justice Story's dictum, altered only by the recognition of Judaism as well as Christianity as a religion which should be recognized and "ought to receive encouragement from the state," is an accurate description of both the principle and the practice of the American nation regarding the place of religion in national concern throughout its history. Is it unfair to add that that is the predominant American attitude today?

The relations which have actually prevailed between government (whether national, state, or local) and religion and church throughout our national history, and which widely prevail today stand at very distant remove from "a wall of separation." On the contrary, state and religion, even state and church, have been and are intimately intermingled at all levels and in a variety of ways.

Some of the ways in which the national government has shown and shows its concern for religion are:

Setting apart of days for national Thanksgiving or prayer.

Provision of chaplains in both Houses of Congress.

Appointment of chaplains in all the Armed Forces of the nation.

Almost universal recognition of God and appeal for Divine assistance on the part of successive Presidents and leaders of government generally.

A few of the ways in which both national and state governments are directly involved in relations with the churches are:

Appointment of chaplains for the Armed Forces.

Appointment of chaplains in penitentiaries, hospitals, and other government-maintained institutions.

Specific exemption of ministers' residences from tax liability, and recognition of contributions to churches as deductible on federal and state personal income taxes.

Perhaps the most widely prevalent and significant way in which state and local governments take cognizance of churches and grant them exceptional recognition is in the exemption of ecclesiastical property from taxation. But the concern of these same agencies of the public for religion is most clearly and significantly revealed in the provisions many of them make for instruction in religion in their educational institutions at both school and college levels—precisely the area of our special concern.

Thus we are brought, at long last, to a direct confrontation of our theme: What *should be* the relation of religion and public education?

Granted that religion, both as a potent historical reality and force and as a continuing and well-nigh universal concern of the human spirit, should find an appropriate place in education, a number of subsidiary queries press for answers.

1. Can religion be taught at a level of scholarly objectivity and competence equal to that demanded of other academic subjects?

2. Can religion be included in the educational program without precipitating contest between the several religions and prejudice and conflict among the pupils?

3. Can religion have a place in *public* education without contravening the basic law of the nation?

Satisfactory assurance with respect to the first two questions may be discovered in the actual teaching of religion in the great bulk of universities and private schools in the land.

The answers to both the major and the subsidiary questions in the context of public education are to be found, not in a theoretical development of what *might* be or in the projection of novelty into the existing structure of American education, but in what actually *is,* in widely prevailing practice, within that accepted structure. What is present practice?

An inquiry conducted in 1939 revealed that among 37 leading state universities (including those of California, Colorado, Connecticut, Florida, Illinois, Indiana, Iowa, Kansas, Kentucky, Louisiana, Maine, Massachusetts, Michigan, Minnesota, Missouri, Nebraska, North Carolina, Ohio, Oklahoma, Pennsylvania, South Carolina, Tennessee, Virginia, Washington, West Virginia, and Wisconsin) 22, or 59.5 per cent, offered courses in religion in their regular curricula, while an additional 8 gave academic credit for courses in religion taught by unofficial agencies near the university. Thus "the grand total for state institutions under examination at which religion is offered for credit, whether or not in the regular curriculum, is 30, or 81.1 per cent." A more comprehensive study, conducted by Dr. Merrimon Cuninggim in 1941, of the 70 state institutions accredited by the Association of American Universities disclosed that 21, or 30 per cent, maintain departments of religion, 35 more offer courses in religion in other departments of the university, while 6 give academic credit for classes taken in off-campus schools or colleges of religion. In brief, students in 62 of the 70 accredited state schools, almost 90 per cent, have the opportunity to elect academically recognized instruction in religion.

Moreover, the evidence is conclusive that these numbers are steadily mounting. "At least a dozen state colleges and universities have established chairs or departments of religion, officially sponsored and financed, since the last War." Thus, in several instances, the state is in direct, active, and apparently mutually satisfactory partnership with the church in the provision of religious instruction for the former's pupils.

Eight state institutions (11.5 per cent of those accredited) maintain compulsory chapel services today, while 11 others (15.7 per cent of the total) hold voluntary chapel.

Nor do these facts regarding chapel services and religious courses exhaust the evidence of state concern for religion and the readiness of publicly supported educational institutions to give all possible aid to the churches and other religious bodies. Among the 37 leading state universities of the 1939 study, while just under a third maintain institutionally sponsored chapel, over 56 per cent hold special religious convocations under college auspices; 45.9 per cent provide official religious leadership (Chaplain, Director of Religious Activities, and so forth) at university expense; and over 40 per cent subsidize voluntary student religious groups such as the Christian Associations.

We have drawn our illustrations from public higher education where full and accurate data are available. Those familiar with the public school system of the nation as a whole could readily adduce essentially parallel instances, although proportionately much less numerous. Perhaps the central issue for our discussion might be put in this query: Should our public schools generally follow the principles and practices with respect to religion which are already widely prevalent in their elder sister institutions at the university level?

Finally, then, these are our conclusions:

1. As to *principle:*

Religion is a perennial, ineradicable, and vital concern of the human spirit. Moreover, religion has been and continues to be one of the formative influences upon every aspect of human culture. Therefore, acquaintance with its history, its literature, and its teaching is a *sine qua non* for the educated man or woman.

More specifically, in Western society in general and in American culture in particular, the Judeo-Christian tradition has furnished the preponderant religions. Therefore, public education is entitled, indeed obligated, to offer its students the best possible instruction in the history, Scriptures and beliefs of the Judeo-Christian heritage; it may well add material on the other major world religions and in comparative religion.

2. As to *practice:*

Teaching of religion may find, or continue to have, an appropriate place within American public education at all levels, provided five conditions are faithfully met—all of them no less mandatory for instruction in any other subject:

a. The program in religion should be determined by the educational authorities and conducted by persons appointed and certified by them.

b. Teaching of religion must meet the standards of objectivity and scholarly competence expected of every other subject.

c. The major religious traditions should be appropriately presented.

d. No student should be *required* to come under instruction contrary to his or his parents' objections.

e. The teaching and practice of religion in public education should not be employed as an instrument of sectarian propaganda. Rather, its aim must be to furnish the youth of the nation with materials which the public, acting through their educational authorities, consider essentials for true education.

BETTER SCHOOLS FOR BETTER TIMES

Most Reverend Joseph M. Marling, C.P.P.S.

What is it that we offer our age? What do we deem essential for the better times of which we speak? It is a Christian philosophy of man and the universe, a philosophy that is God-centered, that acknowledges God as Creator, supreme lawgiver and final end. Such a philosophy accepts the universe for what it is—its vastness and complexity the product of a prolonged evolution, its rich variety subject to rigid chemical and biological classification, its intricate movements expressible in profound mathematical formulas. But it insists that every object that goes to make up that world is a reflection of the beauty, the power, and the wisdom of God. Man, called often and correctly a creature of two worlds, it places at the crown of visible reality, explaining the clash of his flesh and spirit and how it must be resolved. Pleasure, comfort, security, culture, the mastery of his physical environment—these things he may indeed seek, but there are higher goals than those of the temporal order and they concern his immortal destiny. Vast is the interplay of material and human forces that go to make the world, but they blend in harmony and order by reason of the tendency necessarily sown into the texture of every finite object, which St. Thomas describes by the beautiful phrase "assimilari Deo." Everything finite comes from the Hand of God, as the reflection or mirroring of a specific divine perfection. Therefore, its activity is but a return to God as to its final end. In this sense, man and the universe draw meaning, purpose, order, and harmony from the very nature of God.

If it be said that such a view is medieval, fanciful, unreal, and blind to the great political, social and economic problems that characterize our seething century, one can reply that the very criticism is proof of the extent to which our age has lost its vision. To be sound a structure must rest upon a solid foundation. The effort to build our contemporary culture upon the shifting sands of the temporal and empirical must come to grief. The very nature of man creates in him a dual hunger, and each must be sated if he is to enjoy true peace. Bread or even atomic energy may satisfy the one, but never the other. It is in this vein that Peter Wust has written so trenchantly: "Hesse recently typified the outlawed humanity of our day by what is by far the

Reprinted from *National Catholic Educational Bulletin*, Vol. 53, No. 1 (August 1956), pp. 214–221.

most impressive symbol yet conceived. He shows us man under the form of a prairie wolf, roving restlessly hither and thither in the endless and loveless desert that is western civilization, hideously crying his hunger and thirst for Eternity. A howling, hungry wolf is a natural thing, God knows. But a howling, human animal crying for Eternity? . . . Is it not a terrifying metaphysical phenomenon, at which we must shudder with apprehension?"

The Christian philosophy which we regard as essential for the betterment of our times is the very bone and marrow of our educational effort, the key to the existence of our entire Catholic system. Our schools are to be judged, therefore, by the manner in which they embody it, shape their program by it, and endow those whom they train with its force and vitality. The magnitude of the task does not escape us. We must be children of light, yet match in worldly wisdom the children of this generation. Our sight must be focused intently upon eternity, yet miss nothing that is wholesome or essential in the temporal order. Then there is the secularistic spirit which saturates the very air we breathe. It were a miracle if we did not imbibe it in larger draughts than we realize, and thus infected, transmit it to others. In this light we can ponder the oft-repeated truth that a Catholic school, based upon Catholic principles, and with Catholic teachers and pupils, does not necessarily spell Catholic education. To express some of the ways in which we can be truer to our Catholic philosophy of education, and thus build better schools for better times, let us turn to the two chief characters in the drama—the teacher and the pupil.

Progressive educators may boast of the improvement in teaching techniques which they have sponsored, but they have certainly deprived the teacher of the mantle of rank and authority conferred upon him by tradition. Emphasis upon learning through experience and self-activity has tended to deny that he is a true bestower of knowledge and a necessary guide to truth, while stress upon adaptation as synonymous with mental growth has belittled his role as a molder of mind and character. The true cause of knowledge resides in the pupil himself, but education or schooling and the acquisition of knowledge are not the same. As our Holy Father stated recently: "The schoolmaster's function demands something higher and more profound than that of him who merely communicates a knowledge of things. The schoolmaster is a person who knows how to create a close relationship between his own soul and that of the child. He personally devotes himself to guiding the inexperienced pupil toward truth and virtue. It is he, in a word, who molds the pupil's intellect and will so as to fashion, as best he can, a being of human and Christian perfection."

To guide the inexperienced pupil toward truth, to mold the intellect so as to fashion a being of human perfection—such golden objectives demand possession of knowledge and the fullest familiarity with teaching and learning processes. In a word, solid learning and professional skill. Without them the most earnest dedication to the apostolate of education is but a gesture. Nor will basic training suffice. The teacher must grow in his chosen field and in the wider area of knowledge that gives it meaning. With intellect and imagination alert, he must strive for fresh and facile expression so as to present truth in its most alluring form to the restless and distracted minds of our youth.

The effort to produce better schools may well begin with the attempt to raise instruction to the highest possible level. This excellence our recent Pontiffs have requested. "Perfect schools," said Pope Pius XI in his masterly encyclical on Christian Education, "are the result not so much of good methods as of good teachers." In similar vein our present Holy Father has said: "Good teachers should have perfect human formation . . . Good teachers need professional competency, at a minimum above average, and better still, outstanding on all levels of instruction and in each of the specialized fields. . . ." And were His Holiness here this morning, would he not perhaps say to us as he did to the teaching sisters gathered before him in 1951: "Many of your schools are praised and described to us as very good, but not all. It is our fervent wish that all strive to become excellent. This presupposes that your teaching sisters are masters of the subjects they expound."

At the heart of the Catholic instructor's efforts lies the Catholic philosophy of life, voiced formally and explicitly in the religion courses of the secondary schools, implicitly and indirectly in every other subject. Some would see in this animation of professional knowledge by a Christian philosophy of life a puzzling task, one that may readily convert instruction into a kind of dreary preachment. Rather would we stress the impossibility of teaching particular data without investing them with the wider significance which they possess, without indicating their position in that larger frame which we call human life. The teacher is forced to such interpretation by the fact that he is a human being. In this sense he always proposes a creed. The agnostic, the naturalist, the secularist may contradict this, but the very denial is the adoption of an attitude or creed, and in this case, of the most sweeping and dogmatic of all creeds. The Catholic educator proposes the Catholic philosophy of life when, as a proper grasp of truth and reality demands, he locates his subject matter with reference to man's legitimate quest of temporal peace, and his pursuit of eternal happiness.

To accomplish this requires a solid acquaintance with the Christian outlook and serious effort to give it prominence in one's own daily life. Even the pagans knew which would prevail in a contest between word and example. The finest educational efforts will be sterile if they do not go hand in hand with a Christian life. But speculative knowledge of the tenets of Catholic philosophy is equally indispensable. One is tempted at this point to pay tribute to the glorious heritage that is ours. We are heirs to the wisdom of the ages as it has been purified and exalted by contact with the Christian gospel. The mind of every Christian educator should be steeped in this stream. In fact, the right to be called a Christian teacher may be questioned if one lacks this fundamental endowment. Here surely there is opportunity for vast improvement which, if seized, will lead necessarily to better schools and thus to the better times which all men seek.

We do not maintain, of course, that the school is responsible for the total education of our youth. It merely shares with parents the intellectual, emotional and moral training of their children. Between parents and teachers, therefore, should reign a spirit of harmony, sympathy and mutual cooperation. Their common assignment demands a sound working relationship between home and school. Within recent years associations have been wisely formed to bring this about. To them the teacher must give the fullest measure of understanding, and good will, even though they require time and great patience. They tend to prevent the setting before youth of conflicting standards and goals, the gravest obstacle to successful training in character and virtue.

Teachers and parents share a common assignment but their specific duties are quite distinct. The obligations of the parent are not those of the teacher. Consequently, the teacher should neither attempt nor be asked to assume them. One of the grave sins of our day is the shirking of parental obligation. Father and mother are so frequently absent from the home that children seek entertainment and guidance beyond the family hearth. To expect of teachers direction which should stem from parents is to impose burdens that cannot be borne. It is in this connection that all of us can assist. We can lay stress continually upon the sanctity of the home, the God-given rights and duties of parents, the beauty of the family circle, which is such only where parental authority and filial obedience reign. What is done to move parents to exercise conscientiously their natural role as educators, tends indirectly to assist our schools, freeing them from extraneous assignments so that they can give full attention to the highest professional and Christian goals.

There are other ways in which we can lend indirect aid to our educational system. The teacher is to display solid learning and to give rich meaning to his instruction by means of the Catholic philosophy with which his mind and heart are saturated. But he serves in a social role. He is the agent or emissary of society, normally mirroring its mind and will. Whatever he teaches will reflect strain in days of crisis, patriotism in time of war, the national aims in a period of national ambition or expansion. It is thus that our so-called neutral schools reflect the naturalism and secularism that are current today. Christian teachers, we feel, will scarcely rise above the zeal and spirit of the Christian community unless they be exceptional individuals. The more, therefore, that we as a whole seek to exemplify the Christian philosophy in our daily lives, the more central will it become in our schools, the greater the chance that it will become the rich endowment of our youth.

This is a challenge that we may not refuse if it be our sincere yearning to have better schools for better times.

The correlate of the teacher is the pupil, to whom Catholic education with wholeness of vision attributes every essential feature, minimizing in no way his dignity and high calling. It accepts his rich array of natural gifts, his attachment to the temporal order, his affection for his fellowmen, his hunger for temporal happiness and success, as energies capable of great perfection. It sees him primarily, of course, as a child of God, with an immortal destiny, and properly seeks to shape his whole development in accord with this ultimate meaning and purpose. As Pope Pius XI wrote: "The true Christian does not renounce the activities of this life; he does not stunt his natural faculties. But he develops and perfects them by coordinating them with the supernatural. He thus ennobles what is merely natural in life and secures for it new strength in the material and temporal order, no less than in the spiritual and eternal." Thus can he hold: "Christian education takes in the whole aggregate of human life, physical and spiritual, intellectual and moral, individual, domestic and social, not with a view of reducing it in any way, but in order to elevate, regulate and perfect it."

To spurn the temporal order would be to forget the cardinal tenet that grace perfects and builds upon nature, to overlook what has been called the sacramental character of temporal events—the manner in which they signify and manifest the divine government of the world and all reality. In fact, as our civilization advances the temporal sphere makes demands in justice upon the Christian educator. For the good of the whole enjoins that all be somewhat versed, and certain ones highly trained, in the sciences—physical, moral, medical, social and political. The good of the individual requires a general knowledge and specific competence that will enable him to achieve happiness, dignity and security in our complex way of life. But always, as we have stated, as that of a magnet is the attraction of the eternal order felt. Each intellectual and moral enterprise is elevated and enriched by association with the eternal purpose that the individual is to achieve.

The true purpose of man is the formal principle that supplies the Christian philosophy of education with completeness and also with remarkable unity. Lacking such a principle progressive educators fall back upon adaptation as the primary goal of the educative process. The narrowness of this view does not escape us. Man is indeed limited by his environment, but this is outweighed by his enormous ability to rise above his surroundings and mould them according to the ideals which he entertains. Better schools for better times will result when this latent creative power is incessantly called to the pupil's attention and stimulated in every possible fashion. He must be made to see that by joining forces with others of high principle he can help to renovate the face of the earth. Especially is this true in the social and political spheres where the success of secularism poses a threat to the entire social fabric. Blessed indeed is the Christian educator who at least starts his pupils seriously on the steep path that leads to a deep sense of social and political responsibility, a love of social justice, of fraternal charity, and of political understanding and honesty.

If Christian education is to take in the whole aggregate of human life, as Pope Pius XI insists, care must be given to the curriculum and the proper association of discipline with instruction. We are eager to introduce into our educational program every worthwhile discovery of the science of pedagogy, but we rightly guard against trends that have nothing to recommend them in theory or practice. For brevity's sake we may list them under the general heading of soft pedagogy. Little familiarity with human nature is required to know that learning is an arduous process. The effort to render it palatable has resulted in deficiency in basic skills, courses in secondary schools that lead nowhere, a lack of trained individuals for positions of national importance, and concern among parents that their offspring are not being truly educated. When blame for the removal of discipline from the educational process is placed, Freud and his attacks upon frustration and repression must be named, as well as the progressive educators with their identification of learning with the pupil's freedom of choice and expression.

In truth, our young people would not fear discipline or cringe under its restraints. For the springtime of life is an age of daring, of idealism, enthusiasm and heroic dreams. Two world wars have revealed how youth will march into the very jaws of death quietly and without fear, if given a cause for which they can die with dignity and understanding. It is the Christian educator who can hold before youth the noblest and most sacred goals. He must not, therefore, pamper youth in the modern mood, wheedle them to accept responsibility, or dissipate their energies in sports or empty pleasures. Rather will he seek by proper stimulation and fearless restraint to mould them, in the Pauline phrase, "to perfect manhood, to the mature measure of the fullness of Christ."

In training the pupil for later responsibility a familiar difficulty arises. He is an individual, with highly personal needs and capabilities. Yet education has taken on a mass character that, in the light of our growing world, will not diminish but increase. Fortunately aptitudes and degrees of skill can be cleverly measured by modern testing methods, but this will not suffice. Tests must be supplemented by counselling services and programs of skilled vocational and scholastic guidance. The problem may be less acute in secondary than in primary schools, but it is nevertheless challenging. Here, again, the Christian educator is prompted by his Christian outlook to pay grave attention to individual problems. For the individual may indeed be an accident in a philosophy of crass evolution, an insignificant speck in a vast and empty universe. In the Christian scheme of things he is of priceless dignity and worth, since he is made to the image and likeness of God, and, whatever be his accidental status, he is a brother of the Lord Christ.

Another tendency in secondary education that causes serious concern is the glorification of so-called practical or vocational courses at the expense of the basic intellectual disciplines. Sponsors of this training for life or democracy, as it is called, boast that it serves a dual purpose. It adapts pupils to the revolutionary social and economic programs of the era, and it meets the needs of the masses in democratic fashion. Even if we refrain from criticizing the socialistic character of many of the reforms to which students are to be adapted, we must protest vehemently this surrender to mediocrity. With each passing hour the need for extraordinary intelligence grows, for trained statesmen, philosophers, scientists, engineers, historians and men of letters. A system that tends to deplete these ranks by denying to the better pupils the necessary intellectual foundation aims a mortal blow at our country and its leadership of the western world. We have been told on previous occasions that our views are hopelessly antiquated. Let us suffer the charge again if this be the price of unalterable opposition to this prominent phase of progressive education.

It is natural to ask, as we plan for the future, what our schools have accomplished, and what they are achieving today. Quite recently Christopher Dawson has pictured secularism as the great leviathan that swallows our primary and secondary schools without suffering indigestion, and that will be conquered only by our efforts on the highest educational level. How often are we tempted to a like sober judgment. Nevertheless, there are grounds for hope and quiet optimism. Thousands reflect the training they have received at our hands. No difficulty do they encounter in matching the graduates of other schools as citizens, as professional men and women, as fathers and mothers. Love of God and neighbor is discernible in their ways. They are a force for justice and order wherever they live. Because of them the voice of the Church is heard in public life with ever-growing respect. Their loyalty to Christian principles is a force upon which the West may rely in its death struggle with atheistic communism. Humbly but with deep conviction do we say that our glorious country is in genuine debt to our Catholic schools.

We confess that it is a mighty task to cause the Christian philosophy to prevail in our age. But this is our assignment. Let us take courage in the thought that we are asked only to do the sowing. The harvest is in the hands of God. Nor can we ever know just how many, in the divine plan, must be deeply impregnated with Christian ideals before a force is created that the world cannot resist. Genuine and heroic must be our endeavor, but then we may fall back upon the absolute conviction that today, as in apostolic times, if Paul plants and Apollos waters, it is God who gives the growth.

RELIGION IN THE PUBLIC SCHOOL: A NEW APPROACH TO THE JEWISH POSITION

Rabbi Arthur T. Gilbert

Some time ago, in the *Reconstructionist* magazine, I warned the American Jewish community that the rigid, legalistic, and negative position of the Jewish community on church-state problems and religion in public education was seriously damaging our relations with Christian leadership in this country. I called upon the Jewish community to pause and reconsider its position and strategy.

There have been many significant conflicts, legal decisions rendered, and resolutions adopted in this ensuing period. I bring you testimony, however, that the continuous conflict over this issue of religion in public education has not at all clarified our relationship with our Christian neighbors, as some contend. It has not cleared the air. It remains still the most tension-producing issue in our relationship with our American Christian neighbors, and it has provoked terribly bad feeling.

I call upon the Jewish community again not to change its principled position. But rather to consider my hypothesis that were we to use other methods, were we to equip ourselves with a better understanding of what motivates our Christian neighbors, we might achieve a different kind of result in our relationship with them.

I am not questioning the general concern of the Jewish community that religious freedom be maintained. I agree with the position that we have always assumed that the state refrain from the imposition of any sectarian religious rite or obligation upon citizens and particularly upon our children. I think that we shall all agree that the traditional patterns of separation of church and state as practiced in America have enabled all religious groups to grow and flourish and achieve a vitality far greater than in countries where the church is established and where religious freedom is denied for minority groups.

I want now to make these following observations:

1. In the constellation of problems that confront us as citizens and Americans, the question of religion in the public schools is rather insignificant. It is

Reprinted from *Religious Education*, Vol. 56, No. 4 (July 1961), pp. 297–301, 311, by permission of the publisher, the Religious Education Association, New York City.

my general feeling that the Jewish community has exaggerated in importance and provided a priority to this problem far out of all proportion. There are other issues that ought be exercising a Jewish Community Council and Jewish organizations with greater intensity or at least the same degree of emotional involvement. It ought not be our number-one problem nor the issue to which we assign most of the time and energy of our leadership. Problems of disarmament, the world in revolution, aid to countries abroad, new nations of Africa and Asia growing into freedom, the blight of racial prejudice, the sit-ins, the shame of housing discrimination in the lily-white communities in which we live, our relation to these problems are all in my view more basic issues than the religion in the schools' question. The existence of anti-Semitism, Jewish illiteracy, the swastika outbreak, the shocking moral breakdown in America itself, these too are problems that it seems to me ought be exercising the Jewish community first before the question of Channukah or Christmas in the public schools or Bible reading or released time. It is a sad commentary on our narrow provincialism that this is not the case.

2. The problem of church-state relations in this country is broader than religion in the public school. With the revival of interest in religion we have seen efforts made by all religious groups to use the instrumentality of law to establish moral traditions in accordance with their religious judgment. Such issues as Bingo, gambling regulations, magazine and movie censorship, Sunday closing laws, birth control regulations, the religion of a candidate for public office, the continuous claim by the Catholic Church that "distributive justice" calls for some measure of tax relief and support for Catholics who send their children to private schools, bus transportation for private and parochial school students, these too are problems in the church-state area that challenge the American people—indeed, concern them more than the posting of the Ten Commandments in the public school classes. The Jewish community has ducked many of these issues because they are primarily a Protestant-Catholic dispute. We have not with the same intensity involved ourselves in these issues. What results, then, is that we come to a Christian community on the narrower issue of religion in public education, and ask for understanding of our concern, at a time when we have not adequately nor sympathetically come to grips with the broader issues that confront and disturb relations within the Protestant and Catholic community.

Does religion not have anything at all to say to the social situation? May religious groups press for the enactment of social and legal legislation that will conform to their religious moral judgment? Under what circumstances may a religious group use the instrumentality of the state? What are the conditions that justify legislative appeal on one issue by one religious group and make of it "a denial of freedom" when the same technique of pressure politics is used by another religious group? How shall we handle these issues that divide us and on which we make conflicting judgment? I am not aware that the Jewish community in its handling of the problem of Bible reading in the public schools has worked out any clear philosophy on the relations of religious institutions to the state in general that we can apply clearly and intelligently to all these many issues that confront the religious communities of our land.

These two points reflect accurately then my feelings, that this issue of religion in public education is a narrow one and when placed in a proper perspective among the whole constellation of concerns that confront the American Jewish community, ought not be exercising the great degree of emotion and time we have given it.

I

Let me move on. I believe that we have misunderstood the Christian concern for religion in the public school; and because of the misreading of their intention our response to their thrust has been inadequate. We impugn the motive of our Christian neighbors by suggesting that their effort to introduce and maintain religion in the public school represents a desire to evangelize our children. It is suggested that they hope to make Christians of our Jewish children. In my judgment this is not the case. A Christian community that supports a long-established practice of reading Bible verses in the public schools, for example, seeks not through such reading of the Old Testament verse the conversion of the Jewish child to Christianity. This is not the motive of the Christian community. To suggest that every concern on their part that the religious aspect of the heritage of Western civilization be dealt with in the educational program of the public school is a desire to impose Christianity on Jewish or non-religiously affiliated children is completely to misunderstand them; and misunderstanding the Christian's motivation we do not deal adequately with the reality of the situation. We are applying to an American situation the emotions and feelings that derive from our European experience.

It seems to me that what the Christian community is doing is responding in a Christian way to what they feel to be the crucial problems of our time. They are attempting to shore up American democracy in its battle against communism, materialism and secularism by pointing to the theological or religious foundations of our values and our beliefs. "All men are created equal." This concept of creation, of a God who created man equal is an ideal that some Christians would want to teach in the public school in their programs of moral and spiritual values. Their intention in fashioning this program is not to impose Christianity upon our children; rather it is to strengthen American democracy in the crucial struggle that it must face by lifting up the image of God as author of history and source of all values, presumably an image to which Jews ought be able to say "Amen."

They are concerned with the problem of juvenile delinquency and moral breakdown in our community. These are indeed disturbing issues and deserve our attention too. It is out of their Christian pattern, however, that they believe that if children would have before them the Ten Commandments or read the Bible, or hear the Bible read in the morning, or recite a prayer somehow their thoughts would be directed Godward; a proper tone, a reverential tone would be created in the school community.

There is genuine anxiety and fear in the Christian community concerning the moral and spiritual strength of our country. In their judgment the performance of religious rites and practices, the provision of religious instruction, the invocation of religious symbols are methods by which to deal with the sickness of our time. So a Christian community that demands the recitation of the proper creed and the holding aloft of the Christian symbol before the eye of its membership as a sign of "fellowship in the redeemed" inevitably applies the same requirements to our social situation. Thus they look upon these devices as the best way by which to deal with the tensions of our time.

Jews certainly would not use religious ceremonials or symbols in this same way. When we say "no" to their efforts, however, without suggesting a similarly genuine concern for the problems that confront all of us or without offering any other more efficient alternative for dealing with these problems then we commit an irreparable damage. We tear away the defenses that our Christian neighbors have built up to handle their anxieties. Out spills the anger and fear that these defenses have held in check and the anger touches us. The Jews then are identified with those who are against these holy symbols. They are identified in their eyes with the Communist and secularist, with persons blind to the real problems that confront the American community. Our negativism is irritating and it helps not at all to clarify the problems of the time that have provoked recourse to more and more religion in public life including public education. I suggest that we obtain a more sympathetic understanding of the problems that motivate our Christian neighbors as a first step in our communication with them.

II

Furthermore I suggest that Jewish leadership has failed adequately to communicate with the Protestant and Catholic community, not only because we have misread their motivations, but also because the arguments we have used have themselves been secularistic and legalistic. These arguments in my judgment are not the strongest nor the most adequate, nor the most telling that we can use in our dialogue with the Christian community. If we are to speak to the Christian's heart and mind, we must go beyond the law in dealing with this problem. Let me illustrate what I mean.

If we come to the Christian and say to him "we are opposed to released time because it is a violation of the separation of church and state," then he will answer "The Supreme Court of the United States has ruled that released time is not a violation of the principle of separation of church and state. You may in your judgment think that it is a violation of the separation principle and of the First Amendment, but the courts of America do not think so. Furthermore we do not think that the First Amendment was intended to apply to the situation of releasing children from the public school for religious instruction."

If we come to the Christian and say to him that the recitation of prayer in the morning and the reading of the Bible in public schools is a violation of the principle of separation of church and state, then he will answer, "Who told you so? More than half of the states of the United States require or permit the reading of the Bible or the recitation of prayer, and in most of the cases where this has been challenged, the courts have ruled that the reading of the Bible or opening exercises are not a violation of the First Amendment nor of the principle of the separation of church and state particularly when those who so desire may be excused from the practice."

If you come to the Christian and you say to him "If you sing Christmas carols in the public school, and give gifts, and decorate the building with Christmas trees and ornaments, and perform Christmas plays in the public school, you are in violation of the principle of the separation of church and state," he will retort, "If you think so, then test in the court." And in my judgment, there may be no court in the United States that will rule that the celebration of Christmas, the performing of a Christmas play, the singing of Christmas carols or the giving of gifts, or the posting of the Christmas tree on the school lawn is a violation of the First Amendment. I do not believe that any court will see in these actions a violation of our religious liberty.

The courts and the American people have the right at any time to revise, change, deepen, broaden our understanding of what is the proper relationship between the state and religion, between church and state. It is not through the law then that we shall communicate effectively with the Christian community and come to grips with this problem. When we use the argument of "We're for the separation of church and state" it has become almost meaningless. Are we unaware of the fact that every Christian who has suggested that we read the Bible or post the Ten Commandments or institute courses for moral and spiritual values has also claimed "I too believe in the separation of church and state but these practices are not prohibited under the First Amendment?" Do they not rather contend that this is the school's proper way of dealing with the religious aspect of our heritage in Western civilization?

Let us assume that the Jewish community goes to court and that the court rules that the holding of a nativity play in the public school is permissible. The Jewish community may still want to say to the Christian community that although this practice is constitutional, the performing of a nativity play in the public school is not very good practice; and then we shall have to tell the reasons why. The reasons we shall give are not legal. Rather they refer to the experiences of our children and their feelings and thoughts when they are compelled to perform in or observe markedly sectarian Christian rites. We shall explain that our attitudes toward the imposition of such religious rites in the public school arise out of our religious heritage and our understanding of how God's will is to be communicated. Is this not really what we want to tell our Christian neighbors? And I think they will understand us. Instead the Jewish community has rested its case on secularistic and legalistic arguments which are not at all reflective of the spiritual genius and insight within our religious tradition.

In my meetings with church officials, I am painfully aware that they come into the deliberation primed and prepared with an understanding of how it is out of their theology that they have come to their conclusions with regard to the proper relationship of church and state. There is no such developed Jewish philosophy and this is our crying need. This is the language that the rabbis of our country have to develop. We need speak out as rabbis, out of our own Jewish and religious concern, not using the language of law and the interpretation of law but the sense of what it is that the Jewish tradition and Jewish experience has to say on these issues.

This will be no easy task for the Jewish community: to revise our thinking along these authentic lines and to formulate the insight of our religious tradition within the theological framework of contemporary religious thought. For on this issue the Jewish tradition is not that clear. In Israel, where we have some reasonable expectations that a Jewish viewpoint is being fulfilled in the destiny of the country, released time is a part of the official public school program. There it is not considered such a terrible violation of the proper relationship of church and state nor a denial of the religious freedom of Christians, Moslems or non-believers.

III

Finally, I question the technique of the Jewish community which so easily threatens court suit as the most telling weapon in its dialogue with the Christian community on this issue. I suggest that in the area of interreligious relations, the use of the legal process is not the most effective way of dealing with the problem. Communication, discussion and education are more effective and less harmful.

We are dealing here not simply with legal issues but with human relations, the relations between people, the relations of a school to a community, the relations of the Jewish community to the Christian community. In this process more is to be gained through communication and discussion, through an effort to understand what motivates our Christian neighbors and the realization that we too must brush away our stereotyped conceptions concerning them. More will be gained by helping them understand the needs of our children than through the quotation of legal opinion.

We shall have to make accommodations, too, for we live in a pluralistic society. In such a society each group, with the deepest charity and love and respect for the other, must make allowances for each other, for living together in a free society. We must be creative not rigid, affirmative not negative, more trusting and understanding if we are to live happily side by side with our non-Jewish neighbors.

I would suggest, for example, that such an approach to this problem would mean with regard to Christmas celebrations in the public school, that the Jewish community continue to stand firm in its contention that the most blatantly sectarian form of Christological celebration of Christmas is improper in the public school. We can insist that the nativity play is improper in the public school, that the lining up of children in the shape of a cross with lights dimmed and the choir robed and candle in hand is improper. It is a kind of an exercise better befitting a church than a public school. But I warn that the Jewish community ought refrain from objecting to the celebration of Christmas in its entirety in the public schools of the United States. The lighting of the Christmas tree, the singing of carols and the giving of gifts are deep-rooted rituals long embedded in practice and custom in the cultural traditions of the American people. It ill behooves the Jewish community to launch an attack on these practices. We have nowhere been successful in taking Christmas out of the public school. Far better, therefore, that the occasion be used to provide Christian children with an understanding of the celebrations of Jewish children at that time of the year through the observance in the public school of Channukah. Far better if the spirit of good will prevail. Far better, if Jewish children obtain recognition in the public school rather than be compelled by the adult community to become silent martyrs in our principled fight, which we shall never win on this issue. It seems to me that this is a far more constructive approach to our relations with the Christian community than the approaches heretofore adopted by Jewish organizations and agencies.

Furthermore, I contend that through this approach the psychological hurt to Jewish children will be minimized if it exists at all. I am not sure that there will be any hurt to Jewish children in celebrating Christmas in the public school if Channukah is also recognized. My experience has indicated instead that we shall be helping our children gain in self-respect and enable our Christian neighbors to grow in inter-religious understanding.

IV

If our Jewish children are raised in our homes as Jews, if they are provided with the internal strength of positive Jewish commitment and respect for their own identification, then I suggest it will not matter what happens in the public school—and nothing so terrible is going to happen in the public school anyway. Our children educated as Jews will be able to handle any experience of sectarian prayer or teaching in the public school because they will be proud and self-respecting Jews. I recall the story of a six-year-old who attended a private non-sectarian school. One day she came home at the Christmas time and said "Mother, we did the most wonderful thing today. We went to see a manger and there were the animals and the wise men and in the center was the little Jesus child and right next to him were the *Shabbos* candles." It is my conviction that this child, brought up with a proud sense of identification of herself as a Jew will be able to know without any harm or conflict to her self-esteem that the Christian community celebrates its Christian religion. She will be able to understand the school's participation in the Christmas celebration of an entire community and yet she will be faithful to her uniqueness and strong in her identification as a Jew. In no way will she be harmed psychologically or damaged by such practice.

This last assertion is not intended to stop us from holding high the significance of the church-state separation principle for religious liberty nor of remaining eternally vigilant. It is intended, however, to provide us the confidence that in good will, if we are firm in our Jewishness, we can patiently and properly engage the Christian community in forthright conversation on this knotty problem. Hopefully in this confrontation and in the creative resolution of our differences, we shall all grow and deepen in faith and in our joy in the blessing that is democracy.

COMMUNITY EDUCATION: A FUNCTIONAL RELATIONSHIP BETWEEN SCHOOL AND CHURCH

Wesner Fallaw

Children and adolescents need concerted guidance by school and church, two institutions which presently merely take turns with the young, each serving in ways largely unknown to the other; or, if known, scarcely appreciated and sometimes opposed. Due to their alternately conducted programs and inclination to be self-contained, neither school nor church or synagogue takes advantage of what the other knows about a given pupil and his needs, or shows any awareness of what together they might accomplish. The result is disparate guidance and a child often disappearing in the crevices between two presumably self-sufficient institutions. Very likely this will continue to be the situation unless there comes into being a community education transcending the public school system, and unless professionals are trained at the university level for using education and religion to make a co-ordinated impact on the situation.

Co-ordination suggests personal guidance and classroom teaching in school and church or synagogue that would maintain the American system of separate public education and organized religion, while yet establishing a functional relationship between the two. This relationship is herein designated as community education. Community education may be conceived of as embracing public education and religious education without evoking entangling alliances between state and church. Its over-arching objective is the re-evaluation of values that give rise to current thought and conduct; and this means a holistic education that deepens personal religious life and generates spiritually productive social relations.

Public education operates in the implicit belief that its proper service to the individual and society is that of providing a teaching-learning process rooted in and bounded by the natural order. Religion operates in the explicit belief that neither the individual nor society is properly nurtured except by faith in God who is both within and above the natural order. Education and religion

Reprinted from *Religious Education,* Vol. 58, No. 1 (January 1963), pp. 36–43, by permission of the publisher, the Religious Education Association, New York City.

each seeks to effect changes in persons and acts on evidence which shows that learning and faith ought not to be left to chance. The individual needs guidance and instruction. As the instrument of geographic, social, and political community, public education is disposed to care for its own. Similarly, as the servant of the religious community, the church or synagogue is committed to ministering to its own. What school and church have failed to achieve during the past century and more, since the states removed religion from public schools, is a comprehensive education in which the pupil is perceived as a whole, and nurtured in his wholeness: a social, intellectual and spiritual being. Instead of comprehensive or holistic education, we have an education from which religion, as the heart of the culture and the supreme guide of the person, has been severed; one which, being impaired itself, impairs the value system and religious devotions of the young.

This is an anomalous situation, for by tradition Americans are "a religious people." From the time of the Founding Fathers, throughout our civic, legislative, and judicial history until now we have at least paid verbal tribute to religion. Certainly there are many evidences of close ties between the political and religious communities; for example, in the oft-quoted words of the Northwest Ordinance (1787):

> Religion, morality and knowledge being necessary to good government and the happiness of mankind, schools, and the means of education shall be forever encouraged.

And with approximately 63 percent of the population now enrolled in institutional religion (the highest ever), there can be little doubt but that the majority of our citizens would be openminded about a proposal for establishing a working arrangement between public education and institutional religion.

But granted an interested majority, there is still the uninterested and perhaps hostile minority to be reassured that no attempt is to be made to use the public school to enhance sectarian religion. Moreover, there are religionists of various persuasions who are just as quick or quicker than non-believers to forestall possible encroachment by either church or state on the other's sphere. The question is, How are education and religion in America to make a common impact on school-age children and their families and yet guard against breaching the traditional "wall of separation" between church and state?

LOCAL COMMUNITY COUNCIL

Here is a mission awaiting leadership by imaginative citizens aided by a pioneering university through its schools of education and divinity. Experimentation might begin with a local community council composed of public school officials, churchmen and parents who would enlist researchers and advisors from the university for five or more years of testing the validity of the community education idea prior to its possible general adoption. Although an advisory body, careful to respect the autonomy of its supporting institutions, the council might evolve as an agency to give direction for achieving a new dimension in educational and religious development of children and, indirectly, their families.

The council should serve as a kind of broker between the board of public education and institutional religion. In no sense will it displace the board or become an ecclesiastical body. Indeed, its motives may be purer and its effectiveness greater if its members are not officially appointed by school or church groups but are simply gathered as citizens who stand for preservation of the non-sectarian public school and who advocate for each child, whose parents so elect, a comprehensive and manageable schedule that permits him to move back and forth between school and church or synagogue classes as a normal part of his work-week.

Among the tasks of the council are these: (1) Defining a balanced work-week for the child, which is to say, specifying what parts of the child's week belong to the public school, to the church or synagogue, and to the home; (2) providing an integrated schedule for each pupil—whose parents so choose—that envisions the geographic community as a large campus on which the pupil participates in public school, church or synagogue, recreational and home affairs; (3) transmuting the instructional staffs of public schools and religious schools into a community education staff the members of which may view themselves as colleagues who, though operating within their respective organizations of school and church or synagogue, will gain a steady vision of their common educational enterprise; (4) establishing the practice of taking major responsibility for educational, moral and spiritual issues that confront the youth of the community. Consider some of the implications of the above.

I

First, it is to be observed that in addressing itself to the question of what constitutes a balanced work-week for the child, the community council is venturing into an undeveloped area. Doubtlessly an experimental community will be one that believes in good education and therefore has high standards for its public schools. Its elementary schools perhaps occupy 25–30 hours of the week besides requiring home work, while its secondary schools may demand a 40–50 hour week for classes and home work, exclusive of extra-curricular events. It will reflect the fact that quite generally the American academic pace has quickened in recent years, with competition for high school grades and admission to the better colleges exerting unrelieved pressure on secondary school teachers and pupils alike. Moreover, the experimental community will be aware of the recurrent call from certain educationalists for prolonging the school day and year. Hence the questions to be faced by the community council at the outset are these: How far does an extension of the school program go toward actual improvement of teaching and learning? What is the point of no return? And, more difficult yet to answer, Where is a line to be drawn so that religious institutions and homes can have adequate opportunity for dealing with the ultimate concerns of faith and belief?

The council will be mindful that education is no less a process of assimilating meaning and value and channeling devotion toward the highest good than it is a process of accumulating knowledge. Full opportunity needs to be given to spiritual discipline and reflection and to gaining perspective that can hardly be found if citizens allow children's energies and interests to be monopolized by an ever-intensifying and lengthening school day and year.

What is required of a community council and its consultants from the university's School of Education and Divinity School, is sufficient wisdom so to balance academic exertions and spiritual nurture that they may insure a truly holistic education. This achievement depends upon the establishment of a hierarchy of values to guide community educators and pupils as they deal with theoretical and practical issues of learning and living. Failure of genuine education leaves a considerable proportion of school children and their families glorifying prestige symbols, materialism, and entertainment to the detriment of themselves, American society and the religious community. Quite simply, if religious education is important, Protestants, Roman Catholics, Jews, and others need to give their combined support to those citizens and educators who are ready to seek a functional relationship between church and state.

Community education may be expected to appeal to Protestants who perceive the error of relegating church education to such marginal efforts as those represented by the Sunday school and similar amateur teaching programs. Community education may catch the fancy of Roman Catholics who at last are being offered a way to permeate the child's public school experiences with religous meaning, and to do so without having to build and finance more parochial schools. Jews and other minority groups may find that community education strengthens support of the public school—preserving the democratic ideal of schools open to all children of the community—while providing a stimulus for better work by more children in the religious school, and with less sacrifice of athletics and other extra-curricular activities.

If the designers of community education do their job well, either excessive extension or too little support of the schools can be avoided. Furthermore, an effective functional relationship between public schools and religious institutions of the community (the latter acting on behalf of parents who desire religious instruction and guidance for their children) would insure sufficient time and greater prominence for spiritual nurture as an on-going experience during the week. To be sure, the child's time and pursuits are ultimately the responsibility of parents. As citizens, parents have long sanctioned compulsory education requirements by the several states. But as is well known this does not mean (and the Supreme Court has so ruled)[1] that a child has to attend a public, tax supported school. Nor does it signify, presumably, that public schools and religious schools cannot jointly conduct the child's educational program on a basis found to be equitable. It is at this point that Harry L. Stearns' proposal[2] should be examined, although most communities will likely find it simpler for school and church to share the child's time if religious institutions confine their offerings to spiritual guidance and to courses in religion instead of undertaking to teach also such courses as history and literature.

It may be that the community council will need to specify the maximum time properly allocated to public schooling—to instruction and to home work—even as the states of the Union have determined and legalized their respective minimum number of school days and hours per year. To say this is not to censure school authorities for sometimes overworking pupils but rather to acknowledge the reality of a situation partly caused by concern for improving teaching and learning, and more largely caused by churches' and parents' neglecting to think through the problem of providing fruitful religious instruction and home experiences in which the child may, with all his growing knowledge, also get wisdom and understanding. And not least important is the necessity for relieving adolescents from increasing tensions caused by overcompetitiveness and reliance on grades.

II

Second, in the experimental community the child's schedule will enable him to move back and forth between the public school building, the playing field and his chosen church or synagogue as if a student on a large preparatory school or university campus. In the religious institutions, both instruction and personal guidance are to be given by academically qualified men and women paid not by the public school system but by their respective ecclesiastical bodies. Each church and synagogue will look to the community education council and the university's School of Education for formulation of educational standards to be met by the religious mentor who, as teacher and guidance worker, will need the doubly exacting training of theological school and graduate school of education. For no religious institution or teacher of religion can be content with offering any less professionally conducted piece of work than the best offering to which the child is accus-

[1] Pierce et al. v. Society of Sisters (268 U.S. 510), 1925.

[2] "Symposium: Shared Time" in *Religious Education,* January–February, 1962.

tomed in the public school. Participation in religious instruction being a voluntary matter, obviously it is essential that the religious mentor shall be able to attract and hold children by the force of his professional competence and personal magnetism.

One is tempted to add that parental backing will be the decisive factor in pupils' joining and remaining faithful to the religious school. Some parents are able to lend effective support, some are not, among them being those who but faintly honor a religious enterprise. For example, when forced to make a choice between the child's giving himself exclusively to academic work, deemed necessary for entering a prestige college—thereby advancing his social and economic prospects—and less intensive school work that permits regular participation in religious instruction, most parents unhesitatingly by-pass the latter. For them, settling for a modest college is too great a price to pay for religious nurture.

Those who devise a program of experimental community education may well anticipate considerable divergence of opinion as to how frequently a child may be expected to journey from public school to church or synagogue. Perhaps two one-hour periods a week—including travel—for elementary children's classes in religion, and a single two-hour or two-and-a-half-hour block of time for high school pupils' class and study period will prove satisfactory. In addition, particularly for upper elementary and high school pupils, one hour every two or three weeks may be set aside for personal guidance by the religious mentor. Thus, it is implied, at the high school level, religion is to be considered a minor course, an elective which in some states may be counted toward graduation from the public school. And if not, then the church or synagogue can still offer the course and supplement the public school's transcript by informing the college to which a student applies of the work which he has done in religion. Either way, courses studied in church or synagogue are elevated in the minds of school officials, children and parents, and take their rightful place in the total spectrum of the academic week.

Guidance would seem to be an especially rewarding aspect of community education, it being one way in which the overworked public school counselor can be given relief, and being also an area in which pastoral gifts and skills are called for. The administering of objective tests and the keeping of cumulative records would continue to be the responsibility of the public school, as would much of the educational and vocational guidance. But personal guidance involving—as it so often does—sectarian beliefs of the child and his parents would be left to the religious mentor chosen according to the wishes of each family. By training and by virtue of his thorough knowledge of the child's school record and of the child himself, the religious mentor would be prepared to use educational and religious insights as is ordinarily not possible for the public school counselor.

Although it will be more difficult to schedule pupils than religious mentors for journeying between school and church, the American system does not permit doctrinal or sectarian teaching in public schools. Consequently, religious mentors may work with children only off school territory, though as fully qualified educators they may properly confer with their colleagues in the school building, study cumulative records, and familiarize themselves with what is being taught each of their pupils. Indeed, they must take these steps if in the church or synagogue class they are to guide the pupil's public school development into a religious dimension.

Admittedly, there will be those disposed to question any cooperation between church and state, one reason being that the public school might inadvertently influence children of non-believers to take part in religious instruction. But the risk is lessened by staggering the hours, on an individual basis, for scheduling pupils for church or synagogue sessions. For the high school this presents less a problem than for the elementary school, and if by reason of scheduling difficulties young children can only be dismissed by class groups to go at the same hour to the several religious institutions—or to remain in the public school for "busy work"—then it may be better for the experimental community to follow the plan (long used in some places) of ending the elementary school day at noon once or twice a week. Thus each child returns to his home for lunch, and afterwards whether he goes to a religious class, music lesson, or what not, he goes in a way that involves the public school not at all.

As suggested above, the scheduling of pupils on a community basis rather than simply a public school basis offers an opportunity to pattern the child's day of study, worship and play somewhat along the lines followed in the boarding school where class, study hall, chapel and playing field constitute a reasonable and workable balance of activities.

III

Third, the community council will explore the feasibility of so conjoining the work of public school educators and religious educators that they will look upon themselves as a federated community education staff engaged in holistic education. To repeat, staff members will operate in their respective spheres in school and church or synagogue while yet gaining a steady vision of their common purpose and enterprise. These may be defined provisionally as (a) the fullest possible cultural, intellectual, and spiritual development of each individual so that all may hold as primary the giving of the self to the common good, locally, nationally and internationally, and (b) such guidance that those so disposed may center their devotions in the God of a particular religious faith. Obviously both "a" and "b" relate to the work of religious mentors, the "a" part in general and the "b" in particular. Less obvious and probably less permissible is the view that though "a" is the particular province of the public school staff, "b" is not outside its general concern, precisely because by its teaching of history, literature, art and music the public school necessarily accords every pupil the right to respond positively, neutrally, or negatively to the claims of a religion or several religions. Yet it must be added that the public school teacher and administrator may not exceed the privilege which is theirs to teach *about* any or all the major religions. Always they should leave to their colleagues on the community education staff—the mentors in church and synagogue—the more specific task of teaching religion for commitment.

The point needs stressing that community education poses neither threat to institutional autonomy nor to the religious freedom of public school teachers, children and their families. Quite the contrary, for it is in the interest of those whose fundamental allegiance is to God as they know him, that a functional relationship between public education and organized religion is proposed. And no less so it is in the interest of those who want no part of religious faith that the public school and the community council are to respect their wish, the school confining itself to offering relevant information about a given religious heritage when and where it is referred to in the curriculum. Moreover, as an advisory agency on education for the whole community, the council will encourage skeptics and free thinkers who so desire to set up their own instructional program paralleling the programs of the religious bodies. For freedom for religion hinges upon freedom from religion.

Aside from theoretical advantages inherent in systematic study of religion or some other dominant faith, there are several practical reasons why community education ought to be given a trial.

Protestants, whose children constitute the largest number enrolled in American public schools, have never solved the problem of providing first-rate religious education. Roman Catholics, with about half of their children of elementary school age enrolled in parochial schools, in approximately 10,000 of their more than 16,000 parishes with resident priests in the fifty states, are committed to the ideal of a church school for all their children and youth. Unless some alternative to secular education is devised to their satisfaction, their lack of support of the common schools may seriously undermine public education. Like Protestants, Jews tend to be staunch supporters of public education, the difference being that the latter have largely corrected education's religious deficit by establishing professionally conducted religious schools open in late afternoons and on weekends. It is fair to say that once Protestants resolve to take their own instruction as seriously as many Roman Catholics and the Jews take theirs, a decided move will be made toward overcoming Protestantism's proverbial illiteracy. And as members of the three major faiths collaborate on a community education council, there is promise that the public schools' education in moral and spiritual values will be fulfilled in church and synagogue education. So also, the Ethical Culture Society and similar faiths can take their complementary place in community education. Even so short a period as a five-year experiment might well demonstrate that a rewarding advance has been made toward overcoming the depersonalization and materialism of the community.

If it be true that immaturity and delinquency are in part caused by a child's failure to gain an image of a worthy father-figure, by systematically relating children to religious mentors community education will be a fruitful means of fostering maturity and lessening delinquency. For each parson, priest, and rabbi who is both educationally and religiously competent to establish a relationship in which the child learns to admire and therefore to listen to his mentor, will indeed serve as a spiritual father. Knowing the child, staying with him during his growing years, the mentor can guide his moral development, sometimes lift his level of educational and vocational aspiration, and help him make decisions based on faith and reason. And because intelligence, affection and persistent care have validity in counteracting aimlessness and moral and academic flabbiness, obviously there is much practical value to be found in the guidance aspect of community education. Not only so, when through religious instruction youth learns to reckon with the prophetic dimension of the Judeo-Christian tradition, much of the "privatism" and meaninglessness victimizing this generation will yield in favor of social responsibility and personal accountability to God. How else than by teaching of this kind can there be successful wrestling with the evils infecting the American community? Given the vision of what community education purposes to accomplish, financial support and adequate personnel can be supplied for the federated education staff.

Anticipating a time when community education might become a national option, it may be said that Roman Catholics and Jews will have a clear advantage over Protestants with respect to securing funds and teachers. For Catholics, community education actually means expenditure of less money than is required by the present parochial school plan. For Jews, the cost will perhaps be about the same. But for Protestants and others, the staffing of their churches with educationally equipped counselors and teachers will require not only a vastly greater program of recruiting and training personnel but also a marked increase over their customary budgeting. However inexact it may be, the observation deserves making that in some communities, Protestants—by finding money to pay salaries of additional pastor-teachers—might save at least a part of what it would cost them were they taxed to employ public school guidance personnel in sufficient numbers fully to individualize education. In other words, a council on community education will be advised to consider the possibility that though its Protestant constituency will have to provide much more money for education, what is saved by not increasing taxes to support an expansion of public school guidance, may be used by individual Protestants to employ pastor-teachers. And if this is not a strong enough incentive for raising the level of Protestant spending for education, let it be said quite plainly that until communities work out a suitable plan for Roman Catholics to infuse the general education of their children with their doctrinal outlook, the treasuries of many public education systems will be subjected to efforts to divert a portion of public moneys into parochial schools. Not that it is necessarily antithetical to political democracy for Catholics or any religious body to lay claim to a just share of tax funds. At least this is debatable. On the other hand, the principle that gave birth to the common school for all the people is definitely threatened. Consequently, America needs community programs with federated public school, church and synagogue staffs able to articulate and conduct holistic education.

IV

Fourth, with the assistance of university researchers and advisors the council on education in the experimental community may establish the practice of taking major responsibility for dealing with educational, ethical and religious issues confronting learners as they consider both their local and world community responsibilities. Sporadic attempts by sundry civic groups have a place in solving social problems of all kinds, but the genius of a community is hardly expressed other than by advance planning and by setting up a comprehensive body representative of the whole community, one dedicated to continuous work for the general welfare. Caught in a rapidly shifting moral climate, many parents have abdicated. In trying to fill the vacuum they have left, public schools have undertaken more than they can handle. And due to a certain remoteness and irrelevance of much of organized religion, public educators, social workers and guidance clinics find themselves burdened with the task of trying to give individuals personal and social stability. No adequate ethical and deeply grounded interfaith approach has yet developed a clear and manageable system so that confused citizens can visualize it and be disposed to avail themselves of its ministrations. Consequently not only are values fragmented but also social, educational, and religious organizations. The functional relationship, herein advocated, between public education and organized religion is not a super-organization but a working arrangement latent with real possibility for releasing educational and religious resources for the restoration of wholeness to community and to personal life.

The community council on education faces the two-fold task of devising and implementing a unifying and comprehensive philosophy of education. It should be clear that neither the point of view of this writer nor the program implied here so much as hints at uniformity of religious outlook for the community. It should be equally clear that public school educators, religious educators and free thinkers have a common stake in developing persons capable of contributing to the making and realization of national purposes. This means more than education for survival; it means breaking through the provincialism of local community and nation alike and learning how to fashion a world order. And further, it means teachers and pupils who realize that the way in which personal disagreement, racial inequity and injustice of all kinds are faced and resolved in the local community largely determines the way in which the same problems are to be dealt with on a world scale.

A reflective and advisory body, the community council will propagate such summary view-points as these:

It is the task of the public elementary school to provide a climate of good will and mutual respect in which the child masters the tools of learning and practices co-operative and considerate interpersonal relations.

The task of the public high school is to teach pupils according to their ability to be good workmen, thinkers, and eventually, servants of the common good at home and in the world community, overcoming personal narrowness and preoccupation with the acquisition of things.

The task of the religious school is that of so guiding children and youth that they will cherish above all else the ideal of conducting themselves as creatures worthy of their Creator.

Presently the American community does not have a single body whose function is comparable to that of the proposed community council. Given men and women on the council who see education whole, productive experimentation may be expected to follow, giving hope of clear moral purpose, higher educational achievement and firmer religious faith.

To these ends the aid of the university is required beyond research and advice, for public school teachers will need preparation befitting the scope and intention of community education; and pastor-teachers will have to be trained for this new undertaking in which their educational understanding and skills must be no less pronounced than their theological and ecclesiastical qualifications.[3]

In turn, the university dedicated to educating students for humanitarian and public service, needs the experimental community as a laboratory, more specifically for intern opportunities for testing out the professional adequacy of prospective public school and religious school teachers. Indeed, it may be argued that only by coincident development of a new profession—that of religious mentor—and the enlarged outlook of the public-school-educator-become-community-educator, can the local community and the university fulfill their common mission to American society.

[3] Cf. Wesner Fallaw, *Church Education for Tomorrow*, Westminster Press.

Chapter 8

A SYNTHESIS OF VALUES FOR EDUCATION

Ward Madden, *a philosopher, presents a synthesis of the values we find in our religions and in the democratic idea.*

Madden holds that it is possible to abstract from our religions a common core of experience that is free from sectarianism. Since this core represents the experiences of all men, it is therefore available to public education. In this synthesis, it is possible to achieve a rapprochement *of the naturalistic and the supernaturalistic orientations. Madden suggests that, because American society and its institutions are largely secular, a reconstruction of religious values demands that we understand the factors involved in the growth of secularism: the development of modern science, the rise of democracy, and the belief in the integral relation of mind and body. He is convinced that by utilizing all we know about ourselves, we can reconstruct the religious outlook and bring into existence meanings, concepts, and ideologies that will enable all people to live the good life. In this process, the roles and functions of educators, students, and the schools are clearly indicated.*

Madden asserts further that a sociological and psychological study of the purposes of religion leads to an identification of five modes or moods that describe the experiences of all people. These are the valuational, the community, the executive, the esthetic, and the contemplative moods. Central to the functioning of these five modes is the creative social act which "consists of all those interactions of men with one another from which emerge expanding areas of common interest around which activity becomes focused." Madden is convinced that "It is [in] the social act, broadly conceived to include nature as well as man as a participant, that value is created and integrated, community is expanded, the self finds itself and is enriched, the dramatic splendor of life is increased, the most comprehensive consummations are achieved."

For educators, Madden suggests the following principles: (a) the creative social act should be the dominant feature of the curriculum; (b) by means of the social act students can develop a concept of value to be used as a base for daily conduct; (c) through the social act students can develop both a sense of selfhood and a sense of community; (d) involvement in the social act will enable the student to locate the ultimate source of authority; (e) participation in the arguments between those who do and those who do not support the social act can help a student enrich and develop a style of thinking (an esthetic) and strengthen his faith in growth and progress; and (f) the progress made in attaining values through the medium of the social act can stimulate the further pursuit of the desired values.

EDUCATION FOR RELIGIOUS QUALITY IN EXPERIENCE

Ward Madden

There are signs that the next epoch in the history of civilization is going to be one either of synthesis or of quite literal and fairly complete atomization. At the level of world politics, the world hangs in the balance between the two alternatives. A nudge could tip the scales either way. But at the level of ideas—at least in that part of the world still free to have ideas—there remains some possibility of synthesis at certain points. Whether this can be a critical nudge that will make a difference in the whole human situation remains to be seen. Brawn as well as spirit will be required to make a better world. But it is at least hopeful that there are hints of possible integration at some points in man's badly split personality.

What I have in mind particularly is the promise of a rapprochement between the naturalistic and the supernaturalistic approaches to the meaning and control of life. In America, where the naturalism of the leading philosophers has seemed a fruition of the naturalism of the common American mentality, the portents are clear. It is significant that the characteristically American thinker, John Dewey, has seemed to his materialistically minded

Reprinted from *Harvard Educational Review*, Vol. XXI, No. 1 (Winter 1951), pp. 14–31.

critics to be tainted with philosophical idealism, while his idealistic critics see him as a materialist—that the early influences to which he reacted most favorably were Hegelianism on the one hand and Darwinianism on the other.

Historically, religion, supernaturalism and idealism have done the most justice to the creativity in the universe and life, while materialism has done most justice to the natural cause-and-effect relations by which change becomes less mysterious and more explicable. But whereas once we saw a conflict between determinism and creativity, we are now beginning to see mind and purpose as emergent qualities in a determined but not predetermined universe. The frontier edge of the American mentality has outgrown the over-simplified materialism of Newtonian physics, Watsonian psychology, and the acquisitive society, without, however, losing the tough-mindedness of the earlier outlook. We have reached the point where naturalistic philosophers examine myth, not merely for its symbolism, but for its essential truth, and where some religious philosophers and theologians claim that they and their writings are essentially naturalistic in content however supernatural the form. There is both a new naturalism and a new supernaturalism, each of which, as it moves beyond the reductionism and one-sidedness of its ancestry, grows closer to the other.

Yet the synthesis has scarcely begun—the big jobs remain to be done. This is especially true at the only point that really matters—in the life and conduct of the ordinary man. He continues to live in a world split between the uninspired secularism of the workaday world and the sterile spirituality reserved, not just for Sundays, but for Sundays at a given hour.

The secularism of the public school is one of the characteristic manifestations of this state of affairs. This situation in the schools is both praised and condemned, depending, largely, on which side of the naturalistic-supernaturalistic fence the observer stands. On the one hand we are told that the schools are the Godless instrument of Satan, that naturalism is the only "sect" permitted access to the schools. On the other hand, alarms are sounded to the effect that organized religion is out to recapture the schools, and we are told this would mean the smothering of the American mentality by authoritarianism and a pre-scientific outlook.

Of the immediate causes of secularism in the public schools, the most important has been sectarianism. The principle of the separation of church and state originated, not because of any antipathy for religion, but because each sect sought protection from the domination of each other sect. The colonial schools and the schools of the early Republic were essentially religious schools, and there was no widespread serious intention that they should be otherwise. The first amendment to the Constitution and the various state constitutions sought to preserve the right of the people to choose between alternative religious views. The legal effect of these provisions was, and remains to this day, one of excluding sectarian teaching, but not religion itself, from the public schools. But the practical, as distinct from the merely legal, effect has been to exclude religion itself. There has never been agreement among sects sufficient to make the teaching of a common core of religious belief possible.

But the causes of secularism in the schools go even deeper. The schools are secular essentially because contemporary society itself is secular. There are three basic and related trends, aside from sectarianism, which have helped produce our secular civilization and which must be reckoned with in any attempt to make a new approach to religion and education. These are the development of modern science, the rise of democracy, and the belief in the integral relation of mind and body.

If we accept, as I think we must, the basic meaning of these three developments, then we will have to share the common skeptical attitude toward much that has been traditional in religion. The first two of these—science and democracy—are a challenge to all authoritarianism in religion and to all claims to acquaintance with ultimate truth. The third—the belief in the integral relation of mind and body—makes it impossible any longer to think of a world of spirit which is different in kind and separable from the corporeal world.

The acceptance of these ideas confronts us with a choice—shall we reject religion altogether and continue in our secular ways, or shall we seek a reconstruction of the meaning of religion compatible with the democratic-scientific outlook?

It seems strategic that the second choice—the reconstruction of our religious outlook—be made at this time of crisis in world history. There are two compelling reasons.

In the first place, we are in desperate need of moral and spiritual commitments capable of mobilizing our energies for the making of a better world. Men of all persuasions recognize this, and each, whether fascist, communist, democrat or Christian, tries in his own way to meet the need. Though some of these ways are immeasurably better than others, none has proved good enough—a new effort is needed.

In the second place, it is the better part of strategy to make use of the resources we have already developed. Traditional religious outlooks represent judgments based upon ages of religious experience. They command the deepest loyalties of millions of persons. Rather than start with a clean slate, it seems better to make use of the generations of experience and the loyalties which may be used as springboards toward a religious mode of life appropriate to the scientific, democratic, organismic outlook of our age.

It is the purpose in the following pages to suggest the directions that the needed reconstruction of religion may take, and to point out how the public school can help in the process.

It is desirable, first of all, to recall a familiar distinction—the distinction between the function and the structure of religion. The structure of a religion is the body of ritual and doctrine which distinguish it from other religions. The function of religion is the quality with which the daily life and conduct of the devotee becomes suffused. Functionally, religion is a quality of behavior which we seem to recognize in experience even when the structure of a formal religion is absent. We often feel that we recognize something religious in the conduct of a Communist or Nazi, or we say that a man makes a religion of his pursuit of democracy or his pursuit of science. The resemblance between such examples and that which we may be willing to recognize as true religious quality may be superficial; nevertheless the possibility that we may here be sensing something fundamental should not be shrugged off without examination.

Legally, religion could be cultivated in the public schools if a core of meaning common to all sects and religions, a core common even to those who deny the existence of God, could be found. Hitherto all efforts to find such a core have failed. But all, or practically all, such efforts have sought, not a common core of function, but a common core of structure—they have sought common beliefs and rituals, of which there are none. But it is possible there is something functionally religious in the lives even of atheists, that there is a common functional core, a common quality of experience, which all men, Christian and Jew, Buddhist and Confucian, theist and agnostic, can recognize as religious and subscribe to.

It is the belief of the writer that as a matter of fact a sociological and psychological investigation of the function of religion enables one to identify a number of religious modes or moods which characterize the experience of all men whether they embrace a formal religion or not. The existence of such moods in experience is a matter of degree—some men display them so slightly as to be at the foot of a curve of normal probability, while other men display them in the most intense degree. But the occurrence of these moods in some degree is so universal in experience that it seems possible men might agree upon the desirability of cultivating them.

The remainder of these pages will be devoted to identifying and describing these moods, and suggesting how they develop in the experience of the race and may be helped to develop in the experience of children.

While no list of such moods can be exhaustive, and while classification, however necessary to discourse, is always arbitrary, five moods of the religious quality in experience will be discussed. They will be termed the valuational mood, the community mood, the executive mood, the esthetic mood, and the contemplative mood.

The first of these is the valuational mood. When men operate in the valuational mood, they sanctify whatever they take to be the ideal values of existence, and they deify whatever they take to be the source of these values.

The history of religion is essentially the story of man's long struggle to work out his proper relationship to the ideal values which motivate life and to understand the processes by which such values are determinable. What history seems to show is that ideal values originate in experience as mere claims growing out of the ordinary activities and occupations of life. Investigators of primitive societies are able to furnish us examples. For instance, the thirsty and weary savage tries the ground at various places and is finally rewarded by a flow of water into the hole he has made. Overjoyed and awed, he expresses his feelings spontaneously and calls others to witness and enjoy the wonder. Henceforth that particular water place has a name, and the name becomes a deity. In their origins such so-called momentary deities are mere ejaculatory wishes, hopes or fears—claims of the moment rather than established values. But by being named they become objects which remain in the primitive consciousness long after the specific emotions that generated them are forgotten.

When this happens, the momentary god is on the way to becoming a functional god. Functional gods symbolize values which, while they may have originated as spontaneous feeling, enter into the ordered and continuing activities of men. Nearly every department of human activity gives rise to a patron deity. Thus there arise fishing gods for sea-peoples, fertility gods for agriculturists, rain gods for those living in dry areas, war gods for those living among enemies.

As civilizations advance, economic and social specialization and stratification tend to become more intense. Various subcultures, occupational groups and social groups form within the larger group, and each tends to idealize its particular interests and values through religious expression. As this happens, we find the society in question developing a whole pantheon of gods. The Society Islanders, for example, have gods of husbandry, carpentry, forest-work, acting, singing and hairdressing. As in the pantheons of early China, Japan, India, Greece and Rome, the various professional, economic, and social groups within the society tend to stress their preferred deity.

What one discerns in the mentality of man as he moves from momentary to functional or departmental deities is a process of consolidating and integrating what were formerly isolated and even contradictory values. This valuational maturing of man continues, with ups and downs, through the history of religion. Here and there arise deities which unite in themselves a wealth of attributes which originally belonged to departmental gods. This is often accompanied by the phenomenon of polynomy, in which the new god bears all the names of his departmental predecessors. His power is measured by the number of his names. Psychologically, they stand for the multitude of life-values he symbolizes. Thus there appears in Egyptian writings the thousand-named, the ten-thousand-named goddess Isis, while in the Koran Allah's power finds expression in his "hundred names." The Judo-Christian god appears to be an integration of Jahweh, the nomadic Israelites' god of war and fertility, and Baal, the collective name of the agricultural gods of the land-occupying Canaanites.

Analysis of the historical material reveals that man in his religious development has sensed some profound truths. Feeling rather than seeing them, he has expressed them in the symbolic mode. It may well be that the symbolic mode, tapping as it does emotional depths that logical discourse cannot penetrate, will always remain the ultimate mode of religious expression.

Nevertheless, we need at all times to make as concrete an analysis as possible. The rise of monotheism out of polytheism is an expression of several great ideas which need to be better understood. The first of these is that values rise out of experience—out of the acts of men and the suffering and enjoyments that result. The second is that values first enter consciousness as mere claims—claims that must be tested and validated in the light of further experience. The third is that the testing of value-claims results in their integration and consolidation into a coherent value-structure. The fourth is that the only ideal values worthy of our religious devotion—the only ones worthy of having dedicated to their realization the daily conduct of our whole lives—are those values which have stood the test both of experience and of power to be integrated with other values. Monotheism, representing as it does the integration of all partial values into a coherent structure, represents the full maturity of the religious consciousness. Furthermore the monotheistic god, by being conceived as *infinitely* good, leaves the way open for the infinite, i.e., continual, reconstruction of the value-structure in the light of on-going experience. The identification of the monotheistic god with moral or axiological absolutes is a complete reversal of his meaning in racial experience.

This, however, is not all. We return again to the history of religion to find more. It has just been pointed out that religious history shows a process of continual valuational integration. It needs now to be pointed out that, however paradoxical it may seem, this same history also shows an exactly opposed trend—a process of continual valuational differentiation. There is unity and diversity in the same movement. This is particularly seen in each of the great world religions. Even as the people, drawn from various socio-economic groups in the given culture, integrate their values and become united under one god comprehending all value (or one religious "way" in the case of Buddhism), these same people simultaneously re-differentiate themselves in new patterns. They re-divide into special economic and social groups; new beliefs and practices arise in answer to special and local needs.

There are three especially noteworthy socio-economic groups which at various points in the histories of each of the major religions have tended to modify the dominant religious practice in such a way as to express their own values—these are the military, the peasantry, and the bourgeoisie.

The most striking examples in the case of the warriors is perhaps the samurai of Japan, who modified the essentially unwarlike Buddhism to express the ideals that would help make a fierce fighter. As for the peasant, his values have found expression in all the founded religions even though only one of them, Zoroastrianism, was originally born of the soil. This is because the work of the peasant is basic in every economy. Thus we find that the European peasant, nominally a Christian, has in his actual religious practice remained essentially a pagan, with his special values and interests manifested in fertility rites and the worship of the divine manifestations of nature.

The striking phenomenon in the case of the bourgeoisie is that all over the world its members, when they first began to differentiate from the feudal societies in which they originated, formed trade guilds, the secular and religious aspects of which could not be separated. In early China, Japan, and India trade and craft guilds were formed which were prototypes of those of medieval Western civilization. Such guilds tended to find appropriate ways to express their new economic interests religiously, as through patron saints. In the case of the medieval European guilds, the whole ethos of trade and industry became divinely sanctioned. Indeed, in Europe so radical was this religious differentiation from the dominant pattern of Catholicism, that it contributed finally to the breaking away of Protestant groups which expressed better than did Catholicism the developing ethos of capitalism.

Examples of valuational differentiation with corresponding changes in the meaning of dominant religious symbols could be multiplied indefinitely. Thus the god of the American Negro, however nominally Christian and impartial, tends above all to express the Negro's deep yearning to be free of oppression and trouble; while the god of the upper socio-economic classes, including the clergy, of Southern cotton-mill towns defends the paternalistic economic pattern that prevails there, as Liston Pope's famous sociological study shows. Or again, in America's Middletown, middle-class values and manners became a cult subtly associating itself with the official Christian cultus and by contagion taking on the latter's sanctity.

The Roman Catholic devotee in his behavior furnishes another example—all the more striking because here differentiation takes place within a framework which has been so notable for its unity. The worship of the ordinary Catholic is so much directed toward special and local deities that Santayana has called Catholicism the "pagan Christianity." In some Catholic countries every worshipper has his patron, every village its saint, each symbolizing values of special concern to the particular worshipper or group of worshippers.

Thus it appears that in practice religion never escapes the existence of functional gods. We are everywhere confronted by the paradox of monotheism and what amounts to polytheism existing side by side within a single religious faith.

If we analyze this paradox psychologically and sociologically, we are able to understand the process by which man develops his basic life-values and gives his complete loyalty to them. We can, moreover, see the rationale of this process and thereby gain better control over it. The human act is the basis of all valuation. Value-claims, first experienced as consequences of acts, are tested, consolidated, and integrated as further acts reveal the cause-and-effect connections by which values are related to one another. But each new act, in addition to revealing connections which make consolidation possible, also creates a new value-claim. The existing value-structure is the product of innumerable previous human acts—it is the distillation of human experience. Yet every new act, while founded on the existing structure, produces a challenge to the structure itself—produces new claims which may be built into the old structure, not as mere accretions, but as part of a structural reorganization. What we have is an evolving valuational coherence characterized by simultaneous valuational integration and valuational differentiation. The integrating process produces the value-structure to which we give our loyalties and upon which we pin our faith, but the differentiating process is the seminal source of stimulation and fertilization for an infinitely reconstructible structure of value.

Here we encounter a further paradox in the valuational maturing of man. He must, to live a good life, commit himself whole-heartedly to ideal values which are products of experience. But experience is never complete as long as there are men still living; hence the value-structure should always be left open to reconstruction in the light of further experience. Man must be equally committed to a set of limited, partial or finite values and to the necessity of infinite reconstruction of those values. In short, man must commit himself both to the finite and the infinite.

It is the genius of the religious consciousness that it has recognized this paradox and has shown the way to resolve it. The best example is found in Christianity. The Christian God expresses in the symbolic mode the fact of the finite yet infinite nature of value. His dual nature is expressed in the great paradoxes that characterize Christianity. The Christ-God is in history yet transcends it; man is finite yet self-transcendent; the kingdom of God is on earth yet not on earth; man inevitably sins yet is responsible for his sins; God is one yet a trinity, transcendent yet immanent, divine yet human.

An approach to the understanding of these paradoxes can be made by comparing the relative status of God and man. Located as he is in space and time, man does not and cannot see the full implications of his acts. The repercussions of every act spread like a wave through contemporary society and through history in a way no man can foresee or follow. Even the most experienced, astute and enlightened man sees only the circle of events which, in proportion to infinity, is relatively close to him.

God, in contrast, stands outside space and time. Not only is all the universe spread out before him, but so too is all history, future as well as past. It is from the God's eye view alone, then, that the complete and ultimate meaning of the individual acts of man can be seen. Instantaneously God views the whole of history and the fate of the repercussions of a given act.

The Christian message is that man must forever seek to know God but that he can never, short of eternity, know him completely. To pretend to know him completely is to pretend, even while standing in time, to a God-eye view of the universe. This is, in short, to pretend to be God.

Only on this analysis can the meaning of the Christian definition of original sin be understood. To play God, to be deluded into thinking one *is* God, is the sin of sins—the original sin.This is the meaning of the story of Adam and Eve, who tried to partake of forbidden knowledge, and it is the meaning that Christian thinkers from Augustine to Reinhold Niebuhr have given this doctrine. The Christian emphasis upon original sin is a way of saying that while man *must* recognize his limitations, he seldom if ever does. History is a long chronicle of men and groups who believed they found the final word, the last answers, the absolute truth.

It is an irony that the rise of democracy and science, representing as they do the most determined attack upon absolutism ever made, has so often been seen as anti-religious. We find the spokesmen of religion, such as Reinhold Niebuhr, and the spokesmen of the democratic-scientific outlook, such as John Dewey, continually at one another's throats—yet both are trying to say essentially the same thing. In Dewey's language, we need infinitely to reconstruct experience in our quest for a better life, even while we act on our present commitments. In Niebuhr's language, we need to live according to our best present beliefs as to goodness and morality, but to act with the modesty and humility born of our recognition that from the standpoint of eternity those beliefs are partial and incomplete.

Christianity is perhaps the most dramatic and awesome statement ever made bringing attention to the fact that man can expect to find no final answers and must continue to reconstruct his values infinitely. In attempting final judgment upon his own works man presumes to be God in the judgment seat. He presumes from his tiny view of history to enunciate the final meaning of all history. This is sin in its definitive form; and the wages of sin are death, as our present civilization with its various forms of pride, self-righteousness and authoritarianism seems on the verge of demonstrating.

Christianity avoids both absolutism and subjective relativism in valuation by putting the particular into dialectical relationship with the universal in such a way that both are parts of an evolving core of meaning. On the one hand the absolutism of final judgment by men is avoided, yet on the other hand acts are held to be judgable. No act is sufficient to itself; there is no moral anarchy and nihilism. Differences between good and evil, right and wrong, beauty and ugliness, truth and falsity are still relevant; and tentative judgments can be made about them in the light of what small insight into the length and breadth of history man does have. Social justice is still to be sought; the refinement and enrichment of life are still ideals. God demands of man that he seek on earth the Kingdom of God; the only stricture is that man must never pretend to have found it. It would appear that from a Christian standpoint democracy is the only possible ideal society, for it is the only one that insists on its own reconstructibility.

There is profound insight expressed symbolically in the belief that God is the Creator. Man is here worshipping nothing less than the principle of creativity itself, rather than the limited and partial values which are produced by creativity. Here is a recognition, already glimmering at the dawn of history, that when men become enchanted with the worth of what they have already produced and elevate it into ultimate and eternal value, their creative powers weaken and atrophy. There is always the need to press on, to recognize that each new attainment, far from marking the end of human creativity, lifts man to a vantage point from which he can see new horizons to be explored.

What needs to be sanctified are the processes which create value, not merely the values that have thus far been experienced. These processes are embodied in what, generically, may be termed the creative social act.

The creative social act consists of all those interactions of men with one another from which emerge expanding areas of common interest around which activity becomes focused. Since the shared activities of men always go on in a physical, biological and ideational environment, the objects of the environment become involved in the social acts of men and acquire social meaning too. Hence the creative social act is a cooperative event in which living men participate with one another, with the ideas and objects which constitute the culture in which they live, and with nature.

Whenever two or more men come together as equals in the pursuit of any constructive activity or occupation we have a manifestation of the creative social act. Children at play, a man and a woman acting as partners in marriage, a group of men tilling the soil as equals, a family in which democratic, shared activities prevail, a group around a table threshing out an idea, are examples of the creative social act.

Yet the creative social act may be manifested even in the solitary activity of a single man. A man with a book, or a man alone with an idea, great or small, is interacting with something that has been presented to him by his culture. Here the social act is an interaction between a man now living and generations of men who once lived. The same is true of a man alone with nature. He brings to nature ideas, not all of his own invention, which help determine the meaning of whatever relations he has with nature. Even the "man with the hoe," or the woodsman with an axe, however lacking in ideas he may or may not be as he carries on his special transaction with nature, is engaged in an act which is not only productive or creative, but which, by no stretch of the word, is also social, for the implement he uses is a cultural implement, and that which he produces has social meaning.

One of the distinctive characteristics of the social act is that while its participants contribute purposefully to it, none can know or predict the outcome. From the situation of a man wrestling with the ideas in a book there are produced outcomes unforeseen either by the author of the book or by the reader. From a gathering of men come together in some common cause there emerge ways of accomplishing their end which no one had seen in the beginning. Furthermore as new means and instruments are discovered by the group, its very goals and purposes are reconstructed.

Indeed the way—the way of all ways—to destroy the creativity of a group is for any one or more members to try to predetermine the outcome. Equality is destroyed, cooperation gives way to competition, helpfulness becomes blind following, leadership becomes mere arrogance, bent on preserving its own vested interest rather than in releasing creativity. Here is original sin in definitive form operating to destroy creativity—the Creator—itself.

In creative social acts there develops a group spirit which is the invention of no one person and which is larger than any one person. In fact, it is greater than the combined participants if the latter are taken merely additively. The group spirit has qualities which can not be fully accounted for by the individual personal qualities of the participants added together. Somehow, in ways unknown even to them, they develop a morale and an *esprit de corps* which determine the outcome of the common effort even more than do the individual efforts combined.

The spirit of the group sweeps over the participants and lifts their individual spirits to levels not otherwise attainable. The good participant—the one who is neither rigid nor herd-minded—is the one who is able to surrender to this spirit and to let it transform him, even while he does not lose his distinctive individuality. The old self surrenders, but there emerges a new self capable of even more distinctive contributions to the common effort.

Hence the creative social act is seen, God-like, to be an objective existence in the universe. It transcends all particular social events, yet dwells within them. It transcends them because it is the timeless process which creates them. It transcends them because it produces outcomes not explicable in terms of the individual contributing factors. Yet it dwells within all particular and finite social events, for out of the latter generates the transcendent spirit itself.

To sum up, the following can be said of the valuational mood in religious experience:

First, out of the participation of men with one another and with nature—out of the creative social act—there emerge ideal values of existence to which the human participants dedicate the conduct of their lives.

Such acts establish value-claims tested by further acts, which both integrate and differentiate value. Values are integrated when action that is reflected upon reveals the cause-and-effect relations that exist between values as instrumental to one another. But the same acts which integrate values create new, unpredicted values. Differentiation is the seminal source upon which feeds the growing structure of integrated value.

The evolving structure of integrated value is an object of religious devotion. But it must never be taken at any given stage to be the final object of devotion. To pretend to have found, or to be misled into thinking one has found, the final ideal way of life is the height of irreligion.

The ultimate object of religious devotion is the creative social act itself. Broadly defined to include both the interactions of men with one another and the interactions of men with nature, the creative social act is the source of all good, in that it creates, tests, integrates and differentiates value. Thus the creative social act has the requisite attributes of infinite goodness, power and wisdom.

Infinite goodness is the mythological way of expressing the belief that the evolving core of value to which man gives his devotion must forever continue to assimilate new values created in experience.

Infinite power is the mythological way of expressing the belief that all the energies of the universe, physical, social, and psychic, may contribute to the realization of value, and that the power of these energies is unpredictable because the power of the creative social act transcends that of all individual contributions combined, and is unpredictable.

Infinite wisdom is the mythological way of expressing the belief that all value must forever be re-evaluated.

We have now completed a sketchy description of the valuational mood and are ready to make an even briefer outline of the second mood to be considered—the community mood. The comments that have already been made about the creative social act as the source of value provide a springboard for considering the community mood.

The community mood engulfs men when out of the social act there develops a community spirit in which the participants become united as brothers and in which the individual selves lose themselves only to be born again in communion and community.

The spirit of community is a power contributed to by the individual members, yet a power that generates energies which transcend the sum-total of individual contributions—a power that develops qualities that cannot be predicted from the quality of the individual contributions.

The quality and power of the community spirit overwhelms the individual participant and transforms him as a personality. The community is the very source of his being, in that it is the source, as modern social psychology shows, of that which most distinguishes him as a man—his mind.

Because of this the community is an object of religious devotion. But, just as no finite value-system can be taken as finished and the ultimate object of religious devotion, so may no finite community be thus taken. To take any given community as the final object of devotion is another version of original sin and leads to such phenomena as ethnocentrism and absolutistic forms of nationalism which exclude from the value-structure all but a limited set of values and from the community all but a select membership.

The ultimate object of devotion, just as in the analogous case in which values are concerned, is not any existing community, but the social act which creates community. It is this alone which is infinite and unlimited. Devotion to the social act means that one's community is constantly expanding. Beginning with one's mother, immediate family, local community, and local natural environment, one's community may expand to include all men and all the natural universe. But the community can never reach a limit of expansion, either practically or theoretically. Practically, no man can know and understand all others perfectly; and theoretically, the universe can never be regarded as finished. Devotion to the principle of the continual expansion of community comes closer to what is ultimate than does devotion to a given community.

An expanding selfhood is the complement of an expanding community. Walt Whitman expressed deep psychological and religious truth when he identified self and universe in "Song of Myself." The mechanisms by which the self is enriched, expanded, and matured at the same time that the scope of one's effective community is expanded are the cooperative social act, the sharing of experience and role-playing.

There is not space here to review the historical and sociological evidence which shows the essential place of the community mood in religion. Suffice it to cite a few provocative examples. First may be mentioned the practice of totemism, believed to have widely occurred among primitive peoples throughout the world. The verdict of modern scholarship is that the totemic animal worshipped by a given clan was symbolic of the spirit of the tribe. The killing and eating of the ordinarily taboo animal gave the clansman a sense of rebirth and a new strength, as if by so doing he had partaken of and refreshed himself in the strength of the clan itself. The totemistic aspects of the religion of the Semites has been studied by W. Robertson Smith, and there is reason to believe that the sacrificial rites of the Israelites evolved from totemism. In the sacrifice itself we see symbolized the individual person's contribution to the spirit of the community, while in the ritualistic meal we see the communicants refreshing and strengthening themselves in the community spirit. Even today, the rite variously known as the Eucharist, the Lord's Supper and Communion shows an unmistakable emphasis upon the celebration of the brotherhood and comradeship of men.

A second line of evidence has to do with the universal appearance of the golden rule or its equivalent in all the world religions, as in Jesus' doctrine of universal love among men, Confucius' "What you do not want done, do not do to others," and Zoroaster's "Whatever thou dost not approve for thyself, do not approve for anyone else."

A third line of evidence is the existence of the church-type of ecclesiastical organization, in which all men are considered members of a single divine community.

In the Christian view there are two senses—actual and ideal—in which love accounts for the simultaneous realization of individuality and community. The actual loving relations that exist among men promote the individuality of each and the community of all. But love is capable of being extended in a degree and in ways not now realized nor even conceived. We cannot even be sure that what we now recognize as love will be so recognized in the light of further experience. Hence we must infinitely keep moving in the direction of an improved and reconstructed practice and concept of love. This is love in the ideal sense, and is expressed metaphorically in the concept of God as the prototype of love.

In Christianity men must not only love one another, but they must love the ideal of love itself. The brotherhood of man depends upon the fatherhood of God. From a naturalistic standpoint this means that the ideal of love fathers the practice of love.

Having discussed the community mood, we may now proceed to the third of the moods to be considered—the executive mood. Here again the creative social act plays a central role. The ideal values which emerge from the social act mobilize for their realization the full energies and resources of the participants, who dedicate their conduct to that end. Participation in formulating ideals gives those ideals an imperative effect upon the communicant, who sets out to execute the called-for operations. The executive effects of dedication to a set of ideals may be delayed or only unconsciously produced, as when the dedicated group withdraws from the larger community to protect and nurture the values to which it is devoted, as in the case of monasticism or an individual creative worker like Thoreau or Einstein, or when the dedicated group, anxious to preserve the community, involves itself so deeply in the existing order that its motivating values are obscured, as in the case of the Medieval Church. Or, on the other hand, the executive effects may be immediate, as when the militant group intent upon the realization of its ideals does not hesitate to shatter the community in the violence of its attack, as in the case of Communism or the case of the compulsively nonconformist individual. But the executive behavior which is most truly religious is that which seeks to preserve the community and work within it while simultaneously refusing to acquiesce to that conduct of the community which does violence to whatever motivating values are at stake, as in the case of Christian socialism and social democracy.

Any reforming group which makes the latter choice thereby keeps itself in such relation with the larger community that the group continues to share with the community in the social act, with the result that the values of *both* the group and the community change. Complete acquiescence to the prevailing order, on the one hand, and violent militancy that destroys the community, on the other, are alike in that both sin against the social act. Hence neither choice is religious. Both, by destroying creativity, lead to the original sin of absolutism, as numerous historical examples on both sides illustrate.

The fourth mood is the esthetic mood. Though in some respects this mood involves the profoundest meaning of religion, there is time for only the briefest comment. The social act involves all the energies of the individual, non-rational as well as rational, in dramatic conflict between supporting and opposing forces that ends in esthetic consummation. The more comprehensive the range of value satisfied in the consummation, the greater is the religious quality of the experience. The individual identifies himself with an increasingly wide natural and social community, as in the democratic mysticism of Walt Whitman, the intellectual mysticism of Spinoza, and the esthetic mysticism of much Oriental religion.

The fifth mood is the contemplative mood. In this mood the group or community celebrates and commemorates the values with which the group identifies itself, for the purpose of renewing the group's strength and of mobilizing its energies for action. This is a mood which, in the orthodox religions, is associated with prayer, worship and ritual.

Yet it is a mood which appears in the common life of all men whether they recognize it as a religious mood or not. Every well-knit family, every clique of intimate friends, most age, sex, occupation and class groups have innumerable rituals and signs, many of them informal and not consciously recognized to exist, by which the members remind themselves of their belonging to one another and of the values by which the group lives. A father's home-coming whistle, a bobby-soxer's characteristic costume, the type of home furnishings characteristic of members of the middle class, have conscious and unconscious meanings for the persons involved which go far beyond the nominal functions they serve of announcing an arrival, protecting the body, or of making a house livable. They are symbols which evoke in the participants a wide range of feelings and emotions. They somehow sum up and express all the meaning accrued in countless past experiences of living with one's own group—meanings that are non-rational and cannot be expressed in logical discourse.

The rituals and presentational symbols by which a group expresses its consciousness of itself constitute, collectively, the group's cultus. It is possible more or less consciously to plan and choose a cultus which expresses meanings deemed most worthy by the group. This is why it is possible for the ritualism and symbolism of the common life to become refined into the cultus of an established religion. But while rituals and symbols may themselves be consciously chosen, the meanings they express can never be made fully explicit. Though these meanings evolve from common activities and occupations, and hence should be as testable in experience as any other meanings, they cut too deeply into the whole of life, with the latter's inseparable combining of reason and emotion, consciousness and unconsciousness, rationality and irrationality, to be expressible without the aid of the rich resources of music, art, rites, and presentational symbols.

The power of the cultus, whether the latter be consciously planned or a spontaneous growth, to arouse and mobilize for action the full energies of an individual and of a group is enormous. It can tap the deepest well-springs of action and evoke conduct of undreamed vitality and power. Authoritarian states and churches have recognized this and have turned the power of the cultus to their own ends. The result has been a corruption of the cultus which often has impelled free people to turn from the latter in disgust.

But democratic groups and societies must learn that there is nothing inherently evil in the cultus—that it is a power that can and should serve the ends of democratic group living. When the planning and use of the cultus is left in authoritarian hands, it is inevitably put to authoritarian use. But there is no reason why each group, from the smallest and most intimate, such as the family, to the greatest, such as the international community, cannot evolve its own cultus democratically through the contributions of all members on a basis of equality. The cultus should evolve from the common life of the group, and it should constantly change and grow as the experiences of the group call for reconstruction of the evolving structure of integrated value to which the group commits itself. In democratic groups the cultus should operate even more powerfully to mobilize energy for action than in authoritarian groups, for when group members evolve their own symbols and rituals, the meaning of the latter is real and held close to the heart. Furthermore, a democratically achieved cultus, necessarily being a growing thing, cannot degenerate into the meaningless motions which characterize cultic practices grown fixed and stereotyped through the influence of vested interests.

The discussion of how the foregoing five moods originate and develop in experience shows how they may be cultivated in the experience of children. We return now to the educational problem.

It appears from what has been said that the central fact of every religious mood and every religious phenomenon is the creative social act. It is in the social act, broadly conceived to include nature as well as man as a participant, that value is created and integrated, community is expanded, the self finds itself and is enriched, the dramatic splendor of life is increased, the most comprehensive consummations are achieved.

Since the social act is the central fact of religious experience, out of which all aspects of religious life develop, it would seem that this same act should also be the central fact of any system of education which interests itself in the development of religious quality in the conduct and experience of children.

Accordingly, the following principles of education for the religious quality are enumerated:

First, the creative social act should be the characteristic feature of the school curriculum. It should be the basis of every school activity to which it is applicable and should characterize the relations of pupils to one another, of pupils to teachers, of teachers to administrators, and of school to community. The children should participate with one another and with their teachers in choosing, planning and organizing their learning activities. Each learning activity should begin with a problem, enterprise, or undertaking agreed upon by the group (of which the teacher should be considered an integral part) according to criteria cooperatively chosen. The members of the group should together formulate a plan for attacking the problem. Then, pooling their resources and organizing themselves in ways to promote the fullest contribution of every individual, they should cooperatively attack the problem, sharing their difficulties, experiences, findings and successes at every possible point. The measure of the enterprise's success should be the degree to which it ends with a feeling on the part of all, the teacher included, of genuine and significant group accomplishment.

Second, through participation in the social act children should experience, test, integrate, and differentiate value, so that there would develop a growing structure of ideal value to which they could dedicate the conduct of their lives. This process begins with the expression of mere likes and dislikes by the children. But in the cooperative social situation these merely ejaculatory feelings come under the critical scrutiny of the participants, who test their worth and validity in the light of the way they work out when acted upon. Through such experiences of acting upon and then critically evaluating their desires, the children can transform their own desires so that the relations of desires to one another and to the common welfare are taken into account. The difference between ideal values having worth and validity, and mere childish whims, is precisely the difference between desires that have not yet been tested and those that have been acted upon, reflected upon and integrated with one another.

Acting upon their own desires and evaluating the outcome is the primary experience out of which children grow to valuational maturity. Yet it would be irreligious if this process were to ignore the funded experience and judgment of the human race as to what is good and right. The findings of the race as to what is good should be made available to the children and seriously studied by them, so that they can integrate such findings with their own. Yet the conclusions of the race can never be presented to children as being more than value-claims, to be tested by the children in their own experience. The first task of the school, in respect to values, is to develop the child's power to make his own value judgments. If this task is taken seriously, there can be no ethical and axiological absolutes handed down to the child, but rather only claims presented to him for evaluation.

Third, children should be helped to develop an expanding sense of community and selfhood through participation in the social act. Each child should be helped to become a valued member of the group, and to find the fulfillment of his selfhood within the group. As the group's own solidarity increases, it can be helped to identify with various elements of the community of which it is a part. In studying the life of its community, the group can have many opportunities for firsthand contact with and participation in that life. Through dramatization, role-playing and other forms of vicarious experience this participation with the rest of the community can reach out to the whole world and back through all history.

Fourth, involvement in the social act should enable the child to locate properly the ultimate source of value, community and selfhood. His supreme loyalty should be to the social processes which create these. To foster this, it is necessary that the school enable him to work and live according to these processes. The work of the children should be cooperative rather than individualistic and competitive, based upon processes of inquiry rather than upon passive acceptance of authority. From participation in such processes the child should be helped to see that the promotion of the democratic process itself is more important than any particular outcome it may bring, that the preservation of the integrity of human relations is more important than any partial or limited goal upon which the participants may have their minds set, that the processes of objective inquiry are more sacred than any belief, however cherished, those processes may challenge.

Fifth, involvement in the struggle between the forces supporting and those opposing the social act should lead to esthetic consummations which increase the child's faith in the transformability of existence for the better. The activities of the school should be so ordered that a synthesis of challenge and security is achieved by the child. The inquiries, problems, and projects chosen by the group should be of a kind to challenge powers and stretch capacities, yet they should, usually, end in success and emotional consummation. By experiencing difficult challenges ending in success, the child avoids that despair and cynicism which is close to the essence of irreligion, yet acquires the moral fiber and strength of character which enable him to meet life situations with courage and faith.

Sixth, the commemoration and celebration of the ideal values revealed through the social act should be used to mobilize the child's non-rational and rational energies in the pursuit of such values. The children themselves should participate in creating the symbols and rites by which they wish to dedicate themselves to the ideal values they have formulated. Such creative participation would replace the meaningless gestures which now characterize many of the stereotyped ceremonies, such as the flag salute, now carried on in the schools.

The foregoing principles do not embody a new religion to be taught in the schools. Instead they state the conditions by which children, their teachers, and others in the community are enabled to release the religious quality that is potential in their common experience.

The participants in such an enterprise would be embarked upon a new discovery. When individuals become involved in creative social activities there is no knowing what will emerge. Undoubtedly many traditions will be cast aside. Yet the process is essentially constructive, not destructive. The participants draw upon what is already established and stable in the community in order to give their activities and inquiries a foundation, a perspective, the benefit of insight gained through millenia of race experience. The children in our schools are the inheritors of a varied and rich culture which exists by grace of the activities of others. The children's participation in the creative social act enables them to receive the heritage of ideal value which is rightfully theirs. But such participation also enables them to purify and expand that heritage in such a way that it can serve them better than it has ever served men before.

Chapter 9

A BASIS FOR THE TEACHING OF VALUES

The *commitment of educators to support the development of each person to the limit of his ability in a manner consistent with the democratic ethos presupposes that educators: (1) accept moral-ethical and spiritual standards based on verified knowledge; and (2) conduct themselves, singly and collectively, in the light of these standards. Our legal sanctions place the educator in a strategic position because approximately one-fourth of the nation is in school. The educator's responsibility, then, is also an opportunity that invites imagination and dedication. While there are stern guides to be followed, they invite the fullest possible use of the method of intelligence.*

William K. Frankena, a philosopher, offers the thesis that "moral education includes teaching and espousing, not only a particular morality, but the very act or idea of morality itself." He sees the task of helping the immature learn the values of their culture as involving: (a) the transmittal of what constitutes a proper knowledge of morality; and (b) the assurance that all learners will utilize this moral knowledge consistently. For convenience, he refers to these tasks as respectively Moral Education X (MEX) and Moral Education Y (MEY).

According to Frankena, education must teach students certain principles that will guide their conduct in all situations. Education should impart the knowledge required to apply the principles or the techniques that will enable the learner to acquire such knowledge. Basic to the teaching of MEX and MEY is the instructor's obligation to stress both the rationalization, or the "why," and the conclusions, or the "what." This stress upon making MEX and MEY rational should begin when the learner is able to understand the values available to him and to discover how to use them. Facts that will withstand investigation and testing by the learner must support the rationalization process. The teacher cannot use propaganda lest the student lose faith in the meaning of MEX and MEY. The morality taught must express a broad orientation and not a limited rule. It must help the student, as he becomes adult, to resolve moral problems and revise or create principles as circumstances require. In this process, the way the student learns should be consistent with the moral goals he hopes to achieve. He must, at all times, be aware of others and of the effects of his actions upon their welfare.

TOWARD A PHILOSOPHY OF MORAL EDUCATION

William K. Frankena

MEX cannot consist of a long list of specific instructions to our children for all of the situations into which they may fall. It must consist, rather, in teaching them certain principles or ends by which they may guide their conduct in those situations. For teaching these rules or ends either the direct or the indirect methods may be used. That is, we may formulate the rules or ends quite explicitly and seek to inculcate them into our children, as the Israelites were commanded to do by Moses:

> And these words which I command thee this day . . . thou shall teach . . . diligently unto thy children, and shalt talk of them when thou sittest in thine house, and when thou walkest by the way, and when thou liest down, and when thou risest up.

Or we may tell our children or otherwise instruct them, perhaps by example, what to do in this particular case and in that particular case until they begin to discern the rule or the end involved for themselves. Either way, the point is to teach them ends or principles, "that they may do them in the land which I the Lord shall give them," for, like Moses, we shall not be there to lead them.

Yet the point of moral instruction *is* to put the child in the position of being able to decide what he should do in each situation he may come up against; and, for this, it is necessary but not sufficient to teach him the ends

Reprinted from *Harvard Educational Review*, Vol. XXVIII, No. 4 (Fall 1958), pp. 303–312.

or principles involved. We must also supply him with the knowledge required to apply the principle or to realize the end in question, or with the ability to acquire this knowledge for himself. Roughly speaking, as Aristotle and many others have pointed out, the process of determining what one should do takes the form of a "practical syllogism." There is (a) the rule or end, for example, that of keeping one's promises or of not harming anyone. There is (b) the factual knowledge that one has tacitly or openly made a certain promise, or that certain actions will cause harm to certain people. And there is (c) the conclusion that one should or should not do a certain deed. Thus, if our children are to be able to come to right conclusions about what to do, they must have or be able to get the kind of factual knowledge involved in (b). This means that their moral education must include a training in history and science; we must teach them whatever we know that may be relevant to the solution of their moral problems, and train them to go on to find out whatever more they need to know. In this sense at least all intellectual education is moral, as Professor Broudy has remarked in his book,[1] and a moral education includes an intellectual one.

In other words, the task of moral education is not simply to inculcate virtuous principles and good intentions. It is not the road to heaven, but the road to hell, that is said to be paved with good intentions, and the substance of this saying is that we can only be sure of being on the right road when we are guided by factual knowledge as well as by moral principle. As Aquinas puts it, ". . . in order that a choice be good, two things are required. First, that the intention be directed to a due end. . . . Second, that man choose rightly those things which are means to the end. . . ."[2] Russell makes the same point when he says that the good life is one inspired by love and guided by knowledge.[3]

I do not mean to suggest, of course, that the sole ground for an intellectual or scientific education is a moral one; after all, as Matthew Arnold said, morality is only three-fourths of life. But there is a moral justification and need, along the lines just indicated, for a very considerable factual and intellectual training.

So far, however, we have been supposing that the problem in MEX is simply to pass on a set of moral principles which is adequate for all occasions, provided only that we also pass on the knowledge and the intelligence needed to apply them. Actually the problem is much more complex than this.

(1) Whether we use the direct or the indirect method of moral instruction, we can do so in either of two ways. We can simply "internalize" in

[1] H. Broudy, *Building a Philosophy of Education* (New York: Prentice-Hall, 1954), p. 409.

[2] *Summa Theologica,* Pt. I of Pt. II, ch. XII, q. 58. art. 4.

[3] B. Russell, *What I Believe* (New York: Dutton, 1925), ch. II.

our children certain beliefs about how to act, without any indication of any reasons which may lie behind them. That is, we might conceive of moral education in a "Theirs not to reason why" spirit and we might even use such techniques as drill, propaganda, and hidden persuasion. On the other hand, we might take the position that we must teach the reasons as well as the conclusions. Now, there is, no doubt, a period in the life of a child when such appeals to reason are pointless. Says Felix Adler, "The right to reason about these matters cannot be conceded until after the mind has attained a certain maturity. . . . The moral teacher . . . is not to explain [to the child] why we should do the right. . . ."[4] Plato agreed, and thought it the function of a proper education in poetry and music to use this period in schooling the youth to approve what is to be approved and condemn what is to be condemned, "while he is still too young to understand the reason," that "when reason comes, he will greet her as a friend with whom his education has made him long familiar."[5] The question is not whether the introduction of reasons is to begin at birth, but whether it is to begin as soon as it is feasible or is to be put off as long as it can be, perhaps forever.

It should be noted here that to give the child reasons along with his moral instructions does not necessarily entail going on to stimulate in him a full-fledged critical reflection about morality of the sort that G. H. Palmer has in mind when he argues against "ethical instruction" in the schools.[6] This is shown, it seems to me, by the interesting (if sometimes misguided) examples of moral reasoning used on Johnny by his teachers in the NEA booklet on *Moral and Spiritual Values in the Public Schools* (1951), and perhaps even better by the fact that the Navaho almost automatically give reasons along with their prescriptions about what to do, but without any invitation to criticism.[7]

Now, most recent educational philosophy has insisted on the importance in moral as well as in other education of developing and appealing to the child's reason whenever possible. With this I agree, at least to the extent of believing that a reference to reasons in morality must be made in the schools, even if criticism and moral philosophy are to be put off until college, as Aristotle thought. For, as recent ethical writers have been pointing out, it is the very genius of morality to appeal to reason. To make a moral judgment is to claim that it is justified, that a case can be made for it. As Philip

[4] F. Adler, *The Moral Instruction of Children* (New York: D. Appleton, 1901), pp. 13–15.

[5] *Republic,* 402a.

[6] G. H. Palmer, *Ethical and Moral Instruction in the Schools* (Boston: Houghton Mifflin, 1908), Ch. I.

[7] On the Navaho see J. Ladd, *The Structure of a Moral Code* (Cambridge: Harvard University Press, 1957), Ch. XI. They do not, however, offer reasons to children in their early years. Cf. p. 271. The examples in the NEA booklet seem to me misguided because they confuse reasons which are merely motivating (which belong to MEY) and reasons which are morally justifying (which belong to MEX).

Rice writes in *On the Knowledge of Good and Evil*, "Even though the sentence containing the word 'ought' does not itself state the . . . reasons, it suggests that there are reasons, . . . and that the conclusion is dictated by them. . . ."[8] Thus, if the parent, speaking as a moral being, says, "You ought to do so and so," it is appropriate for the child to ask, "Why?", and the parent must be prepared, as soon as the child can understand, with some kind of answer, and not just with any kind of answer but with one which will indicate to him what reasons are supposed to count in morality. R. S. Peters even goes so far as to say, in criticizing Freud, "But customary and obsessive behavior is not morality, for by 'morality' we mean *at least* the intelligent following of rules the point of which is understood."[9]

This point may be pushed a bit farther. It is characteristic of a moral judgment, not only to imply reasons, but to claim a basis in considerations of fact which are objectively valid.[10] Hence the reasons adduced by a teacher must not be recognizable to the pupil as mere propaganda calculated to win his assent; they must be such as will bear whatever investigation the pupil may make, else his adherence to the moral enterprise and his virtue will alike be jeopardized.

Thus, even if MEX cannot be said to call for the handing down of a full-scale philosophical or theological theory of the ultimate grounds of moral obligation, it must involve communicating as early as possible at least some sense of the rationale of our judgments of right and wrong. Else our youth can hardly be expected to recognize reason as a friend, even when she comes, for his education will not have made him familiar with her. "The old-fashioned school," says W. T. Harris, "regarded obedience to authority the one essential; the new ideal regards insight into the reasonableness of moral commands the chief end."[11] On this point, with or without the grace of Dewey, the new school and the new moral philosopher see eye to eye.

This means that we parent-teachers must ourselves have some sense of the rationale of moral commands, and for this we may well go to the moral philosophers, even if our children are to be held back from doing so. We must be prepared, however, to find that they disagree profoundly among themselves about what this rationale is, and, while we can learn much from them, we shall have to a considerable extent to rely on what Rice calls our own "global sense of directedness" which was made a part of our "second nature" by our own teachers and "by long buffeting from the world,"[12] and

[8] P. B. Rice, *On the Knowledge of Good and Evil* (New York: Random House, 1955), p. 111; Cf. K. Baier, *The Moral Point of View* (Cornell University Press, 1958), pp. 222, 280; P. H. Nowell-Smith, *Ethics* (Melbourne: Penguin, 1954), p. 161.

[9] R. S. Peters, *The Concept of Motivation* (London: Routledge, 1958), p. 87.

[10] See M. Mandelbaum, *The Phenomenology of Moral Experience* (Glencoe: Free Press, 1955), pp. 243–57.

[11] Editor's Preface to Adler, *op. cit.*, p. vi.

[12] Cf. Rice, *op. cit.*, pp. 186, 190f., 194f.

without which we shall not be able to benefit from the study of moral philosophy anyway.

(2) The need of building this global sense of moral direction into the second nature of the next generation is reinforced by another consideration, namely, the occurrence of conflicts of duties. Unless the morality which we propose to teach our children is unusually circumspect, it will contain principles which may come into conflict in their experience. In fact, most practical moral problems consist, not simply in applying a given principle, but in resolving conflicts between principles, as in the tragic case of Antigone or in Sartre's example of the young man who "was faced with the choice of leaving for England and joining the Free French Forces . . . or remaining with his mother and helping her to carry on."[13] In such situations, one has one's learned stock of principles. One has also, let us suppose, a well-trained intellect and an excellent supply of relevant information. But, using this information and this intelligence, one still finds a conflict between principles P and Q. If one has also been taught another principle, R, which gives P precedence over Q, all is well, but this is not always the case. Then one must make what Hare calls a "decision of principle"—one must somehow formulate a rule for dealing with the situation in question. This means that we must not only teach our principles and the knowledge required to apply them, but must also prepare the younger generation for a certain creativeness or originality in solving moral problems. We must somehow give them the ability to decide what to do when the answer does not follow from principles learned together with relevant factual information.

(3) This same ability is called for in dealing with another exigency with which new generations are often faced—that of revising or abandoning learned principles in the light of new situations and new knowledge or insight. Perhaps the Socratic-Christian doctrine that it is never right to harm even one's enemies can be regarded as such a revision of a previous rule, or the more recent view that punishment is not retributive but prospective or therapeutic in function. Other reformulations of long-accepted principles may be forced on us by recent work in depth or in social psychology, or even by developments in biophysics. And, unless we mean to leave this sort of moral reform entirely to fortune and sporadic genius, we must try to prepare our successors to sense when such a revision of principle is called for and along what lines.

From these considerations it follows that with all our giving of principles we must give understanding and initiative. We must, in teaching principles, try to communicate a sense of their rationale, and along with this a sense of the direction in which to look in cases of conflict or in the event of radically new knowledge or situation; and, at the same time, as Hare emphasizes, we must provide "ample opportunity of making the decisions—by

[13] J. P. Sartre, *Existentialism* (New York: Philosophical Library, 1947), p. 29.

which [principles] are modified, improved, adapted to changed circumstances, or even abandoned if they become entirely unsuited to a new environment."[14] To do this will not be easy for us, for our own generation seems not to have been adequately prepared by its parent-teachers for coping with the changes which have occurred and are occurring. Our own moral education has been wanting either on the side of moral direction or on the side of opportunity for moral decision or both—as well as in the matter of relevant intellectual discipline and factual knowledge. Else neither the existentialism nor the medievalism which we have with us could have arisen.

(4) There is a fourth complication in the program I am calling MEX, one which is implicit in the three just discussed, namely, that of rearing autonomous moral agents. This notion of autonomy is a difficult one. It seems clear that morality is a guide to life of a peculiar sort in that it allows the individual to be, indeed insists on his being, self-governed in the sense, not only of determining what he is going to do, but of determining what it is that he should do. This feature of morality has been stressed by Kant, Durkheim, and many recent writers. In some of the recent writers, however, this autonomy of the individual is misconstrued; it is taken to mean that the individual can create his own standards, and that there is no sort of authority which he must respect. This is the well-known view of Sartre, but something like it seems to be implied by Nowell-Smith when he concludes his book by saying,

> The most a moral philosopher can do is to paint a picture of various types of life . . . and ask which type of life you really want to lead. . . . The questions 'what shall I do?' and 'what moral principles should I adopt?' must be answered by each man for himself; that at least is part of the connotation of the word 'moral.'[15]

But to say that a developed moral agent must make up his own mind what is right, and not simply accept the dictates of an external authority, is not to say that he can make a course of action right by deciding on it, or that whatever life he chooses or prefers to live can be claimed by him to be *ipso facto* morally right or good; any more than to say that a developed rational man must make up his own mind what is true, and not merely accept the declaration of another, is to say that he can make a statement true by believing it, or that whatever system he chooses or prefers to believe can be claimed by him to be *ipso facto* intellectually justified. Being autonomous does not mean being responsible to no transpersonal standard in morality any more than in science. In both cases one is involved in an interpersonal enterprise of human guidance (in morality of action, in science of belief) in which one is self-governing but in which one makes judgments ("This is right," "That is true") which one is claiming to be warranted by a review

[14] *Op. cit.*, p. 76.

[15] Nowell-Smith, *op. cit.*, p. 319f; cf. Hare, *op. cit.*, p. 77f.

of the facts from the impersonal standpoint represented by that enterprise and shared by all who take part in it—a claim which is not merely an assertion of what one chooses or prefers, and may turn out to be mistaken.

In morality, then, as in science, we must impart to those who come after us a certain difficult but qualified independence or self-reliance of judgment. This and the other three complications in the problem of MEX, however, add up to much the same thing—that there is a Moral Direction or Way which transcends the individual, and within which he stands or claims to stand on his own feet when he makes moral judgments which are not second-hand. I do not conceive of this quite after the manner of C. S. Lewis in *The Abolition of Man*, but with certain judicious modifications much of what he writes about the Tao, as he calls it, seems to me correct, as when he argues that even the moral innovator must speak from within the Tao if what he says is to have any moral force. This Way is for each generation more or less embodied in a set of rules, principles, ideals, or virtues, and this set is what it must proceed to teach to the next generation; but moral education does not consist simply in passing it on intact. Its important task is, rather, in and through the teaching of these ideals or rules, to instill a sense of the Way or Point of View which is involved in morality, and to prepare its pupils to stay self-reliantly within this Way even when the map we have been using turns out to be unclear or inaccurate.

About the nature of this Way recent moral philosophy seems to me in certain respects misleading,[16] but it nevertheless has much to say that is helpful. For example, apart from the existentialists, most writers are agreed that the moral approach to questions about action involves being objective, impartial, fact-facing, willing to see one's maxims acted on by everyone even when this is to one's own advantage, etc., and in this they seem to be correct. Then teaching the Moral Way, insofar as this falls in the province of MEX, must include imparting an intellectual capacity for this kind of open-mindedness with respect to facts and persons. For the rest, it seems to me that Kant came as near to characterizing the Moral Way as anyone has when he stated "the practical imperative" as follows: "So act as to treat humanity, whether in thine own person or in that of any other, in every case as an end withal, never as means only."[17]

In short, if the method of MEX is the teaching of a particular morality, its goal must be to get across a grasp of the art of morality itself which it is the endeavor of moral philosophy to elucidate. Like Zeus in the myth ascribed to Protagoras by Plato (surely one of the neglected classics on our subject),

[16] See my article, "Obligation and Motivation in Recent Moral Philosophy," in *Essays in Moral Philosophy*, ed. by A. I. Melden (Seattle: University of Washington Press, 1958).

[17] I. Kant, *Fundamental Principles of the Metaphysic of Morals* (London: Longmans, Green, 1907), Section II.

each generation must send its Hermes (education) to bring the institution of morality to the next, "to the end that there may be regulation of cities and friendly ties to draw them together."[18] With this, our discussion of MEX has completed its course, and we may take a look at MEY. We must be relatively brief about this, and that is regrettable, for MEY, like the month when this was written or any beautiful woman of the same name, is always an interesting subject.

The object of this part of moral education is to keep the youth from replying, "I can but I won't," when Duty whispers low, "Thou must." In W. T. Harris' words, where the job of MEX is "the formation of right ideas," that of MEY is "the formation of right habits,"[19] that is, the developing of dispositions which will lead one both to ask what the right is and to act accordingly. First among such dispositions are the moral virtues. These, as Aristotle held, are habits of using the "intellectual virtue" or ability developed in MEX to determine what is right, and of choosing it deliberately because it is right. They are of two kinds. There are somewhat restricted first-order ones such as honesty and veracity; and there are more general second-order ones such as conscientiousness, integrity, and moral alertness. Both kinds are acquired by practice; as Aristotle said, "we become just by doing just acts, temperate by doing temperate acts, brave by doing brave acts."[20] Character education, properly so-called, which must be part of what Professor Ducasse calls education of the will, consists of thus building into the young such dispositions as these.

Another kind of disposition must be mentioned, however. Besides these dispositions to act *from* duty, as Kant puts it, or *because* duty requires, there are others which dispose us to do *such actions as* duty requires, or even to do good deeds which are beyond the strict call of duty, but to do them simply because we want to, for instance, benevolence or gratitude. Aristotle would give honor as the chief of these morality-supporting motives. Kant would object to including attention to any such motives as a part of moral education, because he thought a moral man should always act solely from a sense of duty, but to me, as to Friedrich Schiller and so many others, this seems a hard doctrine, and moreover one which somewhat gratuitously increases the chances that our youth will say "I won't." I should hold, therefore, as Russell does, that the cultivation of such dispositions and the weakening of contrary ones (e.g., fear and hatred), so far as this is possible, is a proper part of moral education. It is what Professor Ducasse calls education of the heart, and perhaps he would not agree that it belongs under *moral* education, since he seems to limit this to education in justice, but I am taking it to include education in goodness too.

In addition to cultivating these "internal sanctions" of morality, as Mill

[18] Protagoras, 322c. [19] *Op. cit.*, p. v.
[20] *Nicomachean Ethics*, II, i, 4.

called them, MEY can also make use of such "external sanctions" as punishment or reward (legal, parental, or scholastic) and praise or blame. These are all means of keeping young people on the straight and narrow path, not by changing their motivations, but by using those they already have. To quote Nowell-Smith again, "Pleasure and pain, reward and punishment are the rudders by which human conduct is steered, the means by which moral character is moulded. . . . Moral approval and disapproval play the same role."[21]

This passage makes the point, though it overstates it. The use of the political sanction or power of the state, however, hardly seems a proper part of moral education, for it is of the nature of morality to seek to regulate human behavior without using such power. It may be necessary for the state to back up certain of the demands of morality, but its doing so is not part of the spirit of morality and is necessary only because moral education is not wholly successful. Nowell-Smith, Hare, and others seem to regard punishment of *some* sort as a normal instrument of moral education, but Locke was very chary of its use, as Russell is. It rarely does good and often does harm, he thought; the means to use are praise and blame. "Esteem and disgrace are, of all others, the most powerful incentives to the mind, when once it is brought to relish them."[22] Russell remarks that this relish comes very early, and that "from this moment the educator has a new weapon" which is "extraordinarily powerful," but he adds that "it must be used with great caution."[23] Like most recent educational theorists he prefers to emphasize what Hare, somewhat disparagingly perhaps, calls "other more up-to-date methods."[24]

I shall, however, stick to general theory and not try to evaluate the use of specific kinds of external sanctions. They are all ways of *making* it to an individual's interest to do what is or is regarded as right by some sort of *ad hoc* action, and, while it is clear that morality would like to make its way without them, it is not easy to see how moral education and guidance can get on without anything of the sort. How else, for instance, can it secure the kind of practice which Aristotle says is necessary to produce the habits of justice and temperance, especially when reason cannot yet be used and emulation and generosity do not suffice? We may give up punishment and reward, and limit ourselves to the use of such expressions as "You did right," "But that would be wrong," or "Good boys don't do things like that," but even then we are not simply instructing, we are also appealing to the relishes of esteem and disgrace. This is a sanction which seems almost to be inherent in the use of moral language, and, indeed, Bentham calls it

[21] *Op. cit.*, p. 304. [22] *Op. cit.*, para. 56.

[23] B. Russell, *Education and the Good Life* (New York: Boni and Liveright, 1926), p. 97.

[24] *Op. cit.*, p. 75.

"the moral sanction." That is part of the reason why some contemporary philosophers have been able to make so much of the "emotive meaning" of ethical terms.[25]

Another technique which moralists have often used is not to *make* virtue profitable in this way but rather to *show* that it is profitable or make people *believe* that it is—to prove to the individual, or otherwise lead him to believe, that the world is so constituted as to visit his iniquity, not only on his children and his children's children unto the fourth generation of them that hate morality, but on him. Here enter many gambits which I cannot recite but which are familiar to readers of Plato, Butler, and Hume, as well as of more ordinary moral literature, among them the religious appeal to punishments and rewards in a hereafter. Which of these are sound arguments and which involve what Bergson called myth-making I shall not try to determine. Like Professor Ducasse, I am not convinced that a religious sanction in the form indicated is necessary to morality, and in any case it cannot be appealed to in our public schools. Moreover, I believe that any attempt to prove that being virtuous is always profitable to every individual is and must remain inconclusive, though it may go a long way. But, for so far as it goes, I see no reason why such an attempt should not be included as a part of MEY, at least when it relies on honest argument and not on propaganda—provided that it is not construed as an attempt to give a justification for what is claimed to be right but only as a way of securing the motivation for doing it. Even then, however, it must be made carefully, for the cause of morality will be endangered if the individual is led to think that virtue's promise of profit is its only inducement. That virtue is its own reward is a hoary adage, but it has a present meaning.

Whatever the methods used in MEY, its main concern must not be merely that the individual shall be disposed to act in accordance with certain principles or ideals of right and wrong which have been taught to him in MEX. As the final goal in MEX must be to get across an understanding of the Moral Way and its direction, so the final goal in MEY must be to dispose the individual to follow his Way in spite of contrary temptations, conflicts of duty, or novel situations. Plato thought that we invariably pursue the Idea of the Good, and that our only problem (and hope) in moral education is to understand this Idea or gain true opinion from someone who does. But perhaps there is no such Idea of the *Good* which we can come out of the Cave one day to know in all its glory, and perhaps our problem is rather to understand the Idea of *Morality* as a kind human guidance and to bring about a devotion to it (for such understanding and devotion hardly seem to be natural). It is here that MEX and MEY meet and marry, for of course they are of opposite sexes and bound to fall in love at first sight.

[25] E.g. C. L. Stevenson, *Ethics and Language* (New Haven: Yale University Press, 1944).

This means that, as MEX must not be occupied simply with teaching a specific set of principles like truth-telling and promise-keeping, but especially with developing a "global sense of moral directedness," and an *ability* to think objectively and impartially, so MEY must not be wholly concerned with developing first-order dispositions like honesty, but more generally with cultivating such second-order dispositions as integrity, self-control, and a *readiness* to be governed by impartial and objective thinking and fact-finding.

In saying all this I have been talking as if MEX and MEY are two independent programs of education which meet only at the end. And, indeed, they are distinct and must not be confused. But, of course, they are just two aspects or parts of a single process of moral education, which is going on all the time (just as moral education as a whole is an aspect or part of a yet larger single process of total education), and which has a single ideal of which theirs are components. Really MEX and MEY do not get together only at the end; they are in love and married all the time. Any actual program of moral education must consecrate this marriage at every step, though it must also remember which is husband and which wife.

I have also been talking as if moral education is a log with the older generation at one end and the younger at the other. But, of course, much of it is really a process of self-discipline and self-education.

One thing seems essential if this double program (or "fused curriculum") of moral education is to succeed. This is that we should become aware of others as persons and have a vivid and sympathetic representation in imagination of their interests and of the effects of our actions on their lives.[26] Josiah Royce called this imaginative realization of the feelings of our neighbors "the moral insight," for he believed that one who has it will at once see his duty and feel impelled to act on it. Even his friendly enemy, William James, in "On a Certain Blindness in Human Beings," says much the same thing. "This higher vision of an inner significance in what, until then, we had realized only in the dead external way, often comes over a person suddenly; and, when it does so, it makes an epoch in his history."[27] Earlier we stressed the importance in moral education of factual knowledge and scientific intelligence, but these still proceed in "the dead external way," and something more is needed—a "higher vision" or realizing insight into life which pierces the "great cloudbank of ancestral blindness weighing down upon us." This moral imagination of the lives of others is the one thing needful above all else; perhaps it cannot be taught in any literal sense, but

[26] Cf. D. D. Raphael, *Moral Judgement* (London: Allen and Unwin, 1955), pp. 105–110.

[27] J. Royce, *The Religious Aspect of Philosophy* (Boston: Houghton Mifflin, 1885), Ch. VI, Sect. V; cf. W. James, *On Some of Life's Ideals* (New York: Henry Holt, 1899), pp. 18–20, 45–50, 93–94.

any endeavor of moral education is sadly wanting if it fails to do what can be done to develop it or bring it about. If religion has any direct bearing on moral education, it must be here; James, in fact, calls this "widening of vision" an "increase of religious insight."[28]

[28] *Op. cit.*, p. 64. Cf. pp. 65, 88. The other phrases quoted in this paragraph come from p. 52.

PART THREE

Law and Education

LAW provides the superstructure for American formal education. It mandates the age at which students begin and end education and guarantees to parents the option of utilizing public institutions, secular or sectarian private institutions, or the services of a tutor. The concept of law as an instrument of public policy for the establishment of educational services has always been prominent in American thought. The astuteness of the legal formulations has varied with time and circumstance. From the inception of the first colonies, and especially in Massachusetts, the colonial leaders used law, rather than mores and folkways, to preserve social and cultural values. Interesting evidence of this is the Massachusetts Act of 1647.

It being one chief object of that old deluder, Satan, to keep men from the knowledge of the Scriptures, as in former times by keeping them in an unknown tongue, so in these latter times by persuading from the use of tongues, that so at least the true sense and meaning of the original might be clouded by false glosses of saint-seeming deceivers, that learning may not be buried in the graves of our fathers in the Church and Commonwealth, the Lord assisting our endeavors,

It is therefore ordered, That every township in this jurisdiction, after the Lord hath increased them to the number of fifty householders, shall then forthwith appoint one within their town to teach all such children as shall resort to him to write and read, whose wages shall be paid either by the parents or masters of such children, or by the inhabitants in general, by way of supply, as the major part of those that order the prudentials of the town shall appoint: Provided, *Those that send their children be not oppressed by paying much more than they can have them taught for in other towns; and*

It is further ordered, That where any town shall increase to the number of one hundred families or householders, they shall set up a grammar school, the master thereof being able to instruct youth so far as they may be fitted for the university: Provided, *That if any town neglect the performance hereof above one year, that every such town shall pay five pounds to the next school till they shall perform this order.*[1]

[1] As quoted in Edgar W. Knight, *Education in the United States* (Boston: Ginn & Co., 1934), p. 105.

The commitment to insure the benefits of formal education was also reflected more than a century later in Article 3 of the Ordinance of 1787: "Religion, morality, and knowledge, being necessary to good government and the happiness of mankind, schools and the means of education shall forever be encouraged."

With the founding of the republic, the Constitution, according to the terms of the Tenth Amendment, decreed that "the powers not delegated to the United States by the Constitution, nor prohibited by it to the States, are reserved to the States respectively, or to the people."

Because education is not mentioned in the Constitution, the Tenth Amendment delegated to each state the initial responsibility for the development of educational facilities. As America grew larger and more complex and knowledge increased, men in all walks of life came to agree that tax-supported public education was an instrument necessary for the advancement of civilization. Because each state has accepted responsibility for conducting education, fifty variations of a single theme have been produced in addition to the activities of the Congress in legislating for the District of Columbia. We lack anything resembling national agreement on what constitutes an adequate education because of this diversity.

The evolution of law in reference to education has produced the following legislative hierarchy: United States Constitution, federal statutes, state constitutions, state statutes, regulations of the chief state school officer and the state department of education, local board of education, local superintendent of schools, building principals, and individual teachers. Court decisions, local, state, and federal, have clarified the purpose and intent of the activities of these legislative entities. Law and court decisions, then, supply the basic identifying characteristics of the American educational system.

As knowledge accrues and the social intelligence of the American people enlarges, law will continue to be used, in the form of either legal enactments or court decisions, to assure the benefits of change to succeeding generations. So it is that law serves the dual function of preserving old values and of insuring the adaption of new ones. The Supreme Court desegregation decision of 1954 is an interesting illustration of this purpose.

Chapter 10

LAW INSURES STABILITY AND CHANGE

NEWTON EDWARDS, *a social scientist, is concerned with the significance of the major contributions that law, in all its ramifications, has made to the establishment of stability and change in American education. Edwards suggests that law, in relation to education, performs a dual function: (a) law preserves and conserves social values and can be identified as an instrument of social stability; and (b) law embraces newly defined social values and can be identified as an instrument of social adaption. The interaction of both functions produces gradual change and growth and thus contributes to and insures the stability of both the educational institutions and the other social institutions affected by them.*

Edwards indicates that a number of legal enactments and court decisions have performed the following functions:

(a) The state is supreme in all educational matters defined by the state constitution; (b) the concept that basic educational policy is a state function excludes local communities from this activity; (c) the local school corporation and its officers are agents of the state and subject to state standards; (d) rules of statutory law and of common law govern school boards in reference to the power to tax, to contract for services, to acquire sites for schools, and to determine the use of school facilities; (e) the state is supreme in defining and maintaining standards for teachers; (f) although public school teachers serve as agents of the state, the law does not confer immunity upon them, and they are responsible for any injuries that may occur to students under their supervision.

As instruments of social adaption, legal enactments and court decisions have performed the following functions:

(a) When confronted with a new issue, the courts modify established principles, apply principles contributed by pertinent disciplines, or formulate new principles based upon validated knowledge.

(b) The complexity of modern living has caused a marked change in the belief that policy should be made exclusively by the legislative branch, interpreted by the judiciary, and carried out by the executive branch of government. This system has been replaced by one in which administrative agencies and boards are, within broad limits, vested with legislative, judicial, and executive powers.

(c) Judicial interpretation of the federal Constitution has fundamentally changed traditional conceptions of the locus of power over the American educational enterprise.

(d) The general-welfare clause of the Constitution is interpreted as conferring substantive powers upon Congress.

(e) Recent judicial interpretations of the First, Fifth, and Fourteenth Amendments have been significant for education.

STABILITY AND CHANGE IN BASIC CONCEPTS OF LAW GOVERNING AMERICAN EDUCATION

Newton Edwards

The law is always an important instrument of social policy, and as such it should be sufficiently flexible to make the adaptations required by the changing social context in which it operates. Theoretically and ideally, the law represents a commitment to the value premises of the society in which it operates, and consequently it has a dual function. On the one hand, it is the guardian of the intrinsic values that have stood the test of human experience. Here it is a preservative and conservative influence; it is concerned with stability, with historic continuity in the ordered patterns of human behavior. But, on the other hand, the law is no less concerned with adaptation and change—with the application of old concepts and principles to new social conditions and with the development of new concepts and principles when a new social context requires them.

Reprinted from *School Review,* Vol. 65, No. 2 (Summer 1957), pp. 161–175, by permission of the University of Chicago Press.

The dual function of the law as an instrument of social stability and of social adaptation creates difficulties that cannot be escaped. It means that the various instrumentalities of the political state, be they legislative, executive, administrative, or judicial, must always exercise a very considerable self-restraint regardless of the urge they may have for change, that they must always operate within the confines of historical continuity. As Woodrow Wilson once put it:

> Whatever view be taken in each particular case of the rightfulness or advisability of state regulation and control, one rule there is which may not be departed from under any circumstances, and that is the rule of historical continuity. In politics nothing radically novel may be safely attempted. No result of value can ever be reached in politics except through slow and gradual development, the careful adaptations and nice modifications of growth. Nothing can be done by leaps. . . . Every nation must constantly keep in touch with its past: it cannot run towards its ends around sharp corners. . . . The rule of governmental action is necessary co-operation; the method of political development is conservative adaptation, shaping old habits into new ones, modifying old means to accomplish new ends.[1]

In the area of education, the common law, statutory law, administrative law, and judicial interpretation of the constitution have each made its own contributions to stability or to change, some of which are described below.

Common-law concepts and principles, while exhibiting no inconsiderable flexibility, have been characterized by a high degree of stability. An analysis of court decisions relating to education during the past third of a century and more reveals many areas of stable application of established rules.

The concept of the state's supremacy with respect to all educational policies within the sphere of the state's authority remains unchanged and permeates judicial thinking in a vast number of specific and practical educational problems. Thus the courts uniformly and consistently hold that the creation of a legislative branch of government by constitutional provision confers upon it all legislative powers except such as are expressly withheld. State legislatures, therefore, are vested with plenary powers with respect to educational policy except in those instances where they are expressly or impliedly restrained by some provision in the state or the federal constitution. This means, of course, that a state legislature has a wide choice with respect to educational policies. It means, too, that it has an equally wide choice with respect to the state and local administrative structure it will employ to carry its policy decisions into effect. Subject to constitutional limitations, it may create such state administrative agencies and such local units of administration as it deems wise, and it may confer upon them powers, great or

[1] Woodrow Wilson, *The State* (Boston: D. C. Heath & Co., 1897), pp. 667–68.

small, as policy may dictate. Moreover, all these things it may do with or without the consent of the localities, for in education the state is the unit and there are no legal rights except those that are safeguarded by the state constitution.

In many states, however, the legislature is not vested with the broad powers this discussion has indicated. Not infrequently state constitutions include detailed and restrictive provisions that have no place in fundamental law. It is a mistake to tie up in the constitution, as permanent and fundamental, principles and institutions which, under new conditions, may most need to be changed. And yet the framers of many of our state constitutions have been guilty of this mistake. State constitutions are difficult to change, but even so their educational provisions in many instances afford a fruitful area of reform.

The concept of education as a function of the state excludes the concept of education as a function of municipalities. A school district and a city may embrace exactly the same territory, but they are usually distinct corporations, each with its peculiar function to perform. The school district is a quasi-corporation, created by the state to carry out a state policy at the local level. The city is a municipal corporation, created for governing a locality; it is not created as an instrument of state policy. It follows that education is not essentially or inherently a municipal function and that a city or town possesses no inherent control over the public schools. Whatever powers a city or its officers may possess with respect to education are necessarily conferred by charter or statute. The courts have long been in agreement that municipal officers have only such powers with respect to education as are clearly delegated to them.

When interpreting statutory or charter provisions conferring powers over education on municipalities, the courts apply the rule of strict construction. The presumption always is that the state intended to confer powers over education upon its duly established educational agencies, and that presumption will be overcome only by a clear legislative intent otherwise. Thus it has been held in numerous instances that a city, unless specifically authorized to do so, may not spend its funds for educational purposes. Similarly, municipal officers will not be permitted to exercise any greater degree of control over school finance than that clearly conferred by statutory or charter provision. Power to approve a school budget does not ordinarily mean power to reduce it. Authority on the part of city officials to reduce a school budget must be very clear because, as the courts have repeatedly pointed out, such authority virtually places the control of the schools in the hands of the city officials. And even though the statutes may authorize the city to fix the gross amount to be spent for education, it does not follow that the city authorities may direct how the gross amount may be spent.

Appointment of school-board members by the mayor and council in no way makes them municipal officers, nor does it legally subject them to the control of the mayor.

Home-rule charters making municipalities self-governing and free from legislative interference with respect to matters of local and internal concern do not confer any control over education because education is a state and not a local concern. The only instance in which a city has inherent control over educational policy is in the exercise of its police power. Even here it has been held that a school board may not be required to obey municipal building ordinances unless expressly required by statute to do so. In some instances, however, the courts have ruled that the police power of a city takes precedence over that of the school board when the public safety demands it. Thus it has been held that a city may enforce an ordinance requiring inspection of boilers, smokestacks, and elevators in school buildings. So, too, a city may inspect and regulate lunchrooms and cafeterias maintained by school boards, and its board of health may close schools in the face of an epidemic. Many students of government believe that a closer working relationship should obtain between city governments and school boards, but it seems clear that such a relationship will have to be established by statutory enactment rather than through judicial decision.

Common-law rules relating to school officers have undergone no fundamental change in recent years. School-board members are state officers regardless of the manner of their selection or appointment. Principles of law governing *de facto* officers have remained substantially unchanged. An officer still has the right to hold over until a successor has qualified. Where the term of an appointed officer is fixed by statute, the rule holds that the person or agency appointing the officer may not remove him without cause and without notice and a hearing. An injunction is never granted to test the right of an officer to his office; the mode of attack must be an action in the nature of quo warranto in the name of the state brought by the attorney-general or other officer representing the state.

The law governing the authority of school boards has had many varied and novel applications but has remained substantially unchanged. The local school corporation and its officers are creatures of the state, subject entirely to its will. It follows that they possess no inherent powers whatsoever; such authority as they may exercise is conferred upon them by statute. The courts have long been in agreement that a school district and its officers may exercise the following powers and no others: (*a*) those expressly granted by statute, (*b*) those fairly and necessarily implied in the powers expressly granted, and (*c*) those essential for the accomplishment of the objects of the corporation. And commonly, the courts apply the rule of strict construction; if there is doubt that a school board has the authority to act, the doubt will be resolved against the board and the power be denied. It is not for the courts to exercise the legislative function by enlarging the powers of school boards. And yet it can be said that the courts, in interpreting the implied powers of school boards, do recognize that the school is a social institution subject to change in purpose and function as society itself changes or as ideals and practices in education change, and they recognize that powers which were at one time unnecessary are essential under new conditions.

The law of contracts as it relates to education has remained relatively stable. School boards have, of course, no inherent power to contract. Since they are arms of the state created for the purpose of exercising purely governmental functions, the measure of their contractual power is found in the laws of the state—and in them alone. And all who deal with a school board do so at their peril because they, too, must judge of the powers that have been vested in the board. Moreover, the rule is well established that, where a contractual power is vested in a school board and the mode of making the contract is prescribed, the mode is the measure of power and contracts made in any other mode are void. Thus, where the statutes require that contracts be written, oral contracts are void. So, too, are contracts made without competitive bidding where such mode of making the contract is required. The rule is well established that, where a written contract is clear in its meaning, parol or extrinsic evidence is inadmissible to contradict, vary, add to, or subtract from, its meaning. Contracts which a board had no authority to make or which were made in violation of the statutory mode or in violation of public policy are void, and no recovery can be had upon them in a court of law even though the contract may have been performed. Where property has been delivered to a board under an invalid contract, courts of equity will restore it to the original owner if this can be done without working any injury to the school district. So, too, money paid to school boards for the purchase of illegal bonds will be restored to the original owner if it can still be identified. An illegal contract can be ratified by a school board provided, of course, it had the authority to make the contract in the first instance, and ratification may be by formal resolution or by action that is incompatible with any other assumption than the intent to ratify.

Numerous cases still come into the courts involving the tort liability of school districts, but here again one notes no fundamental changes in the common law. It is true that the doctrine of non-liability has been subjected to criticism by students of the law as illogical and unjust. A number of the courts themselves have expressed dissatisfaction with it on the ground of social policy, but apparently they agree with the Supreme Court of Kansas when it said:

> If the doctrine of state immunity in tort survives by virtue of antiquity alone, it is an historical anachronism . . . and works injustice to everybody concerned . . . the Legislature should abrogate it. But the Legislature must make the change in policy, not the courts.[2]

In some states, notably California and Washington, common-law immunity in tort in the case of negligence has been superseded by statute. But, outside New York, the courts continue to hold to the doctrine of non-liability in the case of negligence causing injuries to pupils, teachers, or to the general public.

Long-established rules of the common law governing authority of school boards to tax, to incur bonded debt, and to acquire and use school property are still applied with few significant modifications. The authority to tax is still strictly construed. Real property is taxable in the state or district in which it is located whether or not the owner is a resident of the state or district. Tangible personal property is taxable at the domicile of the owner, but it may be taxable in the place of its location if it has acquired a business situs there. Intangible personal property may be taxed at the domicile of its owner, or where it has come to acquire a business situs, or in both places. Income may be taxed where it is earned regardless of the domicile of its owner. School money raised by a uniform state tax may be distributed to the various geographical areas of the state, or for the support of special educational services, provided the distribution be made upon the basis of a reasonable classification and provided, too, that it affects alike all in the same class or category.

Authority of school boards to issue bonds continues to be strictly construed. Bonds issued without authority, in excess of the debt limit, or in violation of law do not bind the district, and recovery cannot be had upon them even though they be in the hands of an innocent purchaser. Nor, under such circumstances, may the bond-holder commonly recover on *quantum meruit;* that is to say, the law will not imply a contract and permit recovery for money had and received.

There is still conflict in the law governing the use of school property for other than school purposes, but in recent years the tendency, both of state legislatures and of the courts, has been to liberalize the use of school property for strictly non-school purposes.

During the past few decades a large number of cases have come into the courts involving the administration of the teaching personnel. Here again one notes the application of well-established common-law principles, although in a number of instances they are applied to novel situations. And in some instances one may detect the application of new rules.

[2] *McGraw v. Rural High School District No. 1,* 120 Kan. 413, 243 Pac. 1038.

The state may, of course, require of its teachers such qualifications as public policy may reasonably dictate. The certificate which the state issues to a teacher is a privilege conferred by the state; it is a license and is never regarded as a contract. The state may raise its standards for certification at will or even revoke certificates if it so desires. Boards of education may demand of the teachers whom they employ any reasonable qualifications in excess of those required for certification. Boards of education may employ teachers for any reasonable number of years and for a period of time extending beyond the boards' official term of office. The employment of teachers involves the exercise of discretion, which cannot be delegated to the superintendent or even to a committee of the board itself.

Teacher-tenure legislation is commonly held not to be a contract between the state and the teachers affected by it. A teacher-tenure statute, as in Alabama and Indiana, can be so drawn that it constitutes a contract, but ordinarily the presumption is that a tenure statute is only an expression of current legislative policy, subject to later change. Nor do the courts interpret tenure statutes as conferring upon teachers the right of employment regardless of changing conditions and educational policies. Statutes providing tenure are to be interpreted as only a regulation of dismissal for causes personal to the employee. Where, therefore, it becomes desirable to abolish positions in the interest of economy or for any other good reason, a school board may do so and discontinue the employment of teachers. Tenure statutes commonly stipulate the causes and the procedures to be followed in the dismissal of teachers, and the courts require a strict compliance with the statutes. Tenure statutes do not guarantee teachers the right to hold particular positions in particular schools. School boards may make any reasonable assignments, but the work to which the teacher is assigned must, of course, be of the same grade and rank. Tenure statutes do not prevent school boards from making any reasonable changes in teachers' salaries provided, of course, there is no discrimination as between individual teachers. That is to say, salary schedules may be changed as policy may dictate. It has been held that teachers cannot go on strike, but in Connecticut it has been held that a school board has the implied power to enter into collective bargaining with a teachers' union. Teachers are bound by all reasonable rules that may have been made before or during the time of employment.

Statutes creating a teachers' retirement system may or may not be held to constitute a contract between the state and the teachers affected by it, depending upon the wording of the statute and upon the jurisdiction in which the case arises. Where a statute sets up a retirement system and makes it optional for teachers to come under it and a teacher voluntarily contributes part of his salary to the fund, the statute becomes a contract between the teacher and the state which no subsequent legislature may change. But where the state makes it compulsory upon teachers to have part of their salaries paid into a retirement fund, the courts are divided as to whether a pensionary or contractual relationship is created between the state and the teacher.

Although public school teachers are in the performance of a governmental function, they are not public officers, and they are personally liable for acts of negligence while performing as teachers. A teacher is governed by the common-law obligation that every person must so act or use that which he controls as not to injure another. What the law requires of the teacher is that, in any particular relation to a pupil, he exercise the care and prudence any reasonably prudent person would have exercised in the situation.

Applying established principles to a relatively new situation, the courts have held that school boards do not have the implied power to carry liability insurance and that, where the statutes confer this power, the board's immunity from liability is not waived. Similarly, the principle that a school board may not delegate its discretion to others has been applied to organizations exercising extra-legal controls over education. Thus it has been held that a school board could not delegate to an interscholastic league the authority to make and enforce regulations governing the duties of any of its employees.

So far I have been illustrating how a vast body of well-established common-law principles are applicable to specific educational problems. It must not be supposed, however, that the common law is static. When faced with a novel school situation, the courts modify old principles, apply principles derived from other areas of human behavior, or formulate new rules. Illustrations of the flexibility of the common law may be seen in the interpretation of the implied powers of school boards. It has been held that, under their general powers to erect school buildings, school boards may purchase and maintain gymnasiums, athletic fields, stadiums, and teacherages. It has been held, too, that school boards have the implied power to maintain camps for school pupils, to carry group life insurance for teachers, to maintain a junior college, to spend funds to publicize school-bond elections. Statutes authorizing the creation of a state school-building authority, with power to lease school buildings to local boards for a period of years, the rentals to be paid out of current expenses, have been held constitutional, the rentals not being held to create a debt in excess of the constitutional limit.

It is obvious, of course, that statutory law has provided a wider latitude for policy adaptation than has the common law. But many of the problems of modern life, including those in the field of education, have become so complex and technical that legislative bodies cannot deal with them competently. Members of legislative bodies do not commonly possess the expertness, do not have the intimate knowledge of the intricate web of facts, that are required to deal with many problems of government. The judiciary and the executive are often equally inexpert and equally ignorant of the facts and relationships involved in major contemporary issues. The truth is that, at the operational level of government, at the grass roots, where policy decisions are contantly being made and put into operation, the theory of separation of powers breaks down. It is altogether fallacious to suppose that policy is made exclusively by the legislative branch, interpreted by the judiciary, and carried out by the executive branch of government. The lack of expertness on the part of legislative bodies, the courts, and the executive, in conjunction with the impossibility of separating the powers of government at the operational level, has given rise to the development of administrative agencies and boards which, within broad limits, are vested with legislative, judicial, and executive powers. Within a constantly widening sphere of action, administrative agencies make rules, execute them, and decide the rights of aggrieved parties under them.

The development of administrative agencies and administrative law has gone forward in the field of education as in other areas of public policy. State and local administrative agencies have been created and vested with broad rule-making and rule-executing powers and with power to exercise quasi-judicial functions. A very large percentage of the cases involving education now coming before the courts are cases involving judicial review of discretionary acts of school boards. When called upon to review discretionary acts of school boards, the courts do not, as a rule, try the case *de novo;* they do not weigh the evidence to determine where the preponderance of the evidence lies. If the finding of fact which the school board has made is supported by "substantial" evidence, a court will accept it as conclusive. When an appeal is taken by some aggrieved party to test the legality of board action, the board's action will be overruled only when the board has acted without authority, arbitrarily, under an erroneous theory of the law, or without any substantial basis of fact.

The development of administrative law in the field of education has been of great practical consequence. It has made possible a greater effectiveness of school administration because it has vested power of decision in those who best know the facts. It has contributed much by way of keeping the local school authority the responsible operational unity, and it has permitted local boards to adjust to local conditions and changing social needs.

Written constitutions are designed to give the law a certain permanency, and they provide for adaptability by specific process of amendment. Constitutional law can, of course, undergo profound change by the process of judicial interpretation. During the past half-century or so, and more especially within recent years, judicial interpretation of the federal Constitution has fundamentally changed traditional conceptions of the locus of power over the American educational enterprise.

The general-welfare clause, long uncertain in its precise meaning, has now come to be interpreted as conferring substantive powers upon the Congress without reference to later enumerated powers. The Congress may tax and spend to provide for the general welfare, the only limit on its authority being that the welfare be general and not particular. Certainly the Congress has authority to make any reasonable expenditure of funds for the support of education. Just how far this authority to support education carries with it authority to control education is not yet clear. But since the general-welfare clause has been held to confer substantive powers and since it is a well-established principle that the federal government has the power to employ whatever means may be necessary to carry into effect the powers expressly conferred upon it, it may well be that the Congress is vested with vast powers, not only to support, but to control, education as well.

Recent judicial interpretation of the First and the Fifth Amendments have been significant for education, but less so, I think, than the interpretation given to the Fourteenth Amendment. The clause in the Fourteenth Amendment which declares that no state may deprive any person of life, liberty, or property without due process of law, as now interpreted, confers upon the Supreme Court of the United States power to strike down practically any police legislation passed by the states of which it disapproves. Before the adoption of the Fourteenth Amendment, the states were practically unrestricted in the exercise of their police powers except in two particulars: they could not pass laws impairing the obligations of contracts, and they were restricted in the regulation of foreign and interstate commerce. In his first inaugural message, Abraham Lincoln expressed the prevailing concept of the structure of government with respect to the exercise of the police power on the part of the states. He said:

> The maintenance inviolate of the rights of the states, and especially the right of each state to order and control its own domestic institution according to its own judgment exclusively, is essential to the balance of power on which the perfection and endurance of our political fabric depend.[3]

And for a number of years following the adopting of the Fourteenth Amendment, the Supreme Court was not disposed to assume jurisdiction in cases involving the exercise of the police power on the part of the states. But as state legislatures undertook to control so-called "big business" through regulatory measures and as new judges took seats on the bench, the court reversed its position. Thus as the years have passed, the Supreme Court has not hesitated to strike down legislation passed by the states in the exercise of their police power whenever the court regarded such legislation, in the

[3] Abraham Lincoln Association, Springfield, Illinois, *The Collected Works of Abraham Lincoln,* IV, 263 (New Brunswick, N.J.: Rutgers University Press, 1953).

light of social and economic conditions, as unnecessary, unreasonable, and arbitrary. In the nature of things, the Supreme Court cannot have a ready-made formula that it can apply in determining whether a person has been deprived of liberty or property without due process. Each case has to be determined in terms of the particular web of facts in which it is imbedded.

In the field of education, and indeed in many other aspects of our national life, special significance has become attached to the clause in the Fourteenth Amendment declaring that no state may deprive any person within its jurisdiction of the equal protection of the laws. This prohibition, it will be noted, is directed to the states, and not to private persons and private action. In trying to get some idea of the practical application of this clause, one must try to ascertain the conception of state action which the Supreme Court entertains. An examination of the decisions of the Supreme Court indicates that it is extending its conception to include actions which it previously would have regarded as private action. State action as a legal concept has been relentlessly extending into the area of private action, and today it is extremely difficult to distinguish the two. This extension of the concept of state action has proceeded along two lines.

The first has been designated the "instrumentality theory." The Supreme Court has taken the position that action by private persons or organizations is state action when these persons or organizations perform a function which by its very nature is governmental in character. The thing that makes an action state action is not the agent or agency, but the nature of the action. The theory is that private persons or organizations are instrumentalities of the state when they perform a function that is public and governmental.

The second line along which the concept of state action has been extended has been designated as the "redefinition theory." Here the court has extended its concept of state action to make it include the action of practically all recognized state agencies—the action of the state legislature, the executive branch of government, and indeed the action of state courts. A denial of the equal protection of the law by any of these agencies of the state now comes under the prohibition of the equal-protection-of-the-law clause of the Fourteenth Amendment. More than that, the concept of state action has come to be extended to the actions of local governmental units and their officers.

Finally, it can be said that our system of law governing education has built into its structure and operational procedures the ways and means of maintaining the necessary stability and of making possible adaptation to new social demands. It has been wisely said that experience is the life of the law. Certain it is that the concepts, rules, or principles that make up the common law represent a vast accumulation of experience and wisdom. They insure historical continuity and at the same time provide for some degree of flexibility and adaptation. The development of administrative agencies and administrative law is of profound importance because it utilizes expertness and also makes possible a working combination of legislative, executive, and judicial functions at the operational level. The process of judicial interpretation of the constitution provides a way of adapting the fundamental law to the changing web of social fact. Whether or not, in the words of Woodrow Wilson, we are at present trying to leap towards our future around sharp corners is a matter which one must judge for one's self.

Chapter II

LAW ENRICHES THE CURRICULUM

THE *study of legal literature, in addition to clarifying the teacher's conception of his responsibilities, can also enrich the curriculum, notably in courses dealing with political science, civics, contemporary American history, problems of American democracy, and English. Various court decisions in particular not only serve as examples of clear thinking and writing, but also can introduce students to important current problems, to the ways in which social issues can be resolved through logical and orderly procedures, and to theories about how the conduct of educational institutions can be modified. The legal resolutions of social issues, especially as they pertain to education, serve to highlight the importance of traditional values, provide the opportunities to validate newly defined values, and indicate problems that require further study and clarification. In this respect, an examination of certain majority and dissenting opinions offered by the justices of the United States Supreme Court can make significant contributions to expanding the student's knowledge and inspire him in his search for the uses of intelligence. Harry Kalven, Jr., a lawyer, demonstrates these points by citing portions of Supreme Court decisions in the controversial areas of religious education, segregation, teaching German in elementary schools, and loyalty programs.*

The first decision involves the problems of religious instruction in public schools and represents the majority opinion in McCollum v. Board of Education. *The point at issue was the granting of released time to allow religious instruction to be held in the public school during the school day. The second decision concerns segregated education and represents the unanimous opinion in* Brown v. Board of Education of Topeka. *The point at issue was the validity of "separate but equal" educational facilities. The third decision deals with the power of the state to prohibit the teaching of certain subject matter. The point at issue was the right of the state to prohibit the teaching of Ger-*

man in elementary schools. The fourth decision concerns the problem of loyalty programs and represents a dissenting opinion in Adler v. Board of Education. *The point at issue was the right of the state to determine what organizations it deemed subversive and then to establish regulations whereby membership in such organizations was* prima facie *evidence for barring a teacher from the public schools of the state.*

LAW AND EDUCATION

Harry Kalven, Jr.

The controversy over religious education in the schools has produced a notable series of essays on a troubled theme, with the courts sensitive to the subtle and divisive influences that may come into play. Listen for a moment to Mr. Justice Frankfurter in the *McCollum* case, which involved a released-time scheme:

> Religious education so conducted on school time and property is patently woven into the working scheme of the school. The Champaign arrangement thus presents powerful elements of inherent pressure by the school system in the interest of religious sects. The fact that this power has not been used to discriminate is beside the point. Separation is a requirement to abstain from fusing functions of Government and of religious sects, not merely to treat them all equally. That a child is offered an alternative may reduce the constraint; it does not eliminate the operation of influence by the school in matters sacred to conscience and outside the school's domain. The law of imitation operates, and nonconformity is not an outstanding characteristic of children. The result is an obvious pressure upon children to attend. Again, while the Champaign school population represents only a fraction of the more than 250 sects of the nation, not even all the practicing sects in Champaign are willing or able to provide religious instruction. The children belonging to these nonparticipating sects will thus have inculcated in them a feeling of separatism when the school should be the training ground for habits of community, or they will have religious instruction in a faith which is not that of their parents. As a result, the public school system of Champaign actively furthers inculcation in the religious tenets of some faiths, and in the process sharpens the consciousness of religious differences at least among some of

Reprinted from *School Review,* Vol. 65, No. 3 (Autumn 1957), pp. 291–294, by permission of the University of Chicago Press.

the children committed to its care. These are consequences against which the Constitution was directed when it prohibited the Government common to all from becoming embroiled, however innocently, in the destructive religious conflicts of which the history of even this country records some dark pages.

Or move to the segragation cases, and listen to Chief Justice Warren on the subtle discrimination that persists even where physical facilities are equal:

We come then to the question presented: Does segregation of children in public schools solely on the basis of race, even though the physical facilities and other "tangible" factors may be equal, deprive the children of the minority group of equal educational opportunities? We believe that it does.

In *Sweatt* v. *Painter*, *supra*, in finding that a segregated law school for Negroes could not provide them equal educational opportunities, this Court relied in large part on "those qualities which are incapable of objective measurement but which make for greatness in a law school." In *McLaurin* v. *Oklahoma State Regents*, the Court, in requiring that a Negro admitted to a white graduate school be treated like all other students, again resorted to intangible considerations: ". . . his ability to study, to engage in discussions and exchange views with other students, and, in general, to learn his profession." Such considerations apply with added force to children in grade and high schools. To separate them from others of similar age and qualifications solely because of their race generates a feeling of inferiority as to their status in the community that may affect their hearts and minds in a way unlikely ever to be undone. The effect of this separation on their educational opportunities was well stated by a finding in the Kansas case by a court which nevertheless felt compelled to rule against the Negro plaintiffs:

"Segregation of white and colored children in public schools has a detrimental effect upon the colored children. The impact is greater when it has the sanction of the law; for the policy of separating the races is usually interpreted as denoting the inferiority of the Negro group. A sense of inferiority affects the motivation of a child to learn. Segregation with the sanction of the law, therefore, has a tendency to retard the educational and mental development of Negro children and to deprive them of some of the benefits they would receive in a racially integrated school system."

Whatever may have been the extent of psychological knowledge at the time of *Plessy* v. *Ferguson*, this finding is amply supported by modern authority. Any language in *Plessy* v. *Ferguson* contrary to this finding is rejected.

We conclude that in the field of public education the doctrine of "separate but equal" has no place. Separate educational facilities are inherently unequal.

Or consider Mr. Justice McReynolds on the power of the state to prohibit the teaching of German in elementary school:

Practically, education of the young is only possible in schools conducted by especially qualified persons who devote themselves thereto. The calling always has been regarded as useful and honorable—essential, indeed, to the public welfare. Mere knowledge of the German language cannot reasonably be regarded as harmful. Heretofore it has been commonly looked upon as helpful and desirable. Plaintiff in error taught this language in school as part of his occupation. His right thus to teach and the right of parents to engage him so to instruct their children, we think, are within the liberty of the Amendment.

The challenged statute forbids the teaching in school of any subject except in English; also the teaching of any other language until the pupil has attained and successfully passed the eighth grade, which is not usually accomplished before the age of twelve. The supreme court of the state has held that "the so-called ancient or dead languages" are not "within the spirit or the purpose of the act. . . ." Latin, Greek, Hebrew are not proscribed; but German, French, Spanish, Italian, and every other alien speech are within the ban. Evidently the legislature has attempted materially to interfere with the calling of modern language teachers, with the opportunities of pupils to acquire knowledge, and with the power of parents to control the education of their own.

It is said the purpose of the legislation was to promote civil development by inhibiting training and education of the immature in foreign tongues and ideals before they could learn English and acquire American ideals; and "that the English language should be and become the mother tongue of all children reared in this state." It is also affirmed that the foreign-born population is very large, that certain communities commonly use foreign words, follow foreign leaders, move in a foreign atmosphere, and that the children are thereby hindered from becoming citizens of the most useful type, and the public safety is imperiled.

That the state may do much, go very far, indeed, in order to improve the quality of its citizens, physically, mentally, and morally, is clear; but the individual has certain fundamental rights which must be respected. The protection of the Constitution extends to all—to those who speak other languages as well as those born with English on the tongue. Perhaps it would be highly advantageous if all had ready understanding of our ordinary speech, but this cannot be coerced by methods which conflict with the Constitution—a desirable end cannot be promoted by prohibited means.

Or move to Mr. Justice Douglas, in dissent, discussing the freedom of the teacher under a "loyalty" program:

The very threat of such a procedure is certain to raise havoc with academic freedom. Youthful indiscretions, mistaken causes, misguided enthusiasms—all long forgotten—become the ghosts of a harrowing present. Any organization committed to a liberal cause, any group organized to revolt against an hysterical trend, any committee launched to sponsor an unpopular program becomes suspect. These are the organizations into which Communists often infiltrate. Their presence infects the whole, even though the project was not conceived in sin. A teacher caught in that mesh is almost certain to stand condemned. Fearing condemnation, she will tend to shrink from any association that stirs controversy. In that manner freedom of expression will be stifled.

But that is only part of it. Once a teacher's connection with a listed organization is shown, her views become subject to scrutiny to determine whether her membership in the organization is innocent or, if she was formerly a member, whether she has bona fide abandoned her membership.

The law inevitably turns the school system into a spying project. Regular loyalty reports on the teachers must be made out. The principals become detectives; the students, the parents, the community become informers. Ears are cocked for telltale signs of disloyalty. The prejudices of the community come into play in searching out the disloyal. This is not the usual type of supervision which checks a teacher's competency; it is a system which searches for hidden meanings in a teacher's utterances.

What was the significance of the reference of the art teacher to socialism? Why was the history teacher so openly hostile to Franco Spain? Who heard overtones of revolution in the English teacher's discussion of the *Grapes of Wrath?* What was behind the praise of Soviet progress in metallurgy in the chemistry class? Was it not "subversive" for the teacher to cast doubt on the wisdom of the venture in Korea?

What happens under this law is typical of what happens in a police state. Teachers are under constant surveillance; their pasts are combed for signs of disloyalty; their utterances are watched for clues to dangerous thoughts. A pall is cast over the classrooms. There can be no real academic freedom in that environment. Where suspicion fills the air and holds scholars in line for fear of their jobs, there can be no exercise of the free intellect. Supineness and dogmatism take the place of inquiry. A "party line"—as dangerous as the "party line" of the Communists—lays hold. It is the "party line" of the orthodox view, of the conventional thought, of the accepted approach. A problem can no longer be pursued with impunity to its edges. Fear stalks the classroom. The teacher is no longer a stimulant to adventurous thinking; she becomes instead a pipeline for safe and sound information. A deadening dogma takes the place of free inquiry. Instruction tends to become sterile; pursuit of knowledge is discouraged; discussion often leaves off where it should begin.

This, I think, is what happens when a censor looks over a teacher's shoulder. This system of spying and surveillance with its accompanying reports and trials cannot go hand in hand with academic freedom. It produces standardized thought, not the pursuit of truth. Yet it was the pursuit of truth which the First Amendment was designed to protect.

Chapter 12

LAW FOR EDUCATORS

SINCE *legal enactments and court decisions affect the framework of American education, a general understanding of school law is needed by teachers. Law and court decisions indicate what educators must do, what they might do, and what they cannot do. In addition, since the law is silent on a number of points, teachers must be aware of the areas in which issues have yet to be clarified. Finally, it is important to remember that any change in the basic conception of American education can be accomplished only by a modification of existing law.*

E. Edmund Reutter, Jr., himself a lawyer, recommends that the formal training of the educator include a study of school law. In the following excerpt, Reutter offers what he considers to be the minimum necessary knowledge. He expresses the wish that his ideas will serve as a basis for serious discussion by all those involved in teacher training before this knowledge is incorporated into a formal program.

The following areas of study are suggested: (a) "importance of legal considerations in educational decisions and actions"; (b) "role of law as help or hindrance in achievement of education goals"; (c) "substance and scope of school law"; (d) "general nature of legal knowledge appropriate for educators"; (e) "evolutionary aspects of school law"; (f) "some concepts regarding functioning of courts"; (g) "the 'competing consideration' approach to legal issues"; (h) "basis of authority in school law"; (i) "specific emphases to meet individual needs"; and (j) "sources of assistance in resolving school law matters."

ESSENTIALS OF SCHOOL LAW FOR EDUCATORS

E. E. Reutter, Jr.

1. *Importance of legal considerations in educational decisions and actions.* Public schools are creations of the law. Rights, duties, privileges, and immunities related to public education and the individuals concerned with it are delineated and circumscribed by law. Yet all too frequently the legal ingredient in an educational situation is overlooked. Badly needed is an awareness of the field of school law as a subject for professional inquiry and professional action by educators.

At present there are three all too common and regrettable attitudes about school law among educators. The first is a naive obliviousness to the legal aspects of the education enterprise. This ostrich attitude often constitutes "living dangerously" or, at best, operating at decreased effectiveness. Because there has been no recent "trouble" of a legal nature in connection with one's activities is no more justification for this attitude than is the fact that one has never been hit by a car while crossing a street against a red light. A second attitude is one of baseless fear of the law—seemingly born of unfamiliarity—a definite hindrance to the professional job an educator could and should do. A third attitude is based on an exaggerated delusion of knowledge regarding legal aspects of education. This is especially unbecoming to those in an occupation emphasizing scholarship and responsible for training competent citizens. It is also extremely dangerous, as is the delusion of any type of knowledge. Those who purport to give specific answers to complex legal questions should be treated warily.

There is a legal ingredient in almost every educational decision—whether it involves punishing a pupil, requiring a pupil to take a course, operating a school cafeteria, employing a teacher, using a school building, expending school funds, keeping records, transporting pupils, or reciting the Lord's Prayer in school. In some situations the legal ingredient is the crucial factor; in others it is relatively insignificant. This involvement of the law is similar to that of other facets which should be considered before taking educational action—considerations in such areas as psychology, teaching method, sociology, and community relations. Obviously there are many ideas apparently good educationally or socially which are not legally acceptable, and con-

Reprinted from *Teachers College Record,* Vol. 59, No. 8 (May 1958), pp. 441–449.

versely many things permitted by the law may be undesirable educationally or socially.

2. *Role of law as help or hindrance in achievement of educational goals.* Often the law is used as an excuse for saying no to a new educational idea, and thus is blamed as a blocker of progress. In many cases the charge is justified. However, the law can *help* achieve desirable educational goals. Certification laws for teachers are a good case in point. While they alone cannot assure good teachers, proper certification standards can go far in helping to improve the quality of teaching in the public schools. On the other hand poorly drawn certification regulations can thwart the placing in classrooms of many good teachers. Whereas laws prescribing specific books which must be used in given courses or those establishing unrealistic limitations on school expenditures have impeded educational progress, state minimum salary laws have contributed to the removal of exploitation salaries for teachers, and tenure laws have done much to make the efficient teacher secure in his position.

In terms of a specific item of concern there are four possible legal situations which may prevail. First, the "thing" must be done (for example, American history must be taught). A second possibility is that the "thing" cannot be done (for example, sectarian doctrines must not be taught). A third situation arises when the "thing" is specifically permitted at the option of someone or some body (for example, sabbatical leaves for teachers may be granted at the option of the local school board). The fourth possible situation is the most common one: the law is silent about the item (for example, there is no mention in any source of the law of the uses to which school buildings may be put when school is not in session).

One reason for the prevalence of the last situation is that characteristically the law follows, rather than precedes, experimentation or custom. Theoretically, someone must have an idea and try it out somewhere before it can be specifically treated in a statute or ruled on by a court. Educators should know that historically innovations and progress in education have come as local boards of education and school personnel have decided that some practice would be wise and have experimented with it, other districts have copied the practice, gradually it has become generally accepted throughout the state, and ultimately the practice has found its way into a permissive or mandatory statute.

One of the best ways to promote the spread of a new and desirable educational practice throughout a state is to enact a permissive statute on the point. This will encourage local boards of education to adopt the practice because clearly it is legal, having been stated in a statute. At the same time, the negative effects often concomitant with a requirement that every local school district do something are not included.

3. *Substance and scope of school law.* School law includes much more than the statutes of a state. It comprises all the rules of conduct from any source which are in any way applicable to the schools and which will be enforced by the courts. Some of it is quite elusive, for it cuts across established lines. School law can be categorized in such frameworks as the following: (*a*) level of governmental source, (*b*) branch of governmental source, (*c*) category of law, (*d*) compiled law or common law source.

Viewed by level of governmental source, school law items would range from the Constitution of the United States to the regulations of teachers within their classrooms. The Federal Constitution does not specifically mention public education, and therefore under the Tenth Amendment this function becomes one reserved to the states. However, the increasing number of decisions of the Supreme Court of the United States based on the Federal Constitution indicates the increasingly important role in educational policy played by that document. The First Amendment, for example, is the core of the large amount of litigation concerning church-state-education relationships. The Fourteenth Amendment is the basis of the racial segregation and teacher loyalty decisions. The Fifth Amendment is also pertinent to certain cases involving teacher loyalty. The constitutional provision prohibiting the impairment of contracts by state law is basic to many contract disputes.

Below the Constitution of the United States in the legislative hierarchy come federal statutes. Several of these directly affect education (for example, those pertaining to the school lunch program and to vocational education). On the state level there are four steps of legal authority governing the schools: the state constitution, state statutes, regulations of the state board of education, and regulations of the chief state school officer and the state department of education. It is on the state level that most of the codified law regarding education appears. On the local level are regulations of the local board of education, of the superintendent, of building principals, and of individual teachers. Theoretically, no law or regulation can be contrary to a policy promulgated on any level higher in the hierarchy. In many instances, however, whether a statute or regulation is legal or illegal cannot be finally determined until ruled upon by the courts in an appropriate lawsuit.

Another way to categorize school law is by branch of governmental source—legislative, executive, or judicial. Most of the law, as would be expected, is found in the legislative area, including statutes and regulations of legislatures, state boards of education, and local boards of education. Administrative rules and regulations, whether on the federal, state, or local level are issued by the executive department. The judicial branch plays a critical role in the school law area along two lines: interpreting constitutions, statutes, regulations; and applying common law principles to educational issues.

The traditional categories of law are cut across by school law. Contract law is involved in employment of teachers and in dealing with builders and suppliers. Tort law (civil law not involving contracts) includes such elements involved in operating schools as negligence, trespass, and nuisance. Much school law is found in the law of municipal corporations. The important role of constitutional law in school matters has already been noted. Even criminal law may be involved in such things as enforcement of compulsory attendance laws and assault and battery suits arising out of incidents of corporal punishment.

A fourth way to analyze school law is to classify it in the dichotomy of compiled or written law as found in constitutions, statutes, and regulations, and of common or case law as found in court opinions. One can search the written law relatively easily and find, for example, the subjects that must be taught in the schools. However, the issues involved, for instance, when a pupil is injured on school property, would have to be derived from the case or common law.

4. *General nature of legal knowledge appropriate for educators.* The knowledge of the law that educators should possess is on the level of general understanding and appreciation of broad processes of law—obviously not on the level of the legal practitioner. Perhaps educators' requisite knowledge of law can be characterized as being part of necessary broad, general background. Its type is in many respects analogous to the knowledge of first aid in relation to medical knowledge, or to knowledge about school-building planning in relation to the field of architecture. Educators should know certain overarching principles of the law which are pertinent to educational problems. Furthermore, they should know how these principles have been applied in specific instances involving educational matters. Enough familiarity with law is needed to work effectively in educational areas with legal aspects and to communicate meaningfully with lawyers and legislators. This lack on the part of too many educators is tragically evidenced by the large number of unnecessary court actions and the weakness of rapport between educational groups and legislative agencies in many localities. Rapport on the state level means much more than getting a salary increase voted by the legislature; it involves working with legislators to set up desirable educational policies for the state. On the local level it includes more than winning a lawsuit or staying out of trouble; it encompasses the provision of the best education possible within the existing framework of the law and taking action to change the law where progress is blocked by it.

5. *Evolutionary aspect of school law.* The law affecting schools is not static. It is changed to some extent in each session of the legislature in each

state. Ever-increasing numbers of judicial holdings are continuously contributing to the body of school law. New issues are being litigated, and some old precedents are being superseded by newer judicial points of view. It must be borne in mind that law is a living thing. Furthermore, a given law is not good or bad in the abstract. It is good or bad in relation to how well it achieves its purported purposes. As circumstances change, so should the law.

Most states need thorough examinations of their school law along four lines. Three are essentially of a corrective nature and one is completely creative. Most urgent is the need to eliminate conflicts of law from school codes. Many statutes enacted at different times by different legislators overlap and contain contrary provisions. It should not be necessary to wait for a lawsuit to get the issue resolved.

A second goal should be the removal of vagueness from school law. Most state codes contain many loosely drawn laws. In such instances, too, it would save time and money as well as promote efficiency to have the laws clarified by the legislature, rather than to wait for a judicial interpretation of the legislative intent. It is the legislative function to state the laws clearly, and where legislatures have not done so in statutes pertaining to education it is the educators' responsibility to ask for clarification and to suggest what the clarification should comprise.

A third weakness of most state school codes is the inclusion of obsolescent material. While these provisions may not have been invoked in many years, occasionally they come to light and cause difficulty. The custom of ignoring a law under the assumption that it is obsolete and will not be enforced is not a good one for a democratic society and is particularly inappropriate for those charged with teaching children respect for laws. The proper way to handle the problem is to get the obsolete statute or regulation repealed.

The fourth need is to incorporate in law new ideas and concepts conducive to educational progress. It should be pointed out that putting "good ideas" into mandatory legislation is not necessarily what is meant. Indeed some "good ideas" of by-gone eras or of individuals whose insight was not as great as their enthusiasm or their political skill have resulted in many of the legislative millstones which hang around educators' necks. Good school legislation will evolve only as competent educators and competent legislators work together in a statesmanlike fashion.

6. *Some concepts regarding functioning of courts.* Astonishingly large numbers of educators are ill-informed about the role of courts in relation to the law. Among the basic concepts of the functioning of courts in the American legal system of which educators should be aware are the five briefly discussed below.

The judicial branch of government is not constituted to sit in judgment over the actions of legislative bodies unless a question of constitutionality, state or federal, is raised. That is to say, courts will not pass upon the wisdom of a legislative act so long as it is constitutional or is within the power of the body. Unwise legislative enactments can be set aside only by legislative repeal, which can be brought about by democratic processes of persuasion directed at the legislative body or by action of the electorate at the polls in electing new legislative representatives. The local school board in the governmental structure is essentially a legislative body operating within a limited scope. It sets up rules and regulations to supplement state laws in governing the schools of the district. It has wide discretion. So long as its actions do not violate the law as established by higher legal authority or do not exceed its powers, the local board can be as unwise in its rules as the electorate of the school district will permit. The legal redress of citizens against an unwise school board lies at the polls, and not in the court room. Substantial amounts of money and energy have been wasted by teachers' associations, individual teachers, and citizens-at-large because of failure to understand this keystone of our American democracy.

A second basic concept is that courts are not automatically activated. Also, in general, they do not consider abstract matters. There must be a properly presented controversy in order for a court to decide an issue. Undoubtedly there are many laws and practices in force today which would not stand up in court tests. Thus, because a practice has been in operation for a long time does not mean that it is legal. Rights of teachers, rights of parents and students, rights of taxpayers, and rights of other groups will be secure only so long as these groups are alert to infringements and institute appropriate legal action to protect their rights.

A third important understanding is that each case decided by a court is based on the facts of that specific litigation. Whether the judgment rendered would apply to a different case with changed facts is always problematical (and the facts of no two cases could be absolutely identical). It is here that one can do no more than predict, be he skilled lawyer or legal layman. In a subsequent case one side will endeavor to prove that the facts are so little different from a previously decided case that the same decision should be rendered in the instant case. The other side will argue that the differences in fact are indeed substantial enough to cause a different ruling.

A fourth essential knowledge about the judicial system is that in deciding cases, courts are guided to a large extent by available "precedents" (rules for deciding cases established by courts through the years). Hence, a certain element of stability is incorporated in the judicial process. Also, elaborate appeal channels are set up. Higher courts in effect supervise the decisions of lower courts and are empowered to reverse the judgments of lower courts.

A fifth important understanding is that in theory the courts' function is to interpret the law, not to make it. Thus, within limits, the legislative branch can negate the future effect of a judicial decision by changing the law which was the basis of the decision. Of course the law must be changed in a manner that is not unconstitutional, or the courts will be able to set aside the new law.

7. *The "competing consideration" approach to legal issues.* Contrary to popular lay opinion, the law on most matters is not precise. Many statutes which seem to be concrete are not. For instance a teacher can be dismissed for "incompetence" in any jurisdiction; but whether specific actions constitute "incompetence" is a question for the courts. Also it is clear in the common law that a teacher may be required to respond in damages to a pupil injured through the teacher's negligence; yet whether a specific act is negligent cannot be ultimately determined except through court decision. If the law were as simple as so many legal laymen think it is, there would be little need for highly trained, experienced, intelligent lawyers and judges. Clerks (or even mechanical brains) could match cases with legal rules and have the decisions dropped from a slot.

The question, Is such-and-such legal? generally cannot be answered categorically. Theoretically it could not be answered with finality until ruled on by the highest court having jurisdiction over the matter. Indeed the situation makes the discipline of law much more akin to that of education than most educators realize. Generalizations can be drawn from decided cases, but as in education, differences in individual cases often preclude direct application of general propositions to specific circumstances.

The basis of prophecy as to the likely outcome of a case which may arise is a weighing of the "competing considerations" involved. In some situations, the considerations favoring the likelihood that a court would enter one judgment seem to outweigh greatly the factors favoring the opposite judgment. In other circumstances, the balance appears to be more nearly even. The decision as to whether to pursue a course of action should be made after contemplating the legal eventualities and taking into account non-legal factors, such as educational and social aspects. In many circumstances, the way that something is done determines its legality; that is, a particular goal achieved in one way may be legal and in another way illegal. Therefore, the legally alert educator will take the path most likely to be sustained in the eventuality of a lawsuit. Furthermore, he will be prepared to answer the legal arguments of those who oppose the action.

8. *Basis of authority in school law.* In regard to any item of concern, the effective educator will look for the basis of authority for the prevailing legal situation. His actions if he wished to change a legal situation created by the Federal Constitution should be quite different from the procedure followed

if the legal basis were the regulation of a local administrator. At first glance this point seems completely obvious, yet many educators want to be told specifically whether or not they can do a certain thing. This encourages an uncritical acceptance of statements regarding what the law is on a point. It has already been indicated that, although in some instances a precise answer can be given, definite answers should be accepted with caution. The follow-up question should always be, What is the legal basis for the answer? For example, if one wished not to comply with a United States Supreme Court interpretation of the Constitution, he would have either to convince the Supreme Court that it had erred in its decision and should reverse itself, or to have a constitutional amendment enacted. On the other hand, the provisions of a state statute could more easily be changed, and a local board of education regulation changed still more easily. If the basis of the contrary authority is revealed to be no more than an interpretation by someone in an administrative position, as is often true, there may be no need to have any legal change made before the action can appropriately be taken. Also, as mentioned previously, some statutes now included in school codes would probably be declared unconstitutional if they were challenged, and unquestionably many board of education rules and regulations would likewise not be enforcible in courts.

The legally effective educator should ask himself, therefore, whether he is willing to be blocked on some proposed educational action by the law as interpreted, or should take political steps to have the law changed, or should proceed with his plan and rely on support from the courts in the event that his educational action is challenged. He would want to consider what penalty might be forthcoming if his action were not sustained by the courts. If he could prove that the statute in question is unconstitutional, or that the local board rule is unreasonable, or that the interpretation of the state superintendent of schools is wrong, no legal penalty would result. Intelligent action on a matter often hinges on this point of the basis of authority. If a teacher or a schoolboard is convinced that something should be done in the interests of better education and the statement is made that it cannot be done legally, immediate thought should be given to the legal path to be followed in order to make the educational goal possible of attainment.

9. *Specific emphases to meet individual needs.* A minimum of knowledge by all engaged in the field of education would be required in such substantive areas as: legal structure for education, pupil personnel policies, control of pupil conduct, staff personnel policies, curriculum (broadly defined), and liability. Advanced preparation beyond that required for entrance to the profession would follow two paths: pursuing more deeply the field of school law as part of the general advanced training requisite for better professional effectiveness, and delving deeply into legal areas particularly pertinent to

specialized interests. As illustrations, physical education coordinators should be expert in liability for pupil injuries, those entering guidance work would need more familiarity with compulsory education laws and their enforcement, curriculum coordinators would require extra knowledge of the rights of parents in relation to school studies and activities, business administrators would need considerable work in the area of contracts, personnel administrators would need to know more about the legal aspects of employing and discharging teachers, and those specializing in history or philosophy of education would want to be familiar with the rich source of history and philosophy found in judicial opinions.

10. *Sources of assistance in resolving school law matters.* An educational leader must have a rudimentary knowledge of how to use a law library so that he can utilize primary sources—constitutions, statutes, and judicial interpretations. A great handicap to effective use of the law in education is that too few educators know how to use primary sources and must rely on summaries and interpretations, always abbreviated or paraphrased rather than complete, and sometimes made by individuals not qualified to make them. One does not have to possess a law degree or be a member of the bar to understand the substances of most statutes and court opinions related to educational matters any more than he has to be a licensed physician to understand most reports on prevention of the common cold. This is not to imply, of course, that one should try to be his own lawyer or physician.

Also available in law libraries are key secondary sources which analyze and summarize specific points. The fact that these are written primarily for lawyers makes them no less valuable to the educator possessing the knowledges discussed under the preceding nine points. The educator is looking for a general orientation; he is not preparing a brief in technical legal style. Many procedural questions are essentially for the lawyer. Substantive educational matters, however, treated by statutes or discussed in opinions of courts are understandable to any reasonably intelligent individual.

Other sources of assistance for the educator comprise books written in the area of school law. These tend to summarize and discuss issues from the perspective of the educator. Like writings in any other field, they are of uneven quality, some being clear, accurate, and helpful and others being oversimplified or even misleading. The educator who has the above knowledges will be able to distinguish the good volumes from the poor ones.

In every state the state department of education in one way or another provides guidance on school law matters. Some states are better equipped to do this than are others, but the functions of a state department of education include enforcing the school laws of the state and assisting local districts to comply with them.

An effective local board of education or education association will have available the resources of an attorney skilled in school law matters. Dependent on the size of the district or association and the amount of work, the lawyer may be employed full time or on a retainer basis. A word of caution should be given here. Merely because someone is a member of the bar does not mean that he is well-qualified to give the kind of legal guidance needed by a school system or an education association. The selection of a school board or education association attorney should be made with great care, for his influence will be considerable.

It is hoped that the above ten essentials, offered with the admonition that the list is not all-inclusive, may constitute an approach to answering the question, What should educators know about school law? Many of the reasons for this knowledge have been implied in the foregoing. Four are outstanding, however, and seem to warrant explicit statement. First, educators must equip themselves with the knowledge of the law necessary to accomplish a basic function of the profession—passing on to children the American heritage and helping them to appreciate and improve our way of life within a government of laws. Second, as a matter of enlightened self-interest, educators should know their rights and their responsibilities. They should know enough to prevent unnecessary legal difficulties and thereby save time, money, and mental anguish. Third, as a matter of enlightened professional interest, educators should know enough law to improve the professional status of their occupation—a status greatly dependent upon the law. Fourth, and most important, there is a need for intelligently assessing the legal bases of both everyday and long-range educational policies. Educators must help to make the law work as an instrument in the progress of education. This can be done only if they know enough about school law to communicate effectively with those whose profession is law.

Chapter 13

LAW TO RESOLVE ISSUES

POLITICAL, *social, economic, and cultural change in American society has produced profound and complex problems regarding the conception and administration of education. That the parties to these problems have developed antagonistic approaches has served to dramatize and complicate the progress toward ultimate resolution of the issues. The issues are not restricted to education, for political, economic, and social factors are reflected in each problem. Basically, these difficulties exist because different groups support different approaches to the tasks involved in realizing America's historic objectives. Ultimately, these issues will be resolved only through a modification of existing laws. Before such action, however, full discussion of the ramifications of each issue is necessary.*

Ernest A. Engelbert, a political scientist, in this article presents an interesting résumé of the major problems and the points of conflict. He casts political scientists and educators as the chief protagonists. The following areas of contention are examined: (a) philosophy and the function of education; (b) education and the political process; (c) organization of education; (d) fiscal support of education; (e) training and control of personnel; and (f) success of education.

EDUCATION—A THING APART?

Ernest A. Engelbert

Following is a brief résumé of some of the points of conflict which reflect how difficult any resolution of the controversy has become. There are, to

Reprinted from *National Municipal Review*, Vol. 42 (Fall 1953), pp. 78–82.

be sure, a few educators who will side with political scientists on some of these issues and vice versa. Moreover, this presentation does not purport to represent the thinking of all members of these respective groups.

Philosophy and Function of Education. The disagreements between educators and students of government originate in what are regarded to be differing concepts about the philosophy and function of education in our governmental system. The educators view education as the queen of all governmental services. It is a public responsibility which they feel is so basic to the growth and culture of our civilization and to the values of our democracy that it cannot be treated in the same perspective as other governmental services. Education deals with life's most precious creation—the human being.

It is, therefore, a social and spiritual undertaking which cannot be classified in the same category as public works—utility regulation, police and fire protection—or other governmental undertakings. Educators feel that political scientists are primarily concerned with the structure and organization of education and not with the child. They also feel that the political scientist's interest in all phases of government causes education to be placed in a subordinate role.

Political scientists, on the other hand, counter with the claim that educators have a grossly exaggerated concept of the importance of education in a democracy vis-a-vis other governmental services. They deny that democracy, culture and civilization are primarily the product of our educational system, rather than the product of our total social and economic environment. They point to a number of other public services, such as health and social welfare, which likewise deal directly with the human being and which in many respects could be considered as sacrosanct as education. Political scientists feel that educators have developed a narrow and inbred concept about the function of education which is reducing its potential effectiveness for good government and democracy.

SCHOOLS VS. POLITICS

Education and the Political Process. Educators and political scientists are at odds over what should be the relationships of the educational function to the general political process. Educators look at education as a non-partisan function which should be divorced from the maelstrom of politics. They stress the need for keeping the educational function independent of general government, to protect it from the compromising situations, if not outright corruption, of the political environment.

They maintain that a public school system with independent boards of education elected directly by the voters is not only democratically organized but gives a greater measure of citizen interest and participation in the educational function than would occur if education were integrated into local government. The educators feel that the proposals of the political scientist to bring the function of education into the framework of general government would put education at the disadvantage and mercy of political elements, who would show neither understanding nor sympathy for the goals and needs of the schools.

To this argument the students of government answer that the educators exhibit a distorted and unwholesome attitude to the political process which undermines public confidence in the institutions of government. Political scientists stress the need for bringing the function of education more closely into relationship with other governmental services and the political process generally so that education will be exerting its rightful influence upon the problems and institutions of democracy. They contend that neither the educators nor the public schools make their biggest contribution to democracy by endeavoring to build a Chinese Wall around their function to exclude supposedly contaminating influences of politics.

As a professional group, educators should be the first to know that democracy thrives on participation and criticism, and they should be the first to appreciate that, when education withdraws from the general political process which is the essence of democracy, its chances of becoming a sterile activity with little significance for democratic society are correspondingly enhanced. Furthermore, political scientists point out the danger of building a special citizen clientele whose major interest is to protect politically the function of education. Political scientists maintain that the function of education should be the concern of all citizens, not simply parents or teachers; and that education will be less vulnerable to political attack if support is broadly based.

SCHOOL RECORD BETTER THAN CITY?

Organization of Education. Educators and political scientists are far apart upon the issue of the organization of education in our governmental system. Though educators admit that the educational system is by no means administratively perfect, they stress the fact that the school system has on the whole a far better administrative record than the average city or local government. They contend that the independent school system results in greater organizational effectiveness, in better assurance that the judgments of experts will prevail, in more financial stability, and in better relations between executives and elected officials.

Placing the education function under the city government, in their view, produces political and administrative decisions by persons unfit to make judgments for education, brings in unsympathetic budget scrutiny, leads to interference with teaching personnel and procedures, and breeds unwise competition between education and other public services. Educators point out that political scientists are so obsessed with theories of organization and administrative structure they would force all functions of government into the same mold, irrespective of the unique differences among subject matter fields that may be involved. The political scientist simply does not appreciate that the organization pattern for education cannot be the same as for the fire department.

On the other hand, the political scientist denies that, if separate school districts were abolished and the function of education incorporated into a department of city government, the professional quality of education would suffer. They point to the quality of programs and high administrative standards which are maintained by other governmental services as evidence that administrative integration does not compromise professional values and goals. They contend that independently elected boards of education and separate administrative structures make it difficult for either the people or their elected representatives to make any single effective over-all judgment about all governmental functions and their relationships. They stress the fact that the crying need today is for more responsible government which can come only through integration. Political scientists maintain that the proposals of educators weaken the whole system of state and local government, which in the end weakens the local system of school administration as well.

Fiscal Support of Education. Another area which has given rise to bitter controversy is how education should be supported fiscally. Educators have pressed strongly for complete financial autonomy for the public schools both in the revenue-raising and the expenditure process. At the local level they have fought bitterly to retain tax powers for school districts and freedom from municipal budget review. At the state level they have sought to write into the constitution and into legislation provisions which would guarantee education a fixed percentage of revenues. Educators contend that education suffers more than other governmental services in our uncertain fiscal environment, and that educators as political neophytes are least able to protect their interests in the give and take of the legislative process. Educators contend that political scientists are so absorbed in achieving over-all governmental fiscal harmony and financial review that they are blind to political realities.

Political scientists, contrariwise, state that they are seeking to develop an over-all governmental system which will permit the citizen to make one single intelligent over-all decision about his tax dollar rather than a series of unrelated judgments. They point out that other functions, such as highways and social welfare, are likewise trying to secure financial autonomy and security. This trend they maintain not only weakens the administrative powers of our chief elected officers but in a period of declining revenues leads to financial chaos. On the basis of inadequate teachers' salaries and school facilities, they deny that the function of education has spectacularly prospered as a result of independent financial authority. Political scientists take the position that, if educators had a more wholesome conception of the relative importance of other governmental services, the fiscal fears of the educators would disappear.

EDUCATION PERSONNEL

Training and Control of Personnel. Great division exists between educators and political scientists over the training and control of educational personnel. Educators have fought for an independent school system for the purpose of establishing high standards for the teaching profession. They have fostered the development of teacher training schools in separate professional schools within colleges and universities. Through their numerous professional associations they have exercised powerful influence in legislative halls upon the content of legislation. Through state and local boards of education they have endeavored to set the administrative standards governing the work and conduct of teaching and institutional personnel. Educators contend that only by vigorous surveillance and control of the entire educational system will their profession advance.

Political scientists reply that they heartily favor the professional advancement of education but not at the risk of giving a single profession complete control over a major function of government. They point out that no group, the medical profession not excepted, has gone so far in proposals to insulate its profession. They suggest that there is grave danger that the educational profession will become a hierarchy of inbred personnel. Political scientists recognize the need for a thorough-going merit system in the educational field, but want to insure that the experts will be on tap and not on top.

TO CHANGE OR NOT TO CHANGE

Success of Education. Finally, educators rest their case for an independent school system on the grounds that it has proved successful. Why change a system that has provided the world with the most spectacular educational achievement in the history of civilization? To integrate the school system into city governments as they now exist might retard the advancement of education for decades. Educators contend that, as far as the layman is concerned, the question of an independent school system is a closed issue. Why do not political scientists and others envious of education's status accept the public mandate and turn their efforts to issues of greater importance?

Political scientists reply that educators on this issue at least are living in the past and not in the future. They say that the remedy for advancing the cause of education does not lie in finding historical justification for a continuation of independent organization of the school systems. Educators still conceive of city government in terms of the corruption of the 1890s and ignore the advancements in municipal administration that have taken place in the last half century. Moreover, political scientists contend that educators are failing to interpret properly the crises in which public education finds itself today. The current financial struggles of the public school system, the rise of anti-school campaigns and the growing controversies of public versus private schools, are not coincidental phenomena nor unrelated to this issue. Political scientists contend that educators will need all the help they can get in their fight to protect public education. The first step is to reorganize education out of its independent status into a function that will give it better protection not only from the other institutions of government but the public at large.

Here then are some of the major issues in the controversy between schools and local government. Undoubtedly there are merits in the arguments on both sides. Unfortunately neither the political scientists nor the educators have given this problem sufficient attention. A number of studies urgently need to be undertaken to shed light on this major controversy. Educators and political scientists need to close ranks and restudy afresh the relationships of the public school system to the governmental process.

PART FOUR

Finance and Education

THE FAITH Americans have in the benefits of public education is attested to not only by laws that mandate attendance, but also by a long-standing agreement to finance public schools with tax monies. However, the rising cost of living, the increasing birth rate, the growing realization that formal learning facilitates economic and social mobility, the increasing demand by industry for skilled workers, and the marked decrease in employment opportunities for the unskilled have provoked a lively discussion about the ways in which public monies should be used to obtain a maximum return on the investment.

With the avowed purpose of equalizing educational opportunities, local, state, and national governments at present jointly finance public education. Many local and state governments have said that they cannot increase their contributions to public education and still maintain the other social services required of them. There is the possibility that the federal government may increase its contribution, but with the understanding that local and state governments will continue to meet their responsibilities.

In most states, the burden of maintaining public elementary and secondary schools belongs to the local community. Most states recognize the financial limitations of local communities and offer them aid. Usually, the state, after defining minimum standards for the educational services to be offered by the community, either contributes a lump sum to each community or apportions the money on the basis of student attendance. Of course, local communities are encouraged to exceed the state minima.

Federal assistance for public education is limited to the matching arrangement for vocational education, lunch programs, and projects of a similar nature. For the United States as a whole, the local community provides approximately 56 per cent of the cost of public education, the state approximately 40 per cent, and the federal government approximately 4 per cent. However, it is important to remember that the unequal distribution of wealth throughout the United States and within each state makes for unequal ability to support public education.

Approximately 98 per cent of all local taxes for public schools are derived from a tax on the assessed value of property. Rarely, if ever, is the assessed *value of property equal to the true value. At the present time, the assessed valuation of property for the entire United States is approximately 35 per cent of the true valuation. Furthermore, the tax rate varies from community to community and from state to state. In the United States as a whole the expenditure per pupil for 1960–1961 averaged $390.00. Alabama ranked fiftieth with an expenditure of $217.00 per pupil and Alaska and New York first with expenditures of $585.00 per pupil. Expenditures also vary from community to community within a state. In Connecticut, for example, the range for 1960–1961 was from $580.00 per pupil to $233.00 per pupil.*[1] *Despite a theoretical commitment to equal educational opportunities consistent with individual ability, actual practices leave much to be desired, and one's place of residence will often define what one's child's future will be.*

With the exception of defense expenditures, education in the United States is at present our biggest public enterprise. In comparison with expenditures for personal goods in 1960–1961, the picture was as follows; elementary and secondary schools, approximately 15 billion dollars; recreation, approximately 17 billion dollars; automobiles, approximately 30 billion dollars; alcoholic beverages and tobacco, approximately 15 billion dollars.[2] *It is important to note that the amount of money spent on public education has not kept pace with the growth of our national wealth. It has been pointed out that 35 years ago about 14 per cent of the Gross National Product (GNP) was spent on public services. Today, although about 30 per cent is spent that way, the public schools benefit only slightly. Thirty-five years ago, less than 3 per cent of our total annual wealth was devoted to public education, and today that figure is less than 4 per cent.*

Although the country gives every indication of becoming even wealthier, there is no sign that public education will be supported more generously. What we lack, many well-informed citizens believe, is a grand design to build an education-centered nation and to create a working policy that will achieve this goal. Today, sensitive to the acceleration of social evolution and aware of the apathy displayed by large groups of Americans, public-minded citizens have been pleading for a sustained discussion of the matter. Specifically, marked increases in the school-age population, in construction costs and maintenance, and in the responsibilities assigned the schools, combined with the reluctance of many people to accept additional financial responsibility, have caused these alert citizens to attempt to arouse the public to the significance of the problem.

There are many students of school finance, and their thoughts concerning aspects of the problem are presented under the following topics: need for a policy; general statistics; economics of the problem; income in relation to education; federal aid; and a proposal for financing public education.

[1] *Changing Times—The Kiplinger Magazine*, September 1961, p. 27.
[2] *Ibid.*, p. 26.

Chapter 14

NEED FOR A POLICY

WALTER LIPPMANN, *who is both a philosopher and a political scientist, argues that a strong and prosperous America will continue to exist only if its citizens guarantee, more earnestly than ever, support for programs that will raise the nation's educational level. Lippmann observes that the historic dreams of Americans no longer command the allegiance and respect they should, and the basic tenets of Americanism are often violated by Americans themselves. Although circumstances have elevated our country to a position of leadership, Lippmann is convinced that the nation is unprepared for the new tasks it faces. He suggests that only a drastic revitalization of education will help us become wise and able enough to offer to the world the kind of leadership it needs. He concedes that educational progress across the last century is most impressive. The world we live in has moved, however, even more rapidly. Lippmann identifies basic issues this way: "Why are we not planning to educate everybody as much as everybody can be educated, some much more and some less than others?" After demonstrating that the United States has the necessary wealth and indicating that, in regard to national defense, we have acquired the will to rise above the limitations of circumstance, he states: "In education we have not yet acquired that kind of will. But we need to acquire it, as we have no time to lose. . . . For if, in the crucial years which are coming, our people remain as unprepared as they are for their responsibilities and their mission, they may not be equal to the challenge, and if they do not succeed, they may never have a second chance to try."*

THE SHORTAGE IN EDUCATION

Walter Lippmann

1

What I am going to say is the result of a prolonged exposure to the continuing crisis of our western society—to the crisis of the democratic governments and of free institutions during the wars and revolutions of the twentieth century. Now it does not come easily to anyone who, like me, has breathed the soft air of the world before the wars that began in 1914—who has known a world that was not divided and frightened and full of hate—it does not come easily to such a man to see clearly and to measure coolly the times we live in. The scale and scope and the complexity of our needs are without any precedent in our experience, and indeed, we may fairly say, in all human experience.

In 1900 men everywhere on earth acknowledged, even when they resented, the leadership of the western nations. It was taken for granted that the liberal democracies were showing the way towards the good life in the good society, and few had any doubts of the eventual, but certain, progress of all mankind towards more democracy and a wider freedom. The only question was when—the question was never whether—the less fortunate and the more backward peoples of the world would have learned to use not only the technology of the West but also the political institutions of the West. All would soon be learning to decide the issues which divided them by free and open and rational discussion; they would soon learn how to conduct free and honest elections, to administer justice. Mankind would come to accept and comprehend the idea that all men are equally under the laws and all men must have the equal protection of the laws.

At the beginning of this century the acknowledged model of a new government, even in Russia, was a liberal democracy in the British or the French or the American style. Think what has happened to the western world and to its ideas and ideals during the forty years since the World Wars began. The hopes that men took for granted are no longer taken for granted. The institutions and the way of life which we have inherited, and which we cherish, have lost their paramount, their almost undisputed, hold upon the

Reprinted from *Atlantic Monthly*, Vol. 193, No. 5 (May 1954), pp. 35–38.

allegiance and the affections and the hopes of the peoples of the earth. They are no longer universally accepted as being the right way towards the good life on this earth. They are fiercely challenged abroad; they are widely doubted and they are dangerously violated even here at home.

During this half century the power of the western democratic nations has been declining. Their influence upon the destiny of the great masses of people has been shrinking. We are the heirs of the proudest tradition of government in the history of mankind. Yet we no longer find ourselves talking now—as we did before the First World War—about the progress of liberal democracy among the awakening multitudes. We are talking now about the defense and the survival of liberal democracy in its contracted area.

We are living in an age of disorder and upheaval. Though the United States has grown powerful and rich, we know in our hearts that we have become, at the same time, insecure and anxious. Our people enjoy an abundance of material things, such as no large community of men has ever known. But our people are not happy about their position or confident about their future. For we are not sure whether our responsibilities are not greater than our power and our wisdom.

We have been raised to the first place in the leadership of the western society at a time when the general civilization of the West has suffered a spectacular decline and is gravely threatened. We, who have become so suddenly the protecting and the leading power of that civilization, are not clear and united among ourselves about where we are going and how we should deal with our unforeseen responsibilities, our unwanted mission, our unexpected duties.

It is an awe-inspiring burden that we find ourselves compelled to bear. We have suddenly acquired responsibilities for which we were not prepared —for which we are not now prepared—for which, I am very much afraid, we are not now preparing ourselves.

We have had, and probably we must expect for a long time to have, dangerous and implacable enemies. But if we are to revive and recover, and are to go forward again, we must not look for the root of the trouble in our adversaries. We must look for it in ourselves. We must rid ourselves of the poison of self-pity. We must have done with the falsehood that all would be well were it not that we are the victims of wicked and designing men.

In 1914, when the decline of the West began, no one had heard of Lenin, Trotsky, Mussolini, Hitler, Stalin, and Mao Tse-tung. We have not fallen from our pre-eminence because we have been attacked. It would be much truer to say, and it is nobler to say it, that we have been attacked because our capacity to cope with our tasks had begun to decline.

We shall never have the spirit to revive and to recover so long as we try to console ourselves by shutting our eyes, and by wringing our hands and beating our breasts and filling the air with complaints that we have been weakened because we were attacked, and that we have been making mistakes because we were betrayed.

We must take the manly view, which is that the failure of the western democracies during this catastrophic half of the twentieth century is due to the failings of the democratic peoples. They have been attacked and brought down from their pre-eminence because they have lacked the clarity of purpose and the resolution of mind and of heart to cope with the accumulating disasters and disorders. They have lacked the clarity of purpose and the resolution of mind and of heart to prevent the wars that have ruined the West, to prepare for these wars they could not prevent, and, having won them at last after exorbitant sacrifice and at a ruinous cost, to settle those wars and to restore law and order upon the face of the globe.

2

I have said all this because it is only in the context of our era that we can truly conceive the problem of educating the American democracy. When we do that, we must, I believe, come to see that the effort we are making to educate ourselves as a people is not nearly equal to our needs and to our responsibilities.

If we compare our total effort—in public and private schools, and from kindergarten through college—with what it was fifty years ago, the quantitative increase is impressive. We are offering much more schooling of a more expensive kind to very many more pupils. By every statistical measure, the United States has made striking quantitative progress during the past century towards the democratic goal of universal education. The typical young American is spending more years in school than his father or grandfather; a much higher proportion of young people are going to high school and beyond; and more dollars—even discounting the depreciation of the dollar—are being spent for each person's education.

Now, if it were no more difficult to live in the United States today than it was fifty years ago; that is to say, if life were as simple as it was then—if the problems of private and community life were as easily understood—if the task of governing the United States at home and of conducting its foreign relations abroad were as uncomplicated as and no more dangerous than it was fifty years ago—then we could celebrate, we could be happy, we could be congratulating ourselves that we are making great progress in the task of educating ourselves as a democracy.

But we cannot make that comforting comparison without deceiving ourselves seriously. We cannot measure the demands upon our people in the second half of the twentieth century—the demands in terms of trained intelligence, moral discipline, knowledge, and, not least, the wisdom of great affairs—by what was demanded of them at the beginning of the first half of this century. The burden of living in America today and of governing America today is very much heavier than it was fifty years ago, and the crucial question is whether the increase of our effort in education is keeping up with the increase in the burden.

When we use this standard of comparison, we must find, I submit, that the increase in our effort to educate ourselves is of a quite different—and of a very much smaller—order of magnitude than is the increase in what is demanded of us in this divided and dangerous world. Our educational effort and our educational needs are not now anywhere nearly in balance. The supply is not nearly keeping up with the demand. The burden of the task is very much heavier than is the strength of the effort. There is a very serious and dangerous deficit between the output of education and our private and public need to be educated.

How can we measure this discrepancy? I am sorry to say that I shall have to use a few figures, trusting that none of you will think that when I use them, I am implying that all things can be measured in dollars and cents. I am using the figures because there is no other way to illustrate concretely the difference in the two orders of magnitude—the difference between what we do to educate ourselves, on the one hand, and on the other hand, what the kind of world we live in demands of us.

What shall we use as a measure of our educational effort? For the purpose of the comparison, I think we may take the total expenditure per capita, first in 1900, and then about half a century later, in 1953, on public and private schools from kindergarten through college.

And as a measure of the burden of our task—of the responsibilities and of the commitments to which education has now to be addressed—we might take Federal expenditures per capita, first in 1900, and then in our time, half a century later.

We differ among ourselves, of course, as to whether we are spending too much, too little, or the right amount on defense and on the public services. But these differences do not seriously affect the argument. For all of us, or nearly all of us, are agreed on the general size and the scope of the necessary tasks of the modern Federal government, both in military defense and for civilian purposes. Between the highest and the lowest proposals of responsible and informed men, I doubt that the difference is as much as 20 percent. That is not a great enough difference to effect the point I am making. That point is that the size of the public expenditure reflects—roughly, of course, but nevertheless fundamentally—the scale and scope of what we are impelled and compelled to do. It registers our judgment on the problems which we must cope with.

Now, in 1900, the educational effort, measured in expenditures per capita, was $3.40. The task, as measured by Federal expenditure per capita, was

$6.85. What we must be interested in is, I submit, the ratio between these two figures. We find, then, that in 1900 the nation put out $1 of educational effort against $2 of public task.

How is it now, half a century or so later? In 1953, the educational effort was at the rate of about $76 per capita. Federal expenditures, including defense, had risen to $467 per capita. The ratio of educational effort to public task, which in 1900 was one to two, had fallen, a half century later, to a ratio of one to six.

Perhaps I should pause at this point for a parenthesis to say, for those who may be thinking how much the value of the dollar has depreciated since 1900, that I am aware of that, but for the purposes of this comparison, it makes no difference. For while the dollar was worth probably three times as much in 1900 as in 1953, we are interested only in the relative effort in 1900 and 1953. The ratio would be the same if we divided the 1953 expenditures by three or if we multiplied the 1900 expenditures by three.

You have now heard all the statistics I shall use. The two ratios—the one at the beginning of our rise to the position of the leading great power of the world, and the other the ratio a half century later, when we carry the enormous burden abroad and at home—these two ratios show that the effort we are now making to educate ourselves has fallen in relation to our needs.

3

I must now remind you that this disparity between the educational effort and the public task is in fact greater than the figures suggest. For in this half century there has been a momentous change in the structure of American society, and it has added greatly to the burden upon the schools.

The responsibility of the schools for educating the new generation has become very much more comprehensive than it used to be. Ever so much more is now demanded of the schools. For they are expected to perform many of the educational functions which used to be performed by the family, the settled community, the church, the family business, the family farm, the family trade.

This is a very big subject in itself—much too big for me here—except to mention it as a reminder that the comparison between our real educational effort and our real public need is less favorable than the figures of one to two in 1900, as against one to six today. For the school today has a much larger role to play in the whole process of education than it needed to play in the older American society.

Can it be denied that the educational effort is inadequate? I think it cannot be denied. I do not mean that we are doing a little too little. I mean that we are doing much too little. We are entering upon an era which will test to the utmost the capacity of our democracy to cope with the gravest problem of modern times, and on a scale never yet attempted in all the history of the world. We are entering upon this difficult and dangerous period with what I believe we must call a growing deficit in the quantity and the quality of American education.

There is compelling proof that we are operating at an educational deficit. It is to be found in many of the controversies within the educational system. I am not myself, of course, a professional educator. But I do some reading about education, and I have been especially interested in the problem of providing education for the men and women who must perform the highest functions in our society—the elucidation and the articulation of its ideals, the advancement of knowledge, the making of high policy in the government, and the leadership of the people.

How are we discussing this problem? Are we, as we ought to be doing, studying what are the subjects and what are the disciplines which are needed for the education of the gifted children for the leadership of the nation? That is not the main thing we are discussing. We are discussing whether we can afford to educate our leaders when we have so far to go before we have done what we should do to provide equal opportunities for all people.

Most of the argument—indeed the whole issue—of whether to address the effort in education to the average of ability or to the higher capacities derives from the assumption that we have to make that choice. But why do we have to choose? Why are we not planning to educate everybody as much as everybody can be educated, some much more and some less than others?

This alleged choice is forced upon us only because our whole educational effort is too small. If we were not operating at a deficit level, our working ideal would be the fullest opportunity for all—each child according to its capacity. It is the deficit in our educational effort which compels us to deny to the children fitted for leadership of the nation the opportunity to become educated for the task.

So we have come to the point where we must lift ourselves as promptly as we can to a new and much higher level of interest, of attention, of hard work, of care, of concern, of expenditure, and of dedication to the education of the American people.

We have to do in the educational system something very like what we have done in the military establishment during the past fifteen years. We have to make a breakthrough to a radically higher and broader conception of what is needed and of what can be done. Our educational effort today, what we think we can afford, what we think we can do, how we feel entitled to treat our schools and our teachers—all of that—is still in approximately the same position as was the military effort of this country before Pearl Harbor.

In 1940 our armed forces were still at a level designed for a policy of isolation in this hemisphere and of neutrality in any war across the two oceans. Today, the military establishment has been raised to a different and higher plateau, and the effort that goes into it is enormously greater than it was in 1940.

Our educational effort, on the other hand, has not yet been raised to the plateau of the age we live in. I am not saying, of course, that we should spend 40 billions on education because we spend that much on defense. I am saying that we must make the same order of radical change in our attitude as we have made in our attitude towards defense. We must measure our educational effort as we do our military effort. That is to say, we must measure it not by what it would be easy and convenient to do, but by what it is necessary to do in order that the nation may survive and flourish. We have learned that we are quite rich enough to defend ourselves, whatever the cost. We must now learn that we are quite rich enough to educate ourselves as we need to be educated.

There is an enormous margin of luxury in this country against which we can draw for our vital needs. We take that for granted when we think of the national defense. From the tragedies and the bitter experience of being involved in wars for which we were inadequately prepared, we have acquired the will to defend ourselves. And, having done that, having acquired the will, we have found the way. We know how to find the dollars that are needed to defend ourselves, even if we must do without something else that is less vitally important.

In education we have not yet acquired that kind of will. But we need to acquire it, and we have no time to lose. We must acquire it in this decade. For if, in the crucial years which are coming, our people remain as unprepared as they are for their responsibilities and their mission, they may not be equal to the challenge, and if they do not succeed, they may never have a second chance to try.

Chapter 15

GENERAL STATISTICS

ON AN *annual basis, federal, state, and local expenditures for the maintenance of public elementary and secondary schools amount to approximately 15 billion dollars. The following breakdown of expenditures involving federal contributions; the relation of the federal, state, and local contribution to the growth of the GNP; state and local contributions; and expenditures per pupil comes from a publication of the Department of Health, Education and Welfare entitled "Progress of Public Education in the United States of America, 1962–1963."*

PROGRESS OF PUBLIC EDUCATION IN THE UNITED STATES, 1962–1963

Office of Education,

United States Department of Health, Education and Welfare

Federal Funds for Education. While recognizing the principle that the conduct of public education in the United States is a responsibility of the States and of local districts, the Federal Government provides leadership

Reprinted from *Progress of Public Education in the United States of America, 1962–1963*, FS 5.210:10005-63A (Washington, D.C., U.S. Government Printing Office, 1963), pp. 1–4.

and stimulation in particular fields of education through a wide variety of programs administered by a number of Government agencies. The following figures for 1961, the latest year for which complete data are available, indicate the extent of such aid, by purpose and level of education.

In fiscal year 1961, Federal support of education in educational institutions and agencies amounted to almost $1.5 billion in grants and payments, in addition to loans in the amount of $377.7 million.

SUPPORT OF EDUCATION IN EDUCATIONAL INSTITUTIONS

Grants	$1,481,633,000
Elementary-secondary education	516,411,000
Higher education	757,963,000
Adult education	112,334,000
Not classified by level	94,925,000
Loans	377,673,000
Elementary-secondary education	615,000
Higher education	377,022,000

Federal funds also supported services related to education, such as school lunch programs, and paid for services purchased from educational institutions. Data are not available on all Federal expenditures related to education, but funds for certain categories in this area can be identified as follows for 1961:

Payment for applied research	$680,159,000
Support of related school services	315,796,000
Training of Federal personnel in educational institutions	68,212,000
International education	58,886,000
Other	64,220,000

Relation of Educational Expenditure to Gross National Product. The following table relates the total expenditure for education to the gross national product. It shows that in slightly more than 30 years the percentage of the gross national product increased from 3.10 percent to 5.58 percent. The gross national product in the same period increased almost five times.

Financing Elementary and Secondary Schools. Figure 1 shows that major support of public schools in the United States is at the State and local level, with over half of all revenue receipts coming from local sources. Most funds from local sources are derived from local taxes and appropriations. Less than one-half of 1 percent comes from tuition, transportation fees, and gifts. (See Figure 1.)

Of the total expenditures for public elementary and secondary schools in 1959–60, more than one-sixth was for capital outlay and roughly four-fifths for current expenditures. Instruction—including teachers' salaries, textbooks, library books, and supplies—amounted to approximately two-thirds of the current expenditures. (See Figure 2.)

Expenditure Per Pupil. Expenditures for public elementary and secondary schools in the United States represent approximately five-eighths of the total expenditure for education. The per-pupil expenditure has increased from $313 in 1951–52 to an estimated $539 in 1962–63, an increase of 72 percent.

TABLE 1. GROSS NATIONAL PRODUCT RELATED TO TOTAL EXPENDITURES[1] FOR EDUCATION: UNITED STATES, 1929–30 TO 1961–62

CALENDAR YEAR	GROSS NATIONAL PRODUCT	SCHOOL YEAR	EXPENDITURES FOR EDUCATION	
			TOTAL	AS A PERCENT OF GROSS NATIONAL PRODUCT
1929	$104,436,000,000	1929–30	$3,234,000,000	3.10
1941	125,822,000,000	1941–42	3,204,000,000	2.55
1943	192,513,000,000	1943–44	3,522,000,000	1.83
1945	213,558,000,000	1945–46	4,168,000,000	1.95
1947	234,289,000,000	1947–48	6,574,000,000	2.81
1949	258,054,000,000	1949–50	8,796,000,000	3.41
1951	328,975,000,000	1951–52	11,312,000,000	3.44
1953	365,385,000,000	1953–54	13,950,000,000	3.82
1955	397,469,000,000	1955–56	16,812,000,000	4.23
1957	442,769,000,000	1957–58	21,120,000,000	4.77
1959	[3] 482,783,000,000	1959–60	24,722,000,000	5.12
1960	[3] 503,443,000,000	1960–61	27,300,000,000	5.42
1961	[2] 518,725,000,000	1961–62	[2] 28,962,000,000	5.58

1 Includes expenditures of public and nonpublic schools at all levels of education (elementary, secondary and higher education).

2 Estimate for 50 States and the District of Columbia.

3 Final data for 50 States and the District of Columbia.

NOTE: Unless otherwise indicated, data are for 48 States and the District of Columbia.

SOURCE: U.S. Department of Health, Education, and Welfare, Office of Education, *Biennial Survey of Education in the United States;* U.S. Department of Health, Education, and Welfare, Office of Education, *Digest of Educational Statistics,* 1962; U.S. Department of Commerce, Office of Business Economics, *Survey of Current Business,* July 1958 and July 1962.

FIGURE 1. REVENUE RECEIPTS FOR PUBLIC ELEMENTARY AND SECONDARY SCHOOLS, BY SOURCE: UNITED STATES, 1959–60

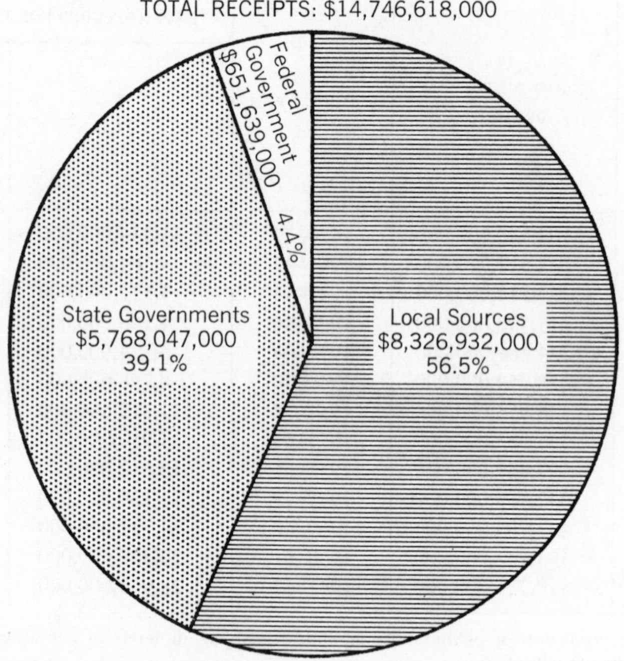

NOTE: Data are for 50 States and the District of Columbia.
SOURCE: U.S. Department of Health, Education, and Welfare, Office of Education, *Statistics of State School Systems, 1959–60*.

TABLE 2. TOTAL AND PER-PUPIL EXPENDITURES FOR PUBLIC ELEMENTARY AND SECONDARY EDUCATION: UNITED STATES, 1939–40 TO 1962–63

SCHOOL YEAR	TOTAL	EXPENDITURE PER PUPIL IN AVERAGE DAILY ATTENDANCE
1939–40	$ 2,344,049,000	$106
1949–50	5,837,643,000	259
1951–52	7,344,237,000	313
1953–54	9,092,449,000	351
1955–56	10,955,047,000	388
1957–58	13,569,163,000	449
1959–60[1]	15,613,255,000	472
1961–62[2]	18,105,285,000	515
1962–63[2]	19,543,692,000	539

1 Data for 50 States and the District of Columbia.

2 Estimates for 50 States and the District of Columbia.

NOTE: Unless otherwise indicated, data are for 48 States and the District of Columbia.

SOURCE: U.S. Department of Health, Education, and Welfare, Office of Education, *Biennial Survey of Education in the United States;* National Education Association, *Estimates of School Statistics, 1962–63.*

FIGURE 2. SUMMARY OF EXPENDITURES FOR PUBLIC ELEMENTARY AND SECONDARY SCHOOLS: UNITED STATES, 1959–60

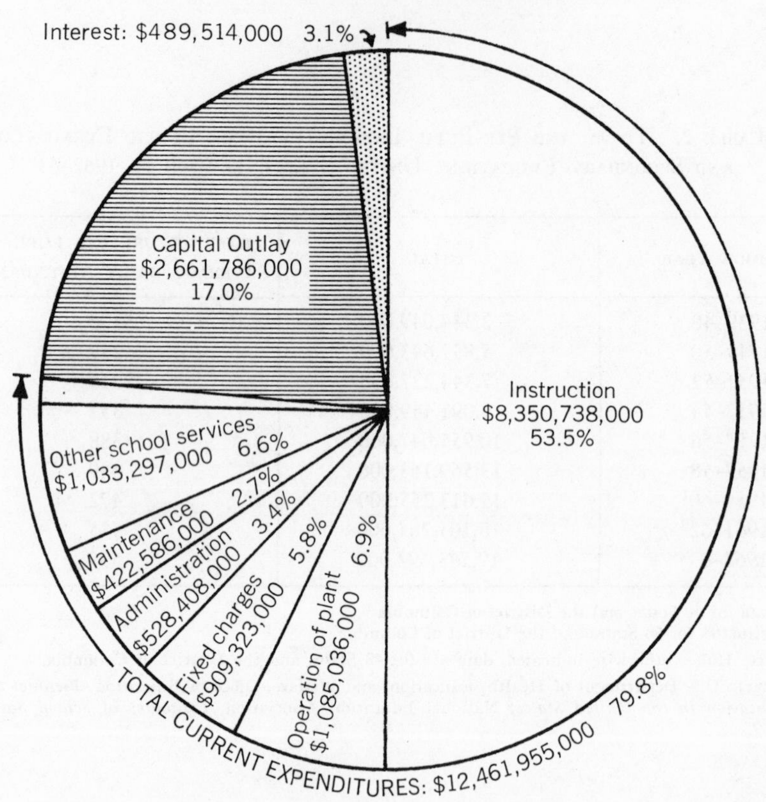

NOTE: Data are for 50 States and the District of Columbia. Because of rounding, detail may not add to totals.

SOURCE: U.S. Department of Health, Education, and Welfare, Office of Education, *Statistics of State School Systems, 1959–60*.

Chapter 16

ECONOMICS OF THE PROBLEM

MANY *economic factors must be considered in any attempt to determine whether our economy today can afford to contribute more to public education. It is worth noting that during the first decade to the twentieth century, approximately 1 per cent of the national income was allocated to public education; during the third decade, approximately 2.5 per cent; at the start of the fourth decade, approximately 3.1 per cent; at the start of the fifth decade, approximately 2.9 per cent; by the close of the fifth decade, approximately 2.5 per cent.*[1] *In light of the marked increase in the Gross National Product and a substantial increase in individual income, such data raise a number of crucial issues: (a) whether the duly elected representatives of the American people feel that the present allocation represents the maximum that the economy can tolerate; (b) whether citizens fully appreciate the economic and social value of education; and (c) whether the level of social thinking of the American people has reached the point where they are willing to develop a new way of tying the nation's economic system to the social services performed by the various federal, state, and local governmental agencies.*

The relationship of the emerging pattern of contemporary American economics to the financing of public education is offered by Proctor Thomson, an economist, in the following article.

[1] As reported in *The New York Times*, August 15, 1960.

ECONOMIC PROSPECTS AND SCHOOL FINANCE

Proctor Thomson

GROWTH IN THE NATIONAL INCOME

The economic prospect. The chief characteristic of the economic life of Western Europe and the Americas for the past century or more has been the regular and cumulative increase in total and per capita real income as a net result of technology plus capital accumulation, in an environment characterized by relatively free trade, private ownership, and emphasis upon individualistic-materialistic norms of conduct. (One of the major forms of "capital accumulation" has been investment in the productive capacity of the human agent; so much so, in fact, that the proportion of national wealth represented by intangible capital in people is probably greater in the advanced industrial economies than in the undeveloped areas of the world.)

Educational implications. Now, by and large, the greater the income per capita, the greater the propensity to save—in other words, the larger the fraction of national income potentially available for capital formation. Assuming that the rate of return on capital will not fall precipitously, or even appreciably, as new increments of investment are added to the existing stocks (assuming, that is, Knight's theory rather than Keynes's theory), additional savings will lead to additional investment at full or substantially full employment. Then, other things being equal, the greater the aggregate of tangible material capital, the greater will be the productivity of human resources complementary to capital and the greater will be the yield of new resources devoted to further education and training. To the extent to which this mechanism is operative, it indicates, in the foreseeable future, that the fraction of the national income devoted to schools, purely as investment, will rise rather than fall.

The effect of technological change may, however, introduce complications. (I defer till later the effect of technology on levels of skill.) In this context the effect depends on the impact that new methods of production will have upon the relative productivities of human versus nonhuman re-

Reprinted from *School Review,* Vol. 60 (October–November 1952), pp. 399–403, 474–480, by permission of the University of Chicago Press.

sources. If inventions are primarily capital-saving and labor-using (raise the marginal product of labor by more than that of "capital"), they will increase the profitability of resources devoted to education and training. But if the inventions are labor-saving, the reverse will be the case.

DIFFERENTIAL RATES OF GROWTH

The economic prospect. Within our own economy the rate of progress has differed widely between regions and communities, with the net result that the differential between the more and the less developed areas has probably increased rather than diminished through time. This is certainly the case if we compare a cross-section in 1800 with 1950 and is probably true for comparisons between 1900 and 1950. Even with relatively free mobility of labor out of, and capital into, these economically disfranchised regions, such as portions of the Southern Appalachians, the cutover Great Lakes area, and areas in which there is much of what passes for subsistence agriculture, cultural and political barriers have proved intractable. To this tendency of an increase in the differential between regions, there are, to be sure, notable and significant exceptions, of which the southern tier of counties in Iowa and the Tennessee Valley region offer outstanding examples. It goes without saying that the same tendency is manifest, but to much greater degree, as between Western Europe plus America as a whole and most of Asia, Africa, and portions of South America as a whole.

Educational implications. Widening the differences in wealth, income, and fiscal capacity of regions probably exerts no direct effect upon the proportional amounts that should be expended for public schools, but it profoundly influences the manner in which the national budget for education should be collected and disbursed. Given our ethical consensus of "equal treatment for equals," individuals with the same income position should bear identical tax burdens and receive an equivalent level of government services no matter where their place of birth or present residence. The ethical criterion of equivalent services has been advancd with particular urgency in the case of education, but no good reason exists for not applying it to other aspects of government as well.

In a federal system, with substantial local and state autonomy, differences in fiscal capacity of districts and states make realization of this criterion extraordinarily difficult; and the prospect that these differentials are widening rather than narrowing increases the need for forging methods of securing fiscal equity within a federal structure of government. In general, a program of inter-area transfer of government funds in the form of federal aid to the states and state aid to the districts is the only feasible method of securing equity without sacrificing the administrative and political advantages of decentralized control. While the claims of public education under this program cannot legitimately be denied, it must be emphasized once again that health, welfare, and local government, in general, should also participate and that it would be eminently desirable to secure a general or block grant-in-aid to be allocated among these different purposes according to the specific consensus of the states and the localities.

CHANGING COMPOSITION OF THE NATIONAL DIVIDEND

The economic prospect. As national income increases, the proportion of the total devoted to primary production (agriculture, forestry, and fisheries) falls cumulatively, the fraction taken up by secondary production (industry) rises and then falls gradually, while the proportion allocated to tertiary production (services of all types) cumulatively rises. An interesting aspect of the changing character of our national output is the increased importance placed on leisure. As productivity rises, workers prefer to take an increasing share of the product in the form of shorter hours per day and fewer work days per year.

Educational implications. The relative decline in primary production, with the concomitant growth of service industries, poses several crucial tasks for public education. In the first place, it is highly probable that service activities require, in general, higher levels of technical skill, adroitness in human relations, and understanding of our cultural heritage than those required by agricultural or factory work. Implications for the educational apparatus are obvious.

In the second place, the declining economic position of the agrarian sector coupled with the relatively high birth rate in rural areas means that migration from farms to cities, in order to equalize earnings of comparable individuals in the two areas, will continue at an accelerated pace. Accordingly, the vocational content of the rural school must be oriented to the possibility that many, perhaps more than half, of the children born on farms will find employment in other sectors of the economy.

Both these factors—increased emphasis on service activities and the reform of the rural curriculum—point to a rising level of expenditures for public education.

The shorter work week and the increased emphasis on leisure set the stage for a rising level of demand for education as a consumption commodity. While this development is not inevitable, depending as it does upon the cultural needs that are satisfied in leisure-time activities, it is at least possible. In particular, it opens up new vistas for the field of adult education, provided that enough adults can be weaned away from their television sets for one or two evenings a week.

CHANGES IN PATTERN OF SKILLS AND ABILITIES OF THE LABOR FORCES

The economic prospect. As a result of the changing composition of the national dividend, the kinds of productive activity engaged in by the labor force have systematically altered. In the long view, the most noteworthy example has been the declining importance of agriculture plus the increasing emphasis on factory work. Somewhat less spectacular, but ultimately of equal importance, is the enhanced role of service activities, such as beauty shops, hotels, and entertainment.

Tendencies toward changes of levels of skill are much more difficult to assess. It has long been a commonplace of economic folklore that the growth of factory technology is responsible for replacing skilled craftsmanship by unskilled machine-tending. But, by the same token, complex mechanical equipment requires engineers and scientists to design it, skilled machinists to fabricate it, and expert mechanics to keep it in running order. Moreover, to the extent to which the new technology is completely automatic, it merely replaces one group of skilled craftsmen (hand fabricators) by another (mechanics and machinists). Evidence as to the net result, or the balance, of these opposing forces is incomplete and fragmentary.

On the other hand, the changing composition of the national dividend, with increased emphasis on service-type industries, places increasing reliance on types of activities in which elements of skill, such as adroitness in human relations, are of conspicuous importance.

Educational implications. While tendencies toward changes of levels of skill are difficult to assess, my presumption that demand is increasing for higher levels of skill and competence means that relatively larger numbers of technical and professional personnel will be turned out by the educational apparatus. It is interesting to note, however, that apprehension is expressed in some quarters that we are producing, for example, too many college graduates or too many engineers and professional men. As evidence, it is pointed out that *relative* (though not, of course, *absolute*) earnings of executives and professional people have been declining within recent decades. To the extent to which this evidence is correct, it may indicate merely that entry into the professional class was artificially restricted by social and other barriers and therefore that the earnings structure did not represent an equalizing differential for the relative abilities actually involved. . . .

CHANGING ROLE OF GOVERNMENT IN THE NATIONAL ECONOMY

The economic prospect. At least four major tendencies can be identified under the changing role of government.

1. Over a period of time, the fraction of the national income devoted to government at all levels has cumulatively risen. In the United States, for example, it has advanced from around 7 percent at the turn of the century to over 30 percent at the present date. In part, this increase merely reflects forces already enumerated under the changing composition of the national dividend, since government in most of its aspects is a service or tertiary industry, but deep-seated changes in the role of the state in national life are also involved. At the same time, the permanent importance of government as a factor in the allocation of resources can easily be overemphasized for the reasons presented in the following paragraph.

One of the major short-run causes for the astronomical size of the federal budget is found in the demands of war and national defense. While the cold war, at varying temperatures, is an outstanding feature of the current political environment and is likely to remain so during our lifetime, war per se is not a permanent and lasting reason for the cumulative increase in the role of government unless, for some reason, the incidence or the intensity of armed conflict among nations is destined to increase cumulatively. For this gloomy possibility, present prospects apart, history provides singularly little evidence. Also, a large share of the nondefense budget of the government, both national and state, is represented by transfer, rather than by resource-using, expenditures. That is to say, the payment of interest on the debt, payment of social security and unemployment compensation, and the like, while not without incidental effects on the allocative mechanism, do not directly result in the production of goods and services by public agencies.

2. The second major tendency which can be identified, with respect to the role of government in the national economy, is the shift from framework or regulatory activities to service and investment activities.

3. Government revenues are increasingly provided by direct taxes rather than by indirect excises. The introduction and gradual extension of the progressive income tax has been one of the major social revolutions of our time. From the point of view of resource allocation, taxation represents payment for the use of goods and services. From the point of view of fiscal policy, taxation is a method of rationing purchasing power. The income tax is an efficient and equitable method of accomplishing both these objectives.

4. Recent decades have witnessed a decline in the relative importance of local government, coupled with rapid increase in the role of the central government. The relative position of state government has diminished slightly. In part, these changes are the result of the assumption of new functions and responsibilities by the central government, but, in part, they also represent delegation upward of some of the activities previously controlled by localities and states. Education has been one of the notable and striking exceptions to this trend.

Educational implications. Education has participated in the general expansion of the scope and role of government during the past several decades. It is impossible to say to what extent the acceleration of other activities of government has aided, and to what extent it has hindered, the growth of public education. Undoubtedly, the general trend in this area provided a more receptive environment for the expansion of the educational apparatus, but at the same time schools were obliged to compete with other government functions for the limited resources of the community.

In and of itself, the shift from indirect to direct forms of taxation should have provided leverage for additional money for public schools, but this potential contribution still awaits the development of adequate and efficient methods of federal aid, since it is the central government which has primary access to direct tax sources.

The declining importance of local government in other areas may significantly infect the vigor and potential of locally administered school systems in that it creates an attitude of indifference toward the functions of local government and an acquiescence toward bureaucratic centralism.

ROLE OF GOVERNMENT AND THE PROCESS OF SOCIAL CHOICE

The economic prospect. As a direct outcome of the vastly augmented role of the state in our national life (but deserving special listing because it raises a special list of problems), the political or group decision-making process has assumed an increasingly prominent part in our social structure. That is to say, the range of issues which are subject to group decision through the political process has widened, while the range of issues that are subject to group decision through other forms of social organization, such as the market mechanism, has considerably narrowed. (In order to clarify the issues, it is important to emphasize that the allocation of resources and the distribution of income via the market is also a form of *social* organization and not, as is sometimes represented, a purely "individualistic" method of dealing with the problems which lie within its scope. The economic organization involves specialization and division of labor; prices of goods and services, on the one hand, and prices of productive factors, on the other hand, are mutually and competitively determined through the mechanism of the market.)

The political process, or the mechanism of social choice as operating through the structure of representative government in a democracy, is complex and devious. It involves the formation of a consensus by the body politic; the balancing of interests at various levels; the interpretation (and reformulation) of the consensus by the representative assembly, together with the enactment of the specific legal and administrative instruments which embody the policy finally agreed upon by the group. It is obvious that the current trend toward transforming economic problems into political problems does not, of itself, mean that the resultant solutions will be more "rational" or even more democratic (in the sense of reflecting an informed consensus) than the solutions resulting from the operations of the market. Indeed, the desirability of the result depends upon the type of the problem in relation to the political decision-making process from which solution emerges. Many economists, for instance, believe that relative income distribution can and should be modified via the political process, as represented by the pattern of taxes and expenditures, but that relative prices are not appropriate candidates for political or administrative decision.

Educational implications. Changes in the relative importance of the political decision-making process present a challenge of the first magnitude for the future of American public education. Widening of the sphere of group action through the legislative machinery demands an alert and informed consensus on problems which are technically complex and are of fundamental importance to the preservation of democratic freedoms. The consensus must be sufficiently detailed to provide a guide for effective action at the legislative level and yet sufficiently flexible to allow for reorientation of policy, especially in the field of foreign relations, when circumstances require. The responsibilities of education, this time from the point of view of schooling as a "consumption" good, are obvious in general, but great care must be exercised in the practical implementation of these responsibilities.

While educational policy demands that the duties of citizenship, in the widest sense, be given increased emphasis at all levels, the frontier of decision will probably have to be made on what is now designated as the area of "higher" education. Specifically, we shall probably have to raise the question: "Does preparation for informed citizenship in a democracy now require universal public education up through, at least, the junior-college level?"

At present, about one-fourth of the population of college age are enrolled in institutions of higher learning. There is no gainsaying the fact that widespread extension of the school-leaving age will be enormously costly, both in terms of direct expense and, more importantly, in the sacrifice of alternative earnings of students whose entry into the labor force will be postponed for an additional two years. Moreover, since the additional schooling will be oriented toward political and social skills rather than toward acquisition of vocational abilities, the productive capacity of the individual will not be appreciably enlarged. The net effect of an affirmative decision to extend compulsory public education by two or more years will be the deduction of the initial two years from the lifetime income stream of the person and his family—a result which will place considerable burden on some of the low- and middle-income groups. Nevertheless, the results may be deemed worth the cost if the survival of democratic citizenship, as effective decision-making, is at stake.

STRATIFICATION AND SOCIAL MOBILITY

The economic prospect. By far the most puzzling and difficult of the tendencies that we have to evaluate is the relative importance of (1) the factors in our society which work toward increasing the flexibility and mobility of individuals in the social structure versus the factors which work toward stratification and (2) the continuance of barriers of caste and class.

So far as the market itself is concerned, the breakdown of regional isolation resulting from the growth of mediums of transportation and communication has surely increased effective competition and mobility during the past century or the past half-century. At the same time, certain types of large-scale financial and industrial organizations have increased in scope —though not nearly to the extent imagined in popular folklore—and this increase has tended to restrict freedom of entry into some fields.

Yet again, the underlying egalitarian tendencies of modern life have made sizable inroads on cultural artifices, such as caste and class barriers, which restrict the mobility of the human agent, though considerable progress here remains to be made. (One of the fascinating paradoxes of the current European scene is the vastly increased emphasis on economic equality, as represented by the redistribution of real income through taxation and controls, coupled with the preservation of social distinctions. For example, exaggerated deference is paid to university professors—a custom which American observers find intolerable and absurd.)

Educational implications. The relation between education, on the one hand, and democracy, citizenship, and social literacy, on the other hand, which has been treated above, is sufficiently obvious to have attracted considerable attention in the literature. Of even more fundamental importance is the contribution of education to social mobility. In this context, education appears primarily as a production good, the major question being the terms on which technical and professional training are accessible to individuals of varying degrees of ability and (family) income. The major restraint to freedom of entry into such training is that individuals of the requisite degree of ability cannot ordinarily borrow or secure capital to make potentially profitable investments in the development of their own productive capacities. The investment is made largely by the family and the community, resulting, under the existing procedures, in undercapitalization in the case of many individuals of high, or even of average, ability.

While the appropriate fiscal and educational policy to remedy this waste of scarce human resources is difficult to prescribe in detail, it must be emphasized that the *profitability* of embarking on this form of capital creation—say, by an expanded program of state or federal scholarships—is, in some sense, a secondary consideration. The primary rationale is the contribution made to social mobility as a dynamic aspect of democratic freedom.

SHORT-RUN ECONOMIC FACTORS

In retrospect, reviewing the conditions arising from the growth in the national income, changes in its composition, and in the composition of the labor force which produces it; problems arising from the expanded role of government and from the increased importance of the political process in the mechanism of social choice; and problems connected with socioeconomic mobility, we have amassed a formidable list of reasons for expecting that public education will, and should, command a larger share of our total resources over the long run. Still, the intractable fact remains that in recent years this fraction has been declining. Our analyses suggest, however, that conditions responsible for this must be sought in the realm of short-run, temporary, and disequilibrating forces in the economy, particularly in the impact of inflation on the revenue sources for public education. A corollary development is the enormous expansion of the defense and foreign-aid budget and the variety of effects which this might have on the community's preference for education.

Inflation. The approximate causes of inflation are everywhere the same, even though the nature of the phenomenon differs from period to period and from place to place. Although the primary cause of cumulative increase in prices is an increase in the stock of money, at a rate faster than the increase (if any) in the flow of goods and services (with or without any accompanying acceleration in velocity as people attempt to reduce the fraction of the income or assets which they hold in liquid form), each inflationary episode has its own peculiarities and its unique features.

With regard to quantitative magnitude, our current inflationary spiral is relatively modest: roughly at a rate of from 6 to 10 percent each year. As a rough forecast, suppose we assume that the maximum figure will be of the order of 10 percent and the minimum 5 percent.

With regard to the direct causes of the phenomenon, the major role has heretofore been played by the rise in bank deposits, with budgetary deficits of the federal government playing a secondary accompaniment, though our forecast is for these roles to be reversed in the immediate future. The increase in bank deposits has been facilitated by government support of the market for government bonds, in order to maintain low interest rates for the United States Treasury on this type of security. This support has the effect of allowing banks to augment their reserves by selling bonds to the Federal Reserve System. A secondary factor in the government support of the bond market has been official uncertainty about the behavior of that market if supports were suddenly withdrawn. Within recent months, this policy has been relaxed, with the result that bond prices have fallen slightly (interest rates have risen) and excess bank reserves have been reduced.

While an excess of expenditures over taxes seems an inevitable result of a federal budget that takes slightly under one-third of the national income, the logic of this procedure is open to serious question in view of the disadvantages of the inflation which arises from the deficit. Inflation, it must always be remembered, *is* a method of taxation. We would not deliberately enact a revenue bill which visits upon our economy the consequences which follow from prolonged inflation. The paradox which cries aloud for explanation, therefore, is why we prefer or allow a portion of our tax bill to be collected through the painful instrumentality of deterioration in the value of money. Perhaps, at the budgetary levels we are now approaching, the political process places a premium on voting "Yes" for every proposal to increase expenditures and "No" for every measure to increase taxes.

Inflation and local school revenue. The effect of inflation upon local school revenue is an oft-told story that may be briefly summed up by the observation that revenue from the local property tax, which is still the mainstay of municipal finance and even more so of school finance, is inflexible and cannot readily be adjusted to changes in the cost of government services. While state aid to school systems has made much headway in the past decade, it has not moved forward rapidly enough to fill the void.

Nevertheless, this obvious and simple explanation requires further clarification in view of the facts that (1) in some inflationary spirals, property values advance about as rapidly as does the index of prices in general (during recent years the sale value of real estate has even moved slightly ahead of the wholesale or retail price level); (2) the proportional share of property and nonproperty income has not materially altered in the course of the recent inflation.

It follows that the economic potential of the property tax has not markedly deteriorated and that the fraction of the national income which could be extracted for state, local, and school purposes without altering the real burden of this levy has not been materially affected by the postwar inflation. Indeed, the trend toward abandonment of this field of taxation by the states has been accelerated so that its potential for local communities and school districts has actually increased.

In spite of the previous statement, the cyclical inflexibility of the property tax is far from being a mere figment of the imagination. The causes of the inflexibility, however, are primarily administrative and political and rest, first, upon the technical difficulty of revising assessed values in line with true values and, second, upon the political unfeasibility of revising nominal rates upward rapidly enough to correct the lag between assessed values and market price. The results are plainly evident in the meager and inadequate programs of the majority of our school districts, in the erosion of the quality and quantity of teaching personnel, and in the antiquated and overcrowded structures which house many of our school children.

Chapter 17

INCOME IN RELATION TO EDUCATION

In our *present industrial-technological order there is a positive relationship between educational attainments and economic rewards. Individuals who can profit from college and post-graduate education will, generally speaking, enjoy a higher income than those with less formal schooling. This does not mean that formal education automatically increases the earning capacity of an individual. In addition to ability and opportunity, such factors as family background, level of aspiration, and level of competence are also significant determinants of one's earning capacity. It is possible, however, to measure the tangible relationship of education to income, despite the other factors. Although Americans claim to live in a classless society, it is interesting to note that we categorize ourselves and others into economic and social groups. It must be reemphasized that while, ideally, the measure of an individual's worth should be neither his economic status nor his social status, undue emphasis is nevertheless placed upon these two factors.*

Formal education, then, in addition to satisfying the needs of individuals in accordance with democratic values, also aids in the development of the talent and knowledge needed to support the economic needs of the industrial, agricultural, and service activities of the society. The fact that education helps increase an individual's earning power makes education both a consumer good and a source of profitable investment. An educated person not only enjoys a high standard of living, but he also pays the increased taxes demanded by a growing society and is able to meet the complex issues of daily living with greater astuteness.

Utilizing data from the 1940 and 1950 decennial censuses and from annual income surveys, Herman P. Miller, who is Special Assistant, Office of the Director, United States Bureau of the Census, discusses the earning capacities in relation to education of men for the period 1938–1958. In his first article his remarks cover the following items: (a) average income by educational level, (b) relation of annual income to age and education, and (c) estimates of lifetime income. In the second article, Miller utilizes the data collected in the 1960 census to bring his thesis up to date. He suggests that money spent on education usually pays a better return than other forms of investment.

MONEY VALUE OF AN EDUCATION

Herman P. Miller

Numerous studies, conducted under varying economic conditions, show that persons with more schooling tend to earn more money. This relationship seems reasonable if it is assumed that more schooling, particularly at the secondary school and college level, in some measure improves the productivity of the individual and thereby compensates for his investment of time, effort, and money.

On the other hand, it is by no means inevitable that money invested in education will pay dividends or that the rate of return will be constant over time. There is always the possibility, indeed the probability, that the higher incomes of those with more years of schooling are due in part to individual differences in intelligence, home environment, family connections, and other factors. It is, of course, almost impossible to measure the extent to which these factors enter into the relationship of education and income. There is, however, some evidence that "ability" as measured by scholastic achievement is highly correlated with earnings.

Since the present study makes no allowance for the personal and social costs incurred in the completion of additional schooling, the income gains associated with greater educational attainment, as shown here, are overstated. However, the available evidence suggests that, even if allowance were made for these costs, an investment in schooling pays, on the average, a better return than many other investments.

Of course, there is no guarantee that an investment in education will be financially profitable in any given case. This fact seems obvious, but it is often ignored. In 1958, for example, about 2.7 million men with college

Reprinted from *Occupational Outlook Quarterly,* Vol. 5, No. 3 (September 1961), pp. 3–10.

degrees had annual incomes under $7,000, whereas 1.9 million high school graduates received more than this amount. How can we explain the fact that so many college graduates had lower incomes than these men with only a high school education? The explanation must be sought in differences in occupations as well as in the quality of education, the abilities and efforts of individuals, and many other forces that impinge on the observed relationship between income and education. For example, many individuals with perhaps average intelligence continue their schooling, whereas many individuals with high intelligence never get as much education as they might assimilate or use to advantage. Furthermore, training completed at inferior schools cannot be equated with equal amounts of time and effort spent in training at excellent schools. For these and many other reasons, it would be fallacious and perhaps even harmful to draw inferences about individual cases from the evidence presented here for the general population.

Although this article deals with the material rewards of an education, this does not imply that the more subtle satisfactions that come with greater educational attainment have been ignored. The cultural and social advantages associated with more schooling may well be worth their cost in time, money, and effort, even if the economic advantages should cease to exist. The only justification for focusing on the economic advantages is that, at present, they are the only ones capable of even approximate measurement.

ANNUAL INCOME

Some of the basic statistics pertaining to the relationship between annual income and educational attainment are presented in Table 1, which shows the variations in average (mean) annual income over the 1939–58 period for men with different amounts of schooling.[1] Women have been excluded because a large proportion of them are not in the labor market and many of those who work are employed on a part-time basis. For these and other reasons, the relationship between their income and education may be distorted in the statistics. In contrast, since practically all adult men are full-time workers, it can be assumed that any advantages gained from more schooling are reflected in their incomes.

In every year for which data are presented, the completion of an additional period of schooling was associated with higher average incomes. This finding supports similar conclusions drawn from numerous other studies dating back to the early part of the century. Although income levels have changed considerably during the past 20 years, the basic relationship between the extent of schooling and income appears to have remained much the same.

[1] Statistics presented in this article are based on data from the 1940 and 1950 decennial censuses of population and the annual income surveys conducted by the U.S. Bureau of the Census since 1945.

TABLE 1. MEAN INCOME (OR EARNINGS)[1] FOR MALES 25 YEARS OF AGE AND OVER, BY YEARS OF SCHOOL COMPLETED, SELECTED YEARS

YEARS OF SCHOOL COMPLETED	1939	1946	1949	1956	1958
Elementary:					
Total	$1,036	$2,041	$2,394	$3,107	$3,096
Less than 8 years[2]	([3])	1,738	2,062	2,613	2,551
8 years	([3])	2,327	2,829	3,732	3,769
High school:					
1 to 3 years	1,379	2,449	3,226	4,480	4,618
4 years	1,661	2,939	3,784	5,439	5,567
College:					
1 to 3 years	1,931	3,654	4,423	6,363	6,966
4 years or more	2,607	4,527	6,179	8,490	9,206

1 Data for 1939 are restricted to persons reporting $1.00 or more of wage or salary income and less than $50 of other income and to native white and Negro males 25 to 64 years old only. Data for 1946 represent total money earnings. Data for 1949, 1956, and 1958 represent total money income.

2 Includes persons reporting no years of school completed, not shown separately.

3 Information not available.

Contrary to the expectations of some analysts, the economic advantages of completing additional years of schooling have not diminished in recent years.

Although income generally tends to increase with education, the attainment of a particular level of schooling (e.g., completing the fourth year of high school) yields a greater return than the completion of any of the years leading up to it. This difference may reflect a selection in terms of ability and application between those who do and those who do not complete their schooling. For example, in 1958, the average annual income for men who started high school but did not graduate was more than $400 more for each additional year of schooling than for men who had completed elementary school only. High school graduates, however, received almost $500 a year more per year of schooling than men who started high school but never graduated. Similarly, men who attended college but did not graduate had, on the average, about $700 more per year of schooling than high school graduates. The comparable differential for college graduates was about $900 per year of schooling.

The educational level of the population has risen considerably during the past generation. The proportion of college graduates in the population has nearly doubled during the period, and the proportion of high school graduates has also risen dramatically. At the same time, the relative supply of workers with only an elementary education has declined. How has this increase in the supply of more highly educated workers affected income differentials? Have the incomes of college graduates, relative to other groups in the population, been pushed down because of the relative increase in their numbers or has the demand for their services increased sufficiently to offset any such tendency?

These questions cannot be answered categorically on the basis of available statistics. There is some evidence that elementary school graduates have had smaller relative gains in income than high school graduates, despite the reduction in their relative numbers. (See Table 2.) In contrast, the relative difference in income between high school and college graduates has not changed much over time, and there is even some evidence that it has increased in favor of college graduates during the past few years.

TABLE 2. MEAN INCOME (OR EARNINGS)[1] BY LEVEL OF SCHOOL COMPLETED, FOR MALES 25 YEARS OLD AND OVER, SELECTED YEARS

YEAR	ELEMENTARY–HIGH SCHOOL DIFFERENTIAL			HIGH SCHOOL–COLLEGE DIFFERENTIAL		
	AVERAGE INCOME		PERCENT DIFFERENCE	AVERAGE INCOME		PERCENT DIFFERENCE
	ELEMENTARY SCHOOL GRADUATE	HIGH SCHOOL GRADUATE		HIGH SCHOOL GRADUATE	COLLEGE GRADUATE	
1939	(2)	$1,661	(2)	$1,661	$2,607	57
1946	$2,327	2,939	26	2,939	4,527	54
1949	2,829	3,784	34	3,784	6,179	63
1956	3,732	5,439	46	5,439	8,490	56
1958	3,769	5,567	48	5,567	9,206	65

1 See footnotes to Table 1.
2 Information not available.

Since 1946, for example, the incomes of high school graduates have risen considerably more, in percentage terms, than those of elementary school graduates. In 1946, the differential between these two groups was only $600, or about 26 percent. By 1958, the differential was about $1,800, or 48 percent. This change is in part related to the fact that a large proportion of the elementary school graduates are employed in occupations such as farmers, farm laborers, and nonfarm laborers which tended to have lower relative income gains in recent years than most other occupations.[2] It is also possible, of course, that even for occupations such as operatives and craftsmen, in which a relatively large number of elementary school graduates are employed, high school graduates received greater increases than persons who never attended high school.

2 Median total money income of employed males increased between 1950 and 1958 by 3 percent for farm laborers, 51 percent for nonfarm laborers, and 27 percent for farmers. In contrast, the increase during this period was 57 percent for professional workers, 54 percent for managers and officials, and 55 percent for craftsmen.

In contrast with the changing relationship between the incomes of elementary school and high school graduates, there has been relatively little change in the income differential between high school and college graduates. In 1939, the average income of college graduates was about $950 more (57 percent) than for high school graduates. In 1956, the absolute difference between the incomes of these two groups increased to $3,050, but the relative difference was unchanged at about 56 percent. By 1958, the absolute difference rose to $3,650, and the relative difference also increased to 65 percent. The data suggest that, during the recession years 1949 and 1958, the incomes of college graduates were less affected than those of other groups, perhaps reflecting a greater tendency for persons with less schooling to be unemployed. There is also some possibility that the income gains for college graduates partly reflect a rise in the proportion of men in this group with graduate school training. The influence of this factor is probably quite small, however, since there is no evidence of a sharp rise in the proportion of college men with graduate training. Moreover, the absolute difference in income between all college graduates and those with graduate training amounted to only about $200 in 1958.

Why has the relative income differential between high school and college graduates been generally maintained, and indeed recently increased, despite the large relative increase in the size of the college-trained population? One explanation may be that the demand for college graduates has kept pace with the supply. Because of the country's changing technology, the demand for trained workers has accelerated since the end of World War II, and industry has absorbed the increased flow of graduates from colleges and universities. The nature of this change is most evident from the sharp rise in the proportion of the labor force engaged in professional and managerial work, the two occupational groups in which the great majority of college graduates are employed. Since 1940, the proportion of men employed in these two groups combined has increased by about 50 percent.

RELATION OF ANNUAL INCOME TO AGE AND EDUCATION

As might be expected, additional years of schooling have little immediate impact on earnings. Inexperienced workers in most occupations start at a relatively low level of earnings which tend to increase as skill and experience are acquired. Therefore, the financial benefits of additional schooling tend to accumulate over time, and the greatest impact is felt during the period of peak earnings. These tendencies are clearly reflected in Table 3 which shows the earnings at an average age of 30 (i.e., after about 10 years of work experience) and 50 (i.e, about the age of peak earnings) for men with different amounts of educational attainment.

TABLE 3. MEAN INCOME (OR EARNINGS)[1] FOR MALES 25 TO 34 YEARS AND 45 TO 54 YEARS OF AGE, BY LEVEL OF SCHOOL COMPLETED, SELECTED YEARS

AGE GROUP AND LEVEL OF SCHOOL COMPLETED	1939	1946	1949	1956	1958
Elementary school graduate:					
25 to 34 years	(2)	$2,011	$2,540	$3,685	$3,663
45 to 54 years	(2)	2,629	3,247	4,289	4,337
Percent change	(2)	31	28	16	18
High school graduate:					
25 to 34 years	$1,335	2,335	3,246	4,813	4,909
45 to 54 years	2,256	3,744	4,689	6,104	6,295
Percent change	69	60	44	27	28
College graduate:					
25 to 34 years	1,956	3,237	4,122	6,307	7,152
45 to 54 years	3,575	5,242	8,116	11,702	12,269
Percent change	83	62	97	86	72

1 See footnotes to Table 1.
2 Information not available.

In view of the limited range of earnings possible in most of the jobs for which elementary school graduates can qualify, it is not surprising that their annual earnings after a lifetime of work are not much higher than their initial earnings. College graduates, on the other hand, tend to choose careers in which the possibilities of high earnings are much greater and therefore have peak earnings which, on the average, far exceed initial earnings.

Since 1939, the differential between initial and peak earnings has decreased considerably for elementary and high school graduates, but has not changed much for college graduates. Evidently, among workers who have not attended college, the younger groups have succeeded in making greater relative gains in earnings than those with more experience. Between 1939 and 1949, these gains were probably due in large measure to reduced unemployment among the younger (and less skilled) groups. The further gains during the past decade may reflect the "across-the-board" wage increases stipulated in union contracts negotiated during the postwar period which resulted in greater relative gains for lower paid workers. They may also reflect the gradual rise in the statutory minimum wage for many industries.

As previously noted, there was no reduction in the incomes of college graduates relative to high school graduates between 1939 and 1958, despite the great rise in the proportion of persons with a college degree. Among men 25 to 34 years old, the proportion of college graduates doubled between 1940 and 1959, whereas the proportion of men who terminated their schooling with elementary school graduation was reduced by two-thirds.

Despite the relative decrease in the number of elementary school graduates 25 to 34 years old since 1946, their earnings have not risen as much as the earnings of high school graduates, and therefore the income differential between these two groups has widened. (See Table 4.) Between 1946 and 1958, the earnings of elementary school graduates increased by about 82 percent, compared with an increase of about 110 percent for high school graduates and 121 percent for college graduates.

TABLE 4. MEAN INCOME (OR EARNINGS)[1] BY LEVEL OF SCHOOL COMPLETED FOR MALES 25 TO 34 YEARS OLD, SELECTED YEARS

YEAR	ELEMENTARY-HIGH SCHOOL DIFFERENTIAL			HIGH SCHOOL-COLLEGE DIFFERENTIAL		
	AVERAGE INCOME		PERCENT DIFFERENCE	AVERAGE INCOME		PERCENT DIFFERENCE
	ELEMENTARY SCHOOL GRADUATE	HIGH SCHOOL GRADUATE		HIGH SCHOOL GRADUATE	COLLEGE GRADUATE	
1939	(2)	$1,335	(2)	$1,335	$1,956	47
1946	2,011	2,335	16	2,335	3,237	39
1949	2,540	3,246	28	3,246	4,122	27
1956	3,685	4,813	31	4,813	6,307	31
1958	3,663	4,909	34	4,909	7,152	46

1 See footnotes to Table 1.
2 Information not available.

LIFETIME INCOME

Estimates of lifetime income provide an insight into the financial returns associated with education which cannot be readily obtained from the annual income data. These estimates are derived from data showing variations in the income of individuals in different age and education groups at a given time, specifically the calendar years for which data are presented. The figures are, therefore, based on incomes of a cross-section of the male population in 1939, 1946, 1949, 1956, and 1958, and do not actually trace an individual's income from the time he starts to work until he retires.

Standard life-table techniques were used in computing the lifetime income figures shown in Table 5. First, an estimate was made of the number of children born in 1939, 1946, 1949, 1956, and 1958 who would survive to each given year of age. By way of illustration, it was estimated from the appropriate life tables that of every 100,000 infants born alive in 1956 about 96,000 would survive to age 18, at which time they would enter the labor market. The basic problem consisted of estimating the life span of these survivors and the amount of income they would receive during their lifetime. For this purpose, it was assumed that survival rates for men in each education group would be the same as for all white males in 1956. On this basis, it was estimated that these 96,000 men would live a total of nearly 5 million man-years between age 18 and the time the last one died. It was further assumed that during each year of life, these men would receive an average income corresponding to that received by men in the same age group with the same amount of education in 1956. For example, as shown in Table 5, it is estimated that a man born in 1956 who subsequently completes high school would receive a lifetime income of $253,631 (computed on the basis of the average income of male high school graduates in 1956).

It should be noted that the estimates presented in Table 5 reflect the economic conditions and other circumstances which existed in each of the years for which data are shown. Some of the differences from year to year may reflect changes in these circumstances. The increase, for example, in the

TABLE 5. ESTIMATED LIFETIME INCOME FOR MALES, BY YEARS OF SCHOOL COMPLETED, SELECTED YEARS

YEARS OF SCHOOL COMPLETED	1939	1949	1956	1958
	INCOME FROM AGE 18 TO DEATH			
Elementary:				
Total	(1)	$113,330	$154,593	$154,114
Less than 8 years	(1)	98,222	132,736	129,764
8 years	(1)	132,683	180,857	181,695
High school:				
1 to 3 years	(1)	152,068	205,277	211,193
4 years	(1)	185,279	253,631	257,557
College:				
1 to 3 years	(1)	209,282	291,581	315,504
4 years or more	(1)	296,377	405,698	435,242
	INCOME FROM AGE 25 TO 64			
Elementary:				
Total	$37,172	91,932	127,047	127,286
Less than 8 years	(1)	79,654	108,310	106,449
8 years	(1)	106,889	148,033	149,687
High school:				
1 to 3 years	53,011	121,943	169,501	175,779
4 years	67,383	148,649	208,322	215,487
College:				
1 to 3 years	73,655	173,166	243,611	269,105
4 years or more	104,608	241,427	340,131	366,990

1 Not available.

value of a college education by about $140,000 between 1949 and 1958 reflects the increase in prices as well as changes in many other economic factors. Moreover, no allowance is made for the possible intrusion of extraneous factors in the relationship between lifetime income and education.

In every year for which data are presented, additional schooling is associated with a very substantial increase in lifetime income. On the basis of conditions in 1958, an elementary school graduate could expect to receive during his lifetime about $52,000 (or two-fifths) more income, on the average, than the person who terminated his formal education before completing the eighth grade. The difference, on the average, between the expected lifetime income of an elementary school and a high school graduate was equally striking. In 1958, an elementary school graduate could expect, on the average, a lifetime income of about $182,000 compared with approximately $258,000 for a high school graduate, a differential of about $76,000, or 42 percent.

Since a college degree is required for many, if not most, high-paying jobs, it should come as no surprise that the greatest income gains associated with additional schooling appear at the college level. On the basis of 1958 data, a college graduate could expect to earn about $435,000 during his lifetime, compared with $258,000 for the high school graduate. It can, therefore, be estimated that the years of schooling beyond the high school level resulted in an increase of about $177,000 in lifetime income, or about $40,000 for each additional year.

Since 1939, the more highly educated groups have clearly made the greater relative gains in expected lifetime income. Thus, for example, in 1946, high school graduates could expect to earn only 35 percent more between the ages of 25 and 64 than elementary school graduates (Table 6). Twelve years later, the differential in favor of the high school graduates

TABLE 6. ESTIMATED INCOME RECEIVED FROM AGES 25 TO 64, FOR MALES, BY LEVEL OF SCHOOL COMPLETED, SELECTED YEARS

YEAR	ELEMENTARY-HIGH SCHOOL DIFFERENTIAL			HIGH SCHOOL-COLLEGE DIFFERENTIAL		
	ELEMENTARY SCHOOL GRADUATE	HIGH SCHOOL GRADUATE	PERCENT DIFFERENCE	HIGH SCHOOL GRADUATE	COLLEGE GRADUATE	PERCENT DIFFERENCE
1939	(1)	$ 67,383	(1)	$ 67,383	$104,608	55
1946	$ 84,687	114,023	35	114,023	168,983	48
1949	106,889	148,649	39	148,649	241,427	62
1956	148,033	208,322	41	208,322	340,131	63
1958	149,687	215,487	44	215,487	366,990	70

1 Information not available.

increased to 44 percent, reflecting the fact that the expected income of high school graduates rose more rapidly during this period.

A comparison of the relative income gains that could be expected by high school and college graduates reveals essentially the same pattern. Evidently, the differential in favor of college graduates dropped from 55 percent in 1939 to 48 percent immediately after the end of the Second World War, probably because a larger proportion of the college graduates continued to serve in the Armed Forces during part of 1946. By 1958, however, the differential between high school and college graduates rose to 70 percent, reflecting a greater relative income gain for the college group. These figures support the conclusion presented earlier that the large increase in the number of college graduates during the postwar period has not adversely affected their income position.

This study raised the question whether or not the marked increase in the number and proportion of high school and college graduates during the past generation has been associated with a reduction in income differentials for these groups. Theoretically, such a reduction could be expected in the long run, assuming no changes in the demand for more highly educated workers. The period under consideration, however, was relatively short and was one in which there were changes in the demand for, as well as in the supply of, such workers. Therefore, no fundamental theoretical issues are involved in this study. The problem is merely one of ascertaining what has taken place and why.

The figures show that the large relative increase in the supply of high school and college-trained workers did not adversely affect their relative income positions. On this basis, it is concluded that the demand for more highly educated workers has kept pace with the increased supply of such workers and, as a result, their relative income position has not changed.

EDUCATION: AN ADVANTAGE FOR A LIFETIME

Herman P. Miller

There are still many in our society who have had little exposure to education, disadvantaged people who cannot see how education can help them or their children. A look at the money value of education may help convince these people that schooling may lead to an improvement in their economic status.

Because the 1961 article [i.e., the previous article. ED.] was based on 1958 data, interest has been expressed in more comprehensive and up-to-date estimates of average lifetime earnings drawn from the 1960 Census of Population. Here are the highlights of these statistics.

Investing in education is somewhat like taking out life insurance. Nobody can tell you exactly how long you are going to live. Neither can anyone tell you how much you will earn in a lifetime. But from your age, sex, occupation, and other items of personal information, your insurance company can judge your chances of living a given number of years. Similarly, the U.S. Bureau of the Census—relying on data gathered in the 1960 Census of Population—has been able to prepare estimates of average lifetime earnings for men, based on educational attainment.

Women have not been included in these estimates because a large proportion of them do not enter the labor market, and many who do, obtain only part-time employment. Although education has a direct impact on the earnings of women employees, its value is much more indirect for the large proportion of them who are not in the labor force. Practically all adult men are employed full time, and the advantages of schooling are reflected more directly in their paychecks.

EDUCATION TALKS

In 1959—the year for which income data were collected in the 1960 Census of Population—a college graduate could look forward to earning about $417,000 during his lifetime, assuming no subsequent drastic changes in economic conditions. (See Table 1.) That would be some $170,000 more than

Reprinted from *Occupational Outlook Quarterly*, Vol. 7, No. 4 (December 1963), pp. 5–8.

the average lifetime earnings of a man whose formal education ended with high school graduation. With lifetime earnings estimated at $247,000, a high school graduate would be $63,000 ahead of an elementary school graduate, who, in turn, would be likely to average $41,000 more than the man who left school before completing the eighth grade.

TABLE 1. ESTIMATED AVERAGE LIFETIME EARNINGS FOR MEN, BY YEARS OF SCHOOL COMPLETED

YEARS OF SCHOOL COMPLETED	LIFETIME EARNINGS FROM AGE 18 TO 64
Elementary school:	
Less than 8 years	$143,000
8 years	184,000
High school:	
1 to 3 years	212,000
4 years	247,000
College:	
1 to 3 years	293,000
4 years or more	417,000

SOURCE: Testimony of Herman P. Miller before Subcommittee on Employment and Manpower, U.S. Senate Committee on Labor and Public Welfare (88th Cong., 1st sess.), July 31, 1963.

A WORD OF CAUTION

Keep in mind that education is only one ingredient, although a very important one. There is no assurance that it alone can pave your way to high earnings. In 1961, about 2.6 million men—46 percent of all college-educated males—had annual incomes under $7,000, whereas 3.3 million men—23 percent of the male high school graduates—earned more than that amount.[1] Responsible for the lower incomes of so many college men are differences in occupations, in social position, in the quality of education, and in the abilities and efforts of individuals. Moreover, many individuals with perhaps no more than average abilities continue their schooling, whereas many highly capable people never get as much formal education as they could assimilate. At the other end of the scale, the lifetime earnings differences between elementary school graduates and those who fail to get through grade school must also be viewed from many angles. Dropping out of the elementary school may often indicate a lack of either capabilities or traits that enable an individual to deal successfully with the workaday world.

[1] Current Population Reports, Consumer Income, Series P-60, No. 39, Bureau of the Census.

A BOON TO ALL

What good is a high school diploma to somebody who is not going on to college, who is going to enter an occupation where the emphasis is on aptitude and know-how—not on formal education? For a clear answer, look at Table 2. Craftsmen and foremen, as a group, average about $36,000 more in a lifetime if they are high school graduates. Even the semiskilled—operatives and kindred workers—stand to earn some $24,000 extra, thanks, at least partly, to a high school diploma.

TABLE 2. ESTIMATED AVERAGE LIFETIME EARNINGS OF ELEMENTARY AND HIGH SCHOOL MALE GRADUATES, SELECTED OCCUPATIONS

OCCUPATION	LIFETIME EARNINGS FROM AGE 18 TO 64		
	ELEMENTARY SCHOOL GRADUATES	HIGH SCHOOL GRADUATES	DIFFERENTIAL
Craftsmen, foremen, and kindred workers			
Average	$207,000	$243,000	$36,000
Brickmasons, stonemasons, and tilesetters	204,000	233,000	29,000
Carpenters	178,000	209,000	31,000
Compositors and typesetters	229,000	254,000	25,000
Electricians	236,000	257,000	21,000
Linemen and servicemen, telegraph, telephone, power	228,000	263,000	35,000
Machinists	215,000	239,000	24,000
Mechanics and repairmen	191,000	216,000	25,000
Painters, construction and maintenance	167,000	189,000	22,000
Plasterers	197,000	239,000	42,000
Plumbers and pipefitters	222,000	252,000	30,000
Toolmakers, and diemakers and setters	264,000	282,000	18,000
Operatives and kindred workers			
Average	186,000	210,000	24,000
Busdrivers	172,000	196,000	24,000
Mine operatives and laborers	173,000	212,000	39,000
Truck and tractor drivers	189,000	212,000	32,000
Operatives and kindred workers	188,000	212,000	24,000
Service workers, including private household			
Average	147,000	181,000	34,000
Barbers	184,000	189,000	5,000
Firemen, fire protection	215,000	244,000	29,000
Policemen and detectives	192,000	230,000	38,000

The reasons are not hard to find. Occupational outlook information shows that employers prefer high school graduates. Take a carpenter, for example. With a high school diploma, he has a better chance to get a regular job with a big and diversified construction firm. Then, rain or shine, he works every day. Unlike the less educated—and often also less trained—carpenter, he may be the last to be laid off in slack times. Or take the busdriver. With a high school diploma, he may be considered for a job by a nationwide carrier—without it, he may need a little luck to turn the wheels for any firm, often at lower pay.

The fact that high school graduates are often preferred for apprentice training also increases the financial benefits of the high school diploma. Intensive and thorough training for skilled occupations may be worth more in the long run than picking up the skills on the job.

A MATTER OF DEGREE

Higher education is practically a "must" nowadays for entry into the professions. For those still in doubt about the monetary value of an education, table 3 should offer final proof. The figures in this table, too, are averages—many men earn more, many make less. Moreover, these are earnings only—not total income. This difference is important for many of the highly paid professional men, especially those who practice independently, who have income from investments, real estate, and other sources.

By far, the highest paid professional men are the doctors, whose average lifetime earnings were estimated at nearly three-quarters of a million dollars. They are closely followed by dentists and lawyers whose respective earnings total about $600,000 each. In the other professions, the earnings level off considerably. Here the remuneration of geologists stands out, mainly because so many of them work for the large oil companies. Since discovery of new oil fields largely depends on their skill, payments for geologists' services tend to be high.

Although it is still possible for exceptional individuals to achieve professional status in some fields without formal higher education, such opportunities are likely to dwindle in the years ahead. Table 3 indicates that in the professions, those whose formal education is limited to high school average consistently less than those with 4 or more years of college. In a profession such as engineering, where a large proportion of the people who identified themselves as engineers in the 1960 Census of Population lacked a college degree, the combination of exceptional ability and extensive experience—in lieu of a college degree—has helped individuals over the hurdles. However, in engineering, as well as in other fields, opportunities to change jobs and earn higher salaries are far better for those with a college background.

It is quite likely that in the future the higher earnings that reward professional careers will be increasingly awarded to those who have at least a bachelor's degree.

TABLE 3. ESTIMATED AVERAGE LIFETIME EARNINGS OF PROFESSIONAL MEN, BY LEVEL OF EDUCATION

OCCUPATION	LIFETIME EARNINGS FROM AGE 18 TO 64		
	AVERAGE	4 YEARS OF HIGH SCHOOL	4 OR MORE YEARS OF COLLEGE
Doctors	$717,000		$721,000
Dentists	589,000		594,000
Lawyers	621,000		642,000
Engineers:			
Aeronautical	395,000	$378,000	418,000
Electrical	372,000	327,000	406,000
Mechanical	360,000	339,000	399,000
Civil	335,000	285,000	380,000
Natural scientists:			
Geologists	446,000		470,000
Physicists	415,000		431,000
Chemists	327,000	274,000	351,000
Biologists	310,000		322,000
Social scientists:			
Economists	413,000		432,000
Psychologists	335,000		345,000
Statisticians	335,000		387,000
Teachers:			
Elementary school	232,000		241,000
High school	261,000		265,000
College	324,000		328,000
Accountants	313,000	286,000	362,000
Clergymen	175,000	156,000	184,000

Chapter 18

FEDERAL AID — CONCEPTS AND ISSUES

THE INCREASING *involvement of the federal government in education has been discussed from many points of view over the years. These discussions have raised issues about the relationship of the individual to the state and to its various levels of government. The need to clarify this relationship requires a reexamination of the values of the society as they affect the responsibilities of the individual, and any new agreements must, of necessity, be reflected in law. This chapter has two purposes. The first is to present, through the medium of a summary of the Report of the Study Committee on Federal Responsibility in the Field of Education, the ideas held by men in government concerned with education. In formulating its position, the committee dealt with issues pertaining to educational responsibility, finances, school lunch programs, vocational education, federally impacted areas, and public libraries.*

The second intention of this chapter is to present a sample of public thought through testimony given to committees of the House of Representatives and the Senate when Congressional hearings were held on federal aid to education.

These were the issues dealt with: "Is federal aid to education necessary?" "Will federal aid mean federal control?" "Should nonpublic schools receive grants or loans from the federal government?" "Would the appropriation of federal funds to the public schools discriminate against those children who attend parochial schools?" "Are parents of parochial school children unfairly subject to double taxation?" "Would federal aid to public schools result in the restriction of religious liberty?" "Is aid to nonpublic schools constitutional?" "Should federal funds be granted to segregated school systems?"

REPORT ON FEDERAL RESPONSIBILITY IN THE FIELD OF EDUCATION

Committee on Federal Responsibility in the Field of Education

1. Adequate education of all American youth is essential to the preservation of the Republic and to the welfare of the Nation in peace and war. The country's most important resource lies in its citizens more than in its soil or climate or extent of territory. Full development of this resource is dependent upon solutions to a number of pressing problems. An unprecedented rise in school enrollment presents a monumental task for our vast elementary and secondary school system; it will in the 1960's pose a problem of similar magnitude to the institutions of higher learning. A current shortage of teachers may become increasingly serious as enrollments grow. Years of depression and war have left a grossly inadequate school plant, and our competition with communism obliges us to utilize our human resources to a greater extent than ever before in our history.

2. These problems combine to emphasize that the financial needs of education are on the rise. We believe that the American people can and will devote an increasing share of their income to education. The question is not whether the United States can afford to spend more on education than it does now, but how the needed funds can best be raised. We have sought the answer to this question within the framework of the traditions of American development though it would have been simpler had we accepted the easier and often urged alternative of passing the problem to the Federal Government for solution. It is necessary to remind ourselves that our primary interest in the immediate schooling of the child must not overwhelm our responsibility to preserve for him a pattern of political and social organization which has values beyond the immediate needs of education. His heritage of individual liberty is a sacred obligation. In seeking solutions to the compelling educational problems of the Nation we have, therefore, attempted to follow these general guides:

Report submitted to the Commission on Intergovernmental Relations by the Study Committee on Federal Responsibility in the Field of Education, June 1955, pp. 5–11.

a. Every child has a right to an education commensurate with his capacity.

b. The purposes of a universal education include not only personal growth but also service to the community and training for responsibility in a free world.

c. Educational responsibility rests initially with the parent, but is shared with the community, the State, and the Nation. It is a function both of government and of private groups. It cannot be allocated to any one level of government, but should be undertaken at the lowest level capable of its satisfactory performance. The presumption must be that responsibility remains within the lesser unit until there is clear demonstration of the necessity of its transfer from one to another.

d. A viable federalism presumes, not only a restraint on the part of the Federal Government, but a full assumption of initiative and responsibility on the part of the parents, the localities, and the States. If there is a disturbing tendency of the Federal Government to assume disproportionate powers, we feel there is an equally dangerous tendency of the States and the communities to neglect, and even abandon, their proper roles. Delinquency in the latter can be quite as serious as an excessive ambition in the former.

e. The educational system, like other institutions in a free society, should be responsive to the desires of the people it serves. Because democracy possesses vitality to the extent that individual citizens are convinced that their choices make a difference, it is most frequently manifested at the local level, where the individual voice has a chance to be heard. Furthermore, the closer the relationship between means and end—between the cost of education and the services received—the greater the sense of responsibility toward both.

f. Fundamental values in our educational system must be a compound of diversity and variety on the one hand and a certain amount of uniformity on the other. The pressures for standardization are clear and often compelling. Yet the traditions of pluralism retain their meaning and essential importance in a democratic society. The preservation of a concept of the multiple sources of truth is peculiarly the responsibility of education, for here we are concerned, not only with the maintenance of diverse points of view in education which is but one area of public policy, but with the preservation of the fundamental concept that a calculated diversity is a major protection against the compulsions of a sterilizing orthodoxy and a paralyzing absolutism. The urgent demand for uniformity of standards must modify rather than parallel this basic pluralist assumption.

g. Extensive citizen participation in public education at the local level provides an important training in self-government. While derivative from the immediate purposes of the educational system, this is nonetheless a feature of our present structure worthy of careful conservation.

h. Governmental structure is not an end in itself, but a vehicle for the realization of community purposes. While it serves its purpose it should be assiduously preserved, but when it is no longer adequate, it must be modified. Preservation of structures and practices as ends in themselves militates against the maintenance of a viable federalism.

i. The tendency of responsible legislators is to attach restrictions to the expenditures of funds they appropriate. To the extent that the Federal Government supplies funds such restrictions are therefore likely to increase.

j. Population mobility, the necessity of reasonable equality in economic position and cultural maturity of residents of the United States, and current international competitive realities have created a national interest in an adequate education for all of our citizens. These same considerations require a higher level of public expenditure for education than has heretofore been made.

k. Fiscal capacity for the performance of a function of government should not be measured in terms of revenues actually available, but in terms of basic resources upon which the unit of government may draw, if it is willing to do so. Nor do we believe that a desirable pattern of governmental activity should be compromised or abandoned because it may be administratively more convenient or publicly more palatable to collect revenues through central facilities.

Education being a function of government which is particularly suited to local control, unused State and local tax capacity and new fiscal resources should be available for educational purposes before being utilized for other functions of government.

3. Every American child has the right to an adequate educational opportunity. That opportunity can be provided by local communities and States more satisfactorily and equitably than by the Federal Government. School boards, in cooperation with State legislatures, are in a better position to determine the adequacy of their schools than Congress or any other agency of the Federal Government.

4. The Federal Government could not achieve universal educational opportunity by appropriating money to the States to be distributed at their discretion. Federal action could bring about universal educational opportunity only if grants-in-aid were conditioned upon control of distribution of both State and Federal funds. Such control is contrary to the established principle of State and local school control and probably unacceptable to the States.

5. The costs of the expansion in enrollment in the next ten years can be taken care of by State and local governments if they continue to increase their school contributions at the rate at which they have been boosting them in recent years. To improve standards at the rate at which they have been advancing in the last few decades will require greater efforts. An effective way in which the Federal Government can aid these efforts is to reduce its tax

bill. Such action should make it easier for State and local governments to raise additional funds for the schools without increasing the total tax burden of their citizens.

6. Research does not sustain the contention that Federal funds are essential to support the elementary and secondary school systems. All economic resources in the United States, all wealth and income, are within the borders of the [50] States and subject to their taxing powers. There is no magic in the United States Treasury. Federal support for education can come, in the last analysis, only from the same basic resources which are available to States and local governments.

The American people have built up over the last century and a half the most extensive school system in the world under State and local responsibility. We believe that this system will continue to grow and show progress.

There are, of course, differences in fiscal ability among States. Those differences have been narrowing considerably in the last two decades; but they are still substantial. Efforts to narrow the gap should aim at raising the economic level and the capacity of the less wealthy States rather than to subsidize them. Existing disparities have been and can continue to be ameliorated by the prudent use of the progressive Federal tax system. State and local government can be more effectively strengthened by taking less money from the States than by taking out more, and returning part of it as a Federal subsidy even with minimum controls attached. Many States and localities are not now utilizing their borrowing capacity to the degree to which they could and should use it to cope with the existing shortages in school plant facilities.

It is our opinion, however, that the appropriation of relatively small sums of Federal aid for school construction—amounting to 10 percent or 20 percent of the present State and local outlay of almost $2 billion a year—may delay rather than advance school construction. Districts not eligible in 1 year may hold off their building plans on the chance of being able to buy their school houses at 50 cents on the dollar a year or two later.

Schools have been State and local responsibility by long-standing and firmly embedded tradition. They should so remain. We have not been able to find a State which cannot afford to make more money available to its schools or which is economically unable to support an adequate school system.

7. States have an obligation to form a genuine partnership with their local communities, to help them discharge their school responsibilities. Differences in economic capacity of local communities within States are often greater than among States. State government's role should be the stimulation of educational programs to meet community needs, and the reduction of the differential between wealthy and less wealthy communities so as to assure a constantly improving overall educational program throughout the State.

State responsibility is not limited to financial support. There are many legal restrictions and other handicaps which hamper an adequate school finance program; they should be corrected.

The most urgently needed measures seem to be these:

a. States should participate in the support of both current operations and capital outlays of the schools where the financing of the needed facilities clearly exceeds the ability of the properly organized districts.

b. Restrictions upon the taxing and borrowing powers of State and local governments should be eased or removed, if they are out of line with contemporary requirements and prevent the financing of adequate service and facilities.

c. State aid should enable every school district to carry on a minimum school program.

d. State laws should facilitate and stimulate organization of school districts through consolidation of small uneconomical districts into larger units which can offer a more complete and diversified school program and have a more adequate tax base.

e. The States should assist local assessors to apply uniform standards of property tax assessment throughout the State in compliance with existing requirements of State constitutions and statutes.

f. States should use their best effort to acquaint their citizens with the needs of the schools and to urge broad participation in school affairs.

Failure of the States to remove these restrictions and obviate these and similar handicaps often forces the people to seek aid of the Federal Government to undertake programs which otherwise could be undertaken by States and localities.

8. The general conclusion is that Federal aid is not necessary either for current operating expenses for public schools or for capital expenditures for new school facilities. Local communities and States are able to supply both in accordance with the will of their citizens.

9. *School Lunch Program.* a. The school lunch program is beneficial to the health and welfare of school children. It should be strengthened and made available to the maximum number of pupils who wish to participate.

b. The distribution for school lunch purposes of surplus commoditites which exist as a result of the farm price support program is justified and desirable, and should be continued as long as such surpluses exist.

c. The program is within the sphere of responsibility of the States and school districts and the parents, and should be carried by them. It is not a Federal responsibility. Federal participation should be gradually tapered off, as State and local communities demonstrate their ability to assume the cost, and as economic conditions warrant.

10. *Cooperative Vocational Education.* a. The teaching of vocational knowledge and skills is an essential part of the general education in our

schools. The vocational education program should be strengthened as an integral part of the high school program.

b. Vocational education, as all education, is a primary responsibility of States and local governments. There is a continuing interest of the Federal Government in vocational education where a clear national interest is involved.

c. In the activities which do not specifically contribute to training for defense there should be a tapering off of Federal grants. State and local governments can and should provide from their own funds an adequate vocational program.

d. In programs where a clear national interest is involved there should be a continuing Federal participation in their financing, so that there will be a hard core of Federal responsibility left which could be expanded in times of emergency. Many of the detailed specifications and minute controls of the existing grant-in-aid programs should be eliminated.

11. *Federally Impacted Areas.* a. There is a clear obligation of the Federal Government to make payments toward the construction and operation of schools in areas where Federal activities have led to an influx of children and thereby imposed a special burden upon communities.

b. Wherever possible the responsibility should be returned to localities as a more adequate tax base is developed.

c. There will be cases where the Federal Government will have to carry the responsibility permanently because of the particular nature of the situation.

12. *Public Libraries.* a. The public library is an important community service and an essential part of overall public education, particularly of adult self-education.

b. The establishment and support of public libraries is a State and local responsibility. It is desirable that States take a more active part in the provision of library service, particularly in the areas which are now inadequately served.

c. The considerations which apply in determining whether Federal grants-in-aid should be given to public schools for operating expenses should also apply to public libraries.

d. Having decided under *b* above that public libraries are primarily a State and local responsibility, and having reviewed the question of whether or not there is such a compelling national interest involved as to justify action by the Federal Government, we have concluded that there is not.

13. The principles which we have outlined earlier in this statement apply at all levels of education, elementary, secondary, and higher. However, there are some special problems in the field of higher education and its relationship to the Federal Government that do not apply to elementary and secondary schools.

The following testimony of various citizens was compiled by William B. Rich, a specialist in the field of state education programs, Division of State and Local School Systems, Office of Education.

FEDERAL AID TO EDUCATION: ISSUES BEFORE CONGRESS

William B. Rich

IS FEDERAL AID TO EDUCATION NECESSARY?

Abraham Ribicoff, Secretary of Health, Education, and Welfare: The United States is the first Nation in history to establish universal public education as its goal. We have demonstrated that education can give each individual a chance to develop his particular talents to the fullest. This kind of educational system is a remarkable and original concept in the perspective of history. This concept, coupled with a concept of educational excellence, represents an essential requirement for our continued progress and survival as a free nation. Our future requires that appropriate educational opportunities be freely available to all children and youth no matter what their background, circumstance, or place of residence.

We have made substantial progress toward meeting this goal, but rising enrollments and increasing costs have placed great pressure upon the States and local school districts. During the past decade, enrollments in public elementary and secondary schools have increased from 25.7 million to 37.6 million, or 46 percent. Annual expenditures have increased during the same period from $6.5 billion to $16.5 billion, or 154 percent. The cost per pupil in our public education system has jumped from $284 a year to $496 per year—an increase of 75 percent.

While Federal tax dollars have increased 85 percent in the postwar years, State and local communities have had to increase their tax revenues by 221 percent. From 1946 to 1959, while the Federal debt increased by 6 percent, State and local debt soared by more than 300 percent. Property taxes, the traditional source of revenue for education, are in many areas rapidly approaching the limits of reasonableness.

Reprinted from *School Life*, Vol. 43, No. 8 (May 1961) pp. 14–18.

Another problem confronting many a school district is the great mobility of our population. Each year more than 5 million people move from one State to another. Today's resident of a high-income State with a better-than-average school system may well find tomorrow that his children must attend a less-than-average school in a low-income State.

Moreover, the States exhibit varying degrees of ability to support education. For example, the State with the highest income enjoys almost four times the income per public school pupil found in the State with the lowest income. On the other hand, the lowest income State has almost 50 percent more children in public schools for each 1,000 population than the highest income State.

The next decade holds no promise of lessened impact upon our resources available for support of education. Enrollments in public elementary and secondary schools will increase from 36 million in 1959–60 to 44 million in 1968–69. These increases in enrollment will require an additional 437,000 instructional personnel and 600,000 new classrooms by the end of the 10-year period. Of more striking importance, however, is the fact that greatest pressure will be placed upon us during the next 5 years. We cannot afford, in my judgment, to permit any of our children to go even one year longer than necessary without adequate instructional staff and classroom facilities.

John B. Swainson, Governor of Michigan: It has become increasingly evident to us in Michigan that the problems confronting education in 1961 must be attacked on all three levels of government. Only by a total mobilization of our Nation's resources can we meet the current and future demands on education.

. . . The sharply unequal educational opportunities within our nation cannot be solved by one State or region. . . .

Our desire is to weld a partnership of public school support that is capable of meeting the educational tasks we, as a nation, face.

Peter T. Schoemann, vice president, AFL–CIO: The real problem facing America today, it seems to us, is whether the National Government is playing its fair part in support of education. We think it is not; we urge that it should. The trade unions of this country have been urging Federal aid to education for many years. We feel that it is essential.

William G. Carr, executive secretary, National Education Association: However, my primary concern is not with economics, but with the improvement of education. I want to emphasize that Federal financial support as proposed in this bill does not bring with it undesirable side effects and that it can strengthen our economy today while strengthening the future of our Nation.

Although we cannot speak of children as "materials," the fact remains that we have been willing to invest more in tangible things than in our human resources. It may be that we, as the largest professional organization of teachers in the country, should be presenting our case more forcefully. We would like to press more research on learning and a greater investment in the proper utilization of these young people so they can help to bring about a stronger nation, a better world, and more satisfying lives for themselves.

We know many of the principles which facilitate learning. Good lighting in the classroom, adequate laboratories and equipment, and moderate-sized classes. Lack of financial support makes it impossible to apply these principles. The citizens of a State may be willing to support good schools but the lack of an adequate tax base at the local and State level makes the job impossible.

Edgar Fuller, executive secretary, Council of Chief State School Officers: The broader and more effective Federal tax system dominates the local and State tax systems, and impinges strongly on local and State tax sources. In spite of the devastating Federal competition, State and local governments have managed to increase their tax revenues much faster than the Federal Government during the past 15 years. During the same period their debt has increased at a rate approximately 39 times faster than the Federal debt. State and local funds are increasingly difficult to obtain. A more equitable allocation of responsibility for the support of public education among the three levels of government is needed.

Harley L. Lutz, government finance consultant, National Association of Manufacturers: (1) Public education is not a Federal responsibility. The sphere of Federal services and functions should be limited to those matters which can be handled only by the National Government. (2) There is no "crisis" in education, present or impending, that would justify assumption by the Federal Government of responsibility for a service completely outside the area of its truly national tasks; (3) The Federal Government is in a precarious financial situation . . . (4) Federal support inevitably leads to Federal control and this control will distort and devitalize the educative process. (5) Federal money cannot buy excellence in learning.

Roger A. Freeman, research associate, Institute for Studies in Federalism, Claremont Men's College (Calif.): . . . the school building situation has shown a tremendous improvement in the past decade and is continuing to improve. States and communities are building classrooms at a more rapid rate than they will need to maintain through the 1960's. Some communities, to be sure, are lagging, particularly those which have for some years been waiting for the Federal Government to do the job for them. Whether that situation would be improved by the enactment of a program at this time remains to be seen.

. . . The public schools have been able to increase their teaching staff proportionately faster than the rise in enrollment, and the number of pupils per teacher was gradually reduced from 35.6 in 1900 to 24.4 in 1961. Meanwhile the educational requirements for teachers were sharply raised and their professional preparation lengthened. Few teachers are hired nowadays who do not, at least, have a college degree, except in the very few States in which a fractionalized school organization survives. The level of teacher compensation has apparently been sufficient to attract a growing number of qualified applicants.

K. Brantley Watson, for the Chamber of Commerce of the United States: The people of the United States have proved that they are more than equal to the challenge to meet their educational needs via local and community action. Their efforts have made it possible for us to boast, proudly, that more Americans receive a better education, are taught by better teachers and do their learning in better facilities than is possible in any nation on earth.

We conclude then with the contention that grant-in-aid legislation like that under consideration of this committee and especially under title I of S. 1021 is not only unnecessary, but might slow down local and State action upon which needed improvements in the quality of education actually depends.

WILL FEDERAL AID MEAN FEDERAL CONTROL?

W. W. Hill, Jr., for Member State Chambers of the Council of State Chambers of Commerce: Federal control will follow Federal aid just as surely as night follows day, but it may not be apparent until the schools are so dependent on Federal support that they cannot conveniently relinquish what appears to be a free subsidy.

Mr. Watson: In the chamber's view, Federal subsidies mean Federal decisions about school problems which should be left to the States or their communities. . . .

Mr. Lutz: Federal support of education means a transfer of responsibility from the home to a bureaucracy; from Main Street to Washington. It means Federal rather than state control, a central regimentation that will eventually extend to curriculum content. . . .

The plain fact is that Federal control and supervision of the educational grants will be both proper and necessary, the most strenuous disclaimers to the contrary notwithstanding. The Congress and the Executive authorities would be guilty of gross neglect if they were to fail in providing for inspection and supervision and, where necessary, the right to direct the use of grant funds, or to withhold them, in order to assure proper application of the money and compliance with the Federal intent. As the grants increase in amount and acquire permanence in duration, Federal control will extend more and more deeply into subject matter. . . .

Mr. Freeman: The significant effect of the grant-in-aid type of bills probably would be a shift in control from general State and local authorities, that is, from State legislatures, parents and communities, in other words from lay persons, to the nationally organized educational administrators at Federal, State, and local levels. . . .

The fact is that most—though not all—of the school administrators who have appeared before congressional committees to testify on Federal aid proposals have spoken in favor of grant programs controlled by State departments of education. When the Governors of the States were polled by the House Committee on Education and Labor in 1959, they spoke overwhelmingly in opposition to Federal aid. None of tens of thousands of State and local boards of education has appeared to testify on behalf of Federal school aid for at least the past 5 years, but some have testified against it. The National School Boards Association has refused to endorse or support Federal aid.

Governor Swainson: This tradition of Federal support to public education has not changed the basic philosophy of local control of education held by the citizens of Michigan. We have at no time seen evidences of Federal control of our educational programs accompanying Federal assistance. We anticipate no difficulties with S. 1021 concerning Federal control. This is not an issue here.

Secretary Ribicoff: These programs of Federal assistance to education have, in my judgment, been administered without evidencing one shred of Federal control. As a former Governor of a State, I have naturally been very sensitive to the question of Federal-State relationships and have been anxious to preserve the rightful responsibility of and independence of action by the States. In my 6 years as Governor of Connecticut, not once has the Federal Government exercised control directly or indirectly over education in my State. I doubt whether you will find any such interference in any of our 50 States.

Benjamin C. Willis, general superintendent of schools, Chicago, and new AASA president: There are some who have equated Federal support with Federal control. The American Association of School Administrators believes in local control; I believe in local control; history has given evidence that local control can be compatible with Federal aid. We have had Federal support of education since the beginning of the Land-Grant Colleges; since 1915, there has been Federal support to vocational education. In this latter case, the program is so local that funds are granted to programs within schools. Recently, millions of dollars have been paid to teachers by the Federal Government while they attended institutes sponsored by universities. The universities select the teachers and determine the course of study; the Federal Government does not.

Dr. Fuller: The respective responsibilities of the three levels of government have been appropriately outlined in S. 1021. Local school districts are required to account to the States for the Federal funds they have received. The States then account to the Federal Government for all Federal funds received by them. The Federal Government cannot control the content of what is taught in the schools under this bill, and it therefore permits no Federal control of education as such control is properly defined.

SHOULD NONPUBLIC SCHOOLS RECEIVE GRANTS OR LOANS FROM THE FEDERAL GOVERNMENT

Frederick G. Hochwalt, director, National Catholic Welfare Conference: Although the parochial schools are not governmentally sponsored and operated, they perform a public function, supplying large numbers of children with an education accepted by the State as fulfilling its requirements of compulsory education and meeting its specific standards.

Walter H. Moeller, Congressman from Ohio: History has been kind to this uniquely American arrangement. Under it, the churches have prospered as nowhere else in the world. They have established their own schools and lived within the framework of the constitutional prohibition against the making of laws "respecting an establishment of religion." However, it must be noted that churches establish parochial schools for one express purpose, namely to propagate the faith of that church. This is the primary reason for church schools on the elementary and secondary level. None dare deny them this right. But with this privilege, also goes the responsibility to maintain such schools. Thus, the use of public funds to aid such schools is helping to advance a particular faith, contrary to the Constitution.

WOULD THE APPROPRIATION OF FEDERAL FUNDS TO THE PUBLIC SCHOOLS DISCRIMINATE AGAINST THOSE CHILDREN WHO ATTEND THE PAROCHIAL SCHOOLS?

Morris Sherer, executive vice president, Agudath Israel of America: It is our view that to deny these tax-paying American citizens of the orthodox Jewish faith the benefit of their taxes in order to help defray the large expense of maintaining the Jewish parochial school system for their children is a discrimination which is not in accordance with basic American ideals. The Jewish parent who sends his child to a parochial school has to make many sacrifices to meet the cost of educating his children, very often at the price of denying for himself and his family some of their own vital needs. These parents should not be unduly penalized for practicing the exercise of their free choice, implicit in the American way of life, to educate their children in accordance with their religious conscience.

Leo Pfeffer, general counsel, American Jewish Congress: There was a time in American history when the demand by Catholics for equality and nondiscrimination was valid. . . .

All this, however, is past history. Today the public school welcomes the Catholic child as a full and equal companion of all children. No religious doctrines contrary to his faith are taught in the public schools, and no religious practices unacceptable to him are carried on there. The anti-Catholic bias in the textbooks has long been eliminated, and the entire atmosphere of the public school is such as to assure the Catholic child a feeling and actuality of full equality.

Where then is the discrimination? Would it not be more accurate to suggest that here too the converse is more accurate? Public schools are supported by all taxpayers regardless of race or religion and are open to all children regardless of race or religion. But church schools are open only to children of the faith that maintains the schools. Does it not constitute discrimination to tax a Protestant parent to support a Catholic school which his child may not enter, or to tax a Catholic parent to support a Jewish school which is closed to his child? Is not this truly discrimination?

ARE PARENTS OF PAROCHIAL SCHOOL CHILDREN UNFAIRLY SUBJECT TO DOUBLE TAXATION?

Msgr. Hochwalt: . . . A great many parents of parochial school children would welcome Federal aid as a necessary help to them in a time of financial strain. They do feel the double burden of supporting two school systems and are apt to inquire much more pointedly now than heretofore why the proponents of Federal aid do not take into consideration their needs. . . .

M. V. Little, consultant on church-state problems, Garden City, N.Y.: The parent who sends his children to a parochial school must realize that the double levy that he takes upon himself is his own free choice. As a citizen, he must support the State and its government. That is his debt to Caesar. The second levy that he incurs is the parochial school fee. He pays this not because he is discriminated against, but because he, himself, discriminates against public education at the behest of his church. He is not a scapegoat when he pays his school tax, but a citizen like his neighbor who has no children.

WOULD FEDERAL AID TO PUBLIC SCHOOLS DENY PARENTS FREEDOM OF CHOICE?

Frank J. Brown, DePaul University: Whatever has happened to parents' rights in education? This principle was a prime ingredient in the foundation upon which this Nation was built, but today it seems to be lost in the welter of talk about a unity and a democracy to be achieved through a government system of education. We remind America that the Supreme

Court has affirmed the rights of parents to direct the education of their children and that it includes therein the right to be free from governmental standardization.

A society cannot claim credit for its devotion to rights if it renders their normal exercise impossible to achieve. We ask the Senate to consider that triple combination of local, State, and federal education taxes imposed on us without any benefits accruing to our children will effectively impair, if not destroy, the economic possibility of many of our families to exercise the right to God-centered education for their children.

Mr. Little: As a matter of fact, here is a paradox: We have a plea for freedom in education by a religious hierarchy . . . [yet] they [Roman Catholic parents] can do nothing but send their children to Roman Catholic parochial schools, unless the diocesan bishop is willing to make an exception.

WOULD FEDERAL AID TO THE PUBLIC SCHOOLS RESULT IN THE RESTRICTION OF RELIGIOUS LIBERTY?

John C. Hayes, president, National Council of Catholic Men (in discussing loans to parochial schools): The providing of routine business services, such as loans, by Government to all schools, including parochial schools (in which provision there is neither net profit for the schools nor net cost to the Government), is, like the providing of general governmental services such as police and fire protection, simply an example of a religiously neutral government dealing with all persons, not as the believers or nonbelievers which they are, but merely as the members of the community, which they also and more pertinently are in respect of such services. To exclude Catholics and Catholic schools from equal participation in those neutral services would be a public disservice, an *unnecessary* discrimination against Catholic schools, and an *unnecessary* substantial impairment of the constitutionally protected rights of Catholic students and their parents to the free exercise of their religion and to the right of parental direction and control of the child's education.

C. Emanuel Carlson, executive director, Baptist Joint Committee on Public Affairs: As we see it, the great American experiment in religious liberty was based on the understanding that religion to be genuine must be voluntary. Free churches and free participation are projected in the First Amendment. The former has been validated by all the religious traditions in their programs and their successes and none of the churches now wish to be tools of national policy. In the success of the churches, however, some have developed a desire to further strengthen their programs by support from tax funds. This means the use of powers properly reserved to the State. The importance of the voluntary quality in religious participation and support is currently obscured by these institutional aspirations. . . .

Max M. Kampelman, counsel, American Jewish Congress: A loan program would still be a use of tax money for the benefit of religious institutions. It would still involve the Government in religious affairs and religion in governmental affairs. It would still be productive of interreligious friction. In short, it would be a breach in the wall of separation [and would carry] with it all the evils which that wall was designed to prevent.

IS AID TO NONPUBLIC SCHOOLS CONSTITUTIONAL?

Mr. Hayes: To tolerate nonpreferential governmental aid to religions as merely incidental to the primarily intended purpose of vindicating the individual's primary right to the free exercise of his religion is an application of the sound policy of avoiding the greater constitutional problem. The one constitutional problem is the nonpreferential extension of aid to all religions, contrary to the "no establishment of religion" clause of the First Amendment as presently construed; the other constitutional problem is the substantial impairment of the individual's right to the free exercise of his religion. As between those problems there can be no doubt which is the more serious. The key freedom of the First Amendment is the free exercise of religion. . . . It would, therefore, be a travesty to permit the prohibition of "an establishment of religion" as presently construed, to operate to impair the very freedom which it was intended to guarantee. Nonpreferential governmental aid to religions may, therefore, simply be tolerated, solely in order to avoid the greater constitutional problem of substantially impairing the individual's right to the free exercise of his religion.

Paul Blanshard, special counsel, Protestants and Other Americans United for Separation of Church and State: The Supreme Court has never *specifically* outlawed *general* loans or grants to sectarian schools by the Federal Government simply because no Congress has been foolish enough to pass such laws. This does not mean that we have a right to trade upon the mere absence of a specific decision. In fact, we have ample precedent in the decisions of the Supreme Court to say that any general appropriation to sectarian schools is in clear violation of the First Amendment. We have three great Supreme Court decisions in the field of public aid to religion at the elementary and high school level, and in all three of these famous decisions the Supreme Court has used language which was clearly intended to erect a financial wall between the public treasury and sectarian education.

SHOULD FEDERAL FUNDS BE GRANTED TO SEGREGATED SCHOOL SYSTEMS?

Clarence Mitchell, director, Washington Bureau, National Association for the Advancement of Colored People: Opponents of this amendment usually assert that its inclusion will kill the bill. Boiled down to its bare bones, their argument is an attempt to persuade the colored citizens of our country to forget that the United States Supreme Court has declared that racial segregation in public schools is unconstitutional. We are asked to step aside and to look in the other direction while millions of tax dollars are used to underwrite the building and operation of public schools that everyone knows will be segregated on the basis of race. Speaking on the basis of 20 years of experience in Washington, I do not know of any other groups of American citizens who have been asked to submit to similar humiliation from the National Government. . . .

. . . we respectfully urge that any bill or bills reported favorably for aid to primary and secondary schools and aid to defense impacted areas include an antisegregation amendment.

Agnes E. Meyer, author and lecturer on education: To those who, like myself, would like to see school desegregation make greater progress, I should like to say that we must not fuse or confuse our purposes. Any revival of what was called the Powell amendment, which refused Federal aid to States that had not yet achieved desegregation, would endanger passage of S. 1021 and . . . be a great disservice to Negro students in Southern States.

Dr. Fuller: It is highly unfair to expect the schools to assume the major effort to enforce desegregation, which is a political, social, and economic problem pervading all aspects of society. The very education needed to reach solutions to this problem would be denied by withholding funds from schools. The problem cannot be solved by such tactics, and public education itself would become the major victim. Violations of civil rights should be dealt with by specialized law enforcement agencies, rather than through punitive and ineffective administrative methods that . . . injure innocent pupils and undermine the schools.

Chapter 19

A PROPOSAL FOR FINANCING PUBLIC EDUCATION

THE FINANCIAL PROBLEMS *of American public education have attracted the attention of a great many people who have discussed them from many points of view. Robert Heller, Chairman, National Citizens Council for Better Schools, makes some far-reaching suggestions that might affect all levels of public education. Heller believes there is substantial agreement that education needs and merits increased financial support and the national economy is capable of meeting such increased financial expenditures. He is of the opinion that "the problem then is not one of resources; it is one of policy." The dimensions of the problem (social, political, economic, and cultural), the resources (both actual and anticipated), and the methods of local, state, and federal financing of public education (past and present) are briefly considered.*

Heller formulates ten principles that could serve as guidelines for the construction of a solution to the problem. He indicates how this formula might be applied to local autonomous school districts, city government, and state government, and describes the effects the implementation of the proposal would have upon federal income tax returns and upon the taxpayer. Because Heller's proposal has produced rather pronounced reactions from school administrators, political leaders, and laymen, his thesis is presented in its entirety.

A PROPOSAL FOR FINANCING TAX-SUPPORTED EDUCATION

Robert Heller

THE PROBLEM

State and local expenditures for public education have increased greatly in recent years, yet the nation is faced with a shortage of classrooms and qualified teachers. The condition has been cumulative, resulting from depression, war, and material shortages. A sharp rise in the number of births during the past decade has made the current problem a serious one, and more acute conditions are forecast for the immediate and long-term future.

In some areas conditions are worse than in others. Heavy population migration has been a complicating factor; the Supreme Court decision on racial segregation created new problems. Taken collectively, the enrollments in the nation's elementary schools have increased 27 percent during the past ten years. There are 33.4 million pupils enrolled in the U.S. public schools this year. By 1960 an additional 3.9 million and by 1965 still another four million are expected to be added to the rolls. [See Chapter 37 of this book for current statistics. ED.]

A few years ago these facts were considered by many leaders to be wild estimates or propaganda of school-minded lobbyists. Today very few education and government leaders at the local, state, and national levels are not mindful of and concerned with the growing needs of the schools supported by taxation.

Recent events have helped our citizens and their leaders to an agreement that good education is essential to the national welfare and that every American child has a right to an adequate educational opportunity. "Adequate" has different meanings to different people, however. To some it is in only a few of the poorer communities of the least wealthy states that "adequate" schools cannot be provided even in these extreme times. To others it is in only a few of the wealthier communities of the wealthiest states that "adequate" education is being provided now.

No matter where "adequate" is placed between these extremes, by 1965 it will require substantially more money than is now being spent for public education. To accommodate increased enrollments without any change in

Reprinted from *Harvard Educational Review*, Vol. 28, No. 3 (Summer 1958), pp. 214–231.

quality will call for an additional annual expenditure of $2.3 billion. To provide funds for public education in all states at the level of expenditure in the state of New York in 1957–58, while providing for the additional school population, would take another $5.9 billion.

But even in New York State many will contend that not enough money is available for education. Many communities within the state now are doing less than the average New York community. So if allowance were made in New York to raise its status to $500 per pupil (currently $482) and all other states brought themselves up to that level it is conceivable that the total annual U.S. public education bill could rise from $9.6 billion to $18.6 billion by 1965.

While there is some difference of opinion as to exactly what the annual expenditure for public education must be to provide "adequate" education, there is no argument that there is a need to spend substantially more than is now being appropriated.

THE RESOURCES

Anticipated resources of the U.S. are expected to rise substantially according to many of the nation's leading economists. Estimates of gross national product in 1965 range between $500 billion and $550 billion. Taking the average of these, $525 billion, which is the same figure as used in "Financing Public Education in the Decade Ahead," a 1954 report of the National Citizens Commission for the Public Schools, this would be an increase of 35 percent over the $390 billion in 1955. An increase of this magnitude, assuming no change in tax rates, could easily result in additional Federal revenue of about $12 billion over 1955.

Assuming even the highest of the possible estimated annual costs for public education by 1965, $18.6 billion or an increase of $9 billion, the anticipated resources of the U.S. will be equal to the burden. In fact, less than 7 percent of the increase in gross national product would be needed for the schools. *The problem then is not one of resources; it is one of policy*. The policies must exist and be effective so that the necessary funds will flow from where they are earned to the thousands of school districts where the children are. It is in this area that something must be done if the national welfare is to be protected.

A brief background of the growth and diversity of our systems of financing public education should be helpful.

The Past

It was not until the decade after the war between the states that people really began to accept their responsibility for education and to replace established funds with local revenue. By 1890, 5.5 percent of public school support came from the federal government, 18.4 percent from the states, and the balance from individual communities. During the next 30 years this trend continued, and by 1920 the federal government was providing 2.7 percent of the support, the states were providing 13.8 percent, and the communities were providing the balance.

In recent years the trend has been reversed, with the states providing a progressively larger share of the school dollar. This has been so for two reasons: first, the state is a better tax gatherer than the locality, having more sources available; and second, there has been a growing awareness of the large economic differentials that exist between wealthy and poor districts. State aid has offered a way of reducing these differentials.

The Present

The estimates for the school year 1957–58 show that the federal government provided 3.6 percent of the school revenues, the state governments 40.6 percent, and the local governments 55.8 percent. The states vary widely, however, both in the proportion of total support they provide and the ways in which they provide it. In Delaware, for example, the state government provides 81.5 percent of public school revenues. In Georgia the state provides 74.2 percent, in North Carolina 73.4 percent. At the other end of the scale, providing 6.1 percent or less, are Nebraska and New Hampshire. These variations have existed for many years. They are due partly to differences in the development of the educational financial systems in the various states, and partly to differences in the philosophy of the people in their home communities as to the location of responsibility for education. Major changes have taken place infrequently, mainly during periods of emergency or when there has been a rapid change in conditions.

LOCAL TAXES

Most of the local revenue for education comes from property taxes, as does county school revenues. Although in 1950 there were 11 states, mostly in the South, where county collections exceeded location collections, in general the county is disappearing as a school tax collector.

Not only is the property tax the main source of local revenue, but also it provides better than half of school revenue from all sources. The schools are so dependent on the property tax that in 1953–54, 24 states used this source for over one-half of their school funds, and the schools of only seven states received less than one-fourth of their revenue by this means. There are, of course, other sources of local revenue, but they are comparatively minor and are usually reserved to counties and the larger cities.

Not only the schools rely upon property taxation. All other local public services depend heavily on it, too, and these services require more money each year. Despite, and perhaps because, most local communities depend on this as a single revenue source, it is regarded by many people as a mixed blessing. The principal objection of taxpayers is that there is little relationship between ownership of property and ability to pay taxes. School finance experts complain that revenue from this source is relatively stable and does not react quickly to economic conditions, although the costs of education do.

Quite aside from these objections, property taxation leads to some major revenue inequities. Assessment practices vary among states and among local districts within states. The ratio between true property value and assessed property value may be four or five times as high in some districts within a state as it is in others. Moreover, the assessed property value per child varies greatly throughout the United States. For example, the U.S. average is $6,959; but in South Carolina the state-wide average is $976, and in Illinois it is $14,069. On a district basis the range is from less than $100 to several hundred thousand dollars per child.

State Taxes

In all but three states (Kentucky, Nebraska and South Dakota) the percentage of school revenue provided by the state government rose sharply in the decade 1940 to 1950. Over-all, the states' portion jumped from 30.3 percent to 42.7 percent, with a particularly sharp rise in Alabama, Arizona, Arkansas, Colorado, Connecticut and Oregon. In recent years, however, the trend has reversed itself in about a third of the states.

The states derived the funds earmarked for the schools from three principal sources: (1) *Permanent school funds and land—1.5 percent.* Thirty-nine of the states distributed some $30 million from this source in 1950. This sum represented earnings on roughly three-quarters of a billion dollars in a variety of permanent trust funds derived chiefly from Federal land grants. (2) *Earmarked taxes—18.2 percent.* Twenty-two states distributed some $364 million from taxes earmarked for schools by constitution or statutory provisions. (3) *General fund appropriation—80.3 percent.* All but Minnesota, New Mexico and North Dakota used this means to help finance public schools from the state level in 1950. Ten of the states used this as their sole method of state school financing. During 1950 these states appropriated $1.6 billion from their general funds which were accumulated from their many income sources.

During the past 30 years the state governments have almost completely relinquished their claim to property tax, turning it over to local taxing bodies. At the close of World War I, over one-half of all state revenue was derived from this source. Now it constitutes but a small percentage of the total. During the same period, the states have found rich sources of revenue in income taxes, sales taxes and gasoline taxes. Most states have taxes on alcoholic beverages, gasoline, insurance, licenses, motor vehicles and payroll.

Some of the most productive state taxes react quickly to changes in economic conditions, in contrast to locally collected property taxes.

Federal Taxes

Although the Federal government contributes only a slight amount to total public expenditures, it does make substantial contributions in certain specified areas. It provided $30 million for vocational education and $69 million for school lunches in 1955. In addition, it has contributed to both construction and operational expenses in federally affected areas under Public Laws 815, 874 and 246.

It is nevertheless easy to underestimate the stake that the Federal government has had in the past and that it now has in education if we consider only the extent to which it supports the schools directly. Its educational investment is far larger than its 2 percent contribution to school revenues would seem to indicate.

For one thing, the Ordinance of 1787 included tremendous land endowments for public education. Over the years the Federal government continued to add to the states' permanent education funds through grants of saline lands, internal improvement lands and swamplands. In recent years, the Federal government has appropriated funds for state colleges of agriculture and mechanical arts, for the Civilian Conservation Corps, and for the National Youth Administration, all of which were public educational projects in the broadest sense. During World War II the Federal government contributed heavily to the training of essential workers. In addition, in the establishment of the U.S. Department of Education in 1867, now the Office of Education in the Department of Health, Education and Welfare, the Federal government gave evidence of its concern for promoting the cause of education throughout the country.

Today, even though the Federal government is giving proportionately less to the operation of the schools than it gave in the past, its financial participation in education as a whole is at an all-time high. In the fiscal year 1955 it spent over $1.6 billion on educational programs. The bulk of this money was spent by the Veterans' Administration, the Federal Security Administration, the Agriculture Department, the Defense Department and the Atomic Energy Commission.

THE CONTROVERSY

Many proposals have been argued in Congress in an effort to find a solution to the problem of channeling more money to the schools. They meet the same fate—no action.

The term "Federal Aid For Education" is widely used and has a generally accepted meaning. It is recognized, however, that the term is a controversial one even though free usage is given to it on the following pages. The following excerpt was taken from a special report on educational issues prepared specifically for the 84th Congress.

Some persons have raised serious objections to the "Aid" concept on the grounds that such "Aid" is not a gratuity from the Federal Government since the funds are drawn from the people in the States. Other persons have objected to the concept on entirely different grounds. These persons contend that the Federal Government inherently bears an obligation to participate in the financing of education, which, they contend, is essential to the discharge of the Federal responsibility for the national defense and for the promotion of the general welfare.

It is a matter of opinion as to whether some of the Federal programs . . . such as the school-lunch program, and the program for the utilization of Federal surplus property, should be regarded as "Federal aid for education." A careful study of the development of these programs clearly indicates that some of them do not represent "Federal aid for education" with respect to either basic purpose or underlying philosophy. However, all of these programs do contribute to the advancement of education.

Many of the educational activities of the Federal Government, such as the numerous and varied forms of training and instruction given in the Armed Forces, have, of course, no place in the concept of "Federal aid for education." These programs are generally administered by the Federal Government, with little or no connection with the educational systems of the States.

The controversy over the significance of the "Federal aid" concept leads to a larger controversy. There is a much greater and more important disagreement among the people over the answers to such questions as: What kind of taxes should or must be used to provide the additional financial support needed for public education—property taxes, or income, or sales taxes? Which level of government should provide the sorely needed funds—local, State, or Federal? Should the whole tax structure of the Nation be revised? If so, what should the new structure be, and can it be built fast enough to meet the emergency needs of the Nation's fast growing school-age population? Should the Federal Government make a larger contribution to the support of education? If so, in what form should it be provided? Particularly, should it be limited to aid to construction of schoolhouses?[1]

There are two main schools of thought regarding Federal financial assistance in meeting the needs of the public schools. Some feel that education is completely a state and local responsibility, and that the quality and characteristics of the schools are subject to the wishes of the people themselves where the children attend school. They believe that the function of the state government should be to insure the provision of a minimum standard of education for all and to help equalize opportunities between the wealthier and poorer areas through state aid programs. As for financing, they insist all

[1] Excerpted from "Educational Issues of Concern to the 84th Congress"—page 10 of a report prepared in the Legislative Reference Service of the Library of Congress by Charles A. Quattlebaum—March 17, 1955.

education costs should be met by taxes levied within the state and that every state can collect enough taxes to provide the funds needed.

Others feel the Federal government has better access to increases in national income, and therefore should raise the additional funds needed. Some disagreement exists within this group, however, on how funds should be distributed to the states for education. Some feel that a form of equalization is necessary and should be based on need and ability to meet need. Others feel that any measures used to determine need and ability would result in federal dominance or control of education. This group favors distribution of Federal money to the states on a per child basis irrespective of need.

The foregoing are, of course, only general remarks about the opposing points of view. Detailed arguments fit within this general framework, however.

Even the most vocal opponents of federal aid to education seem to recognize the need for more financial support for education. An examination of the arguments of these opponents shows that they have one common belief and that is that some tax resources to the federal government should be turned back to the states and communities so that they can support their own educational programs. The following quotes seem to bear this out:

1. Education being a function of government which is particularly suited to local control, unused State and local tax capacity and new fiscal resources should be available for educational purposes before being utilized for other functions of government.

   The costs of the expansion in enrollment in the next ten years can be taken care of by State and local governments if they continue to increase their school contributions at the rate which they have been boosting them in recent years. To improve standards at the rate at which they have been advancing in the last few decades will require greater efforts. An effective way in which the Federal Government can aid those efforts is to reduce its tax bill. It has made an excellent start by the current tax cut of $7.3 billion, which almost equals the sum of all public school revenues in the school year 1953–54. The reduction should make it easier for State and local governments to raise additional funds for the schools without increasing the total tax burden of their citizens.[2]

2. There is strong evidence that there must be an abdication of certain revenue sources by the national government and their assumption by the states. The states must be given the wherewithal to exercise their responsibilities. The pre-emption of revenue sources by the national government has severely limited the capability of the states to develop. We recommend that gift and estate taxation, as a minimum, be turned over completely to the state governments. It is also suggested that study and consideration be given to other tax sources which may be readily transferable.

[2] Commission on Intergovernmental Relations, A Study Committee Report on Federal Responsibility in the Field of Education. June 1955, pp. 7, 97.

. . . There must be a thorough reevaluation of fiscal sources and the restoration of adequate revenue sources to the states. For unless some means are produced to give the states the ability to meet their own problems, it is little more than an academic exercise to talk of transferring functions and responsibilities.[3]

3. How, then, are we going to pay for current educational needs? We know that state governments have been spending record sums for school construction and that these have not been enough. We also know that our economy can afford only so many dollars a year for taxes and that the total tax bill is dangerously high. It follows that the federal tax structure must be reviewed and modified so that the states will again have the opportunity to raise funds for such vital projects as schools.

   To achieve this we must educate people to the fact that 'federal money' is not 'free money'—not a handout from a benevolent Uncle Sam that does not cost us anything the way paying local taxes does. This attitude has led many people to accept the idea of higher federal taxes—part of which will be returned as a 'grant' to the states. That is the path to control.[4]

4. In order that the States and localities may be able to assume this responsibility for a rapid increase in school construction and for other pressing governmental functions, the Governors reaffirm their recommendation that the National Government release to the States the tax on local telephone service and other taxes that can be administered effectively by the States. The Joint Committee directed the staffs to prepare suggested recommendations dealing with school construction and available tax sources and taking into account the current federal review of defense, educational, and revenue policies.[5]

5. It has been suggested that this trend of centralizing fiscal responsibility be reversed by having the federal government turn certain taxes over to the states. More recently interest seems to have shifted to the idea that a reduction in the over-all federal tax burden would enable states to use their own taxing powers more extensively. In 1955, following a major federal tax cut, the states enacted the most substantial tax increases in many years.

   . . . It is unlikely that state and local taxes can be raised substantially if the federal government continues to display a willingness to assume increasing financial commitments in areas of state and local responsibility.[6]

[3] Excerpts from the testimony of Philip M. Talbott, President, Chamber of Commerce of the United States before a House Government Operations Sub-committee, July 30, 1957.

[4] Ernest G. Swigert, President, National Association of Manufacturers. Excerpt from "Professional Teachers for the Nation's Schools," *Teachers College Record,* Vol. 59, No. 1, October 1957.

[5] Excerpts from the Joint Federal–State Action Committee, Progress Report #1, To the President of the United States and to the Chairman of Governors' Conference, Dec. 1957.

[6] Roger A. Freeman, "Crises in School Finance, Part II: How Can Rising School Needs Be Financed?" in *National Tax Journal,* Vol. IX, No. 2, June 1956. Mr. Freeman served in 1954–55 as Director of Research for the Education Committee of the U.S. Commission on Intergovernmental Relations, later in 1955 as consultant on school finance to the Committee for the White House Conference on Education.

6. The responsibility for public schools should continue in the hands of the individual states and their local units. The Federal government, however, can make an important contribution to the solution of the public school problem at the state and local level. First, Federal policy should offer no discouragement to the full development of the economic resources and tax bases of all states. Second, by firmly establishing the format of Federal relationships with state (and local) governments, Federal action should encourage a more definitive pattern of administrative and fiscal responsibility between the states and their local units.

   Increasing the margin of reasonable taxation available to the states and local units is the best course for Federal action in regard to state and local functions, such as public education. An important beginning has been made this year with Federal tax reductions which will amount to approximately $7.5 billion. Local support through local taxation, supplemented by a reasonable and equitable system of state aid, is to be preferred over any system of Federal aid affecting the regular functions of the public schools. The schools, which reflect the economic and social development of their respective areas, must remain primarily a local responsibility if they are to develop consistently with their individual communities and states.[7]
7. Although the report given at the White House Conference on Education representing the distillation of the 166 table reports stated that the Conference was in favor of Federal Aid, an examination of the individual table reports shows that those which were for Federal Aid carried certain qualifications. It is believed that it would be difficult to reconcile these differences. Frequently mentioned by those tables opposing Federal Aid were comments like the following: "If the Federal government will relinquish to the states taxation fields sufficient to provide for school needs there will be no necessity for direct Federal financial assistance."

PROPOSAL

The statements of many groups that the federal government should release its hold on some of the tax resources was kept in mind when seeking a method for education to get its share of available financial resources. It was felt, too, that any proposal should contain the following principles:

1. Should provide encouragement to improve the schools both because of the financial incentives and the implied expression by the Federal government that education *should* be considered a preferential service for the Nation's welfare.
2. Should provide financial assistance only for improvements made, rather than providing encouragement to refrain from improving with the hope that someone else will assume the responsibility.

[7] Excerpt from "Public School Financing 1930–1954" *Project Note No. 36,* The Tax Foundation Inc. New York, September 1954.

3. Should require positive action at local or state level in order to make the proposal operative. In other words, benefits should be available only if school districts or states take the initiative to increase school support.
4. Should be of greater financial assistance to less wealthy individuals and therefore less wealthy states.
5. Should pose no threat to state control of education.
6. Must not present any opportunity for standardization or regimentation of education.
7. Should require no administrative decisions regarding equitable manner of distributing funds.
8. Should avoid all social entanglements.
9. Should not be incompatible with tax systems now in use at any level of government.
10. While the proposal should provide local and state incentive it must contain features which would prevent spending from getting out of control.

The following proposal meets these objectives and should provide a meeting ground for advocates of greater support to education, whether they are for or against "Federal Aid." *The Federal Government should recognize future increase in local and state taxes used for education by giving full credit for such increases against personal and corporate taxes.* Today the Federal Government gives the nation's taxpayers a partial credit for most state and local taxes by allowing their deduction from gross income. This arrangement should be continued. But for all increased school taxes over the current rates taxpayers should be given full credit. In other words, any *increase* in school taxes would be subtracted *in full* by the taxpayer from his federal tax bill. By this simple device the federal government would demonstrate its belief that education is a priority concern of the nation.

MECHANICS OF PROPOSAL

The principle of the proposal is that a taxpayer is permitted to subtract as a credit from his federal income tax *the full amount of any local or state school tax increase* over a base year. He is also allowed to continue taking his base year school taxes as a normal tax deduction from gross income, when computing his federal income tax. The taxpayer whether an individual or corporation, in order to obtain full benefits from this proposal, must know: (1) how much of his local and state taxes are for school, and (2) what portion of these school taxes is an increase over the base year.

To explain how the taxpayer will obtain this information examples are given for three distinct types of tax collecting groups:

1. The local autonomous school district which collects taxes for school purposes only—usually on real estate.

2. The city or county government which levies taxes for other public services as well as schools, and all receipts and expenditures clear through a general fund.
3. The state government which appropriates part of its general fund, drawn from many sources, to the many school districts within the state as well as to other public services.

ILLUSTRATIONS OF PROPOSAL

The examples which follow do not purport to explain every possible case that might arise. The intention is that they serve to explain the principle involved.

Local Autonomous School District

This undoubtedly is the easiest case to explain. It is a case of taxes on real estate only. It is not complicated by many forms of taxes nor is it further confused by having more than education supported by the tax. The following example shows the hypothetical financial highlights of a school district in the base year (1957) and in the two subsequent years. It also brings in a case showing what applies to a taxpayer who acquires additional taxable property.

School District Finance

	BASE YEAR 1957	1958	1959
Total School Budget	$500,000	$550,000[1]	$750,000[2]
Total Assessments	$25,000,000	$27,500,000[3]	$30,000,000[3]
Tax Rate (per thous.)	$20.00	$20.00	$25.00[4]

1 Increase due to rising enrollments.
2 Increase due to rising enrollments and educational improvements.
3 No change in assessment practices. Increase results from new home building.
4 Increase in total assessments not sufficient to bring in enough money for higher budget. Therefore, rate had to be increased.

When Mr. Taxpayer received his *1958* school tax bill it looked like this:

	1958
Assessment—$10,000	Rate $20.00
Base year (1957) tax equivalent $200.00	
School Tax this year—please remit	$200.00

When Mr. Taxpayer filed his federal tax return for 1958 he took $200.00 as a deduction. *He had no increase over the base year so he could not take a credit.*

When the 1959 school tax bills were ready Mr. Taxpayer still owned the house he had in 1958. But in addition he owned and lived in a new and larger home in the same school district. His two tax bills follow:

Home #1	*1959*
Assessment—$10,000	Rate $25.00
Base year (1957) tax equivalent $200.00	
School Tax this year—please remit	$250.00

Home #2	*1959*
Assessment—$16,000	Rate $25.00
Base year (1957) tax equivalent $320.00	
School Tax this year—please remit	$400.00

Because he owned two properties in 1959 he took $200.00 and $320.00 as deductions, and the increases, or $50.00 and $80.00, as credits on his Federal income tax return.

City Government

In this case "school taxes" are not levied as such. The governmental body has fiscal responsibility over all municipal services, including schools. It has several sources of funds and receives and disburses these monies through a General Fund. This method makes the schools' share of taxes less obvious to the taxpayer. However, it is relatively easy for the city government to determine the exact amount which applies to schools, as the following shows:

City Budget

	BASE YEAR 1957	1958	1959
Expenditures (in millions)			
Schools	$ 75	$ 90[1]	$105[2]
Police and Fire	10	10	11
Welfare	10	5	6
Highways	20	20	23
All other Services	35	25	30
Total	$150	$150	$175
Estimated Income (in millions)			
Real Estate Tax	$ 75	$ 75	$ 85[4]
Sales Tax	20	20	20[3]
Wage Tax	50	50	65[5]
Miscellaneous Revenue (Parking meters, etc.)	5	5	5
Total	$150	$150[3]	$175

1 The school budget was increased to accommodate rising enrollments. To provide the extra money non-school services were curtailed. Thus taxes for schools were increased by 10% (from 50% and 60% of the total budget).

2 The school budget was increased partly because of growing enrollments and partly due to improvements. The increase for schools from the base year is 10% (from 50% to 60% of the total budget).

3 No tax rates were increased, and the yield was not expected to rise.

4 Entire increase due to new home building with no increase in tax rate.

5 Increases due mainly to a 20% rise in tax rate and balance because of higher incomes of wage earners.

From the foregoing it can be seen that in 1957, 50% of all taxes went for schools, while in 1958 and 1959 it was 60% each year. In other words, 10% more of a taxpayer's total taxes went for schools than in the base year.

In addition the wage tax rate (municipal gross income tax) was raised by 20% in 1959. Of course this increase went for all services. Since 60% of all taxes were for school purposes, 60% of this rise or 12%, was on account of schools.

The city, therefore, is able to account for school taxes paid by residents, for their federal income tax purposes, as follows:

ACCOUNT TO SHOW PERCENTAGES OF TAXES TO BE USED FOR INCOME TAX CREDIT

	1958		1959	
	BASE YEAR *Equivalent* (Use as Deduction)	EDUCATION *Increase* (Use as Credit)	BASE YEAR *Equivalent* (Use as Deduction)	EDUCATION *Increase* (Use as Credit)
Real Estate Tax	90%	10%	90%	10%
Sales Tax	90%	10%	90%	10%
Wage Tax	90%	10%	78%	22%[1]

1 Consists of 10% due to education's larger share of the budget and 12% due to education's share of the increase in the wage tax rate.

When Mr. Taxpayer receives his 1958 tax bill on his home it will look like this:

1958

Assessment—$20,000 Rate $22.00

Base year (1957) tax equivalents:

For schools (50%)	$220.00
For other services	220.00
Total	$440.00

Tax this year:

For schools (60%)	$264.00	
For other services	176.00	
Total—please remit		$440.00

Mr. Taxpayer therefore took $44.00 as a credit ($264 less $220) and the balance of his total tax, or $396 ($440 less $44), as a deduction on his federal income tax return. Since there was no change in 1959, his real estate tax bill looks just like the one in 1958, and he treats it the same way.

Mr. Taxpayer has estimated that his 1958 and 1959 sales taxes are $100 and $120, respectively. (He has always estimated his sales tax payments because he had no receipts.) The city tax collector had advertised in the local paper each of these years that 10% of sales taxes were considered as increases for schools over the base year, so he was aware of the credits due him. Therefore, when he filed his 1958 federal return, he took $90 as a deduction and $10 (10% of $100) as a credit. Similarly in 1958, he took $108 as a deduction and $12 as a credit (10% of $120).

The City Income Tax office instructed all employers to provide each employee with an annual notice showing:

(1) Total wage tax withheld.
(2) Amount for which deduction is due.
(3) Amount for which credit is due.

Having been informed by the City of the percentage of wage tax (municipal gross income tax) that represents the increase over the base year on account of schools, the employer prepared Mr. Taxpayer's notices as follows:

	1958
Total wages during year	$10,000.00
Wage Tax Withheld	$ 200.00
You are allowed to take as a Federal Income Tax Deduction	$ 180.00
You are allowed to take as a Federal Income Tax Credit	$ 20.00

	1959
Total wages during year	$11,000.00
Wage Tax Withheld	$ 264.00
You are allowed to take as a Federal Income Tax Deduction	$205.92
You are allowed to take as a Federal Income Tax Credit	$ 58.08

State Government

Here again the principle is explained by setting up a hypothetical state budget.

STATE BUDGET

	1957	1958	1959
Expenditures (in millions)			
Schools	$100	$115[1]	$140[2]
General Government	10	10	11
Highways	80	90	95
Police	20	21	22
Welfare	40	42	43
Other Services	50	52	54
Total	$300	$330	$365
Estimated Income (in millions)			
State Income Tax	$100	$119	$142[4]
Licenses	15	16	17 [3]
Gasoline Tax	95	98	102 [3]
Cigarette Tax	20	21	22 [3]
Race Track Revenue	20	21	22 [3]
Miscellaneous Revenue	50	55	60 [3]
Total	$300	$330[3]	$365

1 The schools received 34.8%, or 1½% more of the total budget than in the base year.

2 The schools received 38.5%, or 5% more of the total budget than in the base year.

3 Increase in yields due to rising economy. There were no increases in rates.

4 Increase due partly to rising economy but also because of 10% increase in rates. (Since 38.3% of budget is for schools, 3.8% of increase is on account of schools.)

The State Treasurer is therefore able to inform the Department of Internal Revenue that taxes in his state, for which Federal deduction and credits are allowed, have increased for school purposes as follows:

	1958	*1959*
State Income Tax	1—½%	8.8%
Licenses	1—½%	5 %
Gasoline Tax	1—½%	5 %

It would be a simple matter for the Department of Internal Revenue to include this information for all states, with proper instructions, right in the instruction sheet accompanying the blank tax forms. The taxpayer would, therefore, be easily guided.

The foregoing examples will not cover every tax situation which will arise but it is hoped that they do explain the principle involved in the proposal.

THE EFFECTS

The impact upon taxpayers and upon the federal government is a most important consideration in the evaluation of this proposal.

Upon the Federal Government

Any increase in local and state school taxes affects federal income tax collections because under present tax laws these are allowable deductions. Under present laws an increase of $1 billion in local and state school expenditures reduces federal collections by about $300 million.

Under this proposal, the reduction in federal collections would be increased due to the full credit, for increases, given to the taxpayers. It is estimated that this proposal would reduce federal collections by an additional $350 million for every $1 billion of increased school expenditures.

Upon the Taxpayer

The effect upon the individual or corporate taxpayer is shown below. It can be seen that the proposal is most helpful to the lower income earner and therefore the less wealthy states.

EFFECT OF PROPOSALS ON TAXPAYERS

BASE YEAR

Income	$4,000	$8,000	$10,000	$25,000
Exemptions (wife—3 children)	3,000	3,000	3,000	3,000
Deductions	440	880	1,100	2,500
School Tax (included in above)	100	100	150	300
Taxable Income	560	4,120	5,900	19,500
Present Income Tax	112	826	1,218	5,110
Total Income Tax + School Tax	212	926	1,368	5,410

IF SCHOOL TAXES ARE INCREASED 25%

A. Under Present Tax Laws

Rev. Taxable Income	$535	$4,095	$5,862	$19,425
Federal Income Tax	107	821	1,210	5,085
School Tax	125	125	188	375
Total Income Tax + School Tax	$232	$ 946	$1,398	$ 5,460
Percentage Increase in Total Taxes	9.4%	2.2%	2.2%	1.4%

B. Proposed Tax Credit Revision

Federal Income Tax	$ 87	$ 801	$1,180	$ 5,035
School Tax	125	125	188	375
Total Income Tax + School Tax	$212	$ 926	$1,368	$ 5,410
Percentage Increase in Total Taxes	none	none	none	none

PART FIVE

The Group and Education

IT IS NOW generally accepted by students of human behavior that, in addition to man's biological heritage, environment and day-to-day experiences exert a continuous influence upon the growth and development of personality. The schools are called upon to meet the needs and aspirations of all their students, and educators are required to understand each student's place in our culture (the term culture *is used to denote all the influences that are brought to bear upon the formation of anyone's personality). Since American culture is complex, such influences may or may not help a young person accept the democratic ideas as he grows into adulthood.*

It is also generally accepted that each person is both an individual and a member of many groups. A human being is born into a group and becomes part of the culture as his understanding of the values of that primary group increases. What he learns about the value system of his primary group assists each individual in selecting the other groups he wants to join. By choosing certain groups in preference to others, the individual expresses his understanding, both intellectual and emotional, of the value system into which he was born. This understanding ranges from the significant to the petty and from the rational to the irrational. Sadly, the experiences many groups offer the young fail to contribute to the growth of a commitment to democracy.

In recent years, an increasing number of scholars have tried to describe as accurately as possible the structure of the value systems found in contemporary American culture. Naturally, they offer a number of theses and they do not necessarily agree among themselves. Some urge the acceptance of regional and sectional differences and the clearly recognizable groups and classes that are contained within them. Others argue that, as a result of our economic, political, and social growth, there is a core culture descriptive of the largest part of American society. Still others observe that America is a society in transition and its values are in a state of flux. This section presents a number of interpretations of the nature and influence of the group structures found in American society, and the following section is concerned with the individual as the recipient of group values.

Chapter 20

GROUP VALUES — AMERICAN COMMUNITIES

IT IS ESSENTIAL *to our purpose to describe the cultures of our present-day communities because these communities are the basic units for the transmission of the culture. It is also necessary to indicate, when possible, why these communities are what they are and what significance such data have for the educator. Conrad M. Arensberg, an anthropologist, using the technique of cultural analysis, offers a description of the structure and values of American society. He examines the components of the New England town, the Southern county, and other communities. Arensberg builds his thesis around items common to each community: people, space, time, function, and structure and process.*

AMERICAN COMMUNITIES

C. M. Arensberg

Hundreds of accounts of American communities already exist. They appear in every stage of completeness of description. They come to us from the prolific pages of American censuses, American rural sociology, agricultural and land economics, urban sociology, social-problems literature, archi-

Reprinted from *American Anthropologist,* Vol. 57, No. 6, Part 1 (December 1955), pp. 1145–1160. Footnotes omitted.

tecture and city or community planning, human and urban geography, regional history, local novels, muckraking investigations, as well as from formal "community studies." Our job is less to cite such abundance of data than to order it into sense. We shall content ourselves with drawing upon fairly common knowledge of American life and its local manifestations. Nothing can be more obvious than most of the facts we shall have to use; anthropology can hope to find few esoterica in our own back yards. Nevertheless, if our comparisons order even obvious facts in genuinely universal and cross-cultural ways, then the patterns we discover in American communities will not only be new but they will be important to the perspective of science and to the record of anthropology.

What are the comparative analytic devices of cultural analysis we can put to work on all human communities in general and on American ones in particular? Clearly they must be such as describe all cases in common, yet still combine for useful comparisons. They must be such as go into the building of structural models. Nowadays it is clear that a model rather than a definition serves to represent the complex variables of a complex situation, thing, or process. A model serves better to put together empirical descriptions economically and surely and to handle summarily things of many dimensions, little-known organization, diverse functions and processes, intricate connections with other things. Definitions are too shallow and too full of verbal traps; summaries of propositions are too slow, piecemeal, and cumbersome. And certainly communities are such complex things.

We shall seek here for a family of models comparing all communities to our known American ones. Our models will not be simple ones. Spare as possible, with one term for each attribute and one relation in the model for each relation in the thing, they must still cover the many attributes which communities can be described for. They must cover size, spread, density, land use, traffic flow, population replacement, and so on. They must treat the many functions for individual lives or for society that communities may have: subsistence, defense, sociability, mate choice, trade, social or political control. They must try to cast these attributes and functions into the connections they have in real life. They must go on to trials of forecasting form, structure, and process, since attributes and functions connect in definite ways that have definite products and lawful properties of change. In the last analysis, a model is predictive, as these must be. It is testable in each new prediction. If a new fact can be predicted to fit in just so, with a result upon the model which foretells the outcome in the thing, then the model is correct and the theory upon which it is built is true.

Thus the models we shall need for American communities must rest on the common terms of description which serve for all others. The terms that we must vary as each successive model of the family represents the changed realities of a common experience of all communities in a new particular one must be terms of universal application. The following are the variable comparative terms which apply to all human and animal communities, out of which our models can be built:

(1) Individuals (persons or animals)
(2) Spaces (territory, position, movement)
(3) Times (schedules, calendars, time-series)
(4) Functions (for individual and group life)
(5) Structure and Process

(1) *Individuals.* Our first operation of description and model building for all communities specifies individuals (persons, animals). It answers: Who? With it we treat populations, memberships, exclusions and inclusions. Communities are, of course, collectivities or "social systems" of specific individuals. These have identities, and in description we select some and not others, and specify who is member, to be observed, and who is not. Once identified they can be counted, located, followed. Further, they can be described for the attributes we, observers, select or they, the observed, distinguish: age, sex, color, size, occupation, class, ethnicity, sect, etc. In dealing with human beings and their cultures we learned long ago to treat as significant those categoric attributes which the members of the community and culture inform us they discriminate and to connect these with behavior and organization. In dealing with animals, it is also a truism that behavior varies with category: age, sex, function. Communities, indeed, are unit minima organizing the individuals realizing such categories.

(2) *Spaces.* Communities occupy and use space and its contents, have territories the individuals exploit, create boundaries. They use such space and "environment" differentially. Upon space they produce what the geographer calls culture and the ecologist calls modification of the environment: dumps, blights, houses, canals, roads, harvests, etc. All these are such that maps can record. They assign space differentially to their members, to individuals, to categories of individuals, to functional offices. Thereby they produce settlement patterns, land use and property distributions, assembly points and dispersal zones with tracks between, segregations of sex, age, class, occupation, rank, etc., and the things of each of these. Maps and charts can describe these, and every community and every culture patterns these but patterns them differently, as does every animal species, too. Obviously intricate connections interlace population and space use, (1) and (2) here.

(3) *Times.* Communities occupy their spaces in time. They alternately show dispersal of their persons (to the fields, to the hills, by the season, by day, etc.) with assemblage of them (in sleeping quarters, in ceremonies, in communal efforts, in war). There are climatic and economic rounds, calendars, shorter cycles of euphoria and dysphoria, longer rhythms of generational expansion or colonial budding, monthly, weekly, daily periodicities. There are periodic yields of the community's space and things in crops, in

production, in volume of transactions or of traffic. All these are such that time rates can record. They engage the members differentially, and the description that tells us which members engage when and which do not in this action or that is a necessary complement to our knowing who they are and where the community places them. We cannot compare communities without confronting these periodicities from one community to the next. It is not enough merely to know that we already make imprecise temporal comparisons implicitly: sedentary versus transhumant communities, tight Apollonian sabbatarian ones versus loose Dionysian ones of occasional and irregular celebrations. We must discover in each case explicitly how the community specifically acts out its own sense of time.

(4) *Functions.* Furthermore, communities collectivize in their space; among their members, through their lives (which are generations long and thus longer than those of their members), many gains for individual and for social survival or advantage. We have named some of them already. These too must appear in our models and the gains must be spelled out. But the functions do not define the communities. Any culture has other ways of defense, of mate finding, of socializing, that extend beyond the community or that may supplant the community's. Likewise, communities, like other things, can develop dysfunctions, pain and thwart members, gain or lose functions, without losing identity. Yet some functional reason for any phenomenon's identity certainly exists. In this case the reason seems clear; we will risk repetition to point it out again. The record indicates that some local, continuing grouping of men or animals nearly always comes to exist. Bigger than the family or the mating pair, it insures continuity of the species. Where the species is human—to wit, a culture (for it is only in man that differentiation of kind takes not a genetic but a cultural form)—a characteristic minimal unit of personnel arises, as surely as in its animal counterpart, to subsist in space and endure over lives, sufficient to insure cultural transmission. Thus a human community, specifically, contains within it—and the content gives us both our definition and our problem—roles for every kind and office of mankind that the culture knows: husband, farmer, old man, mother, child, proletarian, priest, etc. A human community does this as surely as does one of ants, which, too, provides a role for every kind of ant the species has evolved: queen, worker, egg, soldier, larva. But the mechanisms, of course, are now known to be quite different.

Tables of functions performed for persons and for groups, then, are quite necessary tools for analysts of this unit of organization and continuity in cultural transmission in man, just as they are for physiologists of cells, organs, and organisms. But they are no more so than the maps and time charts we have already cited.

(5) *Structure and Process.* A model for a community, then, and any models we make for American ones, must put all these things together. It

will represent, and help us explore, the characteristic minimal organization of the bearers of a culture in time and space. How will we put these things together; what devices will best represent them and the whole they make? Trial will tell. We cannot predict in advance, in the abstract. Devices for representing empirical structure and process must be invented, searched out of many prior human experiences, tried and fitted to reality again and again.

Once found, invented, tested, they will fit each community's use of time and space and function and follow each community's organization of roles, institutions, and personnel. The models will have form, carry out functions, show structure, unfold process, like the communities. They will both show the properties we know already and ready us to predict effects and also follow laws we do not yet know are theirs. The double promise of such models is the double promise of science: ordering of the commonplace and unexpected discovery of the unknown.

COMMUNITY PATTERNS IN THE UNITED STATES

Let us now take the known historical communities of the United States and submit them to analysis. We can begin with the New England town.

The New England Town

There is much distinctive about the New England town. First, there is its historical (cultural) descent. I think it unnecessary to go into the long and difficult controversy within American history about the importation or the invention *in situ* of the New England town. Suffice it to say that the eminent colonial historian Wertenbaker accepts the derivation of the New England town from the manorial village of the champion country of East Anglia, whence most of the Puritans came, a derivation established by Homans. In East Anglia that village in turn was a local specialization of the open-field village of the North European plain. It was brought in to newly opened fenlands by Angles and Saxons from the Elbe mouth and was of a settlement pattern, village type, and agriculture quite different from that of once-Celtic western Britain and even from that of nearby once-Belgian and Jutish Kent. Nothing prevents inventors in a New World from elaborating, adapting, formalizing already familiar, even unconscious, heritages. In fact, that is the way anthropology tells us most cultural evolution (*anglice* "invention") proceeds. The urbanizing Puritans rationally planning new settlements in the wilderness were elaborating ancestral cultural materials and, as we shall see, every other American pioneer community did likewise.

Even the distribution of the New England town, its second distinctive trait, confirms its character as culture trait. The town about the green or common, with its centered church and town hall, seats of a single village-wide congregation and town meeting, with its town territory stretching out over fields and woods used by farmers and artisans clustered at the square rather than spread through the open countryside, went only where the New England Yankees went, mixed only where they mixed, survived or died only where they survived or died as a majority. Outside New England, as we know, that is only upstate New York and Long Island; in mixture, the Great Lakes country and the upper Middle West; in descent, Mormon Utah.

Distinctive measures of community use of personnel, space, and time require we create a very special model for the New England town, either for its heyday till the coming of the industrial revolution or for its crippled and dying modern isolated back-country remnant. Take membership first, and let us see who belonged. The nucleated settlement pattern made for close living; the neighbors were fellow-townsmen, visible and ever-present but not necessarily kinsmen. Endogamy, however, was fairly usual and exogamy not obligatory. In this the cultural tradition of the European and Near Eastern but not that of the Indian, Chinese, or African village was preserved, a community pattern which Murdock has mistaken for a kinship form he calls the "deme." Hence, fellows of the town were nearer than kinfolk, and kin moving off to another town soon fell away. The brittle, easily split "nuclear" or "democratic" ("Eskimoan") family, the *famille particulariste* of Le Play, native to North Europe, came with these Yankees from England and fitted well their egalitarian, unstratified farmer-artisan towns.

These Yankee towns were originally single congregations and autonomous villages. They were under the rule of their own householders, as heads of families ("town fathers"), and of their own elders, who hired and fired their own clergy, determined their own orthodoxy, enforced conformity and morality, easily mistaking their own common one-class customs, under a Calvinist Protestantism freed of hierarchical and external control, for exclusive religious truth, through the whole gamut of custom from belief to sumptuary law and sabbath meeting. The same direct democracy among fathers and householders prevailed politically, under the larger framework of inherited English law, at least till the crown reasserted control, and the body of the congregants were also the town meeting, an assemblage of the whole. Church and town hall were one building or, if two, stood side by side on the village common, and only the drop of a gavel might separate religious from secular deliberations.

Only later were there any class distinctions, and these grew up *in situ* among kindred, on a functional basis. Later, on the eve of industrializing, classes and sections were to break away from Yankee equality. Poor pioneers were to break away on the outer western fringe, in the "burnt-over country" of York State, into Mormonism and the evangelical sects of the frontier; merchant patricians on the eastern edge were to give Boston and Unitarianism its distinctive character, in a move which left the Puritans' Congregationalism a core church and subculture, still confined to Puritan middle (and middle-class) territory. But, before all that, Yankees were farmers, artisans, shopkeeper-merchants, seamen and fishermen, without distinction or segregation either in community membership, political right, or use of living space. They were all townsmen together.

It may well be this culturally distinctive use of community space, not any agricultural poverty of New England, which made the Yankee an egalitarian jack-of-all-trades, both individualist in motive and deeply trained in civic co-operation and association. The nucleated village of the open-field agriculture of the North European plain shows many parallels to Yankee tradition, even as far out east as the Russian and Ukrainian *mir*. "National character" studies have still to work out what parallels in social organization and psychological traits in culture respond to substrata of common folk tradition and what to superstructures of state and national institutions of special political and historical development.

Thus, like some other *North* Europeans, these one-congregation, egalitarian villages lived by nuclear families, without much functional extended kinship, with equal division of inheritance, some freedom of divorce, and some ancestral near-equality of the sexes (later to flower in special American feminism). They had the habit of setting up children on their own quite young and of supporting the old and indigent "on the town." They had town officers, such as fenceviewers, weighmasters, etc., remote descendants of the village servants, the gooseherds, cowherds, haywards, and swineherds of the medieval Old World. They displayed, too, the republican tradition of a Roman Cincinnatus, best described as a tendency to assign public office in rotation among "pillars of the community" (and of the church, the same thing) but otherwise to show extreme suspicion of one man's getting ahead of his neighbors, to the point of concealing wealth and understating ability.

Just as the consequences of the New England townsmen's use of space were marked, so were those of their use of time. Frequent daily intercourse of neighbors and townsfolk, continuous contact of the young people among themselves at each age of growing up, as well as enforced frequent sabbatarian communion, meant a dense collective experience, a chance for internalization of these rigidities of repetitive role and habit, a readiness to seek consensus coupled with a stubbornness of egalitarian judgment about which much has long been written. Yet little thought is given, outside the New England heritage, to the rarity of such "town meeting democracy" and "Puritan conscience" in the rest of the American scene. Even the generational rhythm of the New England town, which peopled much of the northern frontier (but far less than is usually assumed), was a use of long-wave time both distinctive and congruent with the nucleated, egalitarian "open-field village" of the cultural past. For it was in New England, and in New England alone, that towns, like Greek cities, sent out whole colonies of surplus young people, newly married church "elders" in their late teens, complete with church, town plan, minister, treasury, etc., in short, a full apparatus for nucleated community living. Only the Mormon community and culture, later-day offshoots of New England, still expands so, in our own present, as they spread up into the Bitterroot Mountains of Idaho, town by town up the mountain valleys.

If this Yankee community, the New England town, is a faithful microcosm in its distinctive pattern of the New England culture in its region and in its epochs of rise and flower, are there other American communities equally distinct? Yes, there are many, as we shall see, and we can find others at once in two other well-known original colonial regions where the first American cultures were established.

The Southern County

For ease of recognition, it is best to turn next to the American Old South, tracing it from its Tidewater beginnings through its Deep South extensions south and west over three centuries of movement toward Texas and California. As we shall see, the original sectionalism, North and South, was a too easy division of the complex country, even in colonial times, but it is so familiar that we can begin with it. We know a great deal about this Old South, counterpoise to the Yankee North, but have we analyzed its historical form of community? Plantations, poor whites, Negro slavery, Anglicanism and Methodism, "Bourbonism" and Fundamentalism, are culture traits we did not need to mention for New England. However, it is not the new traits but their organization into a community of new personnel, space, time, functions, and form that we must specify.

The distinctive community form of the South was and is the county. Dispersed a day's ride in and out around the county seat, that community assembled planter and field- or house-hand from the fat plantations, free poor white or Negro from the lean hills and swamps, for the pageantry and the drama of Saturdays around the courthouse, when the courthouse, the jail, the registry of deeds, and the courthouse square of shops and lawyers' row made a physical center of the far-flung community. This is the American counterpart of the Spanish and Portuguese *municipio*, the French and German *commune* and *Gemeinde*, the rural counterpart of the baroque capital which Mumford called the city of the palace and the parade. It is a product of the same age, the age of the rise of the national state, whose community form it represents.

It is a mistake to treat this county and county seat for its separate parts and to try to find the community in the Old South at any other level. The poor white or Negro hamlets about a country church, set in hill or swamp retreat, the plantation, however large and proud and populous, the county seat as town (older ones seldom had distinctive organs apart from their function as county seat), were and are none of them complete communities. The county itself was the unit of dispersal and assemblage, and it was a two-class community from its inception in the gathering-in of nobles into the king's palace and capital along with *noblesse de robe* and rich *bourgeois*. Formed from the coming together of landowner and *peón*, its pattern of dispersal was a double one, with estates covering the good land, and little men, now clients, now runaways, taking up the leavings in the bad. Nowhere is the church, even the baroque cathedral, the center of this community, either physically or spiritually. There are many churches, and these split along the lines of class or ethnicity: rural chapels in the hamlets and the *barrios*, fundamentalist sectarian or Indianly "superstitious," and city ones, seats of fashion and elegance. The church, both as building and as institution, is overshadowed by another, cynosure of all eyes, seat of power and decision, repository of land grants and commercial debt-bonds: the courthouse, the "palacio."

The county of the Old South, spread across the land to California but purest in the Tidewater and the Black Belt, is the American community form of the Baroque Age. Its distinctly American accents—Methodism, Baptism, and White Supremacy—like the distinct American pattern of race relations to which it gave rise, do not separate it generically from its Latin and Old World counterparts. It received, like the New England town, much of English law and of North European and British Protestantism, two culture elements that never penetrated Latin America, but it reworked these into forms which have no semblance of the forms New England gave these things. In no particular of community form can we find the Southern county like the New England town. Neither in land use, nor in dispersal and assemblage, nor in use of time, nor in deploy of functions, is there anything in which the one community resembles the other, despite their common institutional elements and borrowings. And the cultures were and are just as different as the two communities which miniature them.

These two American communities, then, are easily recognizable and as easily contrasted, and it is not hard to see their reflection of their regional American cultures. It is not hard, either, to make similar recognition of well-documented ethnic-minority communities and their reflected cultures in some other instances. The Spanish–New Mexican culture of the Southwest is mirrored faithfully in such a village as the El Cerrito of Leonard and Loomis, lineal descendant of the Castillian *pueblo*, the centered wheat-village of Spain; the Mormon village of Nelson, descendant of the New England town out of upstate Yankee New York, has already been cited, if its palpable miniaturizing of the Mormon culture is not yet fully spelled out. The Cajun line-village, blood descendant of northern French line-villages of France and Canada, is less well known, beyond Smith's references. This is because the Cajun culture itself is as yet unstudied, though the very form of the line-village would suggest that the *famille souche* way of life that Miner found in St. Denis would hardly fall out of an association with this community which marks the French and their children from Normandy to the bayou country. These minority ethnic communities and cultures of the United States are not unpredictable. It is rather to other cultures or sub-cultures of the "majority" population of the country that we should turn. With them we enter upon scenes less well stereotyped, where our thesis that communities microcosm cultures gets a stiffer test.

Crossroads Hamlets and Main Street Towns

Very much less known are the cultural derivation and continuation, and the communities, of the great American middle country. The American historian Wertenbaker, referred to earlier, reminds us that the Middle Colonies were just that. They were ethnically neither New England Yankee (East Anglian Puritan) nor Southern Cavalier. They were Swedish, Dutch, Quaker English, Welsh, Pennsylvania German, Scots-Irish, and many mixtures of these elements. From the Middle Colonies, too, came two new regions: the Middle West, recipient of streams from all three distinctive seaboard colonial sections but by-and-large continuant of the adjacent Middle Colonies rather than of off-center New England and the South, and the Middle or Appalachian Frontier.

These two new regions, in a historical order the reverse of our naming them here, were the first American regions to stand clear, to rise out of mixture and to shape new and free conditions. They remain distinct today. Any list of American regions must count them in, though the names are various. The best recent treatment of regional cultures still lists them as the Appalachian-Ozark region (i.e., the better-known Hill South) and the Cornbelt. But under any name they must be treated as the full-fledged and distinctive regional cultures that they are. Again, like the original Middle Colonies, that seedbed of mixture that parented them, they still call their majority members by the only possible name: "Americans." Other older regions, where mixture was less, have their own names for such majority members, reminiscent of some degree of common ethnic origin: "Yankees" and "Southerners" of "English ancestry." The majority members of the regions Frontier and Midwest have no such ease in naming themselves. They are only "Americans," not "English stock," except in mix, but as often children of Scots, Welsh, Irish, Germans, Scandinavians, Slavs, Latins, and the endless other in-wanderers since. Only the common name will do. The culture that united and unites under that name the diverse minorities of the great Atlantic migration was a local emergent from such mix, and it still must be recognized in three versions: Middle Colonial (now called Middle Atlantic), Frontier (now Appalachian), and Middlewestern.

Are there, then, three American communities to match these three American cultures of the preindustrial past? Are there three, or more, community forms common to our joint national experience of the United States palpably different from the New England town and the Southern county? Indeed there are. They are dealt with often enough in the literature, both scientific and popular, but they have not been recognized for what they are. Only when we put our comparative tests to work and ask about comparative uses of persons, space, time, function, and form do we see that the differences from New England and Southern experience which we all know mark Middle Atlantic, Appalachian, and Middlewestern life are systematic and thus cultural. Only then do we see that our common experience reflects identifiable community forms, not yet recognized comparatively, and that these forms, like those of the town and the county cited so far, faithfully give body to units of their regional cultures.

First of all, there is the matter of the community's use of space. These three regions, a parent and two offspring, share in common their patterns of dispersal and assemblage, facts better known under the rubric "settlement pattern." The distinctively American settlement pattern, an "open-country neighborhood" (*Einzelhofsiedlung*), marks all three of these regions as it does *not* the Plantation South and New England. Whence came this new, now all-American pattern? Before cultural anthropology flourished, it was all too easy to derive such patterns of land use from the necessities of the frontier, or the rational plans of colonizers and land speculators, or the workings of individual ownership and republican ideals. Cultural anthropology, however, teaches us that we must look for the native covert custom and value that underlie such necessities and rationalities. The human mind (perhaps always) works with some prior experience in adapting to new conditions, not in a vacuum, and it needs some experience other than pure logic to rationalize. Just as it was all too easy to assume, till we learned its Swedish derivation, that the log cabin was a "natural" adaptation to the frontier, so is it all too easy to think this settlement pattern, and the communities which came of it, was "naturally" and not culturally given.

The truth of the matter, however, is cultural. The Middle Atlantic region received as its pioneer settlers, of all those who came to the colonies, the very immigrants who already practiced not village or plantation life but *Einzelhof* dispersal of individual farms. The Dutch, especially the Frisians, already put individual farms on polder plots at home. The Pennsylvania "Dutch" (Palatinate, Swiss, Rhenish, and Westfalian) brought individual *Grossbauer* family farms of mixed, intensive agriculture with them from their homelands to fill up the Appalachian valley floors from the Delaware seaboard to the Susquehanna and thence south up the Shenandoah. And the Scots-Irish, that new English-speaking mix of Celts arising in Ulster and the English frontier in Ireland, a group without a name (except "Orange-men" or "Presbyterian") till William Cullen Bryant invented one here for them in 1870, filled up the mountainsides and the forest coves and clearings beyond the English and Quaker towns, farm by farm, with a few cows and a saddle bag of corn seed, from New Hampshire to the Great Smokies, in a New World repetition of the same Celtic dispersed-farm cattle-and-kitchen-garden agriculture that marks Irish small farms and Scots crofts to this day.

Certainly the Revolutionary Land Grants to soldiers and the later Homestead Acts rationalized and generalized open-country individual farm settlement on the Frontier and in the Old Northwest that soon became a mere "Middle," but the pattern was already laid down in the Middle Colonies. Yankees went to the frontier in wagon trains, to planned villages, and Southerners, some of them, to plantations and county seats cut from the virgin woods, but the Midlanders did neither. They went singly, family by family, into the lands they cleared simply by accretion of farms into "neighborhoods." Their first communities were mere crossroads where scattered neighbors met. Their schools and churches and stores, like their camp meetings and their fairs, were set haphazardly in the open country or where roads met, with no ordered clustering and no fixed membership. But this "pioneer community" is no accident, no "natural" growth of the American frontiers, not even of "isolation" and sparse population. For those who know comparative cultures its Old World origin is plain, and this supposedly "natural," "primitive" pattern is as culturally distinctive and complete as any other.

In such communities the settlers' unit of government, like their point of assemblage, was no town nor *any* fixed place. It was instead a rural "township" or several such diffuse authorities. It was not a single centering but instead a fluid crisscrossing net of emergent countrysides and cantons, variously linking farms in overlapping paths among spreading neighbors, kindred, and fellow-sectarians, about crossroad hamlets or open grounds of infrequent gathering. Even today in the Middle country, from New Jersey to the Rockies, this is the older community form in the countryside, and it persists among the farms despite the growth of towns, burgs, counties, and service centers, marks of later urban consolidation. Even today, in the middle country, the townsman is a separate creature, with no place or vote in the countryside, just as the farmer, chief support of Main Street though he be, is not a citizen of the burg he patronizes but lives and votes beyond the corporate boundaries of the town. Here, in all the middle country, the centered town, either as county seat or as residence of farmers, New England style, is an afterthought. The older communities were the open-country neighborhoods.

Now this sort of community, a rural network of relationships running across countrysides and cantons, round occasional and ephemeral centers of assemblage at shrine or fair or crossroad hamlet, this origin of open-country neighborhoods and townships without urban centering, is honestly come by. As a heritage of culture form it is not unique in the world. To the cultural anthropologist who brings Atlantic Europe into his ken it is very familiar. This is the settlement pattern, community form and cantonal rural republican social organization that marks the fringe of the Atlantic from the Berber country north through "wet Spain" and the Basque and Celtic lands to West Britain, Scotland, and Scandinavia. It is the very community which marked the lands whence the Middle Colonists, so many if not all of them, came. Far older in Europe than the open-field village, or the pueblo, the *latifundium*, and the *municipio*, it is no wonder that its recrudescence and generalization in the English-language cultures' spread across the continent should seem to gentlefolk or pious townsmen a reversion to the primitive. But a submerged culture pattern is not lost, nor is it by reason of submergence any the less capable of further growth. On the Frontier, in the Appalachian region, this community reflected well till just the other day the mostly Scots-Irish-derived culture. Loose, open, Dionysian, kin-based, *famille-souche*, and subsistence farming rather than commercial- or urban-minded, egalitarian through isolation and personal honor rather than through conscience and congregational control, this culture and this community were and are a match. Both are age-long Atlantic European heritages which Americans have not lost and are not likely to lose in the future. This community, like this culture, is as different from either the town or the county we have already named as is sober Saxon different from wild Scot in the British homeland or Andalusian and Gallego in Spain.

When the settled towns did come to the American frontier, as they had come not so long before to the Atlantic European frontiers, they did not change the community forms of the three Middle cultures of the United States out of hand. The new communities that still exist in the Middle Colonies and the Hill South and the Middle West built around urban centers are neither free of the ethnic traditions of those colonies nor deeply planted in older urbanism like the cities that grew up in New England and the Deep South. There has been no final supplanting of this Atlantic-European dispersed-settlement cultural tradition but rather a mingling and borrowing of traits, in which the older traditions have been deepened and transformed. The Hillman and the Midwesterner are not gone, nor are they likely to disappear, and the different continuities they represent back to pre-Roman, pre-German, pre-Christian Atlantic Europe are nonetheless great because anthropology has just barely come to search for them. When today Zimmerman and Du Wors report Middlewestern Cornbelt and Great Plains towns seeking newer industrial and civic forms, commercializing and abandoning the open countryside for in-town residence, the anthropological reader stands before a further cultural succession and adaptation not yet known in any form, transforming an older "Middle America" still little understood.

In all this, however, we must not neglect the great transformations of internal and continuing cultural evolution. New cultures have overtaken the United States, and new cultures, like old ones, must be expected to show in new communities new organization. The cultures and communities of the social organism called the U.S.A. are no longer confined by any means to those brought by the original settlers of either seacoast or frontier.

The great transformations of the industrial revolution, which ushered in our first great new cultural age, brought also a new community. Naturally, if a community microcosms a culture, then so does a cultural revolution bring along as well a revolution in community form, if the correspondence of the two is to keep pace. That such a new community form struck the United States, beginning in New England and spreading slowly west and south, we already know. It remains only to show how the mill town and factory city, which long ago first supplanted and still continue to supplant the New England town, the Southern county seat, and the open-country neighborhoods and crossroads hamlets of older America, are in fact small and big exemplars of a new community form.

Here, of course, I follow the trail that Mumford blazed. He showed graphically the huge revolution in living, in cultural and social organization, that the cities of factory and slum brought in. Park and Burgess went on to show us the form within the outward formlessness of Chicago, the railroad city of concentric zones and dynamic succession and decay, the American industrial city in its heyday of 1905. Later in the early thirties when Lynd went to an American "Middletown" it was to such an industrial town, and when Warner and his students gave us Yankee City and Natchez and Jonesville, in New England, South, and Middle West, it was still to mill towns that they went. For mill towns had invaded and transformed all the older communities, just as the Coal and Iron Age sooted up the older rural culture horizons.

What, then, is a mill town, a factory city, as community form? First, it is a new and distinctive use of space. The new slum-building ("industrial blight"), and the other dynamic succession-and-withdrawal patterns of land and building use in industrial cities, are perfectly lawful and formal patterns, congruent and coincident with the monetarization and the commercialization of the cultural age of the free market and the laissez-faire capitalism they represent. The mill town, born in Britain, has spread, in greater or lesser conjunction with these other patterns of its age, like any other culture wave. It has spread out and around the world for a century and a half, and it is only now in recession and change. In U.S.A. the same mill towns (standard Midwestern American calls them "factory towns") web from New England, whence the New England flavor of their name. Mill towns are dying as captured satellites of a still newer metropolitan community form in the homeland, while they win new territory in continuous diffusion into the Southern and Southwestern and Appalachian regions. In all these spreads and migrations the mill-town forms are constant despite accidents of local circumstance and graft to former patterns.

This use of space is telltale. Far from being merely chaotic and lawless, the "unplanned" form the early industrial cities of America took was a new and distinctive (if unlovely) community form. The new use of space gives us the typical banded and stratified zonal ordering of better and better houses from the slums in the industrial valley, on Water Street and River Street, down by the docks or behind the railroad yards, up to the massed squires' houses on the Hill.

This use of space bands and zones the middle-class dwellings and the middle-class shops in the middle and crams the mills and the warehouses and the industrial warrens of factory workers and immigrant hands in the narrow blighted bottoms which once were the marketplaces and the crossroads of the older towns. It creates a new assemblage center in the railroad station and the "downtown center" about it and a new pattern of withdrawal whereby the same railroad or the avenues—pushing out the "Main Line"—put the better-off and higher occupations of the common factories on which all depend in progressively farther removed residential blocks. It makes visible in external display these graded and successive zones of better or worse neighborhoods and mirrors perfectly an open-class system's scalar stratification of incomes, of power, and of prestige in the zonal successions one sees moving inward from withdrawn garden suburb to blighted tenement district.

The once-new mill town's use of time is of a pattern with this use of space. The commutation lines of streetcar and train and the staggered hours of arrival at work, like the loss of play space and park space to mills, yards, and streets, and the sharp separation of work and leisure, spell out in space and time a community tuned to the factory whistle, stratified according to him who obeys it and him who orders it blown, and united about the mill and its livelihood for worker and owner alike. The mill town is the community of the Victorian industrial age, and it is so much with us, especially in memory and survival, that we need hardly spell it out further. But it is also a community form in perfect harmony with the layered, visible, and pecuniary stratification of its age, with the fluid dynamism of its progressive exhaustion and befouling of an environment which in its heyday, as we now know from a hundred commentators, its people treated first and foremost as a workshop for their machines. It is no wonder, then, that the "open-class system" (or the six-class system, if you prefer Warner) and the "pecuniary civilization" should have a distinctive community form in the mill town and its succession, its blight, and its mechanical massing of visible likes and unlikes.

But the once-new mill town and the sooty, cluttered Pittsburghs and Birminghams of a proud Victorian industrial age are no longer young. They are things in transformation, and a new age, with a new community, has fast supplanted them in its turn. On a hundred fronts the new age of the automobile, of the branch factory with the career manager, of the metropolitan mass-communication city and suburb, of the leveling of incomes and proliferating of "peer groups" and equalized consumptive standards, of the "building back" and clearance of slums and huge desertion of the downtown cities for the Levittowns and highway shopping centers and "rurban fringes" of midcentury, come relentlessly on. The new age is perhaps easiest to see in the new cities and suburbs built since the automobile, like Los Angeles, and hardest to accept in the blighted and abandoned industrial cities of yesteryear. But all the voices agree that it has come.

The new community that corresponds to the newest age is much less understood or even perceived. Yet there is a good deal of writing about it that gives us some evidence of the new form the new metropolitan community has taken or will take. The difficulty is to see the new form whole, rather than in disconnected pieces, and for that, as before, a model must serve.

What are the pieces, then, that we must fit into such a comprehensive model? First, as always, there is the matter of use of space. The new metropolitan community, first charted by McKenzie, is the circle of one and a half to two hours commuting by car from the old downtown railroad center of the city, from which the new mass communications of newspapers, radio, and television now radiate. The various metropolitan district devices and authorities in evolution today, for water, parks, belt highway, and port controls, seem to be political attempts to cope with the metropolis of this huge area and population. With numbers divided in many cases nearly half and half between the outer ring of once independent suburban and satellite settlements and the inner city, neither suburb nor core city will give up the jealous independence of the last century. (New York has not expanded its city's official boundaries since 1895, three generations ago.) Only some new overarching authority can match the new city form.

Within this huge metropolitan space, the new supercity is struggling to take the form of a great wheel of internal traffic arteries and peripheral belts. New factories appear in the empty fields on the outer fringe, where highways and belt roads serve them better than any railroads, and new dormitory suburbs mushroom to bring workers to them or to move workers and white-collars, now less distinguishable, into greener quarters and automotive mobility. At the nodes between artery and belts, between spokes and rims of the great new urban wheel-form, huge new shopping centers arise which duplicate in all particulars, except the centering of mass communications for the whole itself, the erstwhile downtown congestions of traffic, shopping, business, and entertainment. This is the great decentralized city of the automotive age, and no planning can reverse its evolution, just as no plans which belie its form, from traffic roads to slum clearance, can do more than delay or impede its taking its characteristic shape.

In the great and small segments of the huge circle that artery and belt highways cut out, a new urban life—better, a new suburban one—is already well emerged. This is the life of the "peer groups" of the "lonely crowd" which Riesman rightly sees. It is a huge mosaic of massed segregations of age, class, and ethnic group. Because older withdrawn suburbs, new real-estate developments of massed conformity, enclaved factory satellite towns, old slums and factories, and built-back reclaimed areas are all grown together now and stand contiguous in the unbroken urban-suburban expanse, little remains of the old gradations and transitions between house type and house type and class and class. The old graduated concentric zones of the industrial city are fast disappearing. The mosaic that takes their place is a crazy-quilt of discontinuities, where the fault-line between toney garden suburb and Levittown or rich Sutton Place and squalid Dead End is abrupt, sudden, and hostile, sometimes even policed with a guard or marked by a ten-foot fence. It is no wonder that the persons who grow up in such juxtapositions see nothing of the community pattern as a whole, no longer have intimate connection with and reference toward ordered groups a little "better" or a little "worse" than themselves, but turn inward instead to the welter of their peer-group segregations.

This mosaic of discontinuities of age, class, and ethnicity which is the new metropolitan community is a very different one indeed from the visibly hierarchic and mobile community that preceded it. It is not for us here to explore its new features; the subject is doubly difficult because so few people, in or out of social science, have yet learned to look at the metropolitan city whole. Nevertheless, the new cultural form, with its new social and economic traits and problems, is here before us, in the most violent emergence, and the new age has already found its new unit of transmission and organization.

By analyzing studies of acculturation contributed by reputable scholars over a period of years, Leonard Mason, an anthropologist, offers a summary of American cultural values. He describes the commonly accepted beliefs about ethos, economics and technology, social organization, education and welfare, religion and morality, and government and administration.

Mason's summary indicates that, although the prevailing mode of thinking among the scholars cited involves an acceptance of regional and community differences, there is a clear tendency on their part to accept the "core culture" concept (see Chapter 21 for a detailed explanation of this term).

THE CHARACTERIZATION OF AMERICAN CULTURE IN STUDIES OF ACCULTURATION

Leonard Mason

ETHOS

The individual in American society participates in a culture of intricacies and inconsistencies which he is conditioned to accept as normal. Converging lines of development, associated with diverse immigrant strains, conflicting standards of conduct, varied religious sects, and changing economic conditions, have produced a culture that lacks integration. Each individual must regulate his being within a system that separates social, economic, and religious activities, distinguishes between rural and urban and among lower, middle, and upper class, and combines the frontier spirit of Texas with the staid conservatism of New England. He is constantly urged to take the initiative, to assume responsibility, and to consider his own interests above those of his fellows. He may earn approval in so far as he can demonstrate his ability to be resourceful, self-reliant, industrious, and thrifty. He is strongly motivated to achieve personal success, which is measured almost entirely by the income he earns, the property he acquires, and the size of his bank account. Distinction must be achieved within a highly competitive system in which each person tries to do better than his neighbor. An ever-popular theme is the success story of poor boy who became rich by his own efforts and was thereafter the envy of all.

Americans are quick to profess ideals of social democracy, freedom of expression for individual personality, and equality of opportunity unhampered by distinctions of sex, age, race, or religion. The observation that reality often gives the lie to this profession of ideals is perhaps affirmed by the incidence of neuroses among Americans—casualties from the exacting complications of a choice-demanding culture. Some find it difficult to reconcile the aggressive competitiveness essential to the attainment of success with

Reprinted from *American Anthropologist,* Vol. 57, No. 6, Part 1 (December 1955), pp. 1268–1274. Footnotes omitted.

The following sketch of U.S. American culture is based entirely upon characterizations which have appeared in some 65 articles and books written since 1930 by American anthropologists on the acculturation of American Indians and Pacific Islanders who have been exposed in some degree to that culture through the agency of Americans at home or overseas. It thus reflects the manner in which these anthropologists have tended to view their own culture.—*Leonard Mason* the middle-class virtues of honesty, charity, chivalry, and group loyalty. Then, too, Americans have enslaved themselves to the questionable virtue of punctuality and routine, with lives geared to the clock and the calendar. Related to this is an impatience with delay, a penchant for quick and direct action, and a disposition to look to the future and to plan far in advance of present needs.

Science and education are much admired and respected. Physical nature is regarded as something which must be controlled and harnessed to man's advantage. Americans have faith that this can be done through the application of scientific knowledge. Human nature is conceived as being evil though perfectible. Fortified by success in altering their physical surroundings, Americans are equally confident that undesirable social conditions can be remedied just as easily and are confused when such proves not to be the case. Despite a consuming faith in scientific medicine, Americans display considerable anxiety about personal health and make cleanliness a virtue of the highest order.

TECHNOLOGY AND ECONOMICS

The American economic scene has many facets, each variously represented in different sections of the nation. Prominently featured is the agricultural economy, an exploitation of vast lands acquired from the Indians. Homesteading has established many a farming family. Modern farmers invest long hours of daily toil, aided by mechanized equipment and scientific guidance, in anticipation of future rewards when their farm produce is marketed in the cities. Land also provides pasturage for cattle herds and flocks of sheep, which stockmen raise for the same markets. Still other Americans wrest a living from the land through exploitation of its timber and mineral resources.

An equally prominent feature is the capitalistic industrial system based on the concept of credit. Investment and financial promotion are conducted in an atmosphere of competitive individualism where success is measured in dollar profits. Essential to the functioning of this system are the techniques of mass production and a highly specialized labor force. Laborers are required to work regularly and efficiently for sustained periods, for which individual compensation is allowed. Satisfactory conditions of work are maintained by co-operation between management and labor. Individual migration permits a relatively fluid labor supply, which is needed to offset a constantly fluctuating labor market.

Americans have been described as having a "money-gathering economy." Money is the common denominator of exchange by which the relative worth of goods and services is measured. Without it Americans are unable to acquire the material comforts of life. Property, whether personal or real, is held in private (individual) ownership with legal provisions for transfer by sale or by inheritance from a man to his children. Americans commonly furnish their permanent, closed dwellings with beds, tables, chairs, rugs, curtains, clocks, and kitchenware. Homes in rural areas constitute a source of pride and prestige, but in the workaday world of skyscraper cities they tend to become merely places in which to eat and sleep. The American diet, overweighted as it is with carbohydrates, features bacon and eggs, bread, cow's milk, steaks, mashed potatoes, vegetables, and ice cream. Popular as snacks are hamburgers, Coca-Cola, and candybars. For many an American a Sears Roebuck catalog is adequate index to the variety of hats, shoes, shirts, trousers, dresses, cosmetics, and toiletries that are necessary for comfort, modesty, or improvement on nature's handiwork. Thousands of such essential items are offered for sale in the many stores and shops that grace every community. These emporiums, combined with countless beauty parlors, movie theaters, taverns, cafes, and service stations, represent an impersonalized system of commerce that is supported by mechanized transport operating throughout the nation on an elaborate network of roads and rails.

SOCIAL ORGANIZATION

Although social intercourse between the sexes is generally free in both school and home, Americans tend to be prudish about sex itself. In youth they are plagued by ignorance and faulty speculation or by guilty knowledge and the need for secrecy. Sex standards for mature individuals differ widely according to region, social class, and generation. The requirement by most religious sects of chastity before marriage frequently induces frustration among young people who cherish the ideal of romantic love and who are permitted freedom of choice in seeking their mates. The wedding ceremony, which may be civil or religious, sets a public stamp of approval on the sexual relationship. But marriage is more than sex and carries with it economic and other responsibilities. Each spouse regards the arrangement as a partnership in which men treat their wives as equals and bestow small courtesies upon them. Monogamy is mandatory by law, and each party is pledged to remain faithful for life. Personality and circumstance frequently shatter this ideal. In the face of incompatibility some spouses stoically maintain the marriage form for dignity's sake, while others seek a legal divorce which permits each to remarry.

Man and wife and their children form a nuclear family, the most significant American kinship group. Family life is informal, the degree of affection among its members varying with their compatibility. The family is small enough to be easily contained in a single dwelling, which is located usually at some distance from the homes of either parent. Outside the nuclear family, kinship ties are rarely strong, though relatives by blood and by marriage are recognized on both sides. The father's line is slightly favored in that his wife and children take his surname as their own. The father furthermore assumes disciplinary and instructional responsibilities that are considered essential in the socialization of the children at home. In recent years, associated with the rise of a large and complex industrial society, the close social ties within the family group have tended to weaken.

Social relationships outside the family tend to be casual and conventionalized, as epitomized in the average handshake. Business is carried on across the nation by correspondence between persons who never see each other. Radio and television provide communication between regional divisions. Local groups and associations are founded on the basis of common interest and occupation, friendship and congeniality. The individual, and perhaps others of his immediate family, is drawn into the social life of his community by voluntary membership in the Parent Teachers Association, Women's Club, Y.M.C.A., and the Elks.

Americans of Caucasian ancestry are usually ranked in a loosely structured hierarchy of social classes that are based upon differences in occupation, income, education, and social behavior. In older and more settled communities the social restraints between classes are well defined and defy the democratic ideal of social equality, but in smaller, frontier towns a more flexible social code permits considerable personal mobility. Americans of non-Caucasian ancestry, such as Negroes and Orientals, are regarded as minority groups against which discrimination is applied in employment, marriage, and social participation. This race-caste system is characterized by a greater rigidity than are class distinctions among Caucasians, especially in regions where racial groups are in closer contact and where segregation is enforced.

EDUCATION AND WELFARE

Practically from the moment of conception the individual in American society is surrounded with the manifestations of a traditional dread and distaste of dirt and disease. Prenatal clinics, hospital deliveries, and postnatal examinations by the family doctor provide evidence of the belief in pathogenic bacteria and of confidence in the effectiveness of antiseptic, professional assistance. Intimately linked with this preoccupation with cleanliness is the American obsession about schedules, e.g., babies are bathed, nursed, toileted, and put to bed by the clock. This conversion to a life of routine is hastened by intensive disciplinary measures. When a child reaches the age of six, his arena of activity shifts from the sheltered home to the public school. In this important American institution his regular attendance is required for the next ten to twelve years, during which he is taught in a curriculum of decidedly academic character to pursue the goals of good health, good character, and good citizenship.

With all the stress on conformity of behavior, the pupil is also introduced to the value of individual enterprise. His performance in class is graded on the basis of competitive activity. As curriculum planners have come to realize that American culture is not the homogeneous entity once assumed, the child is being educated more in the techniques of adaptation to changing and varied environments. The gulf which had threatened to separate home and school as educational agencies has been narrowed by more effective co-operation between parents and teachers and by an increasing employment of school facilities for community socials and services. When the individual passes from high school to college, if he does not leave school to seek his fortune in the business world, he often views his future education as a means of self-improvement, of "getting on" in life. His behavior may be characterized increasingly as uninhibited, pushing, or climbing and reflects the re-orientation that was achieved probably at great cost after the stormy and perplexing years of adolescence.

The adult frequently faces a major problem in the conduct of his leisure time. As a child he played, as an adult he works, and the transition is not an easy one to make in American culture. Team sports, such as baseball, football, and basketball, may occupy much of his spare time, but his participation is apt to be more that of spectator than of player. Bowling, boxing, tennis, and track emphasize the role of the individual rather than the team. Nearly all sports are conducted in an atmosphere of competition in which a strong desire to win motivates player and spectator alike. Nonathletic recreation frequently follows the spectator theme, as in attendance at movies, plays, symphonies, and art exhibitions. The aggression that is sanctioned in the rivalries of the entertainment world may also be expressed on occasion, at private parties or in public places, through the use of alcoholic beverages, but opinions differ widely among Americans as to standards of indulgence.

RELIGION AND MORALITY

The very first article of the American Bill of Rights guarantees freedom of religious conviction to all within the nation's borders. The separation of church and state is equally important in the American scene. Most church members are Christians, who worship God and Jesus Christ His Son. They believe in a Heaven where happiness after death is promised and in a Hell where the sinful will be punished. Life on earth is viewed as preparation for a spiritual existence in which the personal soul, separated from the body in death, achieves immortality. Though man is held to be conceived in sin, right living may be rewarded by a forgiving God. Chastity before marriage is accorded high honor; individual consciousness of the relation of sex to sin provides support for an inflexible moral code. All people are regarded as the same before God. Brotherly love and the value of human life are religious standards which are difficult to reconcile with the waging of war as a means of resolving international disagreement.

The Holy Bible is the primary source of Christian inspiration and doctrine and must be accepted on faith. Christian principles are taught by professional clergy every Sunday in organized church services which are marked by lengthy sermons, hymn singing, and the collection of money for support of the institution. An important adjunct of the church is the Sunday School class in which children and young adults receive religious indoctrination. During the week, church socials provide opportunity for men, women, and younger people to participate in activities appropriate to their respective interests.

Christianity in the United States commonly takes the form of either Roman Catholicism or Protestantism. The latter is represented by numerous sects. These tend to emphasize the importance of conviction and belief, the sanction of personal conscience, and the evil which attends drinking, gambling, smoking, and swearing. Protestant pastors dress and behave much as other men do but often differ greatly among themselves in their religious policies and predilections, even within the same sect. Catholics give more attention to ceremony and ritual observance, utilizing a host of cult objects, such as the cross, candles at the altar, and sacred pictures and images of Jesus and the Virgin Mother. Catholic priests are readily distinguished by their garb and lead a life of celibacy in the service they have chosen. As individuals they deviate little in the major functions of the church, though differences may be noted among such orders as Jesuit, Franciscan, and Capuchin.

Despite the religious background of American history, the modern trend is toward more emphasis upon the secular. Although Americans generally feel that it is proper or necessary to be baptized, married, and buried with religious ceremony, many act as if religion had little to do with large sections of their life. It is not uncommon for such persons to attend church on Sundays and important holidays, such as Christmas and Easter, but they "turn religion off" at other times.

GOVERNMENT AND ADMINISTRATION

Equality of opportunity is the democratic principle upon which American government was founded. Public officials are elected to legislative and executive posts by universal suffrage, which is intended to insure a representative form of government. Honest, educated, practical, and civic-minded persons are sought for public service and, when elected by majority vote, are assumed to have the respect of their constituents and to exercise some influence over them. Campaigning candidates, generally supported by either Democratic or

Republican political party, provide ample evidence of the competitive aggressiveness that is found in many aspects of American life.

Government as a strictly secular institution has become for most Americans the symbol of formal authority. At the federal, state, and municipal levels this tax-supported structure is comprised of legislative bodies, judicial courts, and administrative agencies charged with the responsibility of making, testing, and implementing the body of law which governs most American activities. With this development have disappeared some of the democratic features that characterized the individualistic society of American pioneers. A relative inflexibility of operation is associated with the hierarchic organization of a centralized bureaucracy bound by civil service regulations and graded job classifications. Officials, eager for personal advancement but operating in limited areas of strict accountability, frequently exhibit a lack of co-operation and integrative capacity that is discouraging to tax-paying citizens.

In administration of dependent peoples, the government has followed a broad policy of intensive acculturation in accordance with the "melting pot" theme in the heritage of Americans. For example, Americans worked diligently to prepare Filipinos for eventual independence by training them in American methods of business, education, and government. Only recently in other areas has there appeared a tendency to interpret alien cultures in terms of their own values and to seek their preservation. Until 1933 the federal Indian Service policy urged the assimilation of Indians as individual wards of the government by the fractionization of their lands, outlawry of tribal ceremonies and substitution of Christianity, and compulsory education of Indian children at government boarding schools. Since that date a reversal of policy has emphasized the development of tribal resources, tribal self-government, and religious and ritual freedom. However, the paternalistic administrator of recent years has been impatient with slow Indian progress toward management of their own affairs. The temptation to be directive and to do things for Indians rather than patiently to encourage them to achieve autonomy has frequently suppressed Indian initiative and strengthened the bonds of dependency.

The prewar Navy Department policy of administering natives of Samoa and Guam combined a benevolent paternalism which sought to protect the islanders from outside exploitation with an authoritarian military regime that was inconsistent with the democratic ideals which were being taught in the local schools. When the Japanese mandated islands of Micronesia were acquired during World War II, Navy administration in all island groups was liberalized in the spirit of trusteeship, although it continued to reflect a duality of purpose that (1) attempted to preserve local custom and (2) encouraged adoption of the "best" in American culture. In the islands and on the reservations today, official policies are at times distorted and unevenly implemented by personnel who have an inadequate conception of cross-cultural administration or who are ill suited to the job because of ignorance and prejudice in dealing with non-Caucasian groups.

Nonofficial intercourse between Americans and dependent peoples is as varied as the heterogeneous background from which Americans spring. Traders and tourists, schoolteachers and scientists, missionaries, farmers and ranchers—each presents a different face to the Indian and Pacific islander. The native in his own environment is commonly cloaked with romance and glamor, but on closer association most Americans regard him as dirty, diseased, lazy, untrustworthy, and biologically inferior. American prejudices about Negroes and Orientals are projected to other dark-skinned peoples, who are then viewed with a contempt that is normally reserved for only the lowest in American society. Caste bars are raised to prevent intermarriage, except among white Americans of low economic and social status who tend to intermingle freely with Indians and especially mixed-bloods. During the war in the Pacific, American servicemen from small midwestern towns distinguished themselves by their informal and egalitarian manner in dealing with the islanders. Their behavior came closest to the American ideal of social democracy and as such constituted a spectacular exception to common practice in American cross-cultural relationships.

Chapter 21

GROUP VALUES — "CORE CULTURE"

WHILE THEY ACKNOWLEDGE *that the classes within each American community have different value systems, a number of anthropologists and sociologists suggest that there is also a "core culture" that represents middle-class values, and they believe these values dominate our community life. This core culture represents the characteristics that a majority of Americans and non-Americans believe best describe contemporary America. It is this system of values that people in strata of society below the core culture aspire to achieve, and strata of the society above the core culture desire to modify, lest their values be endangered. In America today, core culture values are taught in the public schools and in other educational agencies. These values reflect the intellectual, social, moral, and ethical beliefs that the schools and other educational agencies are supposed to transmit, the very beliefs that adults set up as goals for the immature. However, it must be borne in mind that conflicts between theory and practice produce tensions that influence the lives of people in many ways. In addition, the transitional nature of our society, and the role, purpose, and direction of change further complicate the task of organizing and teaching values.*

Cora Du Bois, an anthropologist, presents a description of the core culture. She believes that American culture is a culmination of the development of Western European culture, modified by social, political, economic, geographic, scientific, technical, and industrial factors peculiarly American. On the basis of an examination of the pertinent literature, from de Tocqueville to the present, Du Bois suggests that the value premises of any culture rest upon the assumptions made about man's relation to other men. For the American middle class, it is postulated that: (1) the universe is mechanistically conceived, (2) men are its master, (3) men are equal, and (4) men are perfectible. From these four basic premises many of the focal and specific values, as well as the directives, of the American value system can be derived. Using these postulates, Du Bois describes the core culture created by the middle class under three headings: effort-optimism, material well-being, and conformity.

THE DOMINANT VALUE PROFILE OF AMERICAN CULTURE

Cora Du Bois

EFFORT-OPTIMISM

Work is a specific value in American society. It is not so much a necessary condition of existence as a positive good. It is a specific instrumental value through which man strives to reach not only the goal of his own perfectibility but also the goal of mastering a mechanistically conceived universe. But in values Vaihinger's "law of the preponderance of the means over the ends" is frequently operative. Thus work becomes a goal in itself and in the process may acquire the quality of activity for its own sake. Thus recreation, although theoretically the antithesis of work, nevertheless in its activism shows many of the aspects of work. "Fun" is something that most Americans work hard for and at, so that they must be warned at forty to give up tennis for golf, or hunting trips for painting. Touring, whether at home or abroad, acquires the quality of a marathon. And this in turn is closely associated with another specific value linked with the effort-optimism syndrome, the importance placed on education. However, as we shall see later, the educational effort acquires a particularly American cast when taken in conjunction with the other two focal values, material well-being and conformity. In sum, as many foreigners have observed, American life gives the impression of activism. The directives, as well as the virtues and vices, associated with this optimistic activism are numerous: "If at first you don't succeed, try, try again"; or, in the more contemporary idiom, "Let's get this show on the road." The optimistic quality that pervades the American mood

Reprinted from *American Anthropologist,* Vol. 57, No. 6, Part 1 (December 1955), pp. 1234–1238. Footnotes omitted.

is clearly conveyed by the "bigger ergo better" mentality; the "never say die"; the "up and at 'em."

Vigor, at least as motility, connotes biologic youth. The cult of youthfulness in this society is again a specific value frequently commented upon by foreign observers. This observation is borne out by the popularity of the heroes manufactured in Hollywood and in the world of sports, by the advertisements of styles and cosmetics. As the average age of the population increases, this value is already showing signs of being given new interpretations in terms of geriatrics, etc. This will be alluded to again in following paragraphs.

MATERIAL WELL-BEING

If indeed effort is optimistically viewed in a material universe that man can master, then material well-being is a consistent concomitant value. Not only is it consistent within the value system, but it has been amply demonstrated in our national experience. It has been manifest in the American standard of living. The nation's geographic frontier and its natural resources, combined with an era of invention, have convinced most Americans of the validity of such a proposition. In the American scene progress and prosperity have come to have almost identical meaning. So deeply convinced are most Americans of what is generally called "prosperity" that material well-being is close to being considered a "right" due to those who have conscientiously practiced the specific value of work. The congruence of this view with the new science of geriatrics, social insurance, and the growth of investment trusts is obvious. It represents a consistent adjustment of specific values to a changing situation. However, as the situational context changes it may weaken the present linkage between effort and optimism with the resulting devaluation of both and thereby set up a new strain for consistency that may alter the present configuration of the American value system.

One of the most common stereotypes about the United States is its materialism. Viewed in the context of the value system presented here, materialism is less a value *per se* than an optimistic assertion of two value premises (mastery over material nature and the perfectibility of man) that have operated in a favorable environment. What foreign observers may call materialism, with derogatory or envious innuendos, is to the American a success that carries the moral connotation of "rightness"—of a system that proves itself or, as Americans would say with complete consistency, that "works." Within the frame of American value premises, success phrased as material well-being resolves the material-spiritual opposition and becomes a proof of right-mindedness. "Hard work pays off." The old and widely known proverb that, "Virtue is its own reward" has a particularly American slant, meaning not that virtue is in itself a reward but rather that virtue is rewarded.

If hard work is a "good thing" in a material universe and since it has been rewarded by material well-being, consistency requires that manual labor should be accorded dignity or, at least, should not be considered undignified. Furthermore, manual labor is an unambiguous manifestation of that activism alluded to earlier.

The salience of material well-being as a focal value in American life leads into many by-ways, some of which confuse and confound members of societies founded on a different value configuration. In military terms, for example, Americans are so profoundly convinced of the correctness of the material well-being formula that logistics forms our basic strategy. Personal heroism, though it may amply exist, is not assumed to be the fundamental requisite for victory, as it is in France. In American terms, victory is won by the sheet of matériel laid down in front of advancing infantry and by the lines of supply that must be built up to provide such a barrier between hand-to-hand combat.

In the same vein, there is little room in the American middle-class value system for the realities of physical pain, brutality, and death. Since they are nonetheless natural and undeniable, they are given a highly stylized treatment in detective fiction, newspapers, and movies that provide an acceptable discharge of tension created by the discrepancy between values and reality. Many Americans are alienated and morally repelled when they encounter the poverty and misery prevalent in certain lands. They manage to go through life untouched experientially even by those in our own population who have not succeeded—those who exist hopelessly in rural or urban slums or those who are victims of physical or psychic disasters. We have provided for the latter so effectively that they are whisked away into institutions that our national surpluses permit us to provide comparatively lavishly. Death itself has been surrounded with appurtenances of asepsis. Evelyn Waugh's *The Loved Ones* could never have been written with India as a setting. The compelling quality of this value emerges when we consider world statistics on human welfare facilities. In this respect, the United States is consistently in the lead. Yet, if we compare these statistics with the outbursts of compassion that a newspaper account of a "blue baby" will elicit, we become aware not only of the power of this focal value but also the resultant constellation that might be summarized as compulsive compassionate activism.

CONFORMITY

Viewed historically it seems probable that conformity is a more recent focal value in American culture than effort-optimism and material well-being. It may represent one of the valuational changes induced by the strain for consistency assumed earlier in the paper to be one of the forces that alter value systems. Over a century ago de Tocqueville saw with singular clarity the potential threat to national solidarity inherent in the values of individual liberty, on the one hand, and of the sovereignty of enfranchised masses, on the other hand. In the contemporary American value system, conformity represents an attempt to resolve this dilemma. The France of today, with a comparable dilemma, has still to find a resolution.

If the premises of perfectibility and equality are linked with the focal value labeled effort-optimism, then each middle-class American may legitimately aspire to maximal self-realization. But, if man is to master through his efforts a mechanistic universe, he must co-operate with his fellow-men, since no single man can master the universal machine. In other words, people are individuated and prized, but if they are to co-operate with their fellow-men for mastery of the universe or, in more modest terms, of the immediate physical and socio-political environment, too great a degree of individualization would be an impediment. Also since the American value premises—in contradistinction to much of the rest of the world—include equality, the realization of the self in such a context would not necessarily imply the development of highly personalized and idiosyncratic but rather of egalitarian traits. Self-cultivation in America has as its goal less the achievement of uniqueness and more the achievement of similarity. This is a proposition many Frenchmen, for example, find difficult to grasp. The Japanese, with their stress upon self-cultivation in order more perfectly to discharge the obligations they owe their family and society, might come closer to understanding this American formulation.

The assimilation of diverse immigrant groups to middle-class American values has been one of the remarkable sociopolitical achievements of the nation and testifies to the compelling vigor of its value system. As resources and space were more fully manned, the very lack of tolerance for differences that facilitated assimilation was finally to curtail the admission to this country of those who presented such differences.

Earlier in our history self-reliance and initiative were specific values attached to the focal value of liberty. Today these specific values have a new focus. Individual self-reliance and initiative are attached to the promotion of the commonweal and to the progress of society. Conformity has replaced liberty as a focal value to which these specific entails are attached. Co-operation has been added as a specific value that has facilitated the shift-over. The present American value system manifests a highly effective integration of the individual to society.

The ramification of this nexus into the sphere of education has been alluded to already. Education is envisaged as a means by which all men through effort can realize themselves. But since co-operativeness is a specific value also inserted into this equation, education comes to be envisaged as a means to make more men more effective workers and better citizens. The land-grant colleges, the vast network of public schools, and the system of free and compulsory education with its stress on education for citizenship and on technical skills have set the American educational system apart from that of many other countries. In the American context the linkage between conformity, effort-optimism, and material well-being leads inevitably to mass education with the emphasis on the common man rather than the uncommon man, to its technical and practical cast, to what seems to many observers its low standards. Simultaneously, to many Americans schooling has acquired the weight of a goal rather than a means. A college degree is a "good thing" in itself, whether or not the education entailed is prized. This concatenation does not lead one to expect perfection as a directive for performance in American life.

In a society where co-operation and good citizenship are valued and where the commonweal is served by having each man develop himself through his own efforts, a generous friendliness, openness, and relaxation of interpersonal relations are not only possible but desirable so long as the associated expanding economy furnishes the situational possibilities. Rigid class structures and protective privacies are inconsistent with the values here enumerated. Doors need not be closed to rooms; fences need not be built around properties. The tall hedges of England and the enclosing walls of France are not appropriate to the American scene, where life faces outward rather than inward. If every individual is as "good as" the next and all are good citizens—what is there to hide? The open front yards, the porches, or more recently the picture windows that leave the home open to everyone's view, the figurative and literal klieg lights under which our public figures live are all evidence of the value placed in American life on likeness and the pressure exerted for conformity. This is very different from saying that American middle-class individuals are in fact all alike. It means merely that likeness is valued.

The American hostility to figures in authority has been frequently noted, and in this connection the almost placatory informality and familiarity of American manners that serve to play down status differences have been pointed out. The apparent contradiction between the striving for upward mobility and the distrust of those who achieve pre-eminent positions can now be seen in more balanced terms. If the argument advanced here is correct, upward mobility is valued as successful activity, but when it reaches a point where it outstrips the premise of equality and the focal value of conformity it borders on *hubris*.

In this connection then the relaxed, friendly manner of American life so frequently commented upon by foreign observers can be gauged in the broader context of an adjustment to incompatible values. The search for popularity, the desire to be liked, the wish to be considered a "good fellow," are searches for reassurance that, in striving to achieve all the ends implied by the focal value of effort-optimism, one has not exceeded the bounds set by the other focal value of conformity. That this process can operate at any level of actual achievement, from the presidency of the United States to chairmanship of an Elks Club committee, need not be stressed. It is the boss, the politician, the teacher, the "big shots" who are disvalued figures to the extent that their superordinate position implies authority. It is the movie star and the baseball hero who are valued figures since their pre-eminence connotes no authority but at the same time dramatizes the meteoric rise to fame and popularity through hard work and youthful striving.

Another aspect of American social life is thrown into relief in the effort to balance effort-optimism, material well-being, and conformity and their linked specific values. In the business and financial world, despite conservative tendencies, there has been a steady trend toward consolidation and standardization. Although the familiar and now perhaps inappropriate hue and cry is still raised about monopoly and big business, the latter, at least, serves the greater material well-being of the American mass consumer, whose values are geared to conformity. "Big business" is consonant with the American value system here portrayed so long as the owners of such enterprises are pictured as the American middle class, so long as savings are invested in the stocks and bonds of these enterprises so that the middle class shares "equally" in its successes, and so long as the authorities in such enterprises are presented as servants of the people. In these terms the American value system is served. The dangers of a too extreme individualistic power-centered authority are thus allayed, and competitive rivalry is brought under control.

Chapter 22

GROUP VALUES — "STATUS-GLISSANDO"

In *their study of the development of culture, anthropologists, sociologists, and others have found it desirable to divide each community into a complex of groups. Such divisions are made along social, economic, ethnic, and educational lines. Walter Goldschmidt, an anthropologist, acknowledges that, while this categorizing has been useful, the peculiarly American modifications of our European antecedents have produced marked changes that do not easily lend themselves to typical classifications. Goldschmidt suggests that we describe values, not in terms of groups or class or caste, but as "a chromatic scale of status-glissando." He believes that the previously identified core culture values, formerly associated with the middle class, can be considered to be the values of the entire American society. The current differences among groups can best be described in terms of the differing degrees by which these values are attained. Some people have obtained more and others fewer of the values deemed characteristic of the entire American society. Goldschmidt argues that scholars should attempt to describe American social structure as a single entity, rather than as a whole constructed from individual and related parts. In support of this thesis, Goldschmidt offers a number of pertinent ideas concerning American values.*

SOCIAL CLASS AND THE DYNAMICS OF STATUS IN AMERICA

Walter Goldschmidt

Status distinctions are important in America—and they are exceptionally important—but they do not classify the society into clear social units. Here our language gets in the way, for we have a great tendency to translate infinite variation into discrete and finite categories. The proper figure of speech is not that there are rungs of a ladder; it is rather that there is a chromatic scale of status-glissando.

This the anthropologists must particularly appreciate—as we are committed to definitions of social reality rather than to analytic systems. We do not deal with classes in the sense that there *ought* to be differences of interest, orientation, and identification. We deal rather with some form of social reality, with recognized unities, with the results of empirical investigation. The empirical evidence of status distinction is overwhelming, but the efforts of categorization are the results of an imposed frame of reference.

The apparent paradox of a highly developed concern with social status and the absence of a class system is not a paradox. I suggest that the two are closely and functionally related on the psychological level. Let me develop the logic behind this point.

The American culture is built upon mobility: historical, geographical, philosophical, economic, social. The nation was peopled by humanity on the move. The American culture was built on the frontier, and the frontier is occupied by people on the move; even the frontier shifts. American business is built upon the free movement of labor as much as on the free movement of goods. Furthermore, geographical mobility and social mobility are not just a coming together of words. One leads to the other. The freedom of man to move away from existing tyrannies regularly undermines those tyrannies. Put in terms of American *cliché*, the man who wants to get up in the world gets out from under. Significantly, the caste system of the South was built upon the denial of mobility to the subordinate caste, made possible by the racial "visibility" of the Negro.

Reprinted from the *American Anthropologist*, Vol. 57, No. 6, Part 1 (December 1955), pp. 1213–1216. Footnotes omitted.

This mobility undermines the tendency toward established group identification. The need for such identification is expressed in the great number of voluntary associations—temporary and shifting—that characterizes the American scene. It is also expressed in the strong emotional pull of the "hometown"—which, as we all know, is the place that we have moved away from.

The fundamental dynamic, it seems to me, lies in the assumption that, "You, too, can become president." Behind this phrase stands the assumption not that we can or will enter the White House but that we can and will determine the level of our own status in the American social hierarchy. Our public mythology is replete with models for such an assumption. The "rags to riches" theme enters every phase of our popular literature; our high-school texts are filled with accounts of the careers of Fords and Carnegies.

I am not prepared to defend the thesis that these models are highly influential upon the character of the American individual, though I believe that they are. The modern intellectual scorns this literary pap, reads *Babbitt*, *What Makes Sammy Run*, and *An American Tragedy* rather than Horatio Alger. But there are real-life models: the grandfather who arrived penniless as an immigrant, the uncle who has built—on credit, to be sure—a swimming pool in Hollywood, the boy next door who has worked his way through college.

These more modest models force upon the individual a recognition of both the real possibility of social advancement and the personal responsibility for that advancement. It is in this context that the symbol of the two-tiered desk is important, that the Pontiac is better than the Chevrolet, the Oldsmobile better than the Pontiac, the Buick still better, while the Cadillac tops them all. Indeed, the infinite gradation in cars represented by price-class, lines, and models is symbolic of our sensitivity to the delicate shadings of status that are recognized in the real world of the American culture. The mobile person must be sensitized to the shades of meaning in the symbol system if he is to work his way upward in this scale. Status is generally important just because status is not fixed.

Far from assuming a class position from childhood on, we tend to view our family of orientation as a marker to show the starting place. We measure our own ability not only in terms of where we are, so to speak, but in terms of how far we have moved. And, in like measure, we expect our sons to use us as a point of departure; the "young hopeful" proves himself in terms not of taking over the father's position but of exceeding it. Mead made this point forcibly in *And Keep Your Powder Dry*.

A point of great importance is that status becomes a method for self-evaluation. In a society that determines clearly who you are, you know what you are. If you live in a social system that places you in a caste, in an occupational category, or in a clan (for that matter), your identifications are learned along with your language. Your burden is to learn the role that is expected of you in the status that you are to assume. If it is a taxing role, such as that of the Queen of England, you may well be evaluated in terms of how well you fulfill expectations. But in a society without fixed positions there are no such obvious identifications. Since one has to make one's own status, what one's status is determines what one is. Status becomes a criterion not only by which others evaluate us but by which we evaluate ourselves. We turn around the old saying, "If you're so smart, why aren't you rich?" and measure our "smartness" by our "riches"—always recognizing that smartness stands for a general set of evaluative characteristics and riches for a variety of symbolic representations of status.

The degree to which the foregoing is true varies with respect to time, place, and circumstance in the American scene. It is not without significance that most anthropological studies of class in the community were made during the depression period, when the opportunity for advancement—like the frontier itself—seemed to be closed. (I am aware that my partial reversal of position comes after ten years of prosperity.) There is evidence that the economic distress of that earlier period had less damaging psychological effect than failure does today, because it was so manifestly the result of external factors. It is in this context that there is a growth of conservative voting during times of prosperity, that economic class identification grows fainter when the sense of personal economic opportunity grows brighter. It seems to me that the older communities, and the South in general, have shown greater fixity of social status and that class analyses of the Warner kind are more successful in old Massachusetts and in Mississippi than in the Middle and Far West.

This sense of personal determination of status is less strong at either end of the hierarchy than it is in the middle. The elites assume, as elites always must, that their social position is fixed. The son cannot exceed the father but learns the role he will have to assume. The slum dweller must get relatively little sense for the real models of success, little opportunity for the internalization of the notion that he is what he makes himself. Furthermore, the philosophy of class consciousness exists side-by-side with the philosophy of individualistic social mobility. It has never been entirely lacking. It inspired the early development of unionization and agrarianism and remains strong today. It stands as a secondary rather than a dominant theme, fluctuating in importance inversely with the business cycle. (The separation of dominant and substitutive values is suggested by Kluckhohn).

By focusing attention on the community as a matrix for social action, these dynamic aspects of status are lost. Part of the reason for this is that the social interactions that are community-oriented do partake of a purely local categorization. Few families in Wasco moved upward within the local community, but there are many persons moving in and out of Wasco on their way up. More important is that mobility implies the time dimension, and the community study "stops" the action like a fast shutter. Neither Mead nor Gorer, the only two anthropologists to make broad impressionistic studies of the American scene—nor those older ethnologists like Bryce and de Tocqueville—felt that social classes were important to our culture, though they emphasized status.

In sum, the status system is an important element in American culture, and the dominant cultural motifs of mobility and individual responsibility for social status will bear much fruitful examination. The involvements are widespread, extending from self-attitudes and patterns of anxiety, through the variant symbol systems that are markers in the status game, to the institutional patterns in which these attitudes operate. Studies of the manner in which status concerns are communicated, the nature of the internalization of status demand, the problem of cultural discontinuities that result from differing status roles held by the same individual, the effects on intrafamily tensions associated with the assumption of mobility, the relation of status striving to production performance on the job, and hosts of other problems are associated with this set of considerations.

The anthropological study of the community, with its discussion of social class, has been an important step in the development of these understandings. It is time now to move on. We have come to a growing awareness of the importance of status differentiation, whether or not these differences can be categorized into classes. The next step is to examine the dynamics of status as they affect the personal characteristics and the institutional machinery in modern America.

Chapter 23

GROUP VALUES — "TRADITIONAL TO EMERGENT"

Scholars *repeatedly assert that American society is in a period of transition and that this change is causing a notable shift of the values acceptable to the society. In practice, the shifts in thought and behavior produce anxieties and clashes of personality, with the result that all kinds of people tend to lash out at fancied or actual social inadequacies. Education in general and educators in particular are blamed for a good deal of the trouble, and they are criticized for failing to prepare people to face the issues and problems of the new society.*

George D. Spindler, an anthropologist, believes that major changes are taking place in contemporary American society. These changes make it obligatory for educators to understand the nature and direction of the changes and the manner in which the schools might respond to them. To substantiate his point of view, Spindler utilizes literature from anthropology and sociology, and data obtained from college students. These students ranged in age from nineteen to fifty-seven years, were mainly graduate students in professional education courses, and were drawn from the lower middle to upper middle class.

Spindler assumes that "the middle-class culture is the core of our way of life—the pattern of the norms against which lower- and upper-class cultures are seen as deviations." His primary purpose is to present the major dimensions of cultural change in American society, which he describes as a shift from the "traditional" to the "emergent" values, and to relate this change to the problems and the issues confronting contemporary public education. In elaborating his ideas, he emphasizes the changing conception of the desirable personality, because the formation of personality is identified as a primary responsibility of education. The "traditional" and "emergent" values are defined, and the personnel involved in the educational process are described in relation to the position each occupies in reference to the changes that are taking place. Spindler hypothesizes that educators will fall into one of three possible categories as they adjust to the conditions imposed by social change. His primary concern is not to impose value judgments, but to plead that we use what we know about our society in order to resolve its educational problems.

EDUCATION IN A TRANSFORMING AMERICAN CULTURE

George D. Spindler

I believe it is clear that a major shift in American values has [taken] and is taking place.[1] I find it convenient to label this shift as being from *traditional* to *emergent*. The values thus dichotomized are listed under their respective headings below, with explanatory statements in parentheses.

I believe American Culture is undergoing a transformation, and a rapid one producing many disjunctions and conflicts, from the traditional to the emergent value systems outlined above. It is probable that both value systems have been present and operating in American Culture for some time, perhaps since the birth of the nation. But recently, and under the impetus of World Wars, atomic insecurities, and a past history of "boom and bust," the heretofore latent tendencies in the emergent direction have gathered strength and appear to be on the way towards becoming the dominant value system of American Culture.

Like all major shifts in culture, this one has consequences for people. Culturally transitional populations, as anthropologists know from their studies of acculturating Indian tribes, Hindu villages, and Samoan communities (among others), are characterized by conflict, and in most severe form—demoralization and disorganization. Institutions and people are in a state of

Reprinted from *Harvard Educational Review*, Vol. 25, No. 3 (Summer 1955), pp. 148–156.

[1] I have been particularly influenced by the writings of David Riesman and particularly his *The Lonely Crowd*.

TRADITIONAL VALUES	EMERGENT VALUES
Puritan morality (Respectability, thrift, self-denial, sexual constraint; a puritan is someone who can have anything he wants, as long as he doesn't enjoy it!)	*Sociability* (One should like people and get along well with them. Suspicion of solitary activities is characteristic.)
Work-Success ethic (Successful people worked hard to become so. Anyone can get to the top if he tries hard enough. So people who are not successful are lazy, or stupid, or both. People must work desperately and continuously to convince themselves of their worth.)	*Relativistic moral attitude* (Absolutes in right and wrong are questionable. Morality is what the group thinks is right. Shame, rather than guilt-oriented personality is appropriate.)
Individualism (The individual is sacred, and always more important than the group. In one extreme form, the value sanctions egocentricity, expediency, and disregard for other people's rights. In its healthier form the value sanctions independence and originality.)	*Consideration for others* (Everything one does should be done with regard for others and their feelings. The individual has a built-in radar that alerts him to other's feelings. Tolerance for the other person's point of view and behavior is regarded as desirable, so long as the harmony of the group is not disrupted.)
Achievement orientation (Success is a constant goal. There is no resting on past glories. If one makes \$9,000 this year he must make \$10,000 next year. Coupled with the work-success ethic, this value keeps people moving, and tense.)	
Future-time orientation (the future, not the past, or even the present, is most important. There is a "pot of gold at the end of the rainbow." Time is valuable, and cannot be wasted. Present needs must be denied for satisfactions to be gained in the future.)	*Hedonistic, present-time orientation* (No one can tell what the future will hold, therefore one should enjoy the present—but within the limits of the well-rounded, balanced personality and group.)
	Conformity to the group (Implied in the other emergent values. Everything is relative to the group. Group harmony is the ultimate goal. Leadership consists of group-machinery lubrication.)

flux. Contradictory views of life are held by different groups and persons within the society. Hostilities are displaced, attacks are made on one group by another. And this applies as well to the condition of American Culture—the context of American education.

The traditionalist views the emergentist as "socialistic," "communistic," "spineless and weak-headed," or downright "immoral." The emergentist regards the traditionalist as "hidebound," "reactionary," "selfish," or "neurotically compulsive." Most of what representatives of either viewpoint do may be regarded as insidious and destructive from the point of view of the other. The conflict goes beyond groups or institutions, because individuals in our transitional society are likely to hold elements of both value systems concomitantly. This is characteristic, as a matter of fact, of most students included in the sample described previously. There are few "pure" types. The social character of most is split, calling for different responses in different situations, and with respect to different symbols. So an ingredient of personal confusion is added that intensifies social and institutional conflict.

I hypothesize that the attacks upon education, which were our starting point, and the confusion and failure of nerve characterizing educators today, can be seen in clear and helpful perspective in the light of the conflict of traditional and emergent values that has been described. It is the heart of the matter. The task then becomes one of placing groups, institutions and persons on a continuum of transformation from the one value system to the other. Without prior explanation, I should like to provide a simple diagram that will aid at least the visual-minded to comprehension of what is meant. With this accomplished I will provide the rationale for such placement and discuss the implications of it in greater detail.

The diagram is meant to convey the information that different groups operating in the context of relations between school and community, educator and public, occupy different positions on the value continuum, with

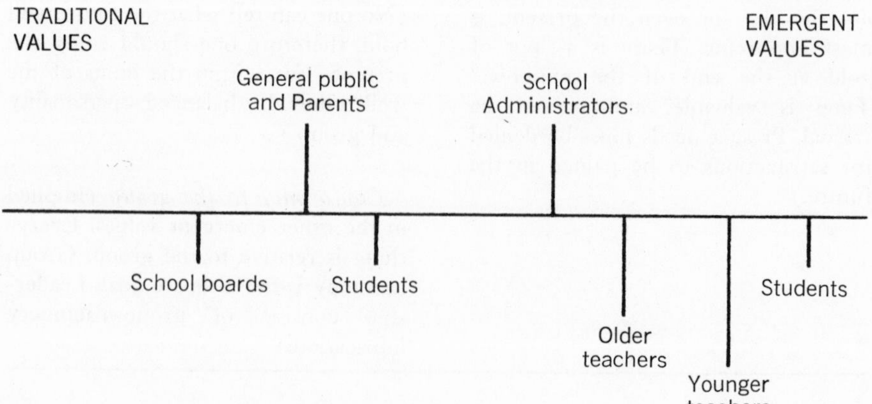

varying degrees and mixtures of traditional and emergent orientations. It should be understood that the placements indicate hypothecated tendencies, that no one group representing any particular institution ever consists of "pure" value types, but that there is probably a modal tendency for the groups indicated to place on the transformation, or continuum line, in the way expressed in the diagram.

The rationale for the placement of the various groups on the value continuum is fairly complex, but let me try to explain some salient points. School boards are placed nearest the *traditional* end of the continuum because such boards are usually composed of persons representing the power, *status-quo*, elements of the community, and of persons in the higher age ranges. They are therefore people who have a stake in keeping things as they are, who gained their successes within the framework of the traditional value system and consequently believe it to be good, and who, by virtue of their age, grew up and acquired their value sets during a period of time when American Culture was presumably more tradition-oriented than it is today.

The general public and parent group, of course, contains many elements of varying value predilection. It is therefore unrealistic to place this public at any particular point in the value continuum. But I hypothesize that the public *tends* to be more conservative in its social philosophy than the professional education set. The placement to the left of center of the continuum ("left" being "right" in the usual sense) takes on further validity if it is seen as a placement of that part of the public that is most vocal in its criticism of educators and education—since most of the criticisms made appear to spring out of value conflicts between traditionalist and emergentist positions. Parents complain that their children are not being taught the "three R's" (even when they are), that educators want to "socialize" the competitive system by eliminating report cards, that children are not taught the meaning of hard work. These all sound, irrespective of the question of their justification or lack of it, like traditionalist responses to change in an "emergent" direction.

Students are placed at two points on the transformation line because it is clear that those coming from traditionalist family environments will tend to hold traditionalistic values, but hold them less securely than will their parents (if our hypothesis for over-all change is valid), while other students who come from emergent-oriented families will tend to place even further, as a function of their age and peer groups, towards the emergent end of the line than their parents would. This is only partially true, indeed, for such a rationale does not account for the fact that offspring in revolt (and many American children from 6 to 16 are in a state of revolt against parental dictums) may go to extremes in either direction.

School administrators, older, and younger teachers, place at varying points on the emergent half of the transformation line. I have placed them there because I believe that the professional education culture (every institution has its own way of life, in this sense) that they have acquired in the schools and colleges of education has a clear bias towards an emergent-oriented ethos. Many of my educationist colleagues will reject this interpretation, and indeed, such interpretations are always guilty of over-generalization. Others of my colleagues will welcome such a characterization, but still question its validity. My case must rest on the basis of contemporary educational philosophy, theory, and practice. The emphasis is on the "social adjustment" of the individual, upon his role as a member of the group and community. Most of the values listed under the *emergent* heading are explicitly stated in educational literature as goals. Some of them, such as conformity to the group, are implicit. This value, in particular, grows out of the others, is more or less unintended, and constitutes a *covert* or *latent* value, by definition. This is, admittedly, a little like accusing a man of hating his mother, but not knowing it, and such accusations are usually rejected, or rationalized out of existence. But I believe that it is literally impossible to hold the other values in this system and avoid placing a strong emphasis on group harmony, and group control of the individual. My data, at least, gathered largely from graduate students in professional education courses, indicate that this is the case.

But educators and schools do not all come off the same shelf in the supermarket. Older teachers will tend, I hypothesize, to hold relatively traditionalist views by virtue of their age, and time of their childhood training (when they acquired their basic values)—a period in American culture when the traditionalist values were relatively more certain and supported than they are at present. Younger teachers were not only children and acquired their personal culture during a relatively more emergent-oriented period of American history, but they have been (I hypothesize) exposed to a professional education culture that has become rapidly more emergent-oriented in its value position. They are therefore placed near the extreme of the transformation line in the emergent direction.

School administrators come from a different shelf in the same section of the supermarket. They, to be sure, range in age from young to old, come from different family backgrounds, and have been exposed in varying degrees to the professional education culture. But sociological and anthropological studies of the influence of status and role on behavior and perception indicate that these factors tend to over-ride others, and produce certain uniformities of outlook. The school administrator's role is a precarious one—as any school principal or superintendent knows. He faces towards several different audiences, each with different sets of demands—school boards, parents, power groups, teachers, and students—as well as other administrators. He has to play his role appropriately in the light of all these demands. The fact that many cannot, accounts for the increasingly short tenure of personages like school superintendents. But to the extent that he plays *across the board* he will place somewhere towards the center of the line of transformation. Furthermore, his dependence upon the school board, and the power groups in the community, in many cases will tend to make his outlook relatively more conservative, and probably more traditionalistic, than that of his teachers—at least the younger ones. There are many exceptions, of course. I am only claiming *tendencies*.

My thesis, I hope, is clear by now. I am attempting to explain, or help explain, the increasingly bitter and strident attacks on schools and educators, and the conflict and confusion within the ranks. I have claimed that this situation can better be understood as a series of complex but very real conflicts in core values. And I have tried to show the direction of the values shift in American culture and place the various actors in the drama upon a transformation line within this shift.

In this perspective, many conflicts between parents and teachers, school boards and educators, parents and children, and between the various personages and groups within the school system (teachers against teachers, administrators against teachers, and so on) can be understood as conflicts that grow out of sharp differences in values that mirror social and cultural transformation of tremendous scope—and for which none of the actors in the situation can be held personally accountable. This is the real, and perhaps only contribution of this analysis. If these conflicts can be seen as emerging out of great sociocultural shifts—out of a veritable transformation of a way of life—they will lose some of their string. To understand, the psychiatrist says, is to forgive.

But now, though it seems indeed improper at this point, permit me to add another complication to an already complicated picture. I have tried to make it clear that not only are there variations in values held by groups and different parts of the social body and school institutions, but that there are also various values, some of them contradictory, held by single individuals as diverse streams of influence in their own systems. This is always true in rapid culture-change situations, as the anthropologist and philosopher know.

This means that the situation is not only confused by groups battling each other, but that individuals are fighting themselves. This has certain predictable results, if the anthropological studies of personal adaptation to culture change have any validity. And I believe that those results can be detected in the behaviors of most, if not all, of the actors in the scene. Let me try to clarify this.

I will deal only with teachers, as one of the most important sets of actors on this particular stage. I hypothesize that the child training of most of the people who become teachers has been more tradition than emergent value-oriented. They are drawn largely from middle to lower-middle social class groups in American society, and this segment of the class structure is the stronghold of the work-success ethic and moral respectability values in our culture (even in a culture that is shifting away from these values). Furthermore, it seems probable that a selective process is operating to draw a relatively puritanistic element into the public school teaching as an occupation. Self-denial, altruism, a moralistic self-concept, seem to be functional prerequisites for the historically-derived role of school teacher in American society (I might have said "school-marm").

If this can be granted, then only one other ingredient needs to be added to explain several persistent types of personal adaptation to value conflicts observable among school teachers. That ingredient is one already spelled out—the relatively heavy emphasis, within the professional education culture, on the emergent-oriented value system. Teachers-to-be acquire their personal culture in a more tradition-oriented familiar environment, but they encounter a new kind of culture when in training to become school teachers —in the teacher-training institutions. There is, in this experience, what the anthropologist would call a discontinuity in the *enculturation* of the individual.[2] This is a particular kind of culture-conflict situation that anthropologists have recently begun to study, but mostly in non-western societies undergoing rapid change towards a western way of life.

On the basis of observation of a fair sample of teachers in coastal communities and in the middle west, I hypothesize that three types of adaptation to this personal culture-conflict situation and experience are characteristic.

Ambivalent: This type is characterized by contradictory and vacillating behavior, particularly with respect to the exercise of discipline and authority. The type tends to be *laissez-faire* in some classroom situations, and authoritarian in others, depending upon which behavior is called into being as a defense against threat of loss of control.

Compensatory: This type is characterized by one of two modes of behavior. The teacher overcompensates consistently either in the direction of the emergent or the tradition-centered values. In the first mode he (or she) tends to become a member of a *group-thinkism* cult—a perversion of progressive educational philosophy in action. The total stress is placed on social adjustment. Individuality is not sanctioned to any significant degree. Conformity to the group becomes the key to success. The type, in its extreme form, is a caricature of the better features of the emergent-centered value set. The second type compensates for internal culture-conflict in the opposite direction, and becomes an outright authoritarian. Tight dominance is maintained over children. All relationships with them are formalized and rigid. No deviation is allowed, so curiously enough, there is a convergence in the end-results of both types. This type is a caricature of the better features of the tradition-centered values set.

[2] *Enculturation* is a new, but useful term being used by social scientists. It stands for the process through which the individual acquires the culture of his group or society.

Adapted: This type can be either traditional or emergent value-oriented. But the compensatory and ambivalent mechanisms operating in the first two types are much less intense, or absent. The teacher of this type has come to terms with the value conflict situation and experience, and has chosen (consciously or unconsciously) to act within the framework of one or the other value set. There is consequently a consistency of behavior, and the mode of classroom management and teacher-student relationship is not a caricature of either value system.

No one is in a position to say which of these types is represented in greatest numbers among American public school teachers today, and there are few "pure" types. Certainly there are many traditional and emergent-oriented teachers who have adapted successfully to the personal culture-conflict situation and discontinuity of enculturative experience described. But equally certainly there are many school teachers who fall more clearly into one or the other typologies. It would be asking too much to suppose that a cultural values-conflict situation as intense as the one transforming American culture could be handled without strain by the key agent of the culture-transmission process—the school teacher. But again, to understand is to forgive.

In any event, it seems clear that if conditions are even partially of the nature described, the group culture-conflict situation resulting in attacks by representatives of those groups upon each other is intensified and at the same time confused by the personal culture-conflict problem. Both processes must be seen, and understood, as resultants of a larger culture-transformation process.

In conclusion to this by-far unfinished analysis (the next 20 years may tell the more complete story), let me make it clear that I am not castigating either the emergentists, or the traditionalists. Value systems must always be functional in terms of the demands of the social and economic structure of a people. The traditional mode has much that is good about it. There is a staunchness, and a virility in it that many of us may view with considerable nostalgia in some future time. But rugged individualism (in its expedient, ego-centered form), and rigid moralism (with its capacity for displaced hate) become non-functional in a society where people are rubbing shoulders in polyglot masses, and playing with a technology that may destroy, or save, with a pushing of buttons. The emergentist position seems to be growing in strength. Social adaptability, relativistic outlooks, sensitivity to the needs and opinions of others, and of the group, seem functional in this new age. But perhaps we need, as people, educators, anthropologists, and parents, to examine our premises more closely. The emergentist can become a group conformist—an average man proud of his well-rounded averageness—without really meaning to at all.

And lastly I would like to reiterate the basic theme of this article. Conflicts between groups centering on issues of educational relevance, and confusions within the rank and file of educators, can be understood best, I believe, in the perspective of the transformation of American culture that proceeds without regard for personal fortune or institutional survival. This transformation, it is true, can be guided and shaped to a considerable degree by the human actors on the scene. But they cannot guide and shape their destiny within this transformation if their energies are expended in knifing attacks on each other in such a central arena as education, or if their energies are dissipated in personal confusions. I am arguing, therefore, for the functional utility of understanding, and of insight into the all-encompassing transformation of American culture and its educational-social resultants.

Chapter 24

THE ROLE OF SOCIAL CLASS IN EDUCATION

WE *have come to know a great deal about the kinds of people who direct the political, social, economic, intellectual, and cultural activities of our society. The members of this "higher" class are the principal architects of the aims and objectives of our educational agencies. By exercising such dominance, this group tends to exclude other classes from participating in the management of education. The public schools can be considered the agency by which this "higher" class perpetuates its values. Examining this cultural development, Leonard Reissman, a sociologist, clarifies the relationship of class, leisure, and social participation as they influence the personality of the members of the "higher" class, the formulation of community aims and objectives, and the aspirational level of this group and of the "lower" class. In particular, he is concerned with these questions: (1) "Can the extent and character of the participation be explained in some measure by the class position of the participants?" and (2) "What differences can be found in the aspirations held by the higher and lower class groups, and how can these differences be related to the information on participation and leisure activity of the two groups?"*

CLASS, LEISURE, AND SOCIAL PARTICIPATION

Leonard Reissman

CLASS AND PARTICIPATION

The present research is based upon a sample of white, male, native-born adults selected from the city of Evanston, Illinois by means of a modified areal sample. One objective of the present paper is to test the relationship between class position and participation along lines of analysis suggested by previous investigations. For the purposes of this analysis, "class" is determined by means of three commonly used variables—occupation, income and education. More specifically, this sample of adults was divided into "higher" and "lower" class groups at the median of each of the three distributions, and then compared, separately for each variable, on a number of items concerned with social participation and leisure activity. The reasoning followed in this comparison can be phrased as follows: If a consistent pattern of differences between the "high" and the "low" class groups is evident regardless of which variable is used, then it might be considered as further support for the conclusions reached by previous studies as discussed above. The relevant information is summarized in Table 1.

A word of explanation is necessary before the information in Table 1 can be evaluated. Most divisions, both in rows and columns, have been made as close to the median as possible for each distribution. "High" and "low" groups for occupational prestige, income and education are based upon the medians of each of these three distributions as indicated in footnotes to Table 1. The "higher participation levels" for each of the eight activities listed in the stub of the table are the upper half of the distribution and are based upon the medians of the entire sample in most instances. In the case of "leadership" and "attendance at organizations," where only two and three response categories respectively were involved, the division was more arbitrarily designated on the basis of the meaning of those categories.

Careful inspection of Table 1 indicates that a relatively consistent pattern of differences in participation and leisure activity is present. In other words, regardless of whether occupation, income or education is used to measure class position, the higher class groups tend to show higher participation

Reprinted from *American Sociological Review*, Vol. 19 (Fall 1954), pp. 79–84. Footnotes omitted.

TABLE 1. A COMPARISON BETWEEN OCCUPATIONAL PRESTIGE GROUPS, INCOME GROUPS, AND EDUCATIONAL GROUPS OF A SINGLE SAMPLE, FOR SELECTED ACTIVITIES

High Participation Levels in:	OCCUPATIONAL PRESTIGE GROUPS[1]			INCOME GROUPS[2]			EDUCATIONAL GROUPS[3]		
	HIGH	LOW	DIFF.	HIGH	LOW	DIFF.	HIGH	LOW	DIFF.
Number of Cases	65	56		61	60		67	54	
	PER CENT	PER CENT	PER CENT	PER CENT	PER CENT	PER CENT	PER CENT	PER CENT	PER CENT
Book reading (2 or more in a 3 months period)	50.8	35.7	15.1	50.8	36.7	14.1	52.2	33.3	18.9*
Magazine reading (4 or more read regularly)	67.7	39.3	28.4*	72.1	36.7	35.4**	67.2	38.9	28.3**
Radio-T.V. listening (5 hours or more per week)	43.1	58.9	15.8	36.1	65.0	28.9**	40.3	63.0	22.7*
Hobbies (Spends 3 hours or more per week)	46.2	46.4	.2	52.5	40.0	12.5	46.3	46.3	0
Church attendance (Several times a month or more)	50.8	30.4	20.4*	44.3	38.3	6.0	46.3	35.2	11.1
Organizations (Belongs to 2 or more)	66.2	39.3	26.9**	59.0	48.3	10.7	56.7	50.0	6.7
Leadership (Holds or has held office in organization)	52.7 (N=55)	33.3 (N=45)	19.4*	57.4 (N=54)	28.3 (N=46)	29.1*	53.6 (N=56)	31.9 (N=44)	21.7*
Attendance at Organizations (Attends "frequently")	47.2 (N=55)	42.2 (N=45)	5.0	46.3 (N=54)	43.5 (N=46)	2.8	53.6 (N=56)	34.1 (N=44)	19.5*

1 Based upon North-Hatt occupational scale. "High" includes scores of 70 and 80, i.e., generally those who are professionals, managers, etc.

2 "High" includes those who earn 125 dollars a week or more.

3 "High" includes any college attendance.

(A single asterisk indicates 5 per cent level of significance, and two asterisks indicate 1 per cent level of significance.)

levels in most of the activities. In only two instances is this not the case. No differences are present between the "high" and the "low" educational groups for time spent in hobbies, and a very slight difference appears between the occupational groups for this activity. Second, more time is spent in radio and television listening by all of the lower class groups than is spent by the higher class groups. Since no information was obtained on the program interests of the different groups, it is impossible to assess this reversal of the general pattern adequately.

The general pattern of dominance by the higher class group, in every instance except the two noted, seems to be more than simply a random one. They read more books and magazines, attend church more frequently, belong to more organizations, attend with greater frequency, and tend more often to hold office in those organizations. This holds true for each of the three variables used to index class position. This finding can be used to substantiate the combined findings of previous studies summarized above. The close similarity between the pattern of participation in this sample and those noted before tends to support the general images of the higher and lower class groups that have been presented.

CLASS AND ASPIRATIONS

The second objective of the present paper is the analysis of information on the aspirations of the higher and lower class groups as an extension of the pattern of differences discussed previously. The suggestion for including such information comes from the article by Knupfer, in which the conclusion is drawn that lower class individuals generally tend to hold lower levels of aspiration to "make life tolerable." The basic information on the aspirations of the present sample has been reported by the writer, and need not be repeated in its entirety. However, the problem now being posed requires a different analytical perspective. The present problem can be phrased as follows: What differences can be found in the aspirations held by the higher and by the lower class groups, and how can these differences be related to the information on participation and leisure activity of the two groups?

The format for the analysis of aspirations follows that presented for the materials on participation and leisure. The sample is again analyzed alternately on the basis of "high" and "low" groups for occupation, income, and education. Eleven items were included in a question asking the respondent to indicate how important each of them would be in considering a possible upward occupational move. These items, as listed in the stub of Table 2, dealt with health, family, leisure time, friendship, and the like. Table 2 summarizes the percentages of each group indicating that the particular item mentioned "wouldn't matter" to them in considering an upward occupational move.

The information that is given in Table 2 is of interest primarily because of the *pattern* of differences it presents rather than the *degree* of difference in individual comparisons. It has been designed primarily to give some insight into the relationship between a series of aspiration choices and class characteristics of this sample. By duplicating the form of analysis used in the earlier section of this paper, it should be possible to include some description of the aspirations of the class groups, whose social participation and leisure activities have been discussed. The central focus here is upon how the different class groups respond to the relative importance of the aspiration items, rather than upon the magnitude of the differences that might occur in individual comparisons.

The class groups were ranked on each of the eleven aspiration items according to the percentages of each group that indicated the particular item "wouldn't matter" to them. The "high" groups in occupation, income and education ranked highest in five of the items. The "low" groups ranked highest in three of the items. For three items, no consistency such as this was found.

A glance at Table 2 indicates that on the following five items the "high" groups for occupation, income and education showed larger percentages than any of the "low" groups of those who said these items"wouldn't matter" to them in considering a possible upward move:

Learn a new routine
Work harder than you are now
Take on more responsibility
Endanger your health
Leave your family for some time

Taken together, these items imply a realistic awareness of what is involved in occupational mobility. The first three—learn a new routine, work harder, take on more responsibility—can be considered as a necessary prerequisite for mobility. Considerations of health and family can be evaluated as possible risks that might have to be undertaken in some situations. In other words, the higher class, in its response to this question, establishes its aspirations on a somewhat more realistic basis than does the lower class. The higher class, either through past experience or through general awareness, seems to hold a standard in its aspirations that reflects some knowledge of the prerequisites for occupational mobility.

The "low" groups for occupation, income, and education, rank highest in the percentages indicating "wouldn't matter" on three of the items listed in Table 2:

Leave your friends
Keep quiet about your political views
Keep quiet about your religious views

TABLE 2. PERCENTAGES OF OCCUPATIONAL, INCOME, AND EDUCATIONAL GROUPS OF A SINGLE SAMPLE INDICATING ITEMS "WOULDN'T MATTER" IN A POSSIBLE OCCUPATIONAL ADVANCE

	OCCUPATIONAL PRESTIGE GROUPS[1]		INCOME GROUPS[2]		EDUCATIONAL GROUPS[3]	
ITEM	HIGH	LOW	HIGH	LOW	HIGH	LOW
Learn a new routine	76.9	67.9	75.4	70.0	79.1	64.8
Leave your community	41.5	48.2	44.3	45.0	44.8	44.4
Leave your friends	41.5	55.4	45.9	50.0	44.8	51.9
Work harder than you are now	69.2	66.1	68.9	66.7	77.6	55.6
Endanger your health	10.8	5.4	9.8	6.7	9.0	7.4
Keep quiet about political views	43.1	51.8	44.3	50.0	44.8	50.0
Leave your family for some time	18.5	17.9	19.7	16.7	20.9	14.8
Move around the country a lot	26.2	35.7	31.1	30.0	26.9	35.2
Take on more responsibility	84.6	75.0	82.0	78.3	90.0	68.5
Give up leisure time	38.5	57.1	50.8	43.3	53.7	38.9
Keep quiet about religious views	46.2	57.1	49.2	53.3	50.7	51.9

1 Based upon North-Hatt occupational scale. "High" includes scores of 70 and 80, i.e., generally those who are professionals, managers, etc.
2 "High" includes those who earn 125 dollars a week or more.
3 "High" includes those with any college attendance.

In other words, the lower class appears to be relatively unconcerned about matters of friendship, politics and religion; considerations upon which the higher class, conversely, places a major emphasis. This indicated unconcern creates an image of the lower class that is noticeably different from the image gained of the higher class. Where the latter expresses realism, the lower class does not. Where the lower class expresses indifference, the higher class shows firmness and conviction. The remaining three aspiration items in Table 2—leisure time, moving around the country, and leaving the community—show no consistent pattern of dominance by either the "high" or the "low" groups on all three variables and therefore are not included in this discussion.

The patterns of preference of the higher class and of the lower class, as they have emerged in this analysis of aspirations, cannot be considered as conclusive. Nevertheless, those patterns do exhibit an intriguing and meaningful consistency that can be related plausibly to the information presented in the first part of this paper. The contrast can be stated simply as follows: The higher class group appears to hold a realistic assessment of what is necessary to achieve upward mobility; the lower class does not. Furthermore, the latter appear to be without ideals in important areas. They would not let friendship be an important consideration in a possible occupational advance, nor would they consider that their political and religious views are important enough to defend in such a situation.

These latter implications bear a suggestive relationship to what has been discussed previously about the participation and leisure activity of the lower class. In the analysis of visiting patterns, it was found that the lower class person had fewer intimate friends than the higher class person. If it can be assumed that this is generally characteristic of the lower class, then it can be seen that a counterpart of this fact is its relative unwillingness to "leave their friends" for a possible upward occupational move.

It was found previously that lower class persons were not as well read nor showed as much knowledge about political affairs as did the higher class. Furthermore, the latter showed more frequent church attendance. Politics and religion would not appear to be as important for the lower class and consequently, tend to be sacrificed more readily in order to take advantage of an upward occupational move. The higher class, on the other hand, appears to hold to a meaningful pattern in its aspirations. Higher class persons show a readiness to undertake the necessary steps for mobility and at the same time hold firm at a point where personal ideals might be endangered. This has been interpreted here to imply that the higher class person is more realistic in assessing his situation and the possibilities within it. The whole pattern of his activity and his aspirations would seem to point to this conclusion.

CONCLUSIONS

Two objectives formed the basis of the present paper. First, it was found that regardless of the variable used to measure class position—occupation, income or education—the higher class shows a higher degree of participation and involvement in the community. That is, individuals in this class read more books and magazines, attend church more frequently, belong to more organizations, and more often hold office in those organizations. The present study thereby lends further support to previous studies on that relationship. Phrased in more general terms, it can be said that the middle class, on the whole, tends to dominate the organizational activity, the intellectual life, and the leadership of the community. Secondly, it was found that the higher class is more realistic in its aspirations, as seen by its greater willingness to recognize the necessary steps for an upward occupational move. The lower class, on the other hand, shows a startling lack of ideals in this matter, part of which might be traced to a lesser degree of involvement in and knowledge of the affairs and social mechanisms of the community. Not only are they less active in the life of the community, but also are more willing to sacrifice their personal views to take advantage of an opportunity for upward mobility. This willingness is misplaced, in a sense, since it does not seem to be founded upon a recognition of the more realistic prerequisites for mobility. An alternative explanation might be that the lower class feels it has nothing at stake in its present situation, that "getting ahead" is all that counts in order to measure up to a satisfactory success ideal. It is, of course, impossible to pin down the validity of either explanation with the data available, yet it might be worth noting that both views connote a somewhat unrealistic attitude—the first in that the lower class does not seem to appreciate sufficiently some of the basic steps for successful mobility; the second in that the lower class has simply subtracted out a single element of the mobility process without due regard apparently for the balance between striving and integrity.

The political and social implications of these differences were mentioned earlier. This is a problem with far too many facets to be resolved in a brief conclusion, although some further mention must be made of it if the information presented in this paper is to cast any light on the far-reaching aspects of the problems it raises. The ideal of a fully democratic process is strongly modified if it can be admitted that a single segment of the population, regardless of its numerical size, retains the effective voice and the intellectual dominance of the American community. In an age when policy often depends upon information which is both subtle and technical, knowledge and not "sympathetic understanding" is a necessary prerequisite for participating in the formation of that policy. It would seem from the information presented here that the higher class (middle class), much more than the lower class, tries to achieve the necessary background. Furthermore, there must also be the willingness to become involved. Here too, the higher class appears to be more fully immersed in the community and shows a greater willingness to exercise leadership and concern with its problems. Perhaps the difficulties of labor union leaders in trying to achieve a measure of coherent political strength at the polls among the membership of their unions is an instance of this point on the relative indifference of the lower class with matters not immediately and directly within its grasp.

Further implications arising from the situation presented are suggested, but can only be noted: (1) How is the content of the mass media affected by the indicated class differences in magazine readership and radio-television listening? (2) What are the consequences for the conduct of community affairs in the light of differential participation by class position? (3) What are the spheres of influence within relevant political groupings based upon social class division? These suggestions are offered, in an admittedly general way, to help point out the questions which might be asked in further research on social class and participation.

Chapter 25

THE ROLE OF THE FAMILY IN EDUCATION

A NUMBER *of the articles and studies previously presented have indicated that the values practiced by the adult members of a family typically become the values of the young people in that family. Although Americans may hope to achieve a set of values common to all, the facts of life make it clear that there is great variety in any catalog of American values. By way of illustration, this chapter will examine the role of the family in relation to the level of educational aspirations and achievement offered to children.*

Current state regulations mandate the maximum number of years that children may attend elementary and secondary schools and the minimum number of years that they must attend school. What that education will be like is left to the discretion of parents. Obviously, many factors enter into a family's decision about the educational aspirations and achievements of its young, and many consequences may follow whatever decision is made. The same educational plan may in one instance serve to stimulate economic and social mobility, while in another instance it may serve as an effective barrier to keep the in-group in and the out-group out.

Three selections will be presented on the role of the family in education. In the first, the influence of class upon the amount and type of education is explored. The second is a brief account of educational attainment in relation to the education of the father and the income of the family. The third examines the personal and social significance of limited educational attainment.

In the first contribution, James S. Davie, a sociologist, suggests that there is a significant relationship between the position of any family in the class structure of the community and the amount and type of educational experiences offered to its children. He examines the following factors: (a) family position in the class structure of the community; (b) the financial position of the family; (c) the manner in which the family is influenced by custom and other families in the same class; and (d) the value that the family places upon education. On the basis of these factors Davie was able to conclude that any child's schooling is partially determined by his birth into a particular social class status. If education is a major determination of any person's future, then a large part of his adult life is set in a cut-and-dried fashion by the accident of birth. Davie's conclusions raise certain serious questions about the waste of intelligence and the ideals we have about human dignity and worth.

In the second contribution, Florence Campi, on the basis of a survey made by the Census Bureau in October 1960, points out that in the United States (a) the educational attainment of the father influences the educational attainment of the male children; (b) family income influences the degree of educational achievement; and (c) the education attained by the children is directly influenced by the education of the father and the family's income.

Along similar lines, the third contribution, by Edward W. Brice and E. E. Huyck, identifies and discusses the plight of persons of lower educational attainment, and emphasizes the social and economic consequences produced in society by limited education.

SOCIAL CLASS FACTORS AND SCHOOL ATTENDANCE

James S. Davie

METHODOLOGICAL PROCEDURES

The study group selected was composed of all children who were sixteen or seventeen years of age as of September 1, 1949, the parents of whom were legal residents of New Haven. This group was considered to meet the theoretical requirements that the children in any group selected be of approximately equal age; that they evidence as many different educational characteristics as could be possibly represented in any group of children drawn from the same population; and that they come from families in all levels of the New Haven class system. A younger group was not selected

Reprinted from *Harvard Educational Review*, Vol. XXIII, No. 3 (Summer 1953), pp. 175–185.

because the state compulsory attendance law is in effect until the child reaches the age of sixteen. An older group was not selected because of the extreme difficulty of obtaining the data necessary to identify such a group.

The group selected for study was readily identified from the records of the New Haven Board of Education which is required by state law to make an annual school census of all New Haven children between the ages of three and eighteen. From these records all the children who met the age and residence requirements were selected as a study group, totaling 3,801. Fifty-one cases who were in either penal institutions or institutions for the physically and mentally abnormal were subsequently discarded, as were fourteen cases found to be in primary school. The latter comprised too small a group to be treated statistically. The tables presented below are based on the remaining 3,736 cases who represent 98.3% of the age group studied.

Educational Classification. The present paper employs six educational categories: non-attendant, trade school, high school, private secondary school, liberal arts college and university, and post-secondary vocational school. The non-attendant category contains all cases listed as not attending school; the trade school category—all cases attending New Haven's one trade school; the high school category—all cases attending either of the city's two public high schools and all cases listed as being in grade nine or above in the city's several junior high schools; and the private school category—all cases attending secondary schools which were not supported by public tax funds. On the post-secondary level, the liberal arts category contains all cases attending post-secondary institutions the main purpose of which was listed by standard educational directories as the provision of a liberal arts education. The vocational category contains all cases attending post-secondary institutions the main purpose of which was the teaching of a practical skill rather than the provision of a general fund of knowledge.

Social Stratification. The families of the children in the study group were stratified socially according to their ecological area of residence. A previous study of New Haven had divided the city into six residential class levels by analyzing land use and population distribution with respect to such social differentia as income, nationality, occupation, delinquency, dependency, social club membership, and inclusion in the social register.[1] Such criteria were found to cluster and to divide the city into more or less "natural" areas, each of which tended to be socially homogeneous. By grouping areas on the basis of their respective similarities and differences, a scale of residential classes was constructed.

Since the criteria used in the determination of the six levels are the same as those which most social class analyses have stressed as important factors

[1] For a detailed statement of the methodology and findings of the original study see Maurice R. Davie, "The Pattern of Urban Growth" in G. P. Murdock (ed.), *Studies in the Science of Society* (New Haven: Yale University Press, 1937), pp. 132–161.

in social differentiation, the author felt that the use of ecological area of residence was a legitimate approximation of a person's position in the class structure of the city. In individual cases, the reliability of such a procedure is admittedly questionable, for in every area of a city one can find people who are sociologically atypical of that area. However, where one is working with mass data and is concerned primarily with broad patterns rather than individual cases, the advantages of an ecological index far outweigh the disadvantages. Space does not permit a detailed description of the residential classes, but some of their more salient characteristics may be sketched.[2]

Class I	Native born of native parentage; professional people or business executives; highest incomes in city; lowest delinquency and dependency rates; greatest representation in social register and leading social clubs; live in one-family houses of highest valuation in city.
Class II	Mixed nativity,[3] minor business executives, dealers and proprietors; less income than Class I but well above the city's median; two- and one-family houses.
Class III	Mixed nativity; office workers, public school teachers, artisans; income around city median; two- and one-family houses.
Class IV	Mixed nativity; artisans and laborers; two-thirds of family incomes below city median; average delinquency and dependency rates; two-family houses of low valuation.
Class V	Mixed nativity; laborers and artisans; four-fifths of incomes below city median; high delinquency and dependency rates; two-family houses of low valuation.
Class VI	Foreign born; laborers; almost all incomes below median; highest delinquency and dependency rates; multi-family dwellings of lowest valuation.

Analysis. Once the children had been classified educationally and their parents stratified socially, the two systems of classification were compared statistically by the use of the chi-square method. A representative sample of families was then drawn from what statistical analysis indicated were key spots in the class structure of New Haven and interviews were held with the families in an attempt to shed further light on the statistical findings.

FINDINGS

When the children in the study group were classified educationally, 52.5% were found in the high school category; 28.2% were listed as non-attendant;

[2] This description is based on conditions existing in the mid-1930's, but subsequent studies of the New Haven community indicate that changes in the character of the residential class areas have not been sufficient to affect the major findings of the present study.

[3] Mixed nativity: native-born of native parentage, native-born of foreign or mixed parentage, and foreign-born.

9.5% were in private secondary schools; 3.4% were in trade school; 3.3% in liberal arts colleges and universities; and 3.1% in higher vocational schools. Were there no relationship between school attendance and social class membership one should expect the children of each social class to be distributed through the six educational categories in these same proportions. However, as Table I indicates, there were striking differences between the classes with

TABLE 1. PERCENTAGE DISTRIBUTION OF SCHOOL ATTENDANCE, BY RESIDENTIAL CLASS LEVEL

CLASS	NON-ATTENDANT	TRADE SCHOOL	HIGH SCHOOL	PRIVATE SCHOOL	LIBERAL ARTS COLLEGE	HIGHER VOCATIONAL SCHOOL	TOTAL	NUMBER IN CLASS
I	1.8	2.4	41.6	33.1	16.3	4.8	100	(166)
II	11.1	0.8	58.0	16.0	10.0	4.1	100	(369)
III	16.9	2.7	55.9	15.4	5.4	3.7	100	(295)
IV	26.0	2.6	57.5	9.1	2.0	2.8	100	(605)
V	29.5	3.4	55.9	6.3	1.8	3.1	100	(1362)
VI	42.6	5.4	43.1	5.9	0.6	2.4	100	(939)
Total	28.2	3.4	52.5	9.5	3.3	3.1	100	(3736)

Chi Square = 539.274 P less than .001

respect to the proportion of children found in the different educational categories. Since such a distribution could arise by chance less than once in a thousand times, one must conclude that the positions the children's parents occupied in the New Haven class system were important determinants of the children's school attendance.

The differences in school attendance by social class level may be pointed up if the data are presented, as in Table II, in terms of quota fulfillment indices which reflect the degree to which the children of a given social level are over- or under-represented in a particular educational category. An index of 100 indicates that one finds the same proportion of children on a

TABLE 2. QUOTA FULFILLMENT INDICES

CLASS	NON-ATTENDANT	TRADE SCHOOL	HIGH SCHOOL	PRIVATE SCHOOL	LIBERAL ARTS COLLEGE	HIGHER VOCATIONAL SCHOOL
I	6	70	79	348	494	155
II	39	24	110	168	303	132
III	60	79	106	162	164	119
IV	92	76	110	96	61	90
V	105	100	106	66	55	100
VI	151	159	82	62	18	77

social level in a given educational category that one finds in the total group. An index of less than 100 indicates that there are disproportionately fewer cases; an index of over 100 that there are disproportionately more cases.

From the two tables one can see not only that there were differences in the amount and type of schooling, but that these factors varied markedly with social level. For example, in the non-attendant category, the lower one goes in the class structure the greater the proportion of children of each level one finds who are not attending school. Only in the Class V and VI areas does one find more non-attendant cases than expected. Class V is slightly over-represented while Class VI is one and one-half times over-represented. Apparently then, it is at the bottom of the class structure where the forces operating to take a child from school after his sixteenth birthday are the strongest.

In the trade school category one finds essentially the same pattern, although by no means statistically uniform. Classes I–IV are under-represented; Class V sends as many children to the trade school as expected; and Class VI is slightly more than one and one-half times over-represented. Interviews with Class V and VI families revealed that were the city to enlarge its trade school facilities there would be a corresponding shift of lower class children from the high school to the trade school. Families on these levels reported that the children would have preferred trade school but that there had not been sufficient facilities to handle the demand.

Within the high school category one notes that on all social levels the greatest percentage of children is found in the public high school but that Classes I and VI, the two extremes, are under-represented. As mentioned above, the Class VI children tended to be in trade school or out of school entirely while the Class I children, as the tables show, tended to be in private secondary schools or in post-secondary schools, particularly liberal arts colleges. Interviews with families of high school students revealed the general tendency for the upper classes to take the college-preparatory course of study; the middle classes to take a general course of study; and the lower classes to take a commercial course of study.

In the private school category one notes that Classes I–III are over-represented and Classes IV–VI are under-represented; that the higher one goes in the class structure the greater the proportion of children one finds in private schools; and that private schooling is most characteristic of children from families living in the Class I areas of the city. There one finds three and one-half times more children attending private school than one would expect on a population basis. Although not reported here, it should be noted that the private school category contains many different types of private schools and that, in general, the upper classes tend to patronize non-denominational boarding and day schools for either boys or girls while the lower classes attend parochial day schools which are co-educational.

On the post-secondary level one notes that the higher one goes in the class structure the greater is the percentage of children one finds attending some type of post-secondary school. Classes I–III are over-represented in both liberal arts institutions and higher vocational schools while Classes IV–VI tend to be under-represented. However, one also notes that in Classes I–III the liberal arts colleges are patronized more than are the higher vocational schools while in Classes IV–VI the reverse is true. There are also differences between the classes with respect to the kinds of colleges and higher vocational schools attended. Children in the upper classes tend to be enrolled at large private eastern universities such as Harvard, Yale, Princeton, Wellesley, Vassar and Smith while children from the lower classes are found overwhelmingly in the state university. Of those attending higher vocational schools, the children from the upper classes tend to enroll at schools of design, art, music, and drama while children from the lower classes tend to enroll at restaurant institutes, physical education schools, business colleges, barber colleges, radio repair schools and the like.

If one looks at each class level in terms of those educational categories in which it is over-represented, the major educational differences between the classes can be most clearly seen. From this viewpoint, each class appears to have its own pattern of educating its children which more or less distinguishes it from other classes. Adjoining classes tend to have similar patterns while classes widely removed from each other tend to have dissimilar patterns. Contrast, for example, Class I with Class VI. Where the former is over-represented in the private secondary and the post-secondary categories, the latter is over-represented in the trade school and non-attendant categories. Viewing the class structure as a whole, one notes a decided shift away from the public high school as one moves from the middle of the class structure toward the extremes. As one approaches Class I, the shift is in the direction of the private school followed by a liberal arts college or university. As one approaches Class VI the shift is in the direction of trade school and non-attendance. In brief, the above tables enable one to assert with some confidence that the position of a family in the social class structure of New Haven exerts a significant influence on the educational characteristics of its children.

Interviews with a sample of families from the study group served to support the patterns revealed by the statistics and to indicate some of the factors which operated on the various class levels to produce the different patterns. In the remaining paragraphs, the six social classes will be sketched in terms of these factors. Because of space limitations, the treatment must be highly generalized and will stress only the dominant educational characteristics of each class and only those factors which seemed most influential in determining the characteristics.

EDUCATIONAL ATTITUDES BY SOCIAL CLASS

The typical family living in the Class I areas of New Haven was most familiar with the pattern of private secondary schooling followed by enrollment at one of the prestigeful private eastern universities. The parents were college graduates as were their circle of friends and quite frequently had attended private secondary schools. The state compulsory attendance law was of no concern to them. Many were unaware that such a law existed. They had assumed their children would be educated as they had been and as the children of their friends were being educated. The children would receive at least a college education, for this was essential for their future psychic and economic welfare. How else could one come to really appreciate life? How else could one understand oneself and others? How else could a man hope to provide a happy, comfortable home and a pleasant life for his family? How else could a woman effectively perform her roles as wife and mother?

Private schooling on the secondary level was frequently regarded as a natural prerequisite to attending a "good" university. The thought of attending a public school had never occurred to several families. Those with children in private schools felt that the public schools were totally inadequate. They tended to be "factories" bogged down with great numbers of students who for one reason or another were not going on to college and who did not have the same interests in education. Also, most of the children in those schools came from different backgrounds and tended to have different values, ambitions, and codes of behavior. It would probably be an interesting and perhaps beneficial experience for a child to mix with other children like that, but his college preparation would suffer. Certainly, private education was expensive, but it was worth it; and it wasn't too much of a burden if one believed in education. Several thousand dollars annually was not an unusual amount to spend for the secondary education of one's children.

For families living in the Class II areas college attendance was also regarded as essential if one wanted to amount to anything more than a clerk. Private education on the secondary level was held better than public education. However, where Class I families accepted it almost without question, Class II families wondered whether it was an entirely necessary and justifiable expense. Their finances were more limited, and after taxes and the expenses of maintaining a comfortable home, only a moderate amount remained for the education of the children. This was earmarked for a college education with the result that there was often the question of whether one could afford private secondary schooling as well. The boarding schools attended by Class I children were too expensive, but the private day school was within the scope of the Class II family budget. If this was still a little too expensive, a small scholarship could usually be obtained to make up the deficit. The other alternative was to send the child to the public high school for the college preparatory course, in which event the parents kept a careful eye on the child's progress, often through the medium of the Parent Teacher's Association. It was a difficult decision to make. Enough of the neighborhood children and enough of the children of one's friends were attending private school to make one seriously consider enrolling one's own children. There was no doubt that the children would be better prepared for college there. Yet it would be a reasonably expensive undertaking. However, no matter what the decision in regard to secondary schooling, the family did not lose sight of its basic conviction that the main purpose of secondary schooling was to prepare the child for admission to the best college the family could afford.

Children from the Class III areas were over-represented in the same educational categories as Class II children, but the pattern was slightly less pronounced. Where Classes I and II had emphasized attendance at specific post-secondary institutions, most usually the large private universities, Class III tended to emphasize the importance of attending *some* school if the family could afford it. Funds for education were more limited, with the result that more of a compromise had to be made between the further training the family wished to provide for its children and the training it could reasonably afford to provide. Thus, on the Class III level, the post-secondary educational horizon seemed to offer three alternatives for those wishing to attend college. One could choose one of the small colleges scattered along the Atlantic seaboard, the state university, or, if one were fortunate to receive a substantial scholarship, one of the large eastern universities. The first two paths seemed most reasonable to follow. In families with several children to educate, limited funds often acted in favor of the boy who received a four-year college program while the girl contented herself with a shorter and less expensive program of study at a state teacher's college, a nursing school or a secretarial school.

Private schooling on the secondary level was regarded as a definite luxury and as something out of the ordinary. The high school was regarded as the natural secondary school to attend. A conscientious child from a good home would do all right there. The trade school was regarded as acceptable but only for that minority of children who for some reason or another didn't "take to bookwork." For them it was better to learn how to be productive rather than to waste their time at something they didn't like or couldn't do. In brief, the Class III family stressed the importance of the child becoming a self-supporting member of society and the educational characteristics of their children reflected this attitude.

On the Class IV level post-secondary education was very much an uncertainty. The biggest educational problem the families reported was that of "getting over the hump" between secondary and post-secondary school.

Considerable "shopping around" was necessary to find some college or vocational school which was not overly expensive or which offered a substantial enough scholarship. Such shopping was difficult, however, for the parents had little knowledge of the variety and costs of post-secondary educational institutions. The Class IV father was typically a skilled artisan who had not been to college. On the one hand, he expressed the desire for his children to go further in life than he had. On the other hand, post-secondary schooling was so much an uncertainty that he found it difficult to advise his children about what to prepare themselves for through their secondary training. One could take the college preparatory course on the gamble that some sort of post-secondary school would be available upon graduation. A safer alternative would be to take the general course of study to prepare themselves for work in the event that further schooling was not available. Then again, a vocationally-oriented course at the trade school or at the high school would best prepare them for earning a living, but this would pretty well close the gate on the possibility of college. Working with things and one's hands, as the father knew, could lead to a comfortable living; but, as he also knew, working with books and ideas and people would probably lead to a better living. Post-secondary schooling was so near and yet so far away that it was difficult to decide what to advise his children.

Families interviewed on the Class V and VI levels felt that one should receive as much education "as one can get." The high school and the trade school were the natural schools to attend. There one should take "something practical" which was defined as "something you can use" or as "something that will get you a good job." A "good job" was generally defined as that of a mechanic, a machine operator, or a similar occupation requiring some degree of manual skill. If one were lucky enough to go beyond secondary school, one could become a clerk or a school teacher or a barber where the work was cleaner and the income more steady.

On the Class V level, life was a little more secure economically. Fewer mothers were working, and thus more could maintain some semblance of a home as well as keep a closer eye on the children. The children could dress a little better and could have a little spending money, but high school was still defined as the end of the educational road for the average child. The same pressures as on the Class VI level operated to remove the child from school before graduation, but the added increment of economic security was often sufficient to allay the forces until the child could finish his secondary schooling.

On the Class VI level, the parents of the children had generally received less than a high school education. Both parents worked in semi-skilled and unskilled capacities to earn enough to pay the rent for their cold-water flat and to keep the family fed. Sickness and industrial accidents often necessitated the children leaving school "to help out." When the children weren't "needed" at home, they often left school anyhow in quest of a job and "some spending money in the jeans" which the parents could not provide. The one positive influence keeping them in school was the knowledge that more and more employers were asking for high school diplomas. However, the attraction of earning one's own money was often too great. Many left school immediately after their sixteenth birthdays only to find the jobs available to them were low-paying ones as bus-boys, waitresses, and pin-boys. The pleasure and sense of accomplishment initially derived from such jobs soon gave way to a sense of discouragement at the lack of remuneration and of future prospects. Hence, it was not unusual to find them holding a succession of jobs which, for the boys in time of peace, was often terminated by enlistment in the armed services as a welcome escape from a drab existence. The girls tended to seek their escape in an early marriage, often to discover later that they had to return to work to keep the family going "when times were tough."

Families frequently reported the children would have left school before their sixteenth birthdays had there been no compulsory attendance law and no careful check on absentees by the city school authorities. With both parents working there was little parental control over the children's behavior and the parents reported that they "couldn't do much with the kids" either before or after their sixteenth birthdays. The chances of post-secondary schooling were seen as minimal. Very few people went. The normal pattern seemed to be to leave school when the rest of the gang did.

SUMMARY AND DISCUSSION

The statistical data presented above have indicated that in a contemporary New England city the social class membership of one's family determines, in part, not only the length of time one will attend school but also the particular type of school attended. The qualitative data from interviews have suggested that behind the observed patterns of school attendance lay a complex of factors which interacted to produce the patterns observed. The description of some of the major educational features of New Haven's six social levels has stressed implicitly three factors which the author felt to be among the more important of those operating. First, and most obvious, is the factor of the family's financial circumstances which influences the extent to which the family can afford to patronize those schools for which some charge is involved or, on the lower levels, the extent to which it can afford to keep the children in the free public schools.

But differences in financial circumstances of the social classes cannot alone account for differences in school attendance. One must consider a second factor of custom which in large part determines how the family will spend whatever funds it has available for education. The factor of custom seemed to influence the family both from within and without. From within, parents tended to educate their children as they had been educated, or perhaps a little better, and to accept this as the natural thing to do. From without, parents tended to educate the children as their friends, neighbors, and social acquaintances were educating their children. Frequent evidence was encountered that the influence of custom in both instances was such that a particular educational pattern was often accepted without question as a minimal desideratum and followed accordingly.

Closely associated with the factor of custom was a third factor: a configuration of beliefs, values and attitudes pertaining to the purpose and value of education. Families on all levels tended to stress the benefits thought to accrue from education and to view education as a means of insuring the future welfare of the individual. Usually, the individual's welfare was defined in economic terms, but the upper classes also stressed the psychic benefits of education. Although families on all levels stressed the economic benefits of education, they differed not only with respect to the particular ends which they considered to be realistic ones for their children but also with respect to the particular amounts and types of education which were seen as necessary means to achieve those ends. The differences between families of various levels were most clearly revealed in the differential evaluation of occupations. What was socially acceptable to one level was often abhorrent to another. On the lower levels it was said that one did not need a college education or sometimes even a high school diploma to get a "good" job in a factory. Secondary schooling, if it was to be worthwhile, should equip the individual to earn a living. On the upper levels one needed a college education if one were to become a successful executive and amount to something more than a clerk. Certainly if one were to enter the professions, one would need college *and* professional training. Private secondary schooling was the perfectly sensible thing to do, since it was oriented toward preparing the child for college as the next step on the road to a happy future.

What implications do these findings have and for whom? They suggest for the child that his pattern of schooling is partially determined by the mere fact of his birth into a family of a particular social class status. If one can assume, with some justification, that an individual's education is a barometer of his future circumstances of life, then a considerable portion of the child's later life as an adult is being influenced in his early years. For the community the differential patronization of schools by the various social classes suggests that the schools function as divisive influences which reduce the amount of interclass contact of children and thereby the broadening benefits such contact is assumed to bestow. In terms of the class system of the community, the school appears to be perpetuating the status of some children by feeding them into occupational pursuits characteristic of the levels from which they come and to be serving as a channel of upward mobility for others.

Finally, the present study along with others serves to bring into question two of America's cherished myths: those of a classless society and of equal educational opportunity for all.

EDUCATIONAL ATTAINMENT AND FAMILY BACKGROUND

Florence Campi

According to a survey taken by the Census Bureau in October 1960, there were 4.7 million men 20–24 years old in the United States. Of this number, 1.7 million had either graduated from college or had some college attendance.

The survey reveals a relationship between the level of education attained by young people and certain factors in their family background. *There is a direct relationship between the college attendance of young men and the education of their fathers.*

College enrollment rates of men in their early twenties whose fathers were college graduates are several times as large as those for persons of the same age whose fathers never finished high school.

When the fathers had completed college, 88 percent of the sons 20–24 years of age had graduated from college or had some college attendance.

In contrast, when the father had completed only high school, 65 percent of the sons had graduated from college or had some college attendance.

In the nonwhite group where the father did not graduate from high school, only 7 percent of the children 16–24 years of age were enrolled in college.

However, in the nonwhite group where the father *did* graduate from high school, 18 percent of the children 16–24 years were enrolled in college.

There is also a direct relationship between high school graduation of young men and education of their fathers.

Where the fathers had graduated from high school, 92 percent of the sons had graduated from high school including 65 percent who had some college attendance.

Reprinted from *New Directions in Health, Education, and Welfare*, United States Department of Health, Education and Welfare, U.S. Government Printing Office, Washington, D.C., 1963, pp. 168–169.

But when the fathers had not completed high school, only 57 percent of the sons graduated from high school including 23 percent who had some college attendance.

Educational attainment is related to family income.

Among the families whose income was less than $5,000 a year, 55 percent of the children 16–24 years old had graduated from high school but only 19 percent went on to college.

Where the families had an income of $10,000 or more per annum, 87 percent of the children had graduated from high school and 60 percent continued on to college.

The educational level which a person attains is a product of both the education of the father and the family income.

Where the father did not graduate from high school and the family income was less than $5,000 only 13 percent of the children had some college attendance.

In contrast, where the father graduated from college and the family income was $10,000 or more, 89 percent of persons aged 16–24 years old had some college attendance.

LIMITED EDUCATIONAL ATTAINMENT: EXTENT AND CONSEQUENCES

E. W. Brice and E. E. Huyck

Persons with low educational attainment have great difficulty in meeting the economic and social needs of modern society. They have limited adaptability to changing requirements for employment, and they frequently are rejected for military service. Those who lack an education extending beyond elementary school are deprived of many opportunities for personal development and participation in community affairs. Often they cannot avoid unemployment and dependency.

Reprinted from *New Directions in Health, Education, and Welfare,* United States Department of Health, Education and Welfare, United States Government Printing Office, Washington, D.C., 1963, pp. 170, 171, 174, 176.

Persons who have less than 8 years of formal schooling thus lack, by and large, the background for effective performance as employees and as citizens. For these reasons they are frequently called "functional illiterates."[1]

ADULTS WITH LESS THAN EIGHT YEARS OF SCHOOL

According to the 1960 Census of Population some 22.1 million persons aged 25 and over—22.2 percent of the adult population—had completed less than 8 years of schooling. Of this number 11.5 million were men and 10.6 million were women.

These "functional illiterates" are concentrated mainly in the following groups: (1) older persons, both white and nonwhite; (2) persons living on farms, especially Negroes; (3) persons with rural backgrounds who have moved to urban centers, including Puerto Rican migrants; and (4) migrant farm workers and other disadvantaged groups, including Spanish-speaking persons in the western and southwestern United States.

Data from the 1960 Census of Population show that:

There are about one million Puerto Ricans in the United States. Some 269,000 of those who are 25 years of age or older live in the five boroughs of New York City. Of these, 53 percent had completed less than 8 years of education. Similar percentages are reported for Jersey City and Philadelphia.

A large number of persons with Spanish surnames live in the five southwestern States. A substantial proportion of them have had less than 8 years of school. Of the 101,000 such persons living in San Antonio, Texas, the rate was 69 percent.

In the United States territories of Guam, Puerto Rico, and the Virgin Islands there are 676,000 persons 25 years of age and older with less than 8 years of school completed. The rate varies from 39 percent in Guam, to 61 percent in the Virgin Islands, and 71 percent in Puerto Rico.

DISTRIBUTION OF FUNCTIONAL ILLITERACY AMONG THE STATES

The problem of limited educational attainment is not, however, limited to particular areas or population groups. Rather it is national in scope. In New York State the number of adults with less than 8 years of schooling is nearly 2,000,000. In Illinois there are 1,048,000 and in California 1,300,000.

[1] "Functional illiteracy" may be contrasted with "illiteracy." The Census Bureau defines an illiterate as "a person who cannot both read and write a simple message either in English or any other language." The ability to read and write is now shared by nearly all persons 14 years old or older; the relatively small number of illiterates is concentrated mostly in the older age groups. Because of the demands of present-day family, community, and national life, this restricted definition of illiteracy is of limited usefulness. More meaningful today is the concept of "functional illiteracy," which is related to low educational attainment as measured by number of years of school completed.

The corresponding numbers in Kentucky, Michigan, New Jersey, and Ohio exceed 500,000, while in Indiana, Maryland, Massachusetts, Missouri, Oklahoma, West Virginia, and Wisconsin the numbers range from 304,000 to over 500,000.

CONSEQUENCES OF LIMITED EDUCATIONAL ATTAINMENT

Lack of schooling results in lower earning capacity, higher rates of unemployment, more dependence on public aid, and higher rejections for military service.

1. *Occupation and Earnings*

A direct relationship exists between an adult's eductional attainment, his occupation, and, consequently, his earnings. The amount of formal schooling a person has received is a major determinant of his occupational group.

Among men 18 years old and over in 1959, 60 percent of the college graduates were in professional and technical fields, and about 20 percent were managers, officials, or proprietors. Among men who completed high school, but did not go beyond, a majority were found in three occupation groups—craftsmen; operatives; and managers, officials, or proprietors. Those with some high school, but lacking four complete years, and men who finished elementary school, but who did not go on to high school, were most likely to have become operatives or craftsmen. Those with lesser amounts of education were most usually found—when employed at all—in farm, service, and unskilled laboring jobs.

Of all employed men, as of 1957, in the age group 35–54 who had completed less than eight years of elementary school, 92 percent earned less than $6,000 per year. In contrast, 65 percent of high school graduates and only 29 percent of college graduates had income below this level.

Employed workers with an eighth grade education or less have 65 percent of the incomes between $1,000 and $1,500, and 61 percent of the incomes between $1,500 and $2,500.

2. *Unemployment and Underemployment*

Unskilled workers have the highest rates of unemployment and the lowest average level of education. A Department of Labor study for March 1959 showed an unemployment rate of 10.0 percent for workers with under 5 years completed, a rate of 9.8 percent for those with 5 to 7 years schooling, 4.8 percent for high school graduates and 1.8 percent for college graduates. These rates had not changed substantially by March 1962.

The rate of unemployment in 1962 among proprietors, managers, professional and technical personnel was between one and two percent. Clerical and sales workers were unemployed at the rate of approximately four percent.

But semi-skilled workers were out of work at the rate of 7½ percent and unskilled workers at the rate of about 12 percent.

3. *Public Assistance*

Recipients of public assistance are more likely to be persons of low educational attainment. A 1957 study in New York, for example, revealed that almost a fifth of the mothers on the aid to dependent children rolls had not gone beyond the fifth grade. This study further showed that among families receiving general assistance half of the family heads had completed no more than six years of schooling. Illinois reported in 1960 that a fifth of their ADC mothers had not gone beyond the sixth grade. In Louisiana, in 1954, half the ADC mothers and three-fourths of the fathers in the home had received only a fifth grade education or less.

4. *Military Service*

In World War II, some 400,000 illiterates were accepted for military service. The armed forces provided these men with the educational fundamentals necessary for useful service. Another 300,000 illiterates—equal to twenty army divisions—were rejected completely.

During the Korean War over 19 percent of all recruits were rejected from military service on grounds of educational deficiencies. Experience showed that many of these men could learn, but overcoming their previous educational deprivations was costly and time-consuming. Draft registrants rejected for "mental reasons," including educational deficiencies, ranged from 56 to 39 percent in the four highest States. Ten other States had rejection rates exceeding 21 percent.

From July 1950 to September 1961, over 900,000 draft registrants out of 6 million examined were rejected on the basis of a mental test alone. This number was almost as many as were disqualified on medical grounds. Low educational attainment was the largest single reason for rejection.

PROJECTED EDUCATIONAL ATTAINMENT OF THE POPULATION

Although lower educational attainment is most prevalent among older persons, the problem will continue for many decades. The Census Bureau estimates that by 1980 there will still be more than 5 million persons 25 years of age and older with less than 5 years of education completed and 21.5 million with less than 8 years if present trends continue.

PART SIX

The Individual and Education

THE RECOGNITION of education as one of society's major socializing agencies demands that educators understand a great deal about the way in which personalities are formed. The fact that, in some ways, all men are the same, some men are the same, and each man is different makes the search for the fullest understanding of human nature enormously complicated. It is commonly accepted that the individual exists and functions as a complete organism, as a total personality, rather than as a personality comprising independent, but related, parts. There is further recognition that the development of personality characteristics involves a subtle interplay between nature (the biological heritage) and nurture (the stimuli, tensions, and pressures of the physical and social environment). As a final point, an account of the factors that contribute to the determination of the individual's personality must include an understanding of the inter-relatedness of man and culture: Just as any person is in an environment, so the environment is built into his reactions. In this conception, the person is not "here" and the environment "there," but the-person-in-the-environment is the culture, a single entity.

This conception of personality and culture as representing a unitary, transactional process, a single entity, is a powerful educational tool. In order to use it, educators need a design for teaching and learning, one whose dimensions will provide an overview of all the factors operating in the formation of personality even as they afford insight into the detailed functioning of each of the factors.

The purpose of this chapter is to explore the factors that contribute to the formation of personality; the function of experience in relation to the growth of personality; the value of planned experience as a recognized means to secure desired behavior; and the significance of encouraging the kinds of personalities that embody the democratic ethos.

Chapter 26

DETERMINANTS AND COMPONENTS OF PERSONALITY

A CONCEPTUAL *scheme designed to answer the question "How do we attain our knowledge of personality?" is offered by Clyde Kluckhohn, an anthropologist, and O. H. Mowrer, a psychologist. They are fully aware of the dangers inherent in any discussion of personality in culture because of the wide-spread tendency to talk about man as a free-floating, generalized abstraction. The authors maintain that "physical-environmental, social, cultural, and biological determinants and their complicated interrelations must all be given due consideration." Personality and culture are accepted as vital interacting parts, and neither can be adequately described without considering the other. The authors maintain that a theory of personality must explain both the similarities and the differences of each personality, and they suggest that the conceptual scheme should incorporate the following generalizations:*

1) All human beings have certain properties of social stimulus value, or personality traits, in common. We shall call these universal traits, or components, and their antecedents universal determinants.

2) The members of any given society tend to share more personality traits with each other than with the members of other societies. We shall call such traits communal traits, or components, and their antecedents communal determinants.

3) Within a society the behavior characteristics of certain groups or categories of persons shows some constancies. The social stimulus value of those who are playing the same role has a common quality. We shall call this the role component and the antecedents of traits dependent upon the roles the role determinants.

4) The members of any given society, even those who are playing similar roles, differ among themselves in social stimulus value. We shall call such distinctive and relatively unique traits idiosyncratic traits or components, and their antecedents idiosyncratic determinants.

5) Certain similarities, other than those common to all humanity, may be observed in the social stimulus value of individuals from different societies even where the personality manifestations for those societies vary widely. The possibility of such similarities is, however, deducible from the fact that idiosyncratic determinants are not society-bounded. Consequently, we need no special designation for nor explanation of such similarities.

In what follows it is important to note that Kluckhohn and Mowrer's thesis consists of two classes of concepts and the interrelationships of the component parts of both concepts. The authors state: "On the one hand, there are the determinants: *those classes of forces which may be abstracted out as influencing social stimulus value. On the other hand, there are the* components *of personality: those facets of the social stimulus value of the individual as an integrate in action which may be regarded as produced primarily by one or another of the classes of determinants."*

In terms of their thesis and their five generalizations, Kluckhohn and Mowrer first discuss the universal, communal, role, and idiosyncratic determinants of personality and then present a discussion of the biological, physical-environmental, social, and cultural determinants of personality. Lest the reader be tempted to accept personality as an entity composed of discrete parts, the authors then present their view of the individual as an integrated whole that functions in a social setting.

CULTURE AND PERSONALITY: A CONCEPTUAL SCHEME

Clyde Kluckhohn and O. H. Mowrer

THE DETERMINANTS OF PERSONALITY

First, we must note that this pie, like all others, can be sliced in more than one way. In speaking of the forces operative in personality formation it has been customary to deal with such abstractions as "the biological," "the cultural," "the environmental," and the like. Such abstractive isolates are useful, but, if the primary purpose is to show how total stimulus value may be segre-

Reprinted from *American Anthropologist*, Vol. 46, No. 1, Part 1 (January–March 1944), pp. 3–9, 11–25. Footnotes omitted.

gated into various facets or components, these are second-order abstractions. That is, such determining forces as "the biological" and "the cultural" are only elements in abstractions such as "universal" and "communal" which may be linked more immediately to the components of personality. No single component can be regarded as the product of forces which are exclusively biological or cultural. But "the communal component" may be directly connected with the partly biological, partly social, partly cultural, partly physical environmental influences which act upon all members of a single society and which hence may be subsumed as the "communal determinants." Let us now examine systematically and in detail the interdigitation of personality determinants classified as "universal, communal, role, and idiosyncratic" with personality determinants classified in a more familiar manner.

We have heard Clark Hull say "In the beginning there is (a) the organism and (b) the environment." Using this dichotomy as a starting point in analyzing the determinants of personality one might say that the *differences* observed in the personalities of human beings are due to variations in their

COMPONENTS OF PERSONALITY

DETERMINANTS	UNIVERSAL	COMMUNAL	ROLE	IDIOSYNCRATIC
Biological	Birth, death, hunger, thirst, elimination, etc.	"Racial" traits, nutrition level, endemic diseases, etc.	Age and sex differences, caste, etc.	Peculiarities of stature, physiognomy, glandular make-up, etc.
Physical-environmental	Gravity, temperature, time, etc.	Climate, topography, natural resources, etc.	Differential access to material goods, etc.	Unique events and "accidents" such as being hit by lightning, etc.
Social	Infant care, group life, etc.	Size, density, and distribution of population, etc.	Cliques, "marginal" men, etc.	Social "accidents" such as death of a parent, being adopted, meeting particular people, etc.
Cultural	Symbolism, tabu on incest and in-group murder, etc.	Traditions, rules of conduct and manners, skills, knowledge, etc.	Culturally differentiated roles	Folklore about accidents and "fate," etc.

For helpful suggestions as to terminology we are indebted to Drs. Leland H. Jenks, Ralph Linton, and John Whiting. For general discussions which have materially assisted in the clarification of this conceptual scheme we are indebted to Dr. Florence Kluckhohn.

biological equipment and in the total environment to which they must adjust, while the *similarities* are to be understood as resulting from biological and environmental uniformities. But such an overly general and overly simple formulation—although useful as a first approximation—will not, unless it be further developed, lead us to hypotheses which have predictive value.

We realize, of course, that even the dichotomy which Hull proposes is an abstraction, for, as Henderson has pointed out, the organism and the environment have a kind of wholeness in the concrete behavioral world which the student loses sight of at his peril. While acknowledging the abstractive nature of the process, it is nevertheless necessary for us to distinguish three aspects of the environment—the physical, the social, and the cultural. The table shows in a schematic way how the two classificatory systems cut across each other in a symmetrical manner.

Although the sixteen cells formed by this two-way system of classification are logically exhaustive, the items which are entered in these cells in the table are, of course, merely illustrative. The following discussion will expand the significance of each cell, indicate the dynamic interrelatedness of the determinants, give some perspective on present knowledge of each, and further develop the logic of the conceptual scheme as a whole.

Universal, Communal, Role and Idiosyncratic Determinants

The *universal* determinants of personality arise out of four facts: (a) man is an animal of distinctive physical appearance and with somewhat distinctive biological equipment, (b) man is a social animal, (c) man is a cultural animal, (d) man lives in a physical world which obeys certain natural laws. All human beings normally have two hands and two feet at birth (not four feet and only most exceptionally one hand or three hands). Such properties as stereoscopic vision which differentiate the human species from most other living organisms immediately imply common features of personality. As animals, all men are also bound to face certain problems: they are born; they must breathe, eat, and excrete; they have imperious sexual and other needs; they grow; they face death. As social animals, they must adjust to dependence upon their society and groups within it. As cultural animals, they must adjust to culturally defined expectations. Finally, all men must adapt themselves to an external physical world.

That these facts do constitute problems for human beings is attested by common experience, yet the import and meaning of these facts have not been fully analyzed from the point of view of personality theory, nor do they seem likely to be in the near future for the reason that, being *universal* determinants, their meaning cannot be demonstrated by the usual methods of contrast and comparison. These are background phenomena, the invariables and inevitables to which man must bow and somehow adjust. That "human nature" would be strikingly different from what it is if the human animal had not assumed upright posture and developed prehensile hands, stereoscopic vision, and a nervous system which makes elaborate speech possible goes without saying; and here we have a clearer perception of the significance of this distinctively human cluster of biological traits since we can see what their absence implies in other animals. Contemporary "super-man" fantasies give us perhaps our only glimpse of what human beings would be like if they lived in a world without gravity, temperature, or time.

Since the universal determinants are relatively constant for all mankind, they provide no explanation either of personality typologies or peculiarities. If, however, we notice how certain universal or almost universal experiences derive a special phrasing from the interaction of the biological determinants with the realities of the social, cultural, and physical environment, we shall begin our systematic understanding of the observed variation in the social stimulus value of individuals.

All men are born helpless; the external impersonal world presents threats to survival; the human species would disappear completely if social life were abandoned. But the human adaptation to the external world depends not merely upon the mutual support which is social life; it also depends upon culture. Many types of insects live socially yet have no culture. They depend for survival upon behavioral dispositions which are transmitted within the germ plasm. Other organisms show great capacities to learn from experience. Human beings, however, learn not only from experience but also from each other. All human societies rely greatly for their survival upon accumulated learning (culture). All human culture is a storehouse of ready-made solutions to problems which human animals face. Into this storehouse are garnered not merely the pooled learning of the men who interact in any one society at any given point in time but also much of the learning of many men long dead, of many men from other societies. This capacity of human beings not only to learn but likewise to teach each other is not the least important of the universal determinants. For example, culture as well as the other three classes of determinants brings it about that throughout the life sequence all men experience both gratifications and deprivations. All persons receive some deprivations and frustrations from the impersonal environment (weather, physical obstacles, and the like interfere with the wishes of men) and from biological conditions (bodily incapacities, illnesses, etc.). Likewise, social life (whether in the ant hill, the beaver colony, the herd, or the human group) means some sacrifice of autonomy, some subordination and superordination. But the pleasure and pain men receive from one another depend not simply on physical facts, biological limitations, and the sheer conditions of social interaction: they depend too upon what the accumulated learning has taught them to expect from one another.

All human personalities are formed under this common condition of demands for conformity to cultural expectation. But the specific character of the cultural expectations varies greatly between different societies and even as between different groups in the same society. This brings us from the universal to the *communal* and *role* determinants. All human beings not only have to be socialized—they are always socialized as members of particular societies and often as members of differentiated categories within the society.

Membership in a society carries with it exposure to determinants of social stimulus value approximately constant for all members of that society. How large or how small a grouping one takes as "a society" is primarily a matter of convenience for the problem in hand. By and large, the physical traits and the total environment of Western Europeans do present a contrast to those of Mohammedans or Eastern Asiatics. White citizens of the United States, in spite of regional, ethnic, and class differences, can usually be distinguished, on the basis of their social stimulus value, from Englishmen, Australians, or New Zealanders. From the point of view of personality formation, there is a hierarchy of "societies" to which any individual belongs, ranging from very large units down to the local community. How inclusive a unit one considers in speaking of communal determinants is purely a function of the level of abstraction at which one is operating at a given time.

Some of the personality traits which the members of the same society have in common but which distinguish them from humanity as a whole unquestionably derive from distinctive biological heredity. Such persons look alike both to each other and to representatives of other societies. This similarity stems in part from uniformity of clothing and other personal artifacts, but the fact that persons who live together are more likely to be related biologically than are persons who live far apart means that "race" is a biological determinant of personality at the *communal* level of analysis. Biological factors common to a given soicety may, of course, manifest themselves, not only in terms of appearance, but also, less directly, in behavior. If the metabolic rate is typically low for one group as contrasted with other groups or if certain types of endocrine inbalance are unusually frequent, the social stimulus value of the members of that society will certainly have distinctive qualities. We have as yet, however, very little unequivocal information on this class of determinants, but their importance in some cases seems unmistakable.

Likewise, we know almost nothing of what the effects of communal constants in the impersonal environment are upon personality. Does living in continually rainy weather make for different social stimulus value from living in a sunny, arid country? What are the differential effects of living in a walled-in mountain valley, on a flat plain, or upon a high plateau studded with wind-sculptured red buttes? Thus far we can only speculate, for we lack controlled data. The effects of climate and even of topography may be considerable, although they have hardly been rigorously explored.

There are certain social, as opposed to cultural, determinants for each society. Thus the size of the society and the density of the population are certainly not culturally prescribed and are not even altogether determined indirectly by the culture, although often conditioned by the interaction between the technological level of the culture and the exigencies of the physical environment. The location of a population is a determining factor—as well as its size and density. Thus the type of social interaction (with its consequences for personality formation) will be different if a village of 1000 persons occupying an area of one square mile is located in central Kansas or within thirty miles of New York City.

The cultural facet of the environment of any society is a signally important determinant both of the content and of the structure of the personalities of members of that soicety. The culture very largely determines what is learned: available skills, standards of value, and basic orientations to such universal problems as death. Culture likewise structures the conditions under which learning takes place: whether from parents or parent surrogates or from siblings or from those in the learner's own age grade, whether learning is gradually and gently acquired or suddenly demanded, whether renunciations are harshly enforced or reassuringly rewarded. To say that "culture determines" is, of course, a highly abstract way of speaking. In the behavioral world what we actually see is parents and other older and more experienced persons *teaching* younger and less experienced persons. We assume that biology sets the basic processes which determine *how* man learns, but culture, as the transmitted experiences of preceding generations (both technological and moral) very largely determines *what* man learns (as a member of a society rather than as an individual who has his own private experiences). Culture even determines to a considerable extent how the teaching that is essential to this learning shall be carried out.

Logically, the role determinants could have been encompassed within the communal, for the reference is again to those determinants of personality which operate upon particular groups. But the fact that every society embraces units of social differentiation is so basic and its consequences for personality formation so tremendous (and so often neglected) that the distinction seemed necessary or, at the least, highly useful. In the personality context, the important criterion is always: to what social categories do the individual and those socializing him have a sense of "belongingness" (or of aspiration)? Certain of the categories are fundamentally biological. In every society the organism is differentially socialized according to sex. In every society different behavior is expected of individuals in different age groups, although where these lines are drawn and what behavioral variations are anticipated differs in different cultures. In all known caste societies physical criteria are to some extent involved, and class differentiations are often also tinged with appearance differences. The correlation of the role and physical environmental determinants rests upon the fact that some categories of persons within a society have differential access to residential locations, house types, and material goods generally. As for the role-social determinants, there are always some social grouping (cliques, for example) of enough permanence to be important for personality formation which are neither rationalized along biological lines nor prescribed by the ideal patterns of the culture. Finally, culture regulates the type of behavior deemed appropriate to individuals of a particular age, sex, and status.

That endless *idiosyncratic* variations can and do occur in the life of each human being hardly requires extensive documentation. A child is born a cripple. He is nearly drowned by a sudden flood in a canyon. If the death of a parent means that an infant goes to live with an aged grandmother, or if the remaining parent takes a new mate with a psychopathic personality, the outcome for the child must necessarily be different than if the original parent had survived. Even casual social contacts of brief duration ("accidental")—not foreordained by the cultural pattern of social interrelations—often seem crucial in determining whether one's life proceeds along one or another of various possible courses. While some cultures do prescribe different treatment for the oldest or youngest child in a series, the fact that a particular child occupies such a distinctive position is an "accident" from the point of view of the cultural system.

Biological, Physical-Environmental, Social and Cultural Determinants

We have now sketched the manner in which universal, communal, role, and idiosyncratic determinants of personality all include biological, physical-environmental, social, and cultural elements. Let us now reverse the emphasis, taking the classes of determinants along the horizontal axis of the table as our point of departure. . . .

Mendelian genetics have taught us that the particular heredity which a new organism gets from the two genetic lines which are crossing depends upon the accidental way in which the two germ cells exchange chromosomes at the time of fertilization. Except for siblings produced from a single fertilized egg, children having the same parents will have a somewhat different heredity. The idiosyncratic biological determinants which we have been discussing thus take their origin in these "accidents" of the genetic processes. Other idiosyncratic biological determinants exert their force as a result of some adventitious circumstance during uterine development.

Some factors that we are likely to pigeonhole all too complacently as "biological" often turn out, on careful examination, to be the products of complicated interactions. A crippling illness, for example, may well be partly the consequence of a constitutional predisposition but partly also the consequence of the individual's participation in a caste or class group where sanitation and medical care are inadequate. A tendency toward corpulence certainly has personality implications as well when it is characteristic for a group as when it distinguishes an individual within a group. But the resources of the physical environment as exploited by the culturally available technology are the major determinants of vitamins, noxiants, and nutrition generally, and it is these which have patent consequences for corpulence, stature, and energy potential. If hookworm is endemic in a population, one will hardly expect vigor to be a striking feature of personality. Yet hookworm is not an ineluctable "given," either environmentally or biologically: the effects and prevalence of hookworm are dependent upon culturally enjoined sanitation facilities and other culturally available types of control.

The same complicated sorts of interrelation may be noted between the physical and cultural environments. On the one hand, the physical environment imposes certain limitations upon the cultural forms which man creates or it constrains toward change and re-adjustment in the culture he brings into an ecological area. There is always a portion of the external environment which man can and does adjust to but which he can only very partially control. On the other hand, a part of even the impersonal environment is man-made and cultural. A culture may provide technologies which permit some alternations in the physical world (for example, by irrigation ditches or by terracing of hillsides). There are also those artifacts (houses, furniture, tools, vehicles) which add to the resources for gratification (and frustration). Most important of all, culture screens man's whole perception of the physical world. Sherif has shown experimentally the effects of social suggestion in setting frames of reference for perception. Hallowell has excellently indicated how culture acts as a set of blinders, or lenses with certain distortions, through which acculturated human beings view the whole world (including other human beings and themselves). Hallowell says:

> Man's psychological responses to the physical objects of his external environment can only be understood . . . in terms of the traditional meanings which these latter have for him. He never views the outer world freshly or responds to his fellows entirely free from the influences which these meanings exert upon his thought and conduct. Celestial and meteorological phenomena, for example, or the plants and animals of man's habitat, even its inanimate forms, are never separated as such from the concepts of their essential nature and the beliefs about them that appear in the ideological tradition of a particular cultural heritage. Man's attitude toward them is a function of reality as culturally defined, not in terms of their mere physical existence. Thus, to treat the physical environment in which a people lives independently of the meaning that its multiform objects have for that people involves a fundamental psychological distortion if we aim to comprehend the universe which is actually theirs. While useful in certain kinds of analysis, even the assertion that two peoples occupy the same natural environment because the regions inhabited by them exhibit the same climatic type, the same typography and biota can only have significance in the grossest physical sense. It is tantamount to ignoring the very data which have the most important psychological significance, namely the differences in meaning which similar objects of the phenomenal world have for peoples of different cultural traditions. Consequently,

the objects of the external world, *as meaningfully defined* in a traditional ideology, constitute the reality to which the individuals habituated to a particular system of beliefs actually respond. As applied to the sphere of ecological relations, for example, an inventory of all the natural resources of a specific human habitat does not necessarily correspond to the "natural resources" of that habitat. The physical objects of the environment only enter the reality-order of the human population as a function of specific culture patterns. It is the knowledge and technological level of the culture of a people that determines their natural resources, not the mere presence of physical objects. To people without a tradition of pottery-making the presence of clay in their habitat is no more a natural resource than was the presence of coal and iron in the habitat of the pre-Columbian Indians of eastern North America.

These words, written by an anthropologist, are readily translatable into psychological terms. They say, in effect, that the perceptual, or sign-function, of natural objects (and persons) is greatly influenced by what these objects do to or for man, and they also say that the sign-function of objects is likewise dependent upon what *other persons* say or do in the presence of these objects or their symbolic equivalents. Thus, if a child learns the name of an object and if the child's parents behave in a characteristic manner (e.g., showing fear, approval, or anger) when the child utters the object's name, the child's future reactions to the object itself are certain to be modified. Hence, Hallowell's emphasis upon the importance of knowing how the physical world is *meaningfully defined* if we are to understand its significance and potentialities for a particular person or group of persons.

Just as there are some features of the physical environment that are common to all human beings and just as there are still other features that are relatively distinctive for a given social group, so also are there physical-environmental determinants of personality that are more or less unique for the individual. The fact that no two human beings can occupy the same point at the same time and that the world is never precisely the same on successive occasions means, as many philosophers have pointed out, that, in detail at least, the physical world is idiosyncratic for each individual. That "accidents," such as being burned or perhaps merely frightened by lightning, being struck by a falling tree, or stumbling over an unseen obstacle, have implications for subsequent personality trends can hardly be doubted. More subtle, cumulative influences stemming from the physical environment may also have distinctive consequences for groups or for particular individuals, but these have not been adequately analyzed.

In some ways, the term "impersonal environment" is preferable to "physical environment" because the latter tends to have the exclusive connotation of topography, weather, and the like, whereas actually dwellings, furniture, and all human artifacts are a very important aspect of the external, objective, and non-human environment. These objects all acquire symbolic (including prestige) value for individuals, for social groups, for whole societies. Both symbolically and in the immediate physical sense they are depriving or frustrating agencies. We often speak as if deprivation and frustration were imposed on children only by their elders, but a high shelf which makes a coveted delicacy inaccessible or a gadget which cannot be manipulated will also interfere with a goal response. Societies and social sub-groups vary widely in respect to the "material culture" sector of their environments.

The effect of the total environment upon personalities may, following Murray, be called the "press." But, in spite of the subtle interactions of different facets of the environment to which we have been drawing attention, the "press" must be broken down into physical-environmental, social, and cultural. Of these abstractions the most elusive is the social. Although intimately interrelated, the *social* determinants of personality must be distinguished from the cultural. Man is, of course, only one of the many social animals, but the ways in which social, as opposed to solitary, life modifies his behavior are especially numerous and varied. The fact that human beings are mammals and reproduce bi-sexually creates a basic predisposition toward at least the rudiments of social living. And the prolonged helplessness of human infants conduces to the formation of a family group. Although more a product of experience than of any inherent biological force, the in-group principle may also be listed as a universal social determinant. Certain universalistic social processes such as conflict, competition, and accommodation are given their specific forms under the influence of communal social determinants and cultural determinants. Thus, while there is a universal process of social interaction whereby the physically strong tend to dominate the weak, this tendency may be checked and even to some extent reversed by a cultural tradition which rewards intellectual strength more richly than physical strength. Or, the operation of the process may be modified by communal and role social determinants: attitudes toward women, toward infants, toward the old, toward the weak will be conditioned by age and sex ratios and the general population equilibrium prevalent in a given society at a particular time.

Analytically, the distinction between the social and the cultural is a most significant one. This is peculiarly true at the level of the idiosyncratic determinants. There are many forces of social interaction which influence personality formation and yet are in no sense culturally prescribed. As Mead has pointed out, all children (unless multiple births) are born at different points in the parental life careers, which means that they have, psychologically speaking, somewhat different parents. Likewise, whether a child is wanted or unwanted and whether it is of the desired sex will also determine the specific ways in which its parents and others will treat it—even though the culture says that all children are wanted and defines the two sexes as of equal value.

In the concrete, however, the social and cultural are, for the most part, almost inextricably mixed. Let us take as an example a case where "accidents" of the life history are superimposed (as idiosyncratic determinants) upon both biological and cultural determinants. Even though identical twins may differ remarkably little from a constitutional standpoint and may also have culturally defined experiences which are very similar, unpredictable factors in the impersonal environment may impinge upon them so that their social interactions are quite different. If, for instance, one of two such twins happened to be injured in an automobile accident and the other was not, and if the injured twin has to spend a year in bed, it is plausible to suppose that marked personality differences might result. But the variations in the social treatment which the bed-ridden twin receives will be partly determined by culture (the extent to which the ideal patterns say that a sick child must be petted etc.), partly by extra-cultural factors: the mother's need for nurturance, the father's idiomatic variant of his culturally patterned role in these circumstances, etc.

"Culture," though definitely an abstraction, is, like "heredity," a highly convenient conceptual construct. Indeed, culture is precisely one form of heredity—social as opposed to biological heredity. Thus, just as we may speak of "constitutional determinants of personality," so equally are we justified in speaking of "cultural determinants of personality." This is not resorting to mysticism or to an abstraction which is not reducible to its behavioral referents. Nothing is more certain and concrete than the fact of human teaching. An example will, however, show the justification for detaching itself from the actual teachers. If a random third of the parents of Cambridge, Massachusetts, were to die tomorrow and their children were to be socialized by their surviving relatives and friends in Cambridge, it may safely be predicted that what these children would learn would be approximately the same—taking the group as a statistical whole—as if their parents had survived. In other words, although culture is always mediated by individuals —and this fact must *never* be forgotten—it does, in a limited sense, have a supra-individual character. The existence and continuity of most of any culture does not depend upon the lives of any *particular* person or persons in that group. Indeed, in moderately stable societies, although the whole population of any one period will, over a period of years, die, the culture will have been transmitted to their descendants and will continue in existence with a modicum of change. One may compare with this the fact that the genes of persons now long dead continue to exert their effects upon the behavior of living descendants.

Anthropology has made what is perhaps its most distinctive contribution by calling attention to the sparsity of *universal* cultural determinants of personality. It has shown that many social values which were formerly assumed to be common to all humanity are functions of a particular culture. But the cross-cultural analyses of the anthropologists have left a few universals. All societies have tabus on incest. All societies teach that it is "wrong" to murder members of one's own social group. And all societies have as part of their culture the precept of loyalty to the in-group.

In order for culture, in the sense of accumulated and transmitted discoveries and skills, to be maximally effective and useful to succeeding generations, its contents must have a certain generality and common applicability. That most of the cultural determinants are of the communal and role types is obvious. Yet, in a sense, certain cultural determinants are idiosyncratic in their reference. In small societies, for example, there may well be but a single dwarf. One culture prescribes that a dwarf shall be laughed at, another that he be regarded with reverence as a supernatural being. Here again we must note the interdependence of the determinants. The effects of "accidents" upon the individual and upon the behavior of others toward him are influenced by culture and indeed by all the communal and role determinants. No society entirely fails to try to prepare individuals for the uncertainties as well as for the culturally predictable "certainties" of life. Most cultures contain preconceptions about the import of "accidents" and "misfortunes." It is, for example, definitely a part of the traditional lore of some societies that disapproved conduct will be punished by "fate" in one way or another. Illness, untimely death, famine, deformity, defeat in war, floods, and other natural catastrophes are interpreted as causally related to previous action on the part of individuals or the group as a whole. In other societies culture may not prescribe that misfortune shall follow socially objectionable behavior, but when misfortunes do occur, such causes may be looked for retrospectively. Still other instances might be cited in which culture provides magical interpretations of uncontrollable events; and each culture must, by virtue of slight uncontrollable and unpredictable deviations in what and how and by whom the individual person is socialized, have for the individual slightly private versions and overtones. But by its very nature culture must be less concerned with the variable than with the relatively constant experiences which human beings encounter, although, as we have seen, it is not entirely meaningless to speak of *idiosyncratic* cultural determinants of personality.

Constants and Variables

While the significance of biological determinants has been, and in popular circles still is, over-estimated, there are some indications that social scientists are tending to give the same misguided unilateral evaluation to culture. The problem must never be structured as biological *or* cultural determinants. The prime point in the foregoing discussion is that physical-environmental, social, cultural, and biological determinants and their complicated interrelations must *all* be given due consideration.

Finally, it must be continually realized that, from the point of view of the vertical columns on page 394, some classes of determinants may be regarded as "constants," others as "variables." The idiosyncratic determinants can be called "variables" in contrast to the other three classes which, with fair precision, may be termed "constants" (either for all men or for social units of men—nations, communities, castes, classes, etc.). Because of personality typologies and folkloristic social stereotypes the constants are not likely to be forgotten. But we sometimes overlook the forces operative in personality formation which cannot be predicted upon the basis of knowledge of a biological stock, a physical environment, the general properties of social interaction, and a given culture. They are the things that "just happen to people"—private to the individual rather than more or less inevitable for all individuals who have a common heredity, share a physical environment, live in a society of a certain size and having other non-cultural determinants of social interaction, and share a common culture. The potentialities for such happenings are obviously present in the system as defined by the communal and role determinants, but they are not prescribed by the total system for all individuals of a certain age, sex, class, or other social category.

Individuals not only have biological and social experiences, but they have experiences which could not have been predicted from the nature of the human body or from membership in a specific society. Putting the conceptual scheme in a manner which cuts across both the constants and the variables we have (a) the organism moving through a field which is (b) structured both by culture and by the physical and social world in a relatively uniform manner but which is (c) subject to endless variation within the general patterning, due to special, or idiosyncratic determinants which are introduced by "accident," or "fate."

THE COMPONENTS OF PERSONALITY

There are fashions in personality. Fashions that vary in time—like crinolines and hobble skirts—and fashions that vary in space—like Gold Coast loin-cloths and Lombard Street tail-coats. In primitive societies everyone wears, and longs to wear, the same personality. But each society has a different psychological costume. Among the red Indians of the Northwest Pacific Coast the ideal personality was that of a mildly crazy egotist competing with his rivals on the plane of wealth and conspicuous consumption. Among the Plains Indians, it was that of an egotist competing with others in the sphere of war-like exploits. Among the Pueblo Indians, the ideal personality was neither that of an egotist, nor of a conspicuous consumer, nor of a fighter, but of the perfectly gregarious man who makes great efforts never to distinguish himself, who knows the traditional rites and gestures and tries to be exactly like everyone else.

European societies are large and racially, economically, professionally heterogeneous; therefore orthodoxy is hard to impose, and there are several contemporaneous ideals of personality. (Note that Fascists and Communists are trying to create one single "right" ideal—in other words are trying to make industrialized Europeans behave as though they were Dyaks or Eskimos. The attempt, in the long run, is doomed to failure; but in the meantime, what fun they will get from bullying the heretics!)

In our world, what are the ruling fashions? There are, of course, the ordinary clerical and commercial modes—turned out by the little dressmakers round the corner. And then *La haute couture. Ravissante personalité d'intérieur de chez Proust. Maison Nietzsche et Kipling: personalité de sport. Personalité de nuit, création de Lawrence. Personalité de bain, par Joyce. . . .* A pragmatist would have to say that Ben Jonson's psychology was "truer" than Shakespeare's. Most of his contemporaries did in fact perceive themselves and were perceived as Humours. It took Shakespeare to see what a lot there was outside the boundaries of the Humour, behind the conventional mask. But Shakespeare was in a minority of one—or, if you set Montaigne beside him, of two. Humours "worked"; the complex, partially atomized personalities of Shakespeare didn't.

In the story of the emperor's new clothes, the child perceives that the great man is naked. Shakespeare reversed the process. His contemporaries thought they were just naked Humours; he saw that they were covered with a whole wardrobe of psychological fancy dress.

Take Hamlet. Hamlet inhabited a world whose best psychologist was Polonius. If he had known as little as Polonius, he would have been happy. But he knew too much; and in this consists his tragedy. Read his parable of the musical instruments. Polonius and the others assumed as axiomatic that man was a penny whistle with only half a dozen stops. Hamlet knew that potentially at least, he was a whole symphony orchestra.

Mad Ophelia lets the cat out of the bag. "We know what we are, but we know not what we may be." Polonius knows very clearly what he and other people *are*, within the ruling conventions. Hamlet knows this, but also what they may be—outside the local system of masks and humours.

To be the only man of one's age to know what people may be as well as what they conventionally are! Shakespeare must have gone through some rather disquieting quarters of an hour.

—ALDOUS HUXLEY (*Eyeless in Gaza*, pp. 105–107)

Although in the literary rather than in the scientific mode, Huxley is here calling attention to certain very real problems in personality theory. If the purpose of the first section was to avoid the pitfalls of an over-simple delineation of the determinants of the social stimulus value of individuals, the purpose of this section is to stress the necessity of treating the individual as an integrate in action. One must not confuse certain limited aspects of social stimulus value with the whole personality. In certain circumstances, we react to men and women, not as unique organizations of experience, but as representatives of a group. In other circumstances, we react to them primarily as fulfilling certain roles. But if at times certain facets draw our attention more than others, we must not lose sight of the fact that the personality, like the organism whose social stimulus value it represents, is a whole. Often the best way to avoid confusing a part with a whole is to become explicitly aware of the specific parts which may be abstracted from the whole.

The Universal Component

In our preoccupation with the interesting differences which we note between individuals and personality types, we tend to forget that the phrase, "a common humanity," is not altogether meaningless. The reaction which any human being produces in other human beings is different from that produced by any other kind of animal or by any sort of inanimate entity or event. The folkloristic saying, "Why, that isn't even *human*," is based, as are so many commonplaces, upon a frequently overlooked but profound truth: the basic uniformities in physical appearance and behavior deeply condition the social stimulus value of all men for all other men. These stem from the universal (biological, physical-environmental, social, and cultural) determinants which have been reviewed in the preceding section and constitute what we may designate as the *universal component* in the personality of all human beings. By using the expression, "all human beings," we tend to exclude from this generalization those individuals who, because of idiocy, physical monstrosity, or social isolation and neglect, fail to qualify for responsible membership in their natural social group. Properly speaking, the universal component of human personality consists of those physical and behavioral traits which are accepted as normal and desirable in *all* human societies. The facts of personality which compose this universal component have been the subject of much speculation, but we have little scientifically verified information concerning them. We mention the universal component of personality in the present context, partly for purposes of conceptual completeness and partly as a means of indicating important lacunae in our knowledge.

The Communal Component

That "the members of any given society tend to share more personality traits with other members of that society than with the members of other societies" is attested by common experience. If we are unfamiliar with Navaho Indians, we are likely to react to them first as Navahos rather than as individuals. Their first social stimulus value is largely in terms of those features of physical appearance, costume, and behavior which sets them off as representatives of a different society from our own. One frequently hears whites who have recently entered the Navaho country say, "I can't tell one Indian from another." Similarly, one hears Navahos who have had little experience with whites saying, "All white women seem alike to me. I just can't recognize one after I have met her."

This diffuse generalization of the social stimulus value of members of a particular out-group certainly rests, in the first instance, upon similarities of total visual (and sometimes olfactory) impression. Such also seems to be the basis of that rather remarkable phenomenon: species cohesion in animals. With human beings, however, the failure to make strictly individual discriminations goes immediately from physical appearance on to behavior, first of all linguistic behavior. Even within a larger social unit the reactor places the actor as the representative of a regional or class group on the basis of "accent." To a considerable degree, physical appearance and accent are reacted to only as symbols of a more thorough-going and deeply felt differentiation. What "sets off" our reaction in the first instance may be a combination of physical traits—but skin color, nose shape, and other physical features are in certain cases closely associated with our experience of certain culturally determined varieties of behavior.

The tendency towards uniformity in social stimulus value may be observed even as between social groups where differences in physique and distinctive costume are slight and inconstant (for example, between Englishmen or Australians and Americans). In this case also, the first contacts with representatives of the alien society are likely to have more the character of culture-defining value than of person-defining value. The statistical prediction can safely be made that one hundred Americans will display particular features of personal organization and behavior more frequently than will a hundred Englishmen of comparable age, social class, and vocational assortment. So great is the influence of culture that there is a grain of truth in Faris' statement that "Culture is the collective side of personality; personality the subjective aspect of culture." But this is rather less than a half-truth. Not only culture but also the other communal determinants—the common forces in the biological heredity and the physical and social environments —bring about that configuration of personality traits which the members of a given society tend to share. Since any organism is a whole and since in the last analysis the social stimulus value of the organism is a totality, we shall not call those *aspects* of social stimulus value which accrue to the individual as a member of a society the "communal personality" but rather the *communal component* of personality.

The Role Component

Still another closely related abstraction must be added if we are not to be misled by certain relatively surface resemblances between personalities. Under the influence of the role determinants the communal component takes many variant forms. It is an induction from common experience that Englishmen occupying different statuses have different social stimulus value for the same persons. The peer's personality is not that of the cab driver nor that of the retired Indian colonel. The personalities of American women tend to be distinguished by certain traits which appear much less frequently in the personalities of American men. When we meet new people at a social gathering, we are often able to predict correctly, "That man is a doctor." "That man certainly isn't a business man—he acts like a professor." "He surely isn't an artist or a writer or an actor."

There is nothing mysterious about all this. As Linton says:

> Each society approves and rewards certain combinations of qualities when they appear in individuals occupying particular statuses. Furthermore, it tries to develop these qualities in all the individuals for whom the particular statuses can be forecast. In other words, each society has a series of ideal personalities which correspond to the various statuses which it recognizes. Such status personalities are not to be confused with psychological types. In their definition societies do not go far below the surface. The status personality does not correspond to the total personality but simply to certain aspects of the content and more superficial orientations of the latter, i.e., to those elements of the total personality which are immediately concerned with the successful performance of the individual's roles.

These considerations explain the observed fact that the account of an individual's personality which we get from equally competent observers who have known him when he was carrying out different roles—in the home, in business, in the clinic, in his lodge—often fail to coincide in important particulars. Few individuals are "single, consistent personalities." Most individuals have "different faces" to put on for each situation that arises. There are not only, as John Dewey says, "occupational psychoses"—there are also "occupational personalities"—which is perhaps but a slightly different way of saying the same thing. Barnard speaks of "organization personality." Merton writes of "bureaucratic personality structure." Landes even talks of the "summer and winter personalities" of the Ojibway Indians. Other writers speak of "age and sex personalities," having in mind such phenomena as the following: the personality of an old doctor is different from that of a young one; the personality of the woman lawyer has typical differences from that of her male colleague.

The differential aspects of personality manifestations which are reacted to and observed when the individual carries out the differing roles of his social life we shall call the *role component*. We shall not speak of the "role personality," for this implies that the personality is divisible, whereas it is a whole, separable only by abstraction. If the terms we use for our abstractions do not imply absolute divisibility but merely facets to which we may differentially react, we are less likely to forget that, when we speak of "personality," we are always necessarily referring to the individual as an integrate in action. The fact that a doctor has a bedside manner does not mean that he ceases to act as an American or in accord with the idiosyncratic core of his personality. We use the term "role" rather than "status" because the distinction which Davis makes between "status" and "office" is a useful one and because, as Davis also points out, the social stimulus value of the individual carrying out a role "is always influenced by factors other than the stipulations of the position itself."

The relative weight of the role component in the social stimulus value of any person varies greatly according to the number of roles defined and the accent of the expectations enjoined by different cultures. Fromm's observations are acute:

> A person [in medieval society] was identical with his role in society; he was a peasant, an artisan, a knight, and not *an individual* who *happened* to have this or that occupation. . . . The "self" in the interests of which modern man acts is the *social* self, a self which is essentially constituted by the role the individual is supposed to play and which in reality is merely the subjective disguise for the objective social function of man in society. . . . The pseudo self is only an agent who actually represents the role a person is supposed to play but who does so under the name of the self. It is true that a person can play many roles and subjectively be convinced that he is "he" in each role. Actually he is in all these roles what he believes he is expected to be, and for many people, if not most, the original self is completely suffocated by the pseudo self. . . . When the general plot of the play is handed out, each actor can act vigorously the role he is assigned and even make up his lines and certain details of the action by himself. Yet he is only playing a role that has been handed over to him.

The Idiosyncratic Component

Alexander remarks that a persistent organization of trends and tendencies of the individual is formed early in life "by a combination of hereditary and domestic influences." He partially recognizes what we should call the "communal component" when he says, "These domestic influences differ enough from family to family to produce a wide variety of personality structures which might be rare in one civilization but common in another." But he correctly points out that only some of the "domestic influences" are "typical of contemporary society rather than peculiar to the individuals, whether parents or siblings, who exercise them." And Alexander is probably right in saying, "The individuality of parents has a greater influence upon the development of their children's personalities than convention and cultural tradition."

Biological, cultural, social, and physical environmental determinants all combine to produce the *idiosyncratic component* of personality. Smith is "stubborn" in his office as well as in his home and in a golf game. He would have been "stubborn" in all social contexts if he had been taken to England from America at an early age and his socialization had been completed there. The idiosyncratic component always tinges the playing of roles. The social stimulus value of different individuals in the same society who occupy the same position (statuses and offices) varies. We verbalize such differences by saying, "Yes, Smith and Jones are both forty-five-year-old Americans, both small business men with about the same responsibilities and prestige—but somehow they are different." Each individual's patterned ways of perceiving, feeling, and behaving do have a characteristic organization which is not precisely paralleled by that of any other individual. For purposes of therapy and for certain research objectives, it is this uniqueness of personality which must be tenaciously accented. But for general scientific purposes both facts must be kept firmly in mind: the uniqueness of personalities and their resemblances. The idiosyncratic features are, as it were, imbedded in a matrix which is more public than private, and only the totality—not any one component—may properly be called the personality. Even though we live in a society where "who you are rather than what you are counts," the role component is only one face of the self. On the other hand, the idiosyncratic component, like the communal and role components, is equally only one part of the individual's total social stimulus value. When Davis and Dollard speak of personality as "that behavior of an individual which distinguishes him from other individuals *trained by similar social controls*," they do violence to the intricate interdependence of the three components.

In the preceding section we called attention to the fact that in addition to universal and communal resemblances in the personalities of different human beings, there is another type of resemblance which cuts across the boundaries of groups but which is due to idiosyncratic rather than to universal determinants. This observation can be concretely illustrated. In general, Hopi Indians and white Americans have very different social stimulus value. But occasionally one meets a Hopi whose behavior, either by total impression or by some single reaction system, reminds one very strongly of the behavior of certain white men or women. Such parallels could originate from a similarity either in biological, physical-environmental, social or cultural idiosyncratic determinants. A Hopi and a white man could have a special endocrine imbalance unusual in the populations of both societies. Or both Hopi and white could have had long childhood illnesses which brought them each an exceptional amount of maternal devotion. While the effects of extra maternal care would have somewhat different effects according to the prevailing constellation of the other determinants, there would remain at least a segmental similarity which might well produce arresting resemblances in the two adult personality structures.

Discrimination of the Components: Actors and Reactors

It is not unenlightening to remember that in early Latin *persona* means "a mask"—*dramatis persona* is thus an actor who wears a mask in a play. Etymologically and historically, then, a personality is the wearer of a mask. For those who are fairly well adjusted in their society, the communal and role components of the personality do tend to constitute disguises. Just as the outer body screens the viscera from view and clothing the genitals, so the "public" facets of personality shield the private personality from the curious and conformity-demanding world of other persons—and usually, also, keep many motivations from the individual's own consciousnes. The person who has painfully achieved some sort of integration and who knows what is expected of him in a particular social situation will produce those responses with only a slight idiosyncratic coloring. This is why the uniformities provided by the communal and role components can, in the case of "normal" individuals, be penetrated only by the long-continued, intensive, and oblique procedures of depth psychology. Only projective techniques will often bring out what the individual does not want to tell about himself and what he himself often does not know.

Some of our analogies perhaps suggest that any personality may be dissected as one peels the layers off an onion. This is a crude and only very partially correct view. Sometimes the communal component is the outer "layer," sometimes the role component. This depends upon who the observer is. For social stimulus value is a function both of actor and of reactor. If the actor is from a society markedly different from that of the observer, his social stimulus value is at first almost completely confused with the communal component. What are actual peculiarities of the individual may be attributed to a stereotype for that society. The role component is hardly perceived at all unless the reactor is familiar with social differentiations in the other society. Roles can be discriminated with refinement only if the "audience" can appreciate differences. The delicacy of "identification" or "placement" depends on this. Thus we see why evaluations of out-groupers as individuals are always more or less inaccurate. Here we have one important aspect of "race prejudice"—individuals are judged on the basis of stereotypes. Discriminations are not sensitive. The kind of person one is taken to be is determined entirely by the kind of people that one habitually has around one.

When one first meets a new person in one's own society, particularly if the person be from an occupational group sharply different from one's own or if the situation be an unfamiliar one, the stimulus value of the person is likely to derive primarily from the role component. If, however, one wants really to comprehend the total personality, one must "get behind" this front, temporarily stripping off (but not forgetting) the outer layer which is the totality of responses expected of the individual (for example, as young man, as lawyer, as lawyer dealing with female client, etc.). Before the student can get to the idiosyncratic component he must also "factor out" the communal component. Apart from the fact that the subject is thirty years old, a man, and a lawyer, he is also an American. Many personality traits he will also share with American men, with American old people, with barbers and factory workers.

Chapter 27

FUNCTION OF EXPERIENCE

THE *concept "experience" plays an important role in any discussion of education. Experience means many things, and educators must be able to follow any meaning to whatever conclusion is called for. In his presidential address to the Eastern Psychological Association, Hadley Cantril suggests that no individual can be understood unless the nature of his previous experiences are revealed. Because many factors operate to influence an individual, the complexity of the task is manifold. For example, not only does the nature of an experience contribute to the formation of personality, but an individual's understanding of what took place is also involved. Whatever is learned from any experience not only influences the present, but also serves to influence the search for and the interpretation of future experience. Furthermore, since each man lives with others, the way an individual shares his experience modifies its significance for him. The meaning any man abstracts from his experience is unique to him: thus, the maturation pattern will vary with each individual. It is through an analysis of this sort that teachers, and those preparing to teach, understand why teaching must be directed to each child, and cut to fit the shape of individual experience.*

AN INQUIRY CONCERNING THE CHARACTERISTICS OF MAN

Hadley Cantril

THE PROBLEM

It is apparent to nearly anyone familiar with attempts to understand man's behavior, whether he is a professional psychologist or not, that the full-bodied experiences of everyday life have in them much more than any "explanatory system" so far seems to take into account. For many of us, no one of them rings quite true. There does not seem to be yet an explanatory system that is intrinsically reasonable in its account of why man's experience is what it is.

The reasons for the apparent inadequacy of the contemporary understanding of experience may be seen by referring back to almost any area of psychological inquiry and seeing how problems have been posed and how research has been conducted. From this some useful lessons should be drawn for the future.

We can use as an illustration the area of psychological inquiry concerned with man's awarenesses: the field technically known as the study of perception. This is a reasonable field to choose since the directions of attack on the ancient problem of how and why man is aware of anything often have been a weathervane in psychology as well as in philosophy.

In studying the way man perceives anything, psychologists concentrated first on the effects on perception when the stimulus was altered or when there were changes in the physiological processes involved. This naturally led to the idea that there was a certain correspondence between the subjective factors in experience on the one hand and the objective and physiological factors on the other hand. And since it was so easy to show how an alteration of "objective" or physiological factors could cause "subjective" effects, the idea was built up that experience could be largely accounted for by corresponding stimulus events and the accompanying physiological disturbances. It was not nearly so easy to demonstrate the reverse effect: the role played by such "subjective" factors as past experience, loyalties, expectancies, and purpose in determining the nature of perception. Furthermore, it was relatively easy to measure and to put in quantitative terms changes in the

Reprinted from *Journal of Abnormal Psychology,* Vol. 45 (July 1950), pp. 492–501. Footnotes omitted.

objective stimulus situation or the physiological factors. But precise measures of past experience and loyalties obviously could be made only in a very crude form.

Of course, normally there is no awareness unless something exists of which to be aware and unless the intricate mechanisms of the body are functioning properly. But this is by no means all of the story. The relations between perception and the physiological processes could be studied forever and still never get at the reason why such relationships seem to exist. The reason why such relationships exist would not be uncovered until the question of what function such relationships serve in the processes of living is asked.

Many of us now share the feeling that psychology has not gone farther in getting at the reasons for man's awarenesses because it has dealt so often with isolated human experience in which isolated physical stimuli are related to isolated sensory processes in an isolated individual usually studied in a situation where his isolation in time and space is not realized. This would mean, too, that while the emphasis of Gestalt psychologists on the interdependence of various parts of a stimulus situation is obviously in the right direction, it still provides no underlying account of *why* "relational determination" functions as it does. No amount of study of the immediate relationship involved in a situation seems to account for the fact that the awareness of *where* a thing is depends on *what* the thing is assumed to be. The why of such relationships can be understood only when the functions such relationships apparently serve are examined in actual transactions of living. Any experience in the "now" cannot be explained without realizing that the "now" is only a transition point carrying the past into the future.

Psychology will meet the challenge it has imposed on itself and which men everywhere expect it to meet only when it becomes fully emancipated from a point of view which permits or encourages the study of isolated individuals, isolated experiences, isolated relationships. Man's thought and behavior can be understood only as *processes* which take place in full-bodied situations. And the cross relationship of factors which must be taken into account becomes complicated indeed as the psychologist tries to account for the experiences of man in his social life, for his family ties, his friendships, his frustrations, ambitions, responsibilities, desire for affection, his strikes and his wars. As Bridgman has recently pointed out, "the world of daily life . . . is obviously enormously more complex than the world of the physicist."

The job is not a simple one of selecting and choosing what appear to be the most significant parts of different explanatory systems and simply adding them together without attempting to understand the cross relationships involved as psychologists labeled "eclectic" would suggest. For this would be failing to make a distinction between taking apart what really belongs together and putting together processes that are inseparable in any actual occasion of life and without which there would be no experience at all. It is because of their failure to make such a distinction that eclectics label anyone a "radical" who adopts a synthesizing explanatory system. Eclecticism by its very nature discourages imagination and leads to sterility.

If the nature of man's everyday life experience is to be fathomed, it is necessary first of all to try to describe man's experience in appropriate terms. Those processes that play significant roles in man's living and their cross relationships must be sought and understood. An account of man's experience will become intrinsically reasonable only in so far as all of those factors are taken into account without which man's experience would not be what it is.

This emphasis may appear to be self-evident. But it is apparently true that the reason why the scientist's understanding of the nature of man's experience and behavior is not greater than it is today is because he has either neglected to search for and discover the characteristics of man's experiences or has deliberately limited those characteristics to a few easy ones psychologists have favored for one reason or another and that still leave much unexplained. Sometimes a psychologist can boast of being scientific only because he is closing his eyes to pressing problems. Obviously such a procedure is not consistent with the spirit of scientific inquiry.

An authority on evolution, G. G. Simpson, has pointed out that "it is important to realize that man is an animal, but it is even more important to realize that the essence of his unique nature lies precisely in those characteristics that are not shared with any other animal." Whitehead has stated as a "general principle" that "low-grade characteristics are better studied first in connection with correspondingly low-grade organisms, in which those characteristics are not obscured by more developed types of functioning. Conversely, high-grade characters should be studied first in connection with those organisms in which they first come to full perfection."

All organisms, including man, are on-going, living processes. And all higher organisms, including man, have biological needs or physiological tension systems that must be satisfied periodically if life and growth are to continue. But there is something about man that is unique. The biologist sees his enormous adaptive and creative abilities; the poet sees his "divine discontent"; the religious prophet sees him searching for the Kingdom of God. Each observer in his own way sees that something has been added in the latest chapter of the long evolutionary story.

It seems hopeless to try to account for man's behavior solely in terms of variables as crude as reflexes, instincts, or physiological tensions. For example, attempts to account for man's motivation in terms of the reduction of physiological tensions seem inadequate to "explain" the many situations in which man's satisfactions and happinesses are actually related to an increase, rather than a decrease, in the state of "tensions" experienced. When a person deliberately undertakes a new task, when he deliberately strives to meet new levels of aspiration he often knows well enough that he will experience new and perhaps more disturbing inner tensions. Man's psychological tensions seem to be more the coproducts of his strivings than basic explanations of them. When the characteristics of individual experiences are observed, their variety and subtlety are apparent. They are by no means all described appropriately by words that may be suitable for lower organisms.

THE QUALITY OF EXPERIENCE

An outstanding characteristic of man is his capacity to sense the value in the quality of his experience. This experienced value attribute is a pervasive and inseparable aspect of every experience. All human wants, urges, desires and aspirations are permeated with some value attribute.

You can see best what is meant by the value attribute in experience by referring to your own experience. A value attribute of a relatively low order is experienced in situations where physical needs are satisfied in a crude and elemental way: *e.g.*, the sense of well-being and taste in the satisfaction of hunger by any kind of food you can get hold of. The satisfying quality of these sensations is apparently the result of some evolutionary process insuring our survival. Man experiences a "higher," subtler, richer, more satisfying value attribute with the satisfaction of his needs in other situations which have become desiderata of civilized men: *e.g.*, satisfaction of hunger with food that is prepared tastefully, served nicely, eaten in attractive surroundings and in the company of congenial people.

You sense the satisfying value of experience from a job well done, from helping to accomplish a community, national or humanitarian task, from having met or exceeded your own expectations or the expectations others have of you. You sense a value attribute in the exhilaration, the sense of well-being you may get from climbing a mountain, from a swim in a lake or the sea, from a good game of tennis or golf. You feel a richness of experience as you watch your children grow and develop. You sense a high quality from the experience of helping a friend or doing a deed which you know is good. You sense a value attribute in creativity whether that creativity involves baking a tasty loaf of bread, making your garden grow, raising hogs, cattle or grain, putting together a homemade radio, repairing a broken machine, painting a picture, or writing a poem or a sonata. You sense a value attribute in experience when you learn something useful for your purposes, when you make sense out of something; and you share the value attributes of a child's experience when you see his sense of satisfaction in learning to tell time, in learning to read, in learning his first simple additions. You sense value attributes in the humble, ordinary activities of life: in saying "hello" to a neighbor, in cleaning your house, in taking a bath after a hard day's work.

You sense the value attributes of disappointment, disturbance, or sorrow when things go wrong.

Man's unusual capacity to sense the value of experience in so many diverse ways provides the possibility of working out a plausible explanation for the many divergent types of activity men seek to repeat. Man tries to recapture qualities he has experienced on previous occasions: in his social gatherings, his ways of satisfying physical needs, his esthetic experiences, his work or his play. He wants to recapture these experiences simply because he enjoys experiencing the value attribute related to them. However, it should be pointed out that in everyday life, situations never repeat themselves identically and, if they tend to, man will often try to create variation, for with the repetition of very similar situations there can be a decreased sense of satisfaction. Habitual activity may become monotonous and boring; or we may become aware of it only subconsciously.

The value attribute that pervades every experience is a crucially important fact. It is the catalyzer needed to produce nearly all of our actions. The sensed value of any experience differs in some subtle way from that of any other experience. To describe the full quality of an experience it is generally necessary to resort to a whole string of adjectives as in describing a person or a landscape. Sometimes analogies are used. Sometimes we think of bits of poetry or passages from a novel where those who are expert in putting our feelings into words have managed somehow to capture, or remind us of, a feeling approximating our own. The value attributes of experience characteristic of man seem to occur largely in what Korzybski has aptly described as "non-verbal," "silent" levels.

We remember the values experienced in life and we store them up, building out of them a standard or system of values which we inevitably, though generally unconsciously, use for later reference. Against this system of values derived from past experiences, we sense the quality of our present experience. It is the only value standard we know. On the basis of our acquired pattern of values we characterize our present experiences variously as "worthwhile," "satisfying," "pleasant," "fruitless," "disappointing," and the like.

It is in terms of the values of experience that the "worthwhileness" of an action is tested. The value of the quality in experience comes into being only in concrete situations. In general it is not subject to recall as are conceptual abstractions.

A sense of quality in experience is achieved only by participating actively in life transactions. And conversely, if no value attribute in action is experienced, there is no participation in the on-going process of living and growing. This is the situation with certain psychiatric patients and with those who live entirely in the past, dreaming of the good old days and wishing they would come again.

The richness and variety of the quality we are able to get out of experience depends on the scope and variety of the life situations in which we can participate, especially with the opportunity we have to share experience with others. The richness of the quality of our experience will depend, too, on the extent to which we can create some order, some meaning, some direction in life situations through our own participation in them.

There is considerable evidence both from the laboratory and from everyday observation that the behavior of animals reflects an increasing sense of value attributes as one moves up the phylogenetic scale. The lowly laboratory rat displays "hierarchies" of path preferences in moving through a maze to a goal. The number and variety of activities shown by a dog in an effort to regain his master's favor suggests a considerable ability to sense value attributes. The descriptions Köhler and Yerkes give of the excited behavior of primates when they reach an insightful solution to a difficult problem leaves no doubt that a fairly high order of value attribute is being experienced. But while the capacity to sense a value attribute of some sort is not peculiar to man's experience alone, the capacity has been developed to such a degree in man that it may be considered sufficiently unique to distinguish man from all other animals. Sensed value attributes characterize all of man's experience.

THE ENHANCEMENT OF THE VALUE ATTRIBUTE OF EXPERIENCE

While the concept of the sensed value attribute of experience seems to me indispensable in providing a toe hold to account for some of the characteristics of man, still it is not enough by itself. On this basis alone it would be impossible to account for man's curiosity and inquiry, for all the new fears and anxieties that beset him, for his self-conscious search to increase the range of the setting in which he can act effectively, for his constant lack of perfect "adjustment," for his will-o'-the-wisp search for peace of mind, or for his feeling of personal development and growth.

This points to the conclusion that the ultimate, the most generalized goal of man is what can be called the enhancement of the value attributes of experience. This can be regarded as the top standard of human experience, a standard in its own right. It is the capacity man has to sense *added* value in his experience that accounts for his ceaseless striving, his search for a direction to his activities, for his characteristic unwillingness to have things remain as they are.

In supposing that the enrichment of the value attributes of experience is the outstanding characteristic of man, there are no teleological implications whatever. There is no implication that the course man's life is pursuing inevitably follows some overall intrinsic design. Neither is there any acceptance of a hedonistic doctrine with its contention that the aim of life is to seek pleasure, nor any thought that the achievement of increments of value attribute means "improvement" or "progress" in any western sense.

The concept of the "enhancement of the value attributes of experience" has been adopted because it seems intrinsically reasonable in itself and because it provides the possibility of explaining plausibly the other characteristics of man's experience. Some such concept must be used and its scientific explanation sought if we are to avoid the inadequacy of any account of man's experience solely in terms of influences that are operating in the "now." For the behavior of the "now" is not something that can be neatly isolated from the past *and* the future.

All observations of man indicate that most people who are attuned to anything approximating normal life will not be satisfied with their role unless it offers some potentiality for one experience to lead to another, for change to occur in some apparent direction. Steinbeck expressed the situation in one of his novels: "For it is said that humans are never satisfied, that you give them one thing and they want something more. And this is said in disparagement, whereas it is one of the greatest talents the species has and one that has made it superior to animals that are satisfied with what they have." It is this characteristic to which the naturalist Coghill referred when he said that his philosophy of life was "not of *being*, but of *becoming;* not of *life*, but of *living*." It is what lies behind the remark I heard a woman make in a crowded railway station, "Most things excite me only once." It lies behind the colloquialisms "It gave me a lift," "I got a kick out of it."

The on-going process described here is distinguished from and should not be confused with the normal "stages of growth" which an individual goes through from conception through birth, adolescence and old age as determined by his chromosome activity and glandular processes. Nor is the process described here to be confused with growth and development in the evolutionary sense.

What is meant by a desired increment in the value attribute of experience can again be seen best by observing one's own life and the lives of others. The skilled worker who gets the job he wants will soon become relatively dissatisfied if it offers no "future"—if there is no chance for increased responsibility, for increased creative effort, or for greater usefulness in his social group. A young woman may have her whole heart set on marriage. But after marriage she will use this new situation as the springboard for obtaining new, emergent qualities of experience through her children, her new social intercourse, her new community responsibilities. Or a farmer's first goal may be to own his own farm. Once he achieves this goal, he will want to "develop" and "improve" his farm. A young man who has acquired the ambition to go to college will rapidly acquire other ambitions as soon as he enters college. He will want to make a certain team or club, or he may strive for a certain academic record. Once he gets into a club or makes a team, the chances are that he will strive within his social groups to raise his status, to become an important member. And once he makes the grades he desires, he will probably raise his sights. Gangsters will strive within the gang of their hearts' desire to "be" somebody.

It should be particularly emphasized that the satisfaction sought in experience is a satisfaction within the particular culture or group of which the individual is a participating member. In western society there is a tendency to think of increased satisfaction in terms of hustling and bustling activities that spell "progress," "wealth," "fame," or "advancement" in terms of our particular norms. It may at first appear, then, that persons in "primitive," "backward," "easygoing," or "static" cultures or groups show no behavior that could properly be described as attempts to experience increments of satisfaction. Yet intimate participation in the social life of any cultural group and an understanding of the significance of individual behavior reveals that the people who compose that group do seek increased satisfactions according to standards and expectancies of their own. While it may appear that the life of a Chinese coolie, a Russian peasant, a South African native, a Navajo Indian in New Mexico, or an Arapesh of New Guinea may go around only in a constant circle, they in turn might wonder what modern Americans could possibly get out of a life that might seem to them a hectic rat-race. Wherever we look in any culture man has aspirations of some kind and never seems completely satisfied with his lot.

An increment of the value of experience is possible only if there is some standard, some form to use as a springboard for emergence. We cannot sense an enhancement of quality in experience if we have no standard as a take-off. It is for this reason that the concept of the value attributes of experience was introduced earlier. Otherwise the concept of an enhanced quality of experience would make no sense. Both are required for an adequate, intrinsically reasonable explanatory system.

The supposition of the enhancement of the value attributes in experience accounts for the aspect of growth. It is dependent on the capacity of man to look into the future as he takes part in and becomes part of emerging situations. What is experienced as an increment of the value today becomes part of the value standard tomorrow if experiences can be repeated in similar future occasions. The process of development in the individual is a constant pyramiding of the set of value standards necessarily used as the test of the next experiences. Participation in any occasion of living alters for good or evil the standard of value built up which provides the only stepping stone for the next participation.

We experience increments of value attributes when we overcome the obstacles facing us constantly in new situations. By the very nature of things, when we overcome one difficulty we are faced with new difficulties which in turn demand resolution and in turn necessitate continued emergence. When our difficulties are of major proportions and when we sense that we are on the way to a better resolution of them, then an increment of value in our experience may have considerable duration. In such cases, we are not bothered by temporary frustrations because we realize we are going on to a richer experience.

Man more than any other animal is faced with the problem of choice. His choice often is between the security he feels fairly certain he can obtain if he does one thing and, on the other hand, the experience of new, emergent quality if he does another thing. For this reason man's judgments are frequently and inevitably tinged with both hope and fear.

Usually man will not choose the path leading to a possible increase in the value attribute of his experience unless a certain minimum feeling of security is guaranteed. Yet it is the nature of man to strive for an increment in the value attribute of his experience even though he may know full well it will involve sacrifice and pain. On the basis of the many cases he has treated, Rogers concludes that "the urge for a greater degree of independence, the desire for a self-determined integration, the tendency to strive, even through much pain, toward a socialized maturity, is as strong as—no, is stronger than—the desire for comfortable dependence, the need to rely upon external authority for assurance. . . . I have yet to find the individual who, when he examines his situation deeply, and feels that he perceives it clearly, deliberately chooses dependence, deliberately chooses to have the integrated direction of himself undertaken by another. When all the elements are clearly perceived, the balance seems invariably in the direction of the painful but ultimately rewarding path of self-actualization or growth."

The whole process of life is dialectical in the sense that the "normal" individual keeps going on to new experiences in so far as his security framework allows. From his observations of children, William Stern concluded that "self-preservation and self-development unite and blend in the process of growth. . . . The activities which first develop are exactly those which are of the most primary importance for self-preservation; and whilst self-development hastens on the ever-new triumphs in the growth of powers and the spiritual conquest of the material, the motive-power and capacity of self-preservation works away in the subconscious with unerring surety of purpose. . . . Each single goal, aimed at by struggling self-development, is no sooner reached than it immediately exists solely to be replaced by others, and not only so, but it becomes a permanent acquirement of the personality. . . . For there is indeed nothing in development of only momentary value, everything keeps on working, even if only as a tool for other efforts, everything heaps up powers, makes reserves, opens roads, that determine future life."

Value attributes and increments of value in experience are always relative. They are unique to the experiencing individual. There are, and can be, no absolute units of the standard of value upon which increments of value are based for *all* individuals. The standard of value for each person is determined by his particular unique biological and life history. There are enormous individual differences in both the quality and the degree of value increment sought. People in lowly stations of life may experience much greater value than persons who are "successful," or "famous." A humble cobbler may "get more out of life," for example, by watching the success of his children as a result of the education he has struggled to furnish them than a millionaire who sees no upward trend in his development as life goes on.

Nor can an increment of value attributes for any single individual be judged in terms of any accepted social standards no matter how these may affect the general direction of a person's activities. Conformity may be only a matter of expediency, not of gratification. There are again huge individual differences. Some people, through circumstance or learning, will place enormous reliance on security, others will more readily take a chance on the satisfaction to be derived from exploring unfamiliar roads. Even within the same culture what one person regards as success, another will regard as failure; what one calls a virtue another will call a vice.

In trying to increase our valueful experiences, we also try, of course, to decrease the number of situations which we know from past experience will either provide no such satisfactions or will keep us from participating in situations that we believe would be satisfying. Similarly, many of us spend a great deal of our lives avoiding situations of various kinds as we attempt to minimize the occasions of life which we predict will give us no increments of value in the immediate or distant future.

The direction any individual's development takes depends largely on the particular situations in which he participates. In the process of development and socialization, specific possibilities providing increments of value to experience are learned. The particular environment through which growth takes place gives a particular individual a particular sense of the direction in which he may look for a richer, more satisfying way of life. Stated somewhat differently, a person's unique environment provides a particular way of instrumenting his pattern of growth with its intrinsic desire for an increment of the value of experience.

Furthermore, it is known from studies of genetics and individual differences that an individual will develop in *his* particular way depending on *his* particular abilities and temperamental traits, *within* the directional framework provided by his participation in a particular social context. Thus, if you are a farmer, your particular abilities and temperamental traits will help determine how good a farmer you will be; if you are a labor leader your abilities and capacities and temperamental traits operating through an environment will largely determine your effectiveness within the situation you face. The same holds true for the talent of a musician or novelist, the creativity of a scientist, the genius of some comedians. The characteristics unique to every person are rooted in his chromosome activity.

A NATURALISTIC BASIS

Why is it that concepts associated with man's capacity to sense a value attribute in experience have not been previously introduced in psychology? It may be due in part to the fact that if such concepts are thought of, they appear to be metaphysical and without any scientific underpinning. But while such concepts, like others in the history of science, may have no explanation today, they are not mystical and by no means outside the bounds of scientific explanation tomorrow. Progress in scientific inquiry can only come about if a notion is postulated that seems to be intrinsically reasonable, whose existence may not be verifiable today but which nevertheless holds out the possibility of yielding to scientific verification in the future. It has been necessary to postulate man's capacity to sense value attributes and an increment of value in experience in order to take into account all of those aspects that characterize man's experience. For if any explanatory system leaves out any characteristic of man's experience then it must itself be ruled out as an adequate account of man.

These concepts have not been pulled out of thin air. What they name are experiences that can be operationally defined as standards that provide man with his most reliable guides for purposeful action. They are the compass which gives man his direction both as to how he should act and what this action is for.

Chapter 28

PLANNED EXPERIENCES AND BEHAVIOR

THE *historic dream of America as a society in which men will rule themselves is in trouble today. We have learned a great deal about human behavior, and countless groups of hidden persuaders work overtime to control the thoughts and actions of others. Even though history is heavily weighted by the record of tyranny over the minds of men, the teacher in America has available to him the relatively new frame of reference provided by the democratic ethos. Our schools can structure experiences that will support the growth of personalities that can think and act democratically.*

Whatever the misuse made of knowledge about human nature, that knowledge can also be utilized to help man remake himself and his society in the image provided by the idea of freedom. The issue involves the degree to which educators can and will accept responsibility to preserve and enlarge an environment in which the values of the democratic ethos will be accepted by a majority. There must be such continued, responsible action or society will be controlled for other ends.

B. F. Skinner, a psychologist, is convinced that the ultimate security of America as a democratic society depends upon the formulation and implementation of a science of man. He suggests that: (a) the concept of freedom and the attitude of Americans toward freedom must be reexamined, especially in reference to what constitutes a proper degree of control over human behavior; (b) the relationship of the control of human behavior to the achievements of cultural evolution should be clarified; (c) the responsibility and authority for the formulation of the design for the control of the individuals in the society must be determined; (d) provision should be made to insure that the control of human behavior will operate in the best interests of the democratic society; and (e) because verified knowledge concerning human behavior makes control over men possible, provision must be made to assure the continuation of the necessary research and the utilization of the results.

FREEDOM AND THE CONTROL OF MEN

B. F. Skinner

Perhaps the most crucial part of our democratic philosophy to be reconsidered is our attitude toward freedom—or its reciprocal, the control of human behavior. We do not oppose all forms of control because it is "human nature" to do so. The reaction is not characteristic of all men under all conditions of life. It is an attitude which has been carefully engineered, in large part by what we call the "literature" of democracy. With respect to some methods of control (for example, the threat of force), very little engineering is needed, for the techniques or their immediate consequences are objectionable. Society has suppressed these methods by branding them "wrong," "illegal" or "sinful." But to encourage these attitudes toward objectionable forms of control, it has been necessary to disguise the real nature of certain indispensable techniques, the commonest examples of which are education, moral discourse, and persuasion. The actual procedures appear harmless enough. They consist of supplying information, presenting opportunities for action, pointing out logical relationships, appealing to reason or "enlightened understanding," and so on. Through a masterful piece of misrepresentation, the illusion is fostered that these procedures do not involve the control of behavior; at most, they are simply ways of "getting someone to change his mind." But analysis not only reveals the presence of well-defined behavioral processes, it demonstrates a kind of control no less inexorable, though in some ways more acceptable, than the bully's threat of force.

Let us suppose that someone in whom we are interested is acting unwisely—he is careless in the way he deals with his friends, he drives too fast, or he holds his golf club the wrong way. We could probably help him by issuing a series of commands: don't nag, don't drive over sixty, don't hold your club that way. Much less objectionable would be "an appeal to reason." We

Reprinted from *The American Scholar*, Vol. 25 (Winter 1955–1956), pp. 54–57, 63–65.

could show him how people are affected by his treatment of them, how accident rates rise sharply at higher speeds, how a particular grip on the club alters the way the ball is struck and corrects a slice. In doing so we resort to verbal mediating devices which emphasize and support certain "contingencies of reinforcement"—that is, certain relations between behavior and its consequences—which strengthen the behavior we wish to set up. The same consequences would possibly set up the behavior without our help, and they eventually take control no matter which form of help we give. The appeal to reason has certain advantages over the authoritative command. A threat of punishment, no matter how subtle, generates emotional reactions and tendencies to escape or revolt. Perhaps the controllee merely "feels resentment" at being made to act in a given way, but even that is to be avoided. When we "appeal to reason," he "feels freer to do as he pleases." The fact is that we have exerted *less* control than in using a threat; since other conditions may contribute to the result, the effect may be delayed or, possibly in a given instance, lacking. But if we have worked a change in his behavior at all, it is because we have altered relevant environmental conditions, and the processes we have set in motion are just as real and just as inexorable, if not as comprehensive, as in the most authoritative coercion.

"Arranging an opportunity for action" is another example of disguised control. The power of the negative form has already been exposed in the analysis of censorship. Restriction of opportunity is recognized as far from harmless. As Ralph Barton Perry said in an article which appeared in the Spring, 1953, *Pacific Spectator*, "Whoever determines what alternatives shall be made known to man controls what that man shall choose *from.* He is deprived of freedom in proportion as he is denied access to *any* ideas, or is confined to any range of ideas short of the totality of relevant possibilities." But there is a positive side as well. When we present a relevant state of affairs, we increase the likelihood that a given form of behavior will be emitted. To the extent that the probability of action has changed, we have made a definite contribution. The teacher of history controls a student's behavior (or, if the reader prefers, "deprives him of freedom") just as much in *presenting* historical facts as in suppressing them. Other conditions will no doubt affect the student, but the contribution made to his behavior by the presentation of material is fixed and, within its range, irresistible.

The methods of education, moral discourse, and persuasion are acceptable not because they recognize the freedom of the individual or his right to dissent, but because they make only *partial* contributions to the control of his behavior. The freedom they recognize is freedom from a more coercive form of control. The dissent which they tolerate is the possible effect of other determiners of action. Since these sanctioned methods are frequently ineffective, we have been able to convince ourslves that they do not represent control at all. When they show too much strength to permit disguise, we give them other names and suppress them as energetically as we suppress the use of force. Education grown too powerful is rejected as propaganda or "brain-washing," while really effective persuasion is decried as "undue influence," "demagoguery," "seduction," and so on.

If we are not to rely solely upon accident for the innovations which give rise to cultural evolution, we must accept the fact that some kind of control of human behavior is inevitable. We cannot use good sense in human affairs unless someone engages in the design and construction of environmental conditions which affect the behavior of men. Environmental changes have always been the condition for the improvement of cultural patterns, and we can hardly use the more effective methods of science without making changes on a grander scale. We are all controlled by the world in which we live, and part of that world has been and will be constructed by men. The question is this: Are we to be controlled by accident, by tyrants, or by ourselves in effective cultural design?

The danger of the misuse of power is possibly greater than ever. It is not allayed by disguising the facts. We cannot make wise decisions if we continue to pretend that human behavior is not controlled, or if we refuse to engage in control when valuable results might be forthcoming. Such measures weaken only ourselves, leaving the strength of science to others. The first step in a defense against tyranny is the fullest possible exposure of controlling techniques. A second step has already been taken successfully in restricting the use of physical force. Slowly, and as yet imperfectly, we have worked out an ethical and governmental design in which the strong man is not allowed to use the power deriving from his strength to control his fellow men. He is restrained by a superior force created for that purpose—the ethical pressure of the group, or more explicit religious and governmental measures. We tend to distrust superior forces, as we currently hesitate to relinquish sovereignty in order to set up an international police force. But it is only through such counter-control that we have achieved what we call peace—a condition in which men are not permitted to control each other through force. In other words, control itself must be controlled.

Science has turned up dangerous processes and materials before. To use the facts and techniques of a science of man to the fullest extent without making some monstrous mistake will be difficult and obviously perilous. It is no time for self-deception, emotional indulgence, or the assumption of attitudes which are no longer useful. Man is facing a difficult test. He must keep his head now, or he must start again—a long way back. . . .

The two great dangers in modern democratic thinking are illustrated in a paper by former Secretary of State Dean Acheson. "For a long time now," writes Mr. Acheson, "we have gone along with some well-tested principles of conduct: That it was better to tell the truth than falsehoods; . . . that duties were older than and as fundamental as rights; that, as Justice Holmes put it, the mode by which the inevitable came to pass was effort; that to perpetrate a harm was wrong no matter how many joined in it . . . and so on. . . . Our institutions are founded on the assumption that most people follow these principles most of the time because they want to, and the institutions work pretty well when this assumption is true. More recently, however, bright people have been fooling with the machinery in the human head and they have discovered quite a lot. . . . Hitler introduced new refinements [as the result of which] a whole people have been utterly confused and corrupted. Unhappily neither the possession of this knowledge nor the desire to use it was confined to Hitler. . . . Others dip from this same devil's cauldron."

The first dangerous notion in this passage is that most people follow democratic principles of conduct "because they want to." This does not account for democracy or any other form of government if we have not explained why people *want* to behave in given ways. Although it is tempting to assume that it is human nature to believe in democratic principles, we must not overlook the "cultural engineering" which produced and continues to maintain democratic practices. If we neglect the conditions which produce democratic *behavior*, it is useless to try to maintain a democratic *form* of government. And we cannot expect to export a democratic form of government successfully if we do not also provide for the cultural practices which will sustain it. Our forebears did not discover the essential nature of man; they evolved a pattern of behavior which worked remarkably well under the circumstances. The "set of principles" expressed in that pattern is not the only true set or necessarily the best. Mr. Acheson has presumably listed the most unassailable items; some of them are probably beyond question, but others—concerning duty and effort—may need revision as the world changes.

The second—and greater—threat to the democracy which Mr. Acheson is defending is his assumption that knowledge is necessarily on the side of evil. All the admirable things he mentions are attributed to the innate goodness of man, all the detestable to "fooling with the machinery in the human head." This is reminiscent of the position, taken by other institutions engaged in the control of men, that certain forms of knowledge are in themselves evil. But how out of place in a democratic philosophy! Have we come this far only to conclude that well-intentioned people cannot study the behavior of men without becoming tyrants or that informed men cannot show good will? Let us for once have strength and good will on the same side.

Far from being a threat to the tradition of Western democracy, the growth of a science of man is a consistent and probably inevitable part of it. In turning to the external conditions which shape and maintain the behavior of men, while questioning the reality of inner qualities and faculties to which human achievements were once attributed, we turn from the ill-defined and remote to the observable and manipulable. Though it is a painful step, it has far-reaching consequences, for it not only sets higher standards of human welfare but shows us how to meet them. A change in a theory of human nature cannot change the facts. The achievements of man in science, art, literature, music and morals will survive any interpretation we place upon them. The uniqueness of the individual is unchallenged in the scientific view. Man, in short, will remain man. (There will be much to admire for those who are so inclined. Possibly the noblest achievement to which man can aspire, even according to present standards, is to accept himself for what he is, as that is revealed to him by the methods which he devised and tested on a part of the world in which he had only a small personal stake.)

If Western democracy does not lose sight of the aims of humanitarian action, it will welcome the almost fabulous support of its own science of man and will strengthen itself and play an important role in building a better world for everyone. But if it cannot put its "democratic philosophy" into proper historical perspective—if, under the control of attitudes and emotions which it generated for other purposes, it now rejects the help of science—then it must be prepared for defeat. For if we continue to insist that science has nothing to offer but a new and more horrible form of tyranny, we may produce just such a result by allowing the strength of science to fall into the hands of despots. And if, with luck, it were to fall instead to men of good will in other political communities, it would be perhaps a more ignominious defeat; for we should then, through a miscarriage of democratic principles, be forced to leave to others the next step in man's long struggle to control nature and himself.

Chapter 29

INTELLIGENCE, IDEAS, AND EDUCATION

THE *primary purpose of focusing education upon the maturation and socialization of personality is to make available to the nation more people than ever who will accept democracy as a way of life. There is no need to elaborate upon the fact that many display a marked reluctance to live democratically. There appears to be an undue emphasis upon techniques of living that get things done, a cheap expediency that has no rationale except immediate, short-range action. There is too much emphasis upon the "what" and too little upon the "why." Since this society has inherited a wealth of ideas from Western culture and has contributed its share of refinements and innovations, there is no absence of ideas in our cultural heritage that could help us remake ourselves and our society.*

We are in trouble, in part, because we have not modified our guiding concepts to keep up with the pace of social change. Any reconstructions of democratic ideals that have occurred have been sporadic and weak. We have not had a design for the continuing reappraisal of our means and ends.

One approach to the problem of remaining true to ideals that are part of a dynamic and changing society is presented by Walter G. O'Donnell, a social scientist. He believes that the enlargement of knowledge in various disciplines affords a base of sufficient magnitude for teachers in contemporary America to design a new series of relationships among certain subject areas. This would be the basis of a science of human relations. Originating in the existing physical, biological, psychological, and social sciences, this new science would organize knowledge and create techniques to help men live effectively in a society pledged to achieve the good life.

SOME PROSPECTS OF A GENERAL SCIENCE OF HUMAN RELATIONS

Walter G. O'Donnell

Science, variations in subject-matter and method notwithstanding, is coming to be recognized as a phase of human experience inseparable from the cultural context and problem-solving purposes of society. In the most advanced sectors of scientific thought there is a growing tendency to define science with reference to a more inclusive range of human activity in which a science is seen as a special case of intellectual controls in the more general exercise of human intelligence. This broader perspective, quite characteristic of twentieth century science, tends to bring out more clearly the integral elements and vital interrelationships among the physical, biological, psychological, and social sciences. If science originated in man's environmental predicaments, it becomes increasingly obvious that society must depend upon science to save its productive artificial structure from destructive convulsions. Science and society have become not only interactive, but interdependent. Max Planck recognizes this important relationship when he writes:

> The roots of exact science feed in the soil of human life. But its link to it is two-fold. For it not only has its source in experience, but also has a retroactive effect on human life, both material and spiritual, and the more freely it can unfold itself, the stronger and more fruitful is this effect.[1]

Science emerges from the problematic situations and generally shared experiences and observations of man-in-action more fundamentally than from the secondary refinements of controlled experiment, statistical induction, and other scientific methods; and human relations, in turn, are largely conditioned by the technological applications of science. A method of intellectual integrity, rather than a rigid content, is coming to characterize modern science. Scientific methods, irrespective of the degree of exactness or strata of phenomena with which they work, when seen as intellectual instrumentalities of modern man used to achieve his purposes and serve his needs, lose their connection with the rigid departmentalism that characterized much of nineteenth century science.

Reprinted from the *American Journal of Economics and Sociology*, Vol. 9, No. 3 (April 1950), pp. 355–356, 357–360, 364–367.

[1] "The Meaning and Limits of Exact Science," (Science, Sept. 30, 1949), p. 319.

Few would openly maintain that any science could develop a useful system of knowledge in a closed framework completely isolated from society, and specialization is generally regarded as a methodological expedient of economy in the use of human resources. Even pure science (which is always short of 100 percent purity) finds its justification in its unforeseen possibilities of social usefulness. Yet, an adamant and officious cult of analytical specialists and pure theorists in social science remains encased in their departmental cocoons, insulating their displays of rationalism from the empirical realities, pragmatic tests, and problematic situations of social life by means of a barrage of far-fetched assumptions and an array of preconceptions that hark back to an earlier stage of scientific and social development. Neglecting life, analytical work of this sort, however attractively garbed in statistical and mathematical techniques, is a reversion to a pre-Darwinian science and Cartesian rationalism in which scientific knowledge was regarded as independent of cultural determinants—residing in an inalterable and autonomous reservoir of natural law which scientists could tap by the logic of pure reason, regardless of creative innovations, significant irregularities, and emergent facts observable in the evolution of sciences and societies. This kind of rigid, rationalistic analysis, in the orthodox style of Newtonian deductive analysis which lends itself to impressive mathematical elaboration is enjoying a resurgence, especially in recent economic and sociological theory. . . .

Twentieth century scientific and philosophic advances embodying a new world view of evolution, relativity, emergence, innovation, organicism, indeterminacy and philosophical naturalism open new prospects for a more effective co-ordination of the physical, biological, psychological, and social sciences in an integrated science of human relations under the auspices of critical philosophy and a newly developing sociology of knowledge. Workers on the frontiers of modern science are drawing closer to a synthetic viewpoint and utilization of their findings. Many of the most significant contributions to recent intellectual development have been made by scientists and philosophers working across the lines of several scientific disciplines. It appears, too, that the urgent procession of socio-economic problems that results from the complicated effects of rapid technological changes attending scientific progress involve such complex elements and diverse ramifications that pooling of various scientific resources is required for reconstructive solutions.

The growing trend toward synthesis through co-operative scientific relationships is evident in many quarters. A glance through the programs of the recent annual meetings of the American Association for the Advancement of Science reveals an increasing cross-fertilization in the various fields of scientific investigation. Educational movements for increased emphasis on "general education" and the rapid spread of "integrative courses" in

American colleges and universities offer evidence that progressive educational institutions are responsive to this felt need for a synthetic approach to the problems of the modern world. The courses in Contemporary Civilization offered at Columbia University for many years, as the outstanding pioneering effort in this timely endeavor, have been conducted co-operatively by the departments of philosophy, economics, sociology, history, and political science, with signal success. Research institutes, such as the Yale Institute of Human Relations, similarly concerned with the co-ordination of investigations in several scientific fields, are being established in increasing numbers. The newly organized Foundation for Integrated Education has brought scholars together in workshops to discuss this general educational problem, and, among other constructive activities, has undertaken a survey of existing efforts to integrate the curricula of American institutions of higher learning. The Philosophy of Science Association, through meetings and its *Journal of Philosophy of Science* has also furthered the integrative trend in scientific circles. The *American Journal of Economics and Sociology* was one of the first of the organized efforts to encourage a wider understanding and application of interrelated sciences. A full survey and objective appraisal of this broad intellectual trend might disclose the promising beginnings of what may become the most vital scientific and cultural achievement of the twentieth century.

A FUNCTIONAL SYNTHESIS OF KNOWLEDGE

Unless the remarkable modern achievements of analytical science and technology are to be dissipated in the confusion of the random forces that they have let loose, new social directives must be constructed from a functional synthesis of modern scientific knowledge. From such a pooling of the cultural heritage of scientific resourcefulness the specific empirical content of normative social standards and human values can be ascertained and society provided with the institutional means for the attainment of these goals of human welfare.

If science is to serve society in this regard, the springs of human action, as well as the constituents of welfare, must receive more intensive study and co-ordinate understanding in several related sciences dealing with human relations. The physical and biological sciences would be included with psychology and the social sciences in such an integrated and objective study of man-in-action as an organism interactive with other organic, ecological, physical, and cultural aspects of the environment. This kind of transactional understanding, with a common root system penetrating several scientific strata, is facilitated by present scientific trends away from the rigorous determinism and separatism of earlier scientific methodology. The fundamental indeterminacy and the statistical conception of probability pervading twentieth century physical and biological science render the findings of these sciences more compatible with the newer conceptions of psychology and social science. Norbert Wiener, one of the frontiersmen of modern science, with a comprehensive sweep of genius, shows the essential identity of action in physical and psycho-biological phenomena and constructs machines that imitate and excel intricate human operations. These may be a decisive measure of progress in this new incentive to create machines in the image of man instead of conceiving of man in terms of machines, for in *Cybernetics*, man is the controller, not the controlled.

Deliberate co-operation among scientists in all fields of investigation in the interest of human welfare is becoming more and more a necessity for the orderly and intelligent reconstruction and control of the artificial and delicately organized environment of civilization. Scientists who work in the isolation of closed systems, apart from other sciences and apart from social necessities, are becoming insupportable luxuries, if not actual dangers, in a modern world in which it is becoming more and more urgent that the power of our scientific resources be directed towards an increasingly creative use of human energy. Pure science, competently organized and responsibly pursued, retains its potential social value, of course, but idle curiosity seeking a discovery of the "laws" of nature can no longer be reasonably regarded as a respectable use of limited resources. This detached attitude is a survival of an aristocratic notion of knowledge seeking as a leisure-time sport of the upper classes, and is consonant only with a social philosophy of privilege and oligarchy which regards things intellectual as best confined to a conspicuous display of time-consuming curiosity and distinctive decoration. Science has become the main instrument with which society deals with its problems, and the whole process, as a part of the cultural heritage, is vested with a public interest which its practitioners can hardly afford to ignore. The reconciliation of the rights of free inquiry and academic freedom with an increased social responsibility of the scientific professions is one of the most insistent problems of our generation. Freedom of scientists from partisan political pressures, organized intellectual intolerance, and character assassination is equally important. . . .

One of the best ways to make the social sciences more workable in the solution of problems confronting the modern world is to synthesize their findings for the intelligent direction of institutional evolution. Departmental divisions among the sciences, largely a matter of accident and convention, cannot be allowed to stand against the current trend toward reintegration, without aggravating the cultural lag as well as the predicament of devaluation in which the social sciences now find themselves. All of the sciences were once included in the general subject of Natural Philosophy, and their boundary lines have shifted from time to time, always overlapping as a matter of fact. Our urgent intellectual need of the present is for a new Natural Philosophy as a framework of reference for the integrated sciences, including a general science of human relations. Such a Philosophy of Science is already in the making.

The insistent pressure of complex problems, which occur more frequently, extend more widely, and penetrate more deeply into the cultural matrix as a result of the highly accelerated rate and widening ramifications of scientific discovery and technological applications, accounts for the present trend toward integration. Modern social problems cannot be thoroughly understood, let alone solved, by reference to a single scientific discipline, and much of the impractical inadequacy of the more rigid types of economic and sociological analysis and theory can be attributed to a failure to consider the whole cultural context of the phenomena with which they deal and the corresponding contributions available from other fields of scientific investigation. Price analysis and theory, for example, reveal merely an instrumental and partial phase of human behavior, and not even an adequate basis for explaining what is conventionally regarded as economic behavior. It is not money, but *men* with—or without—money that require thorough analysis. Under rigid analysis within such a narrow framework of reference, reliable predictions are very improbable. No one scientific discipline is adequate to explain completely any segment of human behavior, and a really workable theory of human relations requires the contributions of all scientific disciplines for its practical development. It is necessary, as a basis for the intelligent solution of modern social problems, to study the manifold aspects of human behavior and its environmental determinants from various scientific viewpoints and with different methods, the findings of analytical investigation to be co-ordinated for synthetic understanding and organic social applications. The analytical process of atomistic vivisection is a necessary method in most scientific investigations, but this process is essentially incomplete, requiring empirical verification or sensible interpretation in the reconstructed synthetic whole. Much of the fragmentary futility of sociological and economic research, especially in dust-gathering dissertations, is due to a ready satisfaction with detached analysis tightly insulated from the changing intellectual climate and the organic environmental pressures.

THE CROSSING OF DEPARTMENTAL BOUNDARIES

The crossing of the boundary lines of the various sciences, even in the analytical stages of investigation, is becoming more common. Foremost scholars starting from different scientific fields, crossing and re-crossing scientific boundary lines, are finding themselves with increasing frequency on common naturalistic grounds or even joining hands in the upper reaches of philosophy. This crossing of departmental lines enriches scientific methodology, and gives a realistic organic perspective and practicality to the content of the sciences. The social sciences, in particular, are in need of this kind of cross-fertilization, but conventional notions of the narrow scope of certain scientific disciplines, and the preoccupation of vested intellectual interests with a rigorous type of theoretical analysis which offers them a continuing opportunity for the display of their logical brilliance, are among the obstacles in the way of a hardy hybridization of the social sciences.

However desirable may be the development of a new science of political economy as a practical move in the direction of a more competent problem-solving social science, the integration of sociology, political science, economics, and other social sciences is no longer to be regarded as an adequate basis for an objective science of human relations. All sciences having a bearing on human behavior and its environmental setting are relevant—and that means practically all of the physical, biological, and psychological sciences as well as the social sciences. All should be available for consultation in the social process of solving problems and guiding public policy. Fundamental scientific concepts, the sources of human motivation and action, and the manifold nature of modern problems require continuous inter-disciplinary consultation and co-operation in order to secure a thorough understanding of human relations and more effective instrumentalities of group action in the interest of human welfare.

Basic terms are used in the propositions of the several sciences with quite different meanings; except where it can be shown that the phenomena dealt with differ substantially, there is no reason for such discrepancies in semantics. Korzybski has done much to clear the air of such terminological confusion. It is known, for example, that economists use such concepts of physical sciences as "equilibrium" in a sense that is nonsense to physicists. Many of the fundamental postulates and preconceptions of the sciences rest upon common foundations in the basic strata of the physical and biological sciences, and unless these are explicity related to the most recent findings in these foundational sciences, the super-structure of social sciences may become distorted by a sinking foundation.

Action, perhaps the great common denominator of all of the sciences, is made meaningful by reference to human motivation and the consequences of combining the two in creative activity. The actual constituents of human welfare and the empirical content of human and social values provide the norms which give direction to individual and collective activities. These changing norms, and the value judgments which are the most active factors in human motivation, deserve thorough empirical analysis and synthesis. Values are of strategic importance in the study of human relations, penetrating not only the whole layer of biological, psychological, and social sciences, but the whole scientific process, studied resistance notwithstanding. Any serious study of values carries the investigator into several related fields of scientific investigation and philosophy.

In addition to these fundamental scientific concepts, a thorough study of any general problem from the standpoint of finding a practical solution will reveal the inter-connection of the sciences. Consider, for example, how many scientific disciplines will have to be utilized in order to plan and administer the proposed Point Four Program to aid the underdeveloped areas of the world. Modern problems call for a new kind of social engineering in which the basic facts of the natural sciences are used in the functional analysis and organic direction of group life by social scientists aware of the attainable empirical content of values, human welfare, and constructive social goals. Scientific versatility is the need of the day. An integral science of human relations embodied in a new natural philosophy is urgent.

By way of brief summary, four reasons for scientific integration are suggested, in conclusion, as worthy of further study and research among social scientists:

1. The composite nature of social problems and their ramifications in several areas of scientific investigation.
2. The manifold aspects of human behavior and relations, including motivation, value judgments, and values.
3. The common and interchangeable facts, concepts, categories, principles, and postulates operative in the several layers of science—physical, biological, psychological, and social.
4. The generally accepted and alternative scientific methods, both analytic and synthetic, atomistic and organic, used or useable in the several fields of scientific inquiry, for methodological enrichment.

New prospects are in evidence for an integrated and objective science of human relations. The real opportunity, the real work, the real prospects of a sound naturalistic social science progressively directed towards the achievement of an increasing degree of human welfare and creative activity lie ahead. The materials are at hand.

PART SEVEN

Educational Specifications

FROM the beginning, the purposes of public education in the United States have been formulated and reformulated by all kinds of people. Such specifications were, usually, scholarly translations of the goals of the society into aims and objectives that educators could follow. The ever-changing social, political, economic, and cultural conditions of America, particularly the dramatic expansion of knowledge during the last century and the increasing sophistication of people, have served to make the clarification of aims and objectives a major responsibility of educators.

It can be argued that the aims and objectives in any society involve what John L. Childs has described as "two basic and interrelated faiths."[1] *The first concerns the modifiability of man and the second describes the opportunity that a group has to control its life in terms of its values. In his passage from animality to humanity, man has moved from educational systems that lacked these faiths to those that seldom thought of doubting them. All the readings that have been presented up to this point stress the ideal possibilities of the democratic ethos: Our society can endure, and will, if its citizens are knowledgeable; and our citizens will be knowledgeable if our society supports each man's growth and development.*

The particular aspect of aims and objectives of interest at this point depends upon an elaboration of the idea of human difference. Although such differences are quite readily acknowledged, there is considerable disagreement over the degree to which such differences should be supported by school programs that are strongly diversified and individualized. The most typical approach to this matter can be found in the general agreement that formal schooling for all individuals should encompass both general education and specific education. General education acquaints the individual with the cultural heritage he must share if organized group life is to be successful. Specific education addresses itself to the unique abilities of the individual and thereby complements and reinforces the values of general education.

[1] J. L. Childs, *Education and Morals* (New York: Appleton-Century-Crofts, 1950), p. 5.

The following examination of education specifications samples what different individuals and groups, all seriously concerned with the operation of education in the American democratic society, have had to say about educational aims and objectives.

Chapter 30

EDUCATIONAL SPECIFICATIONS — AS VIEWED BY A SOCIAL SCIENTIST

George S. Counts, *writing as a social scientist, discusses the following: The control of education rests with the masses of the people, and this control is exercised through state and local boards of education. Although the state is the primary legal authority, the support, control, and general conduct of the public schools is in local hands. The motivating ideas for the operation of education by the society are found in the ethos of the society.*

THE SPIRIT OF AMERICAN EDUCATION

George S. Counts

In the sphere of control authority in the last analysis rests with the people. In spite of the intervention from age to age of privileged groups and classes, whether founded on religion or property, this has always been so. Education

Reprinted from *Teachers College Record*, Vol. 59, No. 8 (May 1958), pp. 451–454.

in the United States has never been imposed from above. First as colonists along the Atlantic coast and later as pioneers in the wilderness of the interior, the people carried their institutions with them wherever they cast their lot. It was in this way that they established their schools, each community or settlement doing as it saw fit. No great statesman, no priesthood, no intellectual class, no committee of wise men, no centralized government devised the American system of education. With whatever merits or defects it may possess, it is the authentic work of the people, with of course the assistance of inspired leaders. Almost universally the conduct of elementary and secondary schools is in the hands of local boards of education chosen in some fashion by the citizens of the community. The boards which control higher schools and universities are ordinarily somewhat further removed from the citizens, but even with them, at least in the case of public education, the contact is fairly close. The development of public education in the United States consequently rests on a sublime faith in the wisdom and virtue of the people.

A word should perhaps be said here about the origin of our people. What is now the United States was populated by the greatest migration of history. From the first colonial settlements, at the beginning of the seventeenth century, down to the present time something like forty million men, women, and children crossed the great oceans to make their homes in this land. Moreover, from beginning to end this great migration was essentially a migration of common people—common in the sense that they were without wealth or social rank. In fact the records show that they came overwhelmingly from the poor, the oppressed, and the persecuted of the Old World. In the colonial period, well over half of the immigrants came as bond servants or Negro slaves. The number of criminals cast on the shores of the thirteen colonies by the mother country far exceeded the renowned migration of English Puritans. To this broad generalization regarding the source of the American people, there are of course many individual exceptions, but the exceptions were generally unsuccessful in the attempt to transport their conceptions of social relations to the New World. As a consequence, feudal institutions and traditions never took root in the colonies. Here, without doubt, is one of the most important and decisive factors shaping the history of the American people. The idea prevails to this day that America is a land without social classes; and anyone who seeks to arouse class antagonisms or even to speak of classes is generally regarded as un-American. It was thus the poor and underprivileged of other countries who in the last analysis built the American Republic and fashioned the system of public education.

In educational matters the people exercise control, for the most part, through state and local boards of education. It should be recalled that when the American Union was formed in the latter part of the eighteenth century the thirteen colonies which entered into the federation regarded themselves as independent states and were exceedingly jealous of their sovereignty. It was in fact only with the greatest difficulty and by means of shrewd political manipulation that they were persuaded to relinquish a portion of this sovereignty and accept membership in the Union. In those days there was a general mistrust of any government far removed from the governed; moreover, whether that government was located in London or in some American city seemed to many a sturdy champion of local rights a matter of little importance. As a consequence, the powers of the Federal Government were carefully listed in the federal constitution, which formed the basis of the Union; and, according to the provisions of the tenth amendment to this document, all other powers were "reserved to the states respectively, or to the people." Since education was not mentioned in the constitution, it thus came to be regarded as an exclusive interest of the separate commonwealths.

Although the Federal Government has played a role in the development of certain aspects of American education and although, ever since the Civil War, organized efforts have been made to secure substantial federal funds for the support of public education, the school remains to this day essentially a function and a responsibility of the individual state. Opposition to federal control is deep-rooted and is shared even by those who seek federal support. According to the American point of view, education is too powerful an instrument over the mind to be placed in the hands of any single authority. The citizens fear that the central government, if it had administrative control over the schools, might fall under the influence of some unscrupulous minority and that the entire educational system from one end of the country to the other might be employed to keep this minority in power and to indoctrinate the coming generation with some authoritarian social philosophy.

Basic to the American system, therefore, is the fact that the individual state is the primary legal authority in the field of education. Yet this statement conveys only a part of the picture. Within the state the local community rather than the central authority has always played the major role in the support, control, and general conduct of the public school. While enforcing minimum standards, promoting diverse limited objectives, and providing a measure of leadership, the state commonly delegates its authority under the federal constitution to the local community. It is in the locality, therefore, that the process of shaping public education is concentrated. And here the people, operating within a framework of traditions, laws, and judicial pronouncements, make decisions governing the establishment and the conduct of their schools. The people do not discharge these functions directly, however. By one means or another, but commonly through popular elections, they create small lay boards of education to which their authority is delegated. It is assumed that at the time of election the broad issues confronting the schools will be thoroughly discussed by the electorate, and that the board members will be chosen on the basis of both their personal qualifications and their announced positions on the issues. It might be assumed further that during their term of office the board members will meet at stated intervals and, free from the pressure of special interests, make decisions respecting the conduct of public education in accord with the expressed mandates of the people.

In actual practice, however, the situation is quite different. In the first place, a large proportion of the people seem to have no interest in education and fail to participate in elections. At the same time, the board of education is rarely permitted to deliberate in solitude, insulated between elections from the play of social forces. And here we encounter a major political reality in the United States. In his study of the American democracy published in 1835, in the period of pre-industrial society, Alexis de Tocqueville observed with astonishment the tendency of Americans to form voluntary organizations. "Americans of all ages, all conditions," he wrote, "constantly form associations. They have not only commercial and manufacturing companies, in which all take part, but associations of a thousand other kinds—religious, moral, serious, futile, general or restricted, enormous or diminutive. . . . If it be proposed to inculcate some truth, or to foster some feeling, by the encouragement of a great example, they form a society. Wherever, at the head of some new undertaking, you see the government in France, or a man of rank in England, in the United States you will be sure to find an association." And so it is today. The battles over the launching and the development of the system of public education in all of its aspects and departments have been conducted by these voluntary and private associations. It is in this way that the active and articulate elements among the people make their views known on every conceivable aspect of education. It is thus in a situation seething with conflict, controversy, and pressure that decisions are made. All of this is in the spirit of American democracy.

The controlling ideas and motivations in American education are many and contradictory. The following five, however, will be briefly developed in this paper: the doctrine of equality, the drive for individual success, the devotion to practical utility, the spirit of pragmatism, and faith in the perfectibility of man. Although each of these ideas or motivations is often observed in the breach, they are all authentic elements in the total spirit of American education. They all have their roots in the long experience of the American people.

At the very base of the theory of education in the United States is a profound faith in the potentialities of the individual human being. Although this faith has been shaken in the twentieth century by the advance of industrialism, the appearance of a highly complex social order, and the results of biological and psychological investigation, the Americans continue to believe in the essential quality of men. They still stoutly maintain in the language of their radical forefathers that the individual is a product of the total influences which play upon him from birth to maturity, and that inequalities are to be explained chiefly in terms of differences in opportunity and of injustices perpetuated by social institutions and conventions. This doctrine, which may be traced to the French philosophers of the period of the Enlightenment, found eloquent expression in the American Declaration of Independence in 1776. Moreover, the citizens of the young republic were revolutionists and, like all revolutionists, had unlimited faith in the power of the environment to transform the individual. They also believed that the conception of equality as a moral idea is one of the truly sublime ideas in the history of the race.

The idea was supported by the great experience of the migration from beyond the Atlantic and across the continent to the Pacific. Here, in an untamed land devoid of historical tradition, whatever artificial social distinctions may have survived the leveling process of migration rapidly melted away. When a man entered this strange new world he was forced to leave his ancestry and family behind him. Indeed, as we have seen, the vast majority of them had no ancestry of distinction or family of social rank. The Americans are ever fond of declaring that their own history is a living refutation of the claims of superiority advanced by privileged classes. Thus the ideas of democracy and popular rule were born. We have an old saying: "One man is just as good as another, if not a little better."

The idea of equality, which is perhaps the most basic idea in democracy, has had a profound impact on the American system of education. It was responsible for the establishment of the *free* school without tuition charges and the *common* school attended by children from all elements of the population. It was also responsible for the development of the *single* educational system—one of the most magnificent achievements of American democracy. Except for the private schools which are permitted under the conception of liberty, the dual system developed in Europe, with its abbreviated program for the masses and its rich offering for the upper classes, has never taken root in the United States, except in the case of the Negro in the southern states, which constitutes our most severe violation of the democratic principle. The sequential organization of institutions, consisting of primary, secondary, and higher schools, is theoretically open to all elements of society and is commonly regarded by the Americans themselves as *their* system of education. The exceptions which exist are usually brushed aside as unimportant or irrelevant.

Chapter 31

EDUCATIONAL SPECIFICATIONS— AS VIEWED BY A PHILOSOPHER

CURT J. DUCASSE *begins his discussion of what philosophy can contribute to educational theory by stipulating that the educational reformer is obligated to know the current status of the educational enterprise; to understand the political, social, and economic aspects of the society in which the educational enterprise operates; to have the authority to accept and use educational innovations; and to have a conception of what the achievement of education should be. Philosophy, and specifically educational philosophy, has a contribution to make to the last point—the conception of education.*

The purpose of education, he writes, is "to lead out or bring out; and that which is to be brought out and developed can only be capacities that man has but that remain more or less dormant or embryonic until something acts upon him that awakens, nourishes, and exercises them." Instruction, training, and indoctrination are the processes through which education is accomplished. Instruction is the process of imparting verifiable knowledge, training is the imparting of skills for the performance of various functions, and indoctrination is the presentation of value systems that enable an individual to live with others. Ducasse here stresses the importance of recognizing a conception of man as the recipient of the educative process. Man is visualized as representing a complex of propensities, which includes cognitive powers, emotional capacities, volitional capacities, physical powers, and social capacities that vary in intensity. Education must utilize all the capacities of each and every individual and achieve, as the ultimate product, an organic unity of personality.

WHAT CAN PHILOSOPHY CONTRIBUTE TO EDUCATIONAL THEORY?

Curt J. Ducasse

Intellectual education. I begin with what ordinarily first comes to mind when education is mentioned, namely, intellectual education. It is the sort of education to which schools, colleges and universities have mainly been instruments, and for which they are the main instruments. It is education of man in the dimension of his nature which consists in knowing and thinking.

One occasionally hears it said nowadays in connection with education of this kind that it does not matter much whether a man acquires any particular stock of information; and that the important thing is that he should learn to think, and develop intellectual initiative and the capacity for independent intellectual exploration. However, I believe this is but an extreme view, excusable at all only as a reaction against the opposing extreme which conceives intellectual education as chiefly the learning of a lot of facts.

To me, the truth seems to be that, for each age and place, there is a minimum amount of information each individual ought to have, and it would be a very good thing if he should have much in addition to this minimum. For, lacking this, he is in life much like a man in a wilderness without a map or compass. His sense of direction, of the resources available to him, of the tasks he should undertake, of the nature of his environment, and so on, is then limited strictly to the relatively small area about him that he can personally explore. I therefore believe that the education of man ought to include acquisition of as large and diverse a stock as possible of what I like to call *map knowledge* or *surface knowledge*. It is knowledge in breadth, not in depth. To seek it is, as the phrase goes, to seek to know something about everything.

The complement of this, of course, is in the corresponding phrase, the attempt to know everything about something; or, more literally, to gain knowledge detailed, precise, and thorough about some things. A certain amount of such knowledge in depth is as necessary as is knowledge in breadth; for after all each mind—however much in need of a map wherewith to orient itself—has a home ground of its own; and, for the work it has to do there, knowledge merely superficial would be of little use.

Reprinted from *Harvard Educational Review,* Vol. XXVIII, No. 4 (Fall 1958), pp. 290–297.

But although acquisition of a stock of knowledge of both the kinds mentioned is an indispensable part of intellectual education, it is neither the whole of it nor its most intimate and abiding part. The latter consists rather in development of the intellectual powers; for example, the power of objective and careful observation and of precise and logically ordered formulation of what has been observed, and of any ideas one may have about it. Again, the power of rigorous inference; practical grasp of the nature of experimental procedure; the habit of verification; the ability to read understandingly and critically; and development of the intellectual independence and initiative which consists so largely in the capacity to think of questions not before raised about matters already familiar.

These are mental powers as distinguished from the mental furniture or material which information constitutes. These powers are developed only through exercise, and the process which exercises them is that of actually searching for knowledge. It is to the development of them that the maxim, "learn by doing," properly applies. This maxim, however, is often unthinkingly taken to mean that learning, in the sense not only of learning how but also of learning facts, is best done by discovering the facts for oneself. But this is of course not true. On the contrary, when important facts which it took hours or days or years to discover can be learned in a few minutes from the records handed down by their discoverers, it would be only stupid not to learn them in this easy way as far as possible. The ability to learn from others is one of the most valuable a man can have; for, as Franklin remarked, "experience [that is, personal experience] keeps a dear school; yet fools will learn in no other."

These remarks on the specific range within which the educational catchword, "learned by doing," is valid, but outside of which it becomes silly, constitute an example of the kind of practical service which philosophical reflection—insisting as it does on always asking where? when? why? and what for?—can render to education. Other stereotypes similarly calling for philosophically critical scrutiny would be "Democracy in education," "Education for adjustment," "The educational process should be made enjoyable," and so on. In what follows, we shall have occasion to comment on some of them.

Physical education. From intellectual education, we may now turn to the education of other aspects of man's nature.

Irrespective of what we may conceive the relation to be between a man's mind and his body, the fact remains that he does have a body, and that his body, like his mind, is capable of education. What physical education, viewed in terms of its contribution to a distinctively human life, should aim at is perhaps best suggested by saying that man's body is the most useful of his domestic animals. It is the physical vehicle and basic implement of all the experiences and undertakings of his life on earth. Physical education should then aim to do in general for the body what the intelligent owner of a valuable horse would do for the horse. On the positive side, this would mean the establishment of physical habits conducive to health and to fitness of the body to do its work, and development of the versatility that renders the body quickly adaptable to the specialized physical tasks or situations which life may thrust upon it. On the negative side, physical education does not mean asceticism, but only restraint of bodily cravings or impulses within the limits compatible with health and bodily efficiency. It means also that such muscular development and agility as those of the fabulous Tarzan might be sensible ideals for apes, but hardly for civilized men. The justification of athletic sports from the point of view of physical education is either, as in the play of children, development of bodily powers needed later; or, as in the play of adults, recreation and maintenance of valuable bodily powers that otherwise would atrophy.

Vocational education. Next to physical education a word should be said about vocational education; but only to point out that it is not education of any specific aspect of human nature, but is essentially development to a high degree of efficiency of such a man's capacities as relate to the particular vocation he proposes to follow. These capacities would be physical ones in the case of a vocation, such as an acrobat's, dependent chiefly on bodily agility, strength, or dexterity; but, for diverse vocations, the capacities to be developed would be of corresponding diversity.

Education in social dexterity. There is a certain human capacity, the educating of which is of considerable importance to man simply as a social being; that is, in his relation with his fellow men. It is difficult to find a suitable name for the dimension of education I am referring to, but it may perhaps be called education in manners, or more comprehensively, education in social dexterity. It is education of an ability usually well developed in politicians, but valuable equally outside of politics; namely, the ability to deal effectively with other human beings *as they are*, in the variety of relations one may have with them—the ability to make contact with them easily, to enlist their good will and cooperation, and to avoid antagonizing them. It is true that there are occasions when competing with others, or opposing them rather than getting along with them, is the task that faces a man; but even then the ability to engage the aid of third parties on his side stands him in good stead.

Education of the will. Another dimension of education, about which in general little is said, was called education of the will by a French writer, Jules Payot, in a book which appeared a good many years ago. What he meant by that phrase was development of the capacity to make oneself do the things which one has the ability to do and desires to do. It is education in the overcoming of inertia, sloth, and procrastination; in perseverance, in firmness of purpose, in courage under difficulties, and in readiness to take pains and to take care. In short, it is education in the translating of dreams into deeds. How important this is, any teacher realizes who has seen highly gifted young men or women, for whom he anticipated a great future, sometimes get nowhere for lack of the capacity to make themselves come through with what they were capable of.

Aesthetic education. Next to be considered, and at somewhat greater length, is what in a broad sense may be called aesthetic education. It includes, for one thing, education of man's capacity for fine discrimination in his sensory impressions. Concerning colors, shapes, tones, textures, odors, and flavors, it is possible to cultivate the ability to discern differences and other relations of which one was before unconscious. Sensitivity to such relations is the very basis of what is called taste or aesthetic appreciation as concerns the various kinds of perceptible objects.

But there is also such a thing as sensitivity and appreciative discernment in matters of human relations. There we give to taste rather the name of tact. What it depends on, however, is not sensory discrimination but comprehensiveness of one's horizon of acquaintance with the immense variety and the subtle nuances of human emotions, sentiments, moods, feelings, and attitudes. For the education of man in this dimension of his being, the most adequate formal instrument consists of literary works—such as novels, poems, dramas, biographies—that depict diverse human characters in situations of various kinds. Into these, the reader can project himself in imagination and, losing for the time being his own identity, he can gain vicariously many experiences which he could neither obtain nor afford in his objective life. Moreover, although the situations depicted in those literary works are lived through by the reader only in imagination, nevertheless the feelings, sentiments, moods, or attitudes thereby generated in him are not imaginary but quite real for the time being, and may constitute emotional insights genuinely novel to him. But these insights, it must be emphasized, result not from reading *about* such literary works, or from dissecting their structure and history, but only from reading the works themselves, and reading them in the manner which consists of intensely living through in imagination the situations they depict.

A similar remark applies to the education of the sensations. For it, the works of painters, of sculptors, of musicians, and of other creative workers in the arts and crafts, are the analogues of what scientific treatises are for education in the sciences. But development of sensitivity to subtle modulations of sensory qualities and of forms results, not from listening to discourses about the technique of art or from reading about the history of art, but from abundant, prolonged, intense, and diversified contemplation of works of art at first hand. This is said not to disparage in any way interest in the history of the arts, in the technical analysis of works of art, or in the lives of their creators, but only to emphasize that interest in *these* matters is essentially intellectual, not aesthetic. It is intellectual interest in aesthetic objects; and this is very different from aesthetic interest in them—as different as, on the other side, aesthetic interest in scientific apparatus would be different from scientific interest in such apparatus. Aesthetic contemplation is something radically different from intellectual curiosity. This greatly needs to be remembered by those who teach courses in the appreciation of the works of the various arts; for aesthetic contemplation is what is directly relevant to aesthetic appreciation; whereas historical and technical knowledge about works of art is at best an aid to aesthetic appreciation, and at worst diverts one's interest altogether from contemplation.

If the term "aesthetic education" is to be taken in the broad sense I have proposed, it must then also cover the active side. It must include cultivation of the capacity to give objective expression to one's insights into the realm of sensations and sentiments; and this means development of the individual's latent artistic abilities. Great natural gifts in this direction are of course as rare as in any other; but the capacity to express oneself in some art medium is no rarer and no more difficult to bring out than is the capacity to express one's ideas in writing exemplified in, for instance, a freshman theme or a letter to a friend. If the capacity for artistic self-expression seems more wonderful, it is only because fewer persons as yet cultivate it. The truth, however, probably is that most of the paintings, music, poems, and other works of art created each day in the land are about on the same level of difficulty, or originality, or of merit as are most of the essays written by students in college.

Much could be said concerning the human importance of aesthetic education. If art and aesthetic experience are thought by many persons to be at best of secondary moment in the life of man, it is I think chiefly because these persons tacitly but mistakenly assume art to be the sort of thing found only in art galleries, studios, museums, concert halls, or the like. The fact, however, is much rather that art and aesthetic experience are among men everywhere and at every moment, and have been so throughout the history of the race. In producing objects of even the most practical utility, men have generally utilized more thought and work than is demanded simply for their practical function. In almost every case, much time, thought and effort have been given also to the attempt to make the object pleasing to the senses. And the consumer willingly pays for this.

Moral and religious education. But there are two other dimensions of education—namely moral education and religious education—on which, because of their importance, it might have been expected that I should have touched before now.

Many persons believe that religion is the indispensable basis of morality, but although this can I think easily be disproved, there is no doubt that a certain close relation often exists between them. For its specific nature to become evident, it is necessary first of all to have a definite idea of what each essentially is; and I shall approach this question through a reference to the contention of Plotinus that, in respect of spiritual worth, men can be divided into three classes. Some, he said, may be described as beasts among men; others, as men among beasts; and others yet as gods among men. But instead of three classes, I shall distinguish four, and describe each in less picturesque but more literal terms.

The lowest class is that of malicious men. Malice is disinterested evil-doing. A man is malicious in so far as he does evil not as a means to advantage of some kind to himself, but for the mere pleasure he finds in doing it, even perhaps sometimes at some cost to himself. The terms "sadism" and "vandalism" describe some of the manifestations of this trait.

Next above the malicious man is the selfish man. He is the man who considers only what benefits him, and strives for it irrespective of what the cost of it to others may be. He does not seek to injure others nor to benefit them, but is quite ready to do either if only it works to his own profit. He does not care what happens to others.

Next higher in the spiritual scale is the moral or righteous man. He is the man whose rule in dealing with others is merely that of justice—or fair exchange or compensation. He is equally scrupulous to give others their due and to demand of them his due. He complies strictly with his obligations and expects others to do likewise; but he feels no impulse to do for others more than his obligations require, or to forgive them any part of what their obligations to him call for. His philosophy is simply that of the square deal.

Duty, justice, or righteousness, in the sense just defined is what I shall here assume to be the province of morality as distinguished from generosity. Morality, as so conceived, is about as much as the laws of the land have generally attempted to codify. It has been the most that a man's fellows felt they had the right to require of him, but it has been also the least they expected of him, since the unrighteous, unjust, undutiful man is in so far a burden or a plague to them. Generosity of spirit is no part of righteousness, which, therefore, does not call forth love; but it rightly calls forth esteem and respect, for it is of great social value. Development of morality is therefore one of the proper objectives of a total education of the individual.

On the other hand, religious education, in so far as it concerns itself with man's disposition towards his fellows, seeks to make him not merely just, but good; that is, freely benevolent. The good man is the man who, going beyond what merely justice or duty requires of him, is kind, merciful, compassionate, helpful. He is the altruistic man, the man who finds his own greatest happiness in bringing happiness to others or in promoting their welfare. He is the polar opposite of the malicious man. The latter does evil disinterestedly, for the sheer love of it. The altruist, on the other hand, does good disinterestedly, for the sheer love of it.

Cultivation in individuals, in social classes, and in nations, of the capacity to interest themselves benevolently and actively in the welfare of others is in our day perhaps the most urgent educational task. The education that undertakes it might be called education of the heart. It is this, I think, which great religious teachers such as the Christ and the Buddha were basically concerned to promote. The particular dogmas of the religions they founded are, from this point of view, significant essentially as premises for arguments in favor of brotherhood among men. Hence, by religious education, I mean in the present context not necessarily instruction in the Scriptures or the beliefs of one or another of the historical religions of mankind; but, essentially, education of the heart—cultivation of altruistic feelings, impulses, and conduct, irrespective of whether this be done by means of indoctrination in the theology of a religion, or in some other way.

In this connection, it is essential to remember that, as a person acts, so does he tend to feel. Hence, in the education of the heart, the first step is to get the person concerned to act beneficently—that is to do good to others—even if he feels no direct impulse to do so. Only in the act of doing good to others can one discover the happiness which resides in the very doing of it. Virtue, we are told, is its own reward; but to discover the reward inherent in altruistic action, it is necessary first to *act* altruistically, that is, in ways that benefit others, even if, to begin with, one so acts out of perhaps remotely egoistic motives, such as hope for a future life in a heaven.

Liberal education. We have now considered the principal aspects of human personality and the corresponding chief possible dimensions of the education of man. When we come to drawing concrete educational counsels from these considerations, however, a number of empirical factors enter the picture. One of them is the fact that, even if all human personalities have all of the kinds of potentialities mentioned, a given man is always more highly gifted with certain ones of them than with certain others. This would, in any given case, influence decision as to which ones of those aspects we ought to select as the ones upon which to concentrate the major part of the limited time and educational resources available in the particular case. The fact that the time and resources to be devoted to a given person's education are always short of what we might wish is thus a second empirical factor. What would in itself be desirable for the fullest development of an individual's potentialities is one thing; but what society, which ultimately pays in one kind of coin or another for his education and for his lack of it, can afford, is another thing. And what is to be done in each concrete case is necessarily a compromise between the two.

Granting this, however, the counsels which would flow from the foregoing analysis of the generic nature of man, would be such, for example, as that the so-called "practical" aims, in education, should not be the only ones taken into account; that the success or failure of an education—or indeed of a life—should not be measured wholly or even mainly in terms of fruits of the conspicuous kinds, such as wealth, honors, position, power, popularity, or renown. Again, that the truly important thing about democracy is not that it performs the objective tasks of government better than could any other system—for this probably is not true—but that it is the one form of government which can in the long run automatically educate the citizen in social and individual responsibility, and which thus tacitly recognizes the fact that the most important thing for him is not that he should be well governed, but that he should have the opportunity to make his own mistakes and to gain wisdom from them. Again, that not only self-expression should be encouraged in the educational process, as has been the fashion in recent years; but also development of the capacity most men are even more likely to need throughout most of their life—namely, the capacity to do and to do well tasks which they perhaps do not like, but which are imposed on them by their own commitments or by the pressure of external necessity.

The essential import of the point of view I have been presenting may perhaps now in the end be summarily put by saying that an education is *humanly* right in proportion as it is as *liberal* as the circumstances of the individual concerned permit.

Essentially, liberal education is *liberating* education. It is not the education of men who are free, but the education that makes men free. More specifically, it is the kind of education designed to free man from his own ignorance, prejudices, and narrowness, by making him aware of them; it aims to give him a comprehensive view of the ranges of human knowledge, human achievements, and human capacities; and to develop in him an appreciative insight into the typical values for which men live. That is, liberal education is education essentially for perspective; and the value of perspective is that it brings freedom of choice of aims, and of judgment. Such freedom consists in awareness of the alternatives there are to choose between. The man who knows but one course, or sees but one aspect of things, or appreciates but a limited range of values, has no choice or but little choice as to the direction he takes. Unaware of his own blind spots and prejudices, he is held by them in an invisible jail. *The task of liberal education is to tear down its walls.*

Chapter 32

EDUCATIONAL SPECIFICATIONS—AS VIEWED BY THE NATIONAL ASSOCIATION OF MANUFACTURERS

Charles R. Sligh, Jr., *Executive Vice President of the National Association of Manufacturers, presents the Association's position concerning the purpose of education and some of its views on the curriculum. Sligh emphasizes the following: The National Association of Manufacturers is concerned with the development of public and private education; the industrialist is in a position to offer good advice to the educator, but he recognizes that final authority for educational decisions rests with school officials; industry must cooperate in providing leadership to secure adequate financial support for education; industry must recognize teaching as one of the great professions; and industry expects the educational enterprise to develop (a) competent citizens, (b) citizens who can make the optimum contribution to the public good, and (c) citizens who are familiar with scientific, technical, and cultural developments. Sligh closes with a plea for the constant evaluation of the offerings of the schools and makes a request that valid, reliable data should be the basis for any reconstruction of the school.*

VIEWS ON THE CURRICULUM

Charles R. Sligh, Jr.

American industry, as represented by the National Association of Manufacturers, has long been interested in educational problems and projects. In the following pages I plan to detail some of my own—and some of the Association's—ideas on how industry can cooperate with education to find solutions to some of the problems of curriculum. Before I do so, however, I want to make it clear that we consider our role to be advisory. We believe:

> That while in the choice of textbooks, determination of curricula, and formulation of teaching methods, interested individuals or lay committees may make a healthy and valuable contribution, final decisions should be left with educational administrators, teachers, or committees of teachers, subject to the general authority of boards of education or of college trustees.[1]

That quotation is from "This We Believe About Education," a 1953 statement. The publication represents the views of NAM's Educational Advisory Committee (members of its Board of Directors) and the Educational Advisory Council (professional educators representing all levels of education, public and private).

The NAM has, through its history, consistently supported education. In 1949, it formally established an Education Department to strengthen and broaden its activities in this field. We feel that the Department, through its publications and the participation of staff members in various professional projects, has done much to make apparent the mutual interests of education and industry.

Where there are mutual interests there are also, of course, mutual responsibilities. It seems to me that industry's first responsibility to public education is to provide leadership in recognizing the necessity for adequate support of schools. As early as 1941, a resolution of the NAM Board of Directors stated: ". . . that the administration and conduct of public education is an essential public service; that its reasonable financial support constitutes a necessary claim upon our American society to which other public services

Reprinted from *Harvard Educational Review,* Vol. XXVII, No. 4 (Fall 1957), pp. 239–245, by permission of the publisher.

[1] National Association of Manufacturers: *This We Believe About Education,* New York, 1953, p. 30.

of lesser value should be subordinated." Later policy statements have repeated and emphasized the point.

Industry's second major responsibility to education is to recognize teaching as one of the great professions. This we have attempted to do in many ways, the latest being the publication of the booklet, *Our Teachers: Their Importance to Our Children and to Our Community.*

Schools and teachers do not command our respect and attention in isolation. They exist to educate our young people to take their place as responsible citizens of the Republic. What, then, should industry—and the community—expect from educators? *First,* we look for the training of *competent citizens* who understand and value the nature of our free, private competitive economy and work for its improvement and preservation. *Second,* industry (and society as a whole) needs men and women who make *optimum contributions to the public good. Third,* we expect our educational institutions to familiarize young people with *scientific, technical* and *cultural developments,* providing them with new experiences and with contemporary outlooks, knowledge and concepts.

I should like now to consider, in turn, the curriculum problems associated with each of these responsibilities which society assigns to educators—attempting to show what the industrial community can do to help educators find solutions to them.

COMPETENT CITIZENSHIP

The definition of competent citizenship is probably a subject which is a perennial on the programs of educators' organization. If it is not, I would like to suggest that it should be. I would, nevertheless, like to offer my own definition. It seems to me that, at this time in our history, the competent citizen has these characteristics:

1. *He (or she) is literate.* This does not mean merely the ability to spell out words in headlines or to sign one's name. It signifies, to me, a person who reads efficiently and whose written communications are clear and understandable.

There is no more universal complaint against young employees, fresh from high school, than "they can't spell." Unless, possibly, it is "they can't add." My college teacher friends, when I tell them this, chime in and say: "They can't read." Taken literally and universally, of course, this is nonsense. But taken in terms of the demands of a job—or of higher education—it cannot be laughed off.

Now I do know enough about the language and techniques of education to know that it is important to motivate youngsters so they will *want* to learn and that one way to do this is to make the subject matter interesting. I would not presume to tell the readers of this article how to apply these principles to the teaching of fundamentals but I know it must be done. Possibly there is something industry can do to help. If there is, we should be told about it because communication is too important a skill for these criticisms to be ignored.

2. *He (or she) is competent to earn a living.* Such competence, it seems to me, comes from a combination of a good general education and such specialized training as is needed for entering the occupation of one's choice. This is, of course, most clearly seen in the learned professions. But the public schools—elementary and secondary—cannot assume that all, or even most, of their students will receive professional education. Statistics tell the story of the large number of dropouts in high school as well as the employment advantages of each year of higher education.[2] Curricula must be planned to provide the dropout with the maximum economic competence he can have *at the time he drops out.*

This *is* an area where industry can help to find solutions. In the first place, establishing programs of cooperative education (work-study courses) at the secondary school level helps keep those youngsters in school who drop out either because of lack of interest in a purely academic curriculum or for financial reasons. Local industry can also help school authorities in planning programs of vocational education which are modern and practical so that the youngster, when he goes to work, has had training which really helps him.

Plant tours, career conferences and vocational guidance materials prepared by industry also help the student to make realistic choices in planning his future. Last year NAM distributed more than a quarter of a million copies of its career planning booklet, *Your Future Is What You Make It.* When industrialists and educators work together on career guidance programs, the businessman is reminded once again that the problems and viewpoints of youth are different—but not so different—from what they were "in his time." The educator learns that industry, unlike industrialists, is always young and growing.

3. *He (or she) understands the nature of our economic system and the importance of freedom in bringing us as far as we have come in our relatively brief national history.*

In my opinion, our national history is one of the fundamentals of any American's education. I recognize that it is widely included in the curriculum. My suggestion, therefore, is not so much for "more history" as for more enthusiastic teaching of history. After all, there is no more glamorous tale of adventure than the history of the United States.

[2] *National Stay-in-School Campaign Handbook for Communities,* sponsored by the U.S. Department of Labor and the U.S. Department of Health, Education and Welfare, in cooperation with the U.S. Department of Defense. Washington, D.C.: Government Printing Office, 1957.

The situation with respect to economics is slightly different because that is a subject which is much less widely taught. In addition to the need for a wider inclusion of economics in the curriculum, it seems to the layman that the problems in teaching this subject fall into two categories: (1) what should be taught and (2) the attitude of the teacher. Let me illustrate what I mean. In planning the curriculum for a course for high school seniors, a decision has to be made as to whether to teach the history of the economy. That is a problem in the first category.

Should the decision be to do so, the rapid industrial expansion of the late nineteenth century would certainly be included. We now are confronted with a problem in the second category. No one can deny that much of what was done by these industrial pioneers would be frowned on today. Nevertheless, I know of no responsible businessman who would suggest that this period should, therefore, not be taught. However, the nineteenth century leaders should be considered in the perspective of their time and their positive contributions should be fully recognized. Even more important, the extent to which their practices differed from those of contemporary industry should be made very clear.

I believe that it is an advantage for every youngster to know and to understand all the phases of our development. However, I think that all fair-minded people expect that each new generation should be permitted to develop justifiable pride in the tremendous story of achievement instead of learning only to fear the motives of industry and business.

Similarly, in teaching the story of freedom, it is not enough to teach the early struggles of the individual against the State as an historical curiosity. Nor are we playing fair with young people in suggesting that political freedom can "stand in" for all freedom. Economic freedom has given us the material standard of living we enjoy today. Only a renewal of the understanding of the interrelationship of all freedoms will allow us to go forward to the even more promising future which is predicted for us.

Stated in another way—there are many schools, or "brands," of economics. These are tied to philosophies, many of which are different from our own—particularly with respect to the concept of the importance of the individual. It is, therefore, not enough to teach *any* economic doctrine. Nor is it sufficient for economic competence to teach only the so-called "consumer economics"—important as it is for young people to have guidance in their own saving and spending habits. It is essential that the people who will make their living in our economy know—and through knowledge learn to appreciate—its fundamentals first. Some of them will later want to make comparative studies and, if their background is good, this can only add to their appreciation of our own economic system.

Conflicts about the economy beset many young intellectuals—young teachers included. Only if they are resolved will the teacher be able to transmit confidence and pride, as well as dates and charts. In the long run, it is much more important for America that young people understand that they have something worth preserving and strengthening than for them to know the definition of an index number.

Industry can help in this connection by presenting its own story—through booklets, films, lectures, plant tours, etc.—positively and clearly and in a form appropriate for the school audience. Such teaching aids will not "convert" the teacher whose pessimism about our potential is deep-rooted but they may help to counteract its influence on the youngsters. They also provide specific information for those teachers who are emotionally "for" the competitive free enterprise system but have had little contact with business or industry and, consequently, do not have a backlog of personal experience to use in illustrating and explaining concepts. The students in our schools will achieve full economic competence only if they know how to interpret their own experiences in the light of an understanding and deep appreciation of private competitive enterprise.

The NAM educational aids are available for teachers to use—how and when they see fit. They have found considerable acceptance in the schools and we attribute this primarily to the fact that they are good educational materials, prepared with the help of educators. If you like, these materials are our "product" in the competition of ideas.

THE INDIVIDUAL AND THE PUBLIC GOOD

The second responsibility industry and the community assign to education is the development of individuals who make optimum contribution to the public good. The choice of the adjective is deliberate. Our society has thrived by emphasizing the individual and it does not seem to me that it is necessarily in the interest of the public good for anyone to become so identified with the group—any group—that his maximum contribution is to it. On the other hand, I believe that the individual who is aware of his identity, his rights—his importance—can make an optimum contribution to society.

This is markedly true of teachers. Although they are, on the whole, a dedicated group, we recognize that they must get individual rewards, attention and recognition if they are to be willing to make their optimum contribution to the community. A recent NAM publication gave this advice to communities:

> However, it is well to remember that "a school is just a school" to an out-of-town teacher fresh out of college, who is looking for a job. Like any other hopeful job aspirant, a teacher seeks career satisfaction and recognition for enthusiasm and initiative. He must be convinced that *your* school district offers these rewards.[3]

[3] *Our Teachers: Their Importance to Our Children and Our Community*, National Association of Manufacturers, New York: 1957, p. 15.

I should imagine that a return to individualism would present as much of a problem to the educational administrators as to the curriculum makers. After years in which educators have stressed "adapting to the group" and being "cooperative instead of competitive," I am suggesting that individual incentives, rewards and recognition should again be emphasized.

This is not an area where industry can present educators with an attractively bound teaching aid. However, I would like you to consider these points:

1. Research findings and experience both show that employees want and need recognition as individuals. Incidentally, about the best way to get "cooperation," whether on a bowling team or a production group, is to offer something worth competing for.

2. Many of you who will read this paper know from your own work experience that individual recognition—whether it takes the form of a pay raise, increased responsibility, or even a compliment—makes you more willing to make your best contribution to the group effort.

3. We are rearing these children to be adult citizens of a Republic whose Constitution is a basic guarantee of individual rights which, of course, have complementary responsibilities. Teachers who subordinate those rights in a classroom—or suggest to the student that he is wrong to think about them—are not giving him a realistic background for adult citizenship.

THE DEVELOPING CULTURE

Lastly, education is expected to familiarize young people with scientific, cultural and technical developments; to provide them with new experiences and with contemporary concepts, knowledge and outlooks. It is important, I think, that in this sense the efforts of the public schools not be limited to the young. The highly dynamic quality of our economy is expanding responsibilities and opportunities in the field of education. As participation in organized educational programs becomes a life-long process for more and more of our citizens, the schools will want to meet the challenge of stimulating and maintaining an interest in learning. They will, of course, also share in the retraining of people whose skills have become out-moded or been displaced.

This third function of education is, of course, closely linked with the details of curriculum. The key words, from industry's point of view, are *developments* and *contemporary*. We can help here by preparing special materials for classroom use. At first these fill the gap until the new developments get into the texts; later they can be revised constantly to illustrate continuing changes. Another function of such materials is to help the teacher relate new concepts to his own store of knowledge. Early in our so-called Atomic Age, a group of high school science students were seriously considering writing a book which would explain atomic energy to adults—particularly their parents and teachers. I understand that they felt a need to reconcile their eagerness to explore the possibilities of this new field with the adults' tendency to be awed—or bored.

Big, medium and small businesses are making it possible for teachers to augment their knowledge by having first-hand experiences in business establishments. This is important not only for the classroom teacher but also for the vocational guidance counselor, who thus becomes familiar with the ever-changing variety of jobs in business and industry.

Experienced industrialists can also help to put new knowledge into perspective by appearing before groups of students and teachers for question and answer periods. Automation is a good illustration of what I mean here. When the word first began to be used, some people erroneously assumed that skills would no longer be needed—"because all you do is push a button." An industrial engineer, who had worked with the new machines, could have told them of the increased need for skills which would accompany this new development.

FOR THE FUTURE

Educators should be the first to ask that curricula be subjected to constant evaluation. Changes should be based on valid research—not on fads or opportunism. Industry has long since discovered the value of research and we have learned that no practice, no matter how time-honored, can automatically be assumed to be efficient or effective. It would seem that significant research is needed on how and where and when to modify educational practices and policies. If such research were to become as generally accepted in education as it is in industry, curricula could be adapted to meet new conditions in community life, business, communications, science and technology.

Above all, the public schools have a responsibility to the young people, whose diverse talents and interests must be accommodated. If we are to develop in each individual his maximum productivity, creativity and skill, curricula and institutions must also be diverse.

If all the wisest men of the past went to work and devised the best curriculum they could, I think the American public schools would be well-advised if they rejected it. Because while we must learn from the past, it is our obligation to teach for the future.

Chapter 33

EDUCATIONAL SPECIFICATIONS—AS VIEWED BY THE AFL–CIO

THE *point of view of the organized labor movement in the United States is presented by Walter P. Reuther, President of the United Auto Workers International Union and Vice President of the AFL–CIO. Reuther discusses the necessity for providing all students with adequate schooling; the importance of emphasizing the discovery and cultivation of the uniqueness common to all; the significance of having the federal, state, and local governments exercise the greatest financial liberality in support of public education; the role of the liberal arts in increasing the student's understanding of American culture and other cultures; the need for educated citizens with a facility in more than one language; the value to be derived from avoiding narrow nationalism and emphasizing international cosmopolitanism. The article closes with a plea for the inclusion of the history of science as a branch of the humanities and the granting of equal weight to the teaching of humanities and technical and vocational studies.*

WHAT THE PUBLIC SCHOOLS SHOULD TEACH

Walter P. Reuther

Perhaps it is too much to expect that our current national preoccupation with costs of school construction will open a new inquiry into the more fundamental question of what to teach.

Americans have been impatient with basic questions. We solved them, presumably, long ago, and have merely been living very well, so to speak, on our original investment.

Yet the era of uncritical optimism and self-confidence is drawing to a close. Whether its formal ending came with the explosion of the first atomic bomb by the United States or the recognition by both this nation and Russia, when they agreed to meet at the summit conference of Geneva, that peace is an absolute condition of survival, is a matter for debate among hissorians.

The fact is we are already living in a new period, and there is a great lag between old assumptions that have hardened into venerable practice and the changing actualities of our lives.

Nowhere is this more true than in the field of education. So while it may seem academic, in the worst sense of that term, to raise fundamental questions about what to teach—which is very close to raising ultimate questions about our views of man—at a time when the financial crisis of our schools is so acute as to involve the viability of the very system, such as it is, there may be a very practical connection between the basic questions and the current financial dilemma.

There is always a smouldering debate, of course, over curriculum, not only among professional educators but also among lay advocates of various attitudes toward retrenchment and reform. The weakness of this debate, in my view, is two-fold.

Among educators, first, the debate seems to lose itself too quickly in considerations of method. Method, of course, is vitally important. It can affect the substance of what is taught to the point of changing it significantly. Yet it cannot replace it, as some educators seem to believe.

Reprinted from *Harvard Educational Review,* Vol. XXVII, No. 4 (Fall 1957), pp. 246–250.

The basic question remains: what to teach. No elaboration of method can evade this question. All the elaboration of method in the world, for example, will not convert a course in business administration into a history of trade-unionism. It is the commitment of our culture at its most articulate and influential levels to a business view of society that accounts for the availability of schools of business administration and for the lack of similar opportunity for study of the nature and purposes of the labor movement.

Proponents of the various views on curriculum, secondly, are in effect quarreling over the distribution of educational scarcity rather than coming to grips with the underlying lack of educational means.

Take, for example, the debate over the education of the so-called gifted child. How, from the standpoint of the average competent and well-intentioned school administrator, can a genuine program specifically devoted to the gifted child be foisted upon a community the majority of whose children are forced, by the current regime of educational scarcity, to submit to part-time schooling by over-worked and underpaid teachers?

The gifted-child approach to curriculum is as much an evasion of the full dimensions of our educational crisis as is the professional obsession with technique. In a regime of educational abundance, where there were enough teachers, enough schools, enough classrooms, where we spent as much on learning as we did on plumbing, the problem of what to teach would not disappear but it would become manageable.

Only under such a regime of educational abundance, as a matter of fact, would it be possible to develop sensible and real programs for gifted children, for only under educational abundance will we be able to pay attention to each child, to recognize the variety of growth patterns, to draw out the latent capacities of children who are not academic front-runners but who may finish strong, to their own and the community's advantage, when we can afford to lavish upon them the attention they will deserve, whatever their record on the I.Q. and aptitude tests.

The subjective bias and cultural preconceptions that permeate these testing devices are considerable, as most educators surely know. A smaller classroom population, leading to more understanding between the teacher and the dullard or eccentric in the corner, will shatter the latest reading of the tests beyond recognition. Each child is unique, we tell each other in our finer democratic moments. Let us believe that enough to create an educational system dedicated in practice as well as in theory to the discovery and cultivation of that uniqueness.

The current advocacy of special programs for the gifted child, when unaccompanied by a concern for the gross lack of educational means, is, it seems to me, an intrusion into the realm of educational discourse of a general view of democracy characteristically held by short-sighted businessmen.

I have myself advocated, and still advocate, a comprehensive federal scholarship program which would have the purpose of developing a civilian corps of men and women trained as technicians and scientists. I believe that such a program is urgently needed to end the senseless pirating of skilled manpower by industry and to put us, domestically, and in terms of our world commitments, in a competitive position to meet the long-term Russian threat.

Yet I do not believe that such a program should be conceived or operated within the present framework of penury and lack. I do not believe in robbing Peter to pay Paul, which is what such a program would amount to if it were not developed as part of a comprehensive federal-state-local program to make public education as central in our budgets as it seems to be in our democratic daydreams and professional doctrine.

Yet the notion of plunging, as it were, on the education of the gifted child is wholly compatible with the current effort of the National Association of Manufacturers and the American Chamber of Commerce to block adequate federal aid to our schools. In this context, the notion is clearly the old class notion of education. The short-sighted businessman is typically interested in two kinds of learning: the best that money can buy for his own children, and a smattering of ignorance mixed with vocational training for other people's children, who will grow up to work for him. Anything else is "frills," or subversive or both, while any departure from use of the local property tax to support public education (except for those vocational supports already forthcoming from the federal government) is anathema, since it would involve the federal taxing power.

The whole nation, of course, ultimately suffers from this niggardly view of our national educational responsibilities. There is a growing awareness now of the domestic and world consequences of the skilled manpower shortage, but it is mostly limited to a concern with this particular shortage; it has not reached the point at which the general insufficiency of our schools will be confronted. To talk of curriculum seriously now is to anticipate that juncture. What to teach must, nevertheless, it seems to me, be seriously discussed now in order that the wisest answers will be available—and in order to hasten the day when the wisest answers may be generally applied. And the leading question, I should say, should be something like the following: How does a technological, business-oriented society, wedded to a utilitarian, vocational concept of education's role, yet willing, despite ingrown anti-intellectualism, to make allowances for subordinate excursions into the liberal arts providing that such flights from "reality" do not divert us from the acquisition and proliferation of material goods—how does such a society cultivate both the necessary special skills and the necessary general culture which alone can save us from the centrifugal pull of specialization?

How do we save, in all its richness and complexity, the general fund of human experience, together with the running commentary on that experience whose continuing availability is our only guarantee of an open society, while at the same time building barriers of specialization across which our most highly trained men and women are finding it increasingly difficult to communicate with each other and with the generality of citizens?

This is not strictly an educational problem; if we ever solve it, it will be solved outside of the schools, in the arenas of our common life. Yet the schools must have their great part in helping to solve it. It will not be solved by timidity, by a stubborn insistence on the life-giving virtues of the local property tax.

I should say that perhaps our first step in solving it would be to understand that all of our particular problems, educational, economic, military, and the rest, are subsumed in the root problem of what man has done to man.

For what man has done to man, once the lament of a poet, has become the basic datum of our situation. Anything we think or do about what to teach must have this moral datum as a point of departure and arrival. Of course, we must "facilitate growth." But we are dealing with human beings, not livestock or hybrid corn. We have to be sure about whether we are facilitating the growth of perfectly-adjusted consumers, sitting ducks for the skilled technicians of motivation research, whether we are facilitating the growth of perfectly-adjusted profit-and-loss reckoners, who know the price of everything and the value of nothing, whether we are facilitating the growth of perfectly-adjusted wage-earners, who will be so coddled and numbed by the personnel department that they will live their lives to its tempo—or whether we are fostering the growth of men and of man.

In the latter case, we must look to much more than the critical shortage of skilled manpower. We must do much more than send the upper percentiles to college, while we shunt the lower percentiles into the vocational schools. Such a course is cynical and defeatist, and what we fondly call the free world can die of it.

I think that we must look to the general disciplines, to the human or humanist disciplines, to the liberal arts. I think we must look to English, to history, to foreign languages, to a study, from what might be called the inside, of other cultures than our own.

I think every American child should learn a second language as well as he learns American English, that this study should begin in the primary grades. I believe that the studies of other countries should be pursued to some extent from the viewpoint of those countries as well as from our viewpoint, while we push the UNESCO and any other fruitful efforts to write histories that are not blinded or misshapen by narrow nationalism.

I think we should teach the history of science as a branch of the humanities, trying to make as much of it as possible available to as many students as possible as early as possible in the primary and secondary grades.

It is my view that the study of the humanities must rank with the vocational and technical studies in our public schools. I think no current or future pressure for skilled manpower should push us into forgetfulness that these general disciplines constitute our long-range hope that, whatever the complexities of a technological society, men will still be knitted together in the creative and truly democratic fellowship of a common awareness of the human record.

These are some of the broad lines along which, in my opinion, the curriculum of our public schools can be strengthened. I am sure, though, that all discussion of curriculum is and will remain "academic" as far as its wholesome effect on most of our children is concerned, as long as we timidly accept the current stranglehold upon education of the penny-wise, democracy-foolish viewpoint fostered by the National Association of Manufacturers and the United States Chamber of Commerce.

Chapter 34

EDUCATIONAL SPECIFICATIONS—AS VIEWED BY THE NATIONAL EDUCATION ASSOCIATION

AMERICAN *educators, as individuals and as members of study groups, committees, and commissions, have made and continue to make notable contributions to a further clarification of educational objectives. The contribution of The Educational Policies Commission, appointed by the National Education Association of the United States and the American Association of School Administrators, represents the point of view of many American educators. On the basis of a careful study of the literature pertaining to this problem and an examination of the development of American society and American education, the Commission prepared the statement that follows.*

THE PURPOSES OF EDUCATION IN AMERICAN DEMOCRACY

Educational Policies Commission, National Education Association

. . . four aspects of educational purpose have been identified. These aspects center around the person himself, his relationships to others in home and community, the creation and use of material wealth, and socio-civic activities. The first area calls for a description of the educated *person;* the second, for a description of the educated *member of the family and community group;* the third, of the educated *producer or consumer;* the fourth, of the educated *citizen.* The four great groups of objectives thus defined are:

1. The Objectives of Self-Realization
2. The Objectives of Human Relationship
3. The Objectives of Economic Efficiency
4. The Objectives of Civic Responsibility.

Each of these is related to each of the others. Each is capable of further subdivision.

THE OBJECTIVES OF SELF-REALIZATION

The Inquiring Mind. The educated person has an appetite for learning.

Speech. The educated person can speak the mother tongue clearly.

Reading. The educated person reads the mother tongue efficiently.

Writing. The educated person writes the mother tongue effectively.

Number. The educated person solves his problems of counting and calculating.

Sight and Hearing. The educated person is skilled in listening and observing.

Health Knowledge. The educated person understands the basic facts concerning health and disease.

Reprinted from *The Purposes of Education in American Democracy* (Washington, D.C.: Educational Policies Commission, National Education Association of the United States and the American Association of School Administrators, 1938), pp. 47, 50, 72, 90, 108.

Health Habits. The educated person protects his own health and that of his dependents.

Public Health. The educated person works to improve the health of the community.

Recreation. The educated person is participant and spectator in many sports and other pastimes.

Intellectual Interests. The educated person has mental resources for the use of leisure.

Esthetic Interests. The educated person appreciates beauty.

Character. The educated person gives responsible direction to his own life.

THE OBJECTIVES OF HUMAN RELATIONSHIP

Respect for Humanity. The educated person puts human relationships first.

Friendship. The educated person enjoys a rich, sincere, and varied social life.

Cooperation. The educated person can work and play with others.

Courtesy. The educated person observes the amenities of social behavior.

Appreciation of the Home. The educated person appreciates the family as a social institution.

Conservation of the Home. The educated person conserves family ideals.

Homemaking. The educated person is skilled in homemaking.

Democracy in the Home. The educated person maintains democratic family relationships.

THE OBJECTIVES OF ECONOMIC EFFICIENCY

Work. The educated producer knows the satisfaction of good workmanship.

Occupational Information. The educated producer understands the requirements and opportunities for various jobs.

Occupational Choice. The educated producer has *selected* his occupation.

Occupational Efficiency. The educated producer succeeds in his chosen vocation.

Occupational Adjustment. The educated producer maintains and improves his efficiency.

Occupational Appreciation. The educated producer appreciates the social value of his work.

Personal Economics. The educated consumer plans the economics of his own life.

Consumer Judgment. The educated consumer develops standards for guiding his expenditures.

Efficiency in Buying. The educated consumer is an informed and skillful buyer.

Consumer Protection. The educated consumer takes appropriate measures to safeguard his interests.

THE OBJECTIVES OF CIVIC RESPONSIBILITY

Social Justice. The educated citizen is sensitive to the disparities of human circumstance.

Social Activity. The educated citizen acts to correct unsatisfactory conditions.

Social Understanding. The educated citizen seeks to understand social structures and social processes.

Critical Judgment. The educated citizen has defenses against propaganda.

Tolerance. The educated citizen respects honest differences of opinion.

Conservation. The educated citizen has a regard for the nation's resources.

Social Applications of Science. The educated citizen measures scientific advance by its contribution to the general welfare.

World Citizenship. The educated citizen is a cooperating member of the world community.

Law Observance. The educated citizen respects the law.

Economic Literacy. The educated citizen is economically literate.

Political Citizenship. The educated citizen accepts his civic duties.

Devotion to Democracy. The educated citizen acts upon an unswerving loyalty to democratic ideals.

Chapter 35

EDUCATIONAL SPECIFICATIONS—AS VIEWED BY A LOCAL BOARD OF EDUCATION

LOCAL *school authorities have found it advantageous to formulate statements of objectives for the orientation and guidance of school personnel, to acquaint the public with the thinking of the school authorities, and to inform other interested communities of the progress being made. An example of this activity is the statement formulated by the Board of Education of New York City.*

AIMS AND OBJECTIVES OF EDUCATION

Board of Education of the City of New York

The fundamental aims and objectives of public education in New York City are in accordance with our democratic traditions and are based on the individual's needs for effective living. To fulfill these broad purposes of education in New York City, the following specific objectives have been accepted:

Reprinted from "Curriculum Development in the Elementary Schools," *Curriculum Bulletin No. 1, 1955–56 Series*, pp. 2–3, by permission of the Board of Education of the City of New York.

Character. To develop the basis for rich, useful, moral and ethical living in a society promoting the common welfare.

Our American Heritage. To develop pride and faith in American democracy and respect for the dignity and worth of individuals and peoples, regardless of race, religion, nationality or socio-economic status.

Health. To develop and maintain a sound body and to establish wholesome mental and emotional attitudes and habits.

Exploration. To discover, develop and direct individual interests, aptitudes and abilities.

Knowledge and Skills. To develop command, in accordance with ability, of the common integrating habits, learnings and skills.

Thinking. To stimulate the inquiring mind and sound thinking functionally necessary for the development of reasoning based upon adequate hypotheses, supported by facts and principles.

Appreciation and Expression. To develop an appreciation and enjoyment of beauty and to develop powers of creative expression.

Social Relationships. To develop desirable social attitudes and relationships within the family, the school and the community.

Economic Relationships. To develop an awareness and appreciation of economic processes and of all who serve in the world of work.

Achievement of these broad objectives is the goal of a curriculum consisting of many worth-while experiences specifically planned to meet the many different needs of each child. The school is concerned with the child's physical self, his social adjustment, his emotional growth, his spiritual attitudes and ethical values, as well as his intellectual development. The responsibility of the school in meeting these needs lies in giving children a sound core of knowledge, understanding, skill and competence, wholesome interests and ideals, and an inquiring mind. Guided by moral and spiritual standards, an inquiring mind and sound thinking are the distinguishing marks of a truly civilized man or woman. It is the inquiring mind of leaders during various periods of world history that has stimulated mankind to take stock of its resources and then to take logical steps forward. Such minds have influenced progress in the arts as well as in the sciences. Linked with sound thinking and under the control of moral and spiritual values, an inquiring mind is our assurance of integrity of character and of dynamic and responsible American citizenship in the best tradition of our founding fathers.

Chapter 36

THE ROLE OF THE STATE

PRIOR *to implementation, the recommendations of individuals, study groups, committees, and commissions must receive the approval of state education officials because primary legal authority for the conduct of public education is vested in the state. The role of the individual state in the operation of education within it raises complex issues. Alonzo G. Grace, an educator, identifies the problem: Does effective democratic action require the centralization of educational organization and administration, or does it require the strengthening of local initiative, responsibility, and control?*

THE STATE'S RESPONSIBILITY FOR A REASONABLE EDUCATIONAL PROGRAM

Alonzo G. Grace

DEMOCRACY MEANS GROWTH FROM THE BOTTOM UP

If public education is to be conceived of as the cornerstone of the democratic order, it is essential that the school system itself be organized on a democratic basis. It is important, too, that local initiative and responsibility be recognized as the central element prerequisite to democratic action. It probably is true that progress may be made more rapidly through centralized procedures. Such progress, however, may not clearly reflect the needs or desires of a people. Efficiency in government involves more than effective management. While it is important that there be efficient organization, it is

Reprinted from *Harvard Educational Review*, Vol. XV, No. 1 (January 1945), pp. 15–21.

infinitely more important that the continued interest of the people be assured, for without the sustained interest of the governed and the intelligent participation of the people in the conduct of government, efficiency is at best but partial. One of the major problems today is that of insuring an intelligent attitude toward the democratic organization. There is no better place to start than in the educational system.

In a democratic organization, the wisdom and intelligence of both citizens and educators should be used to the fullest advantage in the development of an educational program. In order that the public be thoroughly familiar with the need for redirection of a school program, the problems involved, the new procedures recommended, it is equally essential that the lay public be kept informed concerning needed educational changes. It means continued participation in the study and discussion of educational problems by citizens and by educators alike. Growth from the bottom up is infinitely more important than domination from the top down.

The trend in our nation during the past fifty years has been toward the strengthening of state and Federal government at the expense of the local unit. While it is obvious that many units of government conceived during the pioneer era in the evolution of American Democracy no longer are able to provide independently and separately all the services now required for the security of a people, or devised for their security by those who seek the perfect state, the solution does not lie in the creation of a super-state or Federal government. This ultimately would lead to a people of the government, by the government, and for the government.

Toulmin Smith in 1851 defined local self-government and centralization in his treatise on this subject as follows:[1]

> *Local self-government* is that system of government under which the greater number of minds, knowing the most, and having the fullest opportunity of knowing it, about the special matters at hand, and having the greatest interest in its well working, have the management of it or control over it.
>
> *Centralization* is that system of government under which the smallest number of minds and those knowing the least and having the fewest opportunities of knowing it, about the special matter in hand, and having the smallest interest in its well working, have the management of it or the control over it.

The definitions may not reflect the dangers confronting local government. But John Fiske says in his comment on this treatise, "An immense amount of wretched misgovernment would be avoided if all legislators and all voters would engrave these wholesome definitions upon their minds."[2]

[1] John Fiske, *Civil Government in the United States* (Boston: Houghton Mifflin and Co., 1890), p. 274.

[2] *Ibid.*, p. 274.

How much government is essential to protect the sovereign people from their own inadequacies? Are we able to distinguish administration from policy determination? What is the capacity or the ability of people to pay for an adequate system of social control? The solution to America's problem of self-government does not lie solely in effective organization or effective management. *Without the sustained interest of the governed, the policy-determining function which belongs to the people may be absorbed by those not so seriously interested in democracy, by specialists who may be more interested in the area of specialization than in the welfare of the people, or by a great bureaucracy of vested interests.*

The success or failure of government and the quality of service it renders rests, in the last analysis, upon the capacity and the character of the men and women who constitute it. There must be in government men and women who have capacity and character and who believe implicitly in rendering a service rather than in building up a vested interest.

America will preserve local initiative and responsibility only if there be a willingess on the part of all elements locally to improve the local governmental structure in the interests of the whole people instead of permitting aggressive minorities and political expediency to dominate the needs of the group. Unless those locally are willing to assume the responsibility for a more effective organization, for the placement of men and women of character and capacity in positions of government, and for continuous citizen participation in the determination of policy, the trend will be towards units of government far removed from the people.

THE OBLIGATION OF THE STATE

The obligation of the state to establish and to maintain a system of education for all the children of all the people has been accepted as a fundamental principle of American education since the enactment of the Massachusetts school law in 1647. The re-statement of this principle in state constitutions, in the general statutes of the several states, and in decisions of the courts is evidence of the general acceptance of education as a major state responsibility. Public education through the generations, however, has been administered largely through the instrumentality of various local school units. The responsibility not only to provide a system of education but also to designate the means to support and to design the supporting machinery is the indisputable function of the state.

The primary function of a state is to provide sound guidance and leadership in the development of the educational program, to render those services that cannot be provided by individual school systems or which may be supplied more effectively by the state, and to provide research and planning. Let us discuss briefly these three elements in state organizations.

Guidance and Leadership

Wise leadership in a democratic order makes full use of the wisdom of the individual members therein. A leadership of merit insofar as a state department of education is concerned must be based on sound scholarship and upon the general acceptance of certain basic principles. For example, the ideal of quality in educational thinking must supplant past trends toward quantity. An implicit belief in local government as the basic safety valve of democracy must be developed. There must be a willingness to keep the schools close to the people and the people close to the schools.

The consolidation of school districts and schools may serve as an example of educational leadership in some of our communities in many of our states. In some instances, however, consolidation has been sold on the basis of economy. However, it costs more to maintain a consolidated school in the long run than it does to maintain the so-called one-teacher school.

America has attempted to solve the problem of the one-teacher school by one method, namely, by consolidation, rather than to attempt to make the one-teacher school, so-called, an effective part of the educational organization. In many cases, consolidation has done little more than centralize all the existing problems. In other cases, magnificent services and programs are available. There is no general pattern. It may be possible, in many of our states, to create a small attendance area, perhaps with a minimum of two teachers and thirty pupils. A most effective educational experience may result from removing the seventh and eighth grades to regional high schools; eliminating the present grade system; creating a lower elementary school with grades one to three inclusive and an additional year for remedial work for those who are unable to make normal progress; creating an upper elementary school, grades four to six inclusive, with another additional year for those who are unable to make normal progress.

A major problem is to get full value out of every dollar expended. The leadership of a department is important in preventing lag in the educational system and also in making the best possible use of the available resources. The quality of leadership on the part of the state, therefore, must be such that local school systems will have confidence not only in the advice and suggestions which emanate from the state leadership but also in the scholarship and in the ability of the individual members therein. It is important that the contribution of the state be accepted on the basis of its worth. Statutory responsibility should be carried out in a statesmanlike manner. There should not be domination or the superimposing of concepts or the dogmatic and arbitrary administration of the school program. This is not leadership. It is a sort of authoritarian domination feared so much by so many people. There is no substitute for common sense in educational administration. A state's function is to lead, not to dominate.

Service

A second function of the state is to render those services which cannot be provided by individual school systems or which may be supplied more effectively by the state. The service function of a state department should be such as to expedite the work of the local school systems. It should neither impede progress nor should it handicap the effective administrative operation of a school system or the instructional process therein. A service so effective, so valuable, and so close to realism that it makes itself indispensable to local school systems should be the goal of the state. Supervision, for example, is a service of a state department, but too frequently in this country, supervision, instead of becoming an aid to the improvement of instruction, merely becomes an inspectorial or routine procedure of little value in the ultimate progress of a school system. Supervision should be regarded as a scholarly, useful, worth-while aid in the development of an educational program and in the improvement of teaching practices and procedures. Supervision to be effective, therefore, is contingent very largely on the personnel of a department. Unless the individual is accepted because of his ability to contribute to the improvement of a program and to the child's educational opportunity, his service frequently becomes negligible. Too frequently the amount of red tape, misunderstanding, unnecessary services and programs and a host of other problems arise because of those who have not visualized the true significance of service.

Research and Planning

Millions of dollars are spent for research in industry, business, and agriculture. There would be little progress in either were it not for the confidence of our leaders in the value of research in these fields. Research improves processes and products. In agriculture, tremendous sums are invested in the study of plants, animals, soil, poultry, fruit, and in literally hundreds of areas. On the other hand, comparatively small amounts are spent by state and by local boards of education for research or planning. And yet fundamental policies, in many cases, depend upon wise research and planning, as these terms are generally understood. Research and planning on the state level or on the local level, for that matter, can be concerned only with the "here and now problem" or, in other words, with immediate problems. We must develop a close relationship and establish channels to the sources of scholarly research in major universities and colleges that have demonstrated their ability to do basic research.

Do we need more surveys? It seems to me that we have sufficient wisdom and intelligence within our own states to initiate a plan that best fits the needs in each of the several states. It is essential that a state put its own house in order. This is not a criticism of the survey, but we need more than reports now. We need action. We need leadership in our states.

A PROPOSAL FOR ACTION

There must be a complete separation of politics and education. The children of America should not be the victims of changing administrations, of a spoils system, of indiscriminate changes in school systems. An opportunity must be afforded educational leaders to express their judgments courageously on the educational issues that confront our respective states. Courageous administration in many communities of America virtually is impossible, for it means the replacement of the educational leader.

Our boards of education in America have thousands of conscientious, courageous citizens who devote untold time to the establishment of educational policy. The board of education is the most fundamental and important office in the community. Our boards of education should be composed of independent thinking citizens who believe in their community, who believe in the children of the community, and who are willing to see that the citizens of tomorrow are provided every opportunity for the fullest development of their capacities.

The following plan is suggested as one which would retain administration at the local level and which would tend to create a more effective educational structure.

The Development of a National Planning Commission

It is recommended that the National Education Association, American Council on Education, American Vocational Association, the Association of School Administrators, and the U.S. Office of Education develop a national planning commission similar to the organization of education for defense originally initiated by the American Council on Education and ultimately sponsored by all voluntary educational organizations in America. This body subsequently was superseded by the U.S. Office of Education Commission on Education and Wartime Activities.

A national planning institute should be held each year. This congress of American educational organizations should devise a procedure for coordinating efforts, eliminating duplication, and cooperating toward the attainment of the common objectives of education in our country.

RECOMMENDED CHANGES IN STRUCTURE

I. *National Government*

A. *National Board of Education*

There is need for a national board of education which would (1) coordinate all educational matters at the federal level through an interdepartmental education committee; (2) identify problems, collect statistical data, and develop research programs at the national level; (3) advise educational institutions concerning the pertinent research and experimentation in the colleges, universities, business and industry, agriculture, and elsewhere in the country; (4) develop advisory policies with respect to national problems; (5) select the United States Commissioner of Education; (6) appoint an advisory council of American educational organizations—this should be an American council on education or a conference of educational organizations. An independent body of this nature, properly organized, would be an impelling force on the governmental organization, for it would represent all American education—not simply the public enterprise. The functions of such a board could be specifically limited by congressional act. There would be no danger of federal control, or of a ministry of education, or of a great bureaucracy, provided the appointments to the board were on the basis of statesmanship and not political affiliation or partisanship.

It is recommended that a board of nine citizens be appointed by the President of the United States for overlapping terms of nine years. In other words, that each member serve a period of nine years and that the various sections of our country rather than specialized interests be represented on such board. It is further recommended that the board be composed of citizens not associated with the educational enterprise in a professional capacity.

B. *Federal Aid*

There is need for financial aid at the federal level. It is recommended, however, that when federal aid is allocated that thorough consideration be given to the efforts on the part of the state and locality to support an educational program and to the efforts to secure adequate state-aid plans.

II. *The State Structure*

A. *State board of education*

Each state shall provide for a state board of education to be composed of outstanding citizens. A board of seven or nine with overlapping terms is recommended. The functions of this board should be specified by statute. One of its responsibilities should be to select a commissioner of education to serve at the pleasure of the board.

B. *State department of education*

Strong state departments of education, having school personnel selected on the basis of merit, should be developed.

III. *The Local Educational Structure*

A. *Board of education*

The local board of education at the present time really functions as a board of schools. Under the board of education ultimately should be consolidated libraries and recreation programs. Members should be allocated without regard to party label.

B. *A superintendent of education*

It is recommended that there be selected a superintendent of education who would be the administrator of schools, colleges, libraries, recreation programs under public auspices.

C. *The citizens advisory committee*

It is recommended that each board of education through the executive officer appoint a citizen advisory committee representing the various organizations and agencies locally in order that policies suggested by the board may have the benefit of the counsel of the variety of interests represented in the local community.

D. *Democratic administration*

Close the gap between administration and the classroom leader. It is recommended that democratic planning become part of the local school organization procedure. Too frequently, salary schedules or educational programs are adopted by the board upon recommendation of the executive without bringing into the planning procedure the excellent talent available in most school systems.

To accomplish our objective there must be a united American education. No longer can we segregate ourselves into compartments or into vested interests. No longer should there be an education at a state level, education at a local level, education at a federal level. We cannot operate if American education is divided into fifty-seven varieties. We must have a united American education. It is time that we stand together, and dozens of American education organizations of this country can stand together as is being demonstrated now in this war period. There need be no fear as to the development of a fundamental program by educators for the country. We have work to do.

PART EIGHT

Educational Institutions

THERE are fifty-one school systems under public auspices in the United States. In addition, there exists a corresponding complex of schools maintained under private auspices, both secular and sectarian, that also strive to fulfill the commonly accepted goals of American education. The institutional arrangements that have been created for this purpose are many and varied, and their continued growth reflects a deepening public awareness of the significance of education in a democratic society. It is customary today to identify educational institutions as belonging to one of two types: formal institutions and informal institutions. Schools, colleges, and universities are recognized as formal agencies, while the home, church, political clubs, settlement houses, community centers, and mass media of communication are informal. Each in its own way contributes to the maturation and socialization of the individual.[1]

Our discussion at this point deals with the organizational structure and the roles of the formal educational institutions. That formal education in the United States is "big business" is attested by the enrollment figures for the academic year 1964–1965: The United States Office of Education has estimated an enrollment of approximately 65,600,000 students in the public and private elementary and secondary schools, colleges, and universities. It was estimated that approximately 41,200,000 students would be enrolled in kindergarten and grades one through eight; 12,700,000 in grades nine through twelve; and 4,800,000 in colleges and universities. Of the numbers enrolled in kindergarten through twelfth grade, 42,000,000 were expected to attend public institutions, and 11,600,000 pupils were expected to attend private schools.[2]

[1] For a discussion of this influence upon the individual, see R. J. Havighurst, "How Education Changes Society," *Confluence, an International Forum*, Vol. 6 (Spring 1957), 85–96.

[2] As reported in *The New York Times*, September 6, 1964.

Chapter 37

GENERAL STATISTICS

THE *following statistics, a breakdown of the 1962–1963 enrollment, cover enrollments in all types of schools, pupil retention from the fifth grade to entrance into college, percentages of degree-credit students enrolled in higher education, earned degrees conferred by colleges and universities, and teacher-pupil ratio in elementary and secondary schools. The data here are the latest available from governmental agencies.*

ENROLLMENT, 1962–1963

Office of Education,
United States Department of Health,
Education and Welfare

Enrollments in Educational Institutions. Below the college level, education in the United States can best be described as free, compulsory, and nearly universal. Over 96 percent of the total population age 6 through 17 are enrolled in public or nonpublic schools. In the age range 14 through 17, over 90 percent are enrolled in school. Almost 70 percent of the secondary school

Reprinted from *Progress of Public Education in the United States of America 1962–1963,* Office of Education, United States Department of Health, Education and Welfare, U.S. Government Printing Office, Washington, D.C., 1963, pp. 5–9, 11.

age group graduate from secondary schools. Moreover, about half the graduates of secondary schools enter college, and many others continue their education in commercial, trade, and technical schools not associated with colleges or universities.

Pupil Rentention. Up to the fifth grade, it is assumed, State compulsory education laws keep virtually all children in school. The left-hand column of figure 1 shows the retention of fifth grade pupils of the year 1924–25. For each thousand who enrolled in that year, 612 entered high school (ninth grade) in the fall of 1928, 302 graduated from high school in the spring of

TABLE 1. OFFICE OF EDUCATION ENROLLMENT ESTIMATES: UNITED STATES, 1961–62 AND 1962–63

[*Estimates are for total enrollment during the school year. These figure are larger than figures for fall enrollment.*]

TYPE OF SCHOOL, BY GRADE LEVEL	1961–62	1962–63
Total, elementary, secondary, and higher education	49,300,000	51,300,000
Kindergarten through grade 8	34,200,000	35,000,000
Public school system (regular full-time)	28,700,000	29,400,000
Nonpublic schools (regular full-time)	5,300,000	5,400,000
Other schools[1]	200,000	200,000
Grades 9 through 12	10,800,000	11,700,000
Public school system (regular full-time)	9,500,000	10,300,000
Nonpublic schools (regular full-time)	1,200,000	1,300,000
Other schools[1]	100,000	100,000
Kindergarten through grade 12	45,000,000	46,700,000
Public school system (regular full-time)	38,200,000	39,700,000
Nonpublic schools (regular full-time)	6,500,000	6,700,000
Other schools[1]	300,000	300,000
Higher education: Universities, colleges, professional schools, junior colleges, normal schools, and teachers colleges (degree-credit enrollment)	4,300,000	4,600,000

1 Includes Federal schools for Indians, federally operated elementary-secondary schools on posts, model and practice schools in teacher training institutions, subcollegiate departments of colleges, and residential schools for exceptional children.

NOTE: The figures in this table are all estimates for 50 states and the District of Columbia. Those for 1961–62 have been compared with fall 1961 enrollment statistics which have subsequently become available. In the case of nonpublic elementary and secondary schools, the only fall enrollment data come from a sample survey and are subject to sampling variation; consequently the estimates for nonpublic schools require proportionately more revision than do those for public schools or for higher education. The estimates for 1962–63 are derived from the increases expected from population changes combined with the long-run trend in school enrollment rates of the population.

TABLE 2. ENROLLMENT IN GRADES 9–12 IN PUBLIC AND NONPUBLIC SCHOOLS, AND POPULATION 14–17 YEARS OF AGE: UNITED STATES, 1889–90 TO 1962–63

SCHOOL YEAR	ENROLLMENT, GRADES 9–12 AND POSTGRADUATE[1]			POPULATION 14–17 YEARS OF AGE[2]	TOTAL NUMBER ENROLLED PER 100 PERSONS 14–17 YEARS OF AGE
	ALL SCHOOLS	PUBLIC SCHOOLS	NONPUBLIC SCHOOLS		
1889–90	359,949	[3]202,963	[3]94,931	5,354,653	6.7
1949–50	6,453,009	5,757,810	695,199	8,404,768	76.8
1951–52	6,596,351	5,917,384	678,967	[4]8,525,000	77.4
1953–54	7,108,973	6,330,565	778,408	[4]8,878,000	80.1
1955–56	7,774,975	6,917,790	857,185	[4]9,229,000	84.2
1957–58	8,868,586	7,905,569	963,017	[4]10,164,000	87.3
1959–60[5]	9,599,810	8,531,454	1,608,356	11,154,879	86.1
1961–62[6]	10,800,000	9,600,000	1,200,000	12,027,000	89.8
1962–63[6]	11,700,000	10,400,000	1,300,000	12,900,000	90.7

1 Unless otherwise indicated, includes enrollment in subcollegiate departments of institutions of higher education and in residential schools for exceptional children. Beginning in 1949–50, also includes Federal schools.

2 Includes all persons residing in continental United States, but excludes Armed Forces overseas. Data shown are actual figures from the decennial censuses of population unless otherwise indicated.

3 Excludes enrollment in subcollegiate departments of institutions of higher education and in residential schools for exceptional children.

4 Estimated by the Bureau of the Census as of July 1 preceding the opening of the school year.

5 Final data for 50 States and the District of Columbia.

6 Preliminary data for 50 States and the District of Columbia.

NOTE: Unless otherwise indicated, data are for 48 states and the District of Columbia.

SOURCE: U.S. Department of Health, Education, and Welfare, Office of Education, *Biennial Survey of Education in the United States;* Press Release HEW–U98 and unpublished data of the U.S. Office of Education.

1932, and 118 entered college the following school year. For each 1,000 pupils who were enrolled in the fifth grade in 1954, 919 entered high school in the fall of 1958, an increase over the 30 years of more than 50 percent; 636 out of the 1,000 pupils graduated from high school in the spring of 1962, an increase of 110 percent over the number who graduated 30 years earlier; and 336 pupils of the original 1,000 entered college the following year, an increase of 184 percent over the number who entered college in 1932.

Degree-Credit Students in Eight Types of Higher Education Institutions. Seven of the eight types of institutions shown in Figure 2 are known as "4-year" institutions. All except the junior colleges are called 4-year institutions because they grant degrees (or recognition equivalent to degrees) which are based on four or more academic years of college-level work. These

TABLE 3. NUMBER OF HIGH SCHOOL GRADUATES COMPARED WITH POPULATION 17 YEARS OF AGE: UNITED STATES, 1869–70 TO 1961–62

SCHOOL YEAR	POPULATION 17 YEARS OF AGE[2]	HIGH SCHOOL GRADUATES[1]			NUMBER GRADUATED PER 100 PERSONS 17 YEARS OF AGE
		TOTAL	BOYS	GIRLS	
1869–70	815,000	16,000	7,064	8,936	2.0
1939–40	2,403,074	1,221,475	578,718	642,757	50.8
1949–50	2,034,450	1,199,700	570,700	629,000	59.0
1951–52	2,040,800	1,196,500	569,200	627,300	58.6
1953–54	2,128,600	1,276,100	612,500	663,600	60.0
1955–56	2,270,000	1,414,800	679,500	735,300	62.3
1957–58	2,324,000	1,505,900	725,500	780,400	64.8
1959–60[3]	2,862,005	1,864,000	898,000	966,000	65.1
1961–62[3]	2,765,000	1,930,000	940,000	990,000	69.8

1 Includes graduates from public and nonpublic schools.
2 U.S. Bureau of the Census.
3 Preliminary data for 50 States and the District of Columbia.

NOTE: Unless otherwise indicated, data are for 48 States and the District of Columbia.

SOURCE: U.S. Department of Health, Education, and Welfare, Office of Education, *Biennial Survey of Education in the United States.*

4-year institutions confer either bachelor's degrees, or higher degrees, or both. The junior colleges offer at least 2 years of work, but less than 4, and do not grant bachelor's or higher degrees.

A degree-credit student is one whose current program, in a 4-year institution of higher education or a junior college, consists wholly or principally of work which is normally creditable toward a bachelor's or higher degree—either in the student's own institution or by transfer (as from a junior college to a 4-year institution).[1] Only degree-credit students are included in the analysis in Figure 2.

The data for the fall of 1962 are derived from a survey of the 2,043 institutions in the aggregate United States which offer degree-credit programs. The "aggregate United States" includes the 48 contiguous States, the noncontiguous States of Alaska and Hawaii, and the outlying parts; there are institutions of higher education in three of the outlying parts—Canal Zone, Guam, and Puerto Rico.

Earned Degrees Conferred. More bachelor's degrees were conferred in 1949–50 than in any other year, since many veterans of World War II completed their education in that year. The estimated number of bachelor's

1 Students in technical institutes or terminal-occupational programs are not counted as degree-credit students. Students whose work is of the degree-credit type are counted as degree-credit students, whether or not they plan to complete the program required for a degree.

FIGURE 1. APPROXIMATE RETENTION, FIFTH GRADE THROUGH COLLEGE ENTRANCE: UNITED STATES, 1924–32 AND 1954–62

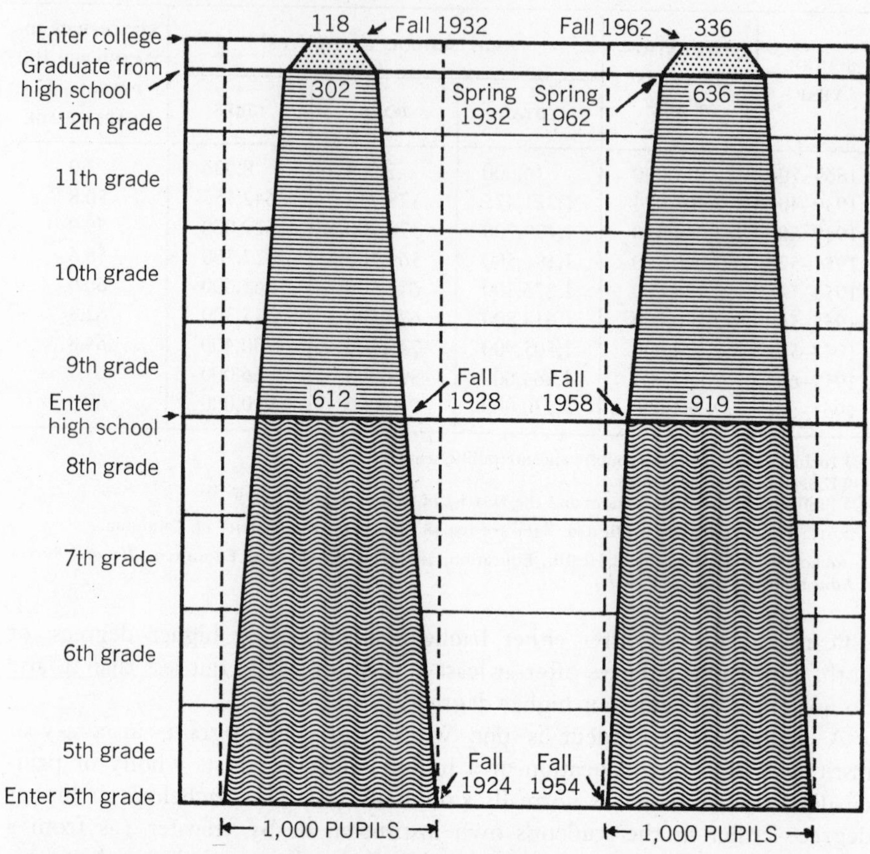

NOTE: Data are for 48 States and the District of Columbia.
SOURCE: U.S. Department of Health, Education, and Welfare, Office of Education, *Biennial Survey of Education in the United States.*

degrees for 1962–63 exceeds by nearly 5,000 the number granted in 1949–50. The number of graduate degrees now being conferred is higher than at any previous time.

TEACHER-PUPIL RATIO

Enrollments and Teacher-Pupil Ratio. In the fall of 1957 the pupil-teacher ratio was 26.2 in public elementary and secondary day schools. By the fall of 1962 the ratio had dropped to 25.7. In the elementary school for the same period, the pupil-teacher ratio dropped from 29.1 to 28.5. In the secondary schools the ratio increased from 21.3 to 21.7.

FIGURE 2. PERCENTAGES OF DEGREE-CREDIT STUDENTS ENROLLED IN THE VARIOUS TYPES OF INSTITUTIONS OF HIGHER EDUCATION: UNITED STATES AND OUTLYING PARTS, FALL 1962

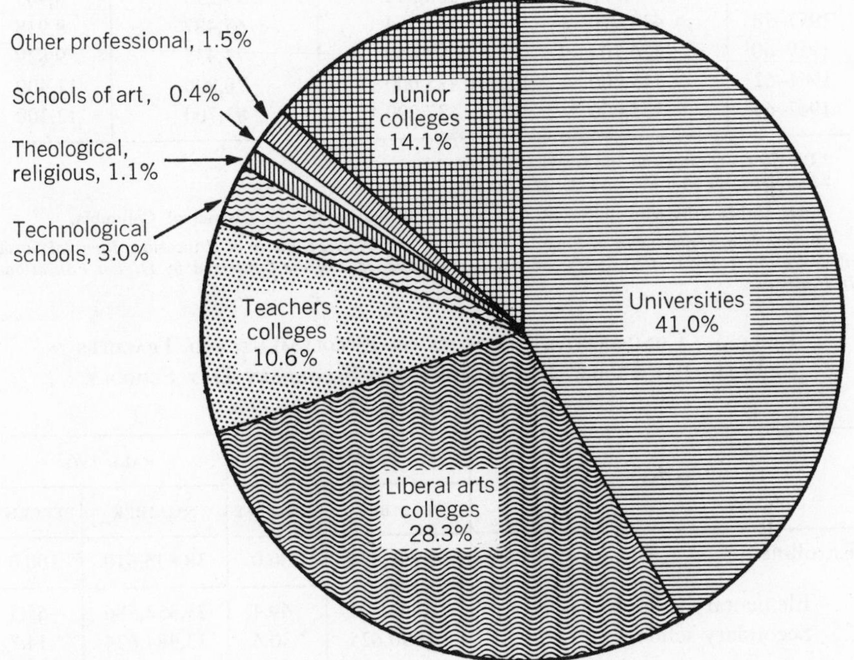

SOURCE: U.S. Department of Health, Education, and Welfare, Office of Education, *Survey of Opening (Fall) Enrollment in Higher Education, 1962.*

TABLE 4. EARNED DEGREES CONFERRED BY INSTITUTIONS OF HIGHER EDUCATION: UNITED STATES, 1869–70 TO 1962–63

ACADEMIC YEAR	EARNED DEGREES CONFERRED			
	ALL DEGREES	BACHELOR'S AND FIRST PROFESSIONAL	MASTER'S, EXCEPT FIRST PROFESSIONAL	DOCTOR'S
1869–70	9,372	9,371	0	1
1949–50	496,874	432,058	58,183	6,633
1951–52	401,203	329,986	63,534	7,683
1953–54	356,608	290,825	56,788	8,995
1955–56	376,973	308,812	59,258	8,903
1957–58	436,979	362,554	65,487	8,938
1959–60[1]	476,704	392,440	74,435	9,829
1961–62[2]	515,200	425,000	78,800	11,400
1962–63[2]	533,000	437,000	83,700	12,300

1 Data for 50 States and the District of Columbia.
2 Estimates for 50 States and the District of Columbia.

NOTE: Unless otherwise indicated, data are for 48 States and the District of Columbia.

SOURCE: U.S. Department of Health, Education, and Welfare, Office of Education, *Biennial Survey of Education in the United States* and circulars on *Earned Degrees Conferred by Higher Educational Institutions.*

TABLE 5. COMPARATIVE STATISTICS ON ENROLLMENT AND TEACHERS IN FULL-TIME PUBLIC ELEMENTARY AND SECONDARY DAY SCHOOLS: UNITED STATES, FALL 1957 AND 1962

ITEM	FALL 1957		FALL 1962	
	NUMBER	PERCENT	NUMBER	PERCENT
Enrollment	32,951,426	100.0	38,836,610	100.0
Elementary schools	22,860,801	69.4	25,352,586	65.3
Secondary schools	10,090,625	30.6	13,484,624	34.7
Pupils in excess of normal capacity	1,953,800	100.0	1,666,711	100.0
Elementary schools	1,341,577	68.7	914,510	54.9
Secondary schools	612,223	31.3	752,201	45.1
Classroom teachers	1,259,206	100.0	1,511,251	100.0
Elementary schools	785,838	62.4	889,012	58.8
Secondary schools	473,368	37.6	622,239	41.2

NOTE: Data are for 50 States and the District of Columbia.

SOURCE: U.S. Department of Health, Education, and Welfare, Office of Education, Press Release HEW–W18, January 9, 1963.

Chapter 38

THE LADDER SYSTEM: THE STRUCTURE OF EDUCATION IN THE UNITED STATES

To serve the 25 per cent of our population who are in school, a plan of organization known as the ladder system of education has come into existence. In an ideal sense, the ladder concept is designed to provide the first twelve years of formal education for all the children of all the people. At the present time, in the majority of American communities, twelve years of formal education are mandatory and are offered at public expense. As a student grows up and successfully completes his studies, he progresses through these twelve years. Naturally, as progress and change modify our social goals, and it becomes clear that the acculturation process must accept new responsibilities, the ladder concept is altered and refined.

The diagram on page 497 illustrates the structure of American education and applies equally to public, private, secular, and sectarian schools. Because of the many variations and exceptions, however, it is possible to describe the structure of education only in general terms.

All communities provide twelve years of schooling, plus the time devoted to kindergarten. The amount of time spent in kindergarten varies from six months to two years. In some communities the child may enter at the age of four; in others at the age of five. Unfortunately, some children are denied a kindergarten experience because certain communities lack funds and space for the program or because parents cannot utilize existing facilities.

The subsequent twelve years of education take a variety of forms, depending upon the judgment of educators. The most commonly used arrangements are: (1) eight years of elementary or primary schooling followed by four years of secondary education; (2) six years of elementary schooling, three years of junior high school, and three years of senior high school; (3) six years of elementary schooling and six years of secondary schooling. A few communities prefer seven years of elementary or primary education and five years of secondary education; still others divide the twelve years into three units of four years each.

In most communities, secondary education is organized in the form of the junior high school and the senior high school. The junior high school generally serves to continue the exploration of individual talents begun earlier. The senior high school offers academic, commercial, and vocational courses of study. In addition, special technical and vocational secondary schools offer courses of study related to the demands of the industrial community. There are high schools devoted to curriculum specialization, generally for the intellectually and creatively gifted students. Although attendance is mandated by state law, whatever the type of school, provision is made for those who, because of economic and social reasons, are forced to withdraw prior to completion of the course of study. In privately sponsored institutions, the concentration is generally upon academic courses of study, with the exception of some private secondary schools, which offer course work in technical and commercial areas.

Attendance in institutions of higher education, whether public or private, secular or sectarian, is voluntary, and completion of the twelve years of mandatory schooling may or may not prepare a student for acceptance into the institutions of advanced learning. Individual ability, financial resources, level of aspiration, and availability of colleges are also determining factors. The ladder diagram indicates the manner in which the years devoted to higher education may be structured. The number of years in attendance are also influenced by the stringency of professional requirements.

At the present time, there is sufficient evidence to indicate that the ladder system of education is undergoing alteration and refinement. In a number of publicly and privately sponsored elementary or primary schools, provision is being made for an expansion of kindergarten experiences to include an increasing number of four-year-olds, and a number of communities are offering nursery education for those three-year-olds who can profit by earlier formal education. There is also a growing demand for the inclusion of the public junior college, or community college. Opportunities for adult education, which exist in most cities and towns, are not indicated in the diagram. Commercial, benevolent, and fraternal organizations also offer opportunities for adult education.

The functions performed by elementary or primary schools, junior high schools, senior high schools, junior or community colleges, senior colleges, universities, and adult education institutions will be discussed in the following chapters.

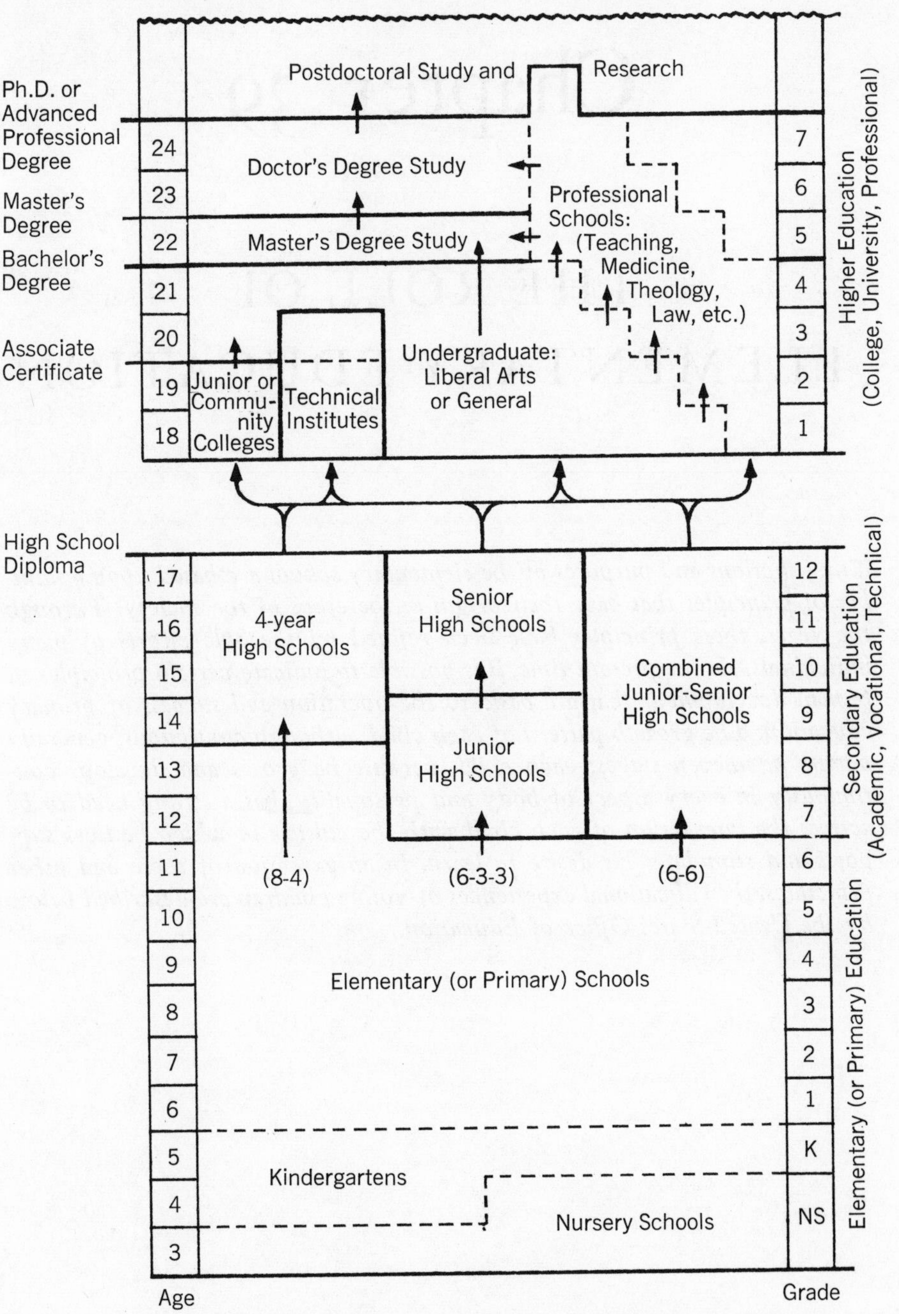

THE STRUCTURE OF EDUCATION IN THE UNITED STATES

Chapter 39

THE ROLE OF ELEMENTARY EDUCATION

THE *functions and purposes of the elementary school are based upon a number of principles that have their origin in the ethos of the society. Through the years, these principles have been refined by the able efforts of many individuals. At the present time, it is possible to indicate certain principles of human development that are basic to the operation and success of primary education: The growth pattern of each child, although continuous, generally occurs in uneven stages; each child, because he grows and develops continuously in every aspect of body and personality, has a strong need to be active; the interaction of each child with the culture in which he lives supports and stimulates his desire to learn. In an extension of these and other principles, the educational experiences of young children are described below by the United States Office of Education.*

FUNCTIONAL SCHOOLS FOR YOUNG CHILDREN

Office of Education,

United States Department of Health, Education and Welfare

EDUCATIONAL EXPERIENCES OF YOUNG CHILDREN

The educational program of young children is planned to foster their total development. They develop their potentials as the result of their experiences. Through their interaction with their environment children grow, and build their concepts, skills, and attitudes. The quality of the environment and the meaning of the experience to the child give direction and depth to his learning and growth.

The program takes all children into account and values each one as a person equally with all other children. The ideas, skills, and products of each are accepted as being worthy. Thus, each child's program of learning furthers his growth toward becoming an effective member of a democratic society. The experiences in the program draw accordingly upon the problems and resources of the community as vital materials of instruction.

AREAS OF THE PROGRAM

Social learnings. Since the child lives in a social world, his program emphasizes understandings and skills in getting along with many kinds of children—in sharing, taking turns, and learning to hold his own with his peers.

The content is in the experiences children have and deals with problems pertaining to the home, school, and expanding community. Each child thus engages in many different activities in which he takes responsibility as well as shares it. Through dramatic play he learns to clarify the work and roles of people he knows—his mother, the doctor, the fireman, and the farmer. He gathers information directly—from objects, neighborhood, and people—and by viewing pictures, charts, and films. He later develops skills in locating

Reprinted from *Functional Schools for Young Children,* Office of Education, United States Department of Health, Education and Welfare, Special Publication No. 8 (Washington, D.C.: U.S. Government Printing Office, 1961), pp. 7–8, 10–12.

and using data from simple maps, globes, and a variety of easy, printed materials.

The organization of his learning is often made through painting, dramatic play, experience charts, or discussions. Other types of activity used for this purpose consist of making layouts and models. For example, a group may use big blocks in building an airport requiring hangars and towers. Later these children use firsthand information in making models or layouts of the community and other areas. Not only do they acquire an orientation to direction, but also they learn about other characteristics of their community. This phase of the program places certain demands on the school facilities.

Science learnings. Young children's concern with their physical and natural environment makes experiences in exploring, manipulating, investigating, and discovering an important phase of their program. Since they perceive their world with all their senses, it is fundamental that they have experiences in touching, manipulating, observing, smelling, and listening. Such experiences are meaningful because they illustrate orderly methods of working and represent scientific approaches to learning and problem solving, abilities with a high priority in our present-day living. Space and materials, therefore, are needed for working and experimenting, which may include such activities as planting and watching things grow and observing and caring for animals at school. Children experiment with water, soil, magnets, and weather instruments, and work with simple machines such as toys and garden tools. The school plant and grounds should thus be planned as laboratories for scientific and creative learning.

Number and space relationships. Children deal with quantity and space because these are realities in all their undertakings. They count objects and people, group and regroup things together, and measure or estimate sizes and the space with which they are dealing. These activities are the bases for acquiring concepts of number relationships involving size, shape, and quantity. Before children are ready to work with symbols, they need to work with objects and materials for counting, grouping, and measuring.

Language. The child's language development grows out of his own firsthand experiences. It develops as a part of the child's total experience as he listens and talks to someone while engaging in an activity. Later on, reading and writing are vital parts of many of his undertakings.

Listening and speaking. The child at school develops further sensitivity and appreciation for the sounds about him. He enjoys experiences with poetry, music, and stories, and learns to listen thoughtfully to conversation and discussions. He participates in dramatic play, storytelling, talking about his experiences, and later makes short reports and explanations to his group. On some occasions he engages in language activities with one or two children; on others, two or more class groups may participate in a "sharing" experience.

Reading and writing. When they have developed the maturity for this task, children begin to read. They begin reading from large experience charts, labels, captions, and lists. Later they go on to both texts and trade books. They work under teacher guidance and also independently. Since young children have varying reading interests and needs, the materials, too, vary in type and use. Thus the environment which best stimulates reading interests and abilities is a flexible one. It includes attractive reading "corners" in the classroom, suitable areas for instruction, and school libraries which invite the young child into the world of books. The reading program also requires that planners of buildings take into account distances, flexibility of equipment, lighting, storage, and comfortable furniture.

Again, when they have acquired sufficient maturity and have a need to communicate in this way, children begin to write. First, they use the chalkboard and large size paper. Crayons, brushes, and pencils are correspondingly large. As children's coordination increases, both reading and writing skills become refined, and the size of print and materials can be reduced.

Art Experiences. Children express their feelings and ideas in many ways —through rhythms, sounds, colors, and touch—by dancing, singing, and making things. They better understand themselves and their own experiences through these creative forms of expression. Since the school nurtures the child's urge to create, its program includes opportunities for rhythms and dancing, painting and modeling, building and manipulating materials. Its environment provides an esthetic climate for encouraging creative responses through harmony of color, line, textures, and spatial proportions. These properties make the child more sensitive to beauty.

Play. Since children are active, developing personalities, the school's program is designed to promote their growth, health, and safety. It includes play and other physical activities—both indoors and out—involving climbing, running, jumping, balancing, lifting, and bending. The proper equipment and space are essential for these activities involving movements which are so fundamental to the development of coordination, poise, and a sense of confidence in the child.

The program likewise must make provision for food, rest, and the safety needs of children and guide them in developing habits and understandings conducive to healthful living.

Sufficient materials and equipment are needed for each child to have reasonable opportunities to use them with satisfaction to himself. Likewise, adequate space is essential to avoid congestion and the resulting tensions from overcrowding. Good mental health conditions include a comfortable climate for living.

In giving consideration to childern as individuals, the school must plan how it will provide for different children: the mentally handicapped, the gifted, and those with physical handicaps. It also resolves in terms of its goals for the education of young children many other issues, including the provisions made for rest periods, outdoor classrooms, libraries, cooking and eating, the kinds and quantity of children's work which is displayed, the kinds of music and art equipment, and the convenience and comfort of the teacher. Answers to these and similar questions will be significant in defining the space requirements for the school program.

If the program is conceived as an on-going dynamic process of learning and growing commensurate with each child's gifts, all who have a part in it are committed to providing the environment which contributes to the full development of all children.

CHILDREN WITH SPECIAL NEEDS

Education of exceptional children has special significance in the years 3 to 8, since identification of these children must start early if their potential for development is to be fully realized. It has been found that children who begin life with physical or mental handicaps can benefit greatly from early educational experiences offered in nursery schools and kindergartens.

In planning school facilities for children who are deaf, blind, crippled or who have speech problems, emotional disorders, or mental retardation, the general principles outlined in meeting the needs of normal children are equally applicable. These children will require adequate space, indoors and outdoors. When their handicap is not too severe, they can be placed in groups with normal children. Their rooms should be located to enable teachers of these groups to provide special instruction planned for them. Children with more acute problems may need a special group placement with teachers especially trained to guide their education, and the rooms for these children should be planned for their needs.

Of course, the particular needs of the exceptional child will require different specifications in some respect from those for normal children. For example, individualized instruction and medical treatment—depending on the child's problem—may be important. Small connecting rooms with a large playroom, which can be used by special teachers—such as teachers for children with speech problems or teachers for children who have poor vision or are hard of hearing—provide a layout which is functional. Special types of equipment to provide training in motor and sensory experiences should be a consideration in planning facilities for exceptional children.

Designing facilities for exceptional children requires the advice of experts who know this field and who will work with the architect. Most State departments of education provide consultative services to local school systems on programs for exceptional children. Several departments have developed suggestions for the planning of facilities for the handicapped, and should be consulted when new plants are being planned. This bulletin can only point out the importance of this growing movement to educate exceptional children in their preschool years and the increasing trend toward including these children in public school programs so that they may live as normal a life as possible.

SCHOOL SERVICES

For meeting the needs of all children, certain school services and facilities are essential. These services and facilities may be used by the entire school but usually are centered in the administrative offices of the school system.

An individual school may have occasion to request the professional services of a visiting teacher, to ask for the help of a school psychologist, to secure the service of a psychiatrist and child guidance clinic. In other instances a child's eyesight or hearing may need to be examined if deficiencies are suspected. Some schools make provision for physical and dental examinations for some children or for all. When these special consultants come to the school on call or on regular assignments, they will need a place for examining individual children. Since space for the consultant helps him to give his best service, a room should be assigned for his use.

If such space would not be in continuous use by a particular consultant, a room or rooms adaptable to various special services could be included in the building. Plans for new school buildings should include space adaptable to services which may be added as school systems grow and employ specialists on their staff.

PARENT-TEACHER RELATIONSHIPS

A good educational program for young children encourages parent-teacher cooperation in guiding a child's learning and development. Teachers profit from the background parents can give them about an individual child. Parents, likewise, feel closer to the school if they know their child's teacher. If teachers and parents plan together, it is possible to achieve mutual understanding which strengthens the educative process.

The effectiveness of the parent-teacher contacts depends to a large extent upon the school's provisions for making parents feel that they are needed in guiding their child's learning. Many types of activities build good parent-teacher relationships. Parents may be encouraged to visit the classroom, to have group and individual conferences with the teacher and principal, to work on school committees, to interpret the work of the school to other citizens, to assist the teacher as resource persons or when children go on trips, and to participate in other parent-teacher programs.

Many new school buildings include special facilities designed for parents. When parents are expected to wait in corridors or to meet in the basement or principal's office, their status in the school system may seem to them rather uncertain. Facilities in the school designed for parents help them work effectively as partners with the school staff.

In some school systems space-facilities should be provided for a parent-education supervisor who is employed to give leadership in developing a program for parents, to organize study groups and various types of parent participation, to help orient new parents and children, and to strengthen the parent-teacher association program. Such a program opens doors for parents to learn about the growth and development of children, to become acquainted with the school, and to understand and support its program. The school can then be said to be a community center to improve family and community life.

Chapter 40

THE ROLE OF THE JUNIOR HIGH SCHOOL

THE *junior high school has been organized to continue the patterns of general education initiated in the elementary schools and to prepare young people for the more advanced learning experiences offered by the senior high schools.*

The children attending junior high school have developmental problems that may have manifested themselves in elementary school, but which now occupy the center of the stage. (Normally, these problems will be adequately resolved before entrance into the senior high school.) The onset of puberty accelerates the intellectual, social, emotional, and physical growth of the individual; therefore, the junior high school is required to place much greater emphasis upon meeting the shifting needs and interests of the individual student. Although the educational program is organized on a group basis, the needs and interests of the individual occupy a very prominent place in the thinking and actions of the faculty. With few exceptions, the junior high school student seeks status in the adult world. Because the growth pattern of each individual is uneven, the period between the attainment of status in the world of the young to the attainment of status in the world of the adult produces a complex of problems of marked intensity. It is these problems which the junior high school must cope with while it continues to stress the values of general education.

Although the individual is still regarded as an integrated entity, a whole personality, the junior high school finds it more effective to deal with the manifestations of the various aspects of personality as separate and distinct provinces. It is through this concern with the aspects of personality that the junior high school seeks to bring about the necessary socialization and maturation. It is anticipated that, through this approach, the senior high school will receive a young adult who has begun to live harmoniously with himself and with his culture.

The following statement of functions to be performed by the junior high school is the work of the Commission on Secondary Schools and the Commission on Research and Service of The Southern Association of Colleges and Schools.

THE JUNIOR HIGH SCHOOL PROGRAM —STATEMENT OF FUNCTIONS

The Southern Association of Colleges and Schools

A major function of the junior high school is to provide for the unique social, emotional and physical needs of the age-group being served. The junior high school must provide experiences and activities which meet the social and emotional needs of early adolescence and late childhood. While a considerable number of these needs are common to other groups, there are many which are unique to young adolescents. Among some of the more apparent needs to be met are (1) a striving for status with their peers, (2) a desire for learning the "niceties" of social relationships, (3) an increasing interest in and desire to belong to social groups and to participate in social activities, (4) an awakened awareness of and interest in the opposite sex, (5) the acquiring of new and more mature relations with age-mates of both sexes, and (6) the desire of this age-group to establish themselves as "normal" in emotional and social behavior.

The proper organization and selection of learning experiences should provide opportunities for early adolescents to deal with their social and emotional problems. Another significant activity for providing rich opportunities for social experiences is the student activity program. The manner in which the school is administered and organized and the degree of responsibility placed on students for the conduct of their affairs influence considerably the degree to which this function is realized.

The mass media of communication—radio, television, movies, inexpensive reading materials and modern transportation—have had a tremendous impact on the early adolescent and bring into focus even more acutely the social and emotional needs of the group. During the two decades, 1910–30, when

Reprinted from "The Junior High School Program" (Atlanta, Ga.: *The Southern Association of Colleges and Schools,* 4th printing, April 1962), pp. 25–34.

the junior high school was created, these mass media did not have the impact on youth that they have today. Furthermore, our complex society makes more demands upon young people today than it did half a century ago. Social mores are changing rapidly, creating confusion and insecurity. These and many other changes make it even more imperative that the modern junior high school recognize its responsibility for fulfilling this function.

The junior high school must share with the family and other community organizations and agencies the responsibility for meeting social and emotional needs. As the characteristics and functions of these agencies change, particularly in the case of the family, the school must continually reappraise its responsibility for fulfilling this function.

It is also the function of the junior high school to provide experiences which will help early adolescents to meet the health and physical needs with which they are and will be confronted. Some of the more common problems and needs about which they are concerned are: (1) loss of muscular coordination, (2) an increasing awareness of their bodies and the anxiety about what is happening to their bodies during pre-adolescent growth spurt, (3) the needs associated with sex awareness, (4) the tendency to go beyond normal fatigue, (5) the earlier maturation of girls compared to boys, and (6) understanding dramatic physical changes such as changes in their voice during the onset of puberty. Severe social maladjustment may result unless the emotional and social stability of the student can be maintained through an understanding of the process of maturation; through a properly conceived environment of physical awareness; and through activities which enable him to meet these problems.

The recognition of these physical needs has particular implications for health instruction, health services, guidance activities, and physical education. Problems such as skin eruptions, awkwardness, physical immaturity and many others are often magnified in importance by early adolescents. Knowledge of causes and proper care may serve to prevent undue concern. An understanding that other people of his or her age share these difficulties may serve to reassure the student about a lot of developmental problems that otherwise would assume more serious proportions.

The junior high school program should emphasize the intellectual growth of young adolescents with particular stress upon continuing improvement in the fundamental skills. As is true at all educational levels one of the primary purposes of the junior high school is to develop the intellectual capacity of each early adolescent to the maximum of his potential. Helping young people grow intellectually involves the development of such abilities and skills as thinking and reasoning, sensing relationships, organizing and evaluating data, and solving problems. Moreover, intellectual growth is facilitated through helping students acquire such abilities as curiosity, desire for continuing intellectual growth, and respect for achievement.

In addition to the skills and abilities which have been cited, there are certain fundamental skills or tools of learning, which often make intellectual growth possible and for which the junior high school must assume continuing responsibility. These are the skills involved in communication (reading, writing, speaking and listening), calculating, and studying. They, of course, are not the only fundamental skills. Equally important are skills in human relations and a host of social skills and attitudes. The need for helping early adolescents develop these essentials skills and attitudes of living has been stressed, forcefully and vividly, in the information about the growth and development of this age group. . . .

It is unrealistic for teachers to assume that all students who enter the junior high schools are at the same level of skill development. . . . it has been shown that early adolescents vary greatly in intellectual, emotional, social and physical growth. In fact, the range of differences is much greater for 12- to 14-year-olds than for any other age group. For example, the reading level of these students may vary as much as seven or eight years and their social skills may range from those common to young children to those of mature adults.

This wide range in skill development provides leads for curriculum content and for ways of working with junior high school students. Teachers must discover the skill achievement level of each student and help him grow to maximum attainment. All students do not have the background and readiness to begin at the same level in the academic curriculum. For example, all students are not ready to understand and master problem solving involving percentage in mathematics. Some will need to begin with addition and subtraction while others can progress far beyond percentage calculations. This means that, while some activities and experiences carried on in the classroom may be profitably participated in by all students, it will be necessary in many learning situations to work with these young people individually and in small groups.

The opportunity to help students who are at varying levels of achievement is particularly favorable in the junior high school. At this stage of development some students who have been slow in learning acquire intellectual maturity and readiness which facilitates and accelerates learning if the teacher begins to work with them at their level of achievement. Moreover, students at average and high learning levels often develop new interests and experience a revival of intellectual curiosity.

It is the function of the junior high school to provide for the continuation and expansion of the general education program. The elementary school program is almost entirely concerned with providing general education experiences for children. The Committee which planned and prepared this publication feels that a major function of the junior high school is also general education. Except for the opportunity provided in the ninth grade for students to choose several electives, the function of the junior high school program is to continue and expand the general education program begun in the elementary school.

A general education program is one in which *common experiences* are provided for *all* students. It is not an elective program, rather it is one required of all students.

There are several schools of thought regarding general education. One contends that there are large, comprehensive areas of content which should be explored and studied by all students. Such areas as communications, social studies, humanities (art, music, literature, foreign languages) and personal-social adjustment are areas commonly used in planning and developing a general education program. Another approach is that of developing a curriculum based upon problems (personal, personal-social, social-civic and economic) which are common and of concern to all students and to society. In either approach the goals to be achieved are changes in behavior (attitudes, habits, skills, appreciations, etc.) which are in harmony with the democratic way of living.

In the junior high school general education includes the core program, mathematics, physical education and a host of exploratory courses and experiences. When students reach the ninth grade, they begin to elect courses based upon needs, aspirations and future vocational plans. Recognition of this by the teachers and other guidance workers should be reflected in the program of guidance.

In the program of general education, provision should be made for the stimulation and development of the natural curiosity of this age group. The problem-solving approach to teaching is an effective way of accomplishing this objective. In the problem-solving approach the student can develop skills in clarifying the problem, setting up hypotheses or "hunches," locating pertinent information which can be used in solving the problem, organizing and evaluating the information, drawing conclusions, and developing a plan of action based upon the conclusions.

In seeking to achieve the goals of general education, opportunities should be provided for the student to develop skill in critical thinking and in ways of evaluating working methods and in appraising his personal progress. These are qualities which must be consciously sought in teaching. Opportunity should be provided for the student to gain skills in group cooperation and skill in living as a part of democratic society. Group activities in the classroom and student activities are the most common vehicles through which these opportunities are provided.

Programs of general education at all educational levels should provide opportunities for creative thinking and the expression of ideas based on sound knowledge. These values have implications not only for the organization of experiences and content but also for the relationship between the student and the teacher and the general tone of the classroom situation. The youth of the junior high school age are, because of their natural curiosity, particularly receptive to teaching which gives them an opportunity for the creation of ideas. All definitions of general education provide for the acquisition of aesthetic values and the development of moral and ethical values. Continued attention to these objectives is a basic part of general education in the junior high school.

It is the function of the junior high school to provide experiences that will assist the early adolescent to make the transition from childhood dependence to adult independence. Since early adolescents are in the beginning stages of the transition from childhood to adulthood, there is an increasing drive to break away from adult control and authority. However, they are not fully capable of assuming the independence of adulthood. Vacillation between childhood and adult behavior is quite common during this period. The child desires independence from adults and yet he constantly is seeking security which many times makes adult control necessary. This need for stability while changing from childhood to adulthood has many implications for such things as self-discipline, student activities, fads in dress, defiance of adults and a host of other behavior problems.

The youth of this age desire the security of a well-defined and understood pattern of behavior, which explains the taboos and rigid rules which teenage groups set up to govern their behavior. If left alone without adult guidance, these youngsters seeking independence and security may well develop rules of behavior which may be ridiculous or even harmful. Under proper guidance of trusted adults, youth can establish rules which are desirable and socially acceptable. While there is, many times because of cultural as well as natural reasons, an increasing tendency to resent adult control, paradoxically, there is a desire for judicious adult guidance. Early adolescents will adopt regulations set by adults if these regulations and the need for such regulations are fair and reasonable and if they are properly interpreted to them or better still if they have a part in developing them. More and more opportunity should be provided these young people to participate in determining codes of conduct and in planning school activities.

Junior high school students can profit from responsibilities. These should be increased as the student develops in age and maturity. Care should be exercised, however, that these responsibilities should not be beyond their capacity and maturity or that they are not increased too rapidly. Such responsibilities will provide opportunities for the student to find an outlet for his energies and help him develop skills, attitudes and other behaviors of adulthood. There is also a need for the school to work with the students to help them make mature decisions and to help them learn that when they participate in making decisions they must accept the consequences of their decisions.

It is the function of the junior high school to provide a program of guidance and personnel services adapted to the needs of early adolescents. Because of the stresses which are a part of his growing into adolescence and the many new problems and concerns which arise during this transitional growth period, the child of this age has particular need for guidance. The guidance program should be organized and administered to assist the student to solve these problems so that he may feel secure and overcome his fears, anxieties and frustrations. The guidance program in the junior high school should provide opportunity both for group and individual guidance.

Group guidance can be carried on best in the classroom. This would involve including, as a regular part of the curriculum experiences, opportunities to consider problems which are of concern to early adolescents and to society. All teachers should assume some responsibility for group guidance but the major responsibility for a group or class of students should be centered in one teacher. In many junior high schools the core teacher serves as the counseling teacher for one and sometimes two core classes. In addition to the group guidance provided in these classes, the counseling teacher works with the students on individual problems.

Early adolescents need contacts with one teacher for a comparatively long period of time during the day. This is necessary so that the teacher may have the opportunity to know the student intimately and to work with him on his problems both through group guidance and individual counseling. Specialized guidance services such as those provided by professional counselors or psychologists should be available to help teachers in working with youth on their problems and to provide the highly specialized services which problem cases require.

Association with the same group of peers for relatively long periods of time makes for a feeling of group belonging and security so necessary for this age group. The traditional organization of the school day into seven or eight periods of forty to forty-five minutes each does not lend itself to this concept. The need for longer periods with the same group can be met through the organization of the curriculum into larger blocks of time. Having the same core or basic studies teacher stay with the same group through the three years of junior high school is essential to continuous, effective guidance.

The guidance program and the services which it provides must create an atmosphere in which the student believes that he is understood by his fellow students and his teachers and that he in turn understands them.

The program of the junior high school should provide those broad exploratory experiences which are necessary in the educational development of early adolescents. Rapid changes, broadened insights and outlook and increased curiosity of early adolescents make possible and necessary school programs which give the student the opportunity to explore and participate in many different kinds of experiences. Young people of this age group are not only curious but they are natural explorers. Creating interest in new things is relatively easy and it is an excellent time in the school program to help the student to pursue and develop these interests.

Exploratory experiences have several very fundamental purposes. *First, they contribute to and are an integral part of the general education program.* The experiences should be those which are valuable and essential for all students. Thus, exploratory experiences should be elective. *Second, they help students develop present and future social and recreational skills and interests.* These would include such experiences as dramatics, social and folk dancing, hobbies (photography, do-it-yourself activities and the like), and individual, and small group sports (golf, tennis, badminton, and many others). *Third, they provide new experiences which broaden the horizons of boys and girls.* Many students entering junior high school have had little or no experience in manual arts, organized science, foreign languages and in working with certain art media. *Fourth, exploratory experiences help students develop new, useful skills* such as those involved in the touch system in typing and the varied skills which are acquired in the manual arts and in homemaking. *Fifth, they assist students in making present and future vocational plans and choices.* Interest in vocations is often developed as students participate in new and varied experiences. A spark of vocational interest may be kindled through well-planned experiences in art, music, manual arts, homemaking, creative dramatics, creative writing, and other exploratory experiences. *Sixth, they provide valuable assistance to students in making choices of future educational experiences.* Many students have preconceived ideas about certain subjects and know little or nothing about other subjects. A student has little basis for election of subjects such as art, music, languages, business, manual arts, science and many others unless he has an experience in each of these subject areas.

Exploration should permeate the entire program of the junior high school. Many experiences such as creative writing, vocational orientation and public speaking can be provided in the core program. Other experiences can be incorporated into the mathematics and physical education curriculums. Still others should be provided in short courses specifically planned and designed for exploratory purposes. Again it should be emphasized that these experiences are valuable for all students and should be included in the general education program.

The junior high school program should help the student to develop vocational consciousness. Closely allied to exploration and guidance, vocational orientation should bring about the beginning of vocational consciousness and an understanding of the world of work. The emphasis here is on understanding, on the knowledge necessary for correct choices, and on an interest in such choices rather than the actual choosing of an occupation. No effort should be made to persuade students to make vocational choices even though some will do so.

Occupational groups or families should be studied along with vital information about them. This study would include conditions of employment, aptitude and training required, relationship of personality to success, and the present and probable future demands for service. Students should also gain an understanding of the significance of work, and of the contributions they can make to society through finding a vocation in which they feel successful and happy. While these experiences should be provided for all students, specialized vocational information should be made available for the individual student who is seeking answers to his personal questions.

The relationship between school activities and ultimate vocational choices should be stressed. Many times it is difficult for youth of this age to see this relationship unless the teacher is consciously helping them to achieve this objective. For the student whose vocational consciousness has been aroused, an understanding of this relationship will create a high level of motivation in his pursuit of learning.

A most productive method of bringing about vocational consciousness is through some form of work experience. Through cooperation with the community many opportunities can be created whereby the students may come to grips with the actual problems of the world of work. Due to the age of the youth, the usual concepts of work experiences may not suffice. Working out of such experiences for these students will call for new approaches and creative thinking on the part of teachers and school officials.

It is the function of the junior high school to provide for the special individual interests and needs of students. Opportunity should be provided in the ninth grade for elective courses or experiences which are attractive to the individual student, or which meet his personal intellectual or aesthetic needs and interests. The major purpose of the junior high school remains general education but all students who attend it have a right to expect an opportunity through specialization to meet their individual needs and interests. This may be done through advanced courses in such areas as art, music, languages, homemaking, science, and mathematics in the ninth grade. It may also be done in core and other general education courses at all grade levels through identifying special interests of students and providing opportunities for them to pursue these interests individually.

Another fruitful area for accomplishing this function is through many of the co-curricular activities to be found in the junior high school program. Club activities and participation in student government afford many opportunities for meeting the individual needs and interests of students. A carefully planned and administered social program also offers many opportunities for meeting individual needs and interests.

It is the function of the junior high school to provide for articulation with the administrative units above and below. The bridging of the gap between the elementary school and the secondary school has been recognized as a major goal of the junior high school since its inception. Unless this is done the establishment of the junior high school may well create two breaks in a child's experience in place of one. The bridging of this gap involves planned articulation with the elementary school below and the senior high school above and calls for a close working relationship with these units.

It is the function of the junior high school to provide the type of program organization and gradually changing experiences which will help the child in making the transition from the self-contained elementary school room with one teacher to the more highly specialized upper secondary school with many teachers. Not only must the transition be made from one teacher to several teachers but from a rather complete pattern of general education to a program of increasingly more specialized subject matter in the senior high school. Transition from the neighborhood school to the community school must also be made. Not only must the student learn to know new teachers but also new surroundings and new students.

The junior high school is concerned with proper articulation with the senior high school just as surely as with the elementary school. Working with the school above on articulation problems poses new approaches but has the same fundamental aspects as working with the elementary school.

Proper fulfillment of the function of articulation with its orientation problems necessitates exchange of information about students, cooperative work on common problems by the faculties of all schools concerned, and inter-school visitation. While the main impact falls on the guidance program, many of the problems are administrative in character.

The significance of functions. Functions, objectives or purposes are fundamental in planning, developing and improving the program for early adolescents. They serve as the basis for determining administrative structure, organization of the program, curriculum design and content, teaching procedures and evaluation of the program. A program for early adolescents cannot be determined intelligently and effectively without agreement upon goals which reflect the needs of the students and of society. Thus, every consideration and action in developing a junior high school program should be based upon carefully formulated, meaningful functions or objectives which are acceptable to all who are planning the program. Moreover, the evaluation of the program should be an appraisal of the degree to which the functions have been achieved.

The responsibility of the faculty. It is rather evident that a faculty which is developing a new program or improving an existing one must, early in the process, agree upon the functions or purposes of a junior high school. If this is done from scratch, the procedure involves arduous, time-consuming study and discussion. When time is available this approach is a most valuable and profitable one. However, many faculties cannot spend an entire year determining objectives and must find a way that involves less time. Such faculties usually study statements of functions such as the one provided here, discussing each until it is clear and meaningful, considering the implications of each function, making modifications and deleting or adding if it is the consensus of the faculty to do so. The end result of this study is faculty agreement on a list of objectives which the members are dedicated to use in developing or improving the program. Only when such understanding and agreement is reached is the faculty ready to work on the specifics of the program.

Chapter 41

THE ROLE OF THE SENIOR HIGH SCHOOL

For the majority of students the years of senior high school bring formal schooling to an end. Since society does not legally require formal schooling beyond this point, the continuation of schooling is left to the discretion of each family. At the high school level, however, not every student can make the most of the opportunities offered him, and for far too many these last school years leave much to be desired. While the curricula offered by our senior high schools represent society's best judgment about the kind of school work this age group needs, many educators are not convinced that society's definition of educational adequacy for this age group is either realistic or valid. There is growing evidence that our academic, technical, and vocational high schools are not attuned to the conditions of contemporary life. The rigidity with which many of these schools are organized and administered places severe limitations upon the opportunities for individual growth for far too many students. The grouping of students on the basis of intellectual ability and vocational aptitude and the induction of students into predetermined and impersonal courses of study certainly suggest that an enormous gap exists between theory and practice at this level of education.

It is generally accepted that the senior high schools are the source of many perplexing educational issues. For example, do the senior high schools, by precept and example, provide a democratic environment for the students? Is the present emphasis upon sharply graded subject matter producing democratically oriented citizens? Are the present courses of study of sufficient range, depth, and flexibility to meet the needs and interests of each student? Can the senior high schools ever realistically service the needs and interests of all students, or will the dropout remain a perennial problem? Are the senior high schools actively contributing to the forces that cause harmonious personal relationships, or are they strengthening the forces that further stratify the American people? These questions are asked in order to encourage a close examination of these institutions, their curricula, and their relationship to society, in order to obtain some insight into their current practices and problems. For this purpose, the following excerpts from a publication issued by the United States Office of Education serve to direct attention toward: (1) some conclusions formulated by acknowledged experts concerning the performance of the high schools; (2) some indications of promising developments in high school education that can conceivably correct inadequacies; and (3) some areas containing unsolved problems.

AN ANALYSIS AND A LOOK AHEAD

H. H. Cummings, et al.

FORCES MOLDING UNIVERSAL SECONDARY EDUCATION

From a busy decade of study and experimentation the educational leaders were able to draw certain tentative conclusions about the program of universal secondary education which was emerging.

1. The secondary school program was not meeting the need of all youth. However, there was a feeling that a new program could be designed which would prepare youth for college as successfully as the traditional academic program. The new program would aim to provide experiences for all youth from which he might learn to live with greater happiness and effectiveness in a free society. The new psychology had suggested certain guide lines for program planners. The ideas of orientation to a changing society, the importance of maturation, and the emphasis on a purpose in learning—clear to the learner—were beginning to be used as criteria for judging proposed programs.
2. The secondary school had not come to grips with real problems of living—in school, in family, or in community. Student government needed greater emphasis. Future citizens should have laboratory practice and work experience in the community, as well as knowledge of the theory and structure of government. With a view to better use, the economic resources of the community should be better understood. Health must be recognized as a

Reprinted from "A Look Ahead in Secondary Education," Office of Education, United States Department of Health, Education and Welfare, Bulletin No. 4 (Washington, D.C., 1954), pp. 75, 77–91.

community as well as a personal matter, and recreation as an important contribution both to the life of the individual and to the general cultural life of the community. Secondary schools should give more emphasis to education for home and family living, making it available to all girls and also to boys.

3. It was apparent that more insight into the problems, needs, interests, motivations, and growth processes of pupils was needed by teachers and administrators as well as psychologists. Especially needed was a better understanding of human behavior in oneself and others in face-to-face relationships. The investigations and experiments had revealed the fact that individual differences were much greater than the visible physical differences and the measurable mental differences of which the schools were somewhat cognizant. The studies of emotional life had discovered that many physical problems were psychosomatic, and that the emotional development of youth was an important and generally neglected phase of education. When the total personality of each individual began to receive consideration, individual differences were seen to be almost infinite.

4. Sociologists, anthropologists, and social psychologists had pointed out the need for a greater perception into the structure and working of community life. Outside investigators were able to discover examples of cruelty, injustice, preventable illness, crippling prejudice, and many other maladjustments about which teachers and administrators with long experience in the community were unaware. The schools in some communities were attempting to educate youth for living in a pattern of social and economic life which had been gradually disappearing from the community and had completely disappeared in more progressive communities.

EMERGING DEVELOPMENTS IN SECONDARY EDUCATION

The following developments in secondary education seem to be under way:

1. *The comprehensive high school.*—The handbooks of the comprehensive high school describe course subjects as academic, vocational, and general. The aim is to provide in a single school all the educational needs of all youth in a community. As new courses have been added, old courses dropped, and requirements altered—by a system of trial and error—the comprehensive high school has evolved.

Most comprehensive high schools of today were either college-preparatory or vocational high schools 20 years ago. The "prep" high school has added a full range of vocational courses to the curriculum. At the same time the "tech" high school has added academic courses. Both types of high schools prepare pupils for college, for skilled trades, and for life in a modern community. In some communities the old names remain over the schoolhouse doors but, inside, the pupils pursue about the same comprehensive or, at least, varied programs of studies.

Some appreciation of what the comprehensive high school is like can be gained by taking a look at what it is not. If secondary education in America had followed the pattern of education developed in Western Europe, each community would likely have four types of schools: a classical high school; a high school emphasizing modern language, science, and mathematics; a commercial high school; and a technical high school. Since coeducation would not be tolerated, the community would have separate high schools for boys and girls or a total of eight high schools instead of the four listed. In addition, vocational schools would provide part-time and continuation-school opportunities for youth not in attendance at the other schools. Vocational schools could exist only in large centers of population, and only a small percentage of the total youth group would be enrolled. Small communities would establish boarding schools. In most instances, decisions regarding the type of high school to be attended would be made at the age of 11. This picture of a fragmentized educational system can be found in many communities of Western Europe today. In fact, several American cities traveled a long way down the same road before the public demand for democratic schools halted them.

The requirements for graduation from secondary schools outlined by State departments of education make up the required subjects which all pupils must take. These lists of subjects vary in number from 5 to 10 in different schools. English, social studies, mathematics, science, and health make up the basic or minimum list of subjects.

The subjects from which each pupil fills out the remaining 16 units required for graduation are usually elective, and depend upon the school's enrollment and resources, together with the imagination, ingenuity, and zeal for serving youth which characterize the staff. The following subjects: agriculture, trade and industrial courses, commercial courses, home economics, and industrial arts, constitute a great part of the list of electives of the majority of high schools. The nonrequired academic subjects—languages, physical sciences, advanced mathematics—complete nearly all lists. Generally speaking, elective subjects still strongly reflect the fact that American secondary schools were designed originally as college-preparatory schools. It was during the first two decades of the 20th century that their curricula were modified to include commercial and vocational education. Music and the fine arts are contributing an increasing number of courses. Industrial arts courses stress the general outcomes of understanding industrial aspects of our culture, exploration of pupil interest, and craftsmanship, rather than the exact skills of specific trades. Homemaking courses, including all aspects of home management, are supplementing the more specialized courses in foods, clothing, and child development. Other shifts from formally organized subjects to courses built around areas of living can be found in many places in the curriculum. Courses in social studies have included consumer economics, human relations, and citizenship education. English has expanded to include the critical study of mass communications media —public speaking, dramatics, journalism, and other phases of language arts. New courses in orientation to school and community life have been added. In the elective offerings of many schools are courses in personal social living. In some schools few pupils graduate without a course in personal typewriting.

While to many educators the rate of change has seemed discouragingly slow, the quality of the changes which have survived the tests of the proving grounds of use in the daily program has been encouraging. Both staff and public have worked to preserve social unity as an outcome of secondary school experience.

In general, special programs for nonacademic pupils have failed. The life adjustment education movement has drawn criticism for its concern for "the 60 percent" when an incomplete reading of the Prosser Resolution has led some educators to believe that a special program was being planned for youth who were to be labeled as noneducable in already established courses. A balance sheet of educational innovation, however, would show solid and numerous—if not widespread—gains for general education. Generally speaking, it can be said that the innovations have provided wider opportunities for youth, and at the same time have encouraged the growth of democratic attitudes and social unity.

The required subjects have been selected with the aim of insuring certain common learnings considered essential for all graduates. In the field of required subjects the shift of content emphasis has been going on gradually since the cardinal principles of education were stated. Program experimentation has been influenced by the more revolutionary proposal to abandon required subjects, and to organize the common learnings necessary for successful living in the modern world into a core curriculum which would be required of all pupils. In general, modifications in the direction of a common learnings extra-class programs of school clubs for French, Latin, and many other subjects have been absorbed into an expanding method of learning. Radio amateurs, photography enthusiasts, and other hobby-interested individuals may pursue their interests during school hours.

Though few educators would label the present program in the comprehensive high school as anything except transitional, there is little inclination to return to the program of earlier years. On the contrary, there is a strong desire to move to an expanded and enriched program which will help a larger number of youth to meet their needs while growing into adult roles in American society. The direction is clear, but the many steps that educators hope will carry the program forward have yet to be taken. Then and only then will the experimenter learn whether the gains he has made are held or lost.

3. *Characteristics of the changing classroom.*—The extent of educational change cannot be measured by counting the titles of new and old courses in the school handbook. Old labels cover a wide variety of new educational experiences. Social studies include current events, use of community resources, consumer education, and many other areas. Science may include health and conservation. English has gone far beyond grammar and rhetoric and a study of the classics. Most school subjects have become broad fields of learning where pupils and teachers work to reach the objectives stated by educational leaders and the public but reconsidered as goals by pupils and teachers planning together.

Once sharply marked, the dividing line between curricular and extracurricular activities has become blurred. The glee club, band, and orchestra have now become a part of the regular curriculum. Student publication activities have been absorbed into journalism courses. The common learnings or core curriculum programs for grades 7, 8, and 9 have increased in numbers. In grades 10, 11, and 12, however, attempts to implement the common learnings idea have been less successful.

The curriculum has increasingly included learning activities carried on outside the school building. Pupils have taken part in studies of the local community, and in social action programs based on their reseach. Work experience for pay, and as community service, has become a part of the school curriculum. Distributive education programs have combined the reality of on-the-job experience with required subjects related to general education as a new phase of the curriculum.

Separate curricula for college preparation, vocational agriculture, and commercial work, which filled the school handbooks in years past, are tending to disappear. In the larger schools, pupils no longer pursue a long sequence of courses which must be completed when they elect one curriculum or another. Each pupil, with the help of teachers, parents, and counselors, selects a progam of studies from the list of required and elective subjects which takes into account his personal interests, needs, aptitudes, and plans for the future. Flexibility, freedom, and a recognition of individual differences have been substituted for rigid patterns of courses designed to achieve standards of academic or vocational specialization.

Daily assignments and recitations in class work have given way to the organization of instruction into large units. The basis for the unit is some major idea, or a cluster of related ideas based on youth needs and interests, which pupils are asked to explore and understand. The unit contains suggested activities which require different abilities and which appeal to different interests of pupils. The monotony of listening to the recitation of lessons is replaced by pupil activity in which ideas learned from many sources are presented for discussion and analysis. The uniform assignment, which was often too easy for the fast learner and beyond the ability of the slow learner, has been replaced by differentiated assignments which challenge the able and give the less talented a chance to learn. The opportunity is given for future workers, farmers, managers, consumers, and professional men and women to have the experience of working together on common problems.

With the introduction of audiovisual aids has come a third change. The increasing use of film strips and recordings has been a major development in the last 10 years. Radio, television, and movie guidance bring current issues into class discussions. However, better techniques for using aids must be perfected to make them of maximum benefit in the classroom and there is a continuing need for content materials of current interest.

A fourth innovation which has modified classroom practice is that of pupil-teacher planning. The need for pupils to understand the purpose of activities and experiences in which they are engaged can be met in part by letting them help plan class undertakings. Planning sessions alternate with small group working sessions and culminate eventually into total-group sessions which may develop the topic or propose a tentative solution for a problem. The formality of the traditional classroom gives way to informal working and planning relationships. Pupil-teacher planning has led to the development of the resource unit to replace the cut-and-dried teaching unit. Since the exact step-by-step details cannot be predicted, the unit becomes a resource for the group to draw up rather than a blueprint to be rigidly followed.

A fifth change has been the development of group work directed by teachers trained in group dynamics. It is important for teachers to understand the interaction of the pupils in the class, the nature of grouping and cliques, and the agreements and disagreements that grow out of personal insecurities. Drives for status, and other factors in the development of personality, are matters of equal importance to teachers.

Over the last 30 years a large body of improved teaching methods has developed, as an outgrowth of experimentation by a whole generation of educators, and much of the practice is still undergoing improvement through experimentation. Two basic sources have furnished ideas and practices: (1) The child growth and development movement in nursery and elementary schools, and (2) the controlled research sponsored by colleges and universities. The techniques used with children have had to be adapted to older youth, and the techniques of scholars (development in universities) to be adapted to younger, less able, and less interested youth. Some basic research on adolescents has been carried on, but more is needed as a basis for the development of even sounder techniques for use in secondary school classrooms.

3. *School services.*—The school staff a generation ago consisted of the principal and a corps of teachers assigned to teach classes in subject fields,

and whatever school services existed were performed by the principal or by teachers. The testing movement of the 1920's brought about the addition of the school psychologist, as a staff member without teaching responsibilities. He was followed by the school doctor, the school nurse, the dietitian, and guidance and counseling workers. These additions to the staff created a problem to secondary administration: that of coordinating the work of the two groups of staff members—service and instruction—to achieve maximum benefit for pupils.

The increasing interest in health education, including mental health, has opened up what is probably the most active field of experimentation in recent years. What is the place of health instruction as a separate subject? As a part of the science course? As an area in home economics? What part should school doctors, nurses, and dietitians play in increasing the sensitivity of teachers and pupils to problems of health and nutrition? How are repetition and overlapping to be avoided in a total school health program? In working out answers to these and many other questions, the school staff is moving toward a program of health education in which responsibility is shared by the total teaching and service staff.

The growth of the guidance movement has raised the same problems of staff cooperation in the whole program of the school. As the addition of counselors trained in psychology increased the amount of information about the personal, social, scholastic, and vocational problems of pupils, the question which immediately appeared was: "How can this knowledge be put to work in administrative policies, curriculum, teaching methods, school-home relationships, and all facets of school life—to improve the learning of pupils?" Having guidance counselors present their own viewpoints in all discussions on school policy is one approach. Increasing the insight of teachers, administrators, and school service workers into the nature of pupil problems and the needs of youth—through experiences where counselors and teachers work together on a specific problem of an individual pupil—is a second approach. It is evident that when classroom teachers in charge of home rooms share in the work of counseling under the direction of guidance-trained personnel they enlarge their viewpoint and give special attention to the relationships between pupil and school. With the development of the guidance movement have come new attitudes toward school discipline, new viewpoints on school-home relationships, and new concepts of pupil appraisal, which will tend to modify school policy and practices in the future.

The guidance movement has helped to focus the attention of school personnel on the growth and development of all pupils. From this new viewpoint in secondary education has developed a new area for school research, the study of "dropouts." The early school-leaver is no longer forgotten as a necessary casualty in the operation of a selective system of education, but is seen as an individual for whom the school failed to provide opportunities to make necessary adjustments. The evaluation of all the pupils' school experiences have been analyzed in followup studies made with graduates and dropouts after they have left school. The points of strength and weakness in their school experiences provide guides for changes in curriculum to strengthen the school program.

4. *Evaluation.*—The steady growth of the testing movement begun during World War I, was encouraged by educational experimentation, by the need to measure general educational achievement for college admission, and by the necessity for proving the effectiveness of new approaches to learning. New tests for knowledges and skills have been developed and some progress has been made in testing of attitudes. Not only have techniques been developed to collect information on the interests of pupils and their problems of personal adjustment, but, also, guidance services have provided the school with personnel better equipped to interpret data from a wider range of evaluation instruments.

The attempt to broaden the field of evaluation from the mastery of school subjects and the measurement of specific skills to as many phases of growth and development as the testmaker's ingenuity can invent is one direction of the testing movement. Another is the attempt to evaluate attributes of the individual pupil other than intelligence. At midcentury, the complexity of the testing process is better recognized than in the period of the early 1920's. Test results are being used with more caution and greater intelligence. There is optimism about the future of evaluation, and school staffs are not only better trained to use tests than at any other period but welcome new developments in the testing field.

5. *Democratic school administration.*—To encourage a more democratic atmosphere in the school, there has been a general change in school policies and administrative practices. Mutual respect characterizes school relationships, and this respect encourages sharing power as far as the laws placing responsibility will permit. The growth of student governments in secondary schools is one evidence of this policy. A second is the practice of operating the school on the basis of policies formed by involving the entire school staff. These changes grew out of the conviction that democracy would not be learned in an institution which was operated under a dictatorship. The fact that the dictator was able, pleasant, intelligent, and kind did not alter the situation. Faith in democratic processes led to the belief not only that decisions would be wise and just when made by the staff, but that the values of staff understanding of problems through the process of decision making were important to successful operation of a social institution such as a school.

The atmosphere of the school is recognized as an important factor in education. To maintain a democratic atmosphere called for continuous study of such factors as the social forces at work in the community, the effect of pupil cliques in school and community life, the place of the teacher in the life of the community, and questions of overemphasis of competitive scholarship and competitive athletics. Respect for the individual, with an absence of bullying and scapegoating, and elimination of community prejudice patterns in school are other aspects. Finally, many situations have to be examined in which it has not been clear whether the school has been helping a pupil to a satisfactory future or merely exploiting some particular ability—usually athletic—for institutional prestige.

6. *Wider school-community relationships.*—The democratic character of universal secondary education has demanded broad and continuous cooperation in school-community relationships. Health, safety, and recreation are three areas where the school and the community by working together have improved the quality of living. Bridging the gap between school and full employment is an unsolved community problem where the school's programs of guidance and work experience need to be supplemented by other means of school-community cooperation. Citizenship at the community level is being taught by laboratory experiences where young citizens and civic leaders work together. Another area in which school, home, and community may work together is that of general cultural improvement. The achievements made to date indicate that a large number of opportunities, not yet developed, remain in the area of school and community cooperation.

The measure of responsibility to be accepted by the school and by community groups has not been clearly defined. The somewhat common assumption that the school is the one institution that reaches all the children and youth, and therefore should assume a position of leadership, overlooks the fact that the school's primary responsibility is the education of its pupils. If the school-community relationship helps the school to do its primary job better, there is no conflict; but there are many tasks in every community where leadership and major responsibility should come from other institutions and agencies.

UNFINISHED BUSINESS OF SECONDARY EDUCATION

1. *The secondary school staffs need to continue their studies of all youth, but especially those now tending to drop out before graduation.*—Since almost one-half of the youth of the United States do not complete grade 12, further improvements should be made in the holding power of secondary schools. General reasons for early school leaving which have been stressed in educational writing include: low family income, lack of success in school work, a low level of educational aspiration, a feeling that the school offers nothing which is of value to the pupil, and the desire for early financial independence. However, general reasons do not apply with equal measure in any given community. A dropout study reveals the reasons boys and girls give for leaving a particular school prior to graduation. These reasons must

be kept in mind when questions of a change in policy or program are considered by the school and community. . . .

Increasingly, schools are using the techniques available for learning more about pupils, and former pupils, and are improving these techniques as a result of experiences.

2. *Educators are working to establish a 14-year sequence of educational experiences which will eliminate the selective character of secondary education.*—Traditionally the secondary school was a separate institution, not a continuation of elementary education. Earlier secondary schoolmasters assumed that entering pupils had mastered reading, writing, grammar, arithmetic, and spelling. Those who did enter without such mastery were not taught these skills; they were eliminated from school. Under present laws each pupil must attend school until the age of 16. If he fails to master the skills of English and arithmetic, he can either be retained in the elementary school with younger children or promoted to the secondary school with his own age group without having mastered these skills. Retention with younger children deprives youth of opportunity for social development, and such a policy often meets opposition from the parents of the children in the lower grades. Too often a policy of drift has allowed pupils to attend classes where they did not have the basic skills to do the work required; and little effort has been made to teach these skills. The teaching of the basic skills should become a matter of primary concern during all the years of compulsory schooling—not during just the first 8 years.

Progress is being made in two areas, the junior high school and the junior college. The transition from a situation where one teacher teaches all subjects in one room, to a program where each subject is taught by a different teacher in a different room, is made less difficult when large blocks of time are given to a teacher for a unified program. The same teacher is in charge of the pupils' home room. The transition from grade 12 to 13 is less sharp when the first 2 years of college are regarded as a continuation of the pupil's education rather than the fresh beginning of a new educational experience, when the junior college or community college is a part of the same system.

Where the secondary schools and colleges are under different authorities, school-college agreements are exploring new ways of dovetailing the 12th and 13th grades to make transition less difficult.

The present requirements for college entrance are being made the subject of careful study. A standard requirement of 12 years of schooling offers little provision for individual differences. Many pupils have demonstrated the ability to begin college work after 10 or 11 years spent in school. In the current experimentation, the age, the aptitude, and the social maturity of the pupil are being studied as factors related to his ability to do creditable college work.

The 14-year sequence would be designed to help children and youth to live in contemporary American society. The education would be general, with specialized education introduced for some pupils at the end of the 10th year. This does not mean that the general education should be uniform. Groups of pupils with different interests may reach the same general objectives by different studies, activities, and experiences. Each student's school program should include experience in: health, safety, leisure-time habits, citizenship, economic competence, general work skills and attitudes, self-understanding, human relations, and home and family—built during each year. The instructional experiences should be discontinued only when a level of competence suitable for American living has been achieved. Such a level of competence is not easy to determine in any of the areas mentioned above. Obviously the schools should not attempt to carry programs of health education, for example, to the point where all graduates would be doctors. However, the levels of desired competence for the laymen in a changing society may vary in different places and times.

At the end of the 10th, 11th, and 12th years, pupils who have demonstrated their maturity and competence to do college work will be transferred to college programs. Other pupils will complete their programs of full-time education with general, commercial, vocational, and technical courses during these years.

3. *In terms of time allotment, an appropriate balance between required and elective subjects or areas of learning has not been adequately determined.*—Secondary schools have experimented with a variety of programs, but the results of the experiments have led to little agreement. At one extreme are groups which would require no subjects at all beyond the eighth grade and make the whole program of 16 units elective. Such a policy would give the guidance counselors room to help each pupil make up a program in which he could develop his interests and aptitudes. There are few who advocate that all 16 units be required subjects, but many would insist upon 11 required units for all pupils, leaving time for 5 units in vocational courses and special interest areas. This large block of requirements is defended as necessary to insure unity for all secondary education. At present, State requirements for graduation range from 5 to 10 units. Pressures from subject groups would add more mathematics, science, and modern language to the present requirements. Health, safety, and practical arts are other areas which are also currently considered necessary, and pressure is being exerted to increase their time allotments.

The basic assumption under the program of required subjects is that a uniform program insures, to some extent, uniform learning results. This assumption has been challenged, and the diverse outcomes from a standard program are sometimes compared with the relatively uniform results of varied programs. Safety may be learned in a variety of experiences and is learned best in situations where the learner is highly motivated. The same may be true of other knowledges, skills, attitudes, and desired outcomes. Problem-solving, with about the same results, may be learned in many courses in agriculture or home economics, or in social studies and a number of other subject fields. The experiences at the workbench in a shop may be more effective in showing many pupils the way to solve a wider range of problems than the assigned reading they do at the table in the library. Further research and the discovery of new teaching techniques are needed for the development of varied approaches to desired learning.

4. *Continued experimentation is needed to provide for greater individualization in instruction by a wide range of methods.*—It is known that pupils learn at varied rates, and pupils with different interests learn from different experiences. Some secondary schools have adapted the methods of research laboratories and college seminars. Public forums have inspired round tables and panels in the classrooms. Emphasis on child development in the elementary schools has furnished basic ideas and techniques which have been adapted for secondary school use. However, there is probably a limit to borrowings from above and below. Although it appears that progress is being made in developing new techniques for teaching pupils in grades 7, 8, and 9, providing educational experiences for the slow learner has remained a persistent problem especially in the upper secondary grades. Individualizing instruction is of special importance in classes where the subject is required of all pupils. In these classes the range of ability is wide, interests are varied, and the socioeconomic background of the pupils reflects a community-wide range of customs and aspirations. The teacher is challenged to provide experiences which will not only encourage the able and interested pupils, but which will also awaken interest in the apathetic and less talented. At the same time he must try to preserve this unity of group discussion. The problem appears in all classes. The idea must be recognized that no two individuals are alike and the idea rejected of imposing conformity through education.

Ability grouping and similar administrative arrangements are no longer embraced as panaceas for solving problems of individual differences. Small schools find the problem of scheduling the different groups impossible. In large schools it is comparatively easy to organize groups on the basis of general intelligence and reading achievement but much more difficult when such additional factors as socioeconomic background, emotional development, and rates of physical maturation are considered.

Experimentation is needed to provide pupils with greater flexibility in planning their programs, which should be made under the guidance of parents and teachers. Some pupils obviously need more knowledge and skill in a given field than others. Some schools, therefore, are frankly offering not one-half units, as has long been done in such fields as music and art, but one-third, one-fourth, or one-fifth credits in a wide variety of subjects.

Other types of flexibility in scheduling are plans whereby pupils study one subject intensively all day or two subjects a half day each for a 9-week span and then go on to the next field of study. Year-round programs divided into quarters are also under experimentation. In these a pupil attends any three of the four quarters. The remaining quarter is devoted to such other purposes as the individual's needs may dictate.

5. *There is need for more experimentation to build a program of work experience.*—At least three goals are to be achieved in the work experience program: (1) Some work experience for all pupils to bring them into contact with business and industry and the problems of preparing for a job; (2) extended work experience for some youth to bridge the gap between school and full-time employment; (3) work that will provide not only experience but also income for youth from families in the lower economic groups. Instruments for evaluating personal growth as an outcome of all work experience, including summer employment, need to be developed. Successive experiences in the work field could then be planned on the basis of strengths and weaknesses revealed by evaluation.

There are many problems which must be solved in cooperation with business and labor leaders. In many cases the most valuable work experiences for youth would cost business and industry more than they would receive in return. Labor leaders will be anxious to guarantee full employment for adult workers. Schools, parents and social agencies will be sensitive to exploitation. However, most citizens believe that there should be no wide gap between full-time schooling and full-time employment for youth. The problem is to translate the conviction into action programs which will be approved by youth, parents, and the major groups with a stake in the problem.

6. *An adequate program for appraising the educational development of individual pupils needs to be developed.*—Instruments entirely adequate for measuring present achievement as an alternative measure to time spent in class have yet to be developed. Devices for predicting future achievement are needed in many areas, and, unfortunately, they are difficult to develop. The use of tests in the armed services, and the growing practice of testing in personnel offices of business and industry, should aid the schools to devise better tests to measure achievement and growth. In addition, the wide use of tests in other areas of American life should develop a public opinion which will accept these means for appraising, for promoting, and for graduating pupils when the schools finally adopt them.[1]

[1] While test development in schools has been the forerunner of test development in the armed services and in industry, school testing programs have always been stimulated when their instruments were adapted and used by other agencies.

The accumulation of a 4-year block of 16 Carnegie units, though deeply entrenched, has become inadequate as a process for gauging a youth's educational growth and development from high-school entrance to graduation. This unit based chiefly upon the time devoted to a given subject was originally devised by college administrators whose purpose was to bring about greater uniformity in the preparation presented by high-school graduates for college entrance. The Tests of General Educational Development which have been used in evaluating the achievements of veterans of the armed services suggest instruments which might supplant or at least supplement the Carnegie unit.

Many important high-school learnings—music, art, physical and health education, school and community service—are not yet fully evaluated in terms of Carnegie units. Now that widespread efforts are being made to further the general education of all youth of high-school age through fusion of courses, core procedures, and common learning programs, the task of assigning values based chiefly upon time units becomes more and more difficult. Increasingly the reliance upon the Carnegie unit as a sole measure of educational achievement has come under scrutiny.

The question of promoting high-school pupils on the basis of chronological age, as has long been done by many elementary schools, is now being boldly faced by the secondary schools. Certificates for early school-leavers which show both the quantity and quality of the work done are being tried out. Schools using this device record all of the significant accomplishment, both class and extraclass, which have been outcomes of the pupils' school experiences.

7. *Secondary school teachers and principals have a contribution to make toward improving programs of teacher preparation.*—Leaders in secondary education for more than a generation have insisted that decisions about secondary education should not be made exclusively by colleges and universities. This attitude has brought secondary school teachers and administrators into the curriculum field, first as partners with college personnel, and increasingly as the group most important in determining the school program. The responsibility of secondary school educators in the field of teacher preparation is receiving more attention from the men and women who are actually doing the job, but there is still a gap between preservice teacher education and the professional needs of teachers who are actually in the classrooms. Such systematic efforts to identify these needs as are represented by the Consensus Studies in the Illinois Curriculum Program[2] should be developed in many places.

When teachers and administrators have been encouraged to pool their ideas in workshops and school staff meetings, they have made useful con-

[2] *Prospectus of the Local Area Consensus Studies,* Bulletin No. 15 (Springfield, Ill., Superintendent of Public Instruction, 1951).

tributions to teacher education. Universal secondary education is being improved by innovations in hundreds of schools and thousands of classrooms. The results of these promising practices reported in educational literature should contribute to the revision and improvement of teacher education.

8. *The problem of school finance remains critical even after the adoption of State equalization programs.*—One foreseeable future need is that of greatly increased expenditures for secondary education to take care of a larger enrollment. There is almost universal agreement on this conclusion, but little consensus on who is to pay the bill. The minority who disapprove of any tax increases for public education might hold the balance of power in some communities and be able to prevent tax increases of any kind.

At an early date the alternatives to increasing school revenues should be clearly presented to the citizens of each community. Over-large classes and half-day sessions are two alternatives, which will cripple the education of youth unless the home supplements the work of the school by a much closer supervision of home study, and unless the community provides a wider range of free cultural and recreational experiences than most homes and communities are providing at present. If the citizens are unwilling to pay for such services, the alternatives are a neglected generation of youth or an increase in the amount and quality of effort spent in the home—supervising intellectual and cultural activities—and time spent as volunteers in the community on group work. On the current budget, no school should promise directly or by implication that it can continue the services, now provided, for twice the number of pupils. A policy of indecision which leads to improvisation in teaching too many pupils, followed by a rationalization that the makeshift operation is "adequate," will be of small service to schools, youth, or community.

Questions relating to the size of secondary school districts are important for better school support and more effective education. Comprehensive high-school programs seem to require a minimum enrollment of about 75 pupils for each grade. Although there is serious doubt as to the effectiveness of many small secondary schools, a program of wholesale consolidation on the basis of size alone would probably violate more principles of sound education than it would serve. Secondary school people cannot justifiably support movements unless they are based on the educational needs of youth. They can support only those which they believe increase the opportunities of youth for better education. Often such a movement has proved to be one which enlarged the administrative area and the financial support of a district and at the same time sustained and strengthened community schools.

9. *The whole question of home-community-school responsibility should be reexamined.*—A reexamination of the home-community-school responsibility may be forced if larger school revenues are not forthcoming. Even if a larger school income appears, the problem is still important and its

solution involves increased participation by noneducators in the determination of educational policies and procedures. The school frequently has assumed, or has been given, an imposing number of responsibilities: insuring safety, good public order, good citizenship, better health, and wholesome recreation; inculcating high moral principles; helping pupils make good decisions; developing sound personalities. Many schools have accepted this enlarged responsibility, but it should be made clear that the school cannot be held solely responsible in all of these areas. The home, voluntary organizations, law-enforcing agencies, social agencies, churches, and the general communities must do their share. Many functions now performed at school might be done as well, or even better, at other places by other community agencies. Social workers have a contribution to make to many aspects of youth adjustment and education. The local community agencies could expand their services in health, guidance, and other areas where the joint efforts of home, school, and community are needed.

The overarching problem which spans all the unfinished business is that of developing in youth the desire for an education that will help him to adjust to a democratic society in an age of science and technology and to take his part in building it. Many of the essentials of such an educational program are not clearly known, and wait for research and mass experimentation. However, the rough sketch available shows that the present organization and machinery are inadequate, and not all teachers and administrators have the vision, education, and training for the job ahead. Educational advancements during the next century, if they are made, will require the professional services of the ablest people. It is no secret that at the present time the chief rewards for such service are the intrinsic satisfactions of teaching. These attract some but not enough of the ablest youth to careers in secondary education. Certainly, the present income and status of many teachers offer little incentives to the best-endowed young men and women. Without some change in public support, the future may see larger numbers of youth receiving little more than custodial care from mediocre teachers lacking in initiative, intelligence, intuition, insight, and imagination. What action programs are needed to keep the gains made for secondary education and to push ahead to complete a program of universal secondary education?

Chapter 42

THE ROLE OF HIGHER EDUCATION

THE *complexities of the political, economic, and social arrangements of the modern world place a premium on formal education. In addition, many Americans find formal education makes economic and social advancement possible. Such factors have brought about a mass invasion of college and other post-high-school institutions. It is anticipated that in the foreseeable future more people than ever will need and want more formal education after high school. It is quite likely that, within a decade, the number of students in such institutions will double, if not triple. This movement has already begun, and it is the rare college that has not grown larger during the last decade.*

These changes have made necessary a reconsideration of the purposes, functions, and responsibilities of our institutions of higher learning. There has already been considerable discussion about the degree to which American higher education supports the growth of intellectual excellence. It is clear that American colleges successfully prepare technicians who can oversee and manage the continued growth of industry. But is this enough? The role of liberal education in a democratic society, and its relationship to technical education, need elaboration. Earlier we suggested that Harold Taylor's concept of the intellectual was important. That was not done to create opposition of any sort between the liberal and technical opportunities of education. Each needs the other if means and ends are to be kept in harmony. This, and other related issues, are explored by Charles Frankel, a philosopher, in the following article.

THE HAPPY CRISIS IN HIGHER EDUCATION

Charles Frankel

The permanent business of higher education is almost always misdefined, it seems to me. Almost every approach to higher education in the United States begins by pointing to the existence of certain problems and asking whether our educational institutions can solve these problems. I don't mean to imply that we don't have problems. I certainly don't mean to imply that colleges and universities have no responsibility to solve them, if they can. But the proper function of higher education, broadly speaking, is not to solve problems; it is to create them. In any free civilization, the college or the university is not simply an instrument of the society to which it belongs; it is one of the special places where we find the meaning of that society. Higher learning is the meaning of a civilization or a considerable part of the meaning or function of the civilization. It represents a society's efforts at self-consciousness. It is an attempt to know the world around it, to know itself, and to stand back and appraise its condition and its commitments.

Reprinted from "The Happy Crisis in Higher Education," *Current Issues in Higher Education* (Washington, D.C.: Association for Higher Education, National Education Association, 1961), pp. 3–11.

If higher education does its job, the society will be aware of problems otherwise unknown. More, the society will have problems, proud problems, the problems of civilized men which it would not have had if higher learning didn't exist. For insofar as institutions of learning raise questions about standards and ideals, they ask men to consider their own conscience. Insofar as universities produce new knowledge, they invite and encourage and cause a collision with traditional pieties, with old institutions. Higher learning in a society means that that society is in a permanent state of disequilibrium, and it is for that reason that higher learning has so often been suspected.

It is the barest of commonplaces that American higher education today is in a condition of crisis; but the commonplace is an ancient one, at any rate as Americans measure time. Those who have been associated with American higher education have almost always thought that our colleges and universities were in a condition of crisis, and they have been right. For higher education, which in most countries has an inherently conservative and backward-looking orientation, has had to be in the United States an instrument for regulating and stabilizing an explosive movement into modernity.

Almost all our problems in higher education, past and present, have arisen out of the fact that the American—the new man, as de Crèvecoeur called him—is the exponent and apostle of modernity, and the problems that our educational systems have rehearsed and are still rehearsing are rapidly becoming today the problems of most educational systems throughout the world. The problems with which we are now concerned, the problems which we seem to think have exploded in our faces, are not in fact new problems. They are old problems simply brought to sharper focus, and they are the problems that are peculiar to a modern culture, a permanently unsettled, heterogeneous, and impious culture: The problem is that of training young men and women in highly specialized skills needed by a modern society while at the same time opening their eyes to what lies outside their specialties; the problem is that of retaining and rebuilding the essentially aristocratic tradition of liberal learning in a democratic climate; the problem is that of connecting technology to the ideals of liberal civilization; and finally, the problem is that of negotiating and mitigating the extraordinary tensions between traditional elements in our culture and the scientific elements.

Let us briefly examine each of these problems. In the first place, we have as part of our unfinished business a kind of chronic disease with which we have to live, the problem of trying to bring together specialized training and broad general education. The problem is aggravated in the United States because our educational system is, in large part, the product of a mismarriage. At the undergraduate level, most of our educational institutions were conceived and created in the Anglo-Saxon mold. At the graduate and professional level most of our educational institutions were conceived in the mold of continental education in France or Germany. Anglo-Saxon education is not, perhaps, a theory of education; it is something even deeper, an inbred habit of thought. I recall the first time that I visited Oxford. I had just left France where I was residing and where I knew a good many teachers and students at the Sorbonne. At Oxford I dropped into a bookstore and among other things bought a little guidebook. The first sentence said, "The University of Oxford exists to train character." I couldn't have imagined finding such a sentence in any book in France on French education.

Anglo-Saxon education is intended to be, as American education is intended, too, not simply a training of the mind but of that impalpable and not easy to locate entity known as character. Anglo-Saxon education had tried to do this in a special way. The differences between John Dewey and his opponents are very slim indeed when looked at against the background of other systems of education. Almost all American schools from the grade school on up have tried to provide the individual student with a special microcosm of the adult world. They have tried to provide the student with something like a planned and total environment. In this environment, the student is expected to rehearse, to practice the skills which he will have to have as an adult. So, he must learn how to get along with the group; he must, of course, learn to read and write, go in for dramatics, journalism, regular exercise, and all the rest.

The American college is student-oriented, it is a home away from home. It is, indeed, more than a home. In its intent it is a community, a sheltered community where people will be hurt, but not hurt very badly, where they can practice most of the skills they will need later on, but not on issues that are really serious or final. So American students are tremendously interested in politics. They are by no means apathetic, but you must see them in their student governments to see their interest in politics. They are not as interested, or at any rate they are not as active, in politics on the streets of great cities as are students in Paris or Cairo. As a result, very often American students show a good deal more practical know-how about political organizations than their Continental counterparts. They know a great deal less, however, about ideology, which may or may not be a good thing.

On the other hand, however, the graduate or professional school brings a different temper and a different spirit into the university atmosphere. It exists not to train individuals as individuals, but to treat individuals as instruments for maintaining a discipline. The graduate school has the attitude of the specialist. A graduate professor looks upon his students as apprentices in his own discipline, as targets for his ideas, as aids in his research. The problem of specialization versus general education, therefore, is a peculiarly difficult problem to solve. It is difficult because we occupy houses that are divided against themselves. The spirit and temper of our universities and our colleges are, as it were, self-alienated. People look in two directions at once, and so it is extremely difficult to come up with any coherent program.

I am not at all sure that this is entirely bad. Like many chronic diseases it probably produces a state of siege, an attitude of sorts. It is a very serious and difficult problem. I think the issue is frequently misstated when it is conceived to be an issue between practical or vocational or professional training on the one side and liberal education on the other. Liberal education is not the same thing as general education. Nor for that matter is general education incompatible with a high degree of specialization in some disciplines. A liberal education is not, in fact, a specific group of subjects; it is not any definite curriculum or program of study. A liberal education is an education conducted in a certain way with a certain purpose from a certain point of view.

The heart of the matter is this. We train people liberally in a subject when at all times we try to expose the working of the human mind in that subject, when we try to show it is an achievement of mind, when we try to expose the elements of logic, of imagination, of historical perspective, or moral meaning in any subject. To do so is an extraordinarily difficult thing to do, but one can teach chemistry liberally, and one can teach English and even philosophy vocationally, professionally, narrowly. The distinction between liberal education and specialized education is not a real distinction. The important distinction is between liberal education and purely vocational education. There are some subjects that have to be vocational and can only be that. Typewriting is an example, but there are very few subjects in college or university curricula that are vocational—doomed as it were to be vocational subjects. If there are, it is the teacher who makes them so. So in a large part the problem is not going to be solved by great sweeping programs. It is going to be solved by getting educated, liberal teachers.

If we can take the specialized discipline, train people in it, but open the windows and the walls of that discipline so, from a given point of view, they can look out on the gardens that are adjacent, we have done what we should do, giving them a solid, civilized education in a specialty and at the same time substantial general or generalizing education.

The second great problem—another problem of unfinished education in America—has to do with the domestication of the liberal arts tradition as a tradition of liberal learning in an essentially democratic environment. This is an extraordinarily difficult thing to do for a number of reasons. The first reason I have already suggested: To teach people liberally requires that we try to fix their minds and imaginations not on what is immediately in front of them, not on some specific practical objective, but on ideas and ideals.

The second reason that we have a very difficult problem here is that the tradition of liberal education is an essentially aristocratic tradition, aristocratic by nature and aristocratic also by historical pedigree. It is aristocratic by nature simply because learning is an arduous thing. No one has really got the spirit of an education, the spirit of learning, unless he has seen the kind of self-mastery and self-discipline that any achievement in the arts and sciences requires.

At the same time, however, we live in an impatient, mobile, restless, democratic environment. I am not sorry about it, and unlike a good many of my colleagues I don't think there is an iron law which says that democracy kills liberal learning. On the contrary, I am rather aware of the fact that in many, many societies, higher education has broken down into a kind of esotericism, a kind of preciosity which is of no service to society and isn't very good higher learning either. So I rather like a society which looks upon intellectuals with a certain measure of scepticism. I live with intellectuals, and with bitter experience I know I look at them with a certain measured and sometimes unmeasured scepticism, myself included. I sometimes think it would be nice to live in a society in which it was habitual to think that a man with a title of professor was really a distinguished man, but I have seen what that habit does to the professor who enjoys it. He thinks he is very distinguished, too, and sometimes without any supporting evidence. A serving of scepticism and even a tiny soupçon of anti-intellectualism is helpful to keep intellectuals on their mettle.

Accordingly, I rather like the tension between democratic tradition and the special aristocratic tradition of liberal learning. There are, of course, very great problems here. In a democratic society education comes to serve very special functions. One of them is that higher education becomes the principal social escalator. The reason most young people are in schools in America is that they hope to get more money as a result, or else to have somewhat higher social positions than their parents did. I don't think that is dishonorable. I think it is not less dishonorable, or no less honorable, than the motive that brought the children of aristocracy to schools a century ago. Wanting money is as honorable as wanting to ride after the hounds. After all, the desires for money and for social position are strong desires and may help students to apply themselves. If we didn't do so much to distract them and perhaps to cushion them, perhaps they would do it. But more important, it is a remarkable evolution in the history of mankind that the major pathway to social advancement should be higher education. That is the problem with which we are faced. I think every professor ought to rejoice, and I think it is one of the reasons we are in the midst of quite a happy crisis in higher education.

At the same time, however, the problem is a serious one. If we try to satisfy all the consumers without erecting very careful safeguards, we will be going in for a species of democratic demagoguery. Very careful safeguards have to be erected if the standards of liberal learning are to be maintained. There has always been a tendency in the United States to survey broadly, to cheapen, to turn learning into the hobby of the dilettante—the democratic dilettante, which almost is a contradiction in its term—and I think that our universities and colleges have to take severe steps to prevent this cheapening process from taking place.

Moreover, there is another issue involved here, that of shifting the perspective of traditional liberal education. No liberal education in a democratic environment can have quite the perspective it once did. In the past, the graduates of a great university went into the elite positions in the nations. They knew they were members of the elite when they entered, and they knew they had a steady and secure position, if they wanted it, when they left. Moreover, they came from backgrounds which had already acquainted them with the world of learning, as such. In contrast, in a democratic environment, most of the young men and young women who go through our schools are going back to relatively modest positions in life. The women in particular are going to spend their most vigorous years largely doing manual work, and we must reflect on the fact that we are now giving collegiate education, and sometimes even graduate education, to people who are then going to go out the next twenty years and be hewers of wood and drawers of water. Now, poverty is one of the indispensable conditions in life. But we are an affluent society and it is harder for many of us to be gentlemen. How can we give a kind of education which will cling and will stick? How can we give a kind of education that will change the perspective of young people when they get it and give them one which will stay with them after they have left?

The problem is a problem of seduction. It is not a problem of fitting their motives, but of using the motives they have and luring them into an appreciation of the broader world of learning.

A third issue is the great problem of maintaining the traditions of higher education in a society that is in love with technology. We have all sorts of contradictory images of ourselves these days; we Americans that don't fuse at all. They tell us we are undisciplined and conformists, sodden with materialism and aching for a cause, and all the rest. The images don't fuse. In particular, we tell ourselves that we are materialists and we point to our booming technology as one of the illustrations or proofs of this point. But, American technology is in its own way not a proof of materialism or even a love of gadgetry. It provides a curiously moral, esthetic, and almost religious sense of proportion to our society and to our institutions of higher learning. In order to provide that civilizing sense of proportion, however, technologists have to be able to keep first things first, to know what their main business is. I don't mean to suggest that specialized research, in space, for example, is not worth doing. It is worth doing in the interest of national defense; it is worth doing in the interest of science. But the most important reason for wanting to do such research is that it contributes to the long-range purposes of science.

This brings us to the final great problem. In the United States, the greatest danger to our conception of the intellectual life comes from our preoccupation with technology. As a result of that preoccupation, we have absorbed the image of science and the image of technology. Until recently, and perhaps even today, most Americans confuse Thomas Edison with a scientist. He was an inventor, but only a scientist of sorts. Science is not organized gadgetry; it exists to provide knowledge for its own sake, to give us some understanding of the order of things insofar as given to us to understand that order.

From this point of view, we come to a fundamentally difficult problem, perhaps not acute in America, but a problem in Western civilization. The college or university that carries on its activity in a climate of freedom is not just an instrument of a free civilization; it is one of the special places where we find the meaning of that civilization. So it is perhaps natural that the deepest intellectual and moral division in our civilization is felt with peculiar intensity on our college and university campuses. I refer to the conflict between means and ends, techniques and values, or science and the humanities. The mere form in which this issue is stated is a reflection of that conflict, a reinforcement of it, and, I think, the expression of a dangerous and exhausting illusion.

The argument, properly construed, is not between those who are engaged in expanding human powers on one side and those on the other who are guardians of the heritage of the human spirit. Science is part of that heritage —an unwelcome part, because it overthrows a good many other parts of the heritage. It is perfectly true that science gives no authoritative or final answer to questions about human values, but then do the humanities? Despite the differences between science and the humanities, both are, or ought to be, examples of disciplined intelligence, of refined analysis, of sober respect for evidence, of taste in the selection of problems and in the organization of them. The real argument is not between subjects. It is between two rather different conceptions of what is the meaning of evidence, what is the nature of intelligence. The source of that argument is the challenge which the scientific style and spirit have presented to those who have traditionally occupied special positions of authority as arbiters of cultural, moral, and social knowledge. The scientific philosopher makes life hard for the metaphysician; the sociologist breaks into the conversation of the teacher of literature and asks for evidence to support the producer of literature's association with our culture.

But the main issue is the question of the nature of intellectual authority, the kind of answer which a society is going to regard as a good answer. The problem that science creates for all of us is a very complicated one. It has two essential features which illustrate its discomfort. The first is that science almost never answers the question the ordinary man and the humanities want answered. So science seemingly is an evasion. But it isn't; it is a triumph over ignorant questions. It is a reformulation of the question. There are some questions, indeed most questions, of common sense which we can't answer, and we can't answer them because they are foolish questions. That hurts, and that is part of the problem.

The second part of the problem is that science almost never gives us an answer that really says something definitely because it doesn't say yes or no. It says "yes, but," or "no, in this respect. . . ." It is really a complicated problem, and it is a dozen problems, and we will have to go after them one by one. We stand by while science is subordinated to the humanities. Science doesn't answer the mystery of life—it has told a lot more about that mystery than it told us 100 years before, but it hasn't solved the mystery. It has insulted our traditional culture in a sense. It wouldn't pay attention to *the* mystery but would look into the mysteries. This is the abominable snowman which Sir Charles Snow has called the conflict between the two cultures. I have considerable sympathy with the view he expressed. Although I am a professor in what conventionally is thought to be one of the new mystic disciplines, I have noted that on the whole my colleagues in the department of literature regard themselves as highly educated men because they read novels and regard scientists as illiterates because they only read books in physics. Whereas, I have noticed that most scientists actually read novels, and they know a good deal beyond the discipline which the average professor of literature thinks is a civilized learning discipline. There is a conflict between two cultures. However, unlike Sir Charles, I don't think that our ability to win the cold war, or even to give aid to underdeveloped nations, depends on our ability to solve this problem. That would be a depressing view of our situation. I think it is unjustified. I don't think the arguments between the scientists and the humanists are going to die in our time. I don't know when, if ever, they are going to die. I rather suspect they will die when men conquer the tendency to go in for wishful thinking and quick answers. Until that happens, I think the conflict will remain.

As long as the argument remains in its present form, however, there is one thing we probably won't do very well. We won't do liberal education very well. We won't do university education very well. As long as the discussion continues to be surrounded by eagerness for the easy, sweeping answer, by arrogance and by a kind of stubborn ignorance, there is very little likelihood that we are going to get very far in dealing with the fundamental issue in liberal education. At the very least, a substantive education in one of the sciences is a prerequisite for any educated man in our society. To give him less than that is to shut the door to his appreciation of some of the most majestic achievements of our culture. In the Middle Ages, things were there for everyone to see. Most people who had experience putting one stone on top of another could understand the kind of achievement the cathedral represented. They couldn't do it, they didn't know how the architect conceived it. But they understood it was quite a glorious achievement. That elementary kind of appreciation is denied to the great majority of educated men in our civilization. The sciences are not more important than the other disciplines, but substantive education in the sciences, education for its own sake in the sciences, is a very high priority matter in the coming decade. And, education ought to begin where most education should begin—with the education of the college and university faculties.

The trouble with the scientists is that life has been so good to them recently that they are no longer interested in teaching. They get better paying jobs, or they can do something else and look as though they are teaching. Scientists have a habit, like other professional groups, of saying they aren't popular. The self-image of professors in America is lower than the image that the outside world has. Sociologists show that the professor is one of the most highly respected people in America. It is the professors who think they are not. We mustn't worry about that, because doctors have a deplorable image of themselves, and lawyers. The members of every group think we don't like them. We are a very self-conscious society. So, scientists complain they are looked upon with suspicion, and, in view of the loud bang some of them are responsible for making, I suppose they are looked upon with mixed feelings. I look upon them too with mixed feelings. They have a major job of education to do. The great imaginative task in the coming decade is that task of liberal education for the laymen in the sciences. Unless a good many scientists make this a major part of their professional commitment, the job is unlikely to be done very well.

Now, let us look briefly at two new issues which I think have not been located or perhaps quite properly defined. A modernist in a society like ours is always in danger of becoming a kind of split personality. This is particularly true when his work becomes more highly specialized in its demands and when on the other side the habit of consuming goes up and up. What is that split personality? On one side, our work sinks into routine. On the other side, our play, our leisure, or what we choose to call our "culture" becomes increasingly disorganized and frivolous. But the sharp division between work and play, machinery and culture, science and the humanities, is itself a sign of man's age-old battle with scarcity—a hangover from that battle. In a society as wealthy as ours, such divisions are increasingly anachronistic. The problem is to unite discipline and spontaneity, usefulness and culture, work, and play.

One of the fundamental problems waged by every society moving toward modernity has been the struggle against illiteracy. The colleges and universities of the United States have in the past been part of that struggle. In the coming decade I think they are going to wage a battle against a new kind of illiteracy—creeping illiteracy of adult human beings in a world in which they have been turned loose with more leisure than before, illiteracy about the uses of leisure or the meaning of leisure. To call the process in which our colleges and universities engage adult education is a misnomer, for education suggests preparation for something, and I am not thinking of preparation. I am thinking of an invitation, as it were, to a consuming and concentrated task. Our society is rich enough and, in terms of its best and most traditional culture, it ought to offer its members a challenge for the kind of play that is the best kind, the kind that is like work or at any rate the best work, disciplined, cumulative, with a chance to perform and to achieve. The colleges and universities are the agencies to perform this task, and they are in the years to come going to have to change themselves over increasingly. Instead of being merely an exclusive training ground for the young, instead of going in for adult education as a form of advertising or an easy form for raising money, they are going to have to take it for granted that they are in America, and have been what the medieval church was in its day—a great shelter for human culture and human achievement.

The process for transforming the lost week ends and lost leisure hours of Americans into something that will help them to demonstrate and find themselves is a process to which I should like to see our colleges and universities commit themselves.

The second new issue is this: The democratic process depends on the state of communication, but communications in our society are warped by the pressures of the market place, burdened by the difficulties of the matters to be communicated, and inherently complicated by the fact that today just to report the news is to make news. An event is not simply what happens, it is what is reported. That plays back on the event, expanding its area and transmuting it into something other than it would have been if it were allowed to play out its career in private. I do not mean to say that the newspapers create events or make them important. I mean to say only that in an open society, in a society in which people want news, the fact that they get the news expands the area of conflict. It is, therefore, terribly important that those who get brought into the conflict by way of communications be reasonably well prepared to understand what is going on. That, of course, is terribly difficult, but it is particularly difficult in a society in which most of our news services, most of our public affairs services, are geared to the moment, the shock, the sensational. Bad news, from a journalist's point of view, is good news; good news is no news. And long-range news is a bore. One cannot understand the nature of the world he inhabits so long as information comes to him in that form and only in that form every day.

I don't know quite how to produce a revolution in this area, but I do think that once again a society as diversified, as plural, as ours ought to be able to provide those citizens who care with other media of communication —media of information that offer an alternative, a standard, a way of judging what they are getting as daily fare. Once again, the colleges and universities have an extraordinary opportunity and responsibility in this area—in radio, in television, in magazines, and in communicating with a large and eager general audience. I don't know whether they can do this individually or regionally or through an association like the Association for Higher Education, but there is a long-range job to be done if the level of communications in the United States is to be raised and once more it looks to me as if the obvious candidate for the job is the higher educational system.

We do, then, have a burdensome, difficult set of issues to deal with, but they are old issues. It is fortunate, it is a happy crisis when we are aware, as we are now aware, that we have these problems. It is also fortunate that, for the first time in the history of American higher education, a very large and broad public is looking upon all of us with considerable curiosity and interest. If we do badly, we will hear about it.

Chapter 43

THE ROLE OF ADULT EDUCATION

THE *notion that a person can learn as long as he lives is a long-established American idea. The dramatic growth of America from an outpost for European colonization to its present position as a world power and the explosion of knowledge now taking place in every field of inquiry make this nation more important than ever. It is the task of adult education, through a variety of private and governmental agencies, to help interested individuals to live with increased effectiveness and meaning.*

Passive acceptance or drift are the only responses that some adults can make to the changing circumstances of life. Others, however, search for and accept the challenges of change, and prepare to meet these challenges by using every formal and informal method of continuous education they can. These methods and experiences may include: seeking a deeper understanding of the self; obtaining a better understanding of the way our domestic society works; obtaining sounder insights into the nature of the international community; fulfilling a desire to become more competent in a particular field of knowledge; refining currently salable skills, or mastering new ones; and refining social graces and accomplishments. The range of desirable learning opportunities moves from the profound to the trivial. While the obligation to provide opportunities for adult education rests with society, the identification of the needs and interests to be satisfied and the utilization of the knowledge gained rests with the individual adult. If one assumes that a person's previous educational experiences contributed to his maturity, then one can assume that an individual who has grown satisfactorily in the past will continue to seek other experiences of greater intensity and significance.

The manner in which adult education developed in the United States, the reasons for this development, and the rationale for its continuation are described by Horace M. Kallen, a philosopher.

THE ADULT AND HIS EDUCATION

Horace M. Kallen

Practically until the turn of the century the prejudice prevailed that education must be for men only, that woman's place is in the home, and that nature, not nurture, fits her for her place. Both the woman's college and the woman's club signalized rebellion against this prejudice, and the more potent of these engines of rebellion was the woman's club. Woman's club and "schoolmarm" develop concurrently. The latter is a recent social type which the "schoolmaster" antedates by millennia. The literature of the race tended, until very recently, to treat both as comic, but comic schoolmasters are ancient perennials; not so schoolmarms. Neither Aristophanes nor Shakespeare has a schoolmarm to hold up to ridicule. Both, together with their many emulators of later generations, made fun of the schoolmaster. The schoolmarm is 19th century woman one step beyond the home. But there were very many places for her to go to catch up with men, and as society had as yet no established institutional vehicles, she, being a full-grown, unschooled, yet socially responsible human person, began by forming her clubs and there taking all culture for her province.

The event introduced a new point of social difference between the sexes. For males, studying and learning were activities identified with school and college and with their authorized modes of acquiring doctrines and undergoing discipline, received from the generations under the sanction of tradition as liberal education. They ceased to be conscious activities when, at graduation, students were dubbed bachelor of arts and admitted to the rights and privileges of "the society of educated men." Some went on to the learned professions, to which teaching was traditionally incidental. Most assumed that their education was now complete. Woman, on the other hand, rarely received anything like the conventional "liberal education," nor did many of them have the privilege of attending finishing schools and acquiring lady-like "accomplishments." They joined their women's clubs, as a rule, after marriage with its adult responsibilities for home and children. Their access to "liberal" disciplines came thus with functional adulthood and their liberal education had a contemporaneity significantly different from that indoctrination concerning the past which the colleges gave their men.

Reprinted from Kallen, Horace. *Philosophical Issues in Adult Education*, 1962, pp. 5–22. Courtesy of Charles C. Thomas, publisher, Springfield, Illinois, and the *Harvard Educational Review.*

In the post-graduate man's world of business, politics and sport where the alumni lived and moved and had their masculine being, there was no place for the professor and pedagogue who had practiced this indoctrination. Teaching, on any level lower than the collegiate, was not appreciated as an occupation for men of character and ambition. It was largely a way of earning money incidental to ambition's larger, nobler ends. The mores somehow joined it to woman's work, and the schoolmasterly expert in culture, to woman's interests. As her place was the home, so his was the academic fane. He could hardly be expected to enter the arena of politics or business and fight a man's fight there. But he did, even as she did. Whatever the cause of his breakthrough, its occasion was the election of a pedagogue to the presidency and the unprecedented problems intrinsic to the First World War. The pedagogue was Woodrow Wilson, whose opponents thought to degrade him by calling him a "mere professor." Wilson's initiative brought, for the first time in our history, economists, historians, psychologists and philosophers out of the academic fanes into the nation's affairs. The need to observe, to think, and to organize scientifically the mobilizing and readying of the men and materiel required to wage a war, into which we had been drawn utterly unprepared, took all sorts and conditions of professors out of their academic seclusion into the hurly-burly of enterprises that included the mental testing of draftees, the analysis and planning of what is nowadays called logistics, and the preparation of the data and program of the peace.

The mobilization of the professorate was later celebrated by at least one of them in the public prints. And justly so. The event signalized a new and unforeseeable diversification of the American people's spiritual economy, a mutation in their institutional mores. Never since has the professorate been segregated to the academic ghetto. Members of it have successfully challenged the "practical" politician and the "realistic" business man on every level and in every branch of government, and have been serving with superior distinction alike in our city councils, our courts and our houses of Congress. The emergence of the professor as citizen, his ingress into public life, exercised a salutary influence on the general idea of education as a continuing concern with the actual present and the nascent future. It contributed something functional and masculine to the developing notion of adult education.

EDUCATION FOR WORKERS; WORKERS' EDUCATION

On this notion the international scene made an especial impact. The American people, safe between two oceans, remote from the fields of battle to which the unwelcome draft had sent their sons, were in sentiment "isolationist." Recognition of the nation's changed role among other, and independent and sovereign, states has taken practically a generation to form. The people's feeling for the future organization of mankind rested, like that of their war-time president, upon their democratic faith, not objective knowledge of the global actualities. As events brought the latter to their attention, a mood set in of disillusionment marked by xenophobia, race prejudice, industrial war, speculation, frivolous violence and cultural escapism. But there was an interlude of hopeful idealism between the armistice and final rejection of the League of Nations and the other terms of the Peace Treaty by the United States Senate under the leadership of Henry Adams' close and rancorous friend, Henry Cabot Lodge. The idealism was signalized by the word "Reconstruction." It came, the writer thinks, from England, where the war had brought the labor movement to unprecedented strength. It had an especially catalytic effect among teachers and students in the colleges. Made aware by the exigencies of war at home and revolution in Europe of the human problems of labor organization they began to reflect upon "industrial democracy," and upon the relation of education to such democracy. It became the vogue for them either to organize "trade union colleges" or to participate in establishments for "labor education" already existing.

The latter had already made spontaneous appearance in the sequence of events that turned the attention of the prevailing craft-unions to reorganization by industries. In this the conscious intent of the unions changed from the defense and advancement of trade-union standards and conditions to a free-enterprise program of democracy in industry. With it went the recognition that in all negotiations over standards and conditions the employers had on their side all the advantages of expert knowledge of the economy of the industry, the advantage being tantamount to a monopoly of knowledge. The unions realized that they must break this monopoly. To do so, they both set up research departments of their own, and launched programs of "labor education." The latter cannot be called autogenous. It is true that immigrant intellectuals, who began their new lives as Americans with manual labor, had at various times initiated educational enterprises. But the ruling hierarchy in the American Federation of Labor had consistently frozen them out, and the American public school system provided at public expense schooling—such as it was—for the nation's children which tended to render private efforts, on whatever level, gratuitous or invidious. Elsewhere, notably in England, such schooling was more conspicuous by its absence than presence. The labor movement was there under the necessity of developing its own standards of culture and instruments of education. The standards were of course drawn from the prevailing climate of cultural opinion. Their carriers were the dons and students of the great universities who, moved by the Christian Socialist tradition deriving from Charles Kingsley and his mates, sought to bring to their under-privileged fellow Britons the Englishman's entire cultural inheritance. Others were Fabians, implementing the practical programs hatched by the Webbs. Still others drew their gospel from John

Ruskin and in the Ruskin College, established at Oxford by Charles Beard and fellow-Americans, undertook to bring to the British workingman the vision and skills that would make him the peer of the British peers.

The overall instrument of this workers' education was the Workers' Education Association. Necessarily the persons whom this association enrolled had to be "adult," if not in years, at least in the fact that they were supporting themselves by their own labor. Their condition gave shape to the Association's goals and methods, if not its means. The education it proffered was, in principle, to be an education which sought, as Robert Peers said, "to help men and women to work out for themselves an effective attitude to life based on wider knowledge, to find their place in the universe, to discover a philosophy which will enable them to face up to life's problems individually and collectively"[1]

This is education as Henry Adams conceived education. It defines the gradient that adult education has been moving on, willy nilly: the formation, by trial and error, of a diversity of free cooperative endeavors after solutions of the joint and several problems of the actual human condition by the persons whose problems they are. In very many instances such persons are unaware of their problems, as contagiously sick people are sometimes unaware of their sickness. Conventionally these problems are not problems in education at all, but problems in political, businesslike, medical or priestly action. Conventionally, education consisted in transmitting the already-known unchanged to those who do not yet know it. Conventionally the method of transmission is indoctrination, not exploration, and its success is measured by precise and accurate reproduction, not recreative use. But for adult education convention could not be sufficient. To function, it had to look not only to new ideas, but to new uses for old ideas under felt exigencies of both the personal and the public life.

THE GLOBAL CRISIS AND THE DISCOVERY OF THE ADULT

In the United States these exigencies carried a mutative import. As if overnight, the unready nation had become practically the foremost power in a world whose war had released passions, initiated transformations, and brought into the foreground of belief and of action designs and dogmas whose propulsions evince no subsidence in the foreseeable future. Already, patriotic scholars, publicists, business men, public servants looked with an anxious eye upon the prospect. Many of them had had no inconsiderable part in the planning of victory and in the endeavor to establish a just peace after victory. They had committed themselves in spirit and in truth to the

[1] Robert Peers, *Adult Education in Practice* (London: Macmillan & Co., Ltd., 1934), p. 10.

idea that the war was a war to "make the world safe for democracy" and to establish for all the world's peoples equal liberty under law. But already in 1919, before peace was yet concluded, they had become aware that winning a war was anything but the same as building a just and lasting peace; they had learned that the responsibilities of peace promised far to outweigh the burdens of war. In their talks together, they came to agreement that the nation's unreadiness was due to a fundamental lack in its educational program. The nation's youth was leaving the nation's schools and colleges unequipped to meet the chronic problems and unexpected contingencies of adult life. They proposed to pioneer with a new kind of school.

"The people of America," they wrote, "as well as those of Europe, now face a tide in the affairs of men such as will scarcely pass without a searching readjustment of the established order of things. In view of the difficult situation in which humanity finds itself, a group of men versed in the various branches of knowledge have drawn together for counsel, for the correlation of their investigations, and the establishment of a center of instruction and discussion where serious-minded and mature students may gather to carry on their studies in the spirit of scientific inquiry."

The work of this center was to be "of post-graduate character." But there were to be no requirements for admission, and no degrees. The only condition was that any person desiring to join the enterprise should be "serious-minded and mature," and that he should be desirous of sharing with his teachers what Charles Beard described as "free, open, unafraid consideration of modern issues in the free spirit of scientific inquiry, and with no commitment to any foregone conclusion."

As a guaranty of this freedom to inquire and to teach, the founders of the center proposed to make it independent of external controls. Many of them felt that they had suffered from the intervention of administrative bureaucrats in scientific procedures and judgments. They had become very sensitive to the workings of economic pressures, and they agreed—it is now clear, mistakenly—that their center should seek no endowments, but should endeavor to pay as it went and make up its deficits through contributions from members and gifts from friends.

Another of its innovations would be to set up no departments. The historians, economists, sociologists, anthropologists, political scientists, philosophers, and psychologists were to join together as the center's permanent staff with the undertaking to pursue their special lines of inquiry in the fellowship and under the critical scrutiny of their colleagues in other fields. They were to work in the faith that the insights they sought could best be pursued through the orchestration of the social sciences.

The Center was set up in the spring of 1919. It is known as The New School for Social Research. In the thirty-three years of its existence it has undergone a good many changes of policy and personnel, some due to illness and death, some to the exigencies of the economic cycle at home, others to the tragedies abroad called the Bolshevik Revolution, Fascism, National Socialism, Falangism. But its overall purpose and program have remained unaltered, giving even the degrees which the New School now awards a special distinction. This derives from the conception of maturity and the idea of adult.

The expression, "adult education" had entered the argot of pedagogy during World War I. For some time before, men and women busy in earning their livings by day, had been attending public schools by night. These "night schools" were simply day-schools in artificial light. Whatever the subject taught—mostly reading and writing—the teachers, the methods, the materials, and the atmosphere prevailing were those of the day schools. For the teacher, night school was an opportunity to eke out a scanty income. For the pupil, if he was an immigrant reading, or wanting to learn English, night school was a necessary activity that did not cost him anything; if he was a youth with ambition, having to earn his living by day, night school was a chance to learn a trade by which he could better himself. There were also varieties of private educational enterprises conducted for profit, whose advertising exploited both this motive and a latent cultural snobism which it endeavored to activate. Correspondence schools offered courses of studies in a great variety of subjects. Institutes, secretarial schools, preparatory schools, all made seductive offers to fill the night-hours with instruction in all knowledge, from improving the memory to profitable story-telling or sleuthing. The educative process of both the public and the private establishments doing night-work was patterned upon that of the day-school, and the psychological assumptions regarding teaching, learning, and their conditions were employed indifferently in both, handling the adult like the youth. Nevertheless, extensive as were the frustrations of the customers, and striking as was the turnover in free as well as paying pupils, the people's hunger for saving, strengthening or profitable knowledge was so great that in 1926 there were five times as many persons taking correspondence courses as there were pupils in all the nation's institutions of higher education.

Unlike the children and youth in schools and colleges, or even the gainfully employed pupils in the public night-schools, the millions who were paying their way were voluntaries. They were buying "education" in an open educational market, where the rule of *caveat emptor* worked with no less effectiveness than in any other market. The appraisal of their intellectual and cultural wants, on which educational goods and services were put on sale, was an appraisal made in terms of the interests and arts of the producer, not the wishes and needs of the customer. The idea "learner" was conformed to the idea "teacher." Because, throughout the educational establishment, the "learners" are a captive audience subject to rule by the teachers, it took a long time for the pundits of pedagogy to realize that learning is independent of teaching, and that as often as not, teaching is the chief obstruction to learning.

In point of fact, the realization owed little to the pedagogic disciplines. It followed from the development of a scientific psychology of learning that started with the study of animal learning and carried on to the processes of human learning. The development is largely attributable to the pioneering inquiries of the late Edward Thorndike, who might be called the father of modern educational psychology. He isolated learning from teaching and treated it experimentally as an independent variable. What is called educational psychology, whatever its denomination, is now in the main a psychology of learning. The discipline now considers the learning of adults as having a configuration of its own. It recognizes that an adult is no more an oversized child than a child is an undersized adult. It recognizes a developmental sequence of mutations and an organic connection between bodily changes and the disposition and powers and relationships of the psyche. If, biologically, adulthood is established by the ripening of sperm and ovum and the ability to beget and bear young—that is, by puberty—its social attainment varies with the determining social institution. In certain family structures adulthood is reached only when the parents die. Religious interests take it at the biological level and set the time for initiation into membership in religious communions at or near puberty. The conventions of the military service put the age of military maturity at eighteen, those of the political order at twenty-one. The learned professions postpone adulthood much longer. Functionally, nevertheless, every individual comes to feel himself adult when he thinks of himself as responsible for himself, to himself; when he maintains himself, materially and spiritually, by his own efforts at his own risk. This may happen before puberty, with puberty, or at shorter or longer stretches of time after puberty. For the social scientist, adulthood or maturity is not a matter of years but of the range and depth of a person's experience in his struggle to survive and to grow in a society of people all different from each other, and having to live together with each other in the many ways that compound into their community.

Some persons are forced into this psychosocial maturity by the time they are ten, others are prevented from acquiring it to the day they die. Marriage used consistently to bring it to women, when it made them responsible for the economy of the common household. Where the homemaker and mother adds to her tasks another than domestic occupation, the experiences compounding into maturity become correspondingly more potent and diversified.

DAYLIFE, NIGHTLIFE, AND EDUCATION

But in our society, the first external sign of social adulthood is earning one's living. To take a job might be to accept excessive demands on the taker's capacity, but it is an initiation of adulthood. It is an entering into a complex of relations with others which are commitments; it sets up responsibilities which are a learning of works and ways that ripens as it continues, and transposes the job-taker from a consumer, into a producer, of community values. Of course it also brings conflicts over rule and status. Earning one's own way makes one independent of family support; contributing to family income alters one's status in the family. The elders may resent the change and parental authority may fight even with fists for its overlordship; parents may never in their hearts surrender their claims. But in living fact they cease to press them, and as often as not acquiesce in the authority of their working children, however young. They acknowledge adulthood.

Perhaps one of the most critical yet obvious and little-heeded of the stigmata laid upon adulthood by our industrial economy is seen in differences between the day life and the night life of adults. Like "adult education," "nightlife" is a comparatively new expression. It names a major trait of our industrial culture. The pre-industrial world did not know it. Lacking the instruments of artificial illumination, its multitudes rose and went to bed with the sun. Worship, play, sport and study as well as work were daytime activities, and whether laborious or free were suffused with similar psychic tones. This is still the case with infants and children, and with all who may live without working and spend without earning. But for the industrial multitudes, daytime is earning time, nighttime is spending time. They earn by day that they may spend by night. By day they work for their livings, by night they live their lives. Whatever any person's occupation, whether that of a guard on a subway train, or a schoolmarm in one of our gargantuan public school buildings, the day's work is routinized, limited, intensive and above all, repetitive. Most have engaged in it by chance or necessity. It is more readily endured than enjoyed, and its consummation is the wage-envelope or salary-check, which the workers consistently would increase, while the hours of work are diminished. It is their gainful occupation, a means to an end other than itself; servile, not free. The free occupations are those of the night; those are not means but ends in themselves. They bring no gain other than the exercises of body and spirit of which they consist. They are the spectacles of the arena, the theatre, the motion picture, the video, the museum, or the street; they are the dancing, the gambling, the bowling, the skating, the wrestling, the boxing and other games and sports one can personally engage in, during the hours between dinner and bed time; they are music heard or made; they are the records and practices of all the arts and sciences, the issues of politics and the arguments, rites and consolations of the cults. In these the person lives his life. By them the flesh of his spirit maintains its health, and the freedom and fulfillment of his spirit magnify.

As against day life, night life is consummatory, restorative and liberating. In terms of education, it enfolds both the matter and the form of liberal education in the truest sense of that much-abused term. Workingmen rarely find their work liberal and liberating. They do not want to make their night life a busman's holiday from their day life. The labor education movement has found consistently that its most welcome programs are those addressed to release from the concerns of the job by means of letters, the arts, the sciences and sports, rather than liberty within the industry, through knowing and understanding with a view to democracy in its entire economy. This disposition is also the tired businessman's; we have noted that it is manifest in the female of the species and it qualifies her duller male no less. The more conspicuous and garish, if less substantial, components of night life bear witness.

LEARNING, UNLEARNING, TEACHING

This is why the chronic problem of the schools of a free society becomes the acute issue of the education of its adults. The problem is always: to transvalue schoolwork from the traditional condition of imposed labor, which teaching under a school system tends to preserve, into a teamplay of free activities, harmonious with the needs and powers of the personality and relevant to the problems of the society of which it is a member. The issue is, how to endow the necessary labors of day life with the actualities of release and restoration intrinsic to night life; how to compenetrate the enfranchisement and consummation of living one's life with the functional relevancies of earning one's living, as livings are earned and lives are lived in a culture like ours. Obviously if the teacher is to think of teaching as a facilitation of learning, *what* is studied becomes of far less importance than *how* it is studied. The adult, unlike youth, studies because he wants to, not because he must. He chooses his field in order to feed some conscious hunger or to gratify some felt, perhaps unarticulated need. This is his *terminus a quo*. Willing or unwilling, his *terminus ad quem* becomes such an ordered conspectus of experience and destiny as would satisfy Robert Peer's definition of the goal of adult education, and Henry Adams' conception of all education—a philosophy of life that a person would bet his life on.

As much as his education would bring the adult to setting the actualities of his life and labor in the perspectives of new knowledge and new insights, it would also achieve his unlearning an immense deal already learned. Indeed, while the education of youth is mostly learning, adult education is very much unlearning, is the liquidation and replacement of habitual rigidities of attitudes, feelings and ways of thought and of work, by a viable configuration of self, society and nature that will nourish and channel curiosity instead of starving it.[2]

[2] What is involved may be inferred from the story of the cobbler of Koepenick, a suburb of Berlin. The tale is that on the afternoon of October 16, 1906, a number of

It was by an insight of this need that the founders of the New School had been moved. In the light of events since their 1919 statement regarding the needs and fields of adult education, that was a piece of successful scientific forecasting; 1952 differs from 1919 mostly by the intensity and spread of the assault upon freedom and upon the peaceful cooperation of free men. Current opinion is disposed to qualify the present age as "the age of anxiety," and anxiety begins in some person's psyche and must then be transposed into the courage which is both wisdom concerning dangers and the readiness to meet them. A democratic philosophy of adult education must needs seek for this courage, taking it as a reasoned faith in freedom based on understanding its nature, its conditions, an insight into dangers, and armed with the knowledge and the knowhow to meet and overcome them. It must seek to convert the unconscious impact of global influences upon personal history into conscious knowledge.

This conversion transforms the spiritual poverty and scarcity we call ignorance into spiritual abundance and simultaneously provides the strategy, the logistics and the tactics of the struggle to defend, to multiply and to enhance the freedoms of a free society. Sometimes it is achievable by the lecture method, by merely communicating information and interpretations. To the adult, fatigued by the day's work and seeking nightly release and restoration, this is often a satisfactory method; least exacting and most complacent. But it is neither the most liberating, nor the most likely to be convertive. That calls for a mode of cooperative inquiry which will lead to new ways and generate new wants, turning desire away from escape and recreation to what might be called self-creation and mastery.

In principle, hence, the teacher of adults is neither schoolmaster nor schoolmarm. He is the captain of a voluntary team going out upon an intellectual exploring expedition. Their inquiry calls for a dual procedure—the art of seeking, and the communication of findings—findings which repeat what has already been found, and findings of what is different, new, and strange. Both procedures call for deliberate comparisons with alternatives present and past, both call for confrontations of alternatives, in a continuous give-and-take that should come to rest in a consensus. In both, inquiry and behavior, thought and action, suffuse each other. The subject of this

---

Wilhelm II's soldiers waiting at the railroad station were accosted by a Prussian army captain who ordered them to follow him. He marched to the town hall, arrested and ordered the burgomaster jailed, examined the financial books, confiscated all the ready cash and disappeared.

Later, it was discovered that the man was no army officer, but a cobbler, Wilhelm Voigt, who played this trick in order to show up the blind response of the Germans to military dress. Voigt was sentenced to four years in prison for impersonating an officer, but his Kaiser pardoned him. This habitual blindness works on every level of every domain of the human enterprise. See William James' essay, "On A Certain Blindness in Human Beings."

action-research may be other people, individually or in groups; it may be nonhuman things and events; it may be a "body of knowledge" in a book. Anything may be taken for subject—a god, a garbage collector, an archaeologist, an advertisement, a poem, a loaf of bread, a jug of wine, or a "thou." Adult education cannot well accept a set curriculum, nor make concessions to the occupational hierarchy, so army-like, characteristic of modern finance-industry. It cannot well concede the invidious distinctions between men and management, the manual occupations and the learned professions, the industrial and fine arts. It must postulate the parity of all occupations, each different from the others, and each exercising some sort of influence upon the others. It must need bring into optimal clearness and distinctness the idea of each and shape the swiftest, simplest, and most effective intercommunication between all in such wise that the singularity of each will be realized as an equally worthy, honorable, and free role in the working and living together of all.

Of course, this is far more an aspiration than an achievement, and not a very general aspiration, at that. Yet the principle is indispensable to adult education in a democratic society struggling to maintain free institutions. Even our military establishment knows this. Authoritarian and hierarchical as the brass imagine a fighting army has to be, the armed forces have devised and managed the most comprehensive work of adult education in the entire United States. Although they postulate that when a citizen becomes a soldier he goes "on leave from democracy," the pretensions by which the military's educational projects are rationalized are strictly democratic. Recently, Mr. Benjamin Fine of the New York *Times,* having made a survey of these projects, took note of the challenging antithesis between pretension and performance. According to the War Department's Technical Manual first produced in the summer of 1945—officers charged with non-military instruction are to develop convinced beliefs in individualism, free enterprise, democracy; to communicate objective analyses of current issues in the light of these qualities of our American way of life. "The United States [believes]" says the manual, "that the soldier's mind should be free, informed, judicious, able to protect itself from sophistry and falsehood, alert and understanding of the problems of command." Considering any and every institution of the nation's life in the light of this article of faith, the observer finds himself forced to conclude, as Mr. Fine concluded from his observation of adult education under military auspices, that the belief is more honored in the breach than the observance.

ADULT EDUCATION: DISENTHRALLMENT FOR SURVIVAL

Such then, is the crux of the problem for both the learner and the teacher in the education of the adult. For the learner it is the consequential development, by acts of well-ordered inquiry, by impartial yet sympathetic scrutiny of alternatives, by such trials as he can make and errors as he can survive, of a vision of existence and destiny which shall with its perspectives ennoble and transvalue the meanest, the most routine and inconsequential events of his day, and then to bet his life on his vision. For the teacher, it is to lead the learner to achieve this development by free exercise of his own powers, at his own risk and on his own responsibility.

Most of what is called adult education does not envisage such a function. Since the expression came into use, it has been applied to every enterprise or activity not included in the acknowledged educational establishments. Semipublic and public institutions such as settlements, churches, Christian and Hebrew Associations, museums, libraries, as well as private undertakings offering instruction for profit, and chambers of commerce, manufacturers associations, *soi-disant* patriotic organizations making their particular propagandas, have all, at one time or another, been said to carry on adult education. So manifold had they become, already in 1924, and so pervasive the sentiment that went with the expression, that the Carnegie Foundation financed an inquiry which produced scores of surveys and reports, and hundreds of definitions of adult education, each expressive of the interests, the faith and the vision of the definers. The following year saw the organization of the American Association for Adult Education, and a multiplication of diversified organizational enterprises, all involving meetings, surveys, publications, a journal, but none reaching to the nuclear problem. Neither did the first world conference on adult education of 1929. The great depression presented the problem to the nation in unforeseen practical form, again with no nuclear rethinking of how to meet the mounting need. For world-events —from Hitler's seizure of Germany to the formation of the United Nations Organization and the conflicts and treacheries its deliberations ironically bring to light—have made the continuing education of the adult an ineluctable national, as it has always been a personal, necessity. The times are replete with signs of an awareness of the need—from the high-powered and well-financed propaganda of "great books" to the observations of the Presidential Commission on Higher Education, the fumblings of UNESCO, and the launching of schools of "general studies" and other night schools as additions to the day time enterprises of colleges and universities. The most recent entrant into the syndrome of anxiety-seeking adult education for assuagement, is the present inquiry into liberal education for adults financed by the Ford Foundation.

The trend suggests a growing awareness not only that knowledge brings power and advantage, but that, insofar as human survival is of another kind than survival of the animal organism, education is survival. Survival is the liberation and exercise of mutually suffusing powers of seeing and understanding and doing that find their way through every frontier which men and nature present. Such liberation and exercise are the same as suffusing the functions of day life with the consummatory values of night life, and validating night life with the functional relevancies of day life. The event would put an end to the long divorce of vocation from culture, the segregation of the past from the present relevancy and future consequences. It would seek to accomplish Henry Adams' aim: "to fit young men in universities and elsewhere [and old men too, as adult education] to be men of the world, equipped for any emergency." And the emergency of free society in our time knows no like. It was during the nation's greatest emergency of freedom, our Civil War, when Henry Adams was himself a youth, that Lincoln had said to the American people: "The dogmas of the quiet past are inadequate to the stormy present. The occasion is piled high with difficulty, and we must rise to the occasion. As our case is new so must we think and act new. We must disenthrall ourselves, and then we shall save our country."

And there is an echo of this requirement to disenthrall ourselves in Adams' conclusion of his old age: "The attempt of the American of 1800 to educate the American of 1900 had not often been surpassed for folly; and since 1800 the forces and their complications had increased a thousand times or more. The attempt of the American of 1900 to educate the American of 2000 must be even blinder than that of the Congressman of 1800, except so far as he has learned his ignorance. . . ."[3]

But: the two disenthrallments postulate irreconcilable goals. With Lincoln, disenthrallment was courage and simply not to yield would have been victory. With Adams it was yea-saying to defeat; and he is remembered as with no present relevance or later consequence, while Lincoln is reverenced for both. The moral and mental antitheses are momentous for the matter, the methods, and the teacher in the education of the adult.

[3] Henry Adams, *The Education of Henry Adams* (Boston: Houghton Mifflin, 1918).

PART NINE

The Educators and Education

THE IMPORTANCE of the roles and tasks performed by educators can hardly be overstated. Education that is designed to guide all the children of all the people to the fullest realization of the democratic ethos requires broad, deep understandings and skills of all teachers. There is no place for halfway measures in this matter, for the goal is the fullest development of every aspect of each individual's personality.

In the ideal sense, the process of becoming educated occurs through meeting, in a democratic manner, the realities of daily experience. It can be said that living and education are two facets of a single goal: the attainment of maturity, for both teachers and students. This requires a design for education that teaches each individual to develop the powers and techniques that make possible the continuous enhancement of maturity. The point to such education is that it is a process that makes further education necessary and possible. As John Dewey has stated: "It [education] is that reconstruction or reorganization of experience which adds to the meaning of experience, and which increases ability to direct the course of subsequent experience."[1]

So far as the preparation of teachers goes, not everyone who desires to teach in schools maintained by a democratically inclined society is the kind of person who can do what is required of him. At the very least, education for democratic living carries with it the obligation to conduct education democratically. It seems quite clear that any number of aspiring teachers can talk about the values of democracy, although they are not able to live by them. Both the aspiring teacher and the college engaged in teacher preparation must face this problem. This has been posed in blunt fashion because in talking about teacher preparation, one of the most perplexing issues in American education, much is said about what teachers should know and not nearly enough about who they must be.

Although it is generally agreed that a well-designed curriculum for teacher education should provide general education and special or professional education, there is much controversy about how to relate liberal and

[1] John Dewey, *Democracy and Education* (New York: The Macmillan Company, 1924), pp. 89–90.

professional studies. While much is made of the educational significance of individual differences, this significance is seldom reflected in the organization of teacher-education curricula. What the appropriate time in the developmental pattern of an individual may be for the introduction of liberal and professional education remains to be clarified. Is it possible or even desirable to design a single curriculum that can be applied in uniform fashion in all institutions maintaining a teacher-training program, or should time, place, and circumstance be determining factors? Whether this education should be under the auspices of a liberal arts institution, a teachers college, or a university has produced strong differences of opinion. Whether the undergraduate years should be devoted solely to general education and the graduate years to professional education with a continuation of general education, or whether a suitable compromise can be effected, requires further clarification. The most appropriate time for the introduction of professional fieldwork that will let the student relate theory and practice is not clearly established.

In the material that follows, various facets of the issue of teacher preparation will be considered. The challenges educators are called upon to resolve in the clash between democratic ideals and the realities of social class are discussed. This sets the stage for an examination of the importance of certain fundamental principles that should support any program of teacher preparation and for a discussion of the role and the responsibility of colleges and other programs of general and professional studies. A plea is then advanced for making the prospective teacher the active center of the educative process rather than the silent, passive recipient of faculty attention. On the basis of this material, a profile is offered of the personality traits a teacher should possess. The last article deals with the significance of academic freedom.

Chapter 44

THE CHALLENGES IN TEACHER PREPARATION

ALTHOUGH we have abstracted from the lives of Americans a group of values that are said to belong to the whole society, the reality of day-to-day living is far more complex. Particular groups have special values, and each child is a protagonist of these values. In addition, the impact each group has upon others produces conflicts that are brought to school where they complicate the tasks of instruction. W. H. Burton, himself an educator, is concerned with the evolution of education in the United States as it serves the needs and interests of different kinds of students and the ever-changing demands of society. In his discussion, Burton describes the principal problems facing the schools and emphasizes the training and responsibilities of teachers. He presents the issues as challenges: (1) "to develop a minimum literacy and simple fundamentals of citizenship," and (2) "to develop cultural unity within a diverse society simultaneously with development of individual talent." A number of highly important questions concerning the future development of schooling as the means to secure democratic values lead Burton to offer eight characteristics he believes should describe the accomplishments of the educator in America. He concludes by raising a number of questions about the nature and purpose of teacher education.

EDUCATION AND SOCIAL CLASS IN THE UNITED STATES

W. H. Burton

THE FIRST CHALLENGE

For the first time in all history a nation and its schools were called upon to educate all the children of all the people—and do it in the school so far designed for the selected few. We accepted the challenge, but not at first.

The first reaction of the school was to maintain the historic and traditional materials and methods. This was education and had been for some centuries. The "best people" had long approved it. If the "new people" now coming to school could not master it, could not learn, they merely represented proof of the ancient belief that the common people were unfit for education. A sad and tragic era ensued. Elimination from school was shockingly great. The army and census figures showed that in 1914 less than fifty percent of adult Americans had finished the sixth grade. The harsh and unsympathetic treatment caused the elimination and must have been a factor also in much delinquency and bad citizenship.

One of the great glories of our democracy and of our educational leadership is that we eventually accepted the challenge to meet this unprecedented situation—to educate all the children of all the people.

The turn of the century saw the development of the first so-called intelligence tests and the first subject matter achievement tests. Faulty as the early instruments were, they opened great new vistas. The huge range and nature of individual differences, commonplace now, gave new purposes and directions to the school. Eventually great amounts of information became available showing that the intellectual ability to handle abstractions was not the only kind of intelligence. Other important mental, social, and motor abilities came in for consideration. The range and complexity of special abilities and of special disabilities was increasingly understood. Diagnostic methods and the increasing knowledge of causes of disabilities encouraged the development of so-called remedial measure.

A great body of new knowledge was also being developed in psychology generally, in learning theory and process particularly. Factors far outside

Reprinted from *Harvard Educational Review,* Vol. XXIII, No. 4 (Fall 1953), pp. 244–256. Footnotes omitted.

the school room were now known to affect achievement in class. Research supplied more new material on personality development, and eventually on causes of personal maladjustment. Controls of behavior such as behavior patterns, constellations of understandings, attitudes, abilities and skills came to be recognized as highly desirable products of education and of learning, along with the typical subject matter outcomes of the traditional school.

The dynamic nature of our democracy, together with far better understanding of democracy, not merely as a political process but as a social theory and way of life, increasingly affected our educational belief and practice.

The educational system of the United States, aided by the great resources in new knowledge met the challenge, namely, to develop an education to serve the wide range of individual differences brought to the school by the influx of all the children of all the people. The most extensive revolution in curriculum content and in methods of instruction ever seen eventually emerged. An important fact, which becomes more important as we consider later the second challenge, is that the answer to the first challenge was aimed at the personal goal of minimum literacy with introduction to citizenship as the only social goal considered. Individual differences between and among persons was the key. This was simple business compared to the new challenge now emerging.

SUCCESS HAS BEEN FAR GREATER ON THE ELEMENTARY LEVEL THAN ON THE SECONDARY

The educational revolution to date is confined largely to the elementary school. The elementary level, both leadership and rank and file, is committed in theory and well on the way in practice to real adjustment to the range of individual differences. Hopelessly unfit curriculums and instructional methods persist but the main battle has been won.

The challenge did not confront the secondary school until the 1930's and stemmed from a set of circumstances different from those which confronted the elementary school. The compulsory attendance laws did affect the secondary schools somewhat, but the huge increase in enrollment followed the depression and the fundamental change in the labor market. The application of the principles of democracy is having some effect but so far chiefly on theory.

The secondary school with approximately seventy percent or more of eligible students enrolled is now challenged as was the elementary school a third of a century earlier. The leadership in American secondary education is keenly aware of the facts and of the situations created. Individual secondary school staffs here and there are making magnificent efforts to meet the challenge. The secondary school generally, however, is relatively untouched by the developments of the first half of the twentieth century. Again we cannot digress into causes; we are concerned for the moment with the facts and possible effects. Conditions within the huge majority of secondary schools are similar to those in the elementary schools before the revolutionary changes. Curriculums and methods are still formal, abstract, verbal, and unrealistic. Students are not introduced in any sensible way to the century in which they live, to its truly great strengths and achievements, to its dangerous tensions, to its imminent and fateful decisions. Certainly they are given no guidance for the second half of the century in which they will live and participate in decisions. So far nothing much has happened beyond tinkering with curriculums and methods. Excellent theoretical proposals are available, but resistance on the practical level is unbelievably stubborn.

The second challenge, discussed below, affects chiefly the secondary school, as the first did the elementary school though both are vitally involved. Failure to meet this challenge may result in (a) the relegation of the present type of secondary school to the status of an extra-curricular activity with a new institution rising to meet the challenge, or (b) in a serious blow to the advancement of democracy in the United States. The first challenge was reasonably well met when all types and conditions of children were given the opportunity to achieve literacy and an introduction to our democratic citizenship. The second challenge is far more complex, aiming at that degree of cultural literacy, moral responsibility, creativity, necessary for the constant upgrading of democracy.

THE SECOND CHALLENGE

The scientific research and philosophic inquiries of the first quarter of the century made us aware of individual differences among learners, of the importance of personality development, and of the principles of democracy as applied to individuals. The second quarter of the century saw the development of another great body of new knowledge, this time in group dynamics, the democratic implications of group discussion and decision, in human relations and particularly in social and cultural anthropology. The anthropologists have demonstrated the social class structure of our society. The implications of these findings raise certain serious questions and present a basic challenge to our society and particularly to the schools.

The people of the United States have been committed from earliest times to a theory of society in which there are no classes, or at least no absolutely insuperable class barriers. Any man, we assert, is free to improve his status, that is, to move upward in the social structure. Education is one of the means, if not the chief means through which the individual may improve himself and his social status. All our far-flung structure of free schools flows from this, plus our insistence enacted into law that all must be exposed to education for a stated number of years.

As we shall see, a number of grave questions arise when we examine theory and practice both in social process and in educational practice. Before proceeding to these questions, let us examine some of the immediate facts, practices, and implications.

THE IMMEDIATE IMPLICATIONS FOR EDUCATION OF THE SOCIAL CLASS STRUCTURE

The culture in general and the particular segment of the culture within which the individual grows up influence learning and behavior in a fundamental manner. Teacher education, until recently, has neglected this vital factor affecting education.

Cultures impose upon their participants a basic set of values and social habits for controlling everyday life activities. Certain general roles are expected of all children as they grow up: a sex role, an age role, and in developed cultures a social class role. A caste role based on race, color, or creed may sometimes be present.

Each child brings to school a collection of values, beliefs, and attitudes, plus behavior patterns through which the values and meanings are expressed. Cultural factors over which he has no control play an important part in making him what he is. These factors are, of course, affected by and affect the biological processes of growth or maturation, the range of individual differences, the interests, purposes, and needs which the individual develops. The constellation of influences playing upon the child is complex; the effects of single components are difficult to trace. Influence is often subtle and hidden from casual observation. Anyone who rears or teaches children must, however, possess such facts as we have at this time. Equally one must be cautious in drawing generalizations, in attributing certain results to one or another factor without reference to the total picture. There is no such thing as "the child." Each one is "a child" with his unique collection of beliefs and behaviors.

The social classes differ materially in approving or stigmatizing certain beliefs, values, and behaviors and in their regard for education. Middle and upper classes particularly stigmatize, in the lower classes, what the upper classes call laziness, shiftlessness, irresponsibility, ignorance, immorality. Within the lower classes, however, some of these are accepted ways of behavior, possessing background and rationale. The lower classes are likely to resent in the upper classes what lower class individuals call "snootiness" or snobbery, good manners, proper language, lack of aggressiveness, or unwillingness to fight.

The middle and the upper-lower classes also believe in and impress on the children the value of "getting ahead" or of "bettering one's self" in life. Children in the middle class largely resist strongly the class values and habits imposed upon them, preferring the less controlled behaviors of the lower classes. Children in the lower classes quite generally accept the values and behaviors of their class. Significantly the latter group is often unaware that its language, manners, and standards are quite unacceptable within other groups.

The efforts of parents and teachers to socialize children precipitates constant conflict between the psychological drives of children and the pressures of the culture. The child's need for physical activity, for sensory enjoyment, for self-direction, and for prestige with age mates fights hard against restraints, controls, and demands for conformance.

Many of the conflicts between parents and children or teachers and children result from grave lack of insight into the nature and effects of constant pressure, open or subtle, to conform to social values and roles. Parents and teachers regard the procedures they use in socializing children as natural and desirable. The *adults* are not even aware that there is any pressure. The *children* are keenly aware of it. The emotional cost to both may be very high. Parents and teachers become irritated and angry. Children become destructive, antagonistic, or sullen, or retreat into periods of negativism. These are not manifestations of "original sin" or of an evil disposition; they are but defenses against the constant "cultural bombardment." The more social the requirements, the more arbitrary and unjust they seem to the "natural" child.

Certain further facts may be summarized briefly as follows:

First, it is important to know that the children in our schools are drawn from the social classes in approximately these percentages: three per cent from the upper class, thirty-eight from the middle class, and fifty-eight from the lower class.

Second, the teaching body, in contrast, is drawn largely from the middle class. Many teachers simply cannot communicate with lower class children and have no idea of the beliefs and motives of these children. The children in turn trying to communicate are abashed at criticism of their language and behavior which is quite acceptable within their own social group.

Third, the school has generally been geared to the aims, ambitions, moral or ethical standards of the white, prosperous middle class, Protestant, Anglo-Saxon population.

Fourth, the school is not organized to capitalize upon the non-verbal types of intelligence often found among children who have not had access to or constant contacts with books. The school often does not recognize the emergence of high intelligence and creative behavior in forms other than the abstract verbal type long fostered by the school.

The school generally attempts to impose middle class values upon huge numbers of lower class children. Problems, assignments, projects set by the school are, therefore, not at all the same problems when tackled simultaneously by upper and lower class children. The motivations are not at all alike.

Many lower class children simply do not value the objectives and processes of the school, hence do not try. The school immediately dubs these children "unintelligent," "uncooperative," or "stubborn." The old class clichés may enter; the children are lazy, shiftless, irresponsible. The facts are that the school often simply does not meet their needs or ambitions, does not operate within their framework of values and motivations. The very tests of intelligence (so-called) and of achievement are now known to be heavily weighted toward middle class experience, knowledge, values, and beliefs. The lower class child, to use his own expression, "Can't win." The school does not give its typical rewards generally to lower class children.

Fifth, the school achievements and the degree of understanding and loyalty to our society and culture are thus definitely affected by the class origins of the children.

The middle class regime simply does not socialize the lower class children. They are neither believers nor participants in the cultural heritage of middle class society. The method of cultural training used by the school has basic effects upon children's *inward acceptance* of cultural objectives, as differentiated from outward conformance. The effects upon morality, delinquency, mental hygiene, and personality development generally are often not what the school thinks they are. We know now that learning situations wherein the child can identify himself with the total social group including adults is far more effective than methods of imposition and pressure.

Sixth, we should note, though this is not strictly a class structure matter, that the gifted child in our schools is often as sadly neglected and unstimulated as is the lower class child.

The school is challenged under the American faith to develop integration and unity within our diverse society; to develop persons possessing, in terms of their capacities, cultural insight, standards, taste, and above all moral responsibility; persons committed to the democratic process in our national life and in the world.

The eight-point discussion which follows is based upon acceptance of the historic American beliefs about society, the individual, and education. Certain very serious questions about the acceptance of these beliefs and the effect of changing beliefs upon education are reserved for the very end of this article.

Detailed development of this challenge would fill a volume. A series of statements with brief supporting discussion must suffice here.

1. All levels of educational workers should be familiar with the structure of our society; particularly with the summaries of the characteristics of the several social classes making up our society.

The process of education, of learning, and of teaching can be based only upon the experiential background, the goals and motivations of the learner.

This is a commonplace. Any extension of experience, improvement of goals and motivations can be achieved only by methods which do not ignore or insult the learner's origins and present value system, thus preserving his security while challenging to growth and improvement.

2. All levels of educational workers should be familiar with the structure of human personality and the conditions of its growth.

3. All levels of educational workers should be sensitive to efforts to state the over-all goal for our society and for education within that society; should constantly engage in critical analysis designed to keep these goals abreast of new knowledge about society and persons.

The desired goals in any dynamic society are in constant need of critical analysis, reassessment, and restatement. A common cultural background making for common aims, beliefs, and loyalties, together with provision for free development of individuality and creativity are essential to any society. The values and beliefs of any one social class cannot be imposed upon the society. Several writers have pointed out that certain values and processes of the lower class, usually ignored, may well possess social value. The characteristics of a desirable personality, of desirable social process, desirable social institutions needs to be restated constantly as new knowledge and insight appear. The implications of the general aim for the more immediate cultural and personal objectives need to be stated in far greater detail than heretofore and far more clearly. We will doubtless always have social classes but equally important is the preservation of upward mobility and the development of necessary cultural integration and unity.

4. All educational workers should be constantly engaged in the reorganization of curriculum materials and instructional processes with special reference to our new knowledge concerning the nature of our society.

The curriculum movement has been under way for some time in our society and will continue under the impetus of new knowledge, which in fact has been the case always.

Several pages could be filled, at this point, with illustrations. Details of curriculum content and instructional procedures could be listed, all showing the almost complete neglect of the facts concerning the structure, problems, tensions, and maladjustments growing out of this special situation.

Books used in beginning reading practically never base content upon the experience known to the whole range of children using the books. The experience of the huge majority is, in fact, usually ignored. The very books designed to teach children to read actually cannot be read by some of the children. Not a single series of readers includes the experience of lower class children. Certain authors of individual books for free reading by children have boldly broken with tradition and are presenting the lives of many different types within our society. Books such as *Steppin' and Family* by Hope Newell, and *Tobe* by Stella Gentry Sharpe tell of the Negro without caricaturing him. *New Broome Experiment* by Adam Allen portrays the stupidity of anti-Semitism, while John R. Tunis, in *The Keystone Kids* aims at breaking down prejudice against any minority. *Blue Willow* by Doris Gate is the story of a family of sharecroppers, while Caroline R. Stone's *Inga of Porcupine Mine* tells of miners' families in Michigan. Eleanor Estes is the author of books dealing with people who are not especially prosperous. These are but promises of what must appear in all subject areas.

History and geography are often presented with no bridge from the backgrounds of meaning possessed by the children. The lack of background necessary to understand is usually ignored. Verbal presentations of places the children will never see are unrelieved by any aids toward reality. Equally, no attention is paid to the possible use and value of these materials in the lives of the particular children being taught.

Details, as stated, could be multiplied indefinitely. The result is an education consisting too largely of verbalisms about the nature and problems of our society, instead of experience with social organization and decision making. The outcomes are glib repetition of the verbalisms with no understanding and certainly no appropriate patterns of behavior.

A sweeping and fundamental revision in curriculum materials and instructional processes is needed. The important curriculum movement already present in our schools needs redirection. The attention given to individual differences in ability, in types of interest and endeavor, in achievement should now be supplemented with attention to the facts concerning differences between and among discernible groups.

The basic revision of the nature and distribution of the rewards of the school, marks, prizes, special recognition of any type, the methods of reporting and using evaluations is a part of this curricular development.

5. All educational workers should study the field and processes of the communication arts, with special reference to communication between and among groups of differing backgrounds, goals, and values.
6. All educational workers should be able practitioners of the group process, and of leadership therein.
7. All educational workers should work for increased school-community interaction.

This has always been important and is doubly so in light of the knowledge about the social structure of the community. Only through genuine interaction can educational workers understand the community (from local to international level), and the community understand classroom procedures and the purposes of education.

8. Education is challenged above all to be real.

An education based on words and gained through words has always been a poor preparation for a world of things and persons. Now it is doubly incompetent. Talking about the tensions and maladjustments of our society, of the effect on our society of differing class values and ambitions is not the same as participating in these problems. The strength and achievements of our society can be learned and will beget loyalty only through participation.

TEACHER EDUCATION AND THE NEW CHALLENGE

The sharpest focus in all this is on teacher education. A number of bold, creative efforts are appearing. New patterns of provocative and promising nature are under trial. In general, however, many engaged in teacher education are incredibly unaware of the nature of the society in which they live, incredibly unaware of the problems of many types of persons trying to live in our changing, insecure, and frightening world. The practice in the field is far too often a soggy mediocrity.

The public does not pay for the teacher or the teaching we need—and thereby may hang a disastrous story in the future. This should not prevent our stating goals and working for them.

The teacher should be an educated person, loyal to his own society but a part of the world society also. A teacher who is to inspire respect for the basic values of the society in which the learner is to live must know and believe in the long cultural history of that society. A teacher who is to aid learners to face courageously our changing, often insecure and frightening world, must know why society is in revolution currently; must know how human beings live and grow, must know their motivations and frustrations, their cultural likenesses and differences. A teacher fundamentally ignorant of the structure of his society, and equally ignorant concerning the growth of human personality, cannot aid individuals to become citizens of their world.

A teacher must not only know the moral and ethical values, the persistent truths of his society but must have actively developed a code of values for himself. A teacher fundamentally ignorant of moral values, who has never developed any values or appreciation of his own cannot possibly contribute to the growth of moral character. Giving devices for the development of "citizenship" to a teacher ignorant of the structure and process of democratic society is absurd.

We seem to be in a world-wide period of what may be called "unmorality." This characterizes many aspects of life from day to day, from person to person relationships to international relations. The struggle within and between groups intensifies all this. Understanding, tolerance, recognition of worth between and among all groups within our society and between societies must be achieved. "Civilization is (in truth) a race between education and disaster."

The most important factor in cultural unity and stability may be moral responsibility. It may even be the crucial factor in the integration or disintegration of a mobile, dynamic society. The teacher needs above all to know the place in life of a philosophy or a religion and to have developed one of his own. Achieving cultural unity within a diverse society is not impossible, but it will not come of itself. The challenge to education and to all agencies of enlightenment is unmistakable and not to be escaped or denied.

The problem is intensified by the world-wide "revolt of the masses." Individuals and groups now sit in places and control operations heretofore controlled by very different persons and groups. The new group brings its values and procedures with it. Condemnation of either group by the other is useless. The development of common values designed to achieve improvement of life for all groups should be our concern.

THE MORE REMOTE AND FATEFUL ASPECTS OF THE CHALLENGE

Education is a part of the social process, the school a part of the social structure. Education and the school cannot ever be free from the influences already at work in society, nor from trends which appear. The school reflects the society and culture within which it operates, and must participate in, and influence, any changes which occur.

The class structure within any society contains a number of factors quite apart from education which also affect mobility upward within society—or downward for that matter. Evidence exists, as stated earlier, that education as administered may actually interfere with social mobility and curtail opportunity—a direct reversal of the original faith and practice.

Educational leaders, both theoretical and practical, must be well informed concerning the life of their society, the factors and trends within it which bear upon the thing education was originally designed to do.

Question. Is education at the mercy of the structure of society? Should we direct education openly toward acceptance of and integration with existing structure? Or, can education do something to influence trends within our society?

The actual situation within society becomes, in the light of these questions, a crucial matter. School leaders, practical and theoretical, are remarkably ill-informed concerning the *actual* philosophy and process of their society.

Question. Should education accept and continue to operate on the basis of the typically accepted American tradition that any and all should aspire to life work within what are usually called the more favorable areas: the professions, skilled technologies, independent enterprise in business, or at least to top level directorial positions in industry and commerce?

Some of these areas are desperately overcrowded. Experience in European countries raises serious questions about the social utility of this procedure. A serious question, stated next, emerges at this point.

Question. Do we as Americans *really* believe in our ancient faith—a relatively classless society, or one at least with relatively easy upward mobility for anyone, and surely with no artificial barriers to individual improvement?

Have we in fact deserted our traditional faith in democracy and in the uniqueness of the individual and accepted uncritically the class structure and the placement of given persons in given classes without opportunity (or possibility) of movement from class to class?

Certain people become furiously angry upon hearing the question. Others cynically regard the question as foolish if to them the obvious answer is that we do not believe in or practice our original philosophy. The reaction of serious and loyal Americans is to look the facts in the face seriously and then to try to develop some answers.

We state *explicitly* in many places and on many occasions that we firmly uphold the faith, but the actual operation of social process and of education within the school gives cause to suspect *implicit* acceptance of a far different social and educational theory.

No one knows the answer but our practices raise serious questions and dilemmas. Educational practices briefly mentioned in earlier pages are illustrations. The differentiation of curriculums which is a prominent characteristic of our secondary schools is ostensibly based on "differences in ability." The ability considered is always but one of the important abilities; namely, that required for abstract, verbal, academic work. Others are ignored. Worse than that, the differentiated curriculums are closely related to class differences within the population. The statement is made openly or by implication that certain individuals are destined for certain levels within society. If this is because of their class origins and not because of their "abilities," then we have a serious interference with democratic process. The cosmopolitan high school with a wide range of courses under one roof is often referred to as a "democratic" school. It is in fact not democratic at all. The basis is a design fundamentally different from democracy as American tradition has upheld it.

The developments in the secondary school have been generally produced by the "practical" schoolman, so-called. The operations of the "practical" man are usually based upon expediency, lack of information, and naive lack of critical insight. The theoretical leaders have also a professional error, namely, the promulgation of doctrinaire solutions due to ignorance of, or failure to recognize, the harsh limitations of reality. *Present unfavorable practices may, therefore, result not from any failure of our faith but from lack of ability and failure to pay attention to such facts as we have.* A number of current proposals by competent theorists and a number of practices developed by competent practical leaders may point the way to a better reassessment of both the extent of our faith and our ability to develop practices in accord with that faith.

Question. Should we not overcome our traditional antagonism to intellectual differences; outgrow our refusal to face the facts of intellectual differences? That is, should we not accept and operate upon knowledge that there are differences in intellectual ability?

Should we not recognize that (a) there are other abilities than the intellectual, with differences here also between persons, and (b) that the other abilities than the intellectual are necessary for the common life?

Granted these facts, we may then attack the two major problems (a) providing general education for all simultaneously with (b) provision for special or differentiated education in terms of individual talents within all of the abilities. One difficulty is to provide general education, common purposes and values thus avoiding artificial divisions within society, and at the same time to maintain a level of quality in the general materials. The other difficulty is to select the various abilities and talents for special training without at the same time unwittingly introducing undesirable group distinctions.

All societies are differentiated except pioneer societies and even there, recognition is given to different contributing groups to the safety and development of the group. We propose here a recognition of differences in capacity on which a democratic system can be built.

Question. Have we the courage and the ability to develop curriculums based not on supposed differences in "ability" but on the hypothesis that we can provide experiences enabling all types and degrees of ability to achieve common cultural understandings, common values, and common understandings of the work of the world?

Have we the courage and the ability to develop curriculums for specialized training and to work for elimination of invidious distinctions between curriculums and their aims?

The answer to those questions turns upon the question that is probably basic to the whole discussion. It is:

Question. Should the leaders of our common life, together with the school workers, stand for a theory of society which would respect and honor any and all types of human endeavor; would regard any contribution to the common life as worthy, regardless of level of difficulty, skill, intangible or material rewards?

The implication is probably nearer to our ancient democratic faith than are most of the current statements and practices. Acceptance of the hypothesis would entail grave responsibilities upon all who participate in any capacity in our social process. Particular responsibility rests upon all who are concerned with processes of enlightenment of any type. A long, slow, tedious process of developing and greatly expanding insights within the body politic is indicated, not to mention the tremendous task within the technical processes of schooling in particular and popular enlightenment in general.

A number of alternative conclusions seem to be apparent. We are now actually operating an educational system based on assertions and assumptions of democracy within society, opportunity for individual advancement, but actually showing practices which deny this. Do we wish to continue this or to substitute something else? The answer will depend upon a far more careful analysis of (1) the actual values and beliefs of our society, (2) the assumptions of our educational sytem, of the practices of that system, and more important, the relation between assumptions and practices.

1. Do we wish to continue a system based on one set of assumptions, but denying these in practice, at least in part?

(The cosmopolitan high school with differentiated courses actually operates on acceptance of the class stratification of society, in large part. The very small high school operates as if there were but one class in society, the others being blithely ignored.)

2. Do we wish boldly and aggressively to reaffirm our original faith in a democratic society, with opportunity and mobility, and then stand up and fight for an educational practice in line with the faith? (This means the rejection of expediency and of the retreat into verbalism, and of the retreat from action. This calls for acceptance of a moral imperative, the avoidance of which will entail severe setbacks to education, and could conceivably contribute ultimately to a social disaster of considerable magnitude.)

3. Do we wish with equal boldness to accept stratification in society with its full and ultimate implications and go boldly about the business of education for it?

The latter would probably be universally condemned by our society—without awareness that we could fall into that very practice for lack of clarifying our assumptions and practices. The only legislative proposal for dual schools ever to emerge in our country aroused such a storm of opposition that it has never seriously appeared again. The practice, however, might easily slip up on us unawares.

Our choices depend upon answers to the several questions propounded. Facts relating to some of the questions do not exist. They will be secured in some instances with great difficulty. The writer does not know the answers. He does believe, however, that answers must be developed. Securing the answers must precede the answering of the great current challenge which is emerging. The rising generation of social and educational leaders will not join the ranks of the unemployed for some time.

Chapter 45

PROFESSIONAL PREPARATION— FUNDAMENTAL POSTULATES

TO MEET *the challenges described by W. H. Burton, educators must be carefully prepared for the complex roles and functions they will perform. To observe that such preparation should include general education, professional education, and related fieldwork is not to offer much help. A detailed analysis of the roles and functions that the teacher will be called upon to perform could provide more reliable clues and insights into teacher education. Such an analysis would disclose that, although the procedures and experiences of teacher education are usually formulated in terms of courses, credits, and degrees, or in terms of the ability to pass examinations, what is of paramount importance is the maturity and integrity of the educator. Unfortunately, it is not possible to insure that each prospective teacher will become a master teacher. The best that can be arranged is to indicate the desirable objectives, provide the necessary training and experiences, and then, through continuous consultation with master teachers, guide the individual toward the greatest possible competence. The final responsibility rests with the individual.*

Robert Ulich, a philosopher, writing on the education of teachers, discusses four ideas fundamental to the preparation of teachers: (1) the teacher as a guide toward better living, (2) teaching and the value of inspiration, (3) the art of conveying, and (4) the teacher as a specialist. In so doing, he indicates the essentials of a meaningful program of teacher education.

ON THE EDUCATION OF TEACHERS

Robert Ulich

However distant the goal may be from present reality, let us contemplate the fundamental postulates on which to build the education of the teacher. If they cannot be materialized fully, at least we can try to avoid as much as possible discordant action stemming from sheer ignorance.

1. *The teacher as a guide toward better living.* A teacher should be the guide of his pupils not only toward more knowledge, but also toward better living. A fully mature understanding of the problems of modern individual and social life cannot be demanded from young people who just enter a vocation. Who, in this sense, is fully mature? However, even a young teacher should look at life with a more developed mind than an adolescent: and, in comparison with older people, he has the advantage of youth. Then, should we not ask to what degree dormitory life in a typical college or teachers' college—with all the advantages springing from communal living—may be too narrow and isolated for developing a young personality? College life today is too narrowly regulated by prescribed courses, credits, and grades. It has little influx from the social and political activities of a normal community where people have to earn their daily bread and are confronted with the changes of employment and unemployment; where old industries go down and new industries arise; where wealth and poverty, love and hatred, responsibility and vice clash with each other. Some colleges have tried to plant their social studies right in the local community, but they are very few, and their attempts have not always been welcomed by the population. Were the respectable citizens afraid that the young teacher could learn too much about social inequality and decide to do something about it?

During the past years more and more voices have been heard that there is too much listening and prescribed reading in our liberal art colleges and too little room for personal initiative. Certainly, the situation is not better in the typical teachers college. The shying away of veterans from these institutions shows that they have little attraction to the more mature mind. The two-year course of the old Normal School has been changed by stretching it across four years, but in spirit many have remained the old "Teacher Seminaries" which a hundred years ago were of inestimable help in the development of the universal public school, but today are obsolete.

Reprinted from *Harvard Educational Review,* Vol. XX, No. 2 (Spring 1950), pp. 71–76.

2. *Teaching and the value of inspiration.* The teaching profession is an inspirational profession which needs inspired men and women, but our teachers' colleges have tended to keep up with the Joneses by aping as much as possible the "scientific method." While the genuine scientist can be a well of inspiration, the person who imitates just his "method" and confuses the method for the total outlook toward life is a source either of dullness or of ridicule. With all this emphasis upon the teaching of experimental psychology, testing, and methods of teaching a dozen subjects, the initiation of the student into the cultural tradition is badly neglected. The great philosophies and religious systems through which man has gradually arrived at an understanding of himself, are mostly unknown. What happened before John Dewey seems not to be worth noticing to a large number of educators, as if Dewey himself could have formed his thought without, though partly in protest against Plato, Hegel, Herbart, Darwin, and Marx. Even Dewey is not really read and understood: only his pedagogical works are touched upon, his more comprehensive philosophical works are "too difficult." Thus some "students of Dewey" state later in a university graduate class that Dewey "believes in a personal God," whereas others say that according to Dewey "relativism" is the only answer, and since we cannot know anything anyhow, we should ask ourselves whether it is desirable for man to think; he may just as well "not think." The people who utter this nonsense are not at all incapable of some philosophical discourse; they are even eager for it. But somehow, all they have to live on are half-digested, philosophically and culturally infantile phrases, defended in the name of "pragmatism," "relativism," some kind of dogmatism, or in the name of "democracy" and "the American way of life." How can people with that muddle in their heads arrive at any substantiated opinion about problems the solution of which determines not only their own philosophy and practice of teaching, but the survival of their country and its culture; problems such as the relation between freedom and authority, self-development and discipline, experience and tradition, self-expression and form, nationalism and internationalism, secularism and religion, individualism and collectivism, science and humanity?

Part of this neglect of the fundamentals of educational philosophy is due to two factors. One, that the teachers of teachers have learned somewhere that metaphysics is an old, obsolete, and subjective discipline of thought. And since even the greatest ignoramus discovers sooner or later that the thorough discussion of any of the problems just mentioned enters into metaphysics, he simply puts them aside. After all, don't we live in an enlightened country and in a scientific era? The second factor is as serious as the first. Our public schools are established on the highly laudable principle of the separation between State and Church. This means that denominational creeds do not belong in the public school. This in turn means that controversial issues of *Weltanschauung* are a hot iron, better to be kept in the distance because a fanatical priest or minister or atheist might complain. Thus the ideal of religious freedom, for which our ancestors in various Western countries have shed their blood, now makes of us cowards in conviction. We arduously concentrate on "facts" and "methods" without any ultimate directives; the only directive left is "democracy." But what makes democracy alive? Absence of faith? Indeed, what a cruel joke of history!

We began this section with the postulate that the teacher should inspire. But whence does the power of inspiration spring? First of all from a person's belief that his saying and doing has some general value. That is the point we have just discussed. But there are others: a person's capacity of inspiring springs also from the cooperation of his imagination with worthwhile mental associations. Imagination without worthwhile associations would be empty; associations without imagination would produce nothing but a chain of dull facts, perhaps not even a chain, but just a jumble.

Now, the source of energy that kindles a person's imagination and produces associations lies mainly in a full life itself. But since, as we said, such fullness cannot be expected in the experiences of young people, they have to be produced vicariously through acquaintance with the great treasures of imaginative creation, such as religion, literature, and the fine arts. Some kind of art every young teacher should try himself, not for the purpose of becoming a musician, or a poet, but because, as in sport, only he can really appreciate another's performance who has somehow participated himself. But how much of this inspiration do our prospective teachers receive in teachers' colleges, liberal arts colleges, and universities?

3. *The art of conveying.* The teacher needs the art of conveying. This is not just a problem in methods of teaching. Nobody can convey effectively what he does not know thoroughly. Therefore, in a good institution for the training of teachers there should not be the artificial separation of subject matter and method; both should go hand in hand. For example, if in a teachers' college the instructor in English literature has a class in Shakespeare he should interpret his work in such a way that he sharpens the student's sensitivity for the art of revealing the inner beauty of literature. As long as we continue the separation of subject matter and method we shall remain in an artificial situation, with all kinds of specialists in methods occupying professorial positions in our teachers' colleges, and the graduates leaving their institutions more and more uneducated. Thus, by the emphasis on courses in method we may do the very contrary of what we intend: we may prevent young people from becoming good conveyors of the values of civilization. But in making this statement I do not wish to join the chorus of the many ignorant writers who believe that a teacher is "born" and does not need any instruction in the art of instructing. Some of the so-called method courses may indeed be unnecessary, even harmful. Still,

who can really believe that a teacher can effectively meet his classes in a big public school just by reciting what he has learned in college?

Only after the art of teaching has been interpreted to the incipient teacher in combination with the active and vital acquisition of the subject matter itself, should methodology of teaching be given in special courses. Such courses should span two poles. One pole should be a thorough discussion of the theory of learning, not only psychologically, but also philosophically, i.e., in relation to the important theories of knowledge from Aristotle through the present. It is tragic to see how psychologists, even in well known university departments, take up problems of the intellectual and ethical behavior of man without the faintest knowledge of a philosophical tradition that could help them to set their experiments into a much more comprehensive context. This is not only the fault of modern psychological training; it is just as much the fault of the philosophy departments which during the past fifty years have practiced the art of self-isolation with unusual success.

It is high time that the centrifugal development which has torn the humanities and social sciences apart be replaced by a new integration. There is hardly a field of study and practice more in need of, and at the same time so well fitted for that purpose than education. In a deeper sense, it cannot be understood without the help of philosophy, psychology, sociology, and history.

The other pole should be observation, experimentation, and the application of theory in direct contact with children, not in a casual way, but extended over a period long enough to make possible real familiarity with the learning process and behavior of young children and adolescents.

4. *The teacher as a specialist.* The teacher must be a specialist. Even if he teaches in the elementary grades where according to modern principles there is no strong articulation of subject matter, he, or in this case, she, has to be trained as a specialist. With respect to psychological and pedagogical problems, the teacher of the very young pupil perhaps needs more professional preparation than the teacher of subject matter in a higher grade who may delude himself into believing that he has done enough when normally gifted boys and girls pass his examinations. Certainly, this was the old, so-called humanist tradition, according to which the learned teacher of Greek and Latin looked down upon the little grade school teacher who, in reality, did not teach more, and often did not know more, than the bare rudiments of reading, writing, and arithmetic. With the recognition of the specific complexities of childhood, and the rise of the prestige of the public schools in democratic societies, this has changed, or, let us speak more carefully, is beginning to change. Even in the older European countries, despite the opposition of the secondary schools, there is a growing tendency toward a unity within the teaching profession.

As everywhere, the consolidation of a profession (which, with respect to the teachers of the United States, is of very late date) goes hand in hand with the establishment of standards and entrance requirements. When in the thirteenth century the universities of France and Italy became established institutions with their own legal rights and seals, they did so by insisting vigorously on definite rites in examinations and procedures of appointment. But when, at the end of the Middle Ages, the professors relaxed, their institutions went down. To be sure, the laxity and corruption in the examination system of this period was but a part of the general disintegration of the medieval guild society and its social and spiritual foundations. However, all historical studies of professions and their preparations point to the fact that without a definite formalism and rigidity in the procedure of selection and appointment, corruption and decay are bound to occur.

There is, however, the reverse danger too. We find it in all nations with a large officialdom and rigid bureaucracy (in other words, nations with which the United States has now joined), namely, the danger of inflexibility and fear of new blood. Such a result is particularly deplorable in the teaching profession. For this profession must be sensitive to intellectual and social changes, and should be open to persons of unusual character and experience, even if they have not received the regular professional training. This should be, in selected cases, possible with the teacher, just as it is possible in public administration. Certainly, the slow development of definite standards for the work in schools is due to the irresponsible opinion that dealing with children is something of lesser importance. Most historians of modern nations, for example, have given no attention to the development of the educational system of their country. The ways by which a people tries to transmit its ideas and ideals to the oncoming generations seemed to the historian of no importance.

But there may also have been a positive reason for the neglect of rigid standards in the teaching profession. Wise people know that a young person learns most from contact with men and women in whom he feels kindness and a wealth of experience. This vicarious participation of a less mature in a more mature life is probably the greatest blessing in human development. From Socrates to Locke this was well known; since then it seems to have been forgotten.

The attraction which youth feel to older people does not necessarily require great intellectual achievement. Unspoiled young people possess an extremely fine sensitiveness for unobtrusive, genuine quality in whatever field it may appear. Hence it would be a pity beyond measure if our new school deprived itself of the cooperation of such superior personalities. Just as it is hardly understandable that our Protestant churches do not invite the cooperation of outstanding men and women in their services, but leave the weekly sermon exclusively to ministers, who, as all human beings, cannot always present to their congregations new bouquets of wisdom.

Though often without success, the school of the future will have to struggle with the problem that confronts the vocational schools in every country, namely, how to find the teacher who combines impressive technical skill with the humanistic quality and methodical art of a good teacher. Often, if the technical knowledge is adequate, the pedagogical quality is not, and vice versa. It is particularly in this area where our teachers' colleges are least efficient and least equipped, for such training is expensive. Therefore, especially for the education of our young workers, let us recruit men and women even without specific pedagogical preparation, provided they can benefit our youth and the nation.

Whatever the special field of a teacher may be, whether mathematics, English, a science, a craft, or a foreign language, one condition should be fulfilled, which for a mass profession may be almost too high an ideal. Though the teacher cannot be a "creative" mathematician, scientist, linguist, or artist in the strict sense of the word—how many of our university professors are?—he should have acquired a sense of the creative process. Of what use is a man who talks about horsemanship, and has never been on a horse? But thousands of teachers talk about science and have never projected themselves into the exciting situation of a great discoverer; others speak about art and seem never to have felt the intensity of experience out of which a work of art arises, if only with the effect that they might have discovered the difference between the mind that creates and the mind that explains.

Today we have become modest with regard to the influence of the school and the teacher upon society. We know that education is much more the determined than the determining factor in human culture. However, to a degree, it is both. For civilization is not a dead mass of material which can be moved like furniture from the house of the deceased into the house of the heirs. While passing from one generation to another, civilization changes its character according to the spirit of those who transmit—for transmission of values is not just a process of "handing down"; it is at the same time re-interpretation; it involves choice and selection; it is continual renascence or it is nothing but a show and a burden. Thus the teacher, who is the transmitter, must also be the interpreter, the selective agent, the reviver and regenerator; otherwise he is not a blessing, but a curse to the younger generation. If he looks at the drama of civilization with lifeless eyes, if he does not feel as one of the actors in this perennial drama, how can his pupils learn from him more than dead knowledge?

Let us never forget this when we speak of the role of the teacher in the culture of nations. Either he is one of its most active participants, or he is one of its destroyers.

Chapter 46

PROFESSIONAL PREPARATION— ROLE OF THE UNIVERSITY

IT IS *the hope of all institutions of higher education that the curricula they offer will turn college freshmen into seniors who are relatively mature young adults. This goal, particularly for those who plan to teach, requires that a good deal of serious thought be given to questions about the relationship of general to professional education. What attention will be devoted to abstract knowledge as compared to concrete applications of that knowledge? How will new contributions from the various disciplines be reflected in general and professional education? Furthermore, what contribution can experience in research, both theoretical and practical, make to the preparation of teachers? What are to be the functions and the responsibilities of a professional school in a university? And finally, what responsibilities should the individual assume in this educative venture? In other words, the preparation of the educator can be regarded as encompassing three interrelated areas: (1) the role of the college or university in the area of general education; (2) the role of the professional school associated with a university, in any area of special education; and (3) the role of the prospective educator in the area of individual development.*

These and similar questions are the concern of Charles Frankel, a philosopher, who discusses the responsibilities of the college or university to its students and to the society and the proper dimensions of general and professional education.

PROFESSIONAL EDUCATION AS UNIVERSITY EDUCATION

Charles Frankel

Mr. Dooley was once asked by Mr. Hennessey whether he would send a boy to college. "Well," said Mr. Dooley, "at the age whin a boy is fit t' be sent to college, he ain't fit t' be kept at home." Universities, like other social institutions, serve many functions that do not fall within their official terms of reference. In the United States, for example, they have been social escalators, convenient forums for retired generals and future presidents, and institutions that have been responsible for important religious ceremonies that take place on Saturday afternoons in the fall. They have provided places in which young people in their adolescent years can engage, under relatively antiseptic conditions, in the personal experiments that are apparently necessary if they are to find themselves. Not least, they have provided refuges for eccentric people like scholars, poets, and intellectuals, who find it difficult to fit into any program of work they have not laid out for themselves. At times they have even re-educated these eccentrics by condemning them to a form of penal servitude known as committee work.

Such functions are important, but I hope you will permit me to pass to other matters that seem to me only a little less important. Among these are the intellectual functions which universities may be expected to serve. In approaching the intellectual function of the university, we can begin, I think, by reminding ourselves of the conditions that call universities into being. Formal education, as everyone knows, arises in certain obvious circumstances. Every human community develops over the course of time a body of skills, ideas, and discriminations which it passes on from one generation to the next and which keep the young, if only they will listen, from living as though no one had ever lived before. When the division of labor within a community reaches a certain stage, however, the process of transmitting such information and attitudes cannot be carried on in an off-hand way or merely as an accompaniment of other activities. Accordingly, schools emerge, and institutions of higher education come into being when the mas-

Reprinted from *The Social Service Review*, Vol. XXXII, No. 3 (September 1958), pp. 237–246, by permission of the University of Chicago Press.

tery of some important skills comes to require a protracted and concentrated course of training.

The mere length of time that goes into training, however, is not enough to explain the special character of higher education. Other special factors intervene, three of which are of special importance. The first is the high degree of abstractness and specialization that marks the materials of higher education. The second is the interlocking and interdependent character of these materials. The third is the necessity constantly to revise and add to them. These three considerations, among others, impose imperatives on higher education which give it its special shape.

Let us first look at some of the implications of the fact that higher education is a response to the emergence within a community of skills, ideas, and discriminations that move on a relatively high level of abstraction. The more complicated a society, the more its crucial activities take on a specialized character for which the ordinary range of everyday experience provides a wholly inadequate preparation. This is true of any sophisticated society with elaborate traditions, but it is especially true of a society which contains institutions for free scientific inquiry, or which governs its activities through impersonal mechanisms like the price-system or the law, which control the relations between individuals by means of abstract rules and symbols. The key activities of such a society depend on highly developed verbal skills, on the construction of specialized and sometimes highly artificial languages, and on the making of discriminations that require considerable sophistication and refinement. Most important, these activities are likely to depend on the use of ideas that have a very broad range of application and that are likely to depart rather radically from the ordinary conventions of common sense.

As a result, institutions of higher education are bound to have a rather distinctive character, if they are to do the job that only they can do. If men and women are to be trained to carry on the refined activities that call institutions of higher education into being, their education has to be at least in part a process of cutting them off from the rough-and-ready world of everyday experience and immersing them in a specialized and artificially constructed world in which they develop habits of thought and imagination they would not otherwise have. Such a process runs evident risks against which safeguards must surely be erected. But it is a strange notion of higher education which, in the name of "practicality," "democracy," or "preparation for life," condemns "artificiality," "specialization," and "abstractness" as evils in a higher educational system. They are, I would say, of its essence. The educational program that stresses the need for connecting the classroom experience with "real life" usually ends both by caricaturing "real life" and by failing to give students the equipment they and their society need if complicated social tasks are to be performed effectively.

There are some possible misinterpretations of what I have just said, however, against which I should like to guard. It is an elementary principle of educational psychology that students will learn more easily and find ideas and facts more exciting if the teacher can connect what they are learning with experiences or thoughts they have already had. And it goes without saying that a person who has been liberally educated can use ideas, not simply to get around effectively within a narrow field, but to illuminate his general experience. Accordingly, I hope that you will not think that I am arguing in favor of insulating education from matters outside the classroom. I have no brief to make for pedantry or bad teaching. I wish merely to say that the university accomplishes its special purpose, not when it cuts its offerings to the measure of the outside world, but when it shows its students that the outside world can be understood better from a perspective they are not likely to find in that world but only within the university.

In the second place, although I would place great importance on the necessary abstractness of higher education, I do not mean to say that a subject like mathematics, for example, should be the paradigm of all study at the university level. I confess that I do think that the importance of mathematics is underestimated and that I find it rather quaint to suggest that mathematics is not a really desirable instrument of education, except for narrowly technical purposes, because it is such an abstract subject. Nevertheless, I do not have any special subjects in mind, but only a special characteristic that might be found in any subject. History, for example, is a very concrete subject, but if it is taught in a university it is clear that it should be more than a series of disconnected anecdotes or a gloss on what can be found in any newspaper. It should be knit togther by abstract ideas that have a larger scope, greater precision, and higher reliability than those we would employ without its aid. These remarks may also help forestall another possible objection to what I have said. In speaking of the need for certain abstract skills, I have not been thinking of "the needs of society" as against "the needs of the individual." The function of an abstraction is to select out of gross experience certain relevant features and to allow us to connect the experience in front of us, by means of these features, with a broad range of other experiences. To know how to use abstractions, therefore, is to know how to give more order and meaning to one's experience. This is a personal good and not simply a socially useful skill.

These remarks bring me to a final misinterpretation which I would hope to prevent. The skills, ideas, and discriminations which it is the business of a system of higher education to transmit are not simply those that are directly useful to some special group in the performance of its economic or social role. There are also a great many that must be generally shared and for which the best educated people in a society must inevitably serve as trustees. To start with something elementary but difficult, such people should be able to speak and write their native language with grace and clarity. If they do not do so, a basic social medium will degenerate. But this example only suggests the general issue. No democratic culture can be governed by men whose *expertise* has cut them off from the memories and aspirations of other men in their society; and no culture worthy of the name can live exclusively in the dimensions of the present. There are, presumably, some things it wishes to preserve, values which it believes are sustained by a long social experience. The proper appreciation of these fundamental elements of a cultural heritage, and the ability to transmit this heritage, much less to add to it, are not skills that develop automatically. They require a long and arduous course of preparation—and one that requires, it should be added, a discipline of the emotions as well as of the mind. One function of the university, plainly, is to provide this kind of training.

This brings me to the second factor that imposes an imperative on programs of higher education. I have stressed the emergence of highly specialized skills as the condition for the emergence of systems of advanced education. But it is a characteristic of the specialized skills which it is the business of universities to keep alive that they tend to hang together and that the lines between them frequently cannot be drawn in a hard and fast way. From the logical point of view, no intellectual discipline is an isolated entity. Economics, for example, may lean on mathematics, literature on history or psychology, biology on chemistry. And there is no telling when developments in one field may not upset conclusions long accepted in another or suggest answers to some of its ancient riddles. Few things have been more detrimental to intellectual progress than the ignorance of misunderstanding of specialists in one field concerning developments in adjacent fields.

Moreover, the evidence is impressive that intellectual versatility and broad sympathies are among the most important psychological sources of creative work. All the fields of inquiry, whether in the natural sciences, the social studies, or the humanities, exhibit certain common patterns. They require, at the least, that the individual have some historical comprehension of the traditions of his subject; they turn on the ability to make generalizations and to apply them; and whether we are thinking of chemistry, social philosophy, or architecture, they demand an imaginative capacity to project alternatives and to choose between them in terms of critical standards. Listening to music, as many have found, may not be wholly irrelevant to the development of one's English prose; the formal systems of mathematics are a species of aesthetic experience; and literature, which exercises our powers of sympathetic projection and takes us into worlds of experience and feeling that are not our own, can be invaluable to the historian, the sociologist, or the social worker. Indeed, the relationship between apparently widely separated fields may be even more intimate. Newton was influenced by theology, Darwin by Malthus.

Accordingly, the initiation of individuals into the traditions and skills of a special discipline will generally be soundest if they are also given some balanced conspectus of other major departments of learning as well. Few people can take a critical or creative view of what they are doing unless they are in a position to look at their subjects from the outside at least occasionally and to see the connections of these subjects with other human activities. This seems all the more important when we recall that those who possess the highly specialized skills are likely to occupy the key positions in modern society and will be called upon to make crucial moral and social decisions that require sensitivity to the variousness of human interests and possibilities.

In general, the undergraduate college, in the American scheme of education, is probably the place where special attention should be paid to this problem. But it would be a mistake to believe that graduate schools can be wholly indifferent to it and an equal mistake to imagine that professional schools can do what they have to do if they have no deliberate interest in producing civilized human beings. The training of young men and women in highly abstract specialties should not be of such a sort that they become intellectual barbarians in the process. A system of higher education that produces experts who are dullards is a scandal.

We come in this way to the final imperative which universities must obey in some way. It is the obviously central commitment to criticism and continuing inquiry. We have been talking of the functions of the university primarily in terms of its teaching responsibilities. But teaching and research are, of course, simply the two sides of the same coin. If those who conduct research love their subject enough to wish to see it continue after they die, teaching is an obvious obligation; and if those who teach believe that an intellectual tradition can be kept alive simply by being transmitted in a frozen form to successive generations, they are gravely mistaken. A system of higher education can try to preserve old dogmas unchanged—but if it does it will almost certainly develop casuistry into a high art. Its criticisms of what it receives from the past may be limited to narrow spheres; its innovations may consist simply in providing new arguments for old absurdities. But in one way or another, a system of higher education can successfully transmit an inherited tradition only by commenting on it, changing it, and adding to it.

In short, the heart of a university, as you do not need to be told, is a community of scholars pursuing new truths. And since all sorts of practical people have recently begun to express rather tender emotions about the importance of fundamental theoretical inquiry, I trust you will permit me to dwell on this theme briefly. I hope too that you will forgive me if I pour a few timid drops of cold water on this budding romance. For I think it only fair that people know what they are getting into when they commit themselves to the support of fundamental theoretical research.

Fundamental theoretical research is wasteful and expensive, it asks for a blank check, and it makes trouble. To be sure, one does not need to be clairvoyant to see that our society is going to become steadily more complex and that a steady supply of new ideas, in science, in technology, and in the human studies, is going to be needed to deal with this complexity. The university, and particularly the non-professional graduate school, must inevitably be a major center for the development of such ideas, and its long-range practical importance from this point of view can hardly be exaggerated. Indeed, the emerging suggestions that leading graduate schools should shift their center of gravity and turn their energies to the training of "college teachers" rather than "research scholars" seems to me very disturbing. But creative research, it must be seen, is in fact inevitably wasteful. High achievement in the arts and sciences is something only a few achieve, and it is built on the disappointments and failures of the many. Moreover, one cannot draw up any simple list of urgent problems, establish their social priority, and tell those engaged in fundamental inquiry to get to work. Such inquiry takes its own course; its practical significance cannot be easily predicted; and much of it, though it is intensely interesting to those who love discovery for its own sake, has no material importance whatsoever. In the long future, fundamental theoretical research will almost certainly be the principal source of major advances in human health, comfort, and convenience. But most fundamental research will simply not pay off in this way.

Worse, such research also causes trouble. In spite of popular demand, there is no way of keeping at least some ideas from being upsetting. And in spite of the long efforts of many members of my own guild, the philosophers, it is not a main function of thought to support either our personal illusions or our vested commitments to the *status quo*. It is a mistake to think that a university can be a center for the search for truth without at the same time serving as an independent center for the criticism of the society in which it exists. Free universities are inevitably sowers of doubt and discontent. If we want them, it is ultimately because we make the moral judgment that it is good to have institutions which represent a society's effort to be self-conscious and to look, with some effort at dispassionateness, at what it believes and what it stands for.

There is one final point, which takes us to the edge of the question of professional schools. Free scholarly inquiry cannot be defined simply in terms of the unhampered search by the scholar for answers to questions the outside world puts to him. Its essence is the search for answers to questions the scholar has chosen for himself. This is why the development of powerful theories that serve as independent matrices for creating problems is the most important sort of achievement in scholarship, and why those disciplines which have achieved such theories represent free inquiry at its best. Accordingly, free scholarly inquiry upsets existing routines in the practical world, not only because it yields new answers to old questions, but because it asks questions which men immersed in practical routines are unlikely to ask. Granting the pettiness and even the hothouse quality of much scholarship, independent scholarly inquiry is important in the last analysis precisely because the questions it pursues may very well seem like impractical questions to practical men.

So we come, by a rather long route, to professional schools and their place in a university setting. I believe you will have begun to suspect my main point. The primary reason for placing a professional school within a university, I would say, is to help a profession become self-conscious about its existing routines. To put the issue maliciously, the purpose of a university education in the professions is to complicate the lives of future members of the professions.

A profession has certain significant characteristics, at any rate when a prima facie case can be made that its centers for education will benefit from association with a university. First and foremost, it is an occupation whose practices lean on the mastery of a body of knowledge of a fairly abstract kind. To some extent this body of knowledge will have been built up out of the practical experience of the profession, but at least to some extent it will also be connected with ancillary bodies of knowledge that have an independent existence among the non-professional arts and sciences. Accordingly, a professional school that justifies its place on the university scene may be expected to carry on active research aimed at bringing the results of inquiry in the fundamental arts and sciences into focus for its own practical use. It may also be expected to turn practical professional experience to theoretical use and to provide information and ideas that enrich learning in other areas. The contribution of clinical experience in medicine to biological knowledge is a case in point.

A second and obvious characteristic of a profession is that it is "client-oriented." It offers techniques and facilities which presumably help laymen solve their problems better than they could if they were forced to proceed on their own. For this reason the professional man does not have customers but clients. They come to him because he knows something they do not know and cannot be expected to know. Consequently, the rule of *caveat emptor* does not apply. The professional man's relationship to his client is not the egalitarian relationship between a seller and a buyer but a hierarchical relationship in which the professional man occupies a position of trust. One must pick one's doctor and be stuck by him.

Accordingly, a third feature of most professions is the possession of an implicit or explicit code of proper conduct. To do his job as he must, the priest, lawyer, or teacher must usually enjoy certain privileges and immunities which those outside the profession do not possess. In compensation for this special status, he is expected to accept certain special rules and responsibilities. Indeed, through accrediting agencies, licensing procedures, professional associations, and the like, professions are frequently assigned a measure of official public responsibility for the governing of their members. In part this reflects the simple recognition of the fact that the outsider is not generally in a position to pass competent judgment on an individual's professional activities. But in part it also reflects the large social importance which is generally assigned to professions, and particularly to those that make their way into universities. One can in fact tell a good deal about a society's fundamental values and about shifts in its fundamental circumstances by charting the rise and fall of given professions. The ascent of journalism toward professional status, for example, is a sign, not only of the increasing complexity of the skills it demands, but also of the importance of media of communication in modern society and of the need to impose some measure of self-control and responsibility in this area. Similarly, the professionalization of social work indicates a fundamental shift in prevailing social attitudes—a shift which is signalized by the verbal change involved in substituting a term like "social services" for a term like "charity."

This brief and familiar list of the marks of a profession carries its own evident implications. There is a difference, plainly, between education in the arts and sciences and education in a profession. The latter is aimed at promoting an individual's ability to deal with specialized problems that others bring him. This is what is meant, I take it, when it is said that professional education is education for practice. Education in the arts and sciences, on the other hand, is primarily an education aimed at developing an individual's ability to ask his own questions and to make his own demands upon his experience. This, I take it, is essentially what is meant by calling it "liberal" education. But though there is a distinction, it is a distinction only in degree and in emphasis. Far from there being any justification for a sharp separation between the programs of the professional and non-professional divisions of a university, the tendency of educational policy in professional schools, I would timidly suggest, should be in the other direction.

The reasons are fairly plain. Professional service involves the ability to make complex practical judgments and to weigh conflicting interests and values. Since most of the key positions in modern society are occupied by members of the professions, such judgments frequently carry far-reaching social implications. The ability to make sensible and sensitive judgments of this character is obviously not the result of abstract classroom instruction alone. It comes usually only with practical experience. But practical experience also has its dangers. It is a characteristic of daily labors in any field that they become habitual, that they give a natural priority to issues that are in the foreground, and that they slowly dull the mind to questions that do not fit the mold of daily routines. This is particularly true when one's work is bureaucratized and formalized. If I may be blunt, "being practical" frequently seems to me to mean simply a willingness to oversimplify a problem in the interest of personal convenience or administrative efficiency. Only an education that has been liberal in its quality, and that has given the individual the habit of looking at his work in a larger setting, can keep him uncomfortable enough to avoid the temptations and seductions of being too practical.

That a properly conceived professional education should have an essentially liberal character is also plain when we reflect on what is involved in saying that the skills of a given profession are embedded in a developing body of knowledge whose roots are in the fundamental arts and sciences. Most professional people cannot be expected, of course, to spend most of their time in research. But it is also true that a good deal of what they learned in professional school—at any rate if they are members of a profession that has some vigor and life—will be questionable ten or fifteen years later. It is for this reason, I think, that a research experience should probably be a central part of the normal student's career in professional school. For the minimal service that a professional school should perform for a student is to give him, first, the habit of keeping in touch with significant developments in theoretical research bearing upon his field and, second, some ability to appraise its usefulness and validity. I would add too that the professional school which gives its students some experience with scholarship for its own sake will do something for which the profession may not thank it, but which any school associated with a university should do. The professions, as you do not need to be told, are not only self-governing bodies serving public functions. Like any other human group, they are also self-regarding bodies whose corporate rules and routines may serve the interests of members of a narrow guild, but at the expense of more generous purposes. The professional school associated with a university has a special opportunity and a peculiar obligation to keep a profession liberated from its own provincialism and prejudices.

These, however, are rather general considerations. I should like to conclude, therefore, with some brief remarks on some of the concrete implications of these principles as I see them.

To begin with, although the purposes I have described seem to me those that should guide educational policy in professional schools, there is not, to my mind, any magic formula which guarantees that they can be achieved. It depends, more than anything else, on who teaches in professional schools and on the perspective they bring to the job. It depends much less on paper plans for the revision of curriculums or on drawing up lists of required courses.

Second, it does not seem to me that the main emphasis should be placed on sending students to take courses in the non-professional faculties. The student's major experience with this kind of work should be at the undergraduate level. Nothing, it seems to me, is more important for a professional school than that it select students who have had a solid and many-sided liberal education. Indeed, if the student has concentrated in any field at the undergraduate level, my own prejudice would be that it be in some other field than those he will cover in professional school. At the post-graduate level, however, new considerations enter. By and large, study in the non-professional faculties is likely to seem off the main path to the majority of professionally oriented students. They should be encouraged to do a little such work, for its values are real, but its lasting impact on most professional students is probably limited.

A major device, it seems to me, is the luring of representatives of the arts and sciences into active participation in the programs of professional schools. This can be done in two ways. Some can be brought into permanent full-time association with the professional school. This has the advantage of focusing the individual's energies entirely on the special problems of professional scholarship and teaching; its disadvantage, of course, is that it may succeed too well and turn a man you originally wanted because he was different into just another member of the guild. A second approach is to bring regular members of the university's non-professional divisions into part-time association with the professional school. This too has its obvious disadvantages, but I think it is probably a useful complement to the first approach. In either case perhaps the most desirable way to use such people, at any rate at the beginning of their association with the professional school, is in the joint course or seminar in which they join forces with a regular member of the professional school's faculty. This, of course, is an expensive procedure. Judging from my own experience and that of many of my colleagues, however, it is also the kind of course which students are likely to find most exciting and which will have the greatest impact upon them—not to mention upon the instructors involved.

This pooling of intellectual resources, indeed, should not take place within the professional school alone. A professional school can make a substantial contribution to a university and can enrich its own program by regularly sending out some of its members to teach and work in other divisions of the university. This has manifest attractions at the graduate level. But its potential usefulness at the undergraduate level should not be overlooked. Courses in the history, problems, and functions of specific professions are, of course, obvious devices for recruitment. But I am not thinking of them primarily from this point of view but rather from the point of view of their usefulness as instruments of undergraduate liberal education. A student who takes a course in religion or in music does not have to approach these subjects as if he were going to be a minister or musician. He can be interested in them as facts of life with which he will have to live.

Similarly, the professions are institutions with a general and significant influence on society, and knowledge about them can be both interesting and important to the layman. Undergraduate courses in the professions should be given, if possible, by members of professional faculties. But they should not be preprofessional courses, useful as they may be for those who are going on to professional school. Their usefulness to the future professional, like their usefulness to the future layman, should reside in the fact that they give students their first acquaintance with a profession, not as a set of technical skills, but as a human institution among other human institutions.

All of this suggests, however, a rather new way of putting a university together. For the most part, each of us who is in a university is immured within a single division, professional or nonprofessional; and, for the most part, this is both inevitable and desirable. If we keep on doing other people's work we shall never do our own. But I am sure that for a good many of us an occasional airing in another climate would be both pleasant and refreshing. The well-organized university that I have in my mind's eye would give us this opportunity. It would see to it that those of us who wished to do so could circulate physically and intellectually within its several divisions. Any professor should have the chance to be a university professor if he desires and if he won't make himself a nuisance. I think we could all have a more exciting time, and educate ourselves better, if such conditions existed.

Finally, there is a simple rule of thumb, I would suggest, which may be a useful guide in setting up the program of a professional school. This rule is that a professional school should not teach anything which a student can reasonably be expected to learn on the job. I would not underestimate the importance of practical and technical skills, but I would suggest that one way in which we can determine what our primary responsibilities are is to ask what it is that it is important to do and that will not be done if we do not do it. I respectfully register my suspicion that if this test were steadily employed a great deal that now goes on in professional schools, including schools of social work, would cease. Professional education as university education is education in the social and moral context of a profession and in the intellectual foundations on which the practice of the profession rests. It should not be training in narrow skills which the student can learn later on and probably—since we may as well be honest—under better conditions.

But I have said so much about the importance of pure scholarly inquiry to professional education that I would wish to end on another note. There is a second sense in which we may speak of professional education as university education. It is the sense in which the professional schools may help educate the rest of the university. Fundamental research, standing apart from the urgencies of the moment, is the heart of a university. But if scholarship is to have an influence, that influence will be exerted largely through the products of professional schools. And if scholarship is to be used for anything else but the amusement of scholars, it cannot be wholly esoteric in the questions it pursues. There is a sense of reality which, as you know, scholars can lose very easily. Scholars who are also members of a profession can call them back to cases. If the non-professional arts and sciences are the heart of a university, the professional schools are its eyes on the world. And I need not tell you that no professional schools are better fitted to serve this function than schools of social work.

Chapter 47

THE PROSPECTIVE TEACHER—"SUBJECT OF EDUCATION"

A GREAT *deal has been said in previous pages about the kind of people who should be teachers in America's schools. The present organization of professional work for teachers in training assumes that the desired results will be achieved through a series of courses. The assumption is also made that, through his previous educational experiences, the student is ready for the new cultural opportunities of higher education. A number of scholars are suspicious of these assumptions, however, and believe that the typical lockstep method of teacher training, although easier on the professional staff, does very little to help the college student grow up. In speaking of the responsibility of the college to the student, Harold Taylor, a philosopher, states: "I speak continually of the needs of the individual student, because I believe that unless we think of the individual, and consider carefully the ways in which we make him an independent and responsible person who thinks and acts for himself, we cannot prepare him to meet his situation in contemporary life." For Taylor, the design of professional education, in addition to reflecting what is known about the cultural heritage of Western man, the psychology of learning, and the psychology of the learner, should put the prospective teacher in the center of the educative process. Since "the student is the subject of education," the offerings of the college should be built around him.*

THE STUDENT AS A RESPONSIBLE PERSON

Harold Taylor

I believe that the present anxiety about the student mind reveals an ignorance of the real situation in which students learn in college, and a lack of respect for the student as a responsible person. It is assumed that, as one educator put it recently in a discussion of these questions, "Students are the objects of education. They are in college to *be* educated." This is a condescending attitude to take towards students. The student is the subject of education, not the object. He is the center of the educational process, the reason for the existence of colleges and universities. If education is conceived as a means of telling students what to think and making sure that they think it, this is the most un-American activity of all, and naturally those who conceive education in this way, would not care to have professors of a dissenting doctrine suggest that students should think differently.

Education is the process by which we and our young people recreate freshly the knowledge and values of each generation. To do so, each one of us, and each one of our students, must think independently, and our whole system of education must be one designed to produce inquiring, informed and responsible students. Our educational plan must be one in which each student is given the chance to *be* independent, in which each is given the responsibility he deserves in forming his own conclusions. It must therefore be a design in which there exists a diversity of controversial opinion. Otherwise, students will never grow to the social maturity they need in order to deal with the political questions of their age.

There are others in America who, in fear, would like to control the thought of the young through regulating the movies, the radio, the press, and the academic profession, into a standard, commercially valuable set of gadgets for saying harmless things over and over. I think this is a very poor and mean way to meet our present social issues. Without a spirit of trust in our colleges and faith in our young people, without a belief that we can settle our affairs through positive, bold, democratic action, we will move from one timid mistake to the next into ultimate failure.

Reprinted from *Harvard Educational Review,* Vol. XIX, No. 2 (Spring 1949), pp. 72–79.

To provide that faith, and to develop young people of creative intelligence, there are great resources available. There is an enormous fund of good will, knowledge, and democratic spirit in the profusion and variety of our colleges, universities, and schools. We have the means, steadily increasing, of meeting the problems of the student's world, and our world, in a forceful way. We know the energies and character of the young American, and the possibilities which lie within him.

I regret, however, that throughout the country, colleges and universities are not taking full advantage of their opportunities. Most of the new plans for higher education are not conceived as attempts to answer the pressing needs of our youth. They serve rather to answer the needs of the faculty, and to provide a set of answers to questions which the youth have not asked. Too few colleges and universities have grasped the essential truth stated by the President's Commission on Higher Education, that the total development of the individual student is the primary concern of the college. The present plans for the reform of higher education have been made with too little reference to the individual student and his place in contemporary life. They have been conceived by members of the academic community, meeting in committee, isolated from the student's world, and accordingly have been conceived in conventionally academic terms. The regular materials of the old college curriculum have now been rearranged in a form which guarantees that every student will be treated to the same intellectual discipline, and will be provided with a set of reports, digests, and surveys of knowledge. This eliminates the organized whimsy of the elective system, but it also eliminates the individual aptitudes, interests, and needs of the students.

It is important to look closely at the way the new college curriculum has been made. The attention of faculty planners has been concentrated on the materials of knowledge and on the question of what young Americans should know. This has led naturally to further concentration on the various departments of knowledge, and there has been a great deal of shifting around of departmental courses. In the absence of a dynamic philosophy, other than the natural cohesion of similar subjects, it has been assumed that the welfare of each department in the college should be the central concern of the planning, and accordingly, representatives of various groups within the faculty have been assembled into committees on curriculum. Often an extra philosopher and psychologist have been added for additional insight. Occasionally a creative writer has been attached, to write the statement of aims, and to make certain that the prose of the report itself is sufficiently abstract to include any point of view favored by the reader. These committee members, together with the dean, and with the general approval of the president, form an interlocking directorate which arranges matters so that due regard is paid to each subject and each department, and a rational order is established for the proper conduct of the business of distributing students fairly throughout the departments. Throughout the country this forms something in the nature of a cartel system, with only a few small businesses, like Sarah Lawrence and Bennington, able to continue in operation outside the monopoly. The students comprise an increasingly large body of consumers, with the difference, as between them and other consumers, that no attention is paid to their individual wants and no market research is considered necessary. The fact that the new curriculum is now in operation from Los Angeles to Boston is a tribute to the seriousness of purpose, ingenuity, diligence, and sound business sense of the American academic community. It preserves intact the heritage of the past, the departmental system, and the authority of the faculty mind over the American student.

But we should remember that that authority is to a high degree illusory. It is based on what I shall call the three illusions of innocence of the American professor. The first of these is the optical illusion. Merely because a body of 100 to 1500 students are sitting in a lecture room all staring in one direction at a man talking, their eyes open, their hair combed, their notebooks in front of them, it is an illusion to believe that anything intellectually profitable is necessarily happening. What usually happens is that the internal life of each student goes along in its own way, alternately dreaming or concentrating; calculations are made about whether anything said will be on any examination; notes are taken such as, "Get laundry tomorrow, see Joe re weekend"; pictures are drawn or elaborate diagrams of concentric circles: I have seen some very careful and delicate drawings of Plato in full color as a result of some of my own classes in philosophy at the University of Wisconsin.

This leads us to the second illusion of innocence—the illusion of the examination. Merely because students are able to pick out the correct words from groups of five possible choices, because they can remember answers and facts for a sufficiently long time to locate them once a week, or once a month, or once a term, it is an illusion to think that the student has therefore shown himself to be educated. What has actually happened is that the student has borrowed someone's notes, looked up past examinations, looked in text books which he underlines interminably, consulted fraternity brothers, and has packed his head hastily with all the odds and ends of information which his preparation has turned up. Once he unpacks his head at the examination it is quite often empty again for some time.

The third illusion is that students are irresponsible, and that since they are still in the process of learning, they do not know how to conduct their own education or to assess the value of the one provided for them. This is the worst illusion of all. Students do know about their university. They can tell anyone who is interested which are the bad teachers, which are the entertainers, which are the good teachers, which are softhearted, which are left or right wing, which are dull, which ones care about students, and which ones they consider useless. The students do this best when they talk among themselves. They advise each other capably and well. In every student group there is a body of knowledge and wisdom about the whole educational system. There is also accurate information provided concerning the various ways to beat the system.

All these sources of educational thought should be tapped for the use of the university. The most important single reform we could undertake to aid the student is to give him responsibility, and greater freedom to carry it out. His courses should be planned by research and discussion with students and faculty together. There should be a recognized student curriculum committee with power to share in the actual construction of the curriculum. In the absence of a recognized student curriculum committee, the students themselves can take the responsibility for forming one, and can help to improve the quality of instruction without waiting to be asked.

The students can aid also in teaching the faculty, by suggesting different forms of examination, by suggesting new ways of conducting the classes, and new student projects related to the classes. There is no basic reason why all the time of classes should be taken up by a professor, unless he is a gifted lecturer whose best mode of communication is in that medium. In many cases it is possible to put the actual conduct of the classes into the hands of the students.

Because of the attitude of educators in the past, there has existed an exclusive concern for storing up knowledge, and for handing it over, intact, as a direct transaction from teacher to pupil, which has led to the many evil practices connected with lectures, textbooks, examining, grading, and the intellectual bullying of the young by the old. Unless the effort of the teacher is in the direction of engaging the student in the process of knowledge, rather than in persuading him to accept the product already made by others, all the reforms of curricula are vain.

I do not think there is a basic distinction to be made between a teacher and a college student, or between a teacher and any other kind of human being who takes seriously his own talents and personal growth. This is a matter of degree. All those who are well educated, or who are becoming well educated, in terms which I should recognize, are people who are seriously interested in life, who enjoy it, who know things, and who want to know more, and to share what they know with others, in as enlightened and persuasive a way as possible. The distinction to be made between the teacher as a person and anyone else, is that the preoccupation with sharing is a little more severe in the case of the teacher. The reason the distinctions between the teacher and the student have become rigidly accepted is because education has been conceived as something which a teacher does to a student, and not something which the student and teacher do together. The reason that college teachers are considered in the public mind as inhabiting a special world of their own is, not only that they are considered to be doing something economically unproductive, but that they themselves conceive knowledge as a rare possession, like housing or old lace, or as a material by which it is possible to make a living. The student and teacher, in their true roles, are actually two students working together, one of whom knows more than the other.

The first need of the student, then, is for an interest in knowing. He needs it because often he does not bring this with him as a part of his native endowment for presentation to the admissions committee. An interest in knowing is a very hard thing either to develop or to discover, since such a quality disguises itself in many ways, and has often been reduced to an absolute minimum through the processes of high school. I do not think that we can investigate intelligently the presence of that interest until we ask the question, *what* is the student interested in knowing? I am prepared to face the fact that throughout the United States, there are large areas of the American student body where there is almost no interest in knowing anything which the academic system has to teach, and the surge towards knowledge moves in the direction of first-hand experience in the various motor skills and emotional responses connected with dating, football, and meeting people who may be useful later on. I do not believe that the way to meet this problem is to take a poor view of students, abolish dating, football, and meeting people, and put in a required curriculum. It consists rather in finding ways in which the student, as an existing reality, complete with faults and virtues of his own and of his society, can be drawn from his absorption in some aspects of life which we consider of lesser value, into other aspects of greater value. The lesser values will not exclude the former, but will be related in a meaningful way.

In any case, the desire to know is not a hot white flame in the American student, except on rare occasions. I do not believe this is a cause for alarm or despair, but I do believe that unless we take account of this fact and the fact that the motivation, interest, and emotional energy of the student is a more significant thing than the rational order in which the materials of knowledge can be organized in a curriculum, we will make only illusory progress in the reform of education. The business of arranging knowledge in orderly sequence is a very simple matter, carried on admirably by good librarians, or curriculum committees. What we must do first of all, is to establish among our students a mood of expectancy, in which the desire to know can be uninhibited and be satisfied, and in which each young person can be given the feeling that he is free to know, and free to say what he knows.

The matter then becomes one of organizing the total educational life of the college in order to achieve the union of all its parts. There is a split in most colleges between the curriculum and the extra-curricular. The student is willing to submit to the tedium of the classroom, as Horace Kallen says, in order to buy with his labor the leisure of his college life. In the ideal college such a split would not exist. I know of colleges where the total education is actually carried on in the bright whirling world of the extra-curricular, and where problems in human relations, emotional adjustment, and moral values, are dealt with exclusively by students in their lives together outside the curriculum.

Often the genuine political education of the young takes place in student clubs and organizations which bear no relation to the work the faculty is doing in political science. Often the materialistic, anti-democratic, and snobbish values, which it is the business of liberal education to eliminate, are taught to students in the fraternity and sorority systems which carry on the social education of the young, unaffected by courses in ethics, philosophy, religion, or social psychology. Very often, the development of democratic attitudes, and the education of the student to face the demands of anti-democratic philosophies, are simply left untouched.

I believe that this has happened because the American educator has been intent on setting the intellect apart from the rest of life. He has been seriously interested not in the aesthetic, personal, or social values of scholarship, but only in its yardage. He has not been seriously interested in the lives, minds, and feelings of the individual students who have come to him for help in personal growth. His conception of the good student is of a diligent, competitive, attentive young person with the combined virtues of a boy scout, a Dale Carnegie, and a quiz kid. The odor of sanctity and piety still lingers in the academies. Somehow the real genius of the democratic American individual, the Tom Sawyer part, has slipped away, or has been educated out of existence by the higher learning. What is needed is a dash of intellectual vitality, of eccentricity, of animal spirits. We must make the life of the student an immersion in a total environment of learning, where the companionship of the scholar, the athlete, the wit, and artist are sought naturally and eagerly at various times and according to various needs.

I believe that it is this ideal environment which the President's Commission has in mind when it repeatedly emphasizes the need for an organic philosophy of education, and the need for following the logic of that philosophy in making the college into a genuine community. We have the chance, in each college, to make a model society, in which discipline in learning and acting will not be imposed, but discovered, as the natural and most fruitful way of behaving. In such a community it would be natural to compose music, to write stories, to perform experiments, to be alive with ideas, to hold belief, to play games, to learn facts, to enjoy life, to govern oneself, and to act cooperatively in the collective government of the community. In such a community, the responsibility of the individual for his society and for himself, is put squarely where it belongs, upon the student himself, and the society aids, rather than hinders, the growth of a genuinely liberal spirit. The ethos of democracy, which is at the heart of the intellectual and personal values we are concerned to develop, cannot be taught from books. It must be known in immediate experience.

The discipline of democracy must be known in the same way. It is something which is achieved, not imposed. It is the discipline which the artist or the scientist imposes on himself, or the discipline which the moral man puts on his actions. Something disciplinary, in a military sense, can be achieved by the conventional college system, but what is needed by our students is a respect for the rules which they themselves make, both in education and social affairs, rules which will be respected because they are valuable and sensible, and because they have been learned. The structure must be set widely, so that mistakes can be made, and yet with sufficient guidance from the teacher, so that the mistake will not be repeated. The student must consistently share in making university policy.

The regular system of lectures, examinations, standard curricula, grades, and the present mechanics of education must, therefore, be radically modified. In their place can be put occasional lectures when considered necessary and desirable by students and teachers, printed or mimeographed material in place of the regular lectures, discussion groups and informal seminars led by students, research projects by students and teachers working together, comprehensive examinations which demand the use of knowledge to answer big questions, and a decentralized system of classes.

The effort here is to make the existing extra-curriculum into the curriculum itself, so that each class becomes a kind of student organization with its own energies, drives, and aims. The dean of the college, whether an academic dean or a director of student personnel, becomes, in this system, not a guardian of intellectual and social virtue, as is usual, but a teacher whose classes are conducted through student meetings, where his role is to help students reach decisions about the educational life of the college. The dean also thinks of his staff and faculty as individuals who share his duties with him, and who carry on the work of advice and help, by example, by leading discussions, and by helping to involve each student in the role of one who makes his own decisions.

I speak continually of the needs of the individual student, because I believe that unless we think of the individual, and consider carefully the ways in which we make him an independent and responsible person, who thinks and acts for himself, we cannot prepare him to meet his situation in contemporary life. The modern citizen needs to be secure enough about his own judgment to face any idea or situation with a confidence that he can form his own conclusion. He needs discipline enough to observe the rights of others, and to aid others to share his privileges. He needs depth enough in his emotional response to enjoy life at its best and to sustain himself at its worst. He needs an aim in life towards which his future is directed, and which his education is helping him to fulfill. He needs teachers, deans, and administrators who realize that universities and colleges exist to help him achieve these qualities by whatever means can be devised. He needs all these things because his world today is confused, overpowering, and tense, and he and his friends, in our anxious age, can help to put it right.

Chapter 48

THE DESIRABLE PERSONALITY TRAITS

As THIS *book has tried to make clear, the obligations of the American teacher make teaching both difficult and complex. The teacher cannot do what is ideally expected of him unless he is more sensitive, more able, and more effective than most people. He does special work and must be a special kind of person. He is not given unusual material rewards, but he must live, in school and out, in an unusual way. He must perform his work with the easy competence and style of a professional, but the work he performs is anything but easy.*

There are not many people like this. Certainly, a young person just beginning to study education displays very few of these characteristics. Even so, the challenge remains.

In the following article, Dana L. Farnsworth, a psychiatrist, writes about ten concepts of personality development. He is interested in teachers, students, and parents, but his major emphasis is on the mental health of the teacher.

EMOTIONS AND LEARNING

Dana L. Farnsworth

Effective teaching is much more a matter of exciting interest and curiosity and a love for learning in the student than imparting facts alone, even though the basic aim of learning includes the assimilation of useful facts.

The most important thing for a teacher to know is himself. The person who can look objectively at his own childhood, understand his relationships with parents and other relatives, and who has worked through the long-term effects of those relationships, is not as easily upset by the curiosity and behavior of children as the one whose defenses are so vulnerable that sensitive areas of personality are disturbed daily. Furthermore, he can understand his pupils better.

From this it follows that such a teacher tends to think of his pupils as active, developing human beings, incomplete but possessed of great potential qualities, who are in a sense a composite of all their previous experiences. He is then in a better position to guide the development of his students than the teacher who thinks of students as young things to be restrained and made to learn.

Instead of trying to cause them to develop along some preconceived pattern, the wise teacher realizes that his function is to cultivate and encourage the traits already possessed by the student, building inner controls as soon as possible, replacing discipline from without with controls from within in the form of integrity, reliability, and a sense of duty and obligation to others. This amounts to saying that the teacher promotes maturity in any and all possible ways both in others and in himself. Maturity is both intellectual and emotional, and is in a sense a by-product in satisfactory living just as happiness and peace of mind should be. There are times, such as this one, when it is worthwhile to look at some of its characteristics.

Like education, maturity is not something one acquires all at once, or completely, nor is it the same in any two individuals. As Dr. Eric Lindemann so clearly states, maturity means different things at different ages, the older and more responsible the person the higher are the standards by which he is judged. What is appropriate at one age may become inappropriate at a later one, but there is always a tendency to revert to an earlier stage when acute

Reprinted from *Harvard Educational Review*, Vol. XXV, No. 2 (Spring 1955), pp. 96–104.

stress is experienced. This regressive behavior may frequently be called "immature." The more that is expected of a person, the more opportunities there are for inappropriate behavior to be observed.

Dr. Lindemann's definition of the mature person is most complete and perceptive:

> He should be able to perform the tasks put before him by himself and his society in such a way to make full use of his capacities without having his efforts hampered by emotional tensions.
>
> He should be able to meet the ordinary stresses of life without disintegration or symptom formation, discharging the tension mobilized by the experience in a relief-producing and ultimately constructive manner.
>
> He can operate without making others sick, either by depriving them of some element of support or freedom needed for their well-being or by so depleting them by his own demands for love or reward that they have little energy left to carry on their own tasks.
>
> He can adapt his perceptions of people and situations to the realities involved rather than falsifying the picture he forms of them by projecting his own needs into it.[1]

He says we must learn to distinguish between maturity and pseudo-maturity which conceals severe developmental flaws under a surface of apparent adequacy. People who seem over-friendly may be wearing a mask which hides hostility or a feeling of emptiness. Others develop the device of martyrdom or willing self-sacrifice in order to control those around them.

He goes on to say that some persons may appear on the surface to be well adjusted, but who are really socially impoverished because of having had an insufficient number of models to love and emulate during the years of personality formation. Such a person might possibly feel comfortable only when he was operating in his own small area of competence, whereas outside that area he might be quite ill at ease in other human relationships. By assuming a superior attitude he could cover up feelings of deep inferiority.

To explore this concept of maturity somewhat further, let us look at it from the administrator's point of view. To him a teacher may be growing, curious, flexible, receptive to new ideas; his point of view cannot be predicted ahead of time; he can see remote as well as immediate reasons for any given act or decision, and he has a concept of discipline based on self-understanding and self-control. On the other hand, another teacher may be very brittle, easily angered, dogmatic in his views; he may take some particular concept and try to make the facts fit it, confuse issues, and have defenses which are obvious to everyone but himself. He makes up his mind quickly and changes

[1] E. Lindemann, "Mental Health—Fundamental to a Dynamic Epidemiology of Health," *Epidemiology of Health,* New York and Minneapolis, Health Education Council, 1953, pp. 109–123.

it only with great difficulty. The second teacher must be treated in an entirely different way from the first one; he is much less mature and suffers from it in failure to achieve as much satisfaction from his work as does the first teacher.

From the pupils' point of view, there are certain general principles that apply to all individuals which the good teacher keeps in mind: (1) people like to be considered a individuals, (2) individuals need a sense of belonging —of team work, (3) sentiments or feelings are facts to be respected, whether based on logical or irrational premises, (4) activity, whether hostile, casual, or friendly, tends to be mirrored or reflected by others, (5) good communication at all levels is fundamental. "No" can be said in a friendly fashion. The teacher is frequently quite unaware of how much time is spent by pupils studying his manner, his attitudes, his way of doing things.

Sometimes it is interesting to hear what the pupils themselves say about the teacher insofar as discipline and attitudes are concerned. For instance, one was observed to say, "I like my teacher because she doesn't pound the desk, scream and holler." Professor Strang[2] of Teachers College, Columbia University, has reported on some of these comments among which were, "I like Mr. E., because he won't let you fool around as much as some of the other teachers do. He is strict, but always ready for a laugh." Another said, "I like my fifth grade teacher when she gets up on the right side of the bed." A sixth grader in a rural community wrote, "My first grade teacher was a very old woman who had never been married. I liked her because she liked children a powerful lot." Another said about her teacher's fairness, "She did not have any one child who was her pet. She always found a way to use pupils, even dumb ones. She would make them feel at home and that they were welcome."

In the background of almost every child who is having trouble with his school work are a number of factors which are monotonously familiar to every experienced teacher, as well as to the psychiatrist. The chief one is almost invariably discord between the parents or parent substitutes. Children have an almost uncanny way of recognizing parental tensions long before the parents themselves think it possible. Furthermore, since the children cannot verbalize their own reactions to this tension, not knowing in many instances what is wrong, they "act out" their feelings more or less unconsciously in the form of reading or scholastic disability, defiant behavior, or other poorly defined aggressive attitudes, bodily symptoms, and in dozens of other ways.

It is the complex of attitudes formed about others in early childhood that determines in large measure whether the adult shall be secure or insecure, able to give and receive affection or be suspicious and self-protective, generally optimistic or pessimistic.

[2] R. Strang, "How Children and Adolescents View Their World," *Mental Hygiene*, Vol. 38, No. 1, January, 1954, pp. 28–33.

If only this one concept could be gotten across to our present-day young people in such a way that they would believe it and act as if they believed it, the problem of the mental health of the next generation would be well on the way to a solution. It is one of the tragedies of this field of the emotions and mental health generally that people tend to learn the principles in a detached intellectual fashion, then when under stress they are apt to behave as if such information had not been acquired.

Other background situations frequently observed in the disturbed or under-achieving child, all related more or less to parental characteristics are (1) faulty discipline, either absent, inconsistent or too authoritarian (2) lack of warm feelings on the part of the parents giving rise to feelings of rejection (3) rigidity in thought and emotional reaction (4) a relative lack of appropriate masculine attributes in the father or feminine traits in the mother (5) distorted or squeamish attitudes about body functions and (6) poor neighborhood environment.

In the attempt to develop children who will at least have the opportunity to acquire mature concepts, behavior, and patterns of thinking, the teacher and the parents encounter many obstacles in the community. We as teachers know that the acquisition of facts is difficult enough even when the facts are constant. How much more difficult it is when the facts change frequently, or the ground rules for interpreting what seem to be facts change. I am referring to a large number of inconsistencies that characterize our behavior but which puzzle children. For example, consider the custom of teaching children that Santa Claus is a real person who comes down all chimneys no matter how small or large, at the same time, and rewards only the good little boys and girls.

Some inconsistencies are presumably desirable in order that a child not be educated for an unreal world—but too many, as Brock Chisholm has observed, are like putting poison in the intellectual soup. Grown-ups often give incorrect answers to children to satisfy their curiosity; or a variation of this, the woman who told her young son she didn't have a quarter when he asked her for one (when he had just seen one in her purse), the child is actually taught that lying is all right when convenient. What can the young boy or girl think when his elders condone lying by a politician but condemn it in others? Or when they see smoking by older people near "No Smoking" signs? They very soon learn who means what he says and says what he means, but equally quickly they learn how to cut corners, how to take ethical short-cuts, and then how to convey false impressions without actually doing any one thing that is out of line. From that we see derived the current morality which seems to stop at the legal level, still somewhat short of a moral level. In the words of a recent *New York Times* article, most people only talk about principle while the rare person tries to defend it. Our children will be like us, only more so, in this regard unless we pay increased attention to consistency, fair play, and the need for honesty in all our dealings with one another.

With our chief agencies of communication, namely the radio, movies and television, we do indeed have a major problem in the attempt to raise the standards of taste of those who plan the programs. A favorite defense of the policy-makers in those fields is that they are giving the people what they want, and they do not want anything serious or educational. H. L. Mencken said a generation ago that no man ever went broke underestimating the tastes of the American public. However, all too often we find the demands of the public being exploited rather than satisfied. A very well known teacher in West Virginia, commenting in his autobiography on the lack of anything but chalk and a piece of sheepskin for an eraser in the school rooms in which he taught his first school, said that modern aids to teaching were not missed because it takes a kind of genius to miss what one does not know about. The tastes of the general public will go up, I believe, when it has the opportunity of continued exposure to programs of good music and other features more desirable than hillbilly songs and soap operas. Experiments such as the new educational television station, Channel 2 in Boston, will be watched, and I hope supported, with much interest.

Mrs. Agnes E. Meyer, writing on "Schoolboy Racketeers" in March, 1954, *Atlantic Monthly* reports with rare insight and perception on some of the social factors which ultimately result in poor school work, juvenile delinquency, and outright criminal behavior. She says our social imagination has failed us in this area largely because the American people, under the lure of materialism, have failed to appreciate the importance of education. We have failed to see that the role of the school is very different in a war-torn, migratory, industrial, urban society than in a more slowmoving, largely agricultural, rural one. As she so eloquently states, "It is high time that we make up our minds what the public schools can and cannot do. For at present the average teacher is expected to be a policeman, a psychiatrist, a public health expert, a doctor, a clergyman, a night club entertainer, and a parent. All this we demand from one underpaid public servant because the nation lacks the wisdom and the will power to face its social problems with honest, effective, and comprehensive insight."

She suggests that true prevention of juvenile delinquency so far as the school's part in this ideal is concerned lies in a greater awareness on the part of the public of the needs of children and teachers together with the willingness to pay them, classes not over 25 in number so teachers can treat pupils as individuals, giving the brighter pupils full scope for their abilities, stopping the practice of promoting by chronological age for political and unwise psychological reasons, closer ties between school and family, and family counseling.

Love and affection always form prominent components of a good home and a good institution just as hatred seems to be associated with crime and delinquency. This emotion and the uses to which it can be put by unscrupulous persons deserves a closer look.

Hatred is a dangerous weapon, always difficult to keep under control. In a social situation filled with stress, demagogues frequently see an opportunity of serving their own special interests in whipping up strong feelings of frenzy, apprehension, fear, and other such reactions, hoping that the people can be molded and controlled by means of hate. Unfortunately hatred is an emotion so strong that it needs a violent outlet, such as war or some equivalent violent conflict. If no outlet is achieved, it tends to turn to some other target, usually inappropriate and hence acts as a divisive force. In our society at present it is dividing us from within rather than uniting us. Frequently hatred and hostility in all their various forms are a means of maintaining personal integrity, even though such emotions are undesired by the individual. This often happens in two married individuals seeking a divorce. Likewise dictators strive to keep their countries united by causing their people to hate other countries, regardless of the logical grounds for enmity. Hatred in the young child, even though not well directed toward any one target, is about as effective a block to learning as any in existence. In a very real sense it is an inverted cry for love. Hatred in the individual blocks his personal development, including learning, just as hatred in a community blocks its social and moral development.

Because hatred is used by so many pressure groups in all societies and tragically in our own, those of us who believe strongly in education, and in the basic decency and good will of mankind generally, must find some antidote for it. Democracy itself, if taught properly, could be the uniting factor behind which all men of good will could exert their strength. As Goethe has said, "Sentiments unite, opinions divide." Ralph Barton Perry has pointed out that Democracy means popular government. It assumes a general confidence in the intellectual and moral capacities of the people. In a social sense it means equal rights and privileges of those who live under government and the spirit of equality that prevails among them.

However, I would like to suggest that Democracy may well mean much more than this. It means a respect for the dignity of the individual. It means freedom accompanied by a sense of responsibility. It presupposes a deep sense of caring for the other person. It requires an awareness, of greater or less degree, of current problems as they arise. It assumes that each person has a duty not only to the community but toward all human beings.

Education contributes toward the maintenance of Democracy and freedom only if it is really free, only if there is room for dissent. The elementary lesson which we have not learned in this country and which is the very essence of Democracy is that one can disagree completely and heartily with one's neighbor and still respect him and cooperate with him on matters of general welfare. Education has thus far failed to live up to all that we have expected of it either because it has not been sufficiently widespread and thorough, or, more probably, because our concept of education has not been as broad as it should have been. It must include the training of the feelings or emotions as well as the intellect. Knowledge without virtue is dangerous, as we have repeatedly learned and as often forgotten.

We have now considered at some length the attitudes and characteristics of the good teacher, some of the social factors which inhibit the growth of maturity, some of the desired goals sought for by the interaction of the teacher and the pupil, and finally some of the specific blocks to the learning process. It is time now to consider some of the positive ingredients in the teacher-pupil relationship which will act to extend the influences of the good home, and to correct in some measure the harmful influences or lack of positive influences in the homes from which some pupils come.

Perhaps the strongest of these influences is that of love and affection. Someone has said that we must learn to love those we do not like. Even Bertrand Russell has conceded that love or compassion, in the Biblical sense, is the one unifying force in a world that is torn apart by dissension and hatreds. "If you feel this, you have a motive for existence, a guide for action, a reason for courage, an imperative necessity for intellectual honesty."[3]

Quite frequently we see the pupil who has an emotional problem, who has struggled against the problem in so many ineffective ways that he has made himself very unpopular in his community so that his friends have turned against him. Yet if he is to be helped to develop in the proper way, the good will and sympathy amounting to real affection of his associates, is usually necessary.

Another very strong factor is that of good communication between the teacher, who represents the school administration, and the pupils. Quite naturally everything that goes on in the school system cannot be passed on to the pupils, but enough can be given them so that they have some sense of participation in the planning of day-to-day activities.

The good teacher also recognizes that the development of attitudes in the pupils is fully as important as the imparting of facts. In fact the pupil with an enormous accumulation of knowledge is not in a position to make good use of it unless he is free enough within his own personality to apply the facts in a logical and social manner. As we have said earlier, the teacher constantly tries to understand the meaning of behavior, while at the same time trying to guide this behavior into proper channels.

From the mental health standpoint discipline is the constant endeavor to transfer authority from without to responsibility and control from within the personality of the young developing student. To assume that discipline

[3] B. Russell, quoted in W. L. Sperry, *Sermons Preached at Harvard,* Cambridge, Massachusetts, Harvard Univ. Press, 1953, p. 131.

means that the pupil does as he is told is to miss the main point. We see many well drilled young boys in military schools or in schools that have a military attitude, but these same youngsters can raise an enormous amount of trouble when out on their own. The most successful discipline is self-discipline. It is based on knowledge and an awareness of one's own place in the scheme of things, and it cannot be transferred in an arbitrary or authoritarian fashion. It seems clear, therefore, that the inculcation of discipline must be done with a permissive attitude, although permissiveness must not be carried to the point where "anything goes." The permissiveness that I speak of is the same kind that the teacher automatically practices in teaching reading, arithmetic, or any of the other school subjects. No one assumes that the young student will get everything right the first time. Similarly one should not assume that all the ethical lessons will be learned equally well at one time. Guidance, not control, thus becomes the central theme.

Last but not least, running through all these general principles must be a strong thread of consistency. We need to keep constantly in mind how things look from the child's point of view. What may seem just to us may seem unfair to the child, and when there is such a paradox, a clear explanation will usually serve to mitigate the sense of injustice felt by the pupil.

I believe we are now ready to come back to the original request from my psychiatrist friend and see if the list of ten concepts valid in psychiatry and useful to teachers can be formulated. It is general, it is philosophical, and it is idealistic, but it must be these if it is also to be practical and inclusive.

(1) The teacher should know himself well, accept his own short-comings and determine to overcome them when possible, and be able to recognize in himself when emotions begin to displace reason. In this way he should not have to work out his own problems at the expense of his students.

(2) He should understand his students in terms of their being products of all their previous experiences, as well as heredity. Each one is, therefore, different, and hence treating them all alike is frequently futile.

(3) The teacher cannot cause growth in his students, but only influence and direct it to a limited extent. He can remove obstacles, add material to make greater growth possible, and aid in every way possible to help the child achieve self-realization of his own potentialities.

(4) Immaturity in all its forms—lack of knowledge, misconceptions, prejudice, sensitivity, tensions between individuals and groups and unreasonable fears—is the reason for the existence of the teacher as a professional person.

(5) Next to mastery of subject matter, the teacher's own attitudes toward students is the most important factor in his success. If he likes them, is consistently firm and patient in applying pressure toward achieving high standards, and can wait patiently for favorable results, his teaching will be successful.

(6) What the teacher *is* and *does* is more influential on students than anything he may say. It is sometimes a shock to teachers to realize how much their students are concerned with what they do, say, read, wear, enjoy, and their manner and behavior generally.

(7) Discipline is a slow process of transferring authority from without (parents, teachers, law enforcement officers) to the individual's own personality (self-discipline, self-control, maturity). The older the student, the greater the proportion of reason and explanation and self-participation in enforcing discipline. Without outside standards at first, self-discipline is nearly impossible.

(8) A permissive attitude coupled with firm discipline is the quickest route to responsibility and self-control, especially when the latter is applied with consistency, kindness, and thoughtfulness.

(9) Authoritarian, inflexible, and impersonal attitudes in the teacher encourage and keep alive rebellion, negativism, and hostility in the pupil.

(10) The good teacher should have a personal philosophy that will tolerate frustration and defeat. He works for the long-run goals. He has the habit of reasonable expectation rather than wishful thinking. He has a respect for, but does not worship facts. He can be uneasy without being unhappy. He can tolerate uncertainty without being paralyzed by anxiety. He can show joy and enthusiasm as well as righteous indignation.

The extension of the teacher's attention to the emotional development of pupils, making the training of feelings as much a part of the teaching and learning process as the training of the intellect, should serve to simplify the task of teaching, rather than complicate it, once the basic assumptions of such a position have been accepted generally. Effective channels of communication for exchanging ideas between teachers, parents and psychiatrists and psychologists are desirable in paving the way for such acceptance. Effective learning is so dependent on proper motivation that no teacher can do his best work or get maximum satisfaction from it without maintaining a lifelong interest in the relationship between emotions and learning.

Chapter 49

ACADEMIC FREEDOM—THE EDUCATOR'S AUTHORIZATION

IN THE *democratic ethos, complete and unrestricted freedom must be accorded to scholars and teachers in their quest for, and utilization of, knowledge. Academic freedom is, in a sense, a gift bestowed by society upon all educators and scholars to help them fulfill their ethical obligations. That academic freedom is often violated is a fact needing no elaboration. In his discussion of academic freedom, Kurt P. Tauber, a social scientist, examines these issues: (1) the relationship of academic freedom to the ethos of society; (2) the trials and tribulations in the evolvement of the theory of academic freedom; (3) the relationship of academic freedom to other value-orthodoxies; (4) what can conceivably occur should the attacks upon academic freedom continue unabated; and (5) what can conceivably occur should academic freedom be fully restored.*

THE FREE UNIVERSITY IN AN OPEN SOCIETY

Kurt P. Tauber

Liberal democracy is primarily characterized by its emergence as an open, pluralistic society; a society, that is, which rests upon the primacy of the values of rationality, tolerance, and the moral autonomy of the individual. Rationality in this sense is not philosophic rationalism as opposed to empiricism; it is rather an attitude, a frame of mind, which combines the rationalist faith in the efficacy of human reason with the humbleness of the empiricist in the face of the contingency of all human knowledge and with his respect for, and discipline in the face of, facts. Rationalism, so understood, is an attitude "of readiness to listen to critical arguments and to learn from experience. It is fundamentally an attitude of admitting that 'I may be wrong and you may be right, and by an effort we may get nearer to the truth.' "

As the rationalist attitude concerns itself with arguments, not with the physical persons propounding them, arguments must be *a priori* accepted as possible sources of reasonable information regardless of their originators. No line whatever can be drawn to exclude anybody from becoming a potential contributor to common knowledge. This necessary implication of tolerance is further strengthened by the empiricist modesty in assessing human knowledge. If, as the empirio-rationalist believes (conscious though he is of the well-known paradox of the liar), all our beliefs are doubtful, no belief has an *a priori* advantage over any other. Tolerance is consequently the only possible rational attitude.

A further corollary of the attitude of empirio-rationalism is the conclusion that insofar as truth-hypotheses are partial, the responsibility for choice among them must remain unequivocably and solely with the individual maker of choices. No dogma, no authority, can remove even for one moment the dread yet ennobling burden of moral choice from the conscience of the more mature individual.

If the ethics of social systems are rated by the demand they make upon the human conscience, then the open society of liberal democracy with its basic values of rationality, tolerance, and individual moral autonomy repre-

Reprinted from *Harvard Educational Review*, Vol. XXIII, No. 1 (Winter 1953), pp. 4–16. Footnotes omitted.

sents the highest level of social responsibility yet achieved. For in this society all the traditional and easy escapes from the tensions and conflicts of life are barred. The romantic flights of political irrationalism, the snivelling retreat to the security of dogmatic authoritarianism, the incantations for lifting the burden of absolute ethical autonomy, all these are inadmissible solutions to trying problems. Liberal democracy makes heavy demands on civilized man for it denies expression to the more primitive and possibly most basic drives of the personality. The will to force, the will to domination and exclusion, the will to self-immolating submission to charisma—all these cannot theoretically be indulged in an open society. Rationalism and the open society are indeed based on a heroic ethics.

Within the limits of the humanitarian ideal (which the tolerance and the idea of the unity of mankind inherent in rationalism demand) any particular system of production and distribution has little to do with the basic requirements of an open society. The open society of a liberal democracy is even less dependent, if possible, on religious foundations, let alone on any particular orthodoxy. It has become fashionable with the critics of a rational society to cite history in support of their contention that the well-being of democracy and that of Christianity necessarily go together. But their partisan appeal is not convincing. Secularism has stood at the cradle of democratic liberty in the thought of the Pre-Socratics, it has attended its re-birth in the 18th Century and was quite marked in the England of the 19th Century which saw the gradual realization of an open society. The goal of liberal, pluralistic democracy is the well-being and happiness of man *on earth*, a thoroughly non-religious fundamental tenet. To the extent to which the open society rests on a faith in rationality it deprecates all attempts of men to solve their problems by appeal to mysticism. The slow emancipation of modern man from the fetters of magic, though often involving prodigious strains in the individual psyche and in the social system which fosters the liberation, represents a singular achievement in man's struggle for inner dignity.

Those who fear the conflicts and the crises which are the normal concomitants of the open society tacitly and erroneously assume that liberal democracy must foster certain substantive values, like Christianity and individualism, which are Truth, and proscribe other values, such as atheism or collectivism, which are Error. However, the values of the open society are not so much substantive as methodological or procedural, if you will. Pluralistic democracy enshrines the value of responsible valuation, it fosters the value of reasonableness and critical intelligence and the value of tolerance precisely because the categories of truth and error are, in a sense, inapplicable to values. Those values can be espoused without self-contradiction because they are methodological and not substantive, because they are permissive, latitudinarian, and not prescriptive or limiting.

Against those who would subvert the free society in the name of preserving it, it is important to stress that faithfulness to the democratic tradition does not forbid the support or encouragement of values antagonistic to one's cherished prejudices. On the contrary, insofar as the primary obligation of the liberal democrat is to the maintenance of a free, pluralistic society he must encourage—not necessarily any particular obnoxious value—but the conditions which make the free expression and propagation of disliked values possible. That is, "faithfulness to the democratic tradition" requires primarily the institutional maintenance of tolerance and of the unhampered exercise of critical reason. The commitment to the maintenance of maximum areas of freedom takes logical and ethical primacy over commitments to substantive partisan values. The primacy is due to the fact that the legitimacy of the propagation of partisan values depends on their compatibility with the moral dignity and autonomy of the individual. This compatibility, however, can be guaranteed only by the continuous existence of real opportunity for the advancement of rival doctrines and values.

But the faint of heart would answer, and they gleefully make that point on every occasion, that even the much vaunted tolerance of liberal democracy must have some limits, which alone is said to prove the speciousness of our argument. Yet the liberal democrat need not deny that tolerance has limits. Unlimited tolerance must paradoxically lead to its own demise. As tolerance is based on the assumption that reasonable arguments must be taken seriously, it cannot tolerate those who refuse to prepare their challenge on the level of rational argument or who denounce all argument as inconsequential. Once the arbitrament of conflicting propositions is removed from the area of rationalism it inevitably devolves upon the guillotine and the gas chamber. This the tolerant has the right, and duty, to prevent even in the name of tolerance. Tolerance, in short, can tolerate everything except the intolerant. Though tolerance admittedly has limits, it is their latitude that really matters. These limits separate not the "good" from the "bad" but the compatible from the incompatible. This is, of course, not to say that tolerance calls for the immediate suppression of incompatible values or intolerant philosophies, for the maximal sufferance even of those values is an important part of tolerance. Where the breaking point comes, where the limits are clearly trespassed, is a matter for the wisdom and tender conscience of the tolerant rationalist. Thus communism is proscribed—if at all—in a pluralistic society not because it is "evil" or "foolish" or "in error," but because its inherent dogmatism, its appeal to authority and, finally, to the arbitrament of fists, are incompatible with the permissive, tolerant bases of a liberal democracy. In short, we must limit tolerance not against what we abhor but against that which would undercut the very basis of our pluralistic society.

The history of the past thirty years seems to have proved to the satisfaction of many that the presumed premise of democracy, the Jeffersonian maxim *Magna est veritas et prevalebit*—Truth is might and will prevail—is unsound. The ideology of liberal democracy, they claim, has been defeated repeatedly when pitted against authoritarian and dictatorial ideologies. To ensure the victory of the former, therefore, such an open battle must not be permitted. False ideologies must be prohibited and outlawed. Democracy can be preserved only by becoming undemocratic vis-à-vis falsehood and error. What we wish to point out here is not that this council of disillusionment is not warranted by the facts, but rather that its very basis is the result of a delusion. For precisely in imputing great significance to the doctrine of *Magna est veritas et prevalebit*—if only negatively for the purpose of disproving it—the defenders of "Americanism" or other orthodoxies once more demonstrate their misconception of the nature of a free society. Such a society, we repeat, does not rest on the acceptance of any substantive doctrine as truth or on the rejection of any other as falsehood. Consequently it is naïve to argue that it relies on the assumption of a victory of truth over error. Much rather, an open society rests on the belief that the struggle between contending doctrines, views and opinions—regardless of its outcome—itself ennobles human life. For such a struggle within the arena of open debate bespeaks tolerance, rationalism, and profound respect for the moral and intellectual personality of one's fellowmen. In this light it is baseless to think that the history of dictatorships furnishes one with evidence of the fact that error sometimes vanquishes truth. The idea that wins out in cases where dictatorships supersede liberal democracies is not any erroneous substantive theory, but the fatal formal theory that proscribes the absolutely free market of ideas. It is not the contempt for "truth" that assures victory to the idolatry of "falsehood," but the contempt for reason and the open society that loses the battle to the irrationalism of the tribe. The problem of the open society is not the problem of error but the problem of intolerance, of limiting the area of free inquiry, free criticism and free choice.

Before discussing some of the implications of the open society for the acquisition of knowledge it seems important to say a word or two about the favorite device of those who would limit academic freedom; they seek to strengthen their argument by pointing out how imperfectly that freedom has been observed even in periods of relative security and peace. This is a mere debater's trick since the recitation of facts is logically irrelevant to their argument, regardless of whether the damaging facts alleged are authentic or not. From the fact that academic freedom is not achieved cannot logically be derived any suggestion for future action which, by its very nature, is normative. Thus, the writer for instance, happens to agree wholeheartedly that there are numerous instances in the recent history of education in the United States which show conclusively that academic freedom on the various levels of education is honored more in the breach than in the observance. No one can read Harold J. Laski's incisive comments on education in America without becoming aware of the often discouragingly uncertain status of freedom of opinion and academic freedom (as well of course of all other liberties). In fact, Laski's analysis leads him to the conclusion that "a high level of academic freedom is not easily compatible with the presidential system," the prevalent mode of university administration in America. These facts, however, demonstrate only the slow and uphill fight for the values of an open society against the inertia and the hostility of the interests and institutions which represent the past and vanishing age. The ethos of the open society is heroic and as the average man is not made of the stuff of heroes, the struggle for greater dignity, for the subordination of instincts and sentiments to the claims of reason cannot be expected to be either effortless or without setbacks and disappointments. But without committing what G. E. Moore has called the "naturalistic fallacy," the recognition of these facts cannot lead to the normative demand that the great fight for liberal democracy should be given up and that modern man should return to the authoritarian obscurantism and dogmatic faith of the Dark Ages.

It is not always clearly recognized that a close relationship exists between the society and its institutions for the acquisition of knowledge which insures that modification in the structure of one will produce changes in the goals of the other, and vice versa. To show this close connection between the structure of society and its attitude toward learning, there follows a very brief sketch of the development of human thought from demoniac animism in the tribal society to truth-hypothetical ratio-empiricism in the open society and a brief description of the rôles of the scholar and the school at each stage of development.

The earliest fully studied social organization of historical man is what might be termed the tribal society. The outstanding feature is its characteristic attitude toward the customs of social life and toward the means of its purposeful direction. As tribal customs are in the form of magical taboos, appeals to their efficacy are almost entirely non-rational. The outside world, under these conditions, is interpretable only as the objectification of mythical forces. The leadership of the closed, tribal society rests largely with the priest-king who propitiates the hostile forces by his magical powers. This function eventually develops into a comprehensive knowledge of sacred lore which it becomes the task of medicine men, magicians, or priests to cultivate and to transmit to successive generations. The priests become the guardians of the entire religious system and sacred schools develop as a matter of social necessity.

The sole function of a scholar in such a closed society is to perpetuate, unchanged, traditional sacred lore. As the knowledge of the scholar is here not considered his own nor the product of his thought, he is neither expected nor allowed to change or modify the received "truths." Teaching and learning under these circumstances are nothing more than the faithful reproduction of those "truths." In an effort to perpetuate the privileges attached to his social rôle by protecting his monopoly position as the keeper of the Truth, the religious scholar establishes as his guiding principle the dogma of obscurantism: "Whatever in the domain of knowledge is verily true cannot be new; whatever is new must be false." The maintenance of authority, dogma, and popular ignorance is the means for the maintenance of the purity of the faith. The schools' purpose in the closed society is to teach the Truth and to forestall all critical reflection on the basic theoretical foundations of the dogma.

Clearly, under these circumstances, critical knowledge in its modern Western meaning cannot be achieved. Nor is it possible for the member of the closed society to achieve a truly ethical life with its characteristic maximal moral autonomy. As long as taboos are uncritically accepted, moral problems cannot even arise. The tribal life does of course offer spiritual and intellectual security, but it is a foetal security. The member of the tribe achieves the security of the foetus at the price of retaining the latter's moral and mental dependence. And the function of the scholar and the school in the closed society is precisely the maintenance of that dependency relation.

In spite of a maximum of thought control, however, small cracks will appear in the solid wall of dogmatic orthodoxy which surrounds the closed society. These cracks are probably caused by the inevitable contacts and conflicts with rival orthodoxies and by those rare individuals whose inquiring minds cannot be sterilized quickly enough by the authorities. Secularism and, closely associated with it, critical thinking make inroads under the guise of demands for critical criteria of truth which rely less on demoniacal "explanations" and the authoritarian dogmatism of tradition than on rational considerations. The changes in the social organization, which spell the beginning of the breakdown of the closed, tribal society are accompanied and partly caused by profound changes in the function of the scholar and of the university in the new environment. The passing of tribalism in the 6th Century B.C. and, sixteen centuries later, the collapse of the Dark Ages by no means meant the Venus-like birth of a full-blown open society, dedicated to the ideal of a humanistic and rational world. The birth was slow and complicated and, as we have seen, the young off-spring is still weak, sickly and in need of continuous and devoted solicitude.

The rise of secularism and philosophical rationalism (realism) replaces sacred Truth (as interpreted by the priest) as the standard of human thought and action with the standard of evident rational certainty. However, the philosophical rationalism (realism) of the transition period, rooted as it is in the sacerdotal dogmatism of the tribal society, is by no means prepared to jettison the centuries-old search for absolute certainty. It merely substitutes for the old ultimate, objective criterion of absolute truth a new criterion—thought to be no less ultimate, objective and absolute. The rationalism of Aristotle and St. Thomas is a typical example of the attempt in the transition period to extend the certainty obtainable in mathematics to knowledge about this world. Syllogistic reasoning from "self-evident" axiomatic truths becomes the main tool of the scholar of the closed transition society. Doubt about the self-evidence of the initial propositions cannot and dare not arise as all "valid" knowledge presupposes those axioms.

The function of the university in this transition stage is the propagation not of traditional sacred lore—as has been the case in the tribal society—but of equally ultimate, objective, and absolute knowledge of a rational character. Doubts are considered the consequence of ignorance which is bound to disappear after a thorough absorption of the teachings of the professor. The rigorously deductive structure of absolutely true knowledge as conceived by the "rationalist" successors of tribal irrationalism does not allow for the admissibility of heterodox "certainties." These are considered dangerous and are outlawed in the universities or fought as "merely" inductive belief—with no claim to inclusion in a system which defines truth by its derivability from "self-evident" principles, without regard to empirical data.

Though it cannot be gainsaid that the philosophy of knowledge and of education outlined above shares some of its most typical attitudes with the tribal society, fundamental and vastly portentous differences do exist. In the first place, the nature of knowledge though still conceived as indubitable truth, is no longer considered holy. Its validity and its imposition can no longer be established by appeal to divine revelation as interpreted by authoritarian dogma, but must rest solely upon human reason. This principle, once established, guarantees the dynamism of the transition, for a secular culture must of needs be a changing culture. The concepts enshrined by the secular neo-tribal society and its theory of knowledge and education vouchsafe their own transitoriness. They carry the seed for their own supersedure by the open society with its epistemology and values. The further importance of this stage of development lies in its recognition and transmission of the vastly significant insight that the prestige of the rôle of the scholar and the status of the institution within which he works depends—in the absence of divine revelation—upon the understanding of and appreciation for scholarship by a more or less large segment of the population. Because of the very dynamism inherent in secular rationalism and the concomitant growth of the open society, the purpose of teaching becomes not so much the inculcation of dogmas and "truths" as the creation of widely held attitudes which make the continued application of creativity to scholarship possible.

Anti-empirical rationalist orthodoxy breaks down by virtue of the dynamism of its own epistemological, educational, and social assumptions. The critical mind, once liberated, can only with difficulty be forced back into the cave of dogma and ignorance. The devastating empiricist criticism of philosophic rationalism, the new distinction between analytic and synthetic propositions and the accompanying democratization of social institutions ushered in the beginnings of the open society. This criticism clarified the necessary distinction between nature as immediately experienced and apprehended and nature as the scientist conceives it in indirectly and experimentally verified theory. The scientific theories themselves emerged from experiments which underscored the rôle of hypotheses in determining the results of scientific investigations and the effect of valuation on scientific method. An analysis of these insights led to a rejection of the category of "self-evidence" as by no means logically respectable and to an appreciation of the relativity—and in some sense even subjectivity—of human knowledge. The new view of knowledge has important implications for the organization and function of a university in the new society. Here we are concerned primarily with the consequences of the new appreciation of the concept of objectivity and the rôle of rigorous criticism.

Philosophical rationalism considers true knowledge to be the product of a process which takes place in the mind of a scientist. True, objective knowledge is true and objective because of the integrity of the deductive system with its self-evident axioms and because of the impartiality and objectivity of the scholar. Modern epistemology and philosophy of science has no difficulty in pointing out the manifold ways in which the subjective values and faculties of the scientist intrude upon his observations. "Pure data" are rationalist abstractions as are the "self-evident" postulates. Subjectivity cannot be left out of the scientific equation. Under these circumstances the objectivity which rationalism values as a prime *desideratum* and as the hallmark of true, public knowledge cannot be guaranteed, as had been thought, by the objectivity of the scholar.

Objectivity in the knowledge of the open society rests on quite other grounds, namely on the social aspect of scientific method, on its intersubjectivity. The necessary requirement for its attainment is the possibility of a maximum of free criticism. The new method not only fosters but rests upon the desirability of criticizing *everything* without regard to its claims to revelationary or other non-rational origin. Once criticism is stopped or otherwise reduced, the whole framework of the new knowledge collapses, for modern science progresses quite as much by the deletion of untenable hypotheses as by the creation of new ones.

An even more important difference between the hypothetical structure of modern science and that of the belief system of dogmatic rationalism is that the former requires for its validation the demonstration of independent evidence in its favor. This is achieved by the most rigorous attempts at falsification of the theories through the choice of new initial conditions which imply predictions in the light of the theory. As there is a fundamental asymmetry of truth and falsehood (from the empiricist point of view) in that the observation and confirmation of predicted events can never "verify" a theory, the total structure of modern science rests on the possibility of refuting inadequate theories. Thus, scientific objectivity is constituted partly by cross-criticism and partly by the testing of theories against the objective materials of scientifically standardized empirical data.

This new concept of scientific objectivity means that the free university with the protection of academic freedom is the necessary precondition to make the progress of reliable new knowledge at all possible. Only the vouchsafing of an arena in which rival theories, ideologies, and views can meet, stripped of all advantage save their inherent theoretical adequacy, can ensure the continued growth of modern science, and hence ultimately, political and social development. The increasingly heard plea for the suppression of heterodoxy and criticism in free universities is consequently incompatible with the continuance of the open, liberal, democratic society. The defender of a value orthodoxy might claim, however, that our historico-theoretical discussion is altogether irrelevant as he is prepared to admit: (a) that the taught orthodoxy should be critically examined "from the heart of an institution" dedicated to its perpetuation, and (b) that the researcher, as against the teacher, can lay claim to an area left untouched by the propagandist of a value orthodoxy. To justify the second admission he would of course have to argue that research is not "inherently related" to teaching and that therefore the freedom necessary to the former cannot be legitimately stretched to encompass the latter.

This possible charge of irrelevance, however, is not substantiated by these admissions for both of them rest on an extremely unsophisticated view of the history of knowledge and of the distinction between the various levels of education. With regard to the first contention, the relevance of our historical discussion is obvious. The similarities between the ideas implied in admission (a) and the assumptions of the epistemology of orthodox rationalism and its demoniacal precursor are striking indeed. In either case the primary assumption is the existence of a pyramidal system of true, substantive knowledge which can be expanded (to include new data) and "refined," but which can never be obliterated. The new generalizations, under this concept of truth, can in no way conflict with the established system for their definition as valid generalizations rests on their compatibility with the original deductive body of "knowledge." Such correction and reduction of inductive generalizations are typical of the dogmatic rationalism of Plato, Aristotle, and the Middle Ages. Insofar as their "truths" rest on an entirely circular procedure which is incapable of testing the *explicandum* with an independent *explicans*, they are "scientific" eyewash and cannot contribute to new insights and knowledge. Secondly, as we mentioned above, modern critical thought has brought out clearly the difficulties and vagaries in the orthodox concept of objectivity and the psychological and logical impossibility of critically examining a proposition from a standpoint which is *a priori* committed to its validity.

The authoritarian's other attempt to extricate himself from the confusions and contradictions of his own position is also unsuccessful. Research, he admits, needs freedom. But teaching, he argues, being merely the skilled transmission of certain doctrines and beliefs to students, may not claim such privileges. Further, he contends, the teacher in a free university is there to satisfy the desires and wishes of the undergraduates, or rather their parents. Both arguments are thoroughly specious.

Teaching at the highest level (to which presumably a free university aspires) is impossible without concomitant research. It is by no means merely the technical transmission of information and beliefs, but rather the presentation of a method of inquiry which guarantees continuous progress in the clarification of problems and of the latest findings within the area of the teacher-scholar's primary interest and research. It is the creative aspect of systematizing and advancing a body of knowledge and the methodology involved which distinguishes teaching at the university level from that done at lower levels.

The peculiar function of the teacher in a university is closely related to the function of the university in contradistinction to the rôle of lower educational institutions. The grammar schools and high schools serve more or less directly the maintenance of the social order. That is, immature minds and personalities are prepared to assume upon maturity the rôles of members of the society of which they are a part. In this respect the school, as is widely recognized, merely supplements the preparation given to the child and adolescent in his family. To be sure, school training involves the imparting of certain minimum theoretic disciplines. Yet the knowledge is imparted because life in a modern society requires it, and not for its own sake or for the sake of clarifying the structure of modern knowledge and of deriving from it certain attitudinal implications.

Whether we think that this function of the high school is adequate and whether the school fulfills it adequately are of no importance here. What is important is to note that it differs drastically from the rôle of a free university. The latter performs the function of an educational institution precisely because its main activities are not social but scientific and methodological. The aim of the free university is not the maintenance of any substantive aspects of the social order but, more significantly, the maintenance of critical knowledge and of the procedural methods which make that maintenance possible. The function of the university in the open society, far from including the physical or moral education of the students or the guidance of their personal development to fit them for social participation, must assume that these processes have been successfully completed before the students' admission to a seat of higher learning. The university's aim on its teaching side, is not to make "good citizens" if that is meant to connote commitment to any particular social, political, or economic theory, but to make intelligent men; to communicate to them the experience of thought and to submit to them (by example and precept) the formal, methodological requirements for the achievement of reliable knowledge, which include the philosophical presuppositions of the open society. The studies, in short, teach respect for critical thought and rational grounds of belief, increase the ability of tolerant discernment, and strengthen the resolve to disbelieve propositions for which there is no reasonable support. But even though the formal, permissive values of critical rationality, tolerance and the moral autonomy of the individual underlie both the new society and the new education, their promotion is only a consequence of university instruction and not the central goal of its effort.

All attempts to subject scholarship and learning to the crude controls of political forces, and even of majority decisions, rest on the fatal shortsightedness of those who are unable to see that a civilization lives by the creative work of those who have the ability to do it, and not by the routine performance of tasks. Once creativity dries out no amount of mere diligence can save that civilization from ceasing to function; it is bound to stagnate and eventually to disintegrate. Because of this vital function of creativity the whole society has an immediate interest in it. Consequently the arguments of the classical economists do not apply to it (even assuming they applied with reasonable adequacy to anything else). In a healthy society the consumer market can no more determine the fate of creative activity than it can determine the fate of other services, essential to human and social well-being, which do not promise sufficient pecuniary returns to attract the private investor. In a free society there must never be unemployment for the trader in ideas or any other creative mind. The penalty for neglecting this requirement would be the disappearance of the free society itself.

In rejecting as fatal to a free university the imposition of any dogma or orthodoxy, the liberal democrat proceeds from an acknowledgment of the very high probability that all our beliefs are doubtful. If we knew the truth, an argument could be made for teaching it. But if it were really true it could be taught without appeal to authority. Whenever there is conclusive evidence in favor of a proposition, authority need not be involved. Now it may be perfectly true that, for instance, Christianity and capitalism is Truth, but teaching them as such is not truthful insofar as a doubtful proposition is misrepresented as certain. The higher education of an open society cannot hope to attain truth but must insist on truthfulness, that is on an attitude of respect for evidence and for holding opinions with a degree of conviction warranted by the evidence. And truthfulness is possible only in the cross-streams of criticism within the free university.

A few words should be said concerning the baneful practical effects of teaching an orthodoxy, quite apart from its profoundly dangerous theoretical effects on the normative and social bases of a liberal democracy. The drive to enforce conformity to a code of conventional thought will exclude from the universities precisely those men who by virtue of their honesty and intellectual vitality are the most sorely needed for the development of scholarship and for the stimulation of the students' minds. Further, even those teachers who are still within the pale will lose their vitally important habit of spontaneity. A vigorous character with a passion for ideas will not accept the humiliating inhibitions which a policy of value inculcation imposes.

From the point of view of the students the practical effects of changing a free university into a doctrinally parochial school are equally disastrous. In such a school, the students' critical faculties will remain undeveloped or might even be thwarted. They will hardly acquire the virtue of skepticism which is crucial for the maintenance of an open society; they are not likely to experience the ennobling emotion of freedom which comes with the awareness of responsibility for the making of decisive value choices, nor will they have learned the sophisticated art of tolerant discernment. Value alternatives will appear to them as clearly black and white, as mutually totally incompatible. Under the aegis of dogmatists university training which normally should represent a period of exhilarating intellectual challenge, an exciting journey into relatively unknown territory with a variety of guides, would become a deadening weeding process in which heterodox ideas are plucked out and replaced by orthodoxy. The regimented university, in short, in encouraging intolerance, ignorance, and a herd instinct, fosters precisely those attitudes which are fatal to the open society.

In conclusion we must touch upon the frequently encountered arguments in favor of alumni control over educational policies. They rest on two assumptions: one is that education is a marketable commodity much like cabbages or electrical engineering which therefore is subject to the classical iron-laws of consumer demand, and, secondly, that the alumni are the consumers of that commodity. Our discussion of the nature of scholarship and of the university shows that both assumptions are erroneous. Education is no more a commodity than national health or social well-being. It is a precondition, and continuously a necessary concomitant, of the healthy society. Without liberal education, which by its teaching ensures its own continuance and the continuance of the open society, and which by its research provides a dynamic social order with the necessary insights and truthful knowledge, a liberal democracy would be impossible and a high level of creative cultural achievement unthinkable. To think of creative knowledge as a commodity is the first step in a series which must lead to making such knowledge impossible. Once creativity is chained to the espousal of any particular doctrine, no matter how noble and desirable that might appear to any or even all people, it not only ceases to exist but even makes reliable knowledge impossible in the absence of the necessary checks, criticism, debate and fundamental re-evaluation. If liberal education is really not a commodity at all, former students (or even present ones) cannot be considered its consumers. The real "consumer" (in a metaphorical sense) is the entire social order, that is *all* the people including those who have never set foot inside a classroom.

The nature of modern knowledge and of its attainment is such that as far as educational and research policy is concerned, only the largely autonomous self-government by the community of scholars will ensure its proper functioning. The flower of free, untrammeled scholarship is too sensitive to be entrusted to the care of anyone but those who have raised it in the first place. The alumni of a liberal educational institution cannot and should not be the ultimate overseer of educational policy—except insofar as the overall policy is restricted to the maintenance of an arena in which the widest and freest exchange and cross criticism of beliefs, opinions and theories are possible.

. . .

The dynamism of the life of an open society—and its very existence—requires of its devotee a readiness to accept the unaccustomed and to be guided by reason and experiment. It requires an attitude which refuses "to confound the new with the dangerous or the traditional with the beneficent." Above all, it requires an education which produces in the students a love and reverence for critical reason, humanistic tolerance, and the heroic struggle of modern man to achieve moral dignity by emancipating himself from the long heritage of ignorance, superstition, and servility. Those who are afraid of the searching light of human reason, who shiver in the open, pluralistic society of free men, who long for a return to the foetal security of the tribe, know that all too well. Should their attack on liberal education prove successful, the end of our open society might well be in sight.

SOME OBSERVATIONS AFTER THE FACTS

You have just finished a big book. As you read, thought, talked, and wrote your way through it, the enormity of your decision to teach must certainly have dawned upon you. Now it is time to suggest how the major thesis presented in the preceding pages can be accepted for action.

You must already have noticed that the introductions and the readings in this book presented many ideas as ideals and still others as practices. You might, had you been so inclined, have posted these ideas in a double-entry ledger and ended up with a balance sheet on the educational state of the nation. Such intellectual bookkeeping would have revealed this: We have been educated well enough to build and operate a complex industrial society, and poorly enough to be capable of destroying ourselves. Our schools, and the other agencies that guide children toward adulthood, have brought us to a crossroads. All that is great and good in us urges us to walk toward a world that would be a golden age the likes of which mankind has dreamed of for thousands of years. And all that is cheap and mean in us prompts us to walk toward a world in which we will hurt and maim the flesh and spirit of the human race in ways that may never be remedied.

The American today finds himself in this dilemma because he is the unwitting inheritor of all the political traditions of the West. While we speak of ourselves as democrats, citizens of a free society, we are equally autocrats and irresponsible, self-seeking individualists. Our characters and our institutions are nowhere as singleminded in their dedication to the idea and practices of freedom as they might be. An institution like the public school, with its teaching and administrative personnel, betrays this fact every day of its existence. One can find in every single school in this country acts of thoughtful consideration, cheap domination, and blatant irresponsibility—often exhibited by a single person.

We live this way because too much of the past has come into the present. We have been sloppy in our estimates of what is of most worth, and crude in our selection of rules of procedure. Our habits, our allegiances, and our purposes are mixed and stained by ideas that are inherently incompatible.

We simply do not think straight long enough and hard enough. For instance, we know that democracy must contain a conception of authority, and that, in the democratic mood, men must know and care enough about themselves in order to find the strength to stand alone when they have to. But we forget that democratic authority is not authoritarian and that independence is not social irresponsibility. This kind of intellectual confusion can never support the growth of healthy, mature personalities.

We understand too much about human behavior to believe that it is easy for people, by taking thought, to stop behaving one way and to begin behaving another. Whether you are a young person in college or an older person adding to your education, all you can do is learn to do a little better some of the things you are already doing well. The point has already been made that we have democratic conceptions about which we say a great deal, and democratic impulses and skills that we act out everywhere and all the time. What we must develop is a more critical understanding of what we believe and a deeper self-consciousness about what we are doing.

The value of these intellectual foundations of education lies in the help they can give to those who are getting ready to teach. Used properly, this book will let us think more critically about our democratic heritage and encourage us to watch our step more sharply. Since there is no trauma involved in this, no one is going to undergo any unusual character reformation. But it is possible, even likely, that if the material in this book is taught and learned with the above goals in mind, everyone involved in its use will become a better democrat.

To be better in the context of this discussion means making the idea of democracy clearer by selecting more focused activities. We need deeds, not more words. As teachers, we must learn to correct the mistakes our students make in ways that will not let them doubt themselves. We need to develop the kinds of programs that clearly help each student know that his skills, understandings, and appreciations are being enlarged. We need to create the kinds of classrooms where students make serious decisions and live by them.

Americans have been behaving this way for the last few hundred years. We need more of the same social evolution, but now the development must be telescoped. We could afford to take our time and make mistakes in the past because there was, in any man's relationships with other men, much margin for error. Now, the margin is smaller. Some people warn us that there is no substantial margin left to rely upon. It is possible, they say, to make a series of economic misjudgments that will stop machines everywhere. It is certainly true that political miscalculations could destroy us and our world.

Are these testable propositions? Many of us think not. The probabilities must be presumed and accepted on faith. We believe that we must try as hard as we can to do the right, as right is defined by the ideals of democracy, as urgently and steadily as we can, and thereby help the human race to choose a proper destiny for itself.

The urban, technological, mass society in which we live does not make it easy for anyone who wants to be a democrat. Its bigness is mechanical and impersonal. It breeds apathy and feelings of inadequacy. What can you do with "them" at city hall? Clearly, there are people who do not want democratic claims to be made and acted upon, for then power would shift away from them. All that one American can say to another is this: What other choice do we have? This generation either chooses to reaffirm the democratic faith, with action and with passion, or it forgets this part of the political tradition of the West in favor of another choice. A century ago, Lincoln reminded us that we could not remain half free and half slave; today, we cannot remain half free.

Most of the children of the nation are enrolled in the public schools of America. Any teacher who chooses to make a difference will make one. To take thought, then, and choose properly are the goals to which *Intellectual Foundations of American Education* addresses itself.

The questions you can ask at this point should guide your inquiries from now on.

SELECTED BIBLIOGRAPHY

The intent of this selected bibliography is to assist readers with diverse interests and backgrounds who wish to obtain a fuller understanding of the role and purpose of contemporary American education. This requires references that refer to two areas of interest: (1) the operation and functioning of American education; and (2) the clarification of the many factors that condition and influence the conduct of education. The two categories, of course, are not mutually exclusive. In other words, attention must be focused upon what education is and why it takes a particular form or design.

The literature dealing with the subject matter of education is voluminous, but not of uniform quality. There appears to be too much emphasis upon describing what is being done or what should be done and too little emphasis upon describing why schooling is conducted as it is and why change should be encouraged. This may be partially explained by the particular orientation of the educator to the complex tasks to be accomplished. The obligation to contribute to the alteration of personality through the medium of ideas and the obligation to impart the knowledge that substantiates the ideas force the educator to concentrate on the "how" and the "what." Too little time and energy are available for a detailed analysis of the "why." As a result the writings of the professional educator all too frequently concentrate upon the mechanics of teaching, and assume a knowledge of the "why." This also may be partially explained by the orientation of the scholar within a particular discipline. The scholar assumes the obligation to advance the frontiers of knowledge in his chosen field, but the relevance the contribution may have for the educator's province of interest may or may not be of value. A new approach seems indicated if any improvement in the quality of the literature of education is to be achieved. Until such time as a comprehensive working arrangement that encourages educators and scholars to participate jointly in formulating research studies of mutual interest is achieved, the student of education will encounter writings that range from those having a deep and vital bearing upon education to those only tangentially related to it.

In the light of these remarks, the bibliographical references have been selected: (1) to reinforce the theses presented in this book; (2) to strengthen the significance of the interdisciplinary approach; (3) to describe what is currently being done in education; and (4) to clarify why Americans use education as an instrument for the attainment of individual and social stability. The selected references for each part are arranged in two groups: The general references emphasize what education is and how it is being conducted, and the special references emphasize why education exists as it does and why change and modification should be encouraged.

I. *Cultural Values and Education*

GENERAL REFERENCES

Berkson, I. A., *The Ideal and the Community*. New York: Harper, 1958. Chapters 5, 9, 10.

Callahan, R. E., *An Introduction to Education in American Society*, 2d ed. New York: A. A. Knopf, 1960. Chapters 5, 7.

Childs, J. L., *American Pragmatism and Education*. New York: Henry Holt, 1956. Chapter 5.

———, *Education and Morals*. New York: Appleton-Century-Crofts, 1950. Chapters 2, 7, 12.

Cox, P. W. L. & Mercer, B. E., *Education in Democracy: Social Foundations of Education*. New York: McGraw-Hill, 1961. Chapters 1, 2.

Dewey, J., *Democracy and Education*. New York: Macmillan, 1924. Chapter 7.

Haan, A., *Education for the Open Society*. Boston: Allyn & Bacon, 1962. Chapter 1.

Morris, V. C., ed., *Becoming an Educator*. Boston: Houghton Mifflin, 1963. Chapters 3, 4.

Thayer, V. T., *The Role of the School in American Society*. New York: Dodd, Mead, 1960. Chapters 1, 16, 17.

SPECIAL REFERENCES

Bay, C., *The Structure of Freedom*. Stanford: Stanford University Press, 1958.

Beck, R. N., *The Meaning of Americanism*. New York: Philosophical Library, 1956.

Cantril, H., *The Politics of Despair*. New York: Basic Books, 1958.

Commager, H. S., *The American Mind*. New Haven: Yale University Press, 1950.

Conant, J. B., *Education and Liberty*. Cambridge: Harvard University Press, 1953.

Cremin, L. A., *The Transformation of the School*. New York: A. A. Knopf, 1961.

Curti, M., *American Paradox: The Conflict of Thought and Action*. New Brunswick: Rutgers University Press, 1956.

Douglas, W. O., *The Right of the People*. New York: Doubleday, 1958.

Havighurst, R. L., & Neugarten, B. L., *Society and Education*, 2d ed. Boston: Allyn & Bacon, 1962. Part 1.

Spindler, G., *Education and Culture*. New York: Holt, Rinehart & Winston, 1963.

Spitz, D., *Democracy and the Challenge of Power*. New York: Columbia University Press, 1958.

II. *Moral-Ethical Values, Spiritual Values, and Education*

GENERAL REFERENCES

Childs, J. L., *Education and Morals*. New York: Appleton-Century-Crofts, 1950. Chapter 9.

Cox, P. W. L. & Mercer, B. E., *Education in Democracy: Social Foundations of Education*. New York: McGraw-Hill, 1961. Chapter 13.

Kneller, G. F., ed., *Foundations of Education*. New York: John Wiley, 1963. Chapter 7.

Mayer, F., *American Ideas and Education*. Columbus, Ohio: Charles E. Merrill, 1964. Chapters 4–10.

SPECIAL REFERENCES

Bower, W. C., *Moral and Spiritual Values in Education*. Lexington, Ky.: University of Kentucky Press, 1952.

Brubacher, J. S., ed., *The Public Schools and Spiritual Values*, Seventh Yearbook, John Dewey Society. New York: Harper, 1944.

Butts, R. F., *The American Tradition in Religion and Education*. Boston: Beacon Press, 1950.

Commager, H. S., *Living Ideas in America*. New York: Harper, 1951.

Dewey, J., *Moral Principles in Education*. New York: Philosophical Library, 1959.

Educational Policies Commission, National Education Association, *Moral and Spiritual Values in the Public Schools*. Washington, D.C., 1951.

Fromm, E., *Man for Himself*. New York: Rinehart, 1947.

Galdston, I., ed., *Panic and Morale*. New York: International Universities Press, 1958.

Hartford, E. F., *Moral Values in Public Education*. New York: Harper, 1958.

McCluskey, N. G., *Public Schools and Moral Education*. New York: Columbia University Press, 1958.

Phenix, P. H., *Education and the Common Good*. New York: Harper, 1961.

III. Law and Education

GENERAL REFERENCES

Callahan, R. E., *An Introduction to Education in American Society*, 2d ed. New York: A. A. Knopf, 1960. Chapter 10.

Kneller, G. F., ed., *Foundations of Education*. New York: John Wiley, 1963. Chapter 8.

Wiggin, G. A., *Education and Nationalism*. New York: McGraw-Hill, 1962. Chapter 8.

SPECIAL REFERENCES

Edwards, N., *The Courts and the Public Schools*, rev. ed. Chicago: University of Chicago Press, 1955.

Hamilton, R. R. & Mort, P. R., *The Law and Public Education*. Brooklyn, N.Y.: Foundation Press, 1959.

Meiklejohn, A., *Political Freedom*. New York: Harper, 1960.

Remmlein, M., *School Law*, 2d ed. Danville, Ill.: Interstate, 1962.

Research Division, National Education Association, *The Teacher and the Law*. NEA School Law Series, Research Monograph 1959–M3, Washington, D.C., 1959.

Smiley, M. B. & Diekhoff, J. S., *Prologue to Teaching*. New York: Oxford University Press, 1959. Part 2.

IV. Finance and Education

GENERAL REFERENCES

Callahan, R. E., *An Introduction to Education in American Society*, 2d ed. New York: A. A. Knopf, 1960. Chapter 11.

Cox, P. W. L. & Mercer, B. E., *Education in Democracy: Social Foundations of Education*. New York: McGraw-Hill, 1961. Chapters 10, 11, 12.

Hillway, T., *Education in American Society*. Boston: Houghton Mifflin, 1961. Chapter 5

Kneller, G. F., ed., *Foundations of Education*. New York: John Wiley, 1963. Chapter 9

Thayer, V. T., *The Role of the School in American Society*. New York: Dodd, Mead, 1960. Chapters 19, 24.

Wiggin, G. A., *Education and Nationalism*. New York: McGraw-Hill, 1962. Chapter 4.

SPECIAL REFERENCES

Benson, C. S., *The Economics of Public Education.* Boston: Houghton Mifflin, 1961.

Havighurst, R. L. & Neugarten, B. L., *Society and Education,* 2d ed. Boston: Allyn & Bacon, 1962. Chapters 11, 16.

Lazarus, R., *We Can Have Better Schools.* New York: Committee for Economic Development, 1960.

National Association of Manufacturers, *Our Public Schools and Their Financial Support.* New York: The Association, 1954.

National Citizens Commission for the Public Schools, *Financing Public Education in the Decade Ahead.* New York: The Commission, 1954.

V. The Group and Education

GENERAL REFERENCES

Callahan, R. E., *An Introduction to Education in American Society,* 2d ed. New York: A. A. Knopf, 1960. Chapter 3.

Childs, J. L., *Education and Morals.* New York: Appleton-Century-Crofts, 1950. Chapters 8, 11.

Cox, P. W. L. & Mercer, B. E., *Education in Democracy: Social Foundations of Education.* New York: McGraw-Hill, 1961. Chapters 3, 4, 5.

Haan, A., *Education for the Open Society.* Boston: Allyn & Bacon, 1962. Chapter 4.

Kallenbach, W. W. & Hodges, Jr., H. M., eds., *Education and Society.* Columbus, Ohio: Charles E. Merrill, 1963. Chapters 1, 2, 4, 7, 8.

Pounds, R. L. & Garretson, R. L., *Principles of Modern Education.* New York: Macmillan, 1962. Chapters 5–7.

Thayer, V. T., *The Role of the School in American Society.* New York: Dodd, Mead, 1960. Chapters 6–8.

SPECIAL REFERENCES

Davis, A., Gardner, B., Gardner, M. R., *Deep South.* Chicago: University of Chicago Press, 1941.

Davis, A., *Social Class Influences on Learning.* Cambridge: Harvard University Press, 1952.

Havighurst, R. L. & Neugarten, B. L., *Society and Education,* 2d ed. Boston: Allyn & Bacon, 1962. Part 2.

Hollingshead, A. B., *Elmtown's Youth.* New York: John Wiley, 1949.

Riesman, D., Glazer, N. & Denney, R., *The Lonely Crowd: A Study of the Changing American Character.* New Haven: Yale University Press, 1953.

Smiley, M. B. & Diekhoff, J. S., *Prologue to Teaching.* New York: Oxford University Press, 1959. Part 4.

Warner, W. L. & Lunt, P. S., *The Social Life of a Modern Community.* New Haven: Yale University Press, 1941.

———, Havighurst, R. L., and Loeb, M. B., *Who Shall Be Educated?* New York: Harper, 1944.

Weiss, T. M., & Hoover, K. H., *Scientific Foundations of Education.* Dubuque: Brown, 1960. Chapters 5–7.

VI. *The Individual and Education*

GENERAL REFERENCES

Childs, J. L., *Education and Morals*. New York: Appleton-Century-Crofts, 1950. Chapter 4.

Cox, P. W. L., & Mercer, B. E., *Education in Democracy: Social Foundations of Democracy*. New York: McGraw-Hill, 1961. Chapters 6, 18, 19.

Grambs, J. D., & McClure, L. M., *Foundations of Teaching*. New York: Holt, Rinehart & Winston, 1964. Chapters 5–8.

Haan, A., *Education for the Open Society*. Boston: Allyn & Bacon, 1962. Chapter 3.

Kallenbach, W. W., & Hodges, Jr., H. M., eds., *Education and Society*. Columbus, Ohio: Charles E. Merrill, 1963. Chapter 3.

Pounds, R. L. & Garretson, R. L., *Principles of Modern Education*. New York: Macmillan, 1962. Chapter 12.

Thayer, V. T., *The Role of the School in American Society*. New York: Dodd, Mead, 1960. Chapters 12–15.

SPECIAL REFERENCES

Hollingshead, A. B., & Redlich, F. C., *Social Class and Mental Illness: A Community Study*. New York: John Wiley, 1958.

Kluckhohn, C., & Murray, H. A., eds., *Personality in Nature, Society, and Culture*. New York: A. A. Knopf, 1953.

Phenix, P. H., *Realms of Meaning*. New York: McGraw-Hill, 1964. Chapters 2–4.

Wallace, A. F. C., *Culture and Personality*. New York: Random House, 1961.

VII. *Educational Specifications*

GENERAL REFERENCES

Butts, R. F., & Cremin, L. A., *A History of Education in American Culture*. New York: Henry Holt, 1953. Chapter 15.

Callahan, R. E., *An Introduction to Education in American Society*, 2d ed. New York: A. A. Knopf, 1961. Chapters 12, 13.

Dewey, J., *Democracy and Education*. New York: Macmillan, 1924. Chapter 8.

Grambs, J. D., & McClure, L. M., *Foundations of Teaching*. New York: Holt, Rinehart & Winston, 1964. Chapters 13, 14.

Hullfish, H. G., & Smith, P. G., *Reflective Thinking*. New York: Dodd, Mead, 1961. Chapters 12, 13.

Thayer, V. T., *The Role of the School in American Society*. New York: Dodd, Mead, 1960. Chapters 2–5, 9.

SPECIAL REFERENCES

Berkson, I. B., *Education Faces the Future*. New York: Harper, 1943. Chapters 12–15.

———, *The Ideal and the Community*. New York: Harper, 1958. Chapters 12–14.

Gross, C. H., Wronski, S. P., and Hanson, J. W., eds., *School and Society*. Boston: Heath, 1962.

Report of the Harvard Committee, *General Education in a Free Society*. Cambridge: Harvard University Press, 1945.

Smiley, M. B. & Diekhoff, J. S., *Prologue to Teaching*. New York: Oxford University Press, 1959. Part 3.

VIII. Educational Institutions

GENERAL REFERENCES

Callahan, R. E., *An Introduction to Education in American Society*, 2d ed. New York: A. A. Knopf, 1960. Chapter 9.

Grambs, J. D., & McClure, L. M., *Foundations of Education*. New York: Holt, Rinehart & Winston, 1964. Chapters 9–12.

Hillway, T., *Education in American Society*. Boston: Houghton Mifflin, 1961. Chapters 6–8.

Kallenbach, W. W., & Hodges, Jr., H. M., eds., *Education and Society*. Columbus, Ohio: Charles E. Merrill, 1963. Chapter 5.

Kneller, G. F., ed., *Foundations of Education*. New York: John Wiley, 1963. Part 4.

Morris, V. C., ed., *Becoming an Educator*. Boston: Houghton Mifflin, 1963. Chapters 6–9.

SPECIAL REFERENCES

A Committee Report by Members of the Faculties of Andover, Exeter, Lawrenceville, Harvard, Princeton, and Yale, *General Education in School and College*. Cambridge: Harvard University Press, 1952.

Alexander, W. M. & Saylor, J. G., *Modern Secondary Education*. New York: Rinehart, 1959.

Caswell, H. & Foshay, A., *Education in the Elementary School*, 3rd ed. New York: American Book, 1957.

Conant, J. B., *Slums and Suburbs: A Commentary on Schools in Metropolitan Areas*. New York: McGraw-Hill, 1961.

———, *The American High School Today*. New York: McGraw-Hill, 1959.

Havighurst, R. L., & Neugarten, B. L., *Society and Education*, 2d ed. Boston: Allyn & Bacon, 1962. Chapters 9, 10, 12–15, 17.

Mayer, F., *American Ideas and Education*. Columbus, Ohio: Charles E. Merrill, 1964. Chapters 32–39.

Sanford, N., ed., *The American College*. New York: John Wiley, 1962.

Van Til, W., Vars, G. F., and Loundsbury, J. H., *Modern Education for the Junior High School Years*. Indianapolis: Bobbs-Merrill, 1961.

IX. The Educators and Education

GENERAL REFERENCES

Berkson, I. B., *The Ideal and the Community*. New York: Harper, 1958. Chapter 15.

Callahan, R. E., *An Introduction to Education in American Society*, 2d ed. New York: A. A. Knopf, 1960. Chapters 17–19.

Childs, J. L., *Education and Morals*. New York: Appleton-Century-Crofts, 1950. Chapter 6.

Grambs, J. D., & McClure, L. M., *Foundations of Teaching*. New York: Holt, Rinehart & Winston, 1964. Chapters, 1–4, 15.

Haan, A., *Education for the Open Society*. Boston: Allyn & Bacon, 1962. Chapter 5.

Hillway, T., *Education in American Society*. Boston: Houghton Mifflin, 1961. Chapters 13, 14.
Mayer, F., *American Ideas and Education*. Columbus, Ohio: Charles E. Merrill, 1964. Chapters 40–43.
Morris, V. C., ed., *Becoming an Educator*. Boston: Houghton Mifflin, 1963. Chapter 11.
Thayer, V. T., *The Role of the School in American Society*. New York: Dodd, Mead, 1960. Chapters 21–23.

SPECIAL REFERENCES

Axtelle, G., ed., *Teachers for Democracy*. Fourth Yearbook, John Dewey Society. New York: Appleton-Century, 1940.
Borrowman, M. L., *The Liberal and Technical in Teacher Education*. New York: Teachers College, Columbia University, 1956.
Chandler, B. J., *Education and the Teacher*. New York: Dodd, Mead, 1961.
Conant, J. B., *The Education of the American Teacher*. New York: McGraw-Hill, 1963.
Havighurst, R. L., & Neugarten, B. L., *Society and Education*, 2d ed. Boston: Allyn & Bacon, 1962. Part 5.
Lindsey, M., ed., *New Horizons for the Teaching Profession*. NEA Commission on Teacher Education and Professional Standards, Washington, D.C., 1961.
McGlothlin, W. J., *Patterns of Professional Education*. New York: Putnam, 1960.
Mead, M., *The School in American Culture*. Cambridge: Harvard University Press, 1951.
Smiley, M. B., & Diekhoff, J. S., *Prologue to Teaching*. New York: Oxford University Press, 1959. Part 1.
Stiles, L. J., *Teacher Education in the United States*. New York: Ronald, 1960.
Ulich, R., *Professional Education as a Humane Study*. New York: Macmillan, 1956.

Index

Academic freedom, 621
attacks on, 75–76
Supreme Court decisions on, 213–14
Acheson, Dean, 428–29
Achievement orientation, 355
Adams, Henry, 548, 553, 557
Adler, Felix, 183
Administration of education, 15–21, 524
See also Professors; Teachers
Adolescents, 337
needs of, 507–8, 511–13
Adult education, 545–57
expenditures for, 246
in military establishment, 555
Affection, importance of, 611
Alumni control, 628–29
American culture, 316–32
activism in, 342–47
anti-intellectualism in, 64–65
children in, 336–37
classes in, *see* Social classes
conformity in, 57–61, 71–78, 344–46, 355
cooperation in, 345–46
equality in, 322, 338, 447
ethos of, 333–34
family in, 335–36
general characteristics of, 333–40
immigrants in, 345
intellectuals in, 64–71
localism in, 445
marriage in, 335
Middle Western, 325–29
morality in, 337–38
New England, 320–23
personality changes in, 74–75
rationalism in, 5–6
religion in, *see* Religion
social mobility in, 349, 352
Southern, 323–25
technology in, 334–35, 539
values of, 333–47, 354–62, 567–69, 572–73
work in, 344
youthful attitudes in, 57–58
American Federation of Labor–Congress of Industrial Organizations (AFL-CIO), 286, 547
educational views of, 466–70
American Jewish Congress, 290, 293
Anti-empirical rationalism, 623–24
Anti-intellectualism, 64–65
Appalachian communities, 325–29
Aptitude tests, 467
Aquinas, St. Thomas, 134, 623
Aristocratic society, 26–27
Aristotle, 38, 188, 623, 625
Art education, 6–7, 452–53
of children, 501
Athens (ancient), public life in, 54
Atomic bomb, 37
Auden, W. H., 59
Audiovisual aids, 522
Authoritarianism, 86, 626
basis of, 16
communistic, *see* Communism
democracy and, 106
effects on students, 615
fascistic, 86
hatred and, 612
Nazi, 43, 50
power basis of, 43
techniques of, 48–49

Beard, Charles, 36, 549
Benjamin, Harold, 76–77
Bible, 142
 influence of, 127
 in public schools, 119, 122, 143
 See also Religion
Bill of Rights, 18
 religion and, 115–17
 See also Constitution; *specific amendments*
Blair bill, 120
Blanshard, Paul, 293
Bode, Boyd H., 86–88
Bokhari, Ahmed, 62
Books
 forbidden, 76
 lower-class children and, 570–71
 in Russia, 62
Brown, Frank J., 291–92
Broudy, H., 182
Buddhists, 164, 166–67
Bureaucracy, 582
Bush, Douglas, 84
Business, American attitudes toward, 336
Butler, Samuel, 190

Carlson, C. Emanuel, 292
Carr, William G., 286
Catholic Church, 106, 290–91, 338
 discipline and, 139
 educational philosophy of, 134–40
 paganism in, 167
 parents in, 137
 progressive education and, 135, 138
 schools of, *see* Parochial schools
 sectarian education and, 119–23
Catt, Carrie Chapman, 48
Chamber of Commerce, 288, 470
 gifted-child approach of, 468
Change
 importance of, 7
 technological, 35–39, 252, 329
Childs, John, 24
Children
 American attitudes toward, 336–37
 attitudes formed by, 609
 conflicts with parents, 568
 delinquency among, 611
 educational experiences of, 499–504
 gifted, 467–70, 502–3
 language and, 500
 maturing of, 510–11
 socializing of, 568
China (ancient)
 guilds in, 167
 religion in, 165
Christian socialism, 547
Christianity
 democracy and, 618
 ethics of, 25
 love ideal of, 174
 nature of, 168–70
 values of, 25
 See also Catholic Church; Protestants
Church-state issue, 579
 Catholic views on, 119–23, 134–40
 Constitutional problems of, 111, 115–17, 130, 211–12, 218
 cooperation on, 155
 Jewish views on, 141–48, 156, 290–91
 local approaches to, 149–59
 origin of, 162
 Protestant views on, 119
 states and, 116–17
 See also Parochial schools; Religion
Cities, *see* Communities; Local agencies
Citizenship, education in, 22, 459–62
Civil liberties
 attacks on, 76
 dangers to, 66
 Supreme Court decisions on, 213–14
 See also Academic freedom; Democracy
Classrooms, shortage of, 286, 296
Closed society, 621–22
Colleges
 attendance at, 56, 375–77
 as communities, 603
 degrees earned from, 494
 enrollment in, 489–93
 entrance requirements for, 526–27
 free, 617–29
 function in open society, 627
 junior, *see* Junior colleges
 land-grant, 289
 personal income of graduates, 263–74
 professional education by, 585–95
 See also Higher education
Common law and education, 199–205
Communications
 breakdown in, 60
 democratic process and, 543
Communism, 34, 86, 106, 144, 214, 356
 changes in, 87
 spread of, 37

Communities, 525
Appalachian, 325–29
colleges as, 603
crossroad, 325–29
declining authority of, 478
educational expenditures of, 296
educational functions of, 229
educational responsibilities of, 282, 284, 477–84
expansion of, 330–32
general features of, 318–20
Middle Western, 325–29
mill town, 329–31
New England, 320–23
powers of, 172–73, 200
Southern, 323–25
suburban, 332
taxation by, 298–99
Community education, 149–59
definition of, 149
Jews and, 152, 156–57
Protestants and, 152, 156–57
public funds for, 157
Competition, 337
Conformity, 57–58, 344–46, 355
break with, 59–61
diversity and, 77–78
freedom and, 71–78
individuality and, 75
Constitution (U.S.), 218, 223
education and, 206–9
religion and, 115–17, 130
See also Bill of Rights; Supreme Court
Control and guidance, 614
Cooperation
in American society, 345–46
education and, 29
importance of, 6
prerequisites of, 103
scientific, 433–38
Courts, functioning of, 220
See also Supreme Court
Creativity, 6
determinants of, 627
Culture
American, *see* American culture
definition of, 403, 408
democracy and, 103–6
developing, 463–64
education and, 25–26, 29
Indian, 405, 407
personality and, 393–412
relativity of, 103–6
religion and, 104
science and, 103–4
subjectivity of, 103
youthful attitudes toward, 57–58
Curriculum
AFL-CIO on, 467–70
balanced, 527–28
of junior high schools, 506–15
NAM's views on, 458–64
in secondary schools, 506–15, 517, 522

Dawson, Christopher, on secularism, 140
Declaration of Independence, 447
Democracy
authoritarianism and, 106
basis of, 16, 444–47
changes in, 87, 444–47, 565
Christianity and, 618
citizenship in, 22
communications and, 543
credo of, 12–21, 632
cultural relativity and, 103–6
decline of, 238–40
demands of, 106, 618
development of, 16
discipline of, 604
dynamic nature of, 565
equality and, 16
falsehood and, 620
human control and, 426–30
liberal education and, 538
methods of, 19, 21
needs of, 84
open societies in, 72–74
opportunities afforded by, 88
parochial schools and, 81
pluralistic society and, 617
popular government and, 612
power in, 20, 41–47, 49
principle of inclusiveness in, 109
private schools, 81
renewal of, 81–82
responsibilities of, 14
training for, 80–91
values of, 12, 103–6
as way of life, 15, 86–88, 90–91
See also Democratic education; Freedom
Democratic education, 28–29
administration of, 15–21, 524
flexibility of, 89–90
goals of, 3, 12

Democratic education (*cont.*)
liberation of intelligence and, 87
open society and, 617–29
premises of, 26–27
public, *see* Public education
scope of, 79–91
See also Democracy
Dewey, John, 84, 161, 169, 184, 535, 579
critics of, 86
definition of democracy, 15–21, 29, 88
on function of education, 561
on personality, 409
on scientific content of education, 3–4
on thought and action, 68–69
Discipline
authority and, 615
Catholic concepts of, 139
democracy and, 604
faulty, 610
nature of, 613–16
Diversity
appreciation of, 6
conformity and, 77–78
in open societies, 73
Douglas, William, 213–14
Dropouts, 525–26

Earnings, *see* Income
Economy, 334–35
differential growth rates of, 253–54
Educational expenditures, *see* Expenditures for education
Effort-optimism, 342–43, 345, 347
Elementary schools
enrollment in, 489–92
expenditures for, 246–50
personal income of graduates, 264–74
revenue sources for, 248
success of, 565
teachers in, 494
time spent in, 495–96
Emotions and learning, 607–15
Empirio-rationalism, 617–24
Employment and educational attainment, 263–74, 384, 386
England, 36
laws of, 321, 324
Equality
in American society, 322, 338, 447
concepts of, 259
democracy and, 16
Esau temptation, 44, 51
Ethics, *see* Morality; Values

Everson case, 111, 117
Expenditures for education, 157, 245–50, 296–300
Experience, value attribute of, 417–24

Fabian socialists, 547
Factory towns, 329–31
Family, 175, 611–12
American attitudes toward, 335–36
disintegration of, 30
educational attainment and, 383–84
educational investment of, 259
Fascism, 86
Federal aid, 285–94, 298, 483
appropriations of, 245–50
increase in, 241–42
limitations of, 233, 242–44
need for, 279, 285
to parochial schools, 120–22
to private schools, 290, 293
religious liberty and, 292–93
to states, 120–22, 279
See also Public funds; Taxation
Federal government
aid to education, *see* Federal aid
economic role of, 255–57
educational responsibilities of, 279–84, 477–84
growing authority of, 478
limitations in, 445
parochial schools and, 120–22, 290–91, 293
secularization of, 338–39
taxation by, 300
Fifth Amendment
education and, 207
teacher-loyalty programs and, 218
Finances for education, 229–33, 245–50
economic growth and, 252–61
First Amendment, 121, 123
church-state issue and, 218
education and, 207
religious freedom and, 115
Fiske, John, 478
Founding Fathers, 27, 69, 119, 150
views on religion, 114–15, 129–30
Fourteenth Amendment
church-state issue and, 116–117
education and, 207–8
racial segregation and, 218
Frankfurter, Felix, 211
Franklin, Benjamin, 69

Free university as open society, 617–29
Freedom
  academic, *see* Academic freedom
  conformity and, 71–78
  human control and, 426–30
  religion and, 113–16, 292–93
  scope of, 17–18
  See also Democracy; Democratic education
Freeman, Roger A., 287–88
Freud, Sigmund, 184
Fromm, Erich, 410
Fuller, Edgar, 287, 288–89
Functional illiteracy, *see* Illiteracy, functional, extent of
Future-time orientation, 355

General-welfare clause, 207
Gifted children, 467–70, 502–3
Goals of education, 3, 12
Greece (ancient), 322–23
  religion in, 165
Gross National Product, 246
Growth
  economic, 253–54
  importance of, 7
Guidance, 523
  control and, 614

Harris, W. T., 184, 188
Hatred, effectiveness of, 612
Hausleiter, Leo, 38
Hayes, John C., 292–93
High schools, *see* Secondary schools
Higher education
  crisis in, 534–43
  federal appropriations for, 246
  See also Colleges
History and education, 25–26
Hitler, Adolf, 50, 239, 429
Hoar bill, 120
Hochwalt, Frederick G., 290–91
Home life, *see* Family
Homestead Acts, 327
Human nature
  American concepts of, 334, 446
  characteristics of, 414–24
  control of, 426–30
Hume, David, 190
Huxley, Aldous, 406
Hydrogen bomb, 37

Illiteracy, functional, extent of, 385–87
Immigrants, assimilation of, 345
Inclusiveness, principle of, 109
Income
  by education, 263–74, 384, 386
  by occupation, 275
India (ancient)
  guilds in, 167
  religion in, 165
Indians, American, 339
  culture of, 405, 407
Individuality, 49, 462–63
  conformity and, 61, 75
  distortion of, 50
  fulfillment of, 25
  ideal of, 14, 355
  in New England, 322
  open societies and, 78
  school instruction and, 528–29
Industrial Revolution, effects of, 329–31
Inflation, effects of, 260–61
Inner-direction, 74
Institutions, educational
  democratic administration of, 21
  operation of, 18
  See also specific educational institutions
Instruction, religious, *see* Religious instruction
Intellectuals
  American society and, 64–71
  definition of, 55–56
  national policy and, 61–63
  responsibilities of, 56–57
  as technicians, 66
Intelligence
  American emphasis on, 5–6
  democratic education and, 87
  liberation of, 87
  pooling of, 17
Intelligence tests, 467
  early use of, 564
Interdisciplinary knowledge, 3–4, 434–38

Jackson, Andrew, influence of, 27–28
James, William, 78, 191
Japan (ancient)
  guilds in, 167
  religion in, 165
Jefferson, Thomas, 119
  educational views of, 27
  on religious freedom, 114–15, 130

Jews, 164
community education and, 152, 156–57
educational views of, 141–48, 156, 290–91
Judeo-Christian tradition, 157
influence of, 126–27
See also Bible; Catholic Church; Jews; Protestants; Religion
Junior colleges, 526
enrollment in, 489–93
Junior high schools, 506–15
Juvenile delinquency, 611

Kallen, Horace, 603
Kampelman, Max M., 293
Kant, Immanuel, 187
Kindergarten
enrollment in, 489
time spent in, 495
Kingsley, Charles, 547

Labor force, changing skills of, 255
Labor unions, 286, 547
educational views of, 466–70
Land-grant colleges, 289
Language, childhood development of. 500
Laski, Harold J., 621
Lasswell, Harold, on human power, 42
Laws
authority of school, 222–23
common, 199–205
constitutional, *see* Constitution (U.S.)
of contracts, 202
education and, 198–209, 216–25
English, 321, 324
evolution of school, 218–20
general nature of school, 219
role of, 217
scope of school, 218
statutory, 205–6
Learning situations, 5
Lewis, C. S., 187
Liberal education, 455–56
democracy and, 538
elitism in, 538
for professionals, 592–95
for women, 545
Life expectancy, increase in, 38
Lincoln, Abraham, 207
Lindemann, Eric, 607
Linton, Ralph, 409
Little, M. V., 291–92
Love
Christian, 174
importance of, 611–12
as unifying force, 613
Lower classes, education for, 570–71
Loyalty programs, 76, 213–14
Fifth Amendment and, 218
Lutz, Harley L., 287

MacLeish, Archibald, 82
Madison, James, 114, 119
Malthus, Thomas, 588
Mann, Horace, 118
Marriage, American concepts of, 335
Mass media
influence of, 77–78
standards of taste and, 611
Maturity, definition of, 7, 608
McCarthyism, 65, 73
McCollum case, 111, 211
McLaurin v. Oklahoma State Regents, 212
McReynolds, James C., 212
Medicine
advance of, 38
public, 31–32
Meiklejohn, Alexander, 57
Merriam, Charles E., 41–43
Meyer, Agnes E., 294, 611
Middle Ages
dogmatic rationalism of, 625
guilds in, 167
social status in, 410
Middle class
educational attitudes of, 567–68
values of, 342–47, 354–62, 567–69
Military establishment
adult education in, 555
illiterates in, 387
promotion of, 243–44
war and, 48
Mill towns, 329–31
Mitchell, Clarence, 293–94
Moeller, Walter H., 290
Morality
in American society, 337–38
Christian, 25
education in, 453–55
human interests and, 99
instruction in, 181–92
meaning of, 97–99
Puritan, 355

Morality (*cont.*)
relativistic, 355
religious sanction and, 97–102
See also Values
Motivation
low, 47–57
research in, 469
Movies
in education, 522
standards of taste and, 611
Mumford, Lewis, 329
Municipalities, *see* Communities; Local agencies

National Association for the Advancement of Colored People, 293
National Association of Manufacturers, 31, 287
educational views of, 458–64, 468
National Education Association, 286, 482
educational views of, 472–74
National income, growth of, 252–53
National Planning Commission, 482–84
Nazism, 43, 50
Negroes, 444
integration of, 212, 218
prejudices toward, 340
racial segregation of, 293–94
religious beliefs of, 167
social status of, 349
in South, 323
See also Racial segregation
New England
community features of, 320–23
conservatism of, 333
individuality in, 322
New School for Social Research, The, 549
New York City
educational objectives of, 475–76
Niebuhr, Reinhold, 169
Night schools, 550
Northwest Ordinance, 150
Nowell-Smith, P. H., 186, 189

Occupation and income, 275
Olds, Leland, 38
Open societies, 72–74
diversity in, 73
dynamism of, 629
ethos of, 621
implications of, 620–29
individuality and, 78
standards of, 617–20
Other-direction, 74

Parents
Catholic, 137
child's conflicts with, 568
double taxation of, 291
rights of, 221
teachers and, 503–4
See also Children; Family
Parochial schools
democracy and, 81
educational philosophy of, 135–40
enrollment at, 156
federal government and, 120–22, 290–91, 293
public funds for, 120–22
taxation and, 291
See also Catholic Church; Religion
Payot, Jules, 451
Peer, Robert, 553
Pennsylvania
"Dutch" culture in, 329
Pericles, 63
on public life, 54
Perry, Ralph Barton, 90–91, 427
Personal income
by education, 263–74, 384
by occupation, 275
Personality
components of, 394, 405–12
culture and, 393–412
determinants of, 393–405
Peters, R. S., 184
Philosophy and educational theory, 22–32, 134–40, 227, 449–56
Physical education, 450–51
Pius XI, Pope, 136, 138–39
Planning, educational, 481
Plato, 26–27, 183, 190, 625
Play, 501–2
Plessy v. Ferguson, 212
Pluralistic society, 617
Political education, 227-28, 603
Pope, Liston, 167
Power
authoritarian, 43
community, 172–73, 200
definitions of, 42–43
democracy and, 45–47, 49
education and, 40–52

Power (*cont.*)
  love of, 46
  low-level, 46
  misuse of, 428
  religion and, 104, 126
  short circuits of human, 44–47
Practices, educational, 4, 522
  over-domination and, 5
Press, influence of, 77–78
Private schools
  aid to, 240
  democracy and, 81
  federal aid to, 290, 293
Professional education, 585–95
Professors, 57
  function of, 626
  limitations of, 86
  self-image of, 541–42
  training of, 590
Progressive education
  Catholic critique of, 135, 138
  See also Dewey, John
Property
  American attitudes toward, 334
  taxes on, 233
Protestants, 338
  community education and, 152, 156–57
  public education supported by, 156
  sectarian education and, 119
Psychology and education, 29
Public assistance, 387
Public education, 22–32, 82
  aid to, 240
  church-state issue in, *See* Church-state issue
  economic growth and, 253–54
  enrollment for, 286, 296, 488–94
  expenditures for, 245–50, 296–300
  government responsibility for, 477–84
  Jewish support for, 156
  ladder system in, 495
  meaning of, 30–32
  non-sectarian, 117–20, 162–63
  philosophical premises of, 22–32
  Protestant support for, 156
  religion and, 124–33
  teachers for, 494
  See also Colleges; Elementary schools; Secondary schools
Public funds
  for community education, 157
  for parochial schools, 120–22
  See also Federal aid; Taxation
Public libraries, 284
Puerto Ricans, functional illiteracy among, 385
Puritans, 320–23, 355, 444

Racial segregation, 340
  court decisions on, 212
  federal aid and, 293–94
  Fourteenth Amendment and, 218
  See also Negroes
Radio
  in education, 522
  influence of, 78
  standard of taste and, 611
Rationalism
  American emphasis on, 5-6
  anti-empirical, 623–24
  dynamism of, 623
  effects of, 622
  empirical, 617–24
  as frame of mind, 617
Reading, childhood knowledge of, 501
Redefinition theory, 208
Reisman, David, 74
Relativism, moral, 355
Released time, 122, 211
Religion
  in American culture, 128–31, 337–38
  Chinese, 165
  Christian, 25, 168–70, 174, 618
  cultural relativity of, 104
  dissension in, 114
  dualities in, 168
  education and, 124–33, 134–40, 149–50 211–12, 453–55
  established, 112, 115–17
  experience of, 99–100
  Founding Fathers on, 129–30
  freedom of, 113–16, 292–93
  Greek, 165
  history of, 165–68
  influence of, 104, 126
  instruction in, 122, 131
  Indian, 165
  Japanese, 165
  Jewish, *see* Jews
  morality and, 97–102
  multiple establishment of, 115
  in New England, 321–22
  released-time for, 122, 211
  Roman, 165

Religion (*cont.*)
sanction of, 99–102
scope of, 125–28
social acts and, 171–72
in Society Islands, 165
in South, 323–24
state and, *see* Church-state issue
taxation and, 117
values and, 161–79
See also specific religions
Religious instruction, in various states, 132
Research, educational, 481
Retirement systems, 204
Revenues
local, 298–300
proposals for, 304–11
See also Taxation
Revolutionary Land Grants, 327
Ribicoff, Abraham, 285, 289
Rice, Philip, 183–84
Rome (ancient), religion in, 165
Routine, American emphasis on, 336
Royce, Josiah, 191
Ruskin, John, 548
Russell, Bertrand, 42, 188–89, 613
Russia, 34, 62

Sartre, Jean-Paul, 185
Schiller, Friedrich, 188
Scholastic achievement and earnings, 263–72
School attendance and social class, 375–77
School boards, 261
authority of, 200–3
educational views of, 475–76
redress against, 221
taxation by, 203
traditionalistic values of, 357
School lunch program, 283
Schools, *see specific schools*
Science, 540–41
advance of, 38
American attitudes toward, 334
childhood interest in, 500
cooperation in, 433–38
cultural relativity and, 103–4
in education, 3
of human relations, 429–38
methods of, 432
pure, 435
values and, 437–38
Secondary schools
attendance in New Haven, 375–77
districts for, 531
dropouts from, 525–26
enrollment in, 490–92
expenditures for, 246–50
failure of, 565
personal income of graduates, 264–75
revenue sources for, 248
role of, 517–32
special programs in, 520, 522–24
teachers in, 494
time spent in, 496
work experience in, 529
See also Junior high schools
Segregation, *see* Racial segregation
Self-discipline, 7, 614
Sex, American attitudes toward, 335, 337–38
Sherer, Morris, 290–91
Shoemann, Peter T., 286
Simpson, G. G., 416
Smith, P. G., 4–5
Smith, Toulmin, 478
Smith-Hughes Act, 121
Snow, Sir Charles, 541
Social acts, creative, 170–72, 178–79
Social classes
in American society, 340, 349–52
American theory of, 566, 574
education and, 378–83, 564–76
in Evanston, Illinois, 364–70
in Middle Ages, 410
mobility of, 349, 352
in New Haven, Connecticut, 373–81
school attendance by, 375–77
Social mobility, 349, 352
Socialism, 547
Society Islands, religion in, 165
Southern communities, features of, 323–25
Soviet Union, 34, 62
Sperry, Dean, on church, 127
States
church-state issue and, 116–17
educational authority of, 207, 218, 445
educational expenditures of, 286, 296, 299–300
educational responsibilities of, 282–84, 477–84
federal aid to, 120–22, 279
growing authority of, 477
religious neutrality of, 123

States (*cont.*)
 taxation by, 299–300
State-church issue, *see* Church-state issue
Status in American society, 349–52
 See also Social classes
Statutory law and education, 205–6
Stearns, Harry L., 153
Strang, R., 609
Students
 disciplining, 613–16
 free university and, 628
 gifted, 467–70, 502–3
 needs of, 602
 political education of, 603
 as responsible persons, 598–605
 rights of, 221
 on teachers, 609
 views of, 57–58, 357
Suburbs, 332
Suffrage, universal, 15, 338
Supreme Court, 207–8, 223, 294
 church-state decisions of, 111, 116–17, 211–12
 civil-liberties decisions of, 213–14
 integration decisions of, 212
 language-instruction decisions of, 212–13
Swainson, John B., 286, 289
Sweatt v. Painter, 212

Taba, Hilda, 6
Taft bill, 122
Taxation
 direct, 256, 298–99
 for education, 233, 291, 298–311
 federal, 300
 increases in, 285
 local, 298–99
 parochial schools and, 291
 property, 298–99
 proposals for, 304–11
 religion and, 117
 by school boards, 203
 sources of, 256, 298–300
 See also Federal aid; Public funds
Teachers, 19
 adult education, 554
 attitude-development and, 613
 Catholic, 137–38
 civil liberties of, *see* Academic freedom
 education of, 572–73, 578–83
 in elementary schools, 494
 function of, 5, 57
 orientation of, 614–15
 over-domination by, 5
 parents and, 503–4
 in public schools, 494
 retirement system for, 204
 in secondary schools, 494
 shortage of, 279
 students on, 609
 tenure legislation for, 204
 training of, 230, 530
 university, *see* Professors
 values of, 358–62, 572–73
Techniques of education, 4–5, 522
Technology
 acceptance of, 104
 American, 334–35, 539
 changes in, 35–39, 252, 329
 demands of, 11
 influence of, 238
Television
 in education, 522
 influence of, 78, 611
Tenure system, 204
Testing programs, 467, 529–30
Thorndike, Edward, 551
Thought
 action and, 68–69
 control of, 39, 49, 622
Tocqueville, Alexis de, 36, 345, 446
Tolerance
 emphasis on, 355
 limits of, 619
Totalitarianism, *see* Authoritarianism
Trade schools, *see* Vocational schools
Truth, 618
 quest for, 124–25

Unemployment and educational attainment, 386–87
Universities, *see* Colleges

Value attributes, 417–24
Values
 absolute, 108
 American, 333–47, 354–62, 567–69, 572–73
 choice of, 103–9
 Christian, 25
 democratic, 12, 103–6
 education and, 96–97

Values (*cont.*)
emergent, 354–62
freedom of, 98
hierarchy of, 107–8
of middle class, 342–47, 354–62, 567–69
pre-industrial, 39
religion and, 161–79
of school boards, 357
science and, 437–38
of students, 357
of teachers, 358–62, 572–73
traditionalistic, 354–62
See also Morality
Vocational schools, 283–84, 451, 513
changing skills and, 255

Warren, Earl, 212
Watson, K. Brantley, 288
Wealth, threats to, 47
Whyte, W. H., 60
Wiener, Norbert, 435
Williams, Roger, 113
Willis, Benjamin C., 289
Wilson, Woodrow, 81–82, 199, 201, 546
Work
American cult of, 344
ethic of, 355
Women, liberal education for, 545
Workers' education, 546–48
Workers' Educational Association, 548
Writing, childhood knowledge of, 501
Wust, Peter, 134–35

Youth, American cult of, 343
See also Children; Students